TE MATATIKI

Contemporary Māori Words

TE MATATIKI

Contemporary Māori Words

MĀORI LANGUAGE COMMISSION

Te Taura Whiri i te Reo Māori

Auckland
OXFORD UNIVERSITY PRESS
Oxford Melbourne New York

OXFORD UNIVERSITY PRESS NEW ZEALAND

Oxford New York
Athens Auckland Bangkok Bombay
Calcutta Cape Town Dar es Salaam Delhi
Florence Hong Kong Istanbul Karachi
Kuala Lumpur Madras Madrid Melbourne
Mexico City Nairobi Paris Singapore
Taipei Tokyo Toronto

and associated companies in
Berlin Ibadan

OXFORD is a trade mark of Oxford University Press

© Te Taura Whiri i te Reo Māori: Māori Language
Commission 1996
First published 1996

All rights reserved. No part of this publication
may be reproduced, stored in a retrieval system,
or transmitted, in any form or by any means,
without the prior permission in writing of Oxford
University Press. Within New Zealand, exceptions
are allowed in respect of any fair dealing for the
purpose of research or private study, or criticism or
review, as permitted under the Copyright Act 1962,
or in the case of reprographic reproduction in
accordance with the terms of the licences issued
by Copyright Licensing Limited. Enquiries concerning
reproduction outside these terms and in other
countries should be sent to the Rights Department,
Oxford University Press, at the address below.

Text designed by Steve Randles
Cover design by Steve Randles
Typeset by Egan-Reid Ltd, Auckland, New Zealand
Printed by McPherson's Printing Group
Published by Oxford University Press,
540 Great South Road, Greenlane, PO Box 11-149,
Auckland, New Zealand

Te Matatiki

He Kupu Whakataki

He Kupu Whakamārama

Nō te tau 1987 i whakamanahia ai e te Ture te Taura Whiri i te Reo Māori me te whakahau i a ia ki te whakapau i ōna kaha e noho mai anō ai te reo Māori hei reo kōrero i ngā kokonga katoa o tōna ao.

E rua ngā huarahi matua e whāia ana e Te Taura Whiri e tutuki pai ai tēnei whakahau. Ko te whāinga tuatahi, ko te pupuri kia pūmau te reo Māori tūturu e noho tonu mai ana i tēnā koko, i tēnā koko, huri i te mata o te whenua. Ko te tuarua, ko te whakawhānui i ngā kupu Māori, ā, e tutuki ai tēnei, kua tīkina atu kia rua, kia toru kupu tawhito, he kupu rānei kua roa e moe ana, ā, kua whakaohohia ake anō, kua kōtuia, kua whiria rānei, e noho mai ai he kupu hou ki te reo Māori.

Te Puku

Nō te tau 1992 i tāia tuatahitia ai *Te Matatiki*, ā, i tēnei te putanga tuarua, e rua ngā rerekētanga matua. Tuatahi, kua hoatu he maramara whakapapa ki ngā kupu katoa e kitea ai te takenga mai o te kupu hou, tuarua, e rua mano neke atu ngā kupu hou e noho mai ana i tēnei o ngā *Matatiki* kāore i roto i te putanga tuatahi.

Kia kaua Te Taura Whiri e horihori nāna katoa ngā kupu hou nei i hanga. Kia tīkina atu ko ngā kupu pāngarau hei whakatauira i tēnei, ā, mei kore ake te rōpū nāna i hanga ngā kupu o *Te Tauākī Marautanga Pāngarau - He Tauira*, i puta i te tau 1994. Kua raua mai ā rātou kupu ki tēnei o ngā *Matatiki* i runga i te tūmanako ka watea ake ki te katoa e manako ana ki te ao pāngarau.

Arā atu anō ngā kupu i hangaia e hinengaro noa atu, ā, kua toro atu te ringa o Te Taura Whiri ki ērā hei pūtakenga mō ētahi o āna kupu. Hei tauira, ko te kupu **rorohiko** tēnā. Kua noho mai te kupu **rorohiko** hei kaui mō te **rorohiko pōnaho**, arā, te rorohiko 'noho ki pona'.

Arā anō ngā kupu kua mārō hītararī te noho mai ki tō tātou reo, ka mutu, mai anō i whakamahia e ngā tīpuna me tā rātou whakanoho tika mai ki tō rātou reo tūāuriuri. Ko te kupu **waka** tērā, ko te kupu **parāoa** tērā. Koinei anō ngā tūmomo kupu kua noho mai hei tāhuhu mō ētahi o ngā kupu hou.

He kupu atu anō kua rokohina atu i roto i ngā ketuketunga pukapuka, ā, kua ūkuia ko te kupu i noho mai ki te tuatahi o ngā *Matatiki*, kua whakanohoia mai he kupu atu anō ki tēnei. I pēnei ai i runga i te whakaaro ka hāngai ake pea te tikanga o tēnei i tērā i te putanga tuatahi.

Kua tūpono atu he kupu Māori kē atu anō e ōrite ana te tikanga ki ētahi atu kupu Māori kua roa e noho mai ana hei hoa mō ētahi kupu Pākehā. Hei tauira, ko te kupu 'kainamu'. Mai anō ko te kupu 'tata' tētahi o ngā kupu e hāngai ana ki ngā kupu Pākehā pēnei i te 'almost' me te 'nearly'. Ehara i te mea e pare atu ana te tuarā ki te kupu 'tata', engari ko te hiahia kē, ko te whakahoki mai i te kupu 'kainamu', me te hiahia anō kia rua, kia toru ngā kupu Māori e hāngai ana te tikanga ki te kupu Pākehā kotahi. He titiro whakamua kei roto i tēnei āhuatanga, arā, ko te tūmanako ka tāia tētahi puna kupu Māori ā taihoa ake nei, arā, i roto i ngā tau tata ki mua.

Kua hoatu anō hoki ki tēnei o ngā *Matatiki* te katoa o ngā ingoa o ngā rā me ngā marama ki te reo Māori, ngā whakamāori anō hoki o ētahi tāone nui, whenua rānei o tāwāhi. Hāngai tonu te whakamāori i ngā tāone me ngā whenua nei i runga i tā te taringa i rongo ai. Waihoki, e mōhio ana Te Taura Whiri ki te kawa o te taringa Māori ki te kupu **Niu Tīreni**, me te reka anō hoki ki te kupu Aotearoa. Kua raua mai anō ngā ingoa o ngā tari Kāwanatanga e whai ingoa Māori ana.

Ngā Tikanga Tuhi

Whai muri tonu mai i te kupu matua, ko te kupu Pākehā e tohu ana i te wāhi e pīkauhia ana e taua kupu i roto i tētahi rerenga kōrero. Ko ngā pīkaunga-kupu e noho mai ana i tēnei o ngā *Matatiki*, kāore e neke atu i ēnei e whai ake nei:

> *kupu ingoa, kupumahi whai hoa, kupumahi takakau, kupu āhua, hikumahi, tīpakonga kōrero*

E kore ake ai te hinengaro e tino whīwhiwhi i te kaha noho mai o te mahi a te pīkaunga-kupu, kei raro katoa ngā kupu ingoa tōpū i te maru o te '*kupu ingoa*'.

He whānui tonu ngā tikanga o ētahi o ngā kupu Pākehā e noho mai ana i te papakupu nei. Mēnā e whēnei ana te āhua, kei konā e taiepa ana te whāitinga o te whakaaro e whāia ana, kei muri tonu mai i te pīkaunga-kupu.

Whai muri tonu mai i ēnei whakawhāitinga, ko te kupu Māori e hāngai ana ki te kupu Pākehā matua me tōna pūtakenga mai. I tīkina atu te nuinga o ēnei takenga mai i te papakupu a Wīremu, ā, ki te kore i reira, i ētahi atu pukapuka, i te reo Māori tonu rānei e kōrerohia nuitia ana huri i te motu.

Te Matatiki

Preface

Objectives

The Māori Language Commission, established in 1987 under the Māori Language Act, has been given the statutory responsibility of promoting Māori as a living language.

The Commission sees itself as having two principal objectives. The first objective is to sustain and nurture the existing language, the second to extend the linguistic range of Māori by weaving together into new combinations current speech, and words and phrases which have fallen out of everyday use, for example:

chilly-bin *noun* tokanga mātao [tokanga W.433 'large basket for food' mātao W.189 'cold']
women's refuge *noun* whare punanga [punanga W.310 'any place used as a refuge for non-combatants in troubled days. Hence kāinga punanga, whare punanga, pā punanga']

Content

Te Matatiki was first published in 1992. This revised edition develops the original in two important respects: it includes over 2,000 previously unpublished terms and each entry is provided with its Māori derivation.

The Commission does not claim to be the originator of all new terms used here. A number of entries, particularly those from specialist areas, have not been previously included in any general dictionary of the Māori language. For example the majority of mathematical terms were produced by the team of Māori mathematicians working on *Te Tauākī Marautanga Pāngarau - He Tauira*, published in 1994. Other words already in common usage have been used to generate new terms and combinations, e.g. **waka** 'vehicle' has been used to form **waka tuarangi** 'spacecraft'; **rorohiko** 'computer' has been used to create **rorohiko pōnaho** 'laptop'.

Similarly, borrowings from English which have become embedded in the language such as **parāoa** 'flour' have been made use of in this way (e.g. kihu parāoa 'spaghetti').

In some instances, on the basis of further research, the Commission has preferred a word or term other than that previously published in *Te Matatiki* for example, **pukepoto** ('a dark-blue earth used as a pigment') is included here for 'dark blue' rather than **ōrangiuri** (a neologism from **ō** 'of' **rangi** 'sky' and **uri** 'dark, deep in colour').

In addition to the main text, an appendix lists the Māori names of Government agencies which have an official Māori name, the Māori names of days and months, as well as a selection of international place names, predominantly derived from English.

Conventions

Ease of use and simplicity have been the determining factors in the arrangement of dictionary entries. Headwords are identified as *noun*, *transitive verb*, *intransitive verb*, *adjective*, *adverb* and *phrase*, compound nouns being included in the general category of *noun*. Where an intransitive verb in Māori is used to perform a transitive function in English, or vice versa, the difference is noted in the text.

Many of the English words which appear in this dictionary have more than one meaning or application. Where the meaning or application of a word is restricted or specialist, clarification is provided by a gloss, followed by the translation of the headword together with its Māori derivation. For example:

crust *noun* (*geology*) kirinuku [kiri W.119 'skin' nuku W.225 'the earth']
hole in one *phrase* (*golf*) kotahi atu, āe [(idiom) kotahi W.147 'one' atu W.20 'to indicate a direction or motion onwards or away from the speaker' āe W.1 'yes']

Most derivations are taken from H.W. Williams *A Dictionary of the Māori Language*. Many words are derived from *Te Matatiki* itself, from common usage, and from a variety of other sources.

A list of abbreviations and sources used in the dictionary is given below.

Best *Astronomical Knowledge*
Best *Games and Pastimes*
Best *Māori Agriculture*
Best *Māori Division of Time*
Best *Māori Religion and Mythology*
Best *Spiritual and Mental Concepts*
Best *Tūhoe, Children of the Mist*
Biggs {*The Complete English-Māori Dictionary*}
Brougham and Reed
common usage {derived from common usage e.g. **waka rererangi** common usage 'aeroplane'}
< Eng. {borrowing from English e.g. **tāke** < Eng. 'tax'}
JB *Māori Plant Names*
Salmond {*Hui*}
Smith *The Lore of the Whare Wānanga*
TM {*Te Matatiki*}
W. {*A Dictionary of the Māori Language*}

In a small number of cases an example has been provided to illuminate Māori usage.

Bibliography

Beever, J.A. *A Dictionary of Māori Plant Names* (Auckland, Auckland Botanical Society, 1991.)

Biggs, B. *The Complete English-Māori Dictionary* (Auckland, Auckland University Press, 1981.)

Brougham, A.E. & Reed, A.W. *Māori Proverbs* (Auckland, Heinemann Reed, 1963.)

Williams, H.W. *A Dictionary of the Māori Language* (Wellington, Government Print, 1985.)

Māori Language Commission *Te Matatiki* (Wellington, Te Taura Whiri i te Reo Māori, 1992.)

Best, E. *The Astronomical Knowledge of the Māori* (Wellington, Government Print, 1978.)

— *Games and Pastimes of the Māori* (Wellington, Government Print, 1976.)

— *Māori Agriculture* (Wellington, Government Print, 1976.)

— *The Māori Division of Time* (Wellington, Government Print, 1986.)

— *Māori Religion and Mythology* (Wellington, Government Print, Wellington, 1925.)

— *Spiritual and Mental Concepts of the Māori* (Wellington, Government Print, Wellington, 1986.)

— *Tūhoe, Children of the Mist* (Wellington, A.H & A.W. Reed, 1925)

Salmond, A. *Hui* (Auckland, Reed Methuen, 1975.)

Smith, S. Percy *The Lore of the Whare Wānanga* (New Plymouth, Thomas Avery, 1913.)

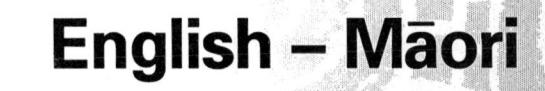

English – Māori
Reo Pākehā – Reo Māori

A

abacus *noun* takatātai [taka W.366 'drop down' tātai TM 'calculate']

abandon *transitive verb* whakarere [W.338 'cast away, reject, leave, forsake']

abdominal exercise *noun* (*sport*) whakapūioio puku [whaka- W.486 'causative prefix' *to make* pūioio W.306 'strong, muscular, sinewy' puku W.308 'abdomen, stomach']

abnormality *noun* pīari [W.279 'deformed, stunted person']

abominable snowman *noun* kōwao puaheiri [kōwao W.152 'living in the woods, wild' puaheiri W.301 'snow']

aborigine *noun* māori [W.179 'person of the native race']

absent-minded *adjective* hinengaro makere [common usage hinengaro W.51 'seat of the thoughts and emotions' makere W.169 'be lost, abandoned, fail, cease']

absolute value *noun* (*mathematics*) uara pū [uara W.465 'value' pū W.300 'origin, source']

absorb *transitive verb* whakawhenumi [whaka- W.486 'causative prefix' *to make* whenumi W.494 'be out of sight, be eclipsed, be consumed' whakawhenumi 'mix up one thing with another']

absorbed, become *intransitive verb* whenumi [W.494 'be out of sight, be eclipsed, be consumed']

abstruse *adjective* ākahukahu [W.6 'indistinct, scarcely visible']

abuse *noun* tūkino [W.450 'ill-treat, use with violence, distressed, in trouble']

abuse, sexual *noun* taitōkai [tai W.361 'anger, rage, violence' tai W.362 'prefix, sometimes with a qualifying force' tōkai W.433 'sexual intercourse']

abuse, solvent *noun* hongi wairou [hongi W.58 'sniff' wai W.474 'liquid, oil etc.' rou W.349 'intoxicated']

accelerate *transitive verb* whakatere [whaka- W.486 'causative prefix' *to make* tere W.412 'swift, moving quickly, active, hasty']

accelerate *intransitive verb* patete [W.271 'move along']

accelerator *noun* (*vehicle*) whakatere [whaka- W.486 'causative prefix' *to make* tere W.412 'swift, moving quickly, active, hasty']

accent *noun* (*mark indicating correct pronunciation*) tohu whakahua kupu [tohu W.431 'mark' whakahua W.64 'pronounce' kupu W.157 'word']

accessory *noun* (*equipment*) tautara [W.403 'fasten, affix']

accessory *noun* (*accompanying item*) whakarawe [W.332 'fitting, furnishing']

accident and emergency unit *noun* taiwhanga mate whawhati tata [taiwhanga TM 'room' mate whawhati tata TM 'emergency']

ACC levy *noun* utu āwhina hunga whara [utu W.471 'price' āwhina W.25 'assist' hunga W.70 'people' whara W.489 'be struck, be hit accidentally']

account *noun* (*statement of expenditure*) kaute [< Eng. 'account']

account, autocall *noun* pūtea tangonoa [pūtea TM 'fund' tango W.380 'remove' noa W.222 'without restraint']

account, bank *noun* pūtea [W.317 'bag or basket of fine woven flax']

account, cheque *noun* pūtea haki [pūtea TM 'account' haki < Eng. 'cheque']

account, joint *noun* pūtea tukutahi [pūtea TM 'account' tukutahi W.452 'together, simultaneous']

account, savings *noun* pūtea penapena [pūtea TM 'account' penapena W.277 'take care of, tend, husband']
account book *noun* pukapuka kaute [pukapuka W.306 'book' kaute common usage 'accounting']
account for *transitive verb* whakamārama [W.180 'make clear, explain']
account payee only *phrase* ki te ingoa e mau nei [ki W.116 'to' ingoa W.78 'name' mau W.196 'fixed']
accounting *noun* (*audit*) mahi kaute [mahi W.163 'work, be occupied with' kaute common usage 'account']
accounting period *noun* wā kaute [wā W.472 'time, interval' mahi kaute TM 'accounting']
accreditation *noun* tohutuku [tohu W.431 'mark, sign, proof' tuku W.451 'present']
accrual accounting *noun* kaute tahua [mahi kaute TM 'accounting' tahua TM 'accumulated funds']
accumulated funds *noun* tahua [W.360 'heap of food, sum of money']
accusation *noun* whakatuaki [TM 'accuse']
accuse *transitive verb* whakatuaki [W.445 'blame']
accused *noun* (*justice*) whakatuaki [W.445 'blame']
achievement *noun* whakatutukitanga [whaka- W.486 'causative prefix' *to make tutuki* W.450 'be finished, be completed']
achiever *noun* ihupuku [W.75 'hesitating, scrupulous, industrious, eager']
acid *noun* waikawa [wai W.474 'water liquid' kawa W.109 'bitter, sour, unpleasant to the taste']
acid, strong *noun* waikawa marohi [waikawa TM 'acid' marohi W.183 'strong']
acid, weak *noun* waikawa ngori [waikawa TM 'acid' ngori W.235 'weak, listless']
acid rain *noun* uakawa [ua W.465 'rain' waikawa TM 'acid']
acidic *adjective* hīmoemoe [hīmoemoe W.50 'acid, sour' moemoe W.205 'sour, acid, i.e., causing one to close the eyes']
acidity *noun* waikawatanga [waikawa TM 'acid']
acrylic *noun, adjective* kiriaku [kiri W.119 'skin' akuaku W.7 'firm, strong']
act *noun* (*theatre*) manga [W.177 'branch of a tree']

acute *noun* (*punctuation*) tohutio [tohu W.431 'mark' tio W.420 'cry']
acute *adjective* (*sudden, of illness, etc.*) pā whakarere [pā W.244 'be struck, overcome' whakarere W.338 'suddenly']
adapt *intransitive verb* urutau [uru W.469 'enter' tau W.396 'settle down']
adaptation *noun* urutaunga [urutau TM 'adapt']
adaptation, behavioural *noun* urutaunga whanonga [urutaunga TM 'adaptation' whanonga W.487 'conduct, behaviour']
adaptation, physiological *noun* urutaunga whaiaroaro [urutaunga TM 'adaptation' whaiaroaro TM 'physiological']
adaptation, structural *noun* (*biology*) urutaunga tinana [urutaunga TM 'adaptation tinana 'body']
adaptive features *noun* āhuatanga urutau [āhuatanga TM 'feature' urutau TM 'adapt']
add *transitive verb* (*mathematics*) tāpiri [W.384 'add']
addict *noun* kiriwara [kiri W.119 'person' waranga TM 'addiction']
addicted *adjective* warawara (ki) [TM 'addiction']
addiction *noun* waranga [W.479 warawara 'crave']
addition *noun* (*mathematics*) tāpiritanga [tāpiri W.384 'add']
adjacent *adjective* pātata [W.270 'near']
adjective *noun* kupu āhua [kupu W.157 'word' āhua W.4 'character, appearance']
adjourn *transitive verb* hiki [W.49 'lift up']
adjourned *adjective* hiki [TM 'adjourn']
adjourned sine die *phrase* waiho kia tārewa [waiho W.475 'let be' tārewa W.391 'hanging, unsettled']
administer *transitive verb* (*manage*) whakahaere [W.30 'conduct any business']
administer *transitive verb* (*give out*) tohungarua [W.431 'dole out']
administer *transitive verb* (*give to patient for consumption*) whāngai [W.488 'feed']
adolescence *noun*, taiohinga [W.364 'young, youthful']
adolescent, female *noun* kōhine [W.125 'girl']
adolescent, female *noun* taitamāhine [W.365 'young woman']

adolescent, male *noun* taitama [W.365 'young man']

advanced *adjective* (*course, qualification etc.*) whatutoto [W.492 'red heartwood of tōtara or matai']

advantage *noun* (*tennis*) tata kaikape [tata W.393 'near' kaikape TM 'game']

advantage line *noun* pae kaneke [pae W.245 'margin, boundary' kaneke W.93 'progress']

adventure *noun* mahi mātātoa [mahi W.163 'occupation, do, perform' mātātoa W.191 'fearless, active, vigorous, energetic']

adventure playground *noun* papa tākaro [papa W.259 'earth floor or site' pukutākaro W.309 'playful, sportive']

adventurous *adjective* mātātoa [W.191 'fearless, active, vigorous, energetic']

adverb *noun* hikumahi [hiku W.50 'tail of a fish or reptile, rear of an army' kupumahi TM 'verb']

advertisement *noun* pānui [pānui W.257 'advertise publicly, publish, public notice']

advertising *noun* pānuitanga [pānui W.257 'advertise publicly, publish, public notice']

advocate *noun* kaitaunaki [kai W.86 'a prefix to transitive verbs to form nouns denoting an agent' taunaki W.400 'support, reinforce'], kaitautoko [W.404 'prop up, support']

advocate *transitive verb* taunaki [W.400 'support, reinforce'], tautoko [W.404 'support']

aerial *noun* hihi irirangi [hihi W.48 'long plume, feelers of crayfish, long slender appendages' reo irirangi W.80 'radio']

aerial *noun* pūhihi [pūhihi W.304 'antennae of insect']

aerobics *noun* haukori [W.40 'move briskly']

aerosol *noun* rehu matūriki [rehu W.344 'spray, fine dust' matūriki TM 'particle'], wainehu [wai W.474 'water, liquid' nehu W.220 'fine powder, dust, spray']

aesthetically pleasing *adjective* rerehua [W.338 'pleasant to the sight, beauty']

aesthetics *noun* taha rerehua [taha W.357 'side' rerehua W.338 'pleasant to the sight, beauty']

affable *adjective* matareka [W.190 'pleasant, like, be fond of']

affidavit *noun* he tikanga, he pononga [W.291 'an expression of emphatic assent, approval or affirmation']

affirm *transitive verb* whakaū [whakaū W.464 'make firm']

affirmation *noun* whakaū pono [whakaū W.464 'make firm' pono W.291 'true']

affix *noun* (*language*) kuhi [W.154 'insert']

afternoon tea *noun* paramanawa [W.264 'refreshment']

agar *noun* maremaretai [W.181 'jellyfish']

agency *noun* pokapū [W.289 'centre'], pūtahi [W.316 'join, meet, as two paths or streams running one into the other']

agenda *noun* rārangi take [rārangi W.324 'line, rank, row' take TM 'matter']

agenda, hidden *noun* take huna [take W.370 'subject of an argument etc.' huna W.69 'concealed'], take atu anō [take W.370 'subject of an argument etc.' atu W.20 'other' anō W.10 'again, also']

agent *noun* (*one who acts on behalf of someone else*) māngai [W.177 'mouth']

aggravated robbery *noun* whānako rupe [whānako W.487 'steal' rupe W.352 'shake violently, treat with violence']

aggregate *transitive verb* whakahiato [W.48 'collect together']

aggregate *noun* hiatonga [hiato W.48 'be gathered together']

agoraphobia *noun* mae ahoaho [mae W.162 'paralysed with fear' ahoaho W.3 'open space']

agricultural *adjective* ahuwhenua [ahuwhenua W.3 'cultivate the soil']

agriculturalist *noun* kaiahuwhenua [kai W.86 'a prefix to transitive verbs to form nouns denoting an agent' ahuwhenua W.3 'cultivate the soil']

AIDS (*acronym*) Mate Ārai Kore [mate W.192 'sickness' ārai W.14 'ward off, screen' kore W.140 'no, not']

aim *noun* (*objective*) whāinga [whai W.484 'follow, pursue, aim at']

aim, take *transitive verb* arotahi [W.17 'look in one direction, look steadily']

air freshener *noun* tāwhiri [W.409 'gum of pittosporum, used as a scent'], tīere [W.414 'scent']

air gun *noun* pū kurutē [pū W.300 'gun' kurutē W.159 'compress (air)']

air waves *noun* (*radio*) aratuku [ara W.13 'way, path, means of conveyance' tuku W.451 'send']

air-conditioning *noun* whāhauhau [whā W.484 'causative prefix' hauhau W.38 'cool']

aircraft carrier *noun* kawe rererangi [kawe W.111 'carry, convey' waka rererangi common usage 'aeroplane']

airforce *noun* tauārangi [taua W.397 'hostile expedition, army' rangi W.323 'sky']

air-mail *noun, adjective* kōpaki rangi [kōpaki TM 'mail' rangi W.323 'sky, heaven']

airport *noun* papa rererangi [papa W.259 'earth floor or site' waka rererangi common usage 'aeroplane'], taunga rererangi [taunga W.396 'resting place, anchorage' waka rererangi common usage 'aeroplane']

airshot *noun* (*golf*) nape [W.218 'make a false stroke with the paddle']

alarm *noun* pūoho [pūoho W.311 'start, take alarm']

albatross *noun* (*golf*) toroa [W.439 'albatross']

albumen *noun* kahu [W.84 'white of an egg']

alcoholic *noun* (*person*) wara waipiro [waranga TM 'addiction' waipiro common usage 'alcohol']

alcoholism *noun* wara waipiro [waranga TM 'addiction' waipiro common usage 'alcohol']

aldehyde *noun* whāparo-tahi [whā W.484 'causative prefix' paro W.268 'dry' tahi W.359 'one']

algae *noun* pūkohu wai [pūkohu W.308 'moss' wai W.474 'water']

algal bloom *noun* pūkohu ngaruru [pūkohu W.308 'moss, mossy' ngaruru W.231 'strong in growth, flourishing']

algebra *noun* mahi taurangi [mahi W.163 'perform, work at' taurangi TM 'variable']

algebraic *adjective* taurangi [taurangi TM 'variable']

algorithm *noun* hātepe [W.38 'proceed in an orderly manner, follow a sequence']

alienated, become *transitive verb* mōriroriro [W.210 'become estranged']

aliphatic *adjective* (*chemistry*) memeka [mekameka W.200 'chain']

alkali *noun* pāpāhua [W.248 'plunder']

alkane *noun* waiwaro tahi [waiwaro TM 'hydrocarbon' tahi W.359 'one']

alkane (*used as suffix*) -waro [waiwaro TM 'hydrocarbon']

alkene *noun* waiwaro rua [waiwaro TM 'hydrocarbon' rua W.349 'two']

alkyne *noun* waiwaro toru [waiwaro TM 'hydrocarbon' toru W.441 'three']

allergic *adjective* pāwera [W.273 'sore, tender to the touch, affected'] *e.g. Pāwera katoa au i te hae.* 'I am allergic to pollen'

allergy *noun* mate pāwera [mate W.192 'sickness' pāwera W.273 'sore, tender to the touch, affected']

alligator *noun* kumi ihupoto [kumi W.156 'a huge fabulous reptile' ihu W.75 'nose' poto W.297 'short']

allowance *noun* (*finance*) utu tāpui [utu W.471 'reward' tāpui W.385 'set aside, reserve']

alloy *noun* pūhui konganuku [pūhui TM 'compound' konganuku TM 'natural metal']

almost *adverb* kainamu [W.88 'be within a little of'] *e.g. Kei te aha te tāima? Kua kainamu ki te whā.* 'What's the time? It's almost four.'

alpha particle *noun* matūriki ārepa [matūriki TM 'particle' ārepa < Eng. 'alpha']

alphabet *noun* wakapū [waka W.478 'canoe' wakawaka 'row' pū TM 'letter of alphabet']

alphabetise *transitive verb* whakarārangi-ā-pū [whakarārangi W.324 'arrange in a line or row' ā W.1 'after the manner of' pū TM 'letter of alphabet']

alphabet, letter of pū [W.300 'base, foundation']

alternating *adjective* hohoko [W.57 'alternate']

altitude *noun* teitei [W.410 'high, lofty']

alto *noun* reo pekerangi [reo W.336 'voice, tone' pekerangi W.276 'a voice pitched above the rest in singing']

aluminium *noun* konumohe [konu- TM 'prefix denoting natural metal' mohe W.205 'soft, yielding']

alveolar *noun* paengao [pae W.244 'gum, border, edge' ngao W.229 'palate']

alveolus *noun* miru [mirumiru Biggs 23 'bubble']

amateur *noun* (*unskilled person*) ringarapa [ringa W.341 rapa W.325 'awkward, unskilful, inexpert']

amateur *adjective* (*unpaid*) utukore [utu 'pay' kore 'no']

ambassador *noun* māngai kāwanatanga [māngai W.177 'mouth' kāwanatanga < Eng. 'government']

ambulance *noun* waka tūroro [waka common usage 'vehicle' tūroro W.460 'sick person']

amendment *noun* (*justice*) ture whakatikatika [ture W.459 'law' whakatika W.417 'correct']

ammeter *noun* ine iahiko [ine W.78 'measure' ia W.74 'current' hiko W.50 'flash, as lightning']

ammonia *noun* haukini [hau TM 'gas' kini W.118 'acrid, pungent']

amniotic fluid *noun* waikahu [wai W.474 'water' kahu W.84 'membrane enveloping foetus']

amniotic sac *noun* kahu [W.84 'membrane enveloping foetus']

ampere *noun* wae iahiko [waeine TM 'unit of measurement' ia W.74 'current' hiko common usage 'electricity']

amphibian *noun* ika oneone [ika W.76 'fish' oneone W.240 'land']

amplifier *noun* tīwerawera [W.427 'loud, intense']

amplify *transitive verb* tīwera [tīwerawera W.427 'loud, intense']

amplitude *noun* kaha tīwera [kaha W.82 'strength' tīwera TM 'amplify']

amputate *transitive verb* pororere [W.295 'cut off, lopped off']

anaesthesia *noun* rehunga [rehu W.334 'render drowsy or unconscious']

anaesthetic, general *noun* rehu tokitoki [rehu W.334 'render drowsy or unconscious' tokitoki W.434 'altogether, without exception']

anaesthetic, local *noun* whakakēkerewai [whaka- W.486 'causative prefix' *to make* kēkerewai W.114 'numb, numbness']

anaesthetist *noun* kairehu [kai W.86 'a prefix to transitive verbs to form nouns denoting an agent' rehu W.334 'render drowsy or unconscious']

analgesic *noun* rongoā patu mamae [rongoā W.346 'remedy' patu W.272 'subdue' mamae W.162 'pain']

analyse *transitive verb* tātari [W.391 'sift, sieve']

analysis *noun* tātaritanga [tātari TM 'analyse']

ancillary *adjective* turuki [W.461 'anything supplementary or by way of support']

angiosperm *noun* whaipua [whai W.483 'possessing' pua W.301 'flower']

angle, acute *noun* koki tāhapa [koki W.129 'angle' tāhapa W.358 'at an acute angle']

angle, co-interior koki tauroto [koki W.129 'angle', tau W.396 'come to anchor, lie to' roto W.348 'the inside']

angle, complementary *noun* koki whakahāngai [koki W.129 'angle' whaka- W.486 'causative prefix' *to make* hāngai TM 'right-angle']

angle, corresponding *noun* koki tūrite [koki W.129 'angle' tūnga W.443 'place of standing' rite W.343 'alike, corresponding']

angle, interior *noun* koki whakaroto [koki W.129 'angle' whakaroto TM 'inwards']

angle, oblique *noun* koki hōtiu [koki W.129 'angle' hōtiu W.62 'oblique, inclined']

angle, obtuse koki hāpūpū [koki W.129 'angle' hāpūpū W.36 'blunt']

angle, reflex *noun* koki mōwaho [koki W.129 'angle' mōwaho W.212 'on the outside']

angle, right *adjective* koki hāngai [koki W.129 'angle' W.34 'at right angles']

angle, supplementary *noun* koki whakarārangi [koki W.129 'angle' whaka- W.486 'causative prefix' *to make* rārangi W.324 'line']

angle, vertically opposite koki tauaro [koki W.129 'angle' tauaro W.397 'facing towards one, opposite']

angle of elevation *noun* koki rewa [koki W.129 'angle' rewa W.339 'be elevated, be high up']

ankle-length skirt *noun* panekoti hauraro [panekoti common usage 'skirt' hauraro W.41 'low down, pendent']

ankylosaurus *noun* mokomakiki [moko W.207 'a general term for lizards, huge mythical creature of lizard-like shape' makiki W.170 'stiff']

annelid *noun* (*biology*) ngunu [W.236 'worm']

annotated diagram *noun* mahere whai whakamārama [mahere W.163 'plan' whai W.484 'possessing, equipped with' whakamārama W.180 'explain, illuminate']

annual *adjective* ā-tau [ā W.1 'after the manner of' tau W.395 'year']

annual leave *noun* whakamatuatanga-ā-tau [whakamatua W.195 'rest, pause, after an effort' ā-tau TM 'annual']

anode *noun* pito-tā [pito W.284 'end, extremity' tā common usage used to indicate indefinite locality]

anorexia *noun* whakatiki hārukiruki [whakatiki W.418 'keep short of food' hārukiruki W.38 'intensive'], mate whakatiki [mate W.192 'sickness' whakatiki W.418 'keep short of food']

answer *noun* (*mathematics*) otinga [oti W.242 'finished']

answer *noun* (*education*) hua [W.64 'fruit, product']

antacid *noun* patu tokopā [patu W.272 'subdue' tokopā W.435 'heartburn, indigestion, belch']

antagonist *noun* kiritautohe [kiri W.119 'person' tautohe W.404 'contend, persist, contest, quarrel']

antelope *noun* koutata [W.151 'smooth, sleek']

antenna *noun* (*aerial*) pūhihi [pūhihi W.304 'antennae of insect']

anther *noun* (*flower*) ketehae [kete W.115 'basket' hae W.29 'pollen']

anthropologist *noun* tohunga tikanga tangata [tohunga TM 'expert' mātauranga tikanga tangata TM 'anthropology'], kaimātai tikanga tangata [kaimātai TM '-ologist' mātauranga tikanga tangata TM 'anthropology']

anthropology *noun* mātauranga tikanga tangata [mātauranga common usage 'knowledge' tikanga 'custom, practice' tangata W.379 'human being']

antibiotic *noun* rongoā paturopi [rongoā W.346 'medicine' paturopi TM 'antibody']

antibody *noun* paturopi [patu W.272 'kill' ropi W.347 'body']

anticyclone *noun* kurahaupō [Best *Astronomical Knowledge* 19 'sign of good weather']

anti-emetic *noun* patu hiaruaki [patu W.272 'subdue' hia W.47 'wish, impulse' ruaki W.350 'vomit']

antigen *noun* akiaki paturopi [akiaki W.7 'urge on' paturopi TM 'antibody']

antioxidant *noun* tāpiri irahiko [tāpiri W.384 'add' irahiko TM 'electron']

anti-perspirant *noun* patu mōrūruru [patu W.272 'strike, subdue' mōrūruru W.210 'odour of human sweat']

antiseptic *noun, adjective* patuero [W.272 'subdue, beat' ero W.28 'putrid']

antitoxin *noun* patu-tāoke [patu W.272 'subdue, beat' tāoke TM 'toxin']

antler *noun* pihi [W.280 'shoot, sprout']

anvil *noun* (*ear*) kurutangi [W.159 'stone beater']

anvil *noun* paekuru [pae W.244 'transverse beam' kuru W.159 'strike, pound']

apartheid *noun* whakatāuke tangata [whaka- W.486 'causative prefix' *to make* tāuke W.399 'apart, separate' tangata W.379 'human being']

apartment block *noun* whaitua noho [whaitua W.485 'region, space' noho W.223 'dwell']

apathetic *adjective* ngākau-kore [W.227 'disinclined, having no heart for anything, dispirited']

apathy *noun* ngākau-kore [W.227 'disinclined, having no heart for anything, dispirited']

aperture *noun* piere [W.279 'cleft, crack, chink']

aphid *noun* ngō [ngongo W.234 'juice of flowers etc., suck']

apiarist *noun* kairaupī [kai W.86 'a prefix to transitive verbs to form nouns denoting an agent' raupī W.330 'take care of, cover up' rau W.328 'gather into a basket etc.' pī < Eng. 'bee']

apiary *noun* pīhaonga [pīhao W.279 'surround' pī < Eng. 'bee' hao W.35 'catch, enclose']

apocalypse *noun* poautinitini [W.286 'tribulation, evil, death']

apologise, I *phrase* taku hē [taku W.374 'my' hē W.43 'error, mistake, fault']

apostrophe *noun* pakini [W.254 'nick, notch']

apparatus *noun* taputapu [W.385 'goods, appliances'], pānga [pā W.243 'be connected with']

appendage *noun* tautara [W.403 'fasten, affix']
appendicitis *noun* hiku whēkau kakā [hiku whēkau TM 'appendix' kakā TM 'inflammation']
appendix *noun* (*written material*) tāpiritanga [tāpiri W.384 'append, supplement']
appendix *noun* (*anatomy*) hiku whēkau [hiku W.50 'tail, rear, tip' whēkau W.493 'entrails']
appetiser *noun* kumamatanga [W.155 'something to tempt the appetite']
appliance *noun* pūrere [pūrere TM 'machine']
applicant *noun* kaitono [kai W.86 'a prefix to transitive verbs to form nouns denoting an agent' tono W.436 'bid']
application *noun* tono [W.436 'bid']
application form *noun* pukatono [puka TM 'form' tono TM 'apply']
apply *transitive verb* (*make relevant*) whakahāngai [whaka- W.486 'causative prefix' *to make* hāngai TM 'relevant']
apply *intransitive verb* (*submit application*) tono [W.436 'bid']
appoint *transitive verb* whakatū [W.443 'set up'], kopou [W.138 'appoint']
appointment *noun* (*employment*) kopounga [kopou TM 'appoint']
apprentice *noun* pia [W.279 'the first order of learners being initiated in esoteric lore']
approach run *noun* whakatata [W. 393 'approach']
approximation *noun* whakaawhiwhitanga [whaka- W.486 'causative prefix' *to make* āwhiwhi W.25 'approximate, resemble']
aqualung *noun* puoto hāora [puoto W.311 'vessel' hāora TM 'oxygen']
aquatic *adjective* rōwai [rō W.344 roto W.348 'in' wai W.474 'water']
arachnid *noun* pūwere [pūwerewere W.318 'spider']
arc *noun* pewa [W.278 'anything bow-shaped']
arch *noun* (*foot*) waerewa [wae W.172 'foot, the middle' rewa W.339 'elevated, raised up']
archaeology *noun* mātai whaipara tangata [mātai W.187 'inspect, examine' whaipara W.485 'remains' tangata W.379 'human being']
architect *noun* kaihoahoa [kai W.86 'a prefix to transitive verbs to form nouns denoting an agent' hoahoa W.54 'plan of a house']
architecture *noun* hoahoanga [hoahoa W.54 'plan of a house']
archive *noun* pūranga [pū W.300 'source, base' pūranga W.312 'heap, lie in a heap']
area *noun* (*mathematics*) horahanga [hora W.59 'spread out']
arithmetic *noun* tauhanga [tau TM 'number' hanga W.34 'make, practise']
armchair *noun* hānea [hāneanea W.33 'pleasant, comfortable']
array *noun* (*mathematics*) mahere huānga [mahere W.163 'plan' huānga W.65 'relative, member of same clan']
arrest warrant *noun* whakamana hopu tangata [whakamana TM 'warrant' hopu W.59 'catch, seize' tangata W.379 'human being']
arrow diagram *noun* hoahoa pere [hoahoa W.54 'lay out, plan' pere W.278 'dart'], kauwhata pere [kauwhata TM 'graph' pere W.278 'dart']
art *noun* mahi toi [mahi W.163 'work, occupation' toi W.431 'art']
art, visual *noun* kōwaiwai [kōwaiwai W.151 'an ancient style of painting for adorning the person and dwellings']
art and craft *noun* kōwaiwai-haratau [kōwaiwai W.151 'an ancient style of painting for adorning the person and dwellings' haratau W.37 'dexterous, suitable, approved']
artery *noun* iatuku [ia W.74 'current' tuku W.451 'send'], ia kawe hāora [ia W.74 'current' kawe W.111 'carry, convey' hāora TM 'oxygen']
artery, cerebral *noun* iatuku roro [iatuku TM 'artery' roro W.347 'brains']
artesian bore *noun* rau matatiki [W.191 'strong gushing spring of water']
arthritis *noun* kaiponapona [kaikōiwi W.88 'rheumatism' ponapona W.291 'joint in the arm or leg']
arthropod *noun* angawaho [anga W.10 'skeleton, shell' waho W.474 'the outside']
article *noun* (*syntax*) kuputohu [kupu W.157 'word' tohu W.431 'show, point out, look towards']
articulate *adjective* wahapū [W.473 'eloquent']

articulated

articulated *adjective* tautō [W.404 'trail, drag']
artificial *adjective* waihanga [waihanga W.485 'make, build, construct']
artificial sweetener *noun* āwenewene [W.24 'very sweet']
artistic *adjective* rerehua [W.338 'pleasant to the sight, beauty']
asbestos *noun* papa kiripaka [papa W.259 'anything broad, flat and hard' kiripaka W.119 'flint, quartz']
asbestosis *noun* mate kiripaka [mate W.192 'sickness' papa kiripaka TM 'asbestos']
asexual *adjective* (*reproduction*) tōkai-kore [tōkai W.433 'copulate' kore W.140 'no, not']
asexual *adjective* (*organism*) taihema-kore [taihema W.363 'genitals of either sex' kore W.140 'no, not']
aspect *noun* (*facet*) āhuatanga [W.4 'likeness']
asphalt *noun* pakakū [W.251 'a bituminous substance found on the beaches']
assess *transitive verb* arotake [aro W.16 'turn towards' take W.370 'reason, base'], aromatawai [aro W.16 'turn towards' matawai W.192 'look closely']
assessment *noun* arotake [TM 'assess']
assessment *noun* aromatawai [TM 'assess']
asset *noun* hua [W.64 'fruit, product' huanga 'advantage, benefit']
asset, current *noun* hua wātea [hua TM 'asset' wātea W.480 'free']
asset, fixed *noun* hua pūmau [hua TM 'asset' pūmau W.309 'fixed']
assimilated *adjective* whenumi [W.494 'be eclipsed, be consumed']
assimilation policy *noun* tikanga whakawhenumi [tikanga W.416 'rule, plan' whakawhenumi W.494 'mix up one thing with another']
assistant *noun* kaiāwhina [kai W.86 'a prefix to transitive verbs to form nouns denoting an agent' āwhina W.25 'assist, benefit'], whakamahiri [W.164 'assist']
associative *adjective* (*mathematics*) herekore [here W.46 'tie, tie up' kore W.140 'no, not']
asterisk *noun* whetūriki [whetū W.496 'star' riki W.340 'small']
asteroid *noun* aorangi iti [aorangi TM 'planet' iti W.80 'small']

astigmatism *noun* (*vision*) arotahi takarepa [arotahi TM 'lens' takarepa W.369 'deficient, imperfect']
astronaut *noun* kaipōkai tuarangi [kai W.86 'a prefix to transitive verbs to form nouns denoting an agent' pōkai W.289 'travel about' tuarangi TM 'outer space']
astronomy *noun* tātai arorangi [W.393 'study the heavens for guidance in navigation etc.']
asymmetric bars *noun* tāuhu karawhiti [tāuhu W.360 'horizontal bar' karawhiti W.99 'uneven, irregular']
at risk *phrase* mōrea [mōrearea W.210 'exposed to danger']
-ate (*chemistry, salt or ester of -ic acid'*) pākawa [pāhare TM 'salt, ester' waikawa TM 'acid']
athlete *noun* kaipara [Best *Games and Pastimes* 23 'athletics']
athletics *noun* kaipara [Best *Games and Pastimes* 23 'athletics']
atlas *noun* pukapuka mahere whenua [pukapuka W.306 'book' mahere TM 'plan' whenua W.494 'land, country']
atmosphere *noun* kōhauhau [kōpaki W.135 'envelop' hau TM 'gas']
atom *noun* ngota [ngotangota W.235 'smashed to atoms']
atomic number *noun* taungota [tau TM 'number' ngota TM 'atom']
atrium *noun* (*heart*) mānawanawa [W.174 mānawanawa 'space' manawa W.174 'heart']
attachment order *noun* whakatau tangomoni [whakatau TM 'decision, settlement' tango W.380 'remove' moni < Eng. 'money']
attack line *noun* (*sport*) pae tuki [pae W.245 'margin, boundary' tuki W.450 'attack, ram']
attentive *adjective* whakarongo pīkari [W.280 '(listen) like nestlings awaiting the parent bird']
attesting witness *noun* kaitaunaki [kai W.86 'a prefix to transitive verbs to form nouns denoting an agent' taunaki W.400 'support, reinforce']
attitude, bad *noun* ngākau kawa [ngākau W.227 'heart, seat of affections or feelings' kawa W.109 'unpleasant to the taste, bitter, sour']
attitude, good *noun* ngākau reka [ngākau

W.227 'heart, seat of affections or feelings' reka W.335 'pleasant, agreeable']
attract *transitive verb* (*physics*) kukume [kumekume W.156 ' draw, attract']
audio-visual *adjective* ataata-rongo [ataata TM 'video' rongo W.346 'hear']
audit *noun, transitive verb* tātari kaute [tātari TM 'analyse' kaute TM 'account']
audit trail *noun* maheu tātari kaute [maheu W.163 'trail or track through fern or scrub' tātari kaute TM 'audit']
auditor *noun* kaitātari kaute [kai W.86 'a prefix to transitive verbs to form nouns denoting an agent' tātari kaute TM 'audit']
auditorium *noun* whare whakarauika [whare W.489 'house' whakarauika W.329 'assemble, gather together']
auditory nerve *noun* iorongo [io W.78 'nerve' rongo W.346 'hear']
autobiography *noun* haukiri [hau W.39 'resound, be published abroad' kiri W.119 'person, self']
automatic *adjective* aunoa [au W.20 'current, whirlpool' noa W.222 'spontaneously']
automatically, switch off *phrase* wetonoa [weto W.483 'be extinguished' noa W.222 'spontaneously']

autopsy *noun* tirotiro tūpāpaku [tirotiro W.424 'investigate' tūpāpaku W.456 'corpse']
available *adjective* wātea [W.480 'unoccupied, free']
avenger *noun* kairanaki [kai W.86 'a prefix to transitive verbs to form nouns denoting an agent' ranaki W.322 'avenge']
average *noun* (*mean*) tau toharite [tau TM 'number' toha W.429 'distribute' rite W.343 'alike']
aversion *noun* konekone [W.133 'repugnance'], anuanu [W.10 'offensive, disgusting']
aversion therapy *noun* tikanga whakakonekone [tikanga W.416 'method' whaka- W.486 'causative prefix' *to make* konekone W.133 'repugnance']
award *transitive verb* whakawhiwhi [W.499 'give, present']
axiom *noun* kupu pono [kupu W.157 'saying' pono W.291 'true']
axiomatic *adjective* he tikanga, he pononga [W.291 'an expression of emphatic assent, approval or affirmation']
axis *noun* tuaka [W.445 'midrib of leaf']
axis of symmetry *noun* tuaka hangarite [tuaka TM 'axis' hangarite TM 'symmetry']
axle *noun* uehā [W.465 'support']

B

baboon *noun* touwhero [tou W.442 'posterior' whero W.495 'red']
baccalaureate *noun* tohu paetahi [tohu mātauranga TM 'qualification' pae W.244 'step, bar' tahi W.359 'one, first']
back *noun* (*rugby*) tuarā [tuarā W.226 'back, support, ally']
back, left *noun* (*rugby*) tuarā mauī [tuarā TM 'back' mauī W.196 'left, on the left hand']
back, right *noun* (*rugby*) tuarā matau [tuarā TM 'back' matau W.192 'right, on the right hand']
back line players *noun* kapamuri [kapa W.95 'stand in a row or rank' muri W.214 'rear, hind part']
back row *noun* (*rugby*) taupuru muri [taupurupuru W.402 'support a person by putting the arm around him' muri W.214 'rear, hind part']
back somersault *noun* pōtēteke whakamuri [pōtēteke W.296 'turning over and over' whakamuri TM 'backwards']
backboard *noun* papamuri [papa W.259 'anything broad, flat and hard' muri W.214 'rear, back']
backhand *noun* tāmuri [tā W.354 'aim a blow at' muri W.214 'backwards']
backpack *noun* peketua [W.276 'supplementary load carried on the back']
backspace *intransitive verb* hoki whakamuri [hoki W.57 'return' whakamuri W.214 'backwards']
backstop *noun* tautopenga [whakatautopenga W.404 'rearguard']
backstroke *noun* kau kiore [Best *Games and Pastimes* 40 'swimming on the back']
backup *noun, transitive verb* (*computer*) tārua [tārua W.392 'repeat any process' tā TM 'print']
backward dive *noun* ruku whakamuri [ruku W.351 'dive' whakamuri TM 'backwards']
backwards *adverb* whakamuri [whaka- W.485 'towards, in the direction of' muri W.214 'the rear, the hind part']
bacteria *noun* kitakita [W.120 'anything very small']
bad debt *noun* nama kāore i utua [nama TM 'debt' kāore W.95 'not' utu 'return, reply']
badminton *noun* pūkura [pūtoi W.317 'bunch' kura W.157 'ornamented with feathers']
badminton player *noun* kaipatu pūkura [kai W.86 'a prefix to transitive verbs to form nouns denoting an agent' patu W.272 'strike, beat' pūkura TM 'badminton']
bag, plastic *noun* kopa kirihou [kopa W.135 'wallet, satchel' kopa whakawiri tītoki 'bag for squeezing the oil from tītoki berries' kirihou TM 'plastic']
bagpipes *noun* pūngawī [pū W.300 'pipe, tube' ngawī W.232 'squeal, howl']
bail *noun* tāhū [W.360 'horizontal rod']
bailiff *noun* kaituku hāmene [kai W.86 'a prefix to transitive verbs to form nouns denoting an agent' tuku W.451 'send' hāmene < Eng. 'summons']
bakery *noun* hereumu [W.46 'cooking shed, kitchen']
baking *noun* tōpīpī [W.437 'small native earth oven, cook in a small oven']
baking tray *noun* paetopī [pae W.245 'open shallow vessel' topī W.437 'cook in a small oven']
balaclava *noun* pōtae pūāhuru [pōtae

W.296 'covering for the head' pūahuru W.302 'close, warm' pū W.300 'source' āhuru W.4 'warm']

balance *noun, transitive verb* (*weighing apparatus*) whārite [W.343 'balance by an equivalent']

balance, electronic *noun* whārite hiko [whārite TM 'balance' hiko TM 'electronic']

balance, spring *noun* whārite whana [whārite TM 'balance' whana TM 'spring']

balance sheet *noun* ripanga kaute [ripanga TM 'spreadsheet' kaute TM 'account']

balcony *noun* parehua [W.266 'terrace, ridge']

ball *noun* (*sport*) poi [W.288 'ball, lump']

ball carrier *noun* kaikawe poi [kai W.86 'a prefix to transitive verbs to form nouns denoting an agent' kawe W.111 'carry, convey' poi TM 'ball']

ballet *noun* ori hīteki [ori W.241 'sway, move about' hītekiteki W.53 'walk on tiptoe']

balloon *noun* pūangi [pū W.300 'tube' angi W.11 'move freely, to float']

ballooning *noun* rere pūangi [rere W.337 'be carried on the wind' pūangi TM 'balloon']

bamboo *noun* inanga [W.77 'grass tree']

banana *noun* maika [< Hawai'i 'banana']

bandage *noun, transitive verb* tākai [W.367 'wrap round, wind round']

banjo *noun* pakakū [W.251 'make a harsh grating sound' kū W.153 'said to have been a one string instrument played by tapping with a stick']

bank card *noun* kāripēke [kāri < Eng. 'card' pēke < Eng. 'bank']

bank statement *noun* pūrongo pēke [pūrongo TM 'report' pēke < Eng. 'bank']

bank teller *noun* kaitatau moni [kai W.86 'a prefix to transitive verbs to form nouns denoting an agent' tatau W.395 'count' moni < Eng. 'money']

bankrupt *noun, adjective* kaihau [W.87 'acquire property without payment or return made']

bankruptcy *noun* kaihau [W.87 'acquire property without payment or return made']

bar *noun* (*weight training*) tautaka [W.404 'pole on which a weight is carried between two persons']

barbecue *noun, transitive verb* hūhunu [W.70 'be charred, scorched']

barbell *noun* (*weight training*) tautaka [W.404 'pole on which a weight is carried between two persons']

baritone *noun* reo mārū [reo W.336 'voice, tone' mārū W.184 'low in tone']

barium *noun* konu-okehu [konu- TM 'prefix denoting natural metal' okehu W.239 'soft white stone']

barium enema *noun* kuhitou konu-okehu [kuhi W.154 'insert, introduce' tou W.442 'anus' konu-okehu TM 'barium']

barium meal *noun* kai konu-okehu [kai W.85 'eat' konu-okehu TM 'barium']

barometer *noun* ine kurahau [ine TM 'meter' kurahau awatea TM 'cyclone' kurahaupō TM 'anticyclone']

barrel *noun* (*gun*) arahāmoa [ara W.13 'means of conveyance' hāmoamoa TM 'bullet'], aramatā [ara W.13 'means of conveyance' matā W.185 'bullet']

barrister *noun* poutoko ture [pou W.297 'expert' toko W.434 'support, prop up' ture W.459 'law']

base *noun* (*number*) kaupapa-ā-tau [kaupapa W.107 'platform, layer' tau TM 'number']

base *noun* (*polygon*) take [W.370 'base of a hill etc.']

base *noun* (*softball*) pūrei [W.313 'isolated rock, patch of anything']

base, first *noun* (*softball*) pūrei tahi [pūrei TM 'base' tahi W.359 'one']

base, home *noun* (*softball*) uta [W.470 'land, as opposed to the sea or water']

base, second *noun* (*softball*) pūrei rua [pūrei TM 'base' rua W.349 'two']

base, third *noun* (*softball*) pūrei toru [pūrei TM 'base' toru W.441 'three']

base umpire *noun* kaiwawao pūrei [kaiwawao TM 'umpire' pūrei TM 'base']

basement *noun* pūwhenua [W.319 'cave used as a dwelling place' pū W.300 'base, foundation' whenua W.494 'ground']

basic facts *noun* meka matua [meka TM 'fact' 'true', matua W.195 'main, important']

basket *noun* (*basketball, structure*) tūkohu [W.451 'cylindrical basket']

basket *noun* (*basketball, point*) paneke [TM 'goal, point']

basketball *noun* poitūkohu [poi TM 'ball' tūkohu TM 'basket']

bass *noun* (*instrument*) panguru [W.258 'bass, gruff']

bass *noun* (*choral singing*) reo nguru [reo W.336 'voice, tone' tanguru W.258 'bass, gruff']

bassinet *noun* pouraka [W.298 'rude form of cradle for infants']

bat *noun* (*cricket*) whiro [common usage 'willow']

bat *noun* (*sport*) rākau [W.321 'weapon']

baton *noun* matire [W.194 'wand, rod']

batsman *noun* kaipatu [kai W.86 'a prefix to transitive verbs to form nouns denoting an agent' patu W.272 'strike, beat']

batter *noun* (*sport*) kaihahau [kai W.86 'a prefix to transitive verbs to form nouns denoting an agent' hahau W.39 'strike, smite']

batter *noun* (*food*) pokewai [pokepoke W.289 'mix up with water of other liquid' waiwai W.474 'watery']

battery *noun* (*electrical*) pūhiko [pū W.300 'source, cause' hiko common usage 'electricity']

batting glove *noun* komonga hahau [komonga TM 'glove' kaihahau TM 'batter']

bayonet *noun* matarere [W.190 'a detachable spear point']

beach skink *noun* mokoone [moko W.207 'a general term for lizards' one W.239 'beach']

beach volleyball *noun* poirewa one [poirewa TM 'volleyball' one W.239 'beach']

beaker *noun* ipurau [ipu W.79 'calabash with narrow mouth, vessel for carrying anything' rau W.328 'lay hold of, handle']

bean, coffee *noun* kanokawhe [kano W.94 'seed' kawhe < Eng. 'coffee']

bean slicer *noun* ripiripi pīni [ripi W.341 'cutting implement, slice off, cut' pīni < Eng. 'bean']

bean sprout *noun* pihi pīni [pihi W.280 'shoot, sprout' pīni < Eng. 'bean']

beans, broad *noun* kanopīni [kano W.94 'seed' pīni < Eng. 'bean']

beans, green *noun* pītau pīni [pītau W.284 'young succulent shoot of a plant' pīni < Eng. 'bean']

bearing *noun* ahunga [ahu W.3 'move in a certain direction']

beat *noun* (*music*) taki [W.371 'tow with a line, lead, bring along' takitaki 'song']

BEDMAS (*abbreviation, mathematics*) raupapa paheko [raupapa TM 'order, sequence' paheko TM 'operation']

beehive *noun* marae o pī [marae W.180 'village common' pī < Eng. 'bee'], wharepī [whare W.489 'habitation' pī < Eng. 'bee']

bee-keeper *noun* kairaupī [kai W.86 'a prefix to transitive verbs to form nouns denoting an agent' raupī W.330 'take care of, cover up' rau W.328 'gather into a basket etc.' pī < Eng. 'bee']

beeper *noun* pūoho [W.311 'start, take alarm']

beet *noun* korare [W.140 'greens, leaves of edible vegetables']

beetroot *noun* rengakura [renga W.336 'mealy fern-root' kura W.157 'red']

beginners' course *noun* pihinga [pihi W.280 'spring up, begin to grow']

behaviour analysis *noun* tātari whanonga [tātari TM 'analyse' whanonga W.487 'behaviour, conduct']

behaviour modification *noun* whakaauraki whanonga [whaka- W.486 'causative prefix' *to make* auraki W.22 'turn aside' whanonga W.487 'behaviour, conduct']

beneficial *adjective* whaihua [whai W.484 'possessing, equipped with' huanga W.64 'advantage, benefit']

beneficiary *noun* (*Government*) kaiwhiwhi takuhe [kaiwhiwhi TM 'recipient' takuhe TM 'benefit']

benefit *noun* (*Government*) takuhe [takoha W.373 'pledge, token, gift']

benefit, domestic purposes *noun* takuhe matua tōtahi [takuhe TM 'benefit' matua W.195 'parent' tōtahi W.441 'single']

benefit, invalid *noun* takuhe hāura [takuhe TM 'benefit' hāura W.41 'sick person, invalid']

benefit, maintenance *noun* takuhe ukauka [takuhe TM 'benefit' ukauka W.466 'bear, support, sustain']

benefit, orphan's *noun* takuhe pani [takuhe TM 'benefit' pani W.257 'orphan']

benefit, sickness *noun* takuhe tahumaero [takuhe TM 'benefit' tahumaero W.361 'sickness, disease']

benefit, supplementary services *noun* takuhe ratonga tāpiri [takuhe TM 'benefit' ratonga TM 'service' tāpiri W.384 'supplement']

benefit, unemployment *noun* takuhe koremahi [takuhe TM 'benefit' kore W.140 'no' mahi W.163 'work']

benefit, unsupported child's *noun* takuhe tamaiti atawhai-kore [takuhe 'benefit' tamaiti W.375 'child' atawhai W.19 'foster' kore W.140 'no']

benefit, widow's *noun* takuhe pouaru [takuhe TM 'benefit' pouaru W.298 'widow, widower']

berry *noun* patatini [pata W.260 'seed' tini W.419 'very many']

beryllium *noun* konuuku [konu- TM 'prefix denoting natural metal' uku W.466 'white clay']

bet *noun, intransitive verb* (*gambling*) takiari [W.372 'omen of a certain class, good or bad']

beta particle *noun* matūriki peta [matūriki TM 'particle' peta < Gk. 'beta"]

between feet *phrase* (*hockey*) wē waewae [wē W.481 'the middle, the midst' waewae W.472 'foot']

biased *adjective* rītaha [W.343 'lean to one side, incline']

biased sample *noun* tīpako rītaha [tīpako TM 'sample' rītaha TM 'biased']

bib *noun* (*netball*) pari tākaro [pari common usage 'bodice' tākaro W.369 'play, sport']

bib *noun usage* (*food*) pari hūhare [pari common usage 'bodice' parahūhare W.33 'scraps of food']

biceps *noun* uarua [ua TM 'muscle' rua W.349 'two']

bicultural *adjective* (*politics*) tikanga-rua [tikanga W.416 'custom, habit' rua W.349 'two']

bicultural person *noun* kākano rua [kākano W.94 'stock, descent' rua W.349 'two']

biculturalism *noun* tikanga-rua [TM 'bicultural']

big screen *noun* pūrangiaho [W.312 'seeing clearly']

bilingual *adjective* reorua [reo W.336 'language' rua W.349 'two']

bilingualism *noun* tikanga reorua [tikanga W.416 'plan method' reorua TM 'bilingual']

bimodal distribution tuari tihirua [tuari common usage 'distribute' tihi W.416 'peak' rua W.349 'two']

binary *adjective* (*number*) kaupapa-ā-rua [kaupapa W.107 'platform, layer' ā W.1 'after the manner of' rua W.349 'two']

binary operation *adjective* paheko-rua [paheko W.247 'join, combine' rua W.349 'two']

bind *noun* (*rugby*) kōtui [W.150 'fasten by lacing']

bind *transitive verb* (*book*) tui [W.449 'sew, fasten by passing a cord through holes']

binding *noun* (*book*) tuinga [W.449 'sew, fasten by passing a cord through holes']

binding machine *noun* (*book*) pūrere tuitui [pūrere TM 'machine' tui W.449 'sew, fasten by passing a cord through holes']

bin-liner *noun* tīrongo [W.424 'slabs of stem of tree fern used for lining a kūmara pit']

binoculars *noun* karurua whakatata [karu W.102 'eye' rua W.349 'two' whakatata W.393 'approach']

biochemistry *noun* matūora [matū TM 'matter' ora W.241 'alive']

biodegradable *adjective* pōpopo [W.292 'rotten, decayed, worm-eaten']

biography *noun* haurongo [hau W.39 'resound, be published abroad' rongo W.346 'tidings, report, fame']

biological principles *noun* mātāpono koiora [mātāpono TM 'principle' koiora TM 'biology']

biologist *noun* kaimātai koiora [kaimātai TM '-ologist' koiora TM 'biology']

biology *noun* mātauranga koiora [mātauranga common usage 'knowledge' koiora W.128 'life']

biosphere *noun* ao koiora [ao W.11 'world' koiora TM 'biology']

biotechnology *noun* hangarau-koiora [hangarau TM 'technology' koiora TM 'biology']

birdie *noun* (*golf*) teo [W.412 'small, of birds']

birth, breech *noun* whānau kōaro [whānau W.487 'be born' kōaro W.122 'inverted, turned right around']

bisect *transitive verb* weherua [weherua W.481 'divided']

bisector *noun* rārangi weherua [rārangi W.324 'line' weherua W.481 'divided']
bisexual *adjective* taera rua [taera W.356 'sexual desire' rua W.349 'two']
bitumen *noun* pakakē [W.251 'a black bituminous substance found on beaches']
bivouac *noun* māhauhau [W.163 'a temporary shelter shed']
black hole *noun* (*astronomy*) hōnea kore [hōnea W.58 'escape' kore W.140 'no']
black-brown *adjective* hāura pango [hāura W.41 'brown' pango W.258 'black']
blacksmith *noun* ringa pīau [ringa W.341 'hand' pīau W.279 'iron']
bleach, chemical *noun* whakatoki [W.343 'bleach']
blender *noun* (*kitchen appliance*) whakahanumi [W.34 'mix, cause to be swallowed up']
blind side *noun* (*rugby*) taha kūiti [taha W.357 'side' kūiti W.154 'narrow, confined']
blind-side *adjective* (*rugby*) kūiti [W.154 'narrow, confined']
blizzard *noun* huka kairākau [W.89 'a very severe front']
block *noun, transitive verb* (*volleyball*) ārau [W.14 'gather, entangle']
block *noun* (*building*) whaitua [W.485 'region, space']
block, illegal *noun* (*volleyball*) ārau hē [ārau TM 'block' hē W.43 'wrong, error']
blockholer *noun* (*cricket*) epawī [epa W.28 'throw, cast' wī TM 'crease']
blood bin *noun* (*sport*) pae hūtoto [pae W.244 'perch, rest' hūtoto W.73 'bloody']
blood pressure *noun* rere o te toto [rere W.337 'flow' toto W.441 'blood']
blood pressure, high *noun* toto pōrutu [toto W.441 'blood' pōrutu W.295 'dashing, surging, of the sea']
blood pressure, low *noun* toto pūroto [toto W.441 'blood' pūroto W.314 'sluggish, of a stream']
blood pressure, normal *noun* toto rōnaki [toto rōnaki W.346 'steady, gliding easily']
blood transfusion *noun* whāngai toto [whāngai W.488 'nourish, feed' toto W.441 'blood']
blood vessel *noun* ia toto [ia W.74 'current' iaia 'veins' toto W.441 'blood']
bloodbank *noun* punatoto [puna W.309 'spring of water' toto W.441 'blood']

blow *noun* (*boxing etc.*) moto [W.211 'strike with the fist']
blue, basic *adjective* ōrangi [ō W.237 'of' te kahu o te rangi W.84 'blue sky']
blue, dark *adjective* pukepoto [W.307 'a dark-blue earth used as a pigment']
blue, light *adjective* ōrangitea [ōrangi TM 'basic blue' teatea W.410 'light in colour']
blue-green *adjective* kānapanapa [W.93 'dark green, as deep water']
blue-grey *adjective* kororā [W.145 'blue penguin, grey'], aumoana [W.22 'blue clay, open sea']
blurred vision *noun* atarua [W.18 'dim-sighted']
board of governors *noun* tumu whakahaere [tumu W.454 'foundation, main post in the palisading of a pā' whakahaere TM 'control']
board of trustees *noun* tumu whakahaere [tumu W.454 'foundation, main post in the palisading of pā, 'whakahaere TM 'control']
boarder *noun* tangata nohoutu [tangata 'person' noho W.223 'dwell, live' utu W.471 'price']
boarding school *noun* kuranoho [kura common usage 'school' noho W.223 'remain, dwell']
boardroom *noun* rūnanga [W.352 'public meeting house']
body bag *noun* puraku [W.312 'coffin or wrap']
body corporate *noun* rangatōpū [ranga W.322 'company of persons' tōpū W.437 'in a body, assembled']
body fluid *noun* wai tinana [wai W.474 'water' tinana W.419 'body']
body language *noun* kōrero tinana [kōrero W.141 'tell, say' tinana W.419 'body']
body protection *noun* ārai tinana [ārai W.14 'ward off' tinana W.419 'body']
bodysuit *noun* kirirua [W.119 'a black thick-skinned species of eel']
bogey *noun* (*golf*) aeha [W.2 'interjection denoting vexation']
bold *adjective* (*printing*) miramira [W.202 'give prominence to']
bolt *noun* (*machinery*) pine [W.281 'close together']
bomb *noun* pahū [W.248 'burst, explode']
bomb *noun* (*rugby*) tīkoke [W.418 'high up in the heavens']

bomb threat *noun* tuma pahū [tuma W.452 'challenge' pahū TM 'bomb']
bombardment *noun* pāhūhū [pahū TM 'bomb']
bone *transitive verb* (*remove bones*) mākiri [W.170 'take the bones out of pigeons, etc.']
bone, alveolar *noun* kauae [kauae W.105 'jaw']
bone, occipital *noun* wheua kōpako [wheua W.496 'bone' kōpako W.135 'back of the head']
bone tissue, cancellate *noun* wheua kakaru [wheua W.496 'bone' kakaru W.102 'spongy matter']
bone tissue, compact *noun* wheua kiato [wheua W.496 'bone' kiato W.116 'compact, in small compass']
bonnet *noun* (*vehicle*) pokiwaka [poki W.290 'cover over' waka common usage 'vehicle']
bonsai tree *noun* rākau tauhena [rākau W.321 'tree' tauhena W.405 'dwarfish, of small stature']
boogie-board *noun* koneke ngaru [koneke W.133 'slide along' ngaru W.230 'wave']
boogie-boarding *noun* eke ngaru [eke W.27 'generally place oneself or be placed upon another object' ngaru W.230 'wave']
book end *noun* tauteka pukapuka [tauteka W.404 'brace, prop' pukapuka W.306 'book']
book review *noun* arotake pukapuka [arotake TM 'review' pukapuka W.306 'book']
boot *noun* (*vehicle*) tauputu [W.402 'lie in a heap']
boron *noun* pūtiwha [pūhui TM 'compound' tiwha W.427 'gleam']
borrow *noun* mino [minono W.202 'beg']
boss *noun* (*science apparatus*) rarawe [W.333 'clasp tightly']
botanical *adjective* huaota [hua W.64 'bear fruit or flowers, abundance' otaota W.242 'herbs in general, vegetation']
botanist *noun* tohunga huaota [tohunga TM 'expert' huaota TM 'botany'], kaimātai huaota [kai W.86 'a prefix to transitive verbs to form nouns denoting an agent' mātai W.187 'inspect, examine' huaota TM 'botany']

botany *noun* mātauranga huaota [mātauranga common usage 'knowledge' hua W.64 'bear fruit or flowers, abundance' otaota W.242 'herbs in general, vegetation']
bottle-brush *noun* (*kitchenware*) taitai pounamu [taitai W.362 'brush' pounamu W.298 'bottle']
bottle-opener *noun* tīkape pounamu [tīkapekape W.417 'move or stir with the point of a stick' pounamu W.298 'bottle']
bounce *transitive verb* tūpana [W.456 'spring up, recoil']
bounce pass *noun* maka tūpana [maka W.168 'throw' tūpana TM 'bounce']
bouncer *noun* epa tūpana [epa TM 'bowl' tūpana W.456 'spring up, recoil']
boundary *noun* tawhā [tapawhā W.381 'four-sided']
boundary line *noun* tawhā [tapawhā W.381 'four-sided']
bow *noun* (*archery*) whana [Best *Games and Pastimes* 183]
bow *noun* (*violin*) whana [Best *Games and Pastimes* 183]
bowels *noun* (*anatomy*) puku hamuti [puku W.308 'stomach, entrails' hamuti W.33 'human excrement']
bowl *noun* (*lawn bowls*) maita [< Hawai'i 'bowls' Best *Games and Pastimes* 173]
bowl *transitive verb* (*lawn bowls*) tuku [W.451 'let go, send']
bowl *noun, transitive verb* (*cricket*) epa [W.28 'throw, cast']
bowl *noun* (*crockery*) oko [W.239 'wooden bowl or other open vessel']
bowl, fast *noun* epa rere [epa TM 'bowl' rere W.337 'rush, hasten']
bowl, seam *noun* epa maurua [epa TM 'bowl' maurua W.198 'seam between two widths of floor mat']
bowl, serving *noun* kūmete [W.156 'wooden bowl or trough']
bowl, slow *noun* epa akitō [epa TM 'bowl' akitō W.7 'be slow, lengthened out']
bowl, spin *noun* epa tāwhirowhiro [epa TM 'bowl' tāwhirowhiro W.409 'whirl spin']
bowled *phrase* (*cricket*) hinga [W. 52 'be outdone in a contest']

bowler *noun* (*lawn bowls*) kaipīrori maita [kai W.86 'a prefix to transitive verbs to form nouns denoting an agent' pīrori W.284 'roll along, as a ball etc.' maita TM 'lawn bowls'], (*cricket*) kaiepa [kai W.86 'a prefix to transitive verbs to form nouns denoting an agent' epa TM 'bowl']

bowling centre *noun* (*lawn bowls*) whare maita [whare W.498 'house' maita TM 'lawn bowls']

bowls *noun* (*sport*) maita [< Hawaii 'bowls']

box *noun* (*sport, protection*) pākai raho [pākai W.251 'shield, screen' raho W.320 'testicle']

box in *transitive verb* awhe [W.24 'hem in, surround']

boxing *noun* (*building*) pākaka raima [pākaka W.251 'surround, hem in, small enclosure' raima common usage 'concrete']

boxing *noun* (*sport*) mekemeke [meke W.200 'strike with the fist, blow with the fist']

boxing glove *noun* komonga mekemeke [komonga TM 'glove' mekemeke TM 'boxing']

bracket *noun* (*printing*) taiapa [W.363 'fence, wall']

Braille *noun* tuhi matapō [tuhi W.448 'write' matapō W.189 'blind']

Braille dot *noun* tongi [W.436 'point, speck']

brain damage *noun* mate roro [mate W.192 'sickness, injury, wound' roro W.347 'brains']

brain scanner *noun* matawai roro [matawai W.192 'look closely' roro W.347 'brains']

brain stem *noun* pūroro [W.300 'foot, base' roro W.347 'brains']

brainstorm *noun* ōhia manomano [ōhia W.238 'think on the spur of the moment' manomano W.176 'innumerable, hoard, swarm']

brainstorming *noun* ōhia manomano [TM 'brainstorm']

brake, foot *noun* tumuwae [tumu W.454 'halt suddenly' wae W.472 'foot']

brake, hand *noun* tumuringa [tumu W.454 'halt suddenly' ringa W.341 'hand']

brake lights *noun* rama tumu [rama W.322 'torch or other artificial light' tumu W.454 'halt suddenly']

bran *noun* pāpapa [W.259 'husk, such as bran chaff etc.']

bran flakes *noun* raupāpapa [rau W.328 'leaf, multitude' pāpapa W.259 'husk, such as bran chaff etc.']

branchlet *noun* rārā [W.319 'twig, small branch']

brand *noun*, *transitive verb* waitohu [W.477 'mark, signify, indicate']

brass *noun* kuratea [konukura TM 'copper' konutea TM 'zinc']

breadbin *noun* taparua parāoa [taparua W.383 'square receptacle for kūmara' parāoa common usage 'bread']

breadboard *noun* papa parāoa [papa W.259 'anything broad, flat and hard' parāoa common usage 'bread']

break away *intransitive verb* (*cycling*) rere whakamua [rere W.337 'rush, hasten, flee' whakamua TM 'forwards']

break down *transitive verb* (*decompose*) whakapopo [whaka- W.486 'causative prefix' *to make* popo W.292 'rotten, decayed, worm-eaten']

break lanes *intransitive verb* (*swimming*) kotiti [kotītiti W.149 'wander about, be irregular']

breakaway *noun* (*rugby*) poutaha [pou W.297 'support, post' taha W.357 'side, edge']

break-dancing *noun* kanikani keretao [kanikani W.93 'dance' keretao W.114 'a grotesque figure with arms moved by a string']

breaststroke *noun* kau āpuru [Best *Games and Pastimes* 40 'breaststroke']

breath freshener *noun* karahā [kakara W.97 'scent, smell, flavour' hā W.29 'breath, taste, flavour']

breathe gently *intransitive verb* hānene [W.33 'blowing gently' hā W.29 'breath, breathe']

breathing, rescue *noun* hā whakaora [hā W.29 'breath, breathe' whakaora W.214 'save, restore to health']

breech birth *noun* whānau kōaro [whānau W.487 'be born' kōaro W.122 'inverted, turned right around']

breve *noun* orowaru [oro W.242 'sound' waru W.480 'eight']

bribe *noun* whakapati [W.271 'induce by means of gifts']

brick *noun* porokere [poro W.294 'block' kere W.114 'clay, earth']

bricklayer *noun* tiri porokere [tiri W.423 'place one on another, stack, place one by one' porokere TM 'brick']

bridal wear *noun* kākahu taumau [kākahu W.84 'garment' taumau W.400 'be betrothed']

bridge *noun* arawhiti [ara W.13 'way, path' whiti W497 'cross over, reach the opposite side']

bridge, bailey *noun* arawhiti rangitahi [arawhiti TM 'bridge' rangitahi W.324 'ephemeral, transient']

briefcase *noun* kopamārō [kopa W.135 'wallet, satchel' mārō W.183 'hard, unyielding']

brigade *noun* ope [W.240 'troop']

bristleworm *noun* weritai [weriweri W.482 'centipede' tai W.361 'coast, sea']

broadcast *intransitive verb, transitive verb* pāpāho [pāho W.248 'be noised abroad']

broadcasting *noun* pāhotanga [pāho W.248 'be noised abroad']

bromine *noun* pūkane [pūhui TM 'chemical compound' kanekane W.93 'pungent']

bronchitis *noun* pūkawe kakā [pūkawe hāora TM 'bronchus' kakā TM 'inflamed']

bronchus *noun* pūkawe hāora [pū W.300 'tube' kawe W.111 'carry, convey' hāora TM 'oxygen']

brontosaurus *noun* mokokairau [moko W.207 'lizard' kai W.85 'eat' rau W.328 'leaf']

bronze *adjective* (*skin-colour*) rauwhero [W.331 'ruddy, brown']

brown, basic *adjective* hāura [W.41 'brown']

brown, dark *adjective* hāurauri [hāura W.41 'brown' uri W.469 'dark, deep in colour']

brown, pale *adjective* hāuratea [hāura W.41 'brown' tea W.410 'light in colour']

Brussels sprouts *noun* aonanī [ao W.11 'bud' nanī W.218 'wild cabbage']

bubble and squeak *noun* tāmahana [W.375 'cook a second time, warm up cooked food']

buckle *noun* tāpine [tā W.355 'prefix having a causative force similar to that of whaka' pine W.281 'close together']

bulb *noun* (*electricity*) pūaho [pū W.300 'source, origin' aho W.3 'radiant light, shine']

bulb holder *noun* (*science*) whakakopa pūaho [whakakopa W.135 'clasp, clutch' pūaho TM 'bulb']

bulimia *noun* pukuruaki [puku W.309 'stomach, secretly' ruaki W.350 'vomit']

bulldog clip *noun* (*documents*) rawhipuka [rawhi W.333 'grasp, hold firmly' pukapuka W.306 'book, paper, letter']

bulldozer *noun* wakapana [waka common usage 'vehicle' pana W.256 'drive away, expel']

bullet *noun* hāmoamoa [W.33 'small spherical stones which were used as bullets']

bullet-proof vest *noun* kahupeka [W.85 'stiff, closely woven mat of flax worn as protection in war, strapped on like the tātua']

bulletin board, electronic *noun* papa pānui rorohiko [papa W.259 'anything broad, flat and hard' pānui W.257 'advertise publicly' rorohiko TM 'computer']

bully off *noun* (*hockey*) hakehakeā [W.31 'facing one, opposite' hake TM 'hockey']

bum-bag *noun* tātua pūpara [W.395 'girdle in which valuables were carried']

bumble-bee *noun* pīrorohū [pī < Eng. 'bee' rorohū W.348 'buzz, buzz about']

bumper *noun* (*vehicle*) pākaituki [pākai W.251 'shield, screen' tūtuki W.450 'strike against another object']

bumper-to-bumper *phrase* piri-ki-tata [piri W.283 'come close, keep close' tata W.393 'near']

bungy-jumping *noun* tirikohu waehere [tirikohu 'dive' wae W.472 'leg, foot' here W.46 'fasten with cord']

bunsen burner *noun* muratahi [mura W.214 'blaze, flame' tahi W.359 'single']

bunt *noun, transitive verb* (*softball*) tuki [W.450 'butt, knock']

bureaucracy *noun* taero [W.356 'obstruction, hindrance']

burette *noun* puoto katirere [puoto W.311 'vessel' katirere TM 'tap']

burner *noun* hatete [W.38 'fire']

bursary *noun* tahua tauira tāpiri [tahua W.360 'fund, sum of money' tauira common usage 'student' tāpiri W.384 'supplement, anything added or appended']

bursary examination *noun* whakamātautau tahua tāpiri [whakamātautau common usage 'examination' tahua tauira tāpiri TM 'bursary']

bus stop *noun* tūnga pahi [tūnga W.443 '(circumstance, time etc.) of standing' pahi < Eng. 'bus']

business *noun (enterprise)* umanga [W.467 'pursuit, occupation, business'], pakihi [kaipakihi W.89 'business, affairs, concerns']

businessman *noun* kaipakihi [W.89 'business, affairs, concerns']

businesswoman *noun* kaipakihi [W.89 'business, affairs, concerns']

butane *noun* pūwaro [pū < Eng. 'bu-' waro TM 'alkane']

butanol *noun* waihā pūwaro [waihā TM 'hydroxide' pūwaro TM 'butane']

butter conditioner *noun* ngehi pata [ngehi W.233 'reduced to a state of softness' pata < Eng. 'butter']

butterfly *noun (style of swimming)* kau aihe [kau W.104 'swim' aihe W.5 'dolphin']

buttock exercise *noun, adjective (aerobics etc.)* whakapūioio remu [whakapūioio W.306 'strong, muscular' remu W.335 'posterior, buttocks']

buyer *noun* kaitango [kai W.86 'a prefix to transitive verbs to form nouns denoting an agent' tango W.380 'take possession of, acquire'], kaihoko [kai W.86 'a prefix to transitive verbs to form nouns denoting an agent' hoko W.57 'buy']

by mistake pokerehū *adverb* [W.290 'unintentional']

bye *noun (sport)* whakanā [W.216 'rest, remain still']

by-law *noun* ture-ā-rohe [ture W.459 'law' ā-rohe TM 'regional']

C

cabbage *noun* nīko [W.222 'wild cabbage'], nanī [W.218 'wild cabbage']
cabin *noun* kōpuha [W.138 'small house']
cable car *noun* waka tautō [waka common usage 'vehicle' tautō W.404 'drag']
cable drum *noun* pōkai waea [pōkai W.289 'coil, roll up' waea < Eng. 'wire']
Caesarian section *noun* motu whakawhānau [motu W.211 'severed, cut, wound' whaka- W.486 'causative prefix' *to make* whānau W.487 'be born']
cafeteria *noun* kāmuri [W.93 'cooking shed']
cake tin *noun* taparua keke [taparua W.383 'a square receptacle for kūmara' keke < Eng. 'cake']
calcium *noun* konupūmā [konu- TM 'prefix denoting natural metal' pūmā W.309 'whitish grey']
calculate *transitive verb* tātai [W.393 'arrange, set in order, measure, be ranged in order']
calculation *noun* tātaitanga [tātai TM 'calculate']
calculator *noun* tātaitai [tātai TM 'calculate']
calculus *noun* tuanaki [W.446 'move with an even motion']
calendar *noun* maramataka [marama W.180 'month' taka W.366 'come round, as a date or period of time']
calibrate *transitive verb* tōkarikari [whakatōkarikari W.443 'cut in notches' tōkari TM 'point on scale']
calibration *noun* tōkarikari [whakatōkarikari W.443 'cut in notches' tōkari TM 'point on scale']
calibre *noun* kūpara [W.157 'size, extent']
calorie *noun* pūngoi [pū W.300 'source, origin' ngoi W.234 'energy']

camera person *noun* kaiwhakaahua [kai W.86 'a prefix to transitive verbs to form nouns denoting an agent' whakaahua TM 'photograph']
camouflage *noun* kirihuna [kiri W.119 'skin' huna W.69 'conceal']
camouflage clothing *noun* weru hunahuna [weru W.482 'garment' hunahuna W.69 'concealed, seldom seen']
can *noun* (*container*) puoto [W.311 'vessel']
canal *noun* kōawa [W.122 'watercourse, narrow gully'], awa [W.23 'channel, river, gorge']
canal, ear *noun* kōawa taringa [kōawa TM 'canal' taringa 'ear']
cancel *transitive verb* whakakore [W.141 'cause not to be']
cancer *noun* mate pukupuku [mate W.192 'sickness' puku W.308 'swelling, tumour, knob']
cancer, cervical *noun* mate pukupuku o te waha whare tangata [mate pukupuku TM 'cancer' waha whare tangata TM 'cervix']
candidate *noun* (*applicant*) kaitono [kai W.86 'a prefix to transitive verbs to form nouns denoting an agent' tono TM 'apply' kaitono TM 'applicant']
candidate, successful *noun* kopounga [kopou W.138 'appoint']
cannabis *noun* whakamāngina [W.178 'floating, fleeting, unreliable']
can-opener *noun* tīwara [W.427 'cleave in twain, split, divide']
canteen *noun* kāmuri [W.93 'cooking shed']
cap, swimming *noun* pōtae kauhoe [pōtae W.296 'cap, hat' kauhoe W.106 'swim']

capacitor *noun* pūranga iahiko [pūranga W.312 'lie in a heap' iahiko TM 'electric charge']

capacity *noun* kahapupuri [kaha W.82 'strength' pupuri W.314 'hold, retain possession of']

capillary *noun (anatomical)* ia tōiti [iatuku TM 'artery' tōiti W.432 'little finger or toe']

capital *noun (accounting)* haupū rawa [haupū W.41 'heap, mound, lie in a heap' rawa W.331 'goods, property']

capital letter *noun* pūmatua [pū TM 'letter of alphabet' matua W.195 'parent, main']

cappucino *noun* kaputino [< Eng. 'cappucino']

captain *noun* kaiurungi [kai W.86 'a prefix to transitive verbs to form nouns denoting an agent' urungi W.470 'steer, rudder']

caravan *noun* whare tāwhai [whare W.489 'hut, habitation' tāwhai W.407 'go forth, travel to a distance']

carbohydrate *noun* warowaihā [waro TM 'carbon' wai W.474 'water' hāora TM 'oxygen']

carbon *noun* waro [W.480 'charcoal']

carbon dioxide *noun* hauhā [hau TM 'gas' whakahā W.29 'emit breath']

carbon monoxide *noun* haukino [hau TM 'gas' kino W.118 'bad']

carbon paper *noun* whārangi tārua [whārangi W.489 'page of a book' tārua W.392 'tattoo a second time']

carbonate *noun* pākawa waro [pākawa TM '-ate' waro TM 'carbon']

carcinoma *noun* mate pukupuku o te kiri [mate pukupuku TM 'cancer' kiri W.119 'skin']

card *noun (stationery)* puka [pukapuka W.306 'book, paper']

cardiac arrest *noun* manawa-hē [manawa W.174 'heart' hē W.43 'in trouble, difficulty']

cardio routine *noun, adjective (aerobics)* whakakakapa manawa [whaka- W.486 'causative prefix' *to make* kakapa W.95 'throb, palpitate' manawa W.174 'heart']

cardiopulmonary resuscitation *noun* whakaora manawa [whakaora W.241 'save alive, restore to health' manawa W.174 'heart']

cardiovascular *adjective* iaia-manawa [iaia TM 'blood vessels' manawa W.174 'heart']

cardiovascular disease *noun* mate iaia-manawa [mate W.192 'sickness' iaia-manawa TM 'cardio-vascular']

carnival *noun* taiopenga [taiope W.364 'gather together']

carnivorous *adjective* kaikiko [kai W.85. 'eat' kiko W.117 'flesh']

carpark *noun* papawaka [papa W.259 'site' waka common usage 'vehicle'], tūnga waka [tūnga W.443 '(circumstance, time etc.) of standing' waka common usage 'vehicle']

carpark entrance *noun* tomokanga papawaka [tomokanga W.435 'entrance, gateway' papawaka TM 'carpark']

carpark exit *noun* putanga papawaka [puta W.315 'pass out of, escape' papawaka 'carpark']

carpus *noun* wheua kawititanga [wheua W.496 'bone' kawititanga o te ringaringa W.111 'wrist']

carrot *noun* uhikaramea [uhi W.471 'root crops' karamea W.98 'red ochre']

cartage *noun* kawekawe [kawe W.111 'carry, convey']

cartilage *noun* wheua ngohe [wheua W.496 'bone' ngohe W.234 'supple, soft']

cartilage, hyaline *noun* wheua ngohe puata [wheua ngohe TM 'cartilage' puata W.303 'clear, transparent']

cartoon *noun* pakiwaituhi [pakiwaitara W.254 'fiction, folklore' tuhi W.448 'draw, adorn with painting']

cartwheel *noun* pōtātaka [pōtēteke W.296 'turning over and over' tātaka W.366 'turn or roll from side to side' cf. TM pōtēteke]

carving fork *noun* mārau [W.181 'fork']

carving knife *noun* māripi [W.182 'cutting instrument, knife']

casein *noun* pūmua kuruwhatu [pūmua TM 'protein' kurukuruwhatu W.159 'curdled, as milk']

cash *noun* ukauka [W.466 'hard'], moni [< Eng. 'money']

cash flow *noun* kapewhiti [W.96 'come and go frequently']

cash register *noun* hake ukauka [hake W.31 'a wooden bowl or trough' ukauka TM 'cash']

casserole dish *noun* tīhake [W.415 'pot, vessel']

castor sugar *noun* huka-one [huka < Eng. 'sugar' one W.239 'sand']

castrate *transitive verb* poka (raho) [poka W.288 'cut out' raho W.320 'testicles']

casual job *noun* mahi waimori [mahi W.163 'work' waimori W.476 'working intermittently'], mahi kōhikohiko [mahi W.163 'work, work at' kōhikohiko W.125 'do irregularly, a bit here and a bit there']

casual worker *noun* kaimahi waimori [kai W.86 'a prefix to transitive verbs to form nouns denoting an agent' mahi W.163 'work' waimori W.476 'working intermittently'], kaimahi kōhikohiko [kai W.86 'a prefix to transitive verbs to form nouns denoting an agent' mahi W.163 'work, work at' kōhikohiko W.125 'do irregularly, a bit here and a bit there']

catalogue *transitive verb* whakarārangi [W.324 'draw up or arrange in a line or row']

catalogue *noun* rārangi [W.324 'line, rank, row']

catalyst *noun* (*chemistry*) whakakōkī [whaka- W.486 'causative prefix' *to make* kōkīkī W.130 'fast']

cataract *noun* mate arotahi [mate W.192 'sickness' arotahi TM 'lens']

catcher *noun* (*softball*) tautopenga [whakatautopenga W.404 'rearguard']

catheter, urinary *noun* pū tōngāmimi [pū W.300 'tube' tōngāmimi W.436 'bladder']

cathode *noun* pito-tī [pito W.284 'end, extremity' tī common usage used to indicate indefinite locality]

catkin *noun* huahae [hua W.64 'product, progeny' hae W.29 'pollen']

caucus *noun* uepū [W.465 'company, party']

caught and bowled *phrase* ika kaiepa [ika W.76 'victim' kaiepa TM 'bowler']

caustic soda *noun* (*sodium hydroxide*) konutai waihā [konutai TM 'sodium' waihā TM 'hydroxide']

cayenne pepper *noun* pūhahana [W.304 'hot to the taste']

cede *transitive verb* tautuku [W.405 'stoop, bend down, so give way']

cell *noun* pūtau [pū W.300 'origin, source' tau W.396 'be able']

cell membrane *noun* kiriuhi pūtau [kiriuhi TM 'membrane' pūtau TM 'cell']

cello *noun* whiranui [whira < Eng. 'fiddle' nui W.244 'large']

cellophane *noun* tākai kōataata [tākai W.367 'wrap up, wrap round' kōataata W.122 'transparent']

cellular phone *noun* waea pūkoro [waea common usage 'phone' pūkoro W.308 'pocket']

cellulose adhesive *noun* kāpia [W.96 'kauri gum, resin']

Celsius *adjective* waeine mahana C [waeine TM 'unit of measurement' mahana W.162 'warm']

central tendency *noun* (*statistics*) wēanga [wē W.481 'the middle' anga W.10 'move in a certain direction']

centre *noun* wēanga [wē W.481 'the middle']

centre *noun* (*agency*) pokapū [W.289 'middle, centre'], pūtahi [W.316 'join, meet, as two paths or streams running one into the other']

centre *noun* (*geometry*) pū [W.300 'heart, centre']

centre *noun* (*lawn bowls*) tawhā waengapū [tawhā TM 'boundary' waengapū W.473 'the midst'], (*netball*) takuahi [W.374 'centre of line of battle as opposed to the paihau'], (*rugby*) topa pū [topa W.436 'soar, swoop' pū W.300 'centre']

centre back *noun* (*soccer*) pūmuri [pū W.300 'centre' muri W.214 'the rear']

centre circle *noun* (*netball*) porohita [W.295 'ring, circle']

centre half *noun* (*soccer*) pū kaunuku [pū W.300 'centre' kaunuku W.107 'centre of any army when formed for a rush, move steadily']

centre line *noun* (*sport*) waenga [W.472 'dividing line']

centre of gravity *noun* pū kume-ā-papa [pū W.300 'centre' kume-ā-papa TM 'gravity']

centre outfield *noun* (*softball*) mokoā wēanga [mokoā W.208 'space' wēanga TM 'centre']

centre spot *noun* (*soccer*) pokapū [W.289 'middle, centre']

centre third *noun* (*netball*) puku [W.308 'stomach']

centrifugal *adjective* whakawaho [whaka- W.485 'towards, in the direction of' waho W.474 'the outside']

cerebellum *noun* (*brain*) roro tuarongo [roro W.347 'brains' tuarongo W.447 'back of the interior of a house']

cerebral haemorrhage *noun* ikura roro [ikura W.76 'haemorrhage' roro W.347 'brains']

cerebral palsy *noun* mate whakatīmohea [mate W.192 'sickness' whaka- W.486 'causative prefix' *to make* tīmohea W.419 'weak, flaccid']

cerebrovascular *adjective* iaia-roro [iaia TM 'blood vessels' roro W.347 'brains']

cerebrovascular disease *noun* mate iaia-roro [mate W.192 'sickness' iaia-roro TM 'cerebro-vascular']

cervical smear *noun* okoi waha whare tangata [okoi W.239 'scrape' waha W.473 'mouth, entrance' whare tangata common usage 'womb']

cervix *noun* waha whare tangata [waha W.473 'mouth, entrance' whare tangata common usage 'womb']

chainsaw *noun* tātaretare [tātare W.395 'a saw-like weapon made from teeth of a shark']

challenging *adjective* (*difficult*) whakatara [W386 'challenge, put on one's mettle']

chamber *noun* (*anatomy*) pakohu [W.255 'cavity']

chamber *noun* (*building*) taiwhanga [W.365 'place locality']

champion *transitive verb* (*support*) kōkiri [W.130 'rush forward, charge, body of men rushing forward']

championship, to win *phrase* eke tangaroa [eke W.27 'come to land' eke tangaroa common usage 'strike home']

chance *noun* heipūtanga [heipū W.44 'hitting exactly']

chance on *transitive verb* heipū [W.44 'coming or going straight towards, hitting exactly']

change, physical *noun* (*biology*) panoni tinana [panoni W.257 'change' tinana W.419 'body']

change down *intransitive verb* (*gear*) whakapūhoi [whaka- W.486 'causative prefix' *to make* pūhoi W.305 'slow']

change ends *intransitive verb* whakawhiti pito [whakawhiti W.497 'cross over' pito W.284 'end, extremity']

change up *noun* (*softball*) epa māminga [epa TM 'pitch' māminga W.172 'use anything for the purposes of deception, feign']

channel, television *noun* hongere (pouaka whakaata) [hongere W.58 'channel' pouaka whakaata common usage 'television'], wāhanga (pouaka whakaata) [wāhanga TM 'division' pouaka whakaata common usage 'television']

character *noun* (*printing*) pū [pū TM 'letter of alphabet']

character reference *noun* taunaki whanonga [taunaki W.400 'support, reinforce' whanonga W.487 'behaviour, conduct']

characteristic *noun* āhuatanga [āhua W.4 'character']

charades *noun* whakatautau [whakatau W.396 'imitate, simulate']

charge *noun* (*justice*) whakapā hē [W.243 'accuse, bring a charge of wrongdoing against anyone']

charge nurse *noun* tapuhi matua [tapuhi TM 'nurse' matua W.195 'chief']

charge sheet *noun* (*justice*) tuhinga whakapā hē [tuhinga TM 'document' whakapā hē TM 'charge']

Charon *noun* Kūwatawata [Smith *The Lore of the Whare Wānanga* 184]

chart *noun* mahere [W.163 'plan']

charter *noun* (*document*) tūtohinga [tūtohi W.462 'indication, point out, direct']

chattel *noun* rawa [W.331 'goods, property']

check *transitive verb* (*inspect*) hihira [W.52 'go over carefully']

cheeseboard *noun* papatīhi [papa W.259 'anything broad, flat and hard' tīhi < Eng. 'cheese']

cheese grater *noun* kuoro tīhi [kuoro W.156 'grate' tīhi < Eng. 'cheese']

chemical *noun* matū [W.195 'gist, kernel, fat']

chemical change *noun* paheko matū [pakeho W.247 'combine, co-operate' matū TM 'chemical, substance']

chemical energy *noun* pūngao matū [pūngao TM 'energy' matū TM 'chemical']

chemical family *noun* uru matū [uru W.469 'grove of trees' matū TM 'chemical']

chemical property *noun* āhuatanga matū [āhuatanga TM 'property' matū TM 'chemical']

chemist *noun* (*science*) kairarau matū [kai W.86 'a prefix to transitive verbs to form nouns denoting an agent' rarau W.328 'lay hold of, grasp, handle' matū TM 'chemistry']

chemist *noun* (*shop*) toa rongoā [toa < Eng. 'shop' rongoā W.346 'remedy, medicine']

chemistry *noun* mātauranga matū [mātauranga common usage 'knowledge' matū TM 'chemical']

chemistry, organic *noun* mātauranga matūwaro [mātauranga common usage 'knowledge' matū TM 'chemical' waro TM 'carbon']

chemotherapy *noun* hahau [W.39 'a charm for curing tumours']

cheque account *noun* pūtea haki [pūtea TM 'fund' haki < Eng 'cheque']

chess *noun* whakarau kīngi [whakarau W.328 'take captive' kīngi < Eng. 'King']

chicken pox *noun* koroputa hei [koroputaputa W.145 'smallpox' heihei W.44 'barnyard fowl']

Chief Judge *noun* Kaiwhakawā Matua [kaiwhakawā W.472 'judge' matua W.195 'main, chief']

chilli *noun* hirikakā [hiri W.53 'brisk, requiring exertion' kakā W.81 'red-hot, glow']

chilly-bin *noun* tokanga mātao [tokanga W.433 'large basket for food' mātao W.189 'cold']

chip *noun, transitive verb* (*golf*) haurewa [hau W.39 'strike, smite' rewa W.339 'float, be high up']

chip basket *noun* (*cooking*) rumaki parai taewa [rumaki W.351 'immerse' W.352 'basket of seed potatoes' parai < Eng. 'fry' taewa W.357 'potato']

chip kick *noun* (*sport*) whana aweawe [whana W.486 'kick' aweawe W.24 'out of reach']

chipboard *noun* papa maramara [papa W.259 'anything hard, broad and flat' maramara W.180 'chip, splinter']

chippies *noun* (*potato*) kotakota rīwai [kotakota W.147 'chips, shavings' rīwai W.344 'potato']

chiropractor *noun* kaikorohiti [kai W.86 'a prefix to transitive verbs to form nouns denoting an agent' korohiti W.147 'jerk, give a sudden impulse to']

chloride *noun* pūhau māota [pūhui TM 'compound' hau māota TM 'chlorine']

chlorine *noun* hau māota [hau TM 'gas' māota W.179 'green']

chlorofluorocarbon *noun* mākōwaro [hau māota TM 'chlorine' hau kōwhai TM 'fluorine' waro TM 'carbon']

chlorophyll *noun* māota [W.179 'green, fresh-grown']

chloroplast *noun* pūmāota [pū W.300 'tube, origin' māota TM 'chlorophyll']

choke *noun* (*vehicle*) natihau [nati W.219 'pinch, contract' W.39 hau 'air']

cholesterol *noun* ngakototo [ngako W.228 'fat' toto W.441 'blood']

chooser *noun* (*computer*) pehutapa [pehu W.275 'dart, spear' tapa W.381 'command, give the word for']

chopping board *noun* papa kotikoti [papa W.259 'anything broad, flat and hard' kotikoti W.149 'cut to pieces']

chopstick *noun* kakape [kape W.96 'pick out, move with the point of a stick']

choral *noun* ngaringari [W.230 'song to make people pull together']

chord *noun* (*mathematics*) aho [W.3 'line']

chordate *noun, adjective* angaroto [anga W.10 'skeleton' roto W.348 'inside']

choroid membrane *noun* koti kamo [koti W.148 'divide' kamo W.92 'eye']

christening *noun* ohorangi [Best *Spiritual and Mental Concepts* 31]

chromate *noun* pākawa konukita [pākawa TM '-ate' konukita TM 'chromium']

chromatography *noun* hīeweewe [W.48 'separated, disengaged, divided']

chrome steel *noun* rinokita [rino W.341 'iron' konukita TM 'chromium']

chromium *noun* konukita [konu- TM 'prefix denoting natural metal' kitakita W.120 'intensely, brightly, of colours']

chromosome *noun* pūira [pū W.300 'tube' ira TM 'gene']

chromosphere *noun* kōhaukura [kōpaki W.135 'envelop' hau TM 'gas' kura W.157 'red']

cigarette lighter *noun* pūahi [pū W.300 'source, tube' ahi W.2 'fire']

circuit *noun* (*cycling, horse-racing*) ara amio [ara W.13 'way, path' amio W.8 'circle round']

circuit *noun* (*electricity*) ara iahiko [ara W.13 'way, path' iahiko TM 'electric current']

circuit, parallel *noun* ara (iahiko) whakarara [ara iahiko TM 'circuit' whakarara TM 'parallel']

circuit, series *noun* ara (iahiko) hātepe [ara iahiko TM 'circuit' hātepe W.38 'follow in regular sequence']

circulation *noun* (*blood*) rere o te toto [toto W.441 'blood' rere W.337 'flow']

circulation, bad *noun* (*blood*) rere pūroto [rere W.337 'flow' pūroto W.314 'sluggish, of a stream']

circulation, good *noun* (*blood*) rere rōnaki [rere W.337 'flow' rōnaki W.346 'gliding easily, steady, continuous']

circumcision, male *noun* poka kirimata [W.288 'cut out' kiri W.119 'skin' mata W.185 'point, extremity']

circumflex *noun* (*printing*) tohu tiorea [tohu W.431 'mark' tohutio TM 'acute' tohurea TM 'grave']

circus *noun* maninirau [manini W.175 'pleasant, agreeable' rau W.328 'hundred, multitude']

cirrhosis, liver *noun* ate ūtonga [ate W.19 'liver' ūtonga W.471 'hard, hardened']

cirrocumulus *noun* māra kūmara a Ngātoro-i-rangi [W.180 'a mackerel sky']

citizen *noun* kirirarau [kiri W.119 'person' rarau W.328 'settle down, remain, take root']

citizenship *noun* raraunga [rarau W.328 'settle down, remain, take root']

civil servant *noun* kaimahi kāwanantanga [kai W.86 'a prefix to transitive verbs to form nouns denoting an agent' mahi W.163 'work, work at, occupation' kāwanatanga < Eng. 'government']

claim *noun* tono [W.436 'bid, demand'], take [W.370 'subject of an argument etc.']

claimant *noun* kaitono [kai W.86 'a prefix to transitive verbs to form nouns denoting an agent' tono W.436 'bid, demand']

clamp *noun* whakakopa [W.135 'clasp, clutch']

clarinet *noun* pūtahoro [W.316 'a long wooden trumpet']

classify *transitive verb* whakarōpū [whaka- W.486 'causative prefix' *to make* rōpū W.347 'company of persons, clump of trees'], kōmaka [W.131 'sort out']

claustrophobia *noun* mae apiapi [mae TM 'phobia' apiapi W.12 'confined, constricted']

clave *noun* (*music*) tīare [tīare W.414 'hollow, empty, void' tītī W.414 'sticks thrown from one player to another in the game of tī rākau']

clay pigeon *noun* tīmori [W.419 'decoy bird']

clean and jerk *noun* (*weightlifting*) hutihiki [huti W.72 'hoist, haul up' hiki W.49 'lift up, raise']

clearance *noun* (*sport*) teitei [W.410 'high']

cleats *noun* matihao [W.193 'claw']

clef *noun* (*music*) tohu [W.431 'mark, sign']

clerk *noun* kaimahi [kai W.86 'a prefix to transitive verbs to form nouns denoting an agent' mahi W.163 'work, work at, occupation']

click on *transitive verb* (*computer*) pāwhiri [pā W.243 'touch' kōwhiri W.153 'select']

client *noun* kiritaki [kiri W.119 'person' apataki W.12 'retinue, following']

client base *noun* apataki [W.12 'retinue, following']

clinic *noun* whare haumanu [whare W.489 'house' haumanu W.40 'restore to health, revive']

clinical services *noun* ratonga haumanu [ratonga TM 'service' haumanu W.40 'revive, restore to health']

clip *noun* rawhi [W.333 'grasp, hold firmly']

clipboard *noun* paparawhi [papa W.259 'anything broad, flat and hard' rawhi TM 'clip']

cloakroom *noun* whata pouheni [whata pouheni W.298 'a pole with branches or pegs on which to hang things']

close *noun* (*computer*) kati [W.103 'close up, shut']

closed curve *noun* ānau kati [ānau W.9 'curve' kati W.103 'closed']

cloth *noun* papanga [papanga-rua W.259 'twofold, of fabric']

clothes-rack *noun* whata pouheni [W.298 'a pole with branches or pegs on which to hang things']

clove *noun* rōkara [rōhutu W.345 'myrtus

obcordata' kakara W.97 'scent, smell, flavour']

clown *noun* hako [whakahako W.32 'bedeck oneself']

clutch *noun* (*vehicle*) whakatanga [whakatanganga W.378 'release from restraint, disengage']

coach *transitive verb* whakaako [whakaako W.7 'teach']

coach *noun* kaiwhakaako [kai W.86 'a prefix to transitive verbs to form nouns denoting an agent' whakaako W.7 'teach']

coach *noun* kaiwhakawaiwai [whakawaiwai W.475 'practise the use of weapons']

coaches' box *noun* nohoanga kaiwhakaako [nohoanga W.223 'seat' kaiwhakaako TM 'coach']

coal mine huke waro [huke W.68 'dig up, expose by removing the earth, excavate' waro W.480 'charcoal, deep hole or pit']

coat-rack *noun* whata pouheni [W.298 'a pole with branches or pegs on which to hang things']

cobble *transitive verb* (*mend*) pūnotinoti [W.310 'stitch roughly, patch up roughly']

cocaine *noun* kukarou [kuka W.155 'dry leaves' rou W.349 'intoxicated, as with tutu juice']

coccyx *noun* timu [W.419 'end, tail']

coefficient *noun* tau whakarea [tau TM 'number' whakarea TM 'multiply']

coelenterate *noun* (*zoology*) wharemoa [W.490 'hollow']

coffee bag *noun* toutou kawhe [toutou W.442 'dip into a liquid' kawhe < Eng. 'coffee']

coffee bean *noun* kanokawhe [kano W.94 'seed' kawhe < Eng. 'coffee']

coffee-grinder *noun* pehukawhe [pehu W.275 'pound' kanokawhe TM 'coffee bean']

coffee-maker *noun* pūrere kawhe [pūrere TM 'machine' kawhe < Eng. 'coffee']

cog *noun* (*individual tooth*) tara [W.386 'tooth of a comb']

cogwheel *noun* kōpaetara [kōpae W.135 'circular' tara TM 'cog']

cohort *noun* aropā [W.17 'clump of one species of tree']

coil *noun* (*intestine*) koru [W.147 'folded, coiled, looped']

coin, dollar *noun* tāra [< Eng. 'dollar']

coin, two dollar *noun* rua tāra [rua W.349 'two' tara < Eng. 'dollar']

coleslaw *noun* roi huamata [roi W.345 'grated kūmara' huawhenua common usage 'vegetable' huarākau common usage 'fruit' mata W.185 'raw, uncooked']

collapsed scrum *noun* taupuru hinga [taupuru TM 'scrum' hinga W.51 'fall from an erect position']

collar *noun* (*weightlifting*) kati [W.103 'closed, close up']

collateral *noun* (*finance*) taituarā [W.365 'support']

colleague *noun* hoamahi [hoa W.54 'friend' mahi W.163 'work']

collectively *adverb* petapeta [W.278 'all at once']

college of education *noun* whare takiura [W.373 'building set apart for instruction in esoteric lore']

colloquialism *noun* kīwaha [kī W.115 'saying' waha W.473 'mouth']

colon *noun* (*anatomy*) kōpiro [W.137 'intestines']

colon *noun* (*punctuation*) kopirua [kopi TM 'full stop' rua W.349 'two']

colon, sigmoid *noun* (*anatomy*) kōpiro whakahume [kōpiro TM 'colon' whakahume W.69 'be drawn between the legs (of the tail of a dog)']

colon, transverse *noun* (*anatomy*) kōpiro pae [kōpiro TM 'colon' pae W.245 'transverse beam']

colony *noun* whenua maru [whenua W.494 'land, country' maru W.184 'shaded, sheltered']

coloured *adjective* (*paper, etc.*) whaikano [whai W.484 'possessing, equipped with' kano W.94 'colour']

colour in *transitive verb* kauruku [W.108 'slightly shaded with colour']

colourless *adjective* kanokore [kano W.94 'colour' kore W.140 'no, not']

coma *noun* mauri ngaro *intransitive verb* [mauri W.197 'life principle, thymos of man' ngaro W.230 'absent, disappeared']

comatosed *adjective* mauri ngaro [mauri W.197 'life principle, thymos of man' ngaro W.230 'absent, disappeared']

combination *noun* kōwhiringa [kōwhiri W.153 'select']

combined doubles *noun* tokowhā tāne, wahine [tokowhā TM 'doubles' tāne W.377 'male' wahine W.474 'woman']
combustion *noun* ngingiha [W.233 'burn']
comedian *noun* pukuhohe [pukukata W.309 'laughing, hilarious' hohehohe W.55 'wrinkled with laughter']
comic *noun, adjective* pukuhohe [pukukata W.309 'laughing, hilarious' hohehohe W.55 'wrinkled with laughter']
comma *noun* piko [W.281 'curve, curved']
commentator *noun* autaua [W.23 'one who announces the approach of a fighting party']
commerce *noun* tauhokohoko [tau- W.397 'prefix denoting reciprocal action' hokohoko W.57 'trade, exchange']
commercial *adjective* arumoni [aru W.17 'follow, pursue' moni < Eng. 'money']
commissary *noun* māngai [W.177 'mouth' TM 'representative']
common *adjective* (*mathematics*) pātahi [pā W.243 'touch, affect' tahi W.359 'together']
common denominator *noun* tauraro pātahi [tauraro TM 'denominator' pātahi TM 'common']
common factor *noun* tauwehe pātahi [tauwehe TM 'factor' pātahi TM 'common']
common multiple *noun* taurea pātahi [taurea TM 'multiple' pātahi TM 'common']
common salt *noun* tote [tote < Eng. 'salt']
community *noun* hapori [W.36 'section of a tribe, family'], tānga whenua [W.378 'people of the place']
community centre *noun* whare tapere [W.383 'house in which the members of the hapū met for amusement etc.']
community service *noun* (*justice*) ngahi hapori [ngahi W.232 'suffer penalty, be punished' hapori TM 'community']
community service *noun* (*organisation*) ratonga hapori [ratonga TM 'service' hapori TM 'community']
commutative *adjective* (*mathematics*) kōrure-kore [kōrure W.147 'change' kore W.140 'no, not']
compact disc *noun* (*music*) kōpaepae pūoru [W.135 'plaited circular band for lining an oven' pūoru TM 'music']
compact numeral *noun* tau kiato [tau TM 'number' kiato W.116 'compact, in small compass']
company *noun* (*commercial enterprise*) umanga [W.467 'pursuit, occupation, business']
comparative adjective *noun* kupu āhua whakataurite [kupu āhua TM 'adjective' whakataurite TM 'compare']
comparative number story *noun* pakitau whakatairite [pakitau TM 'number story' whakatairite whaka- W.486 'causative prefix' *to make* tairite W.365 'like, on a level with']
compare *transitive verb* whakataurite [whaka- W.486 'causative prefix' *to make* taurite W.403 'alike, matching'], whakatairite [whaka- W.486 'causative prefix' *to make* tairite W.365 'like, on a level with']
comparison *noun* whakatauritenga [whakataurite TM 'compare'], whakatairitenga [whakatairite TM 'compare']
compartment *noun* wāhanga [wāhi W.474 'part, portion']
compensate *transitive verb* paremata [W.266 'payment, return']
compensation *noun* paremata [W.266 'payment, return']
competence *noun* tohungatanga [tohunga W.431 'skilled person']
competent *adjective* kaiaka [W.86 'forward in attainments, adept, proficient']
competition *noun* whakataetae [W.356 'try strength, contend']
competition sport *noun* hākinakina whakataetae [hākinakina TM 'sport' whakataetae W.356 'try strength, contend'], hākinakina tauwhāinga [hākinakina TM 'sport' tauwhāinga W.405 'contend, vie']
competitor *noun* māia [W.166 'brave warrior, fellow, bold, capable']
complainant *noun* kaiwhakapae [kai W.86 'a prefix to transitive verbs to form nouns denoting an agent' whakapae W.245 'accuse']
complaint *noun* (*justice*) whakapae [W.245 'accuse, make an accusation']
complement (of set) *noun* (*mathematics*) huinga rāwaho [huinga 'set' rāwaho 'from outside']

composite *adjective* hiato [W.48 'be gathered together']

composite bar graph *noun* kauwhata pou hiato [kauwhata pou TM 'bar graph' hiato W.48 'be gathered together']

compost *noun* wairākau [W.476 'manure']

compound *noun* (*chemistry*) pūhui [pū W.300 'origin, source' hui W.66 'come together, double up']

compound leaf *noun* tawhera [W.408 'leaf']

comprehensible *adjective* mahuki [W.165 'clear, plain']

compress *transitive verb* whakapineke [whaka- W.486 'causative prefix' *to make* pineke W.281 'compressed']

compressed natural gas *noun* (CNG) kapunipuni [kapuni TM 'natural gas' puni W.310 'stopped up, blocked']

compression *noun* pīnekeneke [pineke W.281 'close together, compressed']

compulsory course *noun* (*education*) akoranga me mātua tutuki [akoranga TM 'course' mātua W.195 'first' tutuki W.450 'be completed']

compute *transitive verb* tātai [TM 'calculate']

computer *noun* rorohiko [roro W.347 'brains' hiko common usage 'electric']

computer keyboard *noun* papa pātuhi [papa W.259 'anything broad, flat and hard' pātuhi TM 'key']

computer room *noun* taiwhanga rorohiko [taiwhanga TM 'room' rorohiko TM 'computer']

computer screen *noun* mata rorohiko [mata W.185 'face, surface' rorohiko TM 'computer']

computer terminal *noun* kāpeka rorohiko [kāpeka W.96 'branch of a tree or river' rorohiko TM 'computer']

computing *noun* tātaitanga [tātai TM 'calculate']

concave lens *noun* arotahi hakoko [arotahi TM 'lens' hakoko W.32 'concave']

concave mirror *noun* whakaata hakoko [whakaata TM 'mirror' hakoko W.32 'concave']

concentrate *transitive verb* (*substance*) whakakukū [whaka- W.486 'causative prefix' *to make* kukū TM 'concentrate']

concentrate *noun* (*substance*) kukū [W.153 'thickened, thick liquid']

concentrated solution *noun* wairewa kukū [wairewa TM 'solution' kukū TM 'concentrate']

concentration *noun* (*substance*) kukū [W.153 'thickened, thick liquid']

concept map *noun* mahere ariā [mahere TM 'map' ariā W.15 'notion, idea']

conception *noun* (*idea*) hiringa mahara [hiri W.53 'spring up, rise up, of thoughts' mahara W.163 'thought']

concern *noun* (*issue*) take [W.370 'subject of an argument etc.']

conclude *transitive verb* (*decide*) whakatau [whaka- W.486 'causative prefix' *to make* tau W.396 'come to rest, settle down']

conclusion *noun* (*decision*) whakatau [whaka- W.486 'causative prefix' *to make* tau W.396 'come to rest, settle down']

concurrent *adjective* tautokorua [W.404 'simultaneous, both together']

condiment *noun* whakarehu [W.334 'give a relish to, flavour' rehu W.334 'fine dust']

condition *noun* (*restriction*) here [W.46 'tie up, fasten with cords']

conditional *adjective* tāupeupe [tāupe W.401 'bending, not rigid, variable']

condom *noun* pūkoro ure [pūkoro W.308 'sheath, pocket' ure W.468 'membrum virile']

conduct *transitive verb* (*transmit heat, energy*) kawe [kawe W.111 'convey, carry']

conduction *noun* (*electricity*) kawe iahiko [kawe W.111 'convey, carry' iahiko TM 'electrical current']

conductivity *noun* (*electricity*) kahakawe iahiko [kaha W.82 'strength' kawe W.111 'convey' iahiko TM 'electrical current']

conductor *noun* (*electrical*) kakawe iahiko [kawe iahiko TM 'conduction']

cone *noun* koeko [W.123 'tapering to a point']

cone *noun* (*geometry*) koeko porohita [koeko W.123 'tapering to a point' porohita W.295 'circular']

cone *noun* (*fruit of tree*) koroī [W.144 'fruit of white pine']

confer *transitive verb* whiriwhiri [W.497 'select choose']

confident *adjective* ngākau titikaha [ngākau W.227 'inclination, spirit' titikaha W.425 'steadfast'], ngākau tahi [ngākau W.227 'inclination, spirit']

confidential *adjective* matatapu [matanui W.188 'open, aboveboard' tapu W.385 'inaccessible']

confidentiality *noun* noho matatapu [noho W.223 'stay, remain, lie' matatapu TM 'confidential']

confirm *transitive verb* whakaū [W.464 'make firm, establish'], whakamana [W.172 'give effect to']

congruent *adjective* tairite [W.365 'like, on a level with']

conic section *noun* motunga koeko [motu W.212 'severed, isolated' koeko W.123 'tapering to a point']

conical *adjective* koeko [W.123 'tapering to a point']

conifer *noun* koroī [W.144 'fruit of white pine, the tree itself']

conjunction *noun* (*language*) kupuhoto [kupu W.157 'word' hoto W.62 'join']

conjunctiva *noun* kirikamo [kiri W.119 'skin' kamo W.92 'eye']

conjunctivitis *noun* kirikamo kakā [kirikamo TM 'conjunctiva' kakā TM 'inflammation']

connective *noun* (*language*) kupuhoto [kupu W.157 'word' hoto W.62 'join']

conscientious *adjective* ihupuku [W.75 'hesitating, scrupulous, industrious, eager']

conscious *adjective* (*awake*) mauri ora [mauri W.197 'life principle, thymos of man' ora W.240 'well, in health']

consensus *noun* whakatau a te nuinga [whakatau TM 'decision' nuinga W.224 'majority, larger part']

console *noun* (*control desk*) papatohu [papa W.259 'anything broad, flat, and hard' tohu W.431 'mark, sign, show, point out']

consonant *noun* pūkati [pū TM 'letter, character' kati W.103 'shut, closed, of a passage']

constant *noun* (*mathematics*) tau pūmau [tau TM 'number' pūmau W.309 'constant']

constitutional law *noun* ture kāwanatanga [ture W.459 'law' kāwanatanga < Eng 'government']

consul *noun* kairauhī [kai W.86 'a prefix to transitive verbs to form nouns denoting an agent' rauhī W.329 'take care of, foster, protect']

consul general *noun* kairauhī matua [kai W.86 'a prefix to transitive verbs to form nouns denoting an agent' rauhī W.329 'take care of, foster, protect' matua W.195 'main, chief']

consumer *noun* (*ecology*) whakapeto [whaka- W.486 'causative prefix' *to make* peto W.278 'be consumed']

contend *transitive verb* (*put forward an idea*) whakapae [W.245 'make an accusation']

contest area *noun* (*judo*) wāhirutu [wāhi W.474 'place, locality' rutu W.353 'dash down, overcome']

contestable *adjective* kairapu [W.89 'contend for']

contestant *noun* kaiwhakataetae [kai W.86 'a prefix to transitive verbs to form nouns denoting an agent' whakataetae W.356 'try strength, contend']

context *noun* horopaki [W.61 'surround']

continent *noun* whenua rahi [whenua W.494 'land' rahi W.320 'great']

continental drift *noun* momotunga whenua [momotu W.212 'sever, separate' whenua W.494 'land']

continental shelf *noun* pūkawa raurarahi [pūkawa W.307 'reef' raurarahi W.330 'broad, expansive']

continuing education *noun* mātauranga auroa [mātauranga common usage 'education' auroa W.22 'prolonged, extended']

continuous *adjective* (*mathematics*) motukore [motu W.211 'broken off, separated, anything isolated' kore W.140 'no, not']

continuous data *noun* raraunga motukore [raraunga TM 'data' motu W.211 'broken off, separated, anything isolated' kore W.140 'no, not']

contour line *noun* hua [W.64 'outline, leading line of a pattern in carving']

contraception *noun* ārai hapū [ārai W.14 'ward off' hapū W.36 'pregnant']

contraceptive *noun* ārai hapū [ārai W.14 'ward off' hapū W.36 'pregnant']

contract *noun* (*binding agreement*) kirimana [kiri W.119 'skin, bark' mana W.172 'effectual, binding, authoritative']

contravene *transitive verb* takahi [W.367 'disobey, violate']

control *transitive verb* (*manage*) whakahaere [W.30 'conduct, lead']

control experiment *noun* whakamātau whakatina [whakamātau TM 'ex-

periment' whakatina W.419 'confine, put under restraint']
convalesce *intransitive verb* mātūtū [W.195 'convalescent, not quite healed']
convection current *noun* iakawe mahana [ia W.74 'current' kawe W.111 'convey' mahana W.162 'warm']
conversion *noun* (*computer*) hurihanga [huri W.71 'turn round']
conversion *noun* (*rugby etc.*) whana turuki [whana W.486 'kick' turuki W.461 'come as a supplement, follow']
convert *transitive verb* huri [W.71 'turn round']
conveyor belt *noun* ara nekeneke [ara W.13 'means of conveyance' nekeneke W.220 'move gradually']
cookery book *noun* pukapuka tao [pukapuka W.306 'book' tao W.381 'cook in a native oven']
coolstore *noun* rokiroki mātao [rokiroki W.345 'store, collection of articles, preserve' mātao W.189 'cold']
cooperate *intransitive verb* mahi ngātahi [mahi W.163 'work, work at' ngātahi W.231 'together']
cooperation *noun* mahi ngātahi [mahi W.163 'work, work at' ngātahi W.231 'together']
cooperative *noun* (*venture*) ohu [W.239 'do by aid of a company of volunteer workers']
co-opt *transitive verb* tono kia uru mai [tono W.436 'bid, command' uru W.469 'participate in']
coordinate *transitive verb* ruruku [W.351 'draw together with a cord']
coordinates (*mathematics*) taunga [taunga W.396 'resting place, anchorage']
coordinator *noun* kairuruku [kai W.86 'a prefix to transitive verbs to form nouns denoting an agent' ruruku W.351 'draw together with a cord']
copper *noun* (*metal*) konukura [konu- TM 'prefix denoting natural metal' kura W.157 'red ochre']
copper sulphate *noun* pākawa kura pungawera [pākawa TM '-ate' konukura TM 'copper' pungawera W.311 'sulphur']
copy *transitive verb, noun* (*document*) tārua [tā TM 'print' tārua W.392 'repeat any process']

copyright *noun* manatārua [mana W.172 'authority, power' tārua TM 'copy']
coral *noun* roke kanae [W.345 'a belemnite fossil shell']
cord, extension *noun* taura katete [taura W.402 'cord' katete W.103 'lengthen by adding a piece']
cordial *noun* (*drink*) wainene [W.476 'sweet' wai W.474 'water, liquid']
corduroy *noun* paparai [papanga TM 'cloth' rarai W.321 'ribbed, furrowed']
co-requisite *noun* (*education*) akoranga tautokorua [akoranga TM 'course' tautokorua W.404 'simultaneous, both together']
corkscrew *noun* (*bottle opener*) wairori [W.477 'turn round, twist']
cornea *noun* (*eye*) kirimōwaho [kiriuhi TM 'membrane' mōwaho W.212 'outward, on the outside']
corned *adjective* (*food*) mina-tote [minamina W.202 'affected by' tote < Eng. 'salt']
corner flag *noun* (*sport*) pīwari koko [pīwari TM 'flag' koko W.130 'corner']
corner hit *noun* (*hockey*) patu koko [patu W.272 'hit' koko W.130 'corner']
corner pad *noun* (*boxing*) aupuru koko [aupuru W.22 'cushion or pad under a load to prevent chafing' koko W.130 'corner']
corner post *noun* pou koko [pou W.297 'post' koko W.130 'corner']
cornflakes *noun* kānga rere [kānga < Eng. 'corn' rere W.337 'flow, fall, of rain']
corona *noun* (*solar system*) kurahauao [kurahaupō W.158 'lunar rainbow' ao W.11 'bright']
coroner *noun* kaitirotiro matewhawhati [kai W.86 'a prefix to transitive verbs to form nouns denoting an agent' tirotiro W.424 'investigate' matewhawhati TM 'unexpected death']
corporate *adjective* rangatōpū [ranga W.322 'company of persons' tōpū W.437 'in a body, assembled']
corporate body *noun* rangatōpū [ranga W.322 'company of persons' tōpū W.437 'in a body, assembled']
corporate plan *noun* mahere rangatōpū [mahere TM 'plan' rangatōpū TM 'corporate']

corporate service *noun* ratonga rangatōpū [ratonga TM 'service' rangatōpū TM 'corporate']

corporation *noun* tokapū [toka W.433 'firm, solid' pū W.300 'root, foundation, base']

corrective training *noun* ngahi whakatikatika [ngahi W.232 'suffer penalty, be punished' whakatika W.417 'straighten, correct']

corrode *transitive verb* waikura *intransitive verb* [W.476 'rust, redden']

corrosion *noun* waikura [W.476 'rust, redden']

corrugated *adjective* kōwakawaka [W.152 'grooved, fluted'], rarai [W.321 'ribbed, furrowed']

corrugated iron *noun* piharoa kōwakawaka [piharoa W.279 'iron' TM 'sheet metal' kōwakawaka TM 'corrugated']

corset *noun* koere [W.123 'woven belt or girdle']

cosine *noun* whenu [W.494 'strand of a cord, warp of a flax garment']

cosmetic *noun, adjective* whakanako [W.217 'adorn with fine markings']

cost *noun* utu [W.471 'price']

cost, administrative *noun* utu whakahaere [utu W.471 'price' whakahaere TM 'administer']

cot *noun* (*bassinet*) pouraka [W.298 'rude form of cradle for infants']

cot death *noun* mate pouraka [mate W.192 'dead' pouraka W.298 'rude form of cradle for infants']

cotton fabric *noun* papahune [papanga TM 'cloth' hune W.69 'down, of birds etc., pappus of seeds of raupō']

cotton reel *noun* pōkaimiro [pōkai W.289 'ball of string' miro W.203 'thread']

cotton thread *noun* miro [W.203 'thread']

counsel *noun* (*justice*) waha kōrero [waha W.473 'mouth, voice' kōrero W.141 'speak, address']

counterclaim *noun* tāwari [W.406 'oppose a claim to land etc.']

counting number *noun* tau tatau [tau TM 'number' tatau W.395 'count']

count-out *noun* (*boxing*) tatau waikauere [tatau TM 'number' waikauere W.475 'without energy, subdued']

coup *noun* (*overthrow*) tukipoto [W.450 'sudden attack by a taua']

coup *noun* (*success*) angitu [W.11 'luck, success']

coup d'etat *noun* upokotaua [W.468 'surprise attack']

course, educational *noun* akoranga [W.7 'circumstance of learning']

court *noun* papa tākaro [papa W.259 'site' tākaro W.369 'play, sport']

court *noun* (*justice*) whare whakawā [whare W.489 'house' whakawā TM 'judge']

court, badminton *noun* papa pūkura [papa tākaro TM 'court' pūkura TM 'badminton']

court cost *noun* (*justice*) utu whakawā [utu W.471 'price' whakawā TM 'judge']

cowpox *noun* koroputa kau [koroputaputa W.145 'smallpox' kau < Eng. 'cow']

cox *noun* kaituki [W.90 'the man who gives the time to the paddlers in a canoe']

CPR (*abbreviation*) whakaora manawa [whakaora W.241 'save alive, restore to health' manawa W.174 'heart']

craft *noun* haratau [W.37 'dexterous, suitable, approved']

craftsperson *noun* haratau [haratau W.37 'dexterous, suitable, approved']

crane *noun* (*machine*) wakahiki [waka common usage 'vehicle' hiki W.49 'lift up, raise']

cranium *noun* pakohu roro [pakohu W.255 'cavity' roro W.347 'brains']

cream *adjective* (*colour*) kahotea [kaho W.84 'anything light-coloured' kahotea W.84 'variety of greenstone having light-coloured streaks in it; nearly white']

crease *noun* (*cricket*) wī [TM 'line' see W.284 piro 'out, in games']

crease, bowling *noun* (*cricket*) wī epa [wī TM 'crease' epa TM 'bowl']

crease, popping *noun* wī tarapeke [wī TM 'crease' tarapeke W.388 'spring, leap, jump']

crease, return *noun* wī hoki [wī TM 'crease' hoki W.57 'return']

creation *noun* orokohanga [oroko W.242 'for the first time' hanga W.34 'build, fashion']

creative *adjective* auaha [W.21 'leap, throb, create, form, fashion']

creative therapy *noun* whakaara wairua auaha [whakaara W.13 'raise, rouse, wake' wairua W.477 'spirit' auaha TM 'creative'], whakatō wairua auaha

[whakatō W.428 'introduce, insert, cause to conceive' wairua W.477 'spirit' auaha TM 'creative']
creativeness *noun* auahatanga [auaha TM 'creative']
credit *noun* (*work completed towards university qualification*) waetohu [wae TM 'unit' tohu TM 'degree']
cremate *transitive verb* tahu tūpāpaku [tahu W.360 'set on fire, burn' tūpāpaku W.456 'corpse']
cremation *noun* tahu tūpāpaku [tahu W.360 'set on fire, burn' tūpāpaku W.456 'corpse']
crepe paper *noun* pepamingo [pepa < Eng. 'paper' mingo W.202 'curly, wrinkled']
crime *noun* taihara [tai- W.362 'prefix having no apparent effect on the meaning' hara W.36 'sin, offence']
crime, to commit a *phrase* takahi i te ture [takahi W.367 'disobey, violate' ture W.459 'law']
crime, violent *noun* hara kaikoka [taihara TM 'crime' kaikoka W.88 'violent']
criminal *adjective, noun* taihara [taihara TM 'crime']
criminal justice system *noun* pūnaha ture taihara [pūnaha TM 'system' ture 'law' taihara TM 'crime']
criminal mind *noun* hinengaro taihara [hinengaro W.51 'seat of the thoughts and emotions' taihara TM 'crime']
criminology *noun* mātauranga taihara [mātauranga common usage 'knowledge' taihara TM 'crime']
criterion *noun* paearu [paepae W.245 'beam, bar' aru W.17 'follow, pursue']
crochet *transitive verb* tuimāwhai [tui W.449 'lace, fasten by passing a cord through holes' māwhaiwhai W.198 'spider web']
crocheting *noun* tuimāwhai [tui W.449 'lace, fasten by passing a cord through holes' māwhaiwhai W.198 'spider web']
crockery *noun* okouku [oko W.239 'wooden bowl or other open vessel' uku W.466 'white clay']
crockpot *noun* tāpīpī [W.384 'small earth oven']
crocodile *noun* kumi ihuroa [kumi W.156 'a huge fabulous reptile' ihu W.75 'nose' roa W.344 'long']

croquet *noun* hauwhiti [hau W.39 'strike, smite' whiti W.498 'pass through, hoop']
cross *noun* (*soccer*) whakawhiti [whakawhiti W.497 'convey across']
cross-product *noun* hua whakawhiti [hua TM 'result, product' whakawhiti W.497 'cross over']
crossbar *noun* kaho [W.83 'batten laid horizontally']
cross-section *noun* topenga [tope W.437 'cut, fell' topetope 'cut up, slice, divide']
crossword *noun* pangakupu [panga W.257 'riddle, game of guessing' kupu W.157 'word']
crotchet *noun* orotahi [oro W.242 'sound' tahi W.359 'one']
crowbar *noun* whakatiriwhana [W.424 'prise with a lever']
crown prosecutor *noun* poutoko ture karauna [poutoko ture TM 'lawyer' karauna < Eng. 'crown']
crucial *adjective* matawaenga [W.192 'left in a dilemma']
crucible *noun* (*science*) puoto whakawera [puoto W.311 'vessel' whaka- W.486 'causative prefix' *to make* wera W.482 'heated, hot']
crude *adjective* (*unrefined, in natural state*) urutapu [urutapu W.470 'untouched, in a state of nature, chaste, pure']
crude *adjective* karihika [W.101 'lewd, immoral']
crude oil *noun* hinu urutapu [hinu W.51 'oil' urutapu W.470 'untouched, in a state of nature, chaste, pure']
crust *noun* (*geology*) kirinuku [kiri W.119 'skin' nuku W.225 'the earth']
crustacean *noun* kōurapaka [kōura W.151 'crayfish' pāpaka W.250 'crab']
crystal *noun* (*science*) tioata [tio W.420 'ice' kōataata W.122 'transparent']
crystal *noun, adjective* (*type of glass*) kōataata [W.122 'transparent']
crystalline *adjective* tioata [tio W.420 'ice' kōataata W.122 'transparent']
crystallography *noun* mātauranga tioata [mātauranga common usage 'knowledge' tioata TM 'crystal']
CT Scanner *noun* matawai roro [matawai W.192 'look closely' roro W.347 'brains']
cube *noun* (*non-technical*) mataono [mata W.185 'surface' ono W.240 'six']

cube *noun* (*mathematical*) mataono rite [mata W.185 'surface' ono W.240 'six' rite W.343 'alike']

cubed *adjective* (*mathematics*) pūtoru [pū TM 'power' toru W.441 'three']

cubic *adjective* (*mathematics*) pūtoru [pū TM 'power' toru W.441 'three']

cubic metre *noun* mita pūtoru [mita < Eng. 'metre' pūtoru TM 'cubed'], tuke pūtoru [tuke TM 'metre' pūtoru TM 'cubed']

cuboid *adjective* mataono [mata W.185 'surface' ono W.240 'six']

cucumber *noun* kūkamo [kū- < Eng 'cu-' kamokamo W.92 'fruit of a gourd, possibly from cucumber']

culture *noun* (*biology, nutrient substance*) maremaretai [TM 'agar']

culture *noun* (*biology, micro-organism*) tītipu mōkito [tipu W.457 'grow' mōkitokito W.207 'minute, small']

cumulo-nimbus *noun* okewa whakapipi [okewa W.239 'nimbus, rain cloud' whakapipi W.282 'heap, pile, pile one upon another']

cumulus *noun* kapua whakapipi [kapua W.97 'cloud, bank of clouds' whakapipi W.282 'heap, pile, pile one upon another']

cupboard, kitchen *noun* papatara [W.261 'storehouse, stage for food']

curate *noun* kaiwhakamahiri pirihi [whakamahiri W.164 'assist' pirihi < Eng. 'priest']

curette *noun* tīwani [W.427 'strip, make bare, stripped bare']

curfew *noun* rāhui haere pō [rāhui W.321 'protect by a rāhui' haere W.30 'go' pō W.285 'night']

curriculum *noun* marautanga [marau W.181 'subject of talk']

curriculum vitae *noun* tāhuhu tangata [tāhuhu W.360 'ridgepole of a house, direct line of ancestry, any rod used as stiffener' tangata W.379 'human being']

cursor *noun* (*computer*) pehu [W.275 'dart, spear']

curtail *transitive verb* whāmutu [W.215 'leave off, cause to cease'], tauporo [W.401 'bring to an end, cut short']

cushion *noun* paretua [W.267 'pad under a load to protect the back']

custody *noun* (*children*) mana pupuri tamariki [mana W.172 'authority, control' pupuri W.314 'retain possession of' tamariki W.376 'children']

customer *noun* kiritaki [kiri W.119 'person' apataki W.12 'client base, customers']

customer base *noun* apataki [W.12 'retinue, following']

cutlery *noun* pāokaoka [paoka W.258 'pointed stick, skewer, used for picking up food']

cyclist *noun* kaieke pahikara [kai W.86 'a prefix to transitive verbs to form nouns denoting an agent' eke W.27 'place oneself upon another object' pahikara < Eng. 'bicycle']

cyclone *noun* kurahau-awatea [Best *Astronomical Knowledge* 19 'sign of bad weather']

cylinder *noun* (*container*) puoto [W.311 'vessel']

cylinder *noun* (*mathematics*) rango [W.324 'roller upon which a heavy body is dragged']

cymbal *noun* tīwēwē [W.427 'scream, unrestrained, uncontrolled']

cystitis *noun* tōngāmimi kakā [tōngāmimi W.436 'bladder' kakā TM 'inflammation']

D

dacron *noun* takaaku [taka- < Eng. 'dac-' kaka-aku TM 'textile fibre']
dais *noun* tūāpapa [W.446 'platform, foundation']
dame *noun (title)* kahurangi [W.85 'honourable, distinguished, prized']
danger *noun* mōrearea [W.210 'exposed to great danger']
dangerous criminal *noun* taihara rupe [taihara TM 'criminal' rupe W.352 'treat with violence']
dangerous tackle *noun* tairutu [tai W.361 'anger, violence' rutu TM 'tackle']
daredevil *noun* manawa kai tūtae [W.174 'daring, undaunted']
darn *transitive verb* moanarua [W.204 'repair a garment by weaving a fresh piece']
darning *noun* moanarua [W.204 'repair a garment by weaving a fresh piece']
dart-throwing *noun (game)* toro teka [Best Games and Pastimes 62 'dart-throwing']
dash *noun (punctuation)* āputa [W.13 'causing a gap']
dashboard *noun* papatohu [papa W.259 'anything broad, flat, and hard' tohu W.431 'mark, sign, show, point out']
data *noun* raraunga [rarau W.328 'lay hold of, receptacle']
database *noun* pātengi raraunga [pātengi W.271 'storehouse or pit for kūmara' raraunga TM 'data']
date stamp *noun* pourangi [pou W.297 'fix' rangi W.324 'day']
de facto marriage *noun* moe māori [moe W.204 'marry, sleep together' māori W.179 'freely, without ceremony']
de facto partner *noun* hoa moe māori [hoa W.54 'spouse, husband, wife' moe W.205 'sleep together' māori W.179 'freely, without ceremony']
dead ball *noun (sport)* poihemo [poi TM 'ball' hemo W.45 'miss a mark, die']
dead ball line *noun (sport)* pae poihemo [pae W.245 'margin, boundary' poi TM 'ball' hemo W.45 'miss a mark, die']
dead target *noun (shooting)* moutī [W.212 'decoy kākā']
deafforestation *noun* whakamāmore whenua [whaka- W.486 'causative prefix' *to make* māmore W.172 'without accompaniments or appendages, bare' whenua W.494 'land, country']
dean *noun* manutaki [W.176 'a bird acting as sentry for a flock']
death, sudden *noun* mate ohorere [mate W.192 'death' ohorere W.238 'start suddenly']
death, unexpected *noun* matewhawhati [mate W.192 'death' matawhawhati W.192 'sudden, unexpected']
debt, bad *noun* nama kāore i utua [nama common usage 'debt' kāore W.95 'no, not' utu W.471 'return for anything']
decathlete *noun* kaipara ngahuru [kaipara TM 'athlete' ngahuru W.227 'ten']
decathlon *noun* kaipara ngahuru [kaipara TM 'athletics' ngahuru W.227 'ten']
decelerate *transitive verb* pāitiiti [W.250 'decrease, subside']
deceleration *noun* pāitiiti [TM 'decelerate']
decide *transitive verb, intransitive verb* whakatau [whaka- W.486 'causative prefix' *to make* tau W.396 'come to rest']
deciduous *adjective* tokerauhoro [tokerau W.433 'autumn' rau W.328 'leaf' horo W.60 'drop off']
decimal *adjective* ngahuru [W.227 'ten']

decimal *adjective* tau-ā-ira [tau TM 'number' ā W.1 'after the manner of ira TM 'dot']

decimal, infinite *noun* tau-ā-ira whāioio [tau-ā-ira TM 'decimal number' tau whāioio TM 'infinite number']

decimal, recurring *noun* ngahuru auau [ngahuru TM 'decimal' auau TM 'recurring'], tau-ā-ira auau [tau-ā-ira TM 'decimal' auau TM 'recurring']

decimal fraction *noun* hautau ngahuru [hautau TM 'fraction' ngahuru TM 'decimal'], hautau-ā-ira [hautau TM 'fraction' tau-ā-ira TM 'decimal']

decimal number *noun* tau ngahuru [tau TM 'number' ngahuru W.227 'ten'], tau-ā-ira [tau TM 'number' ā W.1 'after the manner of' ira TM 'decimal point, dot']

decimal point *noun* ira ngahuru [ira TM 'dot' ngahuru TM 'decimal'], ira [TM 'dot']

decimal system *noun* pūnaha ngahuru [pūnaha TM 'system' ngahuru TM 'decimal'], pūnaha tau-ā-ira [pūnaha TM 'system' tau-ā-ira TM 'decimal']

decision *noun* whakatau [whaka- W.486 'causative prefix' *to make* tau W.396 'come to rest']

deck *noun* (*cards*) pūranga [pū W.300 'source, base' pūranga W.312 'lie in a heap, heap']

decking *noun* rueke [W.350 'verandah, porch']

declare *intransitive verb* (*cricket*) whakawātea [whaka- W.486 'causative prefix' *to make* wātea W.480 'clear, free, open']

decompose *transitive verb* whakapopo [whaka- W.486 'causative prefix' *to make* popo W.292 'rotten, decayed, worm-eaten']

decomposer *noun* whakapopo [whaka- W.486 'causative prefix' *to make* popo W.292 'rotten, decayed, worm-eaten']

decontamination *noun* puretumu [W.313 'perform rites to obtain satisfaction for a disaster']

dectane *noun* ngawaro [ngahuru W.227 'ten' waro TM 'alkane']

deep purple *adjective* poroporo [W.294 'solanum nigrum and solanum aviculare, plants']

deep-fry *transitive verb* rumaki parai [rumaki W.351 'immerse' rumaki W.352 'basket of seed potatoes' parai < Eng. 'fry']

deep-fryer *noun* parai rumaki [parai < Eng. 'fry' rumaki W.351 'immerse' rumaki W.352 'basket of seed potatoes']

defamation *noun* heitara [W.44 'accusation, charge, scandal']

defame *transitive verb* heitara [W.44 'accusation, charge, scandal']

default *noun* (*computer*) puta aunoa [puta 315 'come, come forth, come out' aunoa TM 'automatic']

default *intransitive verb* tautuku [W.405 'bend down, so give way']

default summons *noun* hāmene whakaea nama [hāmene < Eng. 'summons' whakaea W.26 'pay for' nama common usage 'debt']

defect *noun* tōrōkiri [W.440 'defect, flaw in timber, due to injury to the growing tree']

defence *noun* kaupare hoariri [kaupare W.107 'turn in a different direction, avert' hoariri W.54 'enemy, foe']; pukumaire [W.309 'a term applied to a line of fortifications']

defendant *noun* whakatuaki [W.445 'blame' TM 'accused']

defender *noun* (*sport*) kaipare [kai W.86 'a prefix to transitive verbs to form nouns denoting an agent' pare W.266 'ward off']

defensive driving *noun* karo aituā waka [karo W.123 'parry, avoid' aituā W.5 'misfortune, trouble, disaster, accident' waka common usage 'vehicle']

definite article *noun* pū tautuhi [pūtohu TM 'article' tautuhi W.405 'indicate, define']

defrost *transitive verb* whakarewa [whaka- W.486 'causative prefix' *to make* rewa W.339 'melt, be or become liquid']

defrost *intransitive verb* rewa [rewa W.339 'melt, be or become liquid']

degree *noun* (*mathematics, unit of angle*) putu [W.317 'lie one upon another']

degree, post-graduate *noun* tohu paerua [tohu mātauranga TM 'degree' pae W.245 'transverse beam' rua W.349 'two']

degree, undergraduate *noun* tohu paetahi [tohu mātauranga TM 'qualification' pae W.244 'step, bar' tahi W.359 'one, first']

degree of difficulty *noun* uaua [W.465 'difficult']

dehydrator *noun* whakamaroke [W.183 'cause to wither'], tauraki [W.402 'dry by exposure to the sun, dried']

delegate *transitive verb* tautapa [W.403 'nominate, designate']

delegate *noun* māngai [W.177 'mouth' TM 'representative']

delegation *noun* apatono [apārangi W.12 'company of persons, especially distinguished persons' tono W.436 'demand']

delineate *transitive verb* whakaahua [W.4 'acquire form']

deliveries *noun* (*goods*) hīkawekawe [hikawe W.49 'carry a burden']

delivery room *noun* (*childbirth*) whare kahu [W.84 'shed erected for childbirth']

delta *noun* pūwaha [W.317 'mouth of a river etc.']

democracy *noun* manapori [mana W.172 'power, control' pori W.294 'people, tribe']

democratic *adjective* manapori [mana W.172 'power, control' pori W.294 'people, tribe']

demographical *adjective* taupori [tau W.395 'count' W.396 'alight, come to rest' pori W.294 'people, tribe']

demography *noun* tatauranga taupori [tatauranga TM 'statistics' tau W.395 'count' W.396 'alight, come to rest' pori W.294 'people, tribe']

denial of liability *phrase* (*justice*) uapare [W.465 'attribute to another what is charged to oneself']

denominator *noun* tauraro [tau TM 'number' raro W.359 'together']

density *noun* kiato [W.116 'compact']

dentine *noun* matūniho [matū W.195 'fat, gist, kernel' niho W.221 'tooth']

dentures *noun* niho more [niho W.221 'tooth' more W.209 'toothless']

deodorant *noun* patu mōrūruru [patu W.272 'strike, subdue' mōrūruru W.210 'odour of human sweat']

deoxyribonucleic acid DNA *noun* pītauira [pītau W.284 'perforated spiral carving, young succulent shoot of a plant, circinate frond of a fern' ira TM 'gene']

dependent partner *noun* hoapori [hoa W.54 'spouse' pori W.294 'dependants']

deposit *noun* (*finance*) moni tāpui [moni < Eng. 'money' tāpui W.385 'set aside, bespeak, reserve']

deposit, long-term *noun* pūtea penaroa [pūtea TM 'account' pena W.277 'take care of, tend, husband' roa W.344 'long']

deposit, short-term *noun* pūtea penapoto [pūtea TM 'account' pena W.277 'take care of, tend, husband' poto W.297 'short']

deposit slip *noun* rau pūtea [rau W.328 'gather into a basket etc.' pūtea TM 'account']

depot *noun* taupuni [W.401 'place of assignation']

depreciation *noun* hekenga uara [heke W.44 'descend, ebb' uara TM 'value']

depression *noun* (*meteorological*) kurahauawatea [TM 'cyclone']

deputy *noun* piki [W.280 'second, support in a duel, assistant']

deranged, temporarily *adjective* keka [W.113 'mentally deranged, beside oneself with grief']

derivative (*mathematics*) pārōnaki [pānga TM 'function' rōnaki TM 'gradient']

dermis *noun* kiri [W.119 'skin']

describe *transitive verb* whakaahua [W.4 'acquire form'], whakamārama [W.180 'illuminate, explain']

desert *noun* koraha [W.139 'open country']

design *noun, transitive verb* hoahoa [W.54 'layout, plan, arrange']

despicable *adjective* whakaharihari [W.340 'disgusting']

dessert bowl *noun* oko purini [oko W.239 'wooden bowl or other open vessel' purini < Eng. 'pudding']

dessert fork *noun* mārau purini [mārau TM 'fork' purini < Eng. 'pudding']

dessert spoon *noun* koko purini [koko W.130 'spoon' purini < Eng. 'pudding']

detector *noun* pūoko [pūrere TM 'machine' oko W.239 'hear']

determine *transitive verb* whakatau [whaka- W.486 'causative prefix' *to make* tau W.396 'come to rest']

detonate *transitive verb* whakapahū [whaka- W.486 'causative prefix' *to make* pahū TM 'explosive']

detonation *noun* whakapahūnga [whakapahū TM 'detonate']

detour *noun* ākau roa [W.6 'circuitous route'], autaki [W.23 'roundabout, circuitous']
detoxification *noun* tangotāoke [tango W.380 'take away, remove' tāoke TM 'toxin, poison']
detoxify *transitive verb* tangotāoke [tango W.380 'take away, remove' tāoke TM 'toxin, poison']
deuce *noun* (*tennis*) haupārua [W.41 'fight with loss on both sides']
develop *transitive verb* (*formulate*) whakahiato [W.48 'collect together']
develop *intransitive verb* (*organism*) whanake [W.487 'grow, spring up']
deviance *noun* kotiti [W.146 'be distorted or displaced']
device *noun* pūrere [pū W.300 'source, base' rere W.337 'fly, flow']
devolution *noun* tuku mana whakahaere [tuku W.451 'allow, let, let go, give up' mana W.172 'authority, power' whakahaere TM 'control, manage']
dextrose *noun* terehuka [tere- < Eng. 'dex-' tere W.412 'swift, active' huka < Eng. 'sugar']
diabetes *noun* matehuka [mate W.192 'sickness' huka < Eng. 'sugar']
diabetic *noun* matehuka [mate W.192 'sickness' huka < Eng. 'sugar']
diabetic and respiratory services *noun* ratonga matehuka, matehā [ratonga TM 'services' matehuka TM 'diabetes' matehā TM 'respiratory disease']
diagnose *transitive verb* whakatau [TM 'conclude']
diagnosis *noun* whakatau mate [whakatau TM 'conclusion' mate W.192 'sickness']
diagonal *noun, adjective* hauroki [hauroki W.41 'the diagonals in measuring the ground plan of a house']
diagram *noun* hoahoa [hoahoa W.54 'plan of a house'], whakaahua [W.4 'acquire form']
diagram, scale *noun* hoahoa taurahi [hoahoa TM 'diagram' taurahi TM 'scale']
dial *noun* mataine [mata W.183 'face, surface' ine W.78 'measure']
diameter *noun* weherua [W.481 'dividing, separating, midnight']
diaphragm *noun* (*anatomy*) pātūpoho [pātū W.272 'screen, wall' poho W.287 'chest, stomach']

diaphragm *noun* (*contraceptive*) pātātea [pā W.243 'block up, obstruct' tātea W.394 'semen']
diary *noun* rātaka [rā W.319 'day' taka W.366 'come round, as a date or period of time']
dichromate *noun* pākawarua konukita [pākawa TM '-ate' rua W.349 'two' konukita TM 'chromium']
dictaphone *noun* hopu kōrero [hopu W.59 'catch, snatch' kōrero W.141 'speak, talk']
dictate *transitive verb* pānui [W.257 'read or speak aloud']
dictation *noun* pānui-ā-waha [pānui W.257 'read or speak aloud' ā W.1 'after the manner of' waha W.473 'voice, mouth']
dictionary *noun* papakupu [papa W.259 'box, chest' kupu W.157 'word']
diet *intransitive verb, noun* nohopuku [W.223 'fast']
diet, crash *noun* whakapuango [W.302 'starve']
difference *noun* (*arithmetic*) huatango [hua TM 'result, outcome' tango TM 'subtract']
differentiate *transitive verb, intransitive verb* wehewehe *transitive verb* [W.481 'sort out, arrange']
digest *transitive verb* nakunaku [W.217 'reduced to fragments, broken in pieces, crushed']
digestion *noun* nakunaku [W.217 'reduced to fragments, broken in pieces, crushed']
digestive tract *noun* roma nakunaku [roma TM 'tract' nakunaku TM 'digest']
digit *noun* (*mathematics*) mati [W.193 'finger']
digraph *noun* (*linguistics*) pūrua [pū TM 'letter' rua W.349 'two']
dilemma *noun* ngākau kōnatunatu [ngākau W.227 'seat of feelings' kōnatunatu W.133 'heart distressed by conflicting emotions']
dinghy, inflatable *noun* pīhau [W.280 'some form of canoe']
dining-room table *noun* paparahua [W.260 'kind of table from which food was eaten']
dinosaur *noun* moko tuauri [moko W.207 'a general term for lizards, huge mythical creature of lizard-like shape' tuauri W.448 'ancient, ancient times']
diphthong *noun* ororua [oro W.242 'sound' rua W.349 'two']

diploma noun tītohu [W.426 'show, display' tohu mātauranga TM 'qualification']

diplomat noun takawaenga kāwanatanga [takawaenga W.366 'go, pass round' waenga W.472 'the middle, the midst' kāwanatanga < Eng. 'government']

directly adverb tauaro [W.397 'straight, direct']

director, assistant noun tuarā tumuaki [tuarā W.446 'assist, ally, support, back' tumuaki W.454 'head, president']

directory noun (computer) rārangi kōpaki [rārangi W.324 'rank, row' kōpaki TM 'folder']

directory, telephone noun rārangi tau waea [W.324 'line, rank, row' tau waea TM 'telephone number']

directory, trade noun rārangi ringarehe [rārangi W.324 'line, rank, row' ringarehe TM 'tradesperson']

directory board noun papatohu [papa W.259 'anything broad, flat and hard' tohutohu W.431 'show, direct, guide']

disable transitive verb whakakaurapa [W.108 'put out of action, unable to swim, cramp in the legs']

disabled adjective hauā [W.39 'cripple, crippled']

disaccharide noun hukarua [huka < Eng. 'sugar' rua W.349 'two']

disarm transitive verb tupe [W.456 'a charm for depriving one's enemies of power, and arresting their weapons']

disarmament noun tupe [W.456 'a charm for depriving one's enemies of power, and arresting their weapons']

discharge transitive verb (release) tuku [W.451 'let go']

discipline noun (field of study) pekanga mātauranga [pekanga W.275 'branch, road' mātauranga common usage 'knowledge']

discipline transitive verb whakatika [W.417 'straighten, correct']

disco noun pekerangi [W.276 'a dance accompanied by song, perform such a dance']

disco-dancing noun pekerangi [W.276 'a dance accompanied by song, perform such a dance']

discourse noun kōrero [W.141 'speak, conversation']

discrete data noun raraunga motumotu [raraunga TM 'data' motumotu W.212 'divided into isolated portions']

discriminate transitive verb (justice) aukati [W.22 'stop one's way, prevent one from passing, line which one may not pass']

discrimination noun (justice) aukati [W.22 'stop one's way, prevent one from passing, line which one may not pass']

discus noun poroāwhio [porohita W.295 'circle, wheel, ring' āwhio W.25 'go round about' āwhiowhio W.25 'whirlwind']

discussion noun matapakinga [matapaki W.189 'make the subject of talk, discuss']

dishcloth noun muku [W.213 'wipe, rub']

dish-rack noun mātiti rerewai [mātiti W.194 'wooden rack or grid on which birds were placed for roasting' rere W.337 'escape' wai W.474 'water']

dishwasher noun (machine) pūrere horoi maitai [pūrere TM 'machine' horoi W.61 'clean, wash, scour' maitai < Eng. 'metal' common usage 'dishes']

dishwashing brush noun taitai [taitai W.362 'brush']

disinfect transitive verb patu kitakita [patu W.272 'kill' kitakita TM 'bacteria']

disinfectant noun patu kitakita [patu W.272 'kill' kitakita TM 'bacteria']

disjoint adjective ritua [W.343 'be divided, be separated']

disk noun (computer) kōpae [kōpaepae W.135 'plaited circular band for lining an oven']

disk-drive unit noun puku rorohiko [puku W.308 'memory, abdomen, stomach' rorohiko TM 'computer']

diskette noun kōpaepae [W.135 'plaited circular band for lining an oven']

dismiss transitive verb pana [W.256 'expel']

display transitive verb whakaatu [W.40 'point out, show']

display noun whakaaturanga [whakaatu W.40 'point out, show']

disqualify transitive verb (vehicle licence) taumanu [W.399 'take possession of another's goods']

disqualify transitive verb (sport) tātāki [W.371 'take to one side, take out of the way']

dissect transitive verb tuaki [W.445 'disembowel fish or birds']

dissection *noun* tuakitanga [tuaki W.445 'disembowel fish or birds']
dissenting *adjective* matangurunguru [W.189 'discontented, disappointed']
dissolution of marriage *noun* tokorau moe [toko rau W.435 'separate, divorce' moe W.204 'marry']
distil *transitive verb* iheu [iheuheu W.74 'separate']
distillation *noun* iheunga [iheuheu W.74 'separate']
distinctive *adjective* kōhure [W.127 'outstanding, conspicuous']
distinguish (between two or more things) *phrase* whiriwhiri (ko tēhea tēhea) [whiriwhiri W.497 'select, choose' tēhea W.410 'which' ko tēhea tēhea common usage 'which is which']
distribution *noun* (*statistics*) tītaringa [tītari W.425 'scatter about, disperse, distribute']
distributive law *noun* (*mathematics*) ture tohatoha [ture W.259 'law' tohatoha W.429 'distribute, disperse']
distributor *noun* (*vehicle*) tīrari [W.425 'distribute']
diurnal *adjective* awatea [W.24 'broad daylight']
divaricating *adjective* (*biology*) rīrapa [W.342 'matted, in close tangled masses']
dive, armstand *noun* ruku porotēteke [ruku W.351 'dive' porotēteke W.295 'turned right over']
diverse *adjective* kanorau [kano W.94 'colour, sort, kind, seed, texture' rau W.328 'multitude']
diversity *noun* kanorau [kano W.94 'colour, sort, kind, seed, texture' rau W.328 'multitude']
divide *transitive verb* (*mathematics*) whakawehe [whaka- W.486 'causative prefix' *to make* wehe W.481 'detach, divide']
dividend *noun* pānga [pā W.243 'be connected with']
diving beetle *noun* tātaka ruku [tātaka W.394 'brown beetle' ruku W.351 'dive']
diving board *noun* kōkiri [Best *Games and Pastimes* 46 'springboard']
diving pool *noun* hāpua ruku [hāpua W.36 'pool, lagoon' ruku W.351 'dive']
division *noun* (*mathematics*) whakawehe [whaka- W.486 'causative prefix' *to make* wehe W.481 'detach, divide']

division *noun* (*part of larger unit*) wāhanga [wāhi W.474 'part, portion']
divisor *noun* tau whakawehe [tau TM 'number' whakawehe TM 'divide']
divorce *transitive verb* tokorau [W.435 'separate, divorce']
divot *noun* (*golf*) poikurukuru [W.288 'lump, clod']
DNA (*abbreviation*) pītau-ira [pītau W.284 'perforated spiral carving, young succulent shoot of a plant, circinate frond of a fern' ira TM 'gene']
doctorate *noun* tohu kairangi [tohu mātauranga TM 'qualification' kairangi W.89 'finest variety of greenstone, anything held in high estimation']
doctrine *noun* whakaakoranga [whakaako W.7 'teach']
document *noun* tuhinga [tuhi W.448 'write']
documentary *noun* motuhenga [W.212 'straight, true, genuine']
doggy lifts *noun* (*aerobics*) hikituri [hiki W.49 'lift up, raise' turi W.459 'knee']
dollar coin *noun* tāra [< Eng. 'dollar']
domain *noun* (*mathematics*) huinga pū [huinga TM 'set' pū W.300 'origin, source, base']
donor *noun* kaituku [kai W.86 'a prefix to transitive verbs to form nouns denoting an agent' tuku W.451 'present, offer']
doorstop *noun* matapipi [W.189 'small entering wedge for splitting timber']
dosage *noun* horopeta [W.61 'bolt, swallow without chewing']
dose *noun* horopeta [W.61 'bolt, swallow without chewing']
dot *noun* ira [W.79 'mole, freckle']
dot plot *noun* (*mathematics*) kauwhata ira [kauwhata TM 'graph' ira TM 'dot']
dotted *adjective* iraira [ira TM 'dot']
double around *intransitive verb* taka mā muri [taka W.366 'undergo change in direction, veer, go around' mā W.161 'by way of' muri W.214 'rear']
double bass *noun* pāngurunguru [panguru W.258 'bass, gruff' TM 'bass (instrument)']
double contact *noun* taupā [W.400 'obstruct, prevent' tau W.397 'prefix denoting reciprocal action' pā W.243 'touch, strike']

double dribble *noun* tūpanapana rua [tūpanapana TM 'dribble' rua W.349 'two']

double fault *noun* haparua [hapa TM 'fault' rua W.349 'two']

double foul *noun* hararua [hara TM 'foul' rua W.349 'two']

double hit *noun* paturua [patu TM 'hit' rua W.349 'two']

double movement *noun* (*rugby*) tororua [toro W.438 'stretch forth, extend' rua W.349 'two']

double play *noun* (*softball*) hingarua [hinga W.52 'be outdone in a contest' rua W.349 'two']

double somersault *noun* pōtēteke rua [pōtēteke TM 'somersault' rua W.349 'two']

doubles *adjective* (*tennis, etc.*) tokowhā [toko W.434 'prefix used with adjectives of number' whā W.484 'four']

down payment *noun* moni tāpui [moni < Eng. 'money' tāpui W.385 'set aside, bespeak, reserve']

Down's syndrome *noun* mate pūira kehe [mate W.192 'sickness' pūira TM 'chromosome' kehe W.122 'an odd number']

downwards whakararo *adverb* [whaka- W.485 'towards, in the direction of' raro W.327 'the bottom, the underside']

draft *noun* (*model*) tauira [W.398 'pattern']

draft *noun* (*preliminary outline*) hukihuki [W.68 'unfinished, incomplete']

drama *noun* whakaari [W.15 'show, expose to view']

draughts *noun* (*board game*) mū [Best *Games and Pastimes* 180 'draughts'], teraku [Best *Games and Pastimes* 181 'draughts']

draw *transitive verb* (*rugby*) pātoi [W.272 'lure, entice']

draw *noun* (*sport, result*) haupārua [W.41 'fight with loss on both sides']

drawer *noun* (*furniture*) hautō [W.42 'draw, drag']

drawing pin *noun* tia [W.414 'stick, peg, drive in peg']

dreadlocks *noun* kōrinorino [W.142 'twist, hank, curl']

dressing *noun* (*medicine*) tāpi [W.383 'apply, as dressings to a wound']

dribble *transitive verb* (*basketball*) tūpanapana [tūpana TM 'bounce']

driftnet fishing *noun* kawau moeroa [W.110 'term applied to eel pots and such nets as are allowed to remain in the water']

drill *noun* (*training*) whakawai [W.474 'practise the use of weapons']

drill *noun* (*tool*) hōrete [W.60 'native drill']

drive *intransitive verb* (*rugby*) kōkiri [W.130 'body of men rushing forward']

drive *noun* (*golf*) haukuru [W.40 'smash']

driver *noun* (*vehicle*) urungi [W.470 'steer, steering, paddle, rudder']

drop *noun* (*softball pitch*) epa taka [epa TM 'pitch' taka W.366 'fall away']

drop *intransitive verb* taka [W.366 'fall off, fall away']

drop goal *noun* (*rugby*) urumaranga [W.470 'surprise in war']

drop out *noun* (*rugby*) whana kōkiri [whana W.486 'kick' kōkiri W.130 'body of men rushing forward']

drop shot *noun* (*tennis*) pao taka [pao W.258 'strike, pound' taka W.366 'fall off, fall away']

drug *noun* (*narcotic*) whakapōauau [whaka- W.486 'causative prefix' to make pōauau W.286 'mistaken, confused']

drum *noun* pahū [W.248 'explode, alarum beaten like a gong']

drum machine *noun* pūrere pahū [pūrere TM 'machine' pahū TM 'drum']

drunkard *noun* porohaurangi [poro W.294 'dazed, half stunned' haurangi W.41 'drunken']

drupe *noun* hua nganga [hua W.64 'fruit' nganga W.228 'stone of fruit']

dual *adjective* tōrua [W.441 'twofold']

duck *intransitive verb* karo [W.101 'parry, avoid a blow']

ductile *adjective* kōngohe [konu- TM 'prefix denoting natural metal' ngohe W.234 'supple, soft']

duet *noun* tōrua [W.441 'twofold']

duet routine *noun* (*ice skating etc.*) whakaatu tōrua [whakaatu TM 'display' tōrua TM 'duet']

duff *noun, transitive verb* (*golf*) pekekiwi [W.276 'strike at random, without effect']

duffel coat *noun* porapora [W.293 'a coarse, shaggy cloak']

dummy *noun* (*rugby*) maka māminga [maka TM 'pass' māminga W.172 'pretend, feign']

dummy-run *noun* whakamāhunga [W.165 'make trial of a new crop']

dune *noun* tāhuna [W.361 'sandbank, seaside, beach']

duplicate *transitive verb, noun* tārua [taruarua W.392 'repeated']

duvet *noun* papangarua [W.259 'twofold, of fabric']

dynamite *noun* taipahū [tai W.362 'prefix, sometimes with a qualifying force' pahū TM 'explosive']

dyslexia *noun* tīpaopao kupu [tīpaopao W.421 'put out of proper sequence' kupu W.157 'word']

E

eagle *noun* (*golf*) kārearea [W.100 'hawk']
ear, inner *noun* taringa roto [taringa W.391 'ear' roto W.348 'inside']
ear, middle *noun* taringa waenga [taringa W.391 'ear' waenga W.472 'the midst']
ear, outer *noun* taringa waho [taringa W.391 'ear' waho W.474 'outside']
ear canal *noun* awa taringa [awa W.23 'channel' taringa W.391 'ear']
earmark *transitive verb* tāpui [tāpui W.385 'set aside, bespeak, reserve']
earmuff *noun* pūāhuru taringa [pūāhuru W.302 'close, warm' pū W.300 'source' āhuru W.4 'warm' taringa W.391 'ear']
earthenware *noun* matapaia [W.189 'clay which when baked hard was used as stone for cooking']
eccentric *adjective* korokē [W.144 'extraordinary, strange, out of the common']
echinoderm *noun* kiritara [kiri W.119 'skin' tara W.386 'point, spike']
eco-funeral *noun* nehu-tōkau [nehu W.220 'bury' tōkau W.433 'plain, devoid of ornament']
ecological diversity *noun* umaraha kaiao [umaraha W.467 'extended, wide' kaiao TM 'organism']
ecological niche *noun* puni kaiao [puni W.310 'place of encampment' kaiao TM 'organism']
ecology *noun* (*organism*) taupuhi kaiao [taupuhi W.401 'lean one on another' kaiao TM 'organism']
ecology *noun* (*study*) mātauranga taupuhi kaiao [mātauranga common usage 'knowledge' taupuhi kaiao TM 'ecology']
economics *noun* ōhanga [ō W.237 'provision for a journey' hanga W.34 'make, build, fashion, business, practice, etc.']
economics *noun* (*study*) mātauranga ōhanga [mātauranga common usage 'knowledge' ō W.237 'provision for a journey' hanga W.34 'make, build, fashion, business, practice, etc.']
economics, principles of *noun* tikanga ōhanga [tikanga W.417 'rule, plan, method' ōhanga TM 'economics']
economy *noun* ao ōhanga [ao W.11 'world' ōhanga TM 'economics']
ecosystem *noun* rauwiringa kaiao [rauwiri W.331 'interlace with twigs' kaiao TM 'organism']
ectopic *adjective* mōwaho [W.212 'outside, on the outside']
eczema *noun* tongako [tongako W.436 'be scabbed, fester']
edition *noun* putanga [puta W.315 'come forth, come out']
editor *noun* kaiwhakatika tuhinga [whakatika W.417 'correct' tuhinga TM 'text'], takatā [taka W.366 'prepare' tā TM 'print']
educate *transitive verb* whakaako [W.7 'teach']
educator *noun* kaiwhakaako [kai W.86 'a prefix to transitive verbs to form nouns denoting an agent' whakaako W.7 'teach']
effect *noun* pānga [pā W.243 'touch, strike']
effects, personal *noun* taonga ake [taonga W.385 'goods, property' ake W.6 'self']
egg *noun* (*human*) kākano [W.94 'seed, stock, descent']
egg-beater *noun* kōheri [W.125 'buffet, whisk']

41

egg-cup *noun* ipuhua [ipu W.79 'vessel for holding anything' hua W.64 'egg of a bird']

egg-ring *noun* awhe hua [awhe W.24 'hem in, encircle' hua W.64 'egg of a bird']

egg-shaped *adjective* matahua [mata W.185 'surface, face' hua W.64 'egg of a bird']

eggshell *noun* pāpapa [W.259 'shell of an egg, crayfish, etc.]

egg-slice *noun* kauhuri hua [kauhuri TM 'flip' hua W.64 'egg of a bird']

ejaculate *intransitive verb* tuha [W.463 'spit, spit out']

elastic *adjective, noun* roroha [roha W.344 'spread out, expanded']

electric balance *noun* whārite hiko [whārite TM 'balance' hiko common usage 'electric']

electric fan *noun* kōkōhiko [kōkō W.121 'wind' hiko common usage 'electric']

electric jug *noun* tīkera (hiko) [tīkera 'kettle' hiko common usage 'electric']

electric shock *noun* hiko [common usage 'electricity']

electrical cell *noun* pūhiko [pū W.300 'source' hiko common usage 'electricity']

electrical connection *noun* hononga hiko [hononga W.58 'splice, join' hiko common usage 'electricity']

electrical cord *noun* taura hiko [taura W.402 'cable, cord' hiko common usage 'electricity']

electrical current *noun* iahiko [ia W.74 'current' hiko common usage 'electricity']

electrical energy *noun* pūngao hiko [pūngao TM 'energy' hiko common usage 'electrical']

electrician *noun* mataaro hiko [mataaro TM 'master' hiko common usage 'electricity']

electrocardiogram *noun* whakaahua hiko-manawa [whakaahua 'picture' iahiko TM 'electrical current' manawa W.174 'heart']

electrocardiograph *noun* ine hiko-manawa [ine W.78 'measure' iahiko TM 'electrical current' manawa W.174 'heart']

electromagnet *noun* aukume-ā-hiko [au W.20 'current, whirlpool' kume W.155 'drag, pull' ā W.1 'after the manner of' hiko common usage 'electricity']

electron *noun* irahiko [ira TM 'particle' hiko common usage 'electricity']

electron microscope *noun* whārahi irahiko [whārahi TM 'enlarge' irahiko TM 'electron']

electronic *adjective* hiko [common usage 'electricity']

electronic data-processing *noun* whāwhā raraunga ā-rorohiko [whāwhā 484 'feel with the hand' raraunga TM 'data' ā W.1 'after the manner of' rorohiko TM 'computer']

electronic mail *noun* karere rorohiko [karere TM 'message' rorohiko TM 'computer']

element *noun* (*chemistry*) pūmotu [pū W.300 'origin, source' motu W.211 'anything isolated']

element *noun* (*mathematics*) huānga [W.65 'member of same hapū']

element *noun* (*stove*) tārahu [W.387 'native oven, heat a native oven']

element *noun* (*oven*) tārahu umu [tārahu W.387 'heat a native oven' umu TM 'oven']

elephantiasis *noun* whekewheke [W.493 'rough, scabrous' fe'efe'e Tongan and Samoan word for elephantiasis]

elevator *noun* ararewa [ara W.13 'means of conveyance' rewa W.339 'be elevated, be high up']

embargo *transitive verb* (*prohibited access*) noho tapu *intransitive verb* [noho W.223 'remain' tapu W.385 'inaccessible']

embargo *noun* (*seize goods etc.*) herepū [W.46 'seize, catch and hold firmly']

embassy *noun* kāinga māngai kāwanatanga [kāinga W.81 'place of abode' māngai TM 'representative' kāwanatanga < Eng. 'government']

embezzlement *noun* raweke pūtea [raweke W.333 'meddle with, disturb, interfere with' pūtea TM 'fund, finance']

embryo *noun* kikiri [W.119 'begin to grow, as a child in the womb']

emergency *noun* mate whawhati tata [mate W.192 'danger, calamity' whawhati tata W.491 'happen suddenly']

emergency service *noun* ratonga mate whawhati tata [ratonga TM 'service' mate TM 'emergency']

emit *transitive verb* pupuha [W.303 'blow, spout']

emotions *noun* kare-ā-roto [W.100 'object of passionate affection']
emphysema *noun* mate miru pupuhi [mate W.192 'sickness' miru TM 'alveolus' pupuhi W.304 'swell']
employer *noun* kaiwhakawhiwhi mahi [kai W.86 'a prefix to transitive verbs to form nouns denoting an agent' whakawhiwhi W.499 'present' mahi W.163 'work'], rangatira [W.323 'master or mistress']
empty set *noun* (*mathematics*) huinga piako [huinga TM 'set' piako W.279 'hollow, empty']
emulsifier *noun* whakaehu [W.26 'disperse']
emulsify *transitive verb* whakaehu [W.26 'disperse']
enamel *noun* kōrahirahi [W.139 'thin, somewhat transparent']
encyclopedia *noun* mātāpunenga [mātā W.185 'receptacle, packed with' punenga W.310 'clever, intelligent, always seeking and acquiring useful knowledge']
endangered *adjective* (*species*) tata wharengaro [tata W.393 'near' wharengaro W.489 'a line or family which has become extinct']
endocrinology *noun* mātai repe [mātai TM 'study' repe W.336 'gland']
endoderm *noun* kiriroto [kiri W.119 'skin' roto W.348 'inside']
enema *noun* kuhitou [kuhi W.154 'insert, introduce' tou W.442 'anus']
energy *noun* pūngao [pū W.300 'source' ngao W.229 'strength, sprout, shoot']
energy, electrical *noun* pūngao hiko [pūngao W.229 'energy' hiko common usage 'electricity']
energy transformation *noun* huringa pūngao [huringa TM 'transformation' pūngao TM 'energy']
enforce *transitive verb* whakaū [whaka- W.486 'causative prefix' *to make* ū W.464 'reach its limit, strike home']
enforcement *noun* whakaū [whaka- W.486 'causative prefix' *to make* ū W.464 'reach its limit, strike home']
engine *noun* pūkaha [pū W.300 'source, origin' kaha W.82 'strength']
engineer, civil *noun* hanga metarahi [hanga W.34 'make, build, fashion, thing' metarahi W.201 'great']
engineer, mechanical *noun* mataaro pūkaha [mataaro TM 'master' pūkaha TM 'engine']
enlarge *transitive verb* whakarahi [whaka- W.486 'causative prefix' *to make* rahi W.320 'great'], whārahi [whā W.484 'causative prefix' rahi W.320 'great']
enlargement *noun* whakarahinga [whaka- W.486 'causative prefix' *to make* rahi W.320 'great']
enlargement, centre of *noun* pū whakarahi [pū W.300 'centre' whakarahi TM 'enlarge']
enlargement, scale factor of *noun* tau whakarahi [tau TM 'number' whakarahi TM 'enlarge']
enrol *intransitive verb, transitive verb* whakauru [whaka- W.486 'causative prefix' *to make* uru W.469 'enter, participate in']
enrolment form *noun* puka whakauru [puka TM 'form' whakauru TM 'enrol']
enterprise *noun* hinonga [W.51 'doing, undertaking']
enterprise, State-owned *noun* hinonga Kāwanatanga [hinonga TM 'enterprise' Kāwanatanga < Eng. 'Government']
entourage *noun* hikuroa [W.68 'train, retinue']
entrepreneur *noun* rakahinonga [raka W.321 'agile, adept, go, spread abroad' hinonga TM 'enterprise']
environment *noun* taiao [W.362 'world, country' taitaiao W. 'dawn']
enzyme *noun* pūmua whakōkī [pūmua TM 'protein' whakōkī TM 'catalyst']
epidemiological *adjective* tahumaero [W.361 'sickness, disease']
epidemiology *noun* mātai tahumaero [mātai W.187 'inspect, examine' W.361 'sickness, disease']
epidermis *noun* kiriwaho [kiri W.119 'skin' waho W.474 'outside']
epididymis *noun* (*testicle*) niko tātea [niko W.222 'form into a bight or coil, go round about' semen W.394 'semen']
epiglottis *noun* kōpani [W.136 'lid of box, etc., shut up, close up']
epilepsy *noun* mate hūkiki [mate W.192 'sickness' hūkiki W.68 'shiver violently']
equal opportunities *noun* ara tautika [ara W.13 'path' tautika W.404 'even, level, straight']

equation

equation noun (*mathematics*) whārite [whā W.484 'causative prefix' rite W.343 'alike']
equator noun weheruatanga o te ao [weherua W.481 'dividing, separating' weherua pō W.481 'midnight' ao W.11 'world']
equatorial adjective weheruatanga ao [weherua W.481 'dividing, separating' weherua pō W.481 'midnight' ao W.11 'world']
equilateral triangle noun tapatoru rite [tapatoru TM 'triangle' rite W.343 'like, alike']
equilibrium noun waikanaetanga [W.475 'peace, tranquility']
equinox noun pahore o Rehua [Best *Tūhoe, Children of the Mist* 819, 820]
equipment noun taputapu [W.385 'goods, property, appliances'], utauta [W.471 'property, accoutrements']
equipment, sports noun taputapu tākaro [taputapu TM 'equipment' tākaro W.369 'sport']
equipment room noun taiwhanga taputapu [taiwhanga TM 'room' taputapu TM 'equipment']
equitable adjective tōkeke [W.433 'just, impartial']
equity noun (*justice*) wairua tōkeke [wairua W.477 'spirit' tōkeke W.433 'just, impartial']
equity noun (*property*) tūtanga [W.462 'portion, division']
equivalent adjective taurite [W.403 'alike, matching']
equivalent fraction noun hau taurite [hau TM 'fraction' taurite TM 'equivalent']
equivalent set huinga taurite [huinga TM 'set' taurite TM 'equivalent']
erase transitive verb ūkui [W.466 'scour, wipe, efface']
ermine noun toritea [tori W.438 'energetic, busy, bustling' teatea W.410 'white or light in colour']
erosion noun horo whenua [horo W.60 'fall in fragments, crumble down' whenua W.494 'land, ground']
erupt intransitive verb (*volcano*) hū [W.64 'hiss, bubble up, any explosive sound']
eruption noun (*volcano*) hūnga [W.64 'hiss, bubble up, any explosive sound']

erythrocyte noun (*anatomy*) ngeniwhero [ngeni W.233 'something small, particle' whero W.495 'red']
escalator noun ara maiangi [ara W.13 'means of conveyance' maiangi W.166 'rise up']
espresso noun kawhe kutē [kutētē W.167 'squeeze fluid out of anything; applied to milking']
espresso machine noun kutētē [kawhe kutē TM 'espresso']
establishment noun (*formation*) orokohanga [oroko W.242 'for the first time' hanga W.34 'build, fashion']
estate noun (*property of deceased person*) pānga tuku iho [pā W.243 'be connected with' tuku W.451 'present, offer' iho W.75 'downwards']
ester noun (*chemistry*) pāhare [W.247 'bitter']
estimate transitive verb, noun whakatau tata [whakatau TM 'conclude' tata W.393 'near']
estimation noun whakataunga tata [whakatau tata TM 'estimate']
ethane noun ewaro [e < Eng. 'e-' waro TM 'alkane']
ethanoic acid noun waikawa ewaro [waikawa TM 'acid' ewaro TM 'ethane']
ethanol noun waihā ewaro [waihā TM 'hydroxide' ewaro TM 'ethane']
ethical adjective matatika [W.191 'right, straight' mata W.185 'face, eye']
ethics noun matatika [W.191 'right, straight' mata W.185 'face, eye']
ethnologist noun kaimātai momo tangata [kaimātai TM '-ologist' mātauranga momo tangata TM 'ethnology']
ethnology noun mātauranga momo tangata [mātauranga common usage 'knowledge' momo W.208 'race, breed, blood' tangata W.379 'human being']
Eustachian tube noun pū taringa [pū W.300 'tube' taringa W.391 'ear']
evade transitive verb karo [W.101 'parry, avoid a blow']
evaluate transitive verb arotake [aro W.16 'consider, think' take W.370 'base, cause, reason'], aromātai [aro W.13 'consider, think' mātai W.187 'inspect, examine']
evaluation noun arotakenga [arotake TM 'evaluate'], aromātai [TM 'evaluate']

even number *noun* taurua [tau TM 'number' rua W.349 'two']

event *noun (sport)* tauwhāinga [W.405 'contend, vie']

event *noun (statistics)* pāpono [pā W.243 'reach, strike' tūpono W.457 'light upon accidentally, chance to hit']

evergreen *adjective* māotaota [maota W.179 'fresh-grown, green']

evidence *noun* taunakitanga [taunaki W.400 'support, reinforce']

evolution *noun* kunenga mai [kune W.156 'swell as pregnancy advances, spring, grow' mai W.166 'indicating a relation or aspect towards the speaker']

example *noun* tauira [W.398 'pattern, copy']

exception *noun* okotahi [W.239 'solitary, few']

excited *adjective* tōiriiri [W.432 'tingle, vibrate']

exclamation mark *noun* tohuhā [tohu W.431 'mark, sign' hā W.29 'interjection What!']

exclusive *adjective (language)* aukati [W.22 'line which one may not pass']

exclusive *adjective (statistics)* tāuke [W.399 'apart, separate']

excrete *transitive verb* papī [W.261 'ooze, leak']

excretion *noun* papī [W.261 'ooze, leak']

exercise, military *noun* whakawai riri [W.474 'practise the use of weapons']

exert oneself *intransitive verb* whakatieke [W.415 'exert one's strength to the full']

exhaust *noun (vehicle)* pūtororē [W.317 'jet of gas from burning wood'], haupara [hau TM 'gas' para W.262 'impurity, waste']

exit *intransitive verb, noun* puta [W.315 'pass through or out']

exit *intransitive verb (computer)* waiho [W.475 'let be']

expand *transitive verb (arithmetic)* whakaroha [whaka- W.486 'causative prefix' *to make* roha W.344 'spread out, expanded']

expanded numeral *noun* tau roha [tau TM 'number' roha W.344 'spread out, expanded']

expenditure *noun* whakapaunga [whaka- W.486 'causative prefix' *to make* pau W.273 'consumed, exhausted']

experiment *intransitive verb, noun* whakamātau [W.192 'make to know, make trial of'], whakamāhunga [W.165 'make trial of a new crop']

expert *noun* tohunga [W.431 'skilled person']

expire *intransitive verb (breathe out)* whakahā [W.29 'emit breath']

explorer *noun* kaihōpara [kai W.86 'a prefix to transitive verbs to form nouns denoting an agent' hōpara W.59 'go about, explore, cover, traverse']

explosion *noun* pahū [W.248 'burst, explode']

explosive *noun* pahū [W.248 'burst, explode']

exponent *noun (mathematics)* taupū [tau TM 'number' pū TM 'power']

export *noun, transitive verb* hoko ki tai [hoko W.57 'barter, buy, sell' ki W.116 'to' tai W.361 'the sea, the other side']

express *transitive verb (liquid)* kutētē [kutētē W.167 'squeeze fluid out of anything; applied to milking']

expression *noun (mathematics)* kīanga [kī W.115 'saying, word']

extension *noun (telephone)* pekanga [peka W.275 'branch of a tree, river etc.']

extension *noun (building)* whakakurepe [W.159 'extend']

extension cord *noun* katete [W.103 'lengthen by adding a piece']

extortion *noun* mure [W.214 'endeavour to obtain by unfair means']

extra *noun (cricket, score)* hemi [hemihemi W.45 'excess over a definite number']

extra time *noun* wā tāpiri [wā W.472 'time' tāpiri W.384 'anything added or appended']

extractor fan *noun* momihau [momi W.208 'suck, suck up, swallow up' hau W.38 'air']

extradite *transitive verb* tūhiti [W.464 'expel, banish']

eyeball *noun* karu [W.102 'eye']

eyedropper *noun* turumata [turu W.460 'leak, drip' mata W.185 'eye']

eyepiece *noun (microscope)* kamo [W.92 'eye']

F

fabric noun papanga [papanga rua W.259 'twofold, of fabric']

face value noun (*mathematics*) uara mata [uara TM 'value' mata W.185 'face']

face-guard noun pātū kanohi [pātū W.272 'screen, wall' kanohi W.94 'face']

face-mask noun kōpare [W.135 'shade or veil the eyes']

facsimile machine noun waea whakaahua [waea common usage 'telephone' whakaahua TM 'picture']

fact noun meka [W.200 'true']

factor noun (*mathematics*) tauwehe [tau TM 'number' wehe W.481 'divide']

factorise transitive verb whakatauwehe [whaka- W.486 'causative prefix' to make tauwehe TM 'factor']

factory noun tohitū whakanao [whare tohitū W.430 'a house with a door at the end' whakanao TM 'produce']

factual adjective meka [TM 'fact']

faculty noun (*university*) manga [W.177 'branch of a river, tree etc.'], wāhanga [TM 'division']

Fahrenheit adjective (waeine) mahana F [waeine TM 'unit of measurement' mahana W.162 'warm']

fair noun (*show*) mataraharaha [W.190 'freedom from care']

fairway noun (*golf*) raorao [W.325 'level or undulating country']

fall of wicket phrase hinganga kaipatu [hinga W.52 'be outdone in a contest' kaipatu TM 'batsman']

falling intonation noun hāheke [hā W.29 'sound, tone of voice' heke W.44 'descend']

Fallopian tube noun pū kākano [pū W.300 'tube' kākano TM 'ovum']

false start noun hēhē [W.43 'wrong, not fulfilling requirements']

falsetto reohori [reo W.336 'voice, tone' hori W.60 'false']

family income noun whiwhinga pūtea ā-whānau [whiwhi W.499 'be possessed of, having acquired' pūtea TM 'fund, finance' ā W.1 'after the manner of' whānau W.487 'family, family group']

family planning noun (*sexual & reproductive health*) oranga taihema [ora W.240 'well, in health, safe' oranga W.241 'welfare' taihemahema W.363 'genitals of either sex']

family planning clinic noun pouāwhina oranga taihema [pou W.297 'support, sustenance' āwhina W.25 'assist' oranga taihema TM 'family planning']

family support noun takuhe whānau [takuhe TM 'benefit' whānau W.487 'offspring, family group']

far post noun (*sport*) poumao [pou W.297 'post, pole' mamao W.178 'distant, far away']

farcical adjective manuware [W.177 'foolish, foolishness']

farmer noun kaiahuwhenua [kai W.86 'a prefix to transitive verbs to form nouns denoting an agent' ahuwhenua W.3 'cultivate the soil']

fashion design noun hoahoa pūweru [hoahoa TM 'design' pūweru W.318 'clothing, garment']

fashion designer noun kaihoahoa pūweru [kai W.86 'a prefix to transitive verbs to form nouns denoting an agent' hoahoa pūweru TM 'fashion design']

fate noun whakatau atua [whakatau TM 'decision' atua W.20 'supernatural being'], okewa [toitoi okewa TM 'tempt fate']

fate, tempt *phrase* toitoi okewa [toitoiokewa W.432 'speak beforehand of game etc., one is going to catch, thereby incurring pūhore' pūhore W.305 'unsuccessful in fishing, an omen of ill success in fishing or fowling']

fats *noun* (*chemistry*) ngako [W.228 'fat']

fatty acid *noun* waikawa ngako [waikawa TM 'acid' ngako TM 'fats']

fault *noun* (*error*) hapa [W.35 'crooked, be in need of anything']

feasible *adjective* ka whaihua [whaihua TM 'beneficial, worthwhile']

feasible, not kāore e whaihua [kāore W.95 'not' whaihua TM 'beneficial, worthwhile']

feature *noun* (*facet*) āhuatanga [W.4 'likeness']

feature, physical *noun* (*biology*) āhuatanga tinana [āhuatanga TM 'feature' tinana W.419 'body']

fee *noun* utu [W.471 'price']

feed *intransitive verb* kai [W.85 'eat']

felt *noun* (*textile*) whītau [W.497 'prepared flax' whīwhiwhi W.499 'entangled']

felt pen *noun* pene whītau [pene < Eng. 'pen' whītau TM 'felt']

female gender *noun* wahine [W.474 'female']

feminism *noun* kōkiri mana wahine [kōkiri TM 'champion' mana W.172 'influence, power, control' wahine W.474 'woman']

feminist *noun* kaikōkiri mana wahine [kai W.86 'a prefix to transitive verbs to form nouns denoting an agent' kōkiri TM 'champion' mana W.172 'influence, power, control' wahine W.474 'woman']

femur *noun* pūkaka [W.306 'long bones of the arm or leg']

fern *noun* (*generic term*) makawe o Raukatauri [W.169 'a fern']

ferret *noun* tori hura [tori W.438 'energetic, busy, bustling' hura W.70 'discover, hunt out']

ferry *noun* waka kōpiko [waka common usage 'boat' kōpiko W.137 'go alternately in opposite directions']

fertilisation *noun* (*reproduction*) whakatō kākano [whakatō TM 'fertilise' kākano TM 'egg']

fertilise *transitive verb* (*reproduction*) whakatō [W.428 'cause to conceive, plant']

fertiliser *noun* (*horticultural*) whakahaumako [whaka- W.486 'causative prefix' *to make* haumako W.40 'rich, fertile']

festival *noun* taiopenga [taiope W.364 'gather together']

fibre *noun* (*synthetic filament*) kaka [W.91 'fibre, single hair']

fibre, animal *noun* kaka kīrehe [kaka W.91 'fibre' kīrehe W.119 'quadruped']

fibre, man-made *noun* kaka waihanga [kaka W.91 'fibre' waihanga W.485 'make, build, construct']

fibre, plant *noun* kaka tipu [kaka W.91 'fibre' tipu TM 'plant']

fibre optics *noun* tuku kōrero ā-kaka [tuku W.451 'send' kōrero 'information' ā W.1 'after the manner of' kaka TM 'fibre']

fibreglass *noun* kaka kōata [kaka W.91 'fibre' matakōata TM 'glass']

fibrin *noun* (*anatomy*) pūtepe [pūmua TM 'protein' tepe W.412 'clot, coagulate']

fibrinogen *noun* (*anatomy*) pūwētoto [pūmua TM 'protein' wētoto TM 'blood plasma']

fibroid *adjective* kākoa [W.92 'full of hard fibres']

fibrous *adjective* kākoa [W.92 'full of hard fibres']

fiction section *noun* wāhanga paki [wāhanga TM 'section' pakiwaitara W.254 'fiction, folk lore'], wāhanga pakimaero [wāhanga TM 'section' pakimaero W.254 'fiction']

field *transitive verb* (*sport*) mau *intransitive verb* [W.196 'caught seized, captured, overtaken']

field *noun* (*sport*) papa hākinakina [papa W.259 'site' hākinakina TM 'sport'], papa tākaro [papa W.259 'site' tākaro W.369 'play, sport']

field *noun* (*data-processing*) āpure [W.13 'patch, circumscribed area']

fielder *noun* (*sport*) ringa tārake [ringa W.341 'hand' tārake W.387 'standing out in the open']

fieldwork *noun* mahi tārake [mahi W.163 'work, work at' tārake W.387 'isolated, standing in the open']

fifth tackle *noun* rutu tuarima [rutu TM 'tackle' tua W.444 'prefix used with numerals to form ordinals' rima W.340 'five']

figure

figure *noun (geometric)* āhua [W.4 'form, appearance']
figure *noun (mathematics, digit)* mati [W.193 'finger']
figure *noun (diagram)* hoahoa [TM 'diagram']
figure, significant *noun* mati tāpua [mati TM 'figure' tāpua TM 'significant']
filament *noun* kakawaea [kaka TM 'fibre' waea < Eng. 'wire']
file *noun (document)* kōnae [W.133 'small basket woven from strips of flax']
file list *noun* rārangi kōnae [rārangi W.324 'line, rank, row' kōnae TM 'file']
filing cabinet *noun* pūpoho kōnae [pūpoho W.311 'wooden trough for holding huahua' kōnae TM 'file']
filing fee *noun (justice)* utu whakatakoto take [utu TM 'cost' whakatakoto W.374 'lay down' take TM 'claim']
fillet *noun, transitive verb (food)* hōripi [W.60 'cut, lacerate, slit']
film *noun* kiriata [kiri W.119 'skin' ata W.18 'shape, semblance, reflected image']
film producer *noun* kaitaki kiriata [kai W.86 'a prefix to transitive verbs to form nouns denoting an agent' taki W.371 'lead, bring along' kiriata TM 'film']
film projector *noun* tukuata [tuku W.451 'send' kiriata TM 'film']
filter *noun, transitive verb* tātari [W.391 'strain, sift']
filter funnel *noun* pūarero tātari [pūarero W.302 'funnel entrance to eel-pot' tātari TM 'filter']
filtrate *noun* wai tātari [wai W.474 'water, liquid' tātari TM 'filter']
final *noun (contest)* tuku mātātahi [W.191 'fight a duel']
final, to win a *phrase* eke tangaroa [eke W.27 'come to land' tangaroa common usage 'God of the sea']
finance *noun* pūtea [TM 'fund']
financial *adjective* pūtea [TM 'fund']
financial liability *noun* taunahatanga [W.400 'bespeak']
financial reform *noun* whakahou tikanga pūtea [whaka- W.486 'causative prefix' *to make* hou W.62 'new' tikanga W.416 'plan, method' pūtea TM 'financial']
financial statement *noun* pūrongo pūtea [pūrongo TM 'report' pūtea TM 'financial']

finding *noun (conclusion)* hua [W.64 'product']
finger bowl *noun* oko koikara [oko TM 'bowl' koikara W.128 'finger']
fingerprint *noun* tapukara [tapuwae W.386 'footprint' koikara W.128 'finger']
finite *adjective* mutu-hengahenga [mutu W.215 'brought to an end' hengahenga W.46 'intensive quite']
finite set *noun* huinga mutu-hengahenga [huinga TM 'set' mutu-hengahenga TM 'finite']
fiord *noun* tai matapari [tai W.361 'sea' matapari W.189 'cliff']
fire alarm *noun* whakahoho [W.55 'a sort of trill to call attention']
fire escape *noun* rerenga ahi [rerenga W.337 'place of escaping' ahi W.2 'fire']
fire exit *noun* rerenga ahi [rerenga W.337 'place of escaping' ahi W.2 'fire']
fire service *noun* ratonga ahi [ratonga TM 'service' ahi W.2 'fire']
fireguard *noun* takuahi [W.374 'stones let into the floor of a house as a fender for fire']
first aid *noun* whakaora whawhati tata [whakaora W.241 'save alive, restore to health' mate whawhati tata TM 'emergency']
first five-eighth *noun* topatahi [whakatopatopa W.437 'give commands' topa 'dart, swoop' tahi W.359 'one']
first half *noun* wāhanga tuatahi [wāhanga TM 'division' tua W.444 'prefix used with numerals to form ordinals' tahi W.359 'one']
first receiver *noun* kaihopu tuatahi [kai W.86 'a prefix to transitive verbs to form nouns denoting an agent' hopu W.59 'catch' tua W.444 'prefix used with numerals to form ordinals' tahi W.359 'one']
first-aid kit *noun* tīpae whawhati tata [tīpae W.421 'small basket' mate whawhati tata TM 'emergency']
first-past-the-post *phrase (electoral system)* mua kai kai ['mua kai kai, muri kai huare' Brougham and Reed 29 'the early ones get the best, the late ones get the spittle']
fish farming *noun* ahumoana [ahuwhenua 'agriculture' ahu W.3 'tend, foster' moana W.204 'sea, lake']

fishing rod *noun* tautara [W.403 'rod to support a line when fishing from a canoe or when fishing for eels'], matira [W.194 'fish with a rod, tilt up, point upwards']

fish-slice *noun* kauhuri ika [kauhuri TM 'flip' ika W.76 'fish']

fission *noun* whakapiere [whaka- W.486 'causative prefix' *to make* piere W.279 'fissure, crack, chink']

fist *noun* ringakuti [ringa W.341 'hand' kuti W.160 'close the hand']

5-foliate *adjective, noun* tawherarima [tawhera W.408 'leaf' rima W.340 'five']

fix *transitive verb* (*correct*) whakatika [W.417 'correct']

fixture *noun* (*building*) tautara [W.403 'fasten, affix']

flag *noun* pīwari [W.285 'wave in the wind']

flagpole *noun* pou pīwari [pou W.297 'pole' pīwari TM 'flag']

flaky pastry *noun* pōhā aparau [pōhā TM 'pastry' apa W.12 'fold, layer' rau W.328 'hundred']

flammable gas *noun* haumura [hau TM 'gas' mura W.214 'blaze, flame']

flan *noun* pararahi [W.264 'flat']

flanker *noun* poutaha [pou W.297 'support, post' taha W.357 'side, edge']

flanker, blind-side *noun* poutaha kūiti [poutaha TM 'flanker' kūiti W.154 'narrow, confined']

flanker, open-side *noun* poutaha takiraha [poutaha TM 'flanker' takiraha W.372 'wide, extended, open space']

flapjack *noun* taringa kurī [W.391 'jew's ear fungus']

flask *noun* kotimutu [W.149 'calabash with small end cut off so as to form a bottle']

flat *adjective* (*tyre*) haukore [hau W.38 'air' kore W.140 'no, not']

flat *noun* (*accommodation*) whare rīhi [whare W.489 'house, habitation' rīhi < Eng. 'lease']

flat *adjective* (*music, key*) taka [W.366 'fall away, fall off']

flaw *noun* tōrōkiri [W.440 'defect, flaw in timber, due to injury to the growing tree']

flawed *adjective* takarepa [W.369 'deficient, imperfect, mutilated']

flawless *adjective* takarepa-kore [takarepa W.369 'deficient, imperfect, mutilated' kore W.140 'no, not']

flex *transitive verb* (*anatomy*) whakawhena [whaka- W.486 'causative prefix' *to make* whena W.494 'stiffen, make taut']

flex the foot *phrase* whakawhena wae [whakawhena TM 'flex' wae W.472 'foot']

flick kick *noun* waepere [wae W.474 'foot' pere W.278 'throw an arrow or dart']

flight path *noun* huanui rererangi [huanui W.65 'road, highway, pathway' waka rererangi common usage 'aeroplane']

flip *transitive verb* kauhuri [W.106 'turn bottom upwards, turn over the soil']

flip chart *noun* mahere hura [mahere TM 'chart' hura W.70 'uncover, expose']

flippers *noun* huirapa [W.67 'having the toes united by a membrane, webbed']

floor, first *noun* papa tuatahi [papa W.259 'earth floor or site' tua W.444 'prefix used with numerals to form ordinals' tahi W.359 'one']

floor, ground *noun* papa whenua [papa W.259 'earth floor or site' whenua W.494 'ground']

floor, top *noun* papa tāuru [papa W.259 'earth floor or site' tāuru W.403 'top of a tree etc.']

floor plan *noun* hoahoa papa [hoahoa W.54 'plan of a house' papa W.259 'earth floor or site of a native house']

floppy *adjective* pītawitawi [W.284 'bending, sagging']

floppy disk *noun* kōpae pīngore [kōpae TM 'disk' pīngore W.282 'flexible, bending']

flow chart *noun* mahere ripo [mahere TM 'chart' ripo W.342 'whirlpool, eddy']

fluorescent *adjective* kōrekoreko [W.141 'dazzled']

fluorine *noun* hau kōwhai [hau TM 'gas' kōwhai common usage 'yellow']

flying fox *noun* taura rere [taura W.402 'cable' rere W.337 'fly']

flying tackle *noun* whakateka [W.410 'fly headlong']

focus *noun, transitive verb* arotahi [W.17 'look in one direction, look steadily']

focus, in *phrase* ngangahu *adjective* [W.226 'sharply cut, clearly seen']

focusing knob, coarse noun (*microscope*) kou whakangahu raunui [kou W.150 'knob, end, protuberance' whaka- W.486 'causative prefix' *to make* ngahu TM 'in focus' raunui W.330 'broad']

focusing knob, fine noun (*microscope*) kou whakangahu rauiti [kou W.150 'knob, end, protuberance' whaka- W.486 'causative prefix' *to make* ngahu TM 'in focus' rauiti W.329 'small, fine, thin']

fodder noun kokinga waru [W.129 'food of indifferent quality, such as is eaten in time of scarcity']

foetus noun kukune [W.156 'swell, as pregnancy advances']

folder noun (*stationery*) kōpaki [W.135 'wrap, envelop, enfold']

follicle noun (*ovary*) ruakākano [rua W.349 'pit, hole' kākano TM 'egg']

follicle, hair noun ruahuru [W.349 'pit, hole' huru W.72 'hair']

font noun (*computer*) momotuhi [momo W.208 'race, breed' tuhi W.448 'write']

food chain noun tāhuhu whakapeto [tāhuhu W.360 'continuous, running in an unbroken line' whakapeto TM 'consumer']

food technology noun hangarau kai [hangarau TM 'technology' kai W.85 'food']

foot-and-mouth disease noun kōmaoa wae, waha [komāoa W.131 'ulcerated' wae W.472 'foot' waha [W.473 'mouth']

footbrake noun tumuwae [tumu W.454 'halt suddenly' wae W.472 'foot']

footer noun (*word-processing*) hiku [W.50 'tail of fish, rear of army etc.']

foot-fault noun hapawae [hapa TM 'fault' wae W.472 'foot']

footnote noun kupu tāpiri [kupu W.157 'word, talk' tāpiri W.384 'add, append, supplement']

foramen noun (*anatomy*) puta [W.315 'hole']

force noun (*physics*) taipana [tai- W.362 'prefix sometimes with a qualifying force' pana W.256 'thrust, drive away, cause to come or go forth in any way']

force, pull noun taipana tō [taipana TM 'force' tō W.428 'drag, haul']

force, push noun taipana ue [taipana TM 'force' ue W.465 'push, shove']

force play *intransitive verb* (*softball*) me mātua oma *phrase* [me W.199 'mild imperative' mātua TM 'must' oma W.239 'run']

forcefield noun mokoā taipana [mokoā W.208 'space, interval' taipana TM 'force']

forecast *transitive verb* matapae [matakite W.188 'one who foresees an event, practise divination' whakapae TM 'contend']

forehand noun tāmua [tātā W.354 'strike, beat with a stick' mua W.213 'front']

foreign language noun reo kē [reo W.336 'language, dialect' kē W.111 'different, of another kind, of non-identity'], reo tauiwi [reo W.336 'language, dialect' tauiwi W.398 'strange tribe, foreign race']

foreskin noun kirimata [kiri W.119 'skin' matamata W.185 'extremity']

forest, virgin noun urutapu [W.470 'untouched in a state of nature']

fork noun (*cutlery*) paoka [W.258 'pointed stick, stab, pierce'], mārau [W.181 'fork, pronged stick for catching eels']

form noun (*document*) puka [pukapuka W.306 'book, paper, letter']

formal *adjective* whai tikanga [whai W.484 'possessing, acquiring the shape or character of' tikanga W.417 'correct, right']

format *transitive verb* (*word-processing*) whakatika i te takoto [whakatika W.417 'straighten, correct' takoto W.373 'lie']

formula noun tauira [W.398 'pattern']

formulate *transitive verb* (*idea, policy*) whakahiato [W.48 'collect together, reduce in size']

fortunately mokori anō *phrase* [W.208 'it is well']

fortune-teller noun matapae [matakite W.188 'seer, one who foresees an event' whakapae TM 'contend']

forward noun (*sport*) takamua [W.368 'fore, front']

forward (*direction*) *adjective, adverb* whakamua [whaka- W.485 'in the direction of' mua W.213 'the front']

forward dive noun tirikohu whakamua [tirikohu common usage 'dive' whaka- W.485 'in the direction of' mua W.213 'the front']

forward pass *noun* maka whakamua [maka TM 'pass' whakamua 'forwards']
forwards whakamua *adverb* [whaka- W.485 'towards, in the direction of' mua W.213 'the front, the fore part']
fossil *noun* roke kanae [W.345 'a belemnite fossil shell']
fossil fuel *noun* kora mātātoka [kora W.139 'fuel' mātātoka TM 'fossilised']
fossilised *adjective* mātātoka [mātā W.185 'heap, layer, deep swamp' mātāniho W.188 'print or mark of teeth' toka W.433 'stone, rock']
foul *noun* (*sport*) hara [W.36 'sin, offence']
foul throw *noun* (*soccer*) maka hara [maka W.168 'throw' hara TM 'foul']
fountain pen *noun* pāhīhī [W.247 'flow in driblets']
foyer *noun* roro [W.347 'front end of a whare']
foyer, main *noun* roro matua [roro TM 'foyer' matua W.195 'main']
fraction *noun* hautau [hau W.39 'excess parts, fraction over any complete measurement' tau TM 'number']
fraction, equivalent *noun* hau rite [hautau TM 'fraction' taurite TM 'equivalent']
fraction, simplest form of *noun* hau rūnā [hautau TM 'fraction' rūnā W.352 'reduce, pare down']
fractional number *noun* hautau [hau W.39 'excess parts, fraction over any complete measurement' tau TM 'number']
frame *noun, transitive verb* (*picture*) tāpare [tāparepare W.383 'be bounded, be enclosed']
frame of reference *noun* pou tarāwaho [W.297 'boundary marks']
framework *noun* pou tarāwaho [W.297 'boundary marks']
frank *transitive verb* (*stamp*) tāpane [tā- W.355 'prefix, having apparently a causative force similar to that of whaka' tā TM 'print' pane kuini common usage 'stamp']
franking machine *noun* pūrere tāpane [pūrere TM 'machine' tāpane TM 'frank']
free *adjective* utukore [utu W.471 'price' kore W.140 'no, not']
free *adjective* (*sport*) pātea [W.270 'unencumbered, freed from burdens']
free kick *noun* whana pātea [whana W.486 'kick' pātea TM 'free']

free throw *noun* maka pātea [maka W.168 'throw' pātea TM 'free']
free translation *noun* whakamāori-ā-wairua [whakamāori TM 'translation' ā W.1 'after the manner of' wairua W.477 'spirit']
freedom of association *phrase* mana whakauru [mana W.172 'power, control' whakauru W.465 'ally oneself to, join']
freedom of speech *phrase* mana whakaputa whakaaro [mana W.172 'power, control' whakaputa W.316 'cause to come forth' whakaaro W.16 'thought, opinion']
freestyle *noun* (*swimming*) kau tāwhai [W.407 'swim, stretching the arms alternately']
freeze *transitive verb* whakatio [whaka- W.486 'causative prefix' *to make* tio W.420 'ice, sharp, piercing, of cold']
freezer *noun* whakatio [whaka- W.486 'causative prefix' *to make* tio W.420 'ice, sharp, piercing, of cold']
freezer bag *noun* kopatio [kopa kirihou TM 'plastic bag' whakatio TM 'freeze']
freezer compartment *noun* wāhanga tio [wāhanga TM 'compartment' whakatio TM 'freeze']
frequency *noun* auau [auau W.21 'frequently, again and again']
frequency chart *noun* tūtohi auau [tūtohi W.462 'point out, indicate' auau TM 'frequency']
frequentative verb *noun* kupumahi auau [kupumahi TM 'verb' auau W.21 'frequently repeated, again and again']
fret *noun* (*music*) tawā [W.405 'ridge']
friction *noun* wakuwaku [waku W.478 'rub, scrape, abrade']
frigate *noun* wakatauā [waka W.478 'canoe in general' tauā W.397 'hostile expedition, army']
frill *noun* pōtete [W.296 'curly, crinkled, puckered up']
frilly *adjective* pōtētete [pōtete W.296 'curly, crinkled, puckered up']
frisbee *noun* ripi [W.341 'small discs of bark thrown by children into the air in some game']
fritter *noun* kao [W.94 'a preparation of kūmara, grated, cooked, and dried in the sun']

front, cold *noun* aro mātao [aro W.16 'front' mātao W.189 'cold']

front, stationary *noun* aro pahoho [aro W.16 'front' pahoho W.248 'still, immovable, quiet']

front, warm *noun* aro mahana [aro W.16 'front' mahana W.162 'warm']

front row *noun* taupuru mua [taupurupuru W.402 'support a person by putting the arm around him' mua W.213 'front']

front-line players *noun* kapamua [kapa W.95 'stand in a row or rank' mua W.213 'the front']

fructose *noun* huahuka [hua W.64 'fruit' huka < Eng. 'sugar']

fruit salad *noun* huarākau haemata [huarākau common usage 'fruit' haemata W.29 'cut up in an uncooked state']

frustrated *adjective* pōkaikaha [W.289 'confused, at a loss, in doubt']

frustrated *noun* kōhukihuki [W.126 'be pressing, make itself felt' kōhuki 'anguish, distress of mind']

fulcrum *noun* kaurori [W.108 'swing, turn on a pivot, as a door']

full court press (*basketball*) kura horahora [W.158 'spread out, extend, applied to a war party']

full stop *noun* (*punctuation*) kopi [W.137 'shut, closed, completed']

full time noun (sport etc.) whakatakupe [W.374 'at ease, pack up']

fullback noun hiku [W.50 'rear of an army on march']

full-length adjective (clothing) hauraro [W.41 'low, pendent']

full-time adjective (occupation) ukiuki [W.466 'lasting, continuous']

function noun (mathematics) pānga [pā W.243 'be connected with, operate on']

fund noun pūtea [W.317 'bag or basket of fine woven flax']

funeral director noun whakatakataka tūpāpaku [whakatakataka W.366 'set anyone on his way, send forth' takataka 'make ready' tūpāpaku W.456 'corpse']

fungi noun (generic term) kōpurawhetū [W.139 'a fungus']

fur noun huruhuru [W.72 'coarse hair, bristles']

furry adjective huruhuru [W.72 'coarse hair, bristles']

fuse transitive verb hono [W.58 'splice, join']

fusion *noun* hono [W.58 'splice, join']

G

gaffer *noun* (*film*) mataaro hiko matua [mataaro hiko TM 'electrician' matua W.195 'main, chief']
galaxy *noun* ikarangi [W.76 'cluster' te ika o te rangi, ika-roa, ika a Māui W.76 'Milky Way' rangi W.323 'sky, upper regions, heaven'], uruwhetū [W.469 'grove of trees, appear above the horizon' whetū W.496 'star']
gallery *noun* (*exhibition*) taiwhanga whakaatu [taiwhanga TM 'room' whakaatu TM 'exhibit']
gallery *noun* (*mezzanine*) huarewa [W.65 'raised aloft']
gallop *intransitive verb* taioma [taioma W.364 'run' tai W.362 'prefix with a qualifying force' oma W.239 'move quickly, run']
gallstone *noun* konga kouawai [konga W.134 'fragment, chip' kouawai W.151 'gall bladder']
game *noun* (*tennis etc.*) kaikape [W.88 'outrun']
game, to win *phrase* (*netball, soccer etc.*) eke panuku [eke W.27 'come to land' panuku W.257 'move on after']
game point *noun* (*tennis etc.*) tata kaikape [tata W.393 'near' kaikape TM 'game']
gamma particle *noun* matūriki kama [matūriki TM 'particle' kama < Eng. 'gamma']
gang *noun* (*workers*) tokomatua [W.434 'company, band of persons']
garlic *noun* kanekane [W.93 'pungent']
garlic crusher *noun* kotē kanekane [kotē W.148 'squeeze out, crush, mash' kanekane TM 'garlic']
gas *noun* hau [W.38 'wind, air']
gas, natural *noun* kapuni [name of gas field]
gas cooker *noun* umu kapuni [umu TM 'stove' kapuni TM 'natural gas']
gas cylinder *noun* puoto kapuni [puoto TM 'cylinder' kapuni TM 'natural gas']
gastroenterology *noun* mātai kōpiro [mātai TM 'study' kōpiro TM 'intestines']
gauge *noun, transitive verb* ine [W.78 'measure']
gauge, petrol *noun* ine hinu [ine TM 'gauge' kōhinu TM 'petrol']
gay *adjective* (*homosexual*) takāpui [takatāpui W.369 'intimate companion of the same sex']
gazebo *noun* pūrori [W.314 'small circular hut']
gear *noun* (*equipment*) taputapu [W.385 'goods, property, appliances']
gear *noun* (*machinery*) nihowhiti [niho W.221 'tooth' whiti W.497 'change, cross over' W.498 'hoop']
gearbox *noun* pōwaka nihowhiti [pōwaka W.299 'wooden chest' nihowhiti TM 'gear']
gearwheel *noun* nihowhiti [TM 'gear']
gelatinous *adjective* hāpiapia [W.36 'sticky, clammy' pia W.279 'gum of trees or any similar exudation']
gelignite *noun* piapahū [pahū TM 'explosive' hāpiapia TM 'gelatinous']
gemstone *noun* mihiwai [W.202 'a kind of stone']
gene *noun* ira [W.79 'life principle']
gene pool *noun* mātāira [mātā W.185 'heap, layer', receptacle' ira TM 'gene']
general enquiry *noun* urupounamu [W.470 'question']
generator *noun* (*electrical*) pukuhiko [puku W.308 'stomach' hiko common usage 'electricity']

genetic engineering *noun* raweke ira [raweke W.333 'manipulate, meddle with, disturb' ira TM 'gene']

genetics *noun* (*study*) mātauranga momo whakaheke [mātauranga common usage 'knowledge' momo whakaheke TM 'inherited characteristics']

genus *noun* puninga [W.310 'tribe, family']

geographer *noun* kaimātai matawhenua [kai W.86 'a prefix to transitive verbs to form nouns denoting an agent' mātai matawhenua TM 'geography']

geography *noun* mātai matawhenua [mātai TM 'study' mata W.185 'surface' whenua W.494 'land, ground']

geologist *noun* kaitātai aro whenua [kai W.86 'a prefix to transitive verbs to form nouns denoting an agent' tātai aro whenua TM 'geology']

geology *noun* tātai aro whenua [tātai W.393 'arrange, set in order' tātai aro rangi W.393 'study the heavens for guidance in navigation' whenua W.494 'ground']

geometry *noun* āhuahanga [āhua TM 'figure' hanga W.34 'make, build, property']

geothermal *adjective* ngāwhā [W.232 'boiling spring or other volcanic activity']

germ *noun* iroriki [iro W.80 'maggot, threadworm, vermin' riki W.340 'small']

German measles *noun* kōpukupuku [W.138 'rash on the skin']

gherkin *noun* kamoriki [kamo W.92 'fruit of the gourd, possibly from cucumber, and restricted to imported gourds' riki W.340 'small']

gib-board *noun* kahupapa [W.85 'layer, matted mass']

gift-wrapping *noun* tākai-koha [tākai W.367 'wrap up, wrap round' koha W.123 'present, gift']

ginger *noun* (*food*) paitu kanekane [paitu W.250 'fern root with coarse fibres' kanekane W.93 'pungent']

give one's all *intransitive verb* (*effort*) whakapau kaha [whakapau W.273 'exhaust' kaha W.82 'strength']

give way *intransitive verb* (*traffic*) tautuku [W.405 'stoop, bend down, so give way']

glacier *noun* awa kōpaka [awa W.23 'river, gully, gorge' kōpaka W.135 'ice, frost']

gland, lachrymal *noun* repe roimata [repe W.336 'gland' roimata W.345 'tears']

gland, parotid *noun* repe hūare [repe W.336 'gland' hūare W.65 'spittle']

gland, pituitary *noun* repe tupu [repe W.336 'gland' tupu W.457 'grow']

gland, prostate *noun* repe ure [repe W.336 'gland' ure W.468 'membrum virile']

gland, sweat *noun* repe werawera [repe W.336 'gland' werawera W.482 'sweat']

gland, thyroid *noun* repe tenga [repe W.336 'gland' tenga W.412 'goitre']

gland, wax *noun* (*ear*) repe tāturi [repe W.336 'gland' tāturi W.395 'wax in the ear']

glass *noun* (*material*) kōata [kōataata W.122 'transparent']

glass *noun* (*drinking vessel*) kōata [kōataata W.122 'transparent']

glass, sheet of *noun* mata kōata [mata W.185 'surface, face' kōata TM 'glass']

glaucoma *noun* papahewa [W.260 'diseased in the eyes']

glaze *noun* (*pottery*) kirimōhinu [kiri W.119 'skin' mōhinuhinu W.205 'shiny, glistening, glossy']

glaze *transitive verb, noun* (*food*) mōhinuhinu [W.205 'shiny, glistening, glossy']

glide reflection *noun* (*mathematics*) whakaata nekehanga [whakaata TM 'reflect' nekehanga TM 'translation']

glider *noun* waka tauihi [waka rererangi common usage 'aeroplane' tauihi W.398 'glide in the air, soar']

glossary *noun* papakupu [papa W.259 'box, chest' kupu W.157 'word']

glottal stop *noun* ngoto [ngotongoto W.235 'make a clicking noise with the tongue' whakangoto 'impress, mark']

glove *noun* komoringa [komo W.132 'put in, insert' ringa W.341 'hand']

glove, oven *noun* komoringa umu [komoringa TM 'glove' umu TM 'oven']

glow brightly *intransitive verb* ramarama [W.322 'gleam']

glow dimly *intransitive verb* kātoretore [W.104 'glimmering, dimly luminous']

glucose *noun* waitī [W.477 'sweet, sweet sap of tī']

glue *noun* kāpia [W.96 'kauri gum, resin']

glue sniffing *noun* hongi kāpia [hongi W.58 'sniff' kāpia TM 'glue']

goal *noun* (*objective*) whāinga [whai W.484 'follow, pursue, aim at']
goal *noun* (*sport, structure*) poutūmārō [pou W.297 'pole, post' tū W.443 'be erect' mārō W.183 'unyielding, hard' poutūmārō W.299 'high, on the meridian']
goal *noun* (*score*) paneke [W.257 'move forwards']
goal attack *noun* poutuki [pou W.297 'support' poutūmārō TM 'goal' tuki W.450 'attack']
goal circle *noun* (*netball*) rohe tītere [rohe W.344 'boundary' tītere TM 'shoot']
goal defence *noun* poupare [pou W.297 'support' poutūmārō TM 'goal' pare W.266 'ward off']
goal line *noun* pae paneke [pae W.245 'margin, boundary' paneke TM 'goal']
goal shoot *noun* ringa tītere [ringa W.341 'hand' tītere TM 'shoot']
goal third *noun* tawhā tītere [tapawhā W.381 'four-sided' tītere TM 'shoot']
goalkeep *noun* tautopenga [whaka-tautopenga W.404 'rearguard']
goalkeeper *noun* tautopenga [whaka-tautopenga W.404 'rearguard']
goalpost *noun* poutūmārō [pou W.297 'pole, post' tū W.443 'be erect' mārō W.183 'unyielding, hard' poutūmārō W.299 'high, on the meridian']
godchild *noun* paruhi [W.269 'favourite, darling']
godparent *noun* whakaparuhi [whaka- W.486 'causative prefix' *to make* paruhi W.269 'favourite, darling']
goggles *noun* mōwhiti [karu mōwhiti W.213 'spectacles']
golf *noun* hahaupōro [hahau W.39 'strike, smite' pōro < Eng. 'ball']
golf bag *noun* pūkoro haupōro [pūkoro W.308 'a long, bag-shaped net for eels' haupōro TM 'golf-club']
golf club *noun* haupōro [hahau W.39 'strike, smite' pōro < Eng. 'ball']
Goods & Services Tax *noun* Tāke Hokohoko [tāke < Eng. 'tax' hoko W.57 'buy, sell']
goosestep *noun* hōkaikai [W.56 'extend and retract alternately, as the legs in swimming']
gossip, subject of *phrase* takawhetanga nā te ngutu [W.370 'something to set the lips moving, subject of free converstion']
government grant *noun* pūtea kāwanatanga [pūtea TM 'fund' kāwanatanga < Eng. 'government']
government superannuation fund *noun* pūtea penihana kāwanatanga [pūtea TM 'fund' penihana < Eng. 'pension' kāwanatanga < Eng. 'government']
grade *noun* (*education*) taumata [W.399 'brow of a hill']
gradient *noun* rōnaki [W.346 'sloping, slanting']
gram *noun* koma [W.131 'a kind of stone']
grammar *noun* wetereo [wete W.483 'untie, unravel' reo W.336 'language']
grammarian *noun* kaiwetereo [kai W.86 'a prefix to transitive verbs to form nouns denoting an agent' wetereo TM 'grammar']
grandstand *noun* karapitipiti [W.99 'put or fasten together side by side']
grant *noun* (*finance*) takuhe [W.374 'secure, without apprehension']
grapevine *noun* (*aerobics*) tiriwae [tiriwā W.424 'plant at wide intervals' wae W.472 'foot']
graph *noun* kauwhata [W.109 'stage of frame for fish etc.']
graph, bar *noun* kauwhata pou [kauwhata TM 'graph' pou W.297 'upright' poupou W.297 'upright slabs forming the solid framework of the walls of a whare', kauwhata io [kauwhata TM 'graph' io W.78 'warp, vertical threads in weaving']
graph, box and whisker *noun* kauwhata kauamo [kauwhata TM 'graph' kauamo W.105 'pole of ladder']
graph, line *noun* kauwhata toro [kauwhata TM 'graph' toro W.438 'stretch forth, creep, extend']
graph, pie *noun* kauwhata porohita [kauwhata TM 'graph' porohita W.295 'circle']
graphics *noun* whakairoiro [W.80 'ornamented']
grappling-iron *noun* kārau [W.99 'dredge for shellfish, grapnel']
grasslands *noun* tahora [W.360 'uncultivated open country']
gratis *adjective* utukore [utu W.471 'price' kore W.140 'no, not']

grave noun (*punctuation*) tohurea [tohu W.431 'mark' rea W.333 'make a low sound']

gravimeter noun (*science*) ine kume-ā-papa [ine TM 'meter' kume W.155 'pull, drag' ā W1 'after the manner of' papa W.259 'earth']

gravimetric analysis noun tātari-kume-ā-papa [tātari TM 'analyse' kume-ā-papa TM 'gravity']

gravity noun kume-ā-papa [kume W.155 'pull, drag' ā W1 'after the manner of' papa W.259 'earth']

green noun (*lawn bowls*) papa maita [papa TM 'field' maita TM 'lawn bowls']

green, basic *adjective* kāriki [kākāriki W.91 'green']

green, bright glossy *adjective* kākāriki [W.91 'small green parrot, parakeet']

green, dark *adjective* kārikiuri [kāriki TM 'green' uri W.469 'dark, green in colour']

green, light *adjective* kārikitea [kāriki TM 'green' tea W.410 'light in colour']

green, pale *adjective* karera [W.100 'light green']

green, sea *adjective* kānapanapa [W.93 'dark green, as deep water']

greenhouse effect noun kati kōtuhi [kati W.103 'close in, barrier, trap' kōtuhi W.150 'hazy, smoky appearance of atmosphere, discoloured']

grey, basic *adjective* kiwi [kiwikiwi W.120 'grey']

grey, dark *adjective* pakohe [W.255 'a dark grey stone']

grey, pale *adjective* kiwitea [kiwi TM 'grey' tea W.410 'light in colour']

grey, whitish *adjective* pūmā [W.309 'whitish, grey']

grey-blue *adjective* kororā [W.145 'blue penguin, grey']

grill noun, *transitive verb* ngunu [W.236 'singe, roast food on glowing embers']

grip noun (*weight-training*) puringa [puri W.314 'hold in the hand']

gross *adjective* (*finance*) peke [W.276 'be all included']

groundsheet noun tīanga [W.414 'mat to lie on']

groundwork noun (*judo*) whātōtō [W.491 'wrestle']

growth hormone noun taiaki whakatupu [taiaki TM 'hormone' whakatupu W.458 'cause to grow']

guarantee noun kupu taurangi [kupu W.157 'anything said, word' kī taurangi W.402 'promise, pledge']

Guaranteed Retirement Income noun Takuhe Whakangā Pūmau [takuhe TM 'benefit' whakangā riro TM 'retire' pūmau W.309 'permanent']

guard noun (*sport*) kaiārai [kai W.86 'a prefix to transitive verbs to form nouns denoting an agent' ārai W.14 'keep off, ward off']

guardian noun matapopore [W.189 'watchful over, careful of, husband, prize'], kairauhī [kai W.86 'a prefix to transitive verbs to form nouns denoting an agent' rauhī W.329 'take care of, tend, foster, protect']

guardianship noun rauhītanga [rauhī W.329 'take care of, tend, foster, protect']

guerilla warfare noun tukipoto [W.450 'sudden attack by a taua']

guessing game noun kai mahara [kai Best *Games and Pastimes* 116 'generic term for guessing games' mahara W.163 'memory, bear in mind, remember']

guest noun tūwaewae [W.463 'visitors, company']

guideline noun aratohu [ara W.13 'way, path' tohu W.431 'show']

guillotine noun, *transitive verb* pororere [W.295 'lopped off, cut off']

guilty, proven *adjective* mau tangetange [mau W.196 'caught, seized captured' tangetange W.379 'forthwith']

gymnasium noun whare pītakataka [whare W.489 'house' pītakataka TM 'gymnastics']

gymnast noun kaipītaka [pītakataka TM 'gymnastics']

gymnastics noun pītakataka [W.284 'tumble about, be constantly on the move, waggle']

gymnosperm noun koroī [W.144 'fruit of white pine, the tree itself']

gynaecology noun mātai āhuatanga wahine [mātai TM 'study' āhuatanga TM 'aspect' wahine W.474 'woman']

H

habit *noun* (*addiction*) waranga [wara W.479 'craving']

habitat *noun* kāinga [W.81 'place of abode']

hacksaw *noun* mira maitai [mira W.202 'a saw-like cutting instrument made by lashing strips of obsidian or shark's teeth to a wooden handle' maitai < Eng. 'metal']

haemodialysis *noun* tātari toto [tātari TM 'analyse' toto W.441 'blood']

haemoglobin *noun* pūtoto [pūmua TM 'protein' toto W.441 'blood']

haemophilia *noun* toto tepekore [toto W.441 'blood' tepe W412 'coagulate' kore W.140 'no, not']

haemorrhage, cerebral *noun* ikura roro [ikura W.76 'haemorrhage' roro W.347 'brains']

haemorrhoids *noun* tero puta [tero W.413 'rectum, anus' puta W.315 'blister, come out']

hair cream *noun* hinu makawe [hinu W.51 'oil' makawe W.169 'hair']

hair gel *noun* pia makawe [pia W.279 'gum of trees or any similar exudation' makawe W.169 'hair']

hair-dryer *noun* whakamaroke makawe [whaka- W.486 'causative prefix' *to make* maroke W.183 'dry' makawe W.169 'hair']

hairspray *noun* rehu makawe [rehu W.334 'spray' makawe W.169 'hair']

half *noun* (*soccer*) takuahi [W.374 'centre of line of battle as opposed to paihau']

half, left *noun* (*soccer*) takuahi mauī [takuahi TM 'half' mauī W.196 'left, on the left hand']

half, right *noun* (*soccer*) takuahi matau [takuahi TM 'half' matau W.192 'right, on the right hand']

half time *noun* (*sport etc.*) whakamatuatanga [W.195 'rest, pause, after an effort']

half volley *noun* (*tennis*) kaku [W.92 'scrape up, scoop up']

halfback *noun* poutoko [poutokomanawa W.297 'post supporting ridge-pole of meeting house']

half-life *noun* (*science*) houanga memeha [houanga W.63 'an interval of time, definite or indefinite' hou W.62 'recent, new, fresh' memeha W.200 'decaying, weak, be dissolved, pass away']

half-twist *noun* (*synchronised swimming*) takawiri haurua [takawiri W.370 'twisted' haurua TM 'half']

half-way line *noun* waenga [W.472 'dividing line']

hallucinogen *noun* whakapohewa [whaka- W.486 'causative prefix' *to make* pohewa W.287 'mistaken, confused, imagine']

halogen lamp *noun* kōnakonako [W.133 'dazzling light, glare']

hamburger *noun* pākī [parāoa < Eng. 'bread' kīnaki W.118 'food which is eaten along with other food' kī W.115 'full']

hammer *noun* (*athletics*) kurutai [kōtaha kurutai W.147 'a stone weapon attached to a cord by which it was recovered after having been thrown at the enemy' kurutai W.159 'a hard, dark-coloured stone used for making weapons']

hammer-thrower *noun* (*athletics*) kaikōtaha [kōtaha kurutai W.147 'a stone weapon attached to a cord by which it was recovered after having been thrown at the enemy']

hammer-throwing *noun* (*athletics event*) kōtaha kurutai [W.147 'a stone weapon attached to a cord by which it was recovered after having been thrown at the enemy']

hamper *noun* (*picnic basket*) tokanga [W.433 'large basket for food']

hamstring *noun* iohere kātete [iohere TM 'tendon' kātete W.103 'leg, the whole leg from the thigh downwards']

handball *noun* (*soccer*) hapa-ā-ringa [hapa TM 'fault' ā W.1 'after the manner of ringa W.341 'hand']

handbasin *noun* kāraha [W.97 'wide and shallow, calabash with a wide mouth, bowl, basin']

handbrake *noun* tumuringa [tumu W.454 'halt suddenly' ringa W.341 'hand']

handcuffs *noun* tūpiki [W.457 'bind securely']

handicap *noun* (*golf*) tohurehe [tohu W.431 'mark, sign' rehe W.333 'expert, deft person']

handlebar *noun* ringa [W.341 'hand']

handout *noun* (*document*) tohanga [tohatoha W.429 'distribute, disperse']

handover *noun* (*rugby, league*) tuku *transitive verb* [W.451 'let go, give up']

hand-over-net *phrase* (*volleyball*) hapa-ā-ringa [hapa TM 'fault' ā W.1 'after the manner of ringa W.341 'hand']

handrail *noun* rōau [W.344 'rail in a fence']

handstand *noun* tūringa [tū W.443 'stand, be erect' ringa W.341 'hand']

handstand vault *noun* kōkiri tūringa [kōkiri TM 'vault' tūringa TM 'handstand']

hang-glider *noun* waka rereangi [waka rererangi common usage 'aeroplane' rere W.337 'fly' angi W.11 'move freely, float']

hang-gliding *noun* rereangi [rere W.337 'fly' angi W.11 'move freely, float']

hangar *noun* tohitū waka rererangi [whare tohitū W.430 'a house with a door at the end' waka rererangi common usage 'aeroplane']

happened upon, be *phrase* rokohanga [W.345 'be found, be come upon']

harass *transitive verb* whakatīwheta [W.428 'make to writhe, torment']

hard copy *noun* (*word-processing*) tānga [tā TM 'print']

hard disk *noun* kōpae matua [kōpae TM 'disk' matua W.195 'main']

hardboard *noun* papamārō [papa W.259 'anything broad, flat and hard' mārō W.183 'hard, solid, unyielding']

hardware *noun* (*computer*) taputapu rorohiko [taputapu TM 'equipment' rorohiko TM 'computer']

harmonica *noun* pūtangitangi [pū W.300 'flute, blow gently' tangi W.379 'sound, give forth a sound']

harmony *noun* (*music*) ōrua [W.242 'coincide, coincide with']

hassle *transitive verb* whakatīwheta [W.428 'make to writhe, torment']

hatstand *noun* whata pouheni [W.298 'a pole with branches or pegs on which to hang things']

hazard *noun* (*golf*) kiri whakatara [kirikiri W.119 'gravel' whakatara W.386 'challenge, put on one's mettle']

hazard *noun* pūmate [pū W.300 'source, origin' mate W.192 'injury, danger, calamity']

head *noun* (*phrase*) rito [W.343 'centre shoot or heart of monocotyledonous plant']

headbin *noun* (*rugby league*) pae hūtoto [pae W.244 'perch, rest' hūtoto W.73 'bloody']

headboard *noun* (*bed*) papahamo [papa W.259 'board' hamo W.33 'back of head']

headbutt *noun, transitive verb* tukirae [tuki W.450 'ram, knock' rae W.320 'forehead']

header *noun* (*sport*) tukirae [tuki W.450 'ram, knock' rae W.320 'forehead']

header *noun* (*document*) pane [W.257 'head']

headgear *noun* (*sport*) papare māhunga [pare W.266 'protection' māhunga W.165 'head']

head-high tackle *noun* porokakī [porokakī W.295 'neck' poro W.294 'strike down']

headlight *noun* (*vehicle*) ramamua [rama W.322 'torch or other artificial light' mua W.213 'the front']

heart, hole in the *phrase* manawa tōrōkiri [manawa W.174 'heart' tōrōkiri W.440 'defect, flaw in timber due to injury to the growing tree']

heart attack *noun* manawa-hē [manawa W.174 'heart' hē W.43 'in trouble or difficulty, fail']

heart murmur *noun* manawa wawaro [manawa W.174 'heart' wawaro W.480 'indistinct sound of voices, murmur']
heartbeat *noun* mokowhiti [W.208 'beat, palpitate'], kapa manawa [kakapa W.95 'throb, palpitate' manawa W.174 'heart, breath']
hearth *noun* tahaahi [W.357 'stones set in the floor of a whare to mark the fireplace']
heat *noun* (*sport*) whiringa aro-ā-kapa [whiriwhiri W.497 'select, choose' aro-ā-kapa W.16 'front rank']
heat capacity *noun* pōkākā [W.289 'hot, heat']
heat energy *noun* pūngao pōkākā [pūngao TM 'energy' pōkākā W.289 'hot, heat']
heat sensor *noun* pūoko pōkākā [pūoko TM 'sensor' pōkākā W.289 'heat']
heater *noun* (*appliance*) whakamahana [W.162 'warm'], hatete [W.38 'fire']
heatwave *noun* hīrangi [W.52 'quivering of atmosphere, from heat']
heavy metal *noun* (*chemistry*) konganuku taumaha [konganuku TM 'metal' taumaha W.399 'heavy']
hedge *noun* pāhuki [W.248 'screen of brushwood']
hedgehog *noun* tuatete [W.447 'furnished with spines']
held ball *phrase* mauroa [mau W.196 'lay hold of' roa W.344 'long, of time']
heliport *noun* taunga waka āwhiowhio [taunga W.396 'resting place, anchorage' waka āwhiowhio TM 'helicopter']
helium *noun* haumāmā [hau TM 'gas' māmā W.161 'light, not heavy']
helix *noun* tōrino [W.438 'twisted spiral']
helmet *noun* pōtae mārō [pōtae W.296 'hat' mārō W.183 'hard, strong, sturdy']
hem *noun* remu [W.335 'lower end of anything']
hemisphere *noun* tuakoi [tuakoi W.445 'boundary, division']
hemisphere, eastern *noun* tuakoi whiti [tuakoi W.445 'boundary, division' whiti W.497 'east']
hemisphere, northern *noun* tuakoi raki [tuakoi W.445 'boundary, division' raki W.322 'north']
hemisphere, southern *noun* tuakoi tonga [tuakoi W.445 'boundary, division' tonga W.436 'south']
hemisphere, western *noun* tuakoi uru [tuakoi W.445 'boundary, division' uru W.469 'west']
hemp *noun* kōaka [W.121 'coarse mat made of flax leaves']
hepatic *adjective* ate [W.19 'liver']
hepatitis *noun* ate kakā [ate W.19 'liver' kakā TM 'inflammation']
heptane *noun* (*chemistry*) hewaro [he < Eng. 'hep-' waro TM 'alkane']
heptathlete *noun* kaipara whitu [kaipara TM 'athlete' whitu W.498 'seven']
heptathlon *noun* kaipara whitu [kaipara TM 'athletics' whitu W.498 'seven']
herb *noun* amiami [W.8 'sweet smelling shrub']
herbicide *noun* patu tarutaru [patu W.272 'kill' tarutaru W.392 'herbage, small vegetation, grass']
herbivore *noun* kaitipu [kai W.85 'eat' tipu TM 'plant']
herbs, dried *noun* amikuka [amiami TM 'herb' kuka W.155 'dry leaves']
herbs, mixed *noun* rauamiami [rau W.328 'leaf, number' amiami W.8 'a sweet-smelling shrub']
hereditary *adjective* he momo *phrase* [W.208 'blood, breed, offspring'] *e.g. He momo tērā. 'That's a hereditary trait.'*
heredity *noun* he momo *phrase* [W.208 'blood, breed, offspring']
heroin *noun* taimiri [tai 362 'prefix, sometimes with a qualifying force' miri W.203 'assuage, tranquillise']
hessian *noun* tāpora [W.384 'a coarse floor mat']
heterosexual man *noun* tāne moe wahine [tāne W.377 'male' moe W.205 'sleep together' wahine W.474 'woman, female']
heterosexual woman *noun* wahine moe tāne [wahine W.474 'woman, female' moe W.205 'sleep together' tāne W.377 'male']
hexagon *noun* tapaono [tapa TM 'side' ono W.240 'six']
hextane *noun* owaro [ono W.240 'six' waro TM 'alkane']
hibernate *intransitive verb* moe hōtoke [moe W.204 'sleep' hōtoke W.62 'winter, cold']
high ball *noun* (*sport*) poi teitei [poi TM 'ball' teitei W.410 'high, lofty']

high board

high board *noun* (*diving*) kōkiri tiketike [kōkiri TM 'diving board' tiketike W.417 'lofty, high']

High Commission *noun* Kāinga Māngai Kāwanatanga [kāinga W.81 'place of abode' māngai TM 'representative' kāwanatanga < Eng. 'government']

High Commissioner *noun* Māngai Kāwanatanga [māngai TM 'representative' kāwanatanga < Eng. 'government']

high jump *noun* (*event*) tūpeke [W.456 'jump, leap']

high jumper *noun* kaitūpeke [kai W.86 'a prefix to transitive verbs to form nouns denoting an agent' tūpeke TM 'high jump']

high kick *phrase* whana tike [whana W.486 'kick' tike W.417 'lofty, high']

high-gloss *adjective* mōhinuhinu [W.205 'shiny, glistening, glossy']

highlight *transitive verb* (*word-processing, text*) tīpako [W.421 'pick out, select']

highlight *transitive verb* miramira [W.202 'give prominence to']

highlighter *noun* miramira [W.202 'give prominence to']

hike *intransitive verb* waeraka [wae W.472 'foot' raka W.321 'go, spread abroad, agile, adept']

hinge *noun* kaurori [W.108 'swing, turn on a pivot'], kauhuri [W.106 'swing on a pivot, as a door']

hire purchase *noun* hoko harangotengote [hoko W.57 'buy' harangotengote W.37 'do piecemeal or by instalments']

historical cost *noun* utu tūturu [utu W.471 'price' tūturu W.460 'fixed, permanent']

history *noun* kōrero o mua [kōrero W.141 'tell, say, story, narrative' mua W.213 'before, formerly']

history, ancient *noun* kōrero nehe [kōrero W.141 'tell, say, story, narrative' nehe W.220 'ancient times']

history, give a *phrase* whakapapa *transitive verb* [W.259 'recite in proper order genealogies, legends etc.']

hit *noun* (*rugby, league*) tuki [W.450 'ram, knock, pound']

hit *noun* (*popular song*) pao [W.258 'sing, strike, as with a hammer']

hit *noun, transitive verb* (*softball, cricket etc.*) haukuru [W.40 'smash']

hit wicket *phrase* (*cricket*) ninipa [W.222 'awkward, unfortunate, unskilful']

hitch-hike *intransitive verb* haere pakituri [W.254 'to go on foot']

HIV (*abbreviation*) whakaruhi ārai mate [whakaruhi W.350 'enervate, weaken, cause anything to exhaust itself' ārai mate TM 'immunity']

hobby *noun* runaruna [W.352 'pastime']

hockey *noun* hake [W.31 'humped, crooked']

hockey-stick *noun* rākau hake [rākau W.321 'stick' hake TM 'hockey']

hoe *noun* tima [Best *Māori Agriculture* 46 'a form of grubber']

hoe-down *noun* (*aerobics*) hōkarikari [W.56 'stretch out one's legs, move anything by stretching out the legs']

hold *noun* (*judo*) mamau [W.196 'grasp, grab, wrestle with']

hole *noun* (*golf*) rua [W.349 'hole'], roherohe [W.344 'mark off by boundaries, separate']

hole in one *phrase* (*golf*) kotahi atu, āe [idiom kotahi W.147 'one' atu W.20 'to indicate a direction or motion onwards or away from the speaker' āe W.1 'yes']

hole punch *noun* weropepa [wero W.482 'pierce' pepa < Eng. 'paper']

holiday *noun* whakamatuatanga [whakamatua W.195 'rest, pause after an effort']

holiday pay *noun* utu whakamatuatanga [utu TM 'pay' whakamatuatanga TM 'holiday']

holocaust *noun* poautinitini [W.286 'tribulation, evil, death']

home base *noun* (*softball*) uta [TM 'home plate']

home plate *noun* (*softball*) uta [W.470 'land, as opposed to the sea or water']

home run *noun* (*softball*) kotahi atu ki uta [idiom kotahi W.147 'one' atu W.20 'to indicate a direction or motion onwards or away from the speaker' uta TM 'home base']

homing device *noun* huriaro [W.71 'turn right round']

homogenise *transitive verb* whakahanumi [W.34 'mix, cause to be swallowed up']

homogenised *adjective* hanumi [W.34 'be merged, swallowed up, be mixed']

homosexual *adjective* takāpui [takatāpui W.369 'intimate companion of the same sex']

homosexual man *noun* tāne moe tāne [tāne W.377 'male' moe W.205 'sleep together' tāne W.377 'male'], tāne takāpui [tāne W.377 'male' takāpui TM 'homosexual']

homosexual woman *noun* wahine moe wahine [wahine W.474 'woman, female' moe W.205 'sleep together' wahine 'woman, female'], wahine takāpui [wahine W.474 'woman, female' takāpui TM 'homosexual']

honeycomb *noun* pīhangaiti [W.279 'be gathered together, compact']

honeysuckle, native *noun* rewarewa [JB *Māori Plant Names* 20]

hook *noun* (*furniture*) tia [W.414 'peg, stake' ara tiatia W.414 'a series of pegs stuck in to assist in climbing a steep ascent']

hook *noun, transitive verb* (*golf*) kōripi whakaroto [koripi W.142 'slice, turn sideways' whakaroto TM 'inwards']

hook and eye *noun* pikopewa [piko W.281 'bent, curved, curve' pewa W.278 'anything bowed shaped']

hook serve *noun* tuku whakarunga [tuku TM 'serve' whaka- W.485 'in the direction of' runga W.352 'the top, upwards']

hooker *noun* waekape [wae W.472 'foot' kape W.96 'pick out']

hopscotch *noun* hītokitoki [W.54 'hop on one foot'], hīkeikei [W.49 'hop']

horizontal bar *noun* tāuhu [W.360 'ridge-pole of a house, any horizontal rod used as a stiffener']

hormone *noun* taiaki [tai W.362 'prefix, sometimes with a qualifying force' akiaki W.7 'urge on']

horn *noun* (*music*) pūtangi [pū W.300 'tube' tangi W.379 'sound']

hors-d'oeuvre *noun* whakapūwharu [W.318 'dainty morsel, titbit']

horticultural *adjective* ahuone [ahu W.3 'tend, foster' oneone W.240 'earth, soil, land']

horticulturalist *noun* ihu oneone [W.75 'soiled face, one who works hard']

horticulture *noun* ahuone [ahu W.3 'tend, foster' oneone W.240 'earth, soil, land']

hostel *noun* kāinga taupua [W.401 'temporary abode']

hotplate *noun* (*cooking*) tārahu [W.387 'native oven, heat a native oven']

hot-water cylinder *noun* kōpapa whakawera wai [kōpapa wai TM 'water tank' whaka- W.486 'causative prefix' *to make* wera W.482 'heated, hot']

house cleaning *noun* whakapai whare [whakapai W.249 'make good, set in order' whare W.489 'house']

hovercraft *noun* waka topaki [waka common usage 'vehicle' topaki W.437 'hover, as a bird']

human immuno-deficiency virus HIV *noun* whakaruhi ārai mate [whakaruhi W.350 'enervate, weaken, cause anything to exhaust itself' W.192 'sickness' ārai mate TM 'immunity']

human resources *noun* pūmanawa tangata [pūmanawa W.309 'natural talents, intuitive cleverness' tangata W.379 'human being']

human rights *noun* mana tangata [mana W.172 'control, power' tangata W.379 'human being']

humble *adjective* māhaki [W.162 'mild, meek']

humorous *adjective* pukuhohe [pukukata W.309 'laughing, hilarious' hohehohe W.55 'wrinkled with laughter']

humour, good sense of *noun* pukuhohe [pukukata W.309 'laughing, hilarious' hohehohe W.55 'wrinkled with laughter']

hurdle *noun* (*athletics*) tāepa [W.363 'fence, wall']

hurdler *noun* kaipeke tāepa [kai W.86 'a prefix to transitive verbs to form nouns denoting an agent' peke W.276 'leap, jump' tāepa TM 'hurdle']

hybrid *noun* kākano whakauru [W.94 'variegated, also applied to a person sprung from two tribes']

hydrant *noun* kōmanawa [W.131 'spring of water']

hydraulic *adjective* waipēhi [wai W.474 'water, liquid' pēhi W.274 'press, weigh down']

hydraulic brake *noun* tumu waipēhi [tumu TM 'brake' waipēhi TM 'hydraulic']

hydrocarbon *noun* waiwaro [wai W.474 'water' waro TM 'carbon']

hydrocephalus *noun* mate wairoro [mate W.192 'sickness' wai W.474 'water' roro W.347 'brains' wairoro W.477 'brains']

hydrogen *noun* hauwai [hau TM 'gas' wai W.474 'water']

hydrometer *noun* ine kiato wai [ine TM 'meter' kiato TM 'density' wai W.474 'water']

hydroponics *noun* whakatipu-ā-wai [whakatipu W.458 'cause to grow' ā W.1 'after the manner of' wai W.474 'water']

hydroxide *noun* waihā [wai W.474 'water' hāora TM 'oxygen']

hyperactive *adjective* takawhita [W.370 'thrown into disorder, anxious, eager']

hyphen *noun* tohuwehe [tohu W.431 'mark, sign' wehe W.481 'divide']

hypnosis *noun* rotu [W.348 'a spell for putting persons in a deep sleep']

hypnotherapy *noun* miri [W.203 'assuage, tranquillize, a karakia, with rites, for soothing pain, grief etc.']

hypnotise *transitive verb* rorotu [rotu TM 'hypnosis']

hypotenuse *noun* tāroa [W.392 'long']

hypothermia *noun* hauhauaitu [W.39 'pinched with cold, listless, weak']

hypothesis *noun* whakapae [TM 'contend']

hypothesise *intransitive verb* whakapae [TM 'contend']

hysterical *adjective* keka [W.113 'mentally deranged, beside oneself with grief']

I

ice-cube *noun* porotio [poro W.294 'block' tio W.420 'ice']
ice-cube tray *noun* paepae porotio [paepae W.245 'open, shallow vessel' porotio TM 'ice-cube']
ice-skating *noun* reti kōpaka [reti TM 'skate' kōpaka W.135 'ice, frost, hail']
icing sugar *noun* puehu huka [puehu W.303 'dust' huka < Eng. 'sugar']
icon *noun* (*computer*) ata [W.18 'form, shape, semblance']
identically equal to *phrase* rite pū [rite W.343 'like, alike' pū W.300 'very, precise, exactly']
identify *transitive verb* tautuhi [W.405 'indicate, define']
identity *noun* (*personal*) tuakiri [W.445 'person, personality']
identity *noun* (*mathematics, set theory*) tūmau [tūmau 'fixed', constant']
idiom *noun* (*local usage*) kīrehu [kī W.115 'saying' rehu W.334 'dimly seen, obscure']
igneous *adjective* ngiha [ngiha W.233 'fire, burn']
ignition *noun* tungi [W.455 'set a light to, kindle']
illegal *adjective* hē ā-ture [hē W.43 'wrong, erring, fault' ā W.1 'after the manner of' ture W.459 'law']
illustrate *transitive verb* (*give example*) whakatauira [whaka- W.486 'causative prefix' *to make* tauira W.398 'pattern, copy']
illustration *noun* (*example*) tauira [W.398 'pattern, copy']
image *noun* (*geometry*) otinga [oti W.242 'used ... to denote the operation is finished']
imitate *transitive verb* pakoire [W.255 'imitate the cry of a bird']

immigrant *noun* manene [W.175 'stranger, one living in a strange country']
immoral *adjective* makihuhunu [W.170 'take an unfair advantage of' maki W.170 'prefix indicating an action is done for one's own benefit' huhunu W.70 'plunder, maltreat']
immunisation *noun* whakatō kano ārai mate [TM 'immunise']
immunise *transitive verb* whakatō kano ārai mate [whakatō W.428 'introduce, insert' kano W.94 'seed' ārai W.14 'ward off, obstruct' mate W.192 'sickness']
immunity *noun* ārai mate [ārai W.14 'ward off, obstruct' mate W.192 'sickness']
imperative *noun* (*grammar*) whakahau [W.38 'command, order, direct']
implant *noun* kuhi [W.154 'insert']
implement *transitive verb* (*policy etc.*) whakatinana [whaka- W.486 'causative prefix' *to make* tinana W.419 'actual, real']
implicate *transitive verb* (*wrongdoing*) whakatuaki [W.445 'blame']
implication *noun* rara [W.326 'effect, repercussion']
import *noun, transitive verb* hoko ki uta [hoko W.57 'barter, buy, sell' ki W.116 'to' uta W.470 'the land, the interior']
impound *transitive verb* (*justice*) taumanu [W.399 'take possession of another's goods']
imprison *transitive verb* mau herehere [mau W.196 'confined, constrained' whare herehere W.46 'prison']
improve *intransitive verb* pai haere [pai W.249 'good' haere W.30 'become'], whakapai ake [whakapai W.249 'make good, set in order' ake W.7 'upwards']
in dribs and drabs *phrase* putuputu [W.317 'frequent, at short intervals']

incense *noun* pawapawa [W.273 'strongly scented' pawa 'smoke']
incident *noun* maiki [W.167 'misfortune']
inclusive *adjective* peke katoa [W.276 'be all included']
income *noun* (*revenue*) moni whiwhi [moni < Eng. 'money' whiwhi W.499 'possessed of, having acquired']
income, prepaid *noun* moni whiwhi tōmua [moni whiwhi TM 'income' tōmua W.435 'early']
incomprehensible *adjective* tē aro [tē W.409 'not' aro W.16 'know, understand'] *e.g.* Tē aro i a au tana reta.
inconclusive *adjective* tārewa [W.391 'unsettled, hanging']
incorporated society *noun* manatōpū [mana W.172 'authority' tōpū W.437 'assembled, in a body']
incorrect *adjective* hē [W.43 'wrong, erring, mistaken']
incorrect feed *noun* (*rugby*) whāngai hē [whāngai W.488 'feed' hē TM 'incorrect']
indefinite article *noun* pūnoa [pūtohu TM 'article' noa W.222 'indefinite']
indent *noun* (*printing*) nuku [W.225 'move']
indent left *noun* nuku mauī [nuku TM 'indent' mauī W.196 'left']
indent right *noun* nuku matau [nuku TM 'move' matau W.192 'right']
indeterminate sentence *noun* (*justice*) whiu tārewa [whiu TM 'sentence' tārewa W.391 'hanging, unsettled']
index *noun* taupū [tau TM 'number' pū 'power']
index *transitive verb* (*publication*) tohu-ā-kupu [tohu W.431 'guide, direct' ā W.1 'after the manner of' kupu W.157 'word']
index *noun* (*book etc.*) kuputohu [kupu W.157 'word' tohu W.431 'guide, direct']
indicator light *noun* rama huri [rama W.322 'torch or other artificial light' huri W.71 'turn']
indict *transitive verb* tāpae tuhinga whakapae [tāpae W.382 'place before a person, present' tuhinga TM 'document' whakapae TM 'accusation']
indictable offence *noun* hara kōti matua [hara W.36 'offence' kōti matua TM 'supreme court']
indictment *noun* tuhinga whakapae [tuhinga TM 'document' whakapae TM 'accusation']

indigenous rights *noun* mana tangata whenua [mana W.172 'control', 'having power' tangata whenua W.494 'natives']
indigo black *adjective* poropango [poroporo TM 'deep purple' pango W.258 'black']
indigo blue *adjective* pororangi [poroporo TM 'deep purple' ōrangi TM 'blue']
indirect free kick *noun* whana autaki [whana W.486 'kick' autaki W.23 'roundabout, circuitous']
indispensable *adjective* tino taonga [tino W.420 'veritable, very' taonga W.381 'anything highly prized'] *He tino taonga taua wahine.* 'That woman is indispensable.'
individual pursuit *noun* (*cycling*) tauwhaiwhai [tau W.396 'prefix denoting reciprocal action' whaiwhai W.485 'chase, hunt']
individual team trial *noun* tauwhaiwhai ā-kapa [tauwhaiwhai TM 'individual pursuit' ā W.1 'after the manner of' kapa W.95 'rank, row']
industrial *adjective* ahumahi [ahu W.3 'tend, foster, fashion' mahi W.163 'work, work at']
industrial relations *noun* mahi ngātahi [mahi W.163 'work, work at' ngātahi W.231 'together']
industrial relations negotiations *noun* matapakinga ahumahi [matapaki W.189 'make the subject of talk, discuss' ahumahi TM 'industry']
industry *noun* ahumahi [ahu W.3 'tend, foster, fashion' mahi W.163 'work, work at']
inequation *noun* whārite kore [whārite TM 'equation' kore W.140 'no, not']
inert *adjective* (*science*) nohopuku [W.223 'be silent, be still']
inertia *noun* (*science*) nohopuku [W.223 'be silent, be still']
inertia *noun* (*of people*) whakapahoho [W.248 'remain listless and inactive']
infer *transitive verb* hīkaro [W.49 'extract, pick out']
inference *noun* hīkaro [TM 'infer']
infighting *noun* riri tara-ā-whare [W.342 'quarrel between sections of the same hapū, civil war']
infinite number *adjective* tau whāioio [tau TM 'number' whāioio W.485 'very, numerous']
infinite set *noun* huinga whāioio [huinga

TM 'set' tau whāioio TM 'infinite number']
infinity *noun* tua whāioio [tua W.444 'the future, the past' whaioio W.485 'very numerous']
infix *noun* kuhiwē [kuhi W.154 'insert' wē W.481 'the middle']
inflamed *adjective* kakā [W.81 'red-hot, glow']
inflammation *noun* kakā [W.81 'red-hot, glow']
inflate *transitive verb* whakamakoha [W.170 'cause to expand']
informal *adjective* kōkau [W.129 'unadorned, without usual preparations']
informant *noun* kaiwhāki [kai W.86 'a prefix to transitive verbs to form nouns denoting an agent' whāki W.486 'reveal, disclose']
information *noun* pārongo [pā W.243 'reach, strike, be connected with' rongo W.346 'tidings, report'], kōrero [W.142 'news, narrative, discussion']
informative *adjective* whaihua [whai W.484 'possessing, equipped with' huanga W.64 'advantage, benefit']
infra-red rays *noun* hihi pōkākā [hihi W.48 'ray' pōkākā W.289 'heat']
infringement *noun* hara [W.36 'sin, offence']
infringement notice *noun* pānui hara [pānui TM 'notice' hara TM 'infringement']
inhaler *noun* ngongō [ngongo W.234 'suck' huangō W.65 'difficulty of breathing, asthma']
inherited characteristic momo whakaheke [momo W.208 'blood, breed, offspring' heke W.44 'descend']
inject *transitive verb* wero [W.482 'pierce, spear, sting of an insect']
injection *noun* wero [W.482 'pierce, spear, sting of an insect']
injunction *noun* whakahōtaetae [W.62 'prevent, obstruct']
injury prevention *noun* ārai whara [ārai W.14 'ward off' whara W.489 'be struck, be hit accidentally']
injury time *noun* wā whara [wā W.472 'time' whara W.489 'be hit, be struck accidentally']
ink, black *noun* wai ngārahu [W.229 'pigment for tattooing']

ink, blue *noun* wai pukepoto [wai W.474 'water, liquid' pukepoto TM 'dark blue']
ink, red *noun* wai hōrū [wai W.474 'water, liquid' renga hōrū W.336 'fine powder of red ochre used as a pigment']
ink pad *noun* hautai [hautai W.42 'sponge']
innings *noun* pāeke [Salmond *Hui* 153 'order of speaking where all the speakers of the local side are followed by the visitors']
innings, bottom of *noun* (*softball*) pāeke whakararo [pāeke TM 'innings' whakararo TM 'lower']
innings, top of *noun* (*softball*) pāeke whakarunga [pāeke TM 'innings' whakarunga TM 'upper']
innovative *adjective* wairua auaha [wairua W.477 'spirit' auaha W.21 'create, form fashion, throb, thrill with passion']
inpatient *noun* tūroro noho hōhipera [tūroro W.460 'sick person' noho W.223 'remain, stay' hōhipera < Eng. 'hospital']
inquest *noun* uiui matewhawhati [uiui W.466 'inquire for, interrogate' matewhawhati TM 'unexpected death']
insecticide *noun* patungārara [patu W.272 'kill' ngārara W.229 'insect']
inside centre *noun* (*rugby*) toparua [topatahi TM 'first five-eighth' rua W.349 'two']
inside centre *noun* (*sport*) pūroto [pū W.300 'heart, centre' roto W.348 'the inside']
inside left *noun* pū mauī [pū W.300 'centre' left W.196 'left']
inside right *noun* pū matau [pū W.300 'centre' matau W.192 'right']
insidious *adjective* kūnāwheke [whakakūnāwheke W.156 'nag, gnaw, work, of suppressed ill-feeling']
inspector *noun* matawai [W.192 'look closely' mata W.185 'eye, face'], whakatewhatewha [W.413 'investigate, examine']
inspiration *noun* (*breathe*) whakangā [W.225 'take breath']
inspiration *noun* hiringa [W.53 'energy, determination']
instep *noun* kapuwae [kapu W.97 'sole of the foot, hollow of the hand' wae W.472 'foot']

institute *noun* pūtahi [W.316 'join, meet, as two paths or streams running one into the other']
instrument *noun* (*music*) taonga pūoru [taonga W.381 'property, anything highly prized' pūoru TM 'music']
instrument, string *noun* autangi [au W.20 'string, cord' tangi W.379 'sound, give forth a sound']
insulate *transitive verb* tauārai [W.397 'screen, barrier']
insulation *noun* tauārai [W.397 'screen, barrier']
insulation *noun* (*building*) tīrepa [W.423 'line with reeds the roof of a native house']
insulator *noun* tauārai [W.397 'screen, barrier']
insulin *noun* taiaki huka [taiaki TM 'hormone' huka < Eng. 'sugar']
insurance *noun* rīanga [rī W.339 'bond, screen, protect' rīanga W.339 'screen']
insurance, car *noun* rīanga waka [rīanga TM 'insurance' waka common usage 'vehicle']
insurance, house *noun* rīanga whare [rīanga TM 'insurance' whare W.489 'house']
insurance, life *noun* rīanga tangata [rīanga TM 'insurance' tangata W.379 'human being']
inswinger *noun* epa tataha whakaroto [epa TM 'bowl' tataha W.357 'swerve' whakaroto TM 'inwards']
integer *noun* tau tōpū [tau TM 'number' tōpū W.437 'assembled, in a body']
integrate *intransitive verb* kōmitimiti [W.132 'mingle' te komititanga o ngā wai W.132 'the junction of the waters']
intellectual property rights *noun* mana whakairo hinengaro [mana W.172 'authority, control' whakairo W.80 'ornament with a pattern, used of carving, tatooing, painting, weaving' hinengaro W.51 'seat of the thoughts and emotions']
intellectually handicapped *adjective* hinengaro hauā [hinengaro W.51 'seat of the thoughts and emotions' hauā W.39 'lame, crippled']
intensive care *noun* wāhanga whāomoomo [wāhanga TM 'unit' whāomoomo W.239 'tend an invalid']
intentional foul *noun* hapa pokerenoa [hapa TM 'fault' pokerenoa W.290 'wilful, reckless']
intercept *noun* (*mathematics*) haukoti [W.40 'intercept, cut off']
interchange bench *noun* (*sport*) pae whakahirihiri [pae W.244 'perch, rest' whakahirihiri TM 'reserve, substitute']
interdependence *noun* taupuhipuhi [W.401 'lean on one another, support a person by placing the arm around him']
interest *noun* huamoni [hua W.64 'fruit' huanga W.64 'advantage, benefit' moni < Eng. 'money']
interject *intransitive verb* aruaru [W.17 'interrupt']
intermediate *adjective* (*level*) māhuri [W.165 'young tree, sapling']
international affairs *noun* take tāwāhi [take TM 'issue, matter' tāwāhi W.406 'the other side of the sea']
international law *noun* ture o te ao [ture W.459 'law' ao W.11 'world']
internet *noun* (*computer*) ipurangi [whakaipurangi W.79 'head or source of a stream, a small storehouse on a single post' ipu W.79 'vessel for holding anything' rangi W.324 'heaven, upper regions, abode of supernatural beings']
interruption *noun* pōrearea [W.293 'tiresome, importunate']
intersection *noun* (*mathematics*) pūtahitanga [pūtahi W.316 'join, meet']
interview *noun, transitive verb* patapatai [W.269 'question, inquire']
interviewer *noun* kaipatapatai [kai W.86 'a prefix to transitive verbs to form nouns denoting an agent' patapatai W.269 'question, inquire']
intestine, large *noun* kōpiro [W.137 'intestines']
intestine, small *noun* kōpiro koromeke [kōpiro W.284 'intestines' koromeke W.144 'in loops, coils, or kinks']
intonation *noun* tangi [W.379 'sound, cry of things animate or inanimate']
intra-uterine device *noun* rore ārai hapū [rore W.347 'ensnare, impede' ārai hapū TM 'contraceptive']
intransitive verb *noun* kupumahi takakau [kupumahi TM 'verb' takakau W.368 'free from the marriage tie, at leisure']
in-tray *noun* (*office equipment*) pae reta mai [pae W.246 'dish' reta < Eng. 'letter' mai

W.166 'indicating a relation or aspect towards']

introvert *noun* nguengue [W.235 'quiet, silent, reserved']

introverted *adjective* nguengue [W.235 'quiet, silent, reserved']

intuitive *adjective* ihumanea [W.466 'knowing, clever']

invaluable *adjective* tino taonga [tino W.420 'veritable, very' taonga W.381 'anything highly prized'] *He tino taonga tana āwhina mai.* 'His assistance was invaluable.'

invariant *adjective* pūmau [W.309 'fixed, constant']

invariant property *noun* āhuatanga pūmau [āhuatanga TM 'characteristic' pūmau TM 'invariant']

inventory *noun* (*equipment etc.*) rārangi taputapu [rārangi TM 'list' taputapu W.385 'goods, property, appliances']

inverse *noun, adjective* (*mathematics*) kōaro [W.122 'inverted, turned right round, upside down']

inverse operation *noun* (*mathematics*) paheko kōaro [paheko TM 'operation' kōaro TM 'inverse']

invertebrate *noun, adjective* hātaretare [W.38 'slug or snail']

invest *intransitive verb* (*finance*) haumi [W.40 'reserve, lay aside, lengthen by addition']

investigator *noun* whakatewhatewha [W.413 'investigate, examine']

investment *noun* (*finance*) haumi [W.40 'reserve, lay aside, lengthen by addition']

investment, long-term *noun* (*finance*) haumi roroa [haumi TM 'investment' roa W.344 'long']

investment, short-term *noun* (*finance*) haumi popoto [haumi TM 'investment' poto W.297 'short']

invoice *noun* nama [common usage 'account']

inwards *adverb* whakaroto [whaka- W.485 'towards, in the direction of' roto W.348 'the inside']

ion *noun* ngota katote [ngota TM 'atom' katote W.104 'not fixed, displaced, quake, shake']

IRD number *noun* tau tāke [tau TM 'number' tāke < Eng. 'tax']

iris *noun* (*eye*) mata-ā-ruru [W.185 'eye, rings of pāua shell inserted in carved work'], tiwha [W.427 'rings of pāua shell inserted in carved work, generally as eyes, spot' titiwha W.427 'show out, gleam']

iron *noun* (*golf*) rino haupōro [rino W.341 'iron' haupōro TM 'golf club']

ironic *adjective* korokē [W.144 'extraordinary, strange, out of the common']

irradiate *transitive verb* patu ā-iraruke [patu W.272 'kill' ā W.1 'after the manner of' irarukeTM 'radiation']

irreconcilable breakdown *noun* kaikiri [W.88 'cherish hostile feelings, quarrel']

irregular *adjective* (*shape*) hikuwaru [W.50 'crooked, asymmetrical'], tipihori [W.422 'askew, placed irregularly']

irresponsible *adjective* tōtōā [W.441 'wasteful, use carelessly, disrespectful']

irrigate *noun* hāwaiwai [whā W.484 'causative prefix' wai W.474 'water']

ischaemic *adjective* rere pūroto [rere W.337 'flow' pūroto W.314 'sluggish, of a stream']

ischaemic heart disease *noun* manawa toto pūroto [manawa W.174 'heart' toto W.441 'blood' pūroto W.314 'sluggish, of a stream']

isosceles triangle *noun* tapatoru waerite [tapatoru TM 'triangle' waerite TM 'isosceles']

issue *noun* (*publication*) putanga [puta W.315 'come forth, come out']

issue *noun* (*concern*) take [W.370 'subject of an argument etc.']

issues desk *noun* (*library*) wāhituku [wāhi W.474 'place, locality' tuku W.451 'allow, let']

isthmus *noun* kūititanga [W.154 'narrow, confined']

italic *adjective* tītaha [W.424 'slant, be on one side']

-ite (*chemistry, salt or ester of '-ous' acid*) pākati [pāhare TM 'salt, ester' kakati W.103 'sting, bite']

J

jack *noun* (*lawn bowls*) maitamā [maita TM 'bowl' mā W.161 'whiti']
jack *noun* (*vehicle*) hikiwaka [hiki W.49 'lift up, raise' waka common usage 'vehicle']
jam *noun* (*basketball*) haukuru [W.40 'smash' kuru W.159 'strike with the fist, thump']
javelin *noun* (*event*) hōreke [W.60 'throw a spear']
javelin *noun* (*equipment*) tao [W.380 'spear']
javelin thrower *noun* kaihōreke [kai W.86 'a prefix to transitive verbs to form nouns denoting an agent' hōreke W.60 'throw a spear']
jelly *noun* (*dessert*) wai petipeti [wai W.474 'water' petipeti W.278 'jellyfish']
jigsaw puzzle *noun* tāpaepae [tāpae W.382 'transverse, lay across' kaiwhakatāpaepae W.90 'the name of a game']
job scheme *noun* kaupapa whakawhiwhi mahi [kaupapa TM 'scheme' whaka- W.486 'causative prefix' to make whiwhi W.499 'possessed of, having acquired' mahi W.163 'work']
jockstrap *noun* tātua raho [tātua W.395 'girdle' raho W.320 'testicle']
jog *intransitive verb* toitoi [W.432 'move quickly, trot']
joinder *noun* hono [W.58 'join']
joint *adjective* (*combined*) tautokorua [W.404 'simultaneous, both together'], tukutahi [W.452 'together, simultaneous']
journal *noun* hautaka [hau W.39 'be published abroad, report' taka W.366 'come round, as a date or period of time etc.']
judo *noun* nonoke [W.223 'struggle together, wrestle']

judoist *noun* kainonoke [kai W.86 'a prefix to transitive verbs to form nouns denoting an agent' nonoke TM 'judo']
jug *noun* takawai [W.370 'calabash used as a water bottle']
jumbo *noun* (*aviation*) waka ruarangi [waka rererangi common usage 'aeroplane' ruarangi W.350 'large, robust']
jump ball *noun* (*basketball*) tauhonehone [W.398 'snatch or pull from one another']
junction *noun* (*electricity*) ūngutu [W.468 'place with the ends touching or converging, meet together, converge']
jungle gym *noun* tīrewa [W.423 'scaffolding or raised frame for hanging things upon']
junket *noun* waiū pupuru [W.315 'curdled milk' pupuru W.315 'thick, stiff, semi-solid']
jurisdiction *noun* mana [W.172 'authority, control']
jury *noun* hunga whakawā [hunga W.70 'company of persons' whakawā W.472 'adjudicate on']
justice *noun* (*equity*) haepapa [W.30 'straight, correct']
justice *noun* (*legal*) ture [W.459 'law']
Justice of the Peace *noun* Kaiwhakawā Tūmatanui [kaiwhakawā W.472 'judge' tūmatanui TM 'public']
justice system *noun* (*legal*) ture [W.459 'law']
justify *noun* whakamārama [whakamārama W.180 'illuminate, explain'] *e.g. Tēnā whakamārama mai he aha i pau ai tērā nui o te moni. 'Justify spending that amount of money.'*
justify *transitive verb* (*printing*) whakatautika [whaka- W.486 'causative prefix'

to make tautika W.404 'even, level, boundary']

justify, left *transitive verb* (*printing*) whakatautika maui [whaka- W.486 'causative prefix' to make tautika W.404 'even, level, boundary' maui W.196 'left']

justify, right *transitive verb* (*printing*) whakatautika katau [whaka- W.486 'causative prefix' to make tautika W.404 'even, level, boundary' katau W.103 'right']

jute *noun* hipora [W.52 'a coarsely made mat, a rough basket, a rough flax cape']

juvenile *adjective* pūhouhou [W.305 'young, youthful']

K

kaftan *noun* pūweru ruarangi [pūweru W.318 'clothing generally, garment' ruarangi W.350 'large']
kaleidoscope *noun* takawhīwhiwhi [W.370 'entangled, interlaced']
kayak *noun* kōreti [W.142 'a small canoe']
keen-sighted *adjective* kanohi hōmiromiro [W.58 'said of one who has sharp sight for very small objects']
key *noun* (*computer*) pātuhi [pā W.243 'touch' tuhi W.448 'write']
key *noun* (*music*) orooro [oro W.242 'clump, sound']
key signature *noun* (*music*) tohu orooro [tohu W.431 'mark sign' oro W.242 'clump, sound']
keyboard *noun* papa pātuhi [papa W.259 'anything broad, flat and hard' pātuhi TM 'key']
keyboard *noun* (*music*) tāwakawaka [tāwakawaka W.406 'striped, banded, a cloak of dressed flax made in black and white stripes']
keyhole *noun* (*basketball*) rohe tītere [rohe W.344 'boundary' tītere TM 'shoot']
kick, bicycle *noun* whana korowhiti [whana W.486 'kick' korowhiti W.146 'bent round, like a hoop']
kick, corner *noun* (*soccer*) whana koko [whana W.486 'kick' koko W.130 'corner']
kick, drop *noun* whana taka [whana W.486 'kick' taka W.366 'fall off']
kick, free *noun* whana pātea [whana W.486 'kick' pātea W.270 'unencumbered, free from burdens']
kick, goal *noun* whana tautopenga [whana W.486 'kick' tautopenga TM goalkeeper]

kick, grubber *noun* whana ripi [whana W.486 'kick' ripi W.341 'glance off, skim along the surface']
kick, overhead *noun* whana korowhiti [TM 'bicycle kick']
kick, penalty *noun* whana tautuku [whana W.486 'kick' tautuku TM 'penalty']
kick, place *noun* whana tū-ā-nuku [whana W.486 'kick' tū W.443 'stand' ā W.1 'after the manner of nuku W.225 'the earth']
kick, round-the-corner *noun* whana tāwhe [whana W.486 'kick' tāwhe W.408 'go round, turn a corner']
kick, tap *noun* whana whakatau [whana W.486 'kick' whakatau W.396 'feign, simulate']
kick, torpedo *noun* whana tōkiri [whana W.486 'kick' tōkiri W.434 'thrust lengthwise']
kicker *noun* wae whana [wae W.472 'leg, foot' whana W.486 'kick']
kickoff *noun* tīmata [W.418 'begin']
kidney disease *noun* mate tākihi [mate W.192 'sickness' tākihi W.372 'kidney']
kidney-shaped *adjective* matatākihi [mata W.185 'face, surface' tākihi W.372 'kidney']
kilogram *noun* koma-mano [koma TM 'gram' mano W.176 'thousand']
kindergarten *noun* kura pūhou [kura < Eng. 'school' pūhou W.305 'young']
kindling *noun* kōetoeto [W.123 'dry twigs']
kinetic energy *noun* pūngao konikoni [pūngao TM 'energy' konikoni W.134 'move, alter one's position']
kingdom *noun* (*biology*) mātāmuatanga [mātāmua W.188 'first']

kiosk *noun* wharau hoko [wharau W.489 'temporary shed or booth' hoko W.57 'sell']

kiss *noun* ūngutu [W.468 'place with the ends touching or converging' ngutu W.236 'lip']

kitchen bench *noun* raumanga [W.330 'platform for storing food']

kitchen hand *noun* ringawera [ringa W.341 'hand' wera W.482 'hot']

kitchen hand *noun* kanohi wera [kanohi W.94 'face' wera W.482 'hot']

kitchen table *noun* paparahua [W.260 'kind of table from which food was eaten']

kitchen whizz *noun* tāwhirowhiro [W.409 'whirl, whizz']

kiwifruit *noun* huakiwi [hua W.64 'fruit' kiwi < Eng. 'kiwi (fruit)']

kleptomania *noun* mate ringarau [mate W.192 'sickness, disease' ringa 'W.341 'hand' rau W.328 'hundred' rarau W.328 'lay hold of, grasp']

kleptomaniac *noun* ringarau [mate ringarau TM 'kleptomania']

knee-jerk *adjective, noun* turi tāmaki [turi W.459 'knee' tāmaki W.375 'start involuntarily']

knickerbockers *noun* tarau turipona [tarau common usage 'trousers' turipona W.459 'knee joint']

knife, bread *noun* mira parāoa [mira W.202 'a sawlike cutting instrument lashed to a wooden handle' parāoa < Eng. 'bread']

knife, paring *noun* pīauau [W.279 'cutting instrument, knife']

knife, serrated-edge *noun* mira [mira W.202 'a sawlike cutting instrument lashed to a wooden handle']

knife-sharpener *noun* whakakoi māripi [whakakoi W.127 'sharpen' māripi W.182 'knife']

knight *noun* kaiaka [W.86 'forward in attainments, adept, proficient, man, adult']

knitting-needle *noun* patui whatu [patui W.272 'needle of bone or wood' whatu W.492 'weave garments']

knock-on *noun* (*rugby*) taka whakamua [taka W.366 'fall off, fail of fulfilment' whakamua TM 'forwards']

knock-out *noun* horotete [W.62 'exhausted, prostrated']

L

label *noun* tapanga [tapa W.381 'call, name']

laboratory *noun* taiwhanga pūtaiao [taiwhanga TM 'room' pūtaiao TM 'science']

labour *noun* (*birth*) whakamamae [W.162 'feel pain'], whakawhānau [W.487 'come to the birth']

labour force *noun* hunga mahi [hunga W.70 'company of persons, people' mahi W.163 'work, work at']

lactation *noun* whakangote [W.235 'suckle, cause to suck']

lactose *noun* reihuka [rei W.335 'breast, chest' huka < Eng. 'sugar']

ladybird *noun* ngoikura [ngoi W.234 'creep, crawl' kura W.157 'red, precious']

lamp *noun* rama [W.322 'torch or other artificial light']

lamp-post *noun* pourama [pou W.297 'post, pole' rama TM 'lamp']

land, industrial *noun* papa ahumahi [papa W.259 'earth floor, site' ahumahi TM 'industry']

land, reclaimed *noun* papatai [papa W.259 'earth' tai W.361 'the sea, the coast']

land anemone *noun* humenga uta [humenga W.69 'sea anemone' uta W.470 'the land, the interior']

landing pad *noun* tauranga [W.396 'resting place, anchorage']

landlord *noun* rangatira [W.323 'chief, master or mistress']

language laboratory *noun* whakawaiwai reo [whakawai TM 'practise' reo W.336 'language']

lap scorer *noun* kaituhi huringa [kaituhi TM 'scribe' huringa TM 'revolution']

laptop *noun* (*computer*) rorohiko pōnaho [rorohiko TM 'computer' pōnaho W.291 'diminutive, small']

larder *noun* pātaka [W.270 'storehouse for storing food']

larynx *noun* pokorua [W.290 'pit, hollow']

laser *noun* taiaho [taiahoaho W.362 'very bright']

laser beam *noun* hihi taiaho [hihi W.49 'ray of the sun' taiaho TM 'laser']

laser printer *noun* tā taiaho [pūreretā TM 'printer' taiaho TM 'laser']

last *adjective* whakamutunga [W.215 'concluding']

late tackle *noun* rutu tōmuri [rutu TM 'tackle' tōmuri W.435 'late']

latex *noun* tawau [W.407 'milky juice of plants']

latex *noun* (*rubber*) tawau rapa [tawau W.407 'milky juice of plants' rapa < Eng. 'rubber']

latitude *noun* ahopae [aho W.3 'string, line, cross threads of a mat' pae W.244 'horizontal ridges, circumference']

laundromat *noun* whare horoi kākahu [whare W.489 'house, hut, shed' horoi W.61 'cleanse, wash' kākahu W.84 'garment']

laundry-hand *noun* ringahopi [ringa W.341 'hand' hopi < Eng. 'soap']

lawnmower *noun* pōtarotaro [W.296 'cut close, cropped']

lawyer *noun* poutoko ture [pou W.297 'expert' toko W.434 'support, prop up' ture W.459 'law']

laxative *noun* whakatiko [whaka- W.486 'causative prefix' to make tiko W.418 'evacuate the bowels']

lay-by *noun* (*commerce*) hoko tāpui [hoko W.57 'buy' tāpui W.385 'set aside, bespeak, reserve']

layout *noun* takoto [W.373 'lie, be in a position']

leach *transitive verb* (*earth*) whakapākeka [whaka- W.486 'causative prefix' *to make* pākeka W.252 'land that has been exhausted by cultivation']

leaflet *noun* (*biology*) tawheraiti [tawhera W.408 'leaf' iti W.80 'small']

leathery *adjective* pakaua [W.252 'muscular, brawny, sinewy, wiry']

lecturer *noun* pūkenga [W.307 'skilled in, versed in, repository']

leek *noun* rikiroa [riki common usage 'onion' roa W.344 'long, tall']

left-handed *adjective* hemarehe [W.45 'left hand' rehe W.333 'expert, neat-handed, deft person']

left-winger *noun* paihau mauī [TM 'left wing']

leg *noun* (*athletics*) tūāoma [W.446 'stage of a journey']

leg before wicket *phrase* wae tūtuki [wae W.472 'leg' tūtuki W.450 'strike against an object']

leg biceps *noun* (*anatomy*) uarua kātete [uarua TM 'biceps' kātete W.103 'leg']

leg slip *noun* (*cricket*) kōripi wae [kōripi W.142 'cut, slice, turn sideways' wae W.472 'leg']

legal *adjective* ture [W.459 'law']

legal process *noun* hātepe ture [hātepe TM 'process' ture TM 'legal']

legal system *noun* tikanga ture [tikanga W.416 'rule, method, plan' ture TM 'legal']

leg-bye *noun* ripiwae [ripi W.341 'glance off' wae W.472 'leg']

leggings *noun* (*tights*) taraupiri [tarau < Eng. 'trousers' piri W.283 'stick, adhere, cling']

leg-side *noun, adjective* taha wae [taha W.357 'side, edge' wae W.472 'leg']

leg-spinner *noun* epa tāwhiro wae [epa TM 'bowl' tāwhirowhiro W.409 'turn, whirl, spin' wae W.472 'leg']

lemon squash *noun* waipē rēmana [wai W.474 'water, liquid' pēpē W.274 'crushed, mashed' rēmana < Eng. 'lemon']

lemon-squeezer *noun* kotē rēmana [kotē W.148 'squeeze out' rēmana < Eng. 'lemon']

lend *transitive verb* (*used by person giving*) hoatu taurewa [hoatu W.55 'give, away from speaker' taurewa W.402 'not paid for, unrequited']

length and breadth *phrase* whānui, whāroa [whānui W.487 'broad, wide' whāroa W.490 'long-continued']

lens *noun* arotahi [W.17 'look in one direction, look steadily']

leotard *noun* kahupiri [kahu W.84 'garment' piri W.283 'stick, adhere, cling']

lesbian *noun* wahine moe wahine [wahine W.474 'female' moe W.205 'sleep together' wahine W.474 'female'], wahine takāpui [wahine W.474 'female' takāpui TM 'homosexual']

lesson *noun* akoranga [ako W.7 'learn, teach']

let *noun* (*squash, tennis etc.*) tukurua [W.452 'repeat an operation. do a second time']

letter *noun* (*alphabet*) pū [W.300 'main stock, origin, source']

letterhead *noun* ūpoko reta [ūpoko W.468 'head, upper part' reta < Eng. 'letter']

letter-opener *noun* huaki reta [huaki W.65 'open' reta < Eng. 'letter']

leucocyte *noun* (*anatomy*) ngenimā [ngeni W.233 'something small, particle' mā W.161 'white']

leukaemia *noun* mate ruru toto [mate W.192 'sickness' ruru W.352 'attack invade' toto W.441 'blood']

level *noun* taumata [W.399 'brow of a hill']

liability *noun* taunaha [W.400 'bespeak']

liaise *intransitive verb* takawaenga [W.370 'go-between, mediator']

liaison *noun* takawaenga [W.370 'go-between, mediator']

lid *noun* (*kitchenware*) kōmutu [W.133 'calabash with top cut off and used as a lid']

lien *noun* here [W.46 'tie, tie up']

life cycle *noun* mataora [W.189 'living, alive']

lifesaving stroke *noun* kau tāhoe [Best Games and Pastimes 40 'sidestroke']

life-support system *noun* (*medicine*) manapou hiko [W.173 'anything to support life' hiko common usage 'electric']

lift *noun* (*elevator*) ararewa [ara W.13 'means of conveyance' rewa W.339 'be elevated']

lift *noun* (*gymnastics*) teitei [W.410 'high, lofty']

lift lobby *noun* roro ararewa [roro W.347 'front end of a whare' ararewa TM 'lift']

lifter *noun* (*weightlifting*) kaihiki [kai W.86 'a prefix to transitive verbs to form nouns denoting an agent' hiki W.49 'lift up, raise']

ligament *noun* nape [W.218 'ligament of a bivalve']

light sensor *noun* pūoko aho [pūoko TM 'detector' aho W.3 'radiant light']

light-dependent resistor *noun* (*science*) ārai-ā-ngaoaho [ārai W.14 'ward off' ā W.1 'after the manner of' ngao W.229 'strength, energy' aho W.3 'radiant light']

lighthouse *noun* tīramaroa [W.423 'a term applied to some light, like a torch, seen on mountain tops']

limestone cave *noun* ana pākeho [ana W.9 'cave' pākeho W.252 'limestone']

limit *noun* (*restriction*) here [W.46 'tie up, fasten with cords']

limited liability taunaha tāpui [taunaha TM 'liability' tāpui W.385 'set aside, reserve']

limited liability company umanga taunaha tāpui [umanga TM 'company' taunaha TM 'liability' tāpui W.385 'set aside, reserve']

limited speed zone *noun* *usage* rohe āta haere *phrase* [rohe W.344 'boundary' āta W.17 'slowly' haere W.30 'go']

line *noun* (*text*) ripa [W.341 'row, rank, line, furrow']

line *noun* (*sport, athletics etc.*) wī [*Best Games and Pastimes* 165 'a circle marked on the ground around which players stand']

line, number *noun* (*mathematics*) rārangi tau [rārangi W.324 'line, row' tau TM 'number']

line ball *noun* (*tennis*) tau tapa [tau W.396 'alight, come to rest' tapa W.381 'margin, edge']

line graph *noun* (*mathematics*) kauwhata rārangi [kauwhata TM 'graph' rārangi W.324 'line']

line of symmetry *phrase* (*mathematics*) rārangi hangarite [rārangi W.324 'line' hangarite TM 'symmetry']

linear accelerator *noun* whakatere matūriki iraruke [whakatere TM 'accelerate' matūriki TM 'particle' iraruke TM 'radiation, radioactive']

linear function *noun* pānga rārangi [pānga TM 'function' rārangi W.324 'line']

linen *noun* papamuka [papanga TM 'fabric, textile' muka W.213 'prepared fibre of flax']

lineout *noun* (*rugby*) āpititū [āpititū W.13 'fight at close quarters']

lineout, short *noun* (*rugby*) āpiti poto [āpititū TM 'lineout' poto W.297 'short']

linesman *noun* kairota [kai W.86 'a prefix to transitive verbs to form nouns denoting an agent' rotarota W.348 'sign with the hands']

linesman's flag *noun* haki kairota [haki common usage 'flag' kairota TM 'linesman']

linguist *noun* tohunga wetereo [tohunga W.431 'skilled person' wete W.483 'untie, unravel' reo W.336 'language']

linguistics *noun* mātauranga wetereo [mātauranga common usage 'knowledge' wete W.483 'untie, unravel' reo W.336 'language']

lining *noun* (*building*) pairi [pairi ponga W.250 'slabs of tree-fern trunks used in building of huts and for lining store pits']

link *noun* hoto [W.62 'join']

linoleum *noun* takitahi [W.373 'an inferior kind of floor mat']

lipstick *noun* pani ngutu [pani W.257 'paint, besmear' ngutu W.236 'lip']

list *noun* rārangi [W.324 'line, rank, row']

literal translation *noun* whakamāori-ā-kupu [whakamāori TM 'translation' ā W.1 'after the manner of' kupu W.157 'word']

litmus *noun* tohu waikawa [tohu W.431 'mark, proof' waikawa TM 'acid']

litre *noun* kīaka [W.116 'calabash' kī W.115 'full']

loaded bases *noun* (*softball*) pūrei kapi [pūrei TM 'base' kapi W.96 'be covered, be occupied']

loan *noun* (*financial*) pūtea taurewa [pūtea TM 'fund' taurewa W.402 'not paid for']

lob *noun, transitive verb* tīkoke [W.418 'high up in the heavens']

lobby *noun* (*building*) roro [W.347 'front end of a whare']

local *adjective* ā-rohe [ā W.1 'after the manner of' rohe W.344 'boundary']

local authority *noun* mana-ā-rohe [mana

W.172 'authority, control' ā W.1 'after the manner of' rohe W.344 'boundary']

local community *noun* tānga whenua [W.378 'people of the place']

local non-commercial fishing zone *noun* āpure ika [āpure W.13 'patch, circumscribed area' ika W.76 'fish']

locative noun *noun* kupu ingoa wāhi [kupu ingoa TM 'noun' wāhi W.474 'place, locality']

lock *noun* (*wrestling, judo etc.*) nanati [W.219 'pinched, constricted']

lock *noun* (*rugby*) kaiwhītiki [kai W.86 'a prefix to transitive verbs to form nouns denoting an agent' whītiki W.498 'tie, bind, gird']

locus *noun* (*mathematics*) huanui [W.65 'path, pathway']

lode *noun* awahuke [awa W.23 'furrow, channel' huke W.68 'dig up, expose by removing the earth, excavate']

logarithm *noun* taupū kōaro [taupū TM 'exponent' kōaro W.122 'inverted']

logo *noun* waitohu [W.477 'mark, signify, indicate']

long ball *noun* (*soccer*) whana roa [whana W.486 'kick' roa W.344 'long']

long wave *noun, adjective* (*radio*) aratuku roa [aratuku TM 'frequency' roa W.344 'long']

long-distance run *noun* oma hauroa [oma W.239 'run' hauroa W.41 'long']

long-distance runner *noun* waetea hauroa [W.473 'good runner, one of strong foot' hauroa W.41 'long']

long-drop *noun* paepae whakaheke [W.245 'horizontal beam of a latrine']

longitude *noun* ahopou [aho W.3 'line' poupou W.297 'perpendicular, upright']

longitudinal *adjective* ahopou [TM 'longitude']

long-jump *noun* (*sport*) kairērere [Best Games and Pastimes 30]

long-jumper *noun* (*sport*) kairērere [kairērere TM 'long-jump']

long-run roofing *noun* piharoa [W.279 'iron']

long-sighted *adjective* kanohi kāhu [kanohi W.94 'eye' kāhu W.84 'hawk']

loose forward *noun* poutaka [pou W.297 'support, post' taka W.366 'range, roam at large, undergo change in direction']

loosehead prop *noun* (*rugby*) poumua mauī [poumua TM 'prop' mauī W.196 'on the left hand']

loot *noun* parakete [W.263 'booty']

lose *intransitive verb* mīere [W.201 'become powerless, be exhausted'], hinga [W.52 'be outdone in a contest']

loser *noun* wairuatoa [W.477 'unlucky']

loss *noun* hinga [W.52 'be outdone in a contest']

lost property bin *noun* paekura [W.246 'lost property']

lounge suite *noun* hāneanea [W.33 'pleasant, comfortable']

low tackle *noun* rutu kātete [rutu TM 'tackle' kātete W.103 'the whole leg from the thigh downwards']

lower *adjective* whakararo [whaka- W.485 'towards, in the direction of' raro W.327 'the bottom, the underside']

lower bar *noun* (*gymnastics*) tāuhu whakararo [tāuhu TM 'bar' whakararo TM 'lower']

lowercase letter *noun* pūriki [pū TM 'letter of alphabet' riki W.340 'small']

lunge *intransitive verb* tītaha [W.424 'lean to one side']

lymph *noun* waitinana [wai W.474 'water, liquid' tinana W.419 'body']

lymph node *noun* tīpona waitinana [tīpona W.422 'form a swelling or knot' waitinana TM 'lymph']

lymphocyte *noun* ngeni waitinana [ngeni W.233 'something small, particle' waitinana TM 'lymph']

M

macaroni *noun* tīkohu parāoa [tīkohu W.418 'hollowed out, bent, curved' parāoa < Eng. 'flour']
machine *noun* pūrere [pū W.300 'source, foundation, base' rere W.373 'flow, fly']
machine-gun *noun* pū tiripapā [pū W.300 'gun' tiripapā W.423 'explode in succession']
macron *noun* tohutō [tohu W.431 'mark, sign' tō W.428 'drag']
macula *noun* tongi [W.436 'speck']
magazine *noun* (*book*) puka maheni [pukapuka W.306 'book' maheni W.163 'smooth, sleek']
magic *noun* tūmatarau [tūmatapōngia, tūmatawarea W.453 'a charm to render oneself invisible to one's foes' rau W.328 'hundred, multitude']
magnesium *noun* konupora [konu- TM 'prefix denoting natural metal' pora W.293 'a white stone']
magnet *noun* aukume [au W.20 'current' kume W.155 'pull, drag']
magnetic *adjective* aukume [TM 'magnet']
magnetic field *noun* mokowā aukume [mokowā W.208 'space' aukume TM 'magnet']
magnetic force *noun* aukume [TM 'magnet']
magnifying glass *noun* karu whakarahi [karu W.102 'eye' whakarahi TM 'enlarge']
maiden over *noun* paiepa omakore [paiepa TM 'over' oma W.239 'run' kore W.140 'no']
mail *noun* kōpaki [W.135 'envelope, wrap, envelop']
mailroom *noun* kōmiringa kōpaki [kōmiri W.132 'sort out' kōpaki W.135 'envelope, wrap, envelop']

main entrance *noun* kūaha matua [kūaha W.154 'entrance' matua W.195 'main']
mainframe *noun* (*computer*) rorohiko matua [rorohiko TM 'computer' matua W.195 'main, chief']
mainstream *transitive verb* whakarīroa [whaka- W.486 'causative prefix' *to make* rīroa TM 'mainstream']
mainstream *noun* rīroa [W.323 'main pathway in a pā']
majority rule *noun* whakatau a te nuinga [whakatau TM 'decision' nuinga W.224 'majority, larger part']
male gender *noun* tāne [W.377 'male']
malleable *adjective* māngohe [W.178 'soft']
malnourished *adjective* pohokore [W.287 'starved, emaciated']
malnutrition *noun* pohokore [W.287 'starved, emaciated']
mammal *noun* whakangote [W.235 'suckle, cause to suck']
mammogram *noun* whakaata ū [whakaata roto TM 'x-ray' ū W.464 'breast']
mammography *noun* matawai ū [matawai W.192 'look closely' ū W.464 'breast']
man to man *phrase* (*basketball*) kura horahora [W.158 'spread out, extend, applied to a war party']
management *noun* (*employment*) tumu whakahaere [tumu W.454 'main post in the palisading of a pā' whakahaere TM 'manage, administer']
manager *noun* tumu [W.454 'main post in the palisading of a pā'], kaiwhakahaere [kai W.86 'a prefix to transitive verbs to form nouns denoting an agent' whakahaere TM control, administer']
mandate *noun* mana kōkiri [mana W.172 'authority, control' kōkiri W.130 'rush forward, charge']

mandible *noun* kauwae [W.105 'jaw']
man-made *adjective* waihanga [waihanga W.485 'make, build, construct']
mannequin *noun* ropi pūeru [ropi W.347 'body, figure' pūeru W.318 'clothing generally, garment']
manoeuvre *noun* nekeneke [W.220 'move gradually']
manufacture *transitive verb* whakanao [W.218 'make, manipulate, operate on']
map *noun* mahere whenua [mahere W.163 'plan' whenua W.494 'land, country']
mapping skills *noun* pūmanawa whai mahere whenua [pūmanawa TM 'skill' whai W.484 'follow' mahere whenua TM 'map']
maraca *noun* māpara [W.179 'pieces of wood used as castanets']
marathon *noun* oma taumano [oma W.239 'run' taumano W.399 'for a long time']
marathon runner *noun* waetea taumano [W.473 'good runner, one strong of foot' taumano W.399 'for a long time']
margin of error kotiti [W.149 'be distorted or displaced']
marijuana *noun* whakamāngina [W.178 'floating, fleeting, unreliable']
marina *noun* herenga waka [here W.46 'tie, tie up, fasten with cords' waka common usage 'boat']
marinade *noun* whakapūkara [whaka- W.486 'causative prefix' *to make* pūkarakara W.307 'fragrant, well flavoured']
marinate *transitive verb* pūkarakara [W.307 'fragrant, well flavoured']
marine reserve *noun* āpure moana [āpure W.13 'patch, circumscribed area' moana W.204 'sea, lake']
mark *transitive verb* (*rugby*) whakareke [whakarekenga W.335 'mark made by stamping on the ground' rekereke W.335 'heel']
marker *noun* (*bowls*) kaituhi [TM 'scribe']
marksman *noun* whakakeko pū [W.113 'take aim']
markswoman *noun* whakakeko pū [W.113 'take aim']
marmite *noun* īhipani [īhi TM 'yeast' pani W.257 'spread']
marquee *noun* atorua [W.20 'a long temporary house used for a feast']
marriage, de facto *noun* moe māori [moe W.204 'marry, sleep together' māori W.179 'freely, without ceremony']
marshall *noun* atoato [W.19 'marshal, regulate the formation of a corps on the march']
mass *noun* (*science*) papatipu [W.261 'solid mass']
mass number *noun* tau papatipu [tau TM 'number' papatipu W.261 'solid mass']
master *noun* (*trade*) mataaro [mata W.185 'eye, face' aro. W.16 'be inclined, be disposed']
masturbate, of female *intransitive verb* pīkoikoi [atua pīkoikoi W.281 'clitoris']
masturbate, of male *intransitive verb* tītoi [W.426 'retract the prepuce']
match *noun* (*sport*) whakataetae [W.356 'try strength, contend']
match, to win *phrase* (*sport*) eke panuku [eke W.27 'come to land' panuku W.257 'move on after']
match point *noun* tata toa [tata W.393 'near' toa W.428 'victorious'], tata piro [tata W.393 'near' piro W.284 'victory in a game']
material *noun* (*fabric*) papanga [papangarua W.259 'twofold, of fabric']
material *noun* (*teaching*) rauemi ako [rauemi TM 'resource' ako W.7 'teach, instruct, advise']
material *noun* (*textual*) rauemi tuhi [rauemi TM 'resource' tuhi W.448 'delineate, draw']
maternity ward *noun* whare kōhanga [W.124 'house to which mother and new-born child were removed']
mathematics *noun* pāngarau [pa W.243 'touch, be connected with' rau W.328 'hundred, multitude']
matricide *noun* kaikaiewe [kaikaiwaiū W.87 'one who turns traitor, generally from having relatives among the enemy' ewe W.28 'placenta, afterbirth, mother, womb']
matrimonial property *noun* rawa mārena [rawa W.332 'goods, property' mārena < Eng. 'marriage']
matron *noun* kaiwhakahaere tapuhi [kaiwhakahaere TM 'manager' tapuhi TM 'nurse']
matt finish *noun* mōhanihani [W.205 'smooth']

matter noun matū [W.195 'gist, kernel, of a matter']
matter noun (*issue*) take [W.370 'subject of an argument etc.']
mattock noun wauwau [W.480 'a pole used to loosen the earth for making earthworks, cultivation etc.']
maul *transitive verb, intransitive verb, noun* (*rugby*) kaunuku [W.107 'centre of an army when formed for a rush, move steadily, large splitting wedge']
maul, rolling noun kaunukunuku [kaunuku TM 'maul' nuku W.225 'move, extend']
mauve adjective porotea [poroporo TM 'deep purple' teatea W.410 'light in colour']
maxilla noun (*anatomy*) kauwae whakarunga [kauwae W.105 'jaw' whakarunga TM 'upper']
maxim noun mātāpono [mātāpuna W.190 'source of a river' pono W.291 'true']
maximum security prison noun wharehere whakatiki [whare herehere W.46 'prison' whakatiki W.417 'tie up, keep in confinement']
mayonnaise noun wairanu huamata [wairanu TM 'sauce' huamata TM 'green salad']
mayor noun kahika [W.83 'chief']
mayoress noun kahika [W.83 'chief']
maypole noun moari [Best *Games and Pastimes* 48 'swing']
maze noun pāwhatiwhati [ara pāwhati W.274 'track marked by breaking branches']
mean, arithmetic noun (*average*) tau toharite [tau TM 'number' tohatoha 429 'distribute' rite W.343 'alike']
measurement noun inenga [ine W.78 'measure']
measuring spoon noun kokoine [koko W.130 'spoon' ine W.130 'measure']
measuring tape noun taura tīeke [W.415 'line for measuring the diagonals of a house']
mechanic noun kaiwhakatikatika pūkaha [kai W.86 'a prefix to transitive verbs to form nouns denoting an agent' whakatika TM 'fix' pūkaha TM 'engine']
medal noun tohutoa [tohu W.431 'mark, sign, proof' toa W.428 'victorious, brave']
medal presentation noun whakatāhei tohutoa [whaka- W.486 'causative prefix' to make tāhei W.358 'wear anything suspended from the neck' tohutoa TM 'medal']
medal presenter noun kaiwhakatāhei tohutoa [kai W.86 'a prefix to transitive verbs to form nouns denoting an agent' whakatāhei tohutoa TM 'medal presentation']
medal round noun (*competition sport*) whiringa toa [whiriwhiri W.497 'select, choose' toa W.428 'victorious']
medallist noun toa [W.428 'victorious, brave']
medallist, bronze noun toa mātāmuri [toa W.428 'victorious, brave' mātāmuri W.188 'last, latter']
medallist, gold noun toa mātāmua [toa W.428 'victorious, brave' mātāmua W.188 'first']
medallist, silver noun toa mātāwaenga [toa W.428 'victorious, brave' waenga W.472 'the middle, the midst']
media noun hunga pāpāho [hunga W.70 'company of persons, people' pāpāho TM 'broadcast']
media coverage whakaatu pāpāho [whakaatu W.20 'point out, show, call attention to' pāpāho TM 'media']
median noun (*triangle*) weherua tapatoru [weherua TM 'bisector' tapatoru TM 'triangle']
median noun (*statistics*) tau waenga [tau TM 'number' waenga W.472 'dividing line']
medical school noun kura rata [kura < Eng. 'school' rata W.327 'doctor']
medication noun rongoā [W.346 'drugs, medicine']
medicine cabinet noun tīpae rongoā [tīpae W.421 'small basket' rongoā W.346 'medicine']
medium of exchange noun taonga tauhokohoko [taonga W.381 'property, anything highly prized' tauhokohoko TM 'commerce']
medium security prison noun wharehere whakaita [whare herehere W.46 'prison' whakaita W.80 'hold fast, restrain']
medley noun pāhekoheko [pāhekoheko W.247 'join, combine']
meiosis noun (*biology*) rūnā pūira [rūnā W.352 'reduce, pare down' pūira TM 'chromosome']

melancholy noun, adjective matapōuri [W.189 'sad, gloomy']
melanoma noun tonapuku [tona W.435 'excrescence, wart, corn, etc.' puku W.308 'swelling, tumour']
member noun (*mathematics*) huānga [W.65 'relative, member of same hapū']
membership fee noun utu whakauru [utu TM 'fee' whaka- W.486 'causative prefix' to make uru W.469 'associate oneself with, participate in']
membrane noun kiriuhi [kiri W.119 'skin' uhi W.471 'cover']
membrane, cell noun kiriuhi pūtau [kiriuhi TM 'membrane' pūtau TM 'cell']
membrane, semi-permeable noun kiriuhi hītari [kiriuhi TM 'membrane' hītari W.53 'sieve']
memento noun manatunga [W.173 'keepsake']
memoirs noun ripoinga [W.342 'haunts' ripoi 'go, travel']
memory noun (*computer*) pūmahara [W.309 'memories']
meningitis noun kiriuhi ua kakā [kiriuhi TM 'membrane' ua W.465 'backbone, neck, back of the neck' kakā TM 'inflammation']
meninx noun kiriuhi ua [kiriuhi TM 'membrane' ua W.465 'backbone, neck, back of the neck']
menopause noun koero [W.123 'sickness, particularly later stage of menstruation']
menstrual cycle noun awa wahine [awa W.23 'river' wahine W.474 'woman'], awa o te atua [awa W.23 'river' atua W.20 'menses']
menstruation noun rerenga awa wahine [rere W.337 'flow' awa W.23 'river' wahine W.474 'woman'], rere o te awa atua [rere W.337 'flow' awa W.23 'river' atua W.20 'menses']
mental health noun hauora hinengaro [hauora W.41 'health, vigour' hinengaro W.51 'seat of the thoughts and emotions']
menu noun (*computer*) rārangi tono [rārangi W.324 'line, rank, row' tono W.436 'bid, command']
menu noun rārangi kai [rārangi W.324 'line, rank, row' kai W.86 'food']
mercury noun konuoi [konu- TM 'prefix denoting natural metal' oi W.238 'move continuously']

merge transitive verb (*computer*) hanumi [W.34 'be merged or swallowed up']
mesoderm noun kiriwai [W.119 'inner skin']
mesosphere noun (*science*) kōhauwaenga [kōpaki W.135 'envelop' hau TM 'gas' waenga W.472 'the middle, the midst']
message noun karere [W.100 'messenger']
metabolism noun matūriaka [matū TM 'matter' riaka W.339 'put forth strength, energy']
metacarpus noun wheua kapu [wheua W.496 'bone' kapu W.97 'hollow of the hand']
metal, natural noun konganuku [kongakonga W.134 'fragment, chip' nuku W.225 'the earth']
metal, natural (*used as prefix*) konu- [kongakonga W.134 'fragment, chip' nuku W.225 'the earth']
metal alloy noun koranu [konu- TM 'prefix for natural metals' ranu W.322 'mix']
metal detector noun pūoko maitai [pūoko TM 'sensor, detector' maitai < Eng. 'metal']
metamorphic adjective kāhuarau [kāhua W.85 'form, appearance' rau W.328 'number']
metamorphosis noun kāhuarau [kāhua W.85 'form, appearance' rau W.328 'number']
metaphor noun kupu whakarite [kupu W.157 'word, saying' whakarite W.343 'make like, liken']
metatarsus noun wheua kapuwae [wheua W.496 'bone' kapu W.97 'hollow of the hand, sole of the foot' wae W.472 'foot']
meteorologist noun matahuarere [mata W.185 'eye, face' huarere TM 'weather']
meteorology noun mātai huarere [mātai TM 'study' huarere TM 'weather']
meter noun ine [W.78 'measure']
methane noun mewaro [me < Eng. 'me-' waro TM 'alkane']
methanoic acid noun waikawa mewaro [waikawa TM 'acid' mewaro TM 'methane']
methanol noun waihā mewaro [waihā TM 'hydroxide' mewaro TM 'methane']
method noun huarahi [W.65 'road, highway']
methodical adjective hakune [W.32 'be deliberate, be careful']

methylated spirits *noun* wai ewaro [wai W.474 'water, liquid' ewaro TM 'ethane']

meticulous *noun* mārehe [W.181 'painstaking, deft']

metre *noun* tuke [W.450 'a measure of length from one elbow to the fingers of the other extended arm']

metric system *noun* pūnaha rau [pūnaha TM 'system' rau W.328 'hundred'], pūnaha tuke [pūnaha TM 'system' tuke TM 'metre']

mezzanine *noun* huarewa [W.65 'raised aloft']

microcomputer *noun* rorohiko mōkito [rorohiko TM 'computer' mōkitokito W.207 'minute, small']

micro-organism *noun* moromoroiti [moroiti W.210 'small']

microbe *noun* mororiki [W.210 'small']

microbiology *noun* mātauranga koiora mororiki [mātauranga common usage 'knowledge' koiora TM 'biology' mororiki TM 'microbe']

microfiche *noun* kiriata mororiki [kiriata TM 'film' mororiki W.210 'small']

microfilm *noun* kiriata mōkito [kiriata TM 'film' mōkitokito W.207 'minute, small']

microphone *noun* hopuoro [hopu W.59 'catch' oro W.242 'rumble, sound']

microscope *noun* karu whakarahi [karu W.102 'eye' whakarahi TM 'enlarge']

microscope, binocular *noun* karurua whakarahi [karu W.102 'eye' rua W.349 'two' whakarahi TM 'enlarge']

microscope slide *noun* tawhera whakarahi [tawhera W.408 'leaf' whakarahi TM 'enlarge']

microscope tube *noun* pū whakarahi [pū W.300 'tube' whakarahi TM 'enlarge']

microscopic *adjective* mōkitokito [W.207 'minute, small']

microwave *noun* (*kitchenware*) ngaruiti [ngaru W.230 'wave' iti W.80 'small']

middle-distance run *noun* oma taitua [oma W.239 'run' taitua W.365 'distant']

middle-distance runner *noun* waetea taitua [W.473 'good runner, one strong of foot' taitua W.365 'distant']

midfielder *noun* takuahi [W.374 'centre of line of battle as opposed to the paihau']

military strategist *noun* pūkenga kawe-ā-riri [pūkenga W.307 'skilled in, versed in, repository' kawe-ā-riri W.111 'warfare, battle']

milli- (*prefix*) haumano [hautau TM 'fraction' mano W.176 'thousand']

milligram *noun* koma haumano [koma TM 'gram' haumano TM 'milli-']

millilitre *noun* kīaka haumano [kīaka TM 'litre' haumano TM 'milli-']

millimetre *noun* tuke haumano [tuke TM 'metre' haumano TM 'milli-']

mimic *transitive verb* pakoire [W.255 'imitate the cry of a bird']

mimicry *noun* whakatau [W.396 'imitate, make believe, simulate'], pakoire [W.255 'imitate the cry of a bird']

mince *noun, transitive verb* nakunaku [W.217 'reduce to fragments, broken in pieces, crushed']

mine *transitive verb* huke [W.68 'dig up, expose by removing the earth, excavate']

mine *noun* waro [W.480 'deep hole or pit, abyss']

mineral *noun* manawa whenua [W.174 'from the bowels of the earth']

mineral water *noun* puna manawa [W.174 'a spring from the heart of the earth']

miniature *adjective* tauhena [W.405 'dwarfish, of small stature']

mini-bin *noun* taiaroa para [taiaroa W.362 'basket, receptacle' para W.262 'impurity, refuse, waste']

minimum *noun* iti [W.80 'small']

minimum security prison *noun* wharehere pupuri [whare herehere W.46 'prison' pupuri W.314 'detain, press to remain']

miniskirt *noun* hikupeke [W.50 'hanging down a short distance']

minor offence *noun* hara namunamu [hara W.36 'sin, offence' namunamu W.217 'small, diminutive']

minority *noun, adjective* (*group*) tokoiti [toko W.434 'prefix used with adjectives of number' iti W.80 'small']

mint *transitive verb* (*coinage*) whakanao [TM 'produce']

minute-taker *noun* (*meeting*) kaiāmiki [kai W.86 'a prefix to transitive verbs to form nouns denoting an agent' āmiki TM 'minute-taking']

minute-taking *noun* (*meeting*) āmiki [W.8 'tell a story without omitting any particular']

mirror *noun* whakaata [W.18 'reflect, as water']
mirror, concave *noun* whakaata hakoko [whakaata TM 'mirror' hakoko W.32 'concave']
mirror, convex *noun* whakaata koropuku [whakaata TM 'mirror' koropuku W.145 'convex']
mirror line *noun* (*mathematics*) rārangi hangarite [rārangi W.324 'line' hangarite TM 'symmetry']
miscellaneous *adjective* maramara *noun* [W.180 'piece, bit, portion']
misconduct *noun* reho [W.334 'bad']
misfire *intransitive verb* hori [W.60 'mistake, misjudge']
miss a target *phrase* tohipa [tohipa W.430 'pass on one side']
mitochondrian *noun* (*biology*) pata pūngao [pata W.269 'seed, grain, numerous' pūngao TM 'energy']
mitosis *noun* (*biology*) pūmau pūira [pūmau W.309 'fixed, constant' pūira TM 'chromosome']
mitt *noun* komoringa [TM 'glove']
mitten *noun* pūāhuru ringa [pūāhuru W.302 'close, warm' pū W.300 'source' āhuru W.4 'warm' ringa W.341 'hand']
mixed doubles *noun* tokowhā tāne, wahine [tokowhā TM 'doubles' tāne W.377 'male' wahine W.474 'woman']
mixed member proportional representation MMP *noun* (*electoral system*) whirirua [whiriwhiri W.497 'select, choose' rua W.349 'choose']
mixed number *noun* tau hanumi [tau TM 'number' hanumi W.34 'be mixed']
mixing bowl *noun* okopoke [oko W.239 'wooden bowl or other open vessel' pokepoke W.289 'mix up with water or other fluid']
mixture *noun* (*liquid*) raranu [ranu W.322 'mix' whakaranu W.322 'gravy, juice of anything']
mixture *noun* (*solid*) pokepoke [W.289 'mix up with water or other fluid']
mobile *noun* (*decoration*) kaui [W.106 'cord or stick on which articles are strung']
mobile *adjective* nekeneke [neke W.220 'move']
mode *noun* (*mathematics*) tauputu [tau TM 'number' putu W.317 'lie in a heap' pūputu 'frequent']

model *noun* tauira [W.398 'pattern, copy']
model *transitive verb* (*clothing*) whakaatu [whakaatu W.20 'call attention to, show']
module *noun* (*unit*) kōwae [W.151 'divide, part']
molecule *noun* rāpoi ngota [rāpoi W.326 'cluster' ngota TM 'atom']
mollusc *noun* kaiwhao [W.90 'a mollusc']
momentum *noun* torohaki [W.439 'impel, push, thrust']
monitor *noun* (*computer*) kaupane [W.107 'head, upper end']
monitor *transitive verb* aroturuki [aro W.16 'consider, think' turuki W.461 'come as a supplement, follow, reinforce']
monk *noun* moke [W.207 'solitary person']
monomer *noun* (*chemistry*) waetahi [wae TM 'unit' tahi W.359 'one, single']
monopoly *noun* mana tokitoki [mana W.172 'power, control, authority, influence' tokitoki W.434 'altogether, without exception']
monosaccharide *noun* hukatahi [huka < Eng. 'sugar' tahi W.359 'one']
moose *noun* pihiringa [pihi W.280 'shoot, sprout' ringa W.341 'hand(-like)']
moral *adjective* matatika [W.191 'right, straight' mata W.185 'face, eye']
mordant *noun* (*colour-fixing*) tūmau kano [tūmau W.453 'fixed, constant, permanent' kano W.94 'colour']
morning tea *noun* paramanawa [W.264 'refreshment']
morpheme *noun* wetenga [wete W.483 'untie, unravel']
morphology *noun* wetekupu [wete W.483 'untie, unravel' kupu W.157 'word']
mosasaur *noun* mokotai [moko W.207 'a general term for lizards, huge mythical creature of lizard-like shape' tai W.361 'the sea']
motivate *transitive verb* toitoi manawa [toitoi W.432 'encourage, incite' manawa W.174 'mind, spirit']
mouli *noun* kūoro [toitoi W.156 'grind, rub down, grate']
mousetrap *noun* tāwhiti [W.409 'snare, trap']
mousse *noun* (*hair*) huka makawe [huka W.67 'foam, froth' makawe W.169 'hair']
moustache *noun* whenguwhengu [W.494 'tattoo marks on the upper lip']

mouth freshener *noun* karahā [kakara W.97 'scent, smell, flavour' hā W.29 'breath, taste, flavour']
mouth guard *noun* whakapuru waha [whakapuru W.314 'cram, protect with a pad' waha W.473 'mouth']
muesli *noun* patahua [pata W.269 'seed, grain' hua W.64 'fruit']
muffler *noun* whakakōmau [W.132 'repress, stifle']
muggy *adjective* haitutu [W.31 'close, oppressive, of atmosphere']
multicoloured *adjective* ōpurepure [W.240 'varied with patches of colour']
multiple *noun* taurea [tau TM 'number' whakarea TM 'multiply']
multiple, common *noun* taurea pātahi [taurea TM 'multiple' pātahi TM 'common']
multiple foul *noun* hapawene [hapa TM 'foul' wene W.482 'many, numerous']
multiple sclerosis *noun* roro tapepe [roro W.347 'brains, marrow' tapepe W.383 'stumble, make a mistake, speak inarticulately']
multiplication *noun* whakarea [whaka- W.486 'causative prefix' *to make* rea W.333 'multiply'], whakarau [W.328 'multiply']
mumps *noun* repe hūare pupuhi [repe W.336 'gland' hūare W.65 'spittle' pupuhi W.304 'swell']
muscle *noun* ua [uaua W.465 'sinew, strenuous, vigorous']
muscle, biceps *noun* uarua [ua TM 'muscle' rua W.349 'two']
muscle, brachioradialis *noun* ua kawiti [ua TM 'muscle' kawititanga o te ringaringa' W.111 'wrist']
muscle, buccinator *noun* ua pāpāringa [ua TM 'muscle' pāpāringa W.260 'cheek']
muscle, deltoid *noun* ua pakihiwi [ua TM 'muscle' pakihiwi W.254 'shoulder']
muscle, digitorum *noun* ua matitoro [ua TM 'muscle' mati W.193 'finger' toro W.438 'stretch forth, extend']
muscle, erector spinae *noun* ua tuaiwi [ua TM 'muscle' tuaiwi W.445 'back, backbone']
muscle, extensor pollicis longus *noun* ua kōnui toro [ua TM 'muscle' kōnui W.134 'thumb', great toe' toro W.438 'stretch forth, extend']

muscle, flexor digitorum superficialis *noun* ua mati whati [ua TM 'muscle' mati W.193 'finger' whawhati W.491 'bend at an angle, fold']
muscle, flexor pollicis brevis *noun* ua kōnui whati [ua TM 'muscle' kōnui W.134 'thumb, great toe' whawhati W.491 'bend at an angle, fold']
muscle, gastrocnemius *noun* ateate [W.19 'calf of the leg']
muscle, gluteus maximus *noun* ua kōtore [ua TM 'muscle' kōtore W.150 'buttocks']
muscle, gluteus medius *noun* ua kumu [ua TM 'muscle' kumu W.156 'posterior, buttocks']
muscle, latissimus dorsi *noun* ua rara [ua TM 'muscle' rara W.326 'rib']
muscle, levator scapulae *noun* ua hiki pākoukou [ua TM 'muscle' hiki W.49 'lift up, raise' pākoukou W.255 'shoulder-blade']
muscle, masseter *noun* ua ngaungau [ua TM 'muscle' ngau W.230 'bite, gnaw']
muscle, nasalis *noun* ua ihu [ua TM 'muscle' ihu W.75 'nose']
muscle, occipitofrontalis *noun* ua rae [ua TM 'muscle' rae W.320 'forehead']
muscle, orbicularis oculi *noun* ua karu [ua TM 'muscle' karu W.102 'eye']
muscle, orbicularis oris *noun* ua kati waha [ua TM 'muscle' kati W.103 'shut, close up' waha W.473 'mouth']
muscle, pectoralis major *noun* ua rei [ua TM 'muscle' rei W.335 'breast, chest']
muscle, quadriceps *noun* ua whā [ua TM 'muscle' whā W.484 'four']
muscle, sartorius *noun* ua tūturi [ua TM 'muscle' tūturi W.459 'bend the legs, draw up the knees' turi 'knee']
muscle, serratus anterior *noun* ua kaokao [ua TM 'muscle' kaokao W.94 'ribs, side of the body']
muscle, sternocleido-mastoid *noun* ua rūrū māhunga [ua TM 'muscle' rūrū W.349 'wave about' māhunga W.165 'head']
muscle, temporalis *noun* ua rahirahinga [ua TM 'muscle' rahirahinga W.320 'temple of the head']
muscle, tibialis anterior *noun* ua takakaha [ua TM 'muscle' takakaha W.368 'shinbone']
muscle, trapezius *noun* ua paemanu [ua

TM 'muscle' paemanu W.246 'collarbone']
muscle, triceps *noun* ua tengi [ua TM 'muscle' tengi W.412 'three']
muscular dystrophy *noun* mate horokiwa [mate W.192 'sickness' horokiwa W.61 'wasting away of the body in disease']
muscular system *noun* ua tōpū [ua TM 'muscle' tōpū W.437 'assembled, in a body']
music *noun* pūoru [W.311 'sound']
musical instrument *noun* taonga pūoru [taonga W.381 'property, anything highly prized' pūoro TM 'music']
must *auxiliary verb* mātua [W.195 'first'] e.g. *me mātua haere* 'must go'

mustard *noun* panikakā [pani W.257 'smear, spread' kakā W.81 'red-hot']
mustard powder *noun* rehukakā [rehu W.334 'fine dust' kakā W.81 'red-hot']
mustard seed *noun* patakakā [pata W.269 'seed, grain' kakā W.81 'red-hot']
mutate *transitive verb, intransitive verb* iranoi [ira TM 'gene' nonoi W.223 'disfigured']
mutation *noun* iranoi [TM 'mutate']
mutiny *noun* whana [W.486 'revolt, rebel']
myriapod *noun* waengero [wae W.472 'leg' ngero W.233 'very many']
mystery *noun* pirikoko [piri W.283 'stick, adhere, cling' piringa 'hiding place' koko W.130 'corner, recess']

N

nappy *noun* kope [W.136 'soft mosses used as wrappers or absorbents']
narcissism *noun* (mate) whakaataata [mate W.192 'sickness' whakaata W.18 'look at one's reflected image, in water or in mirror'], whakatāupe [W.401 'regard oneself with admiration, i.e. bend over the wai whakaata']
narcotic *noun* whakapōauau [whaka- W.486 'causative prefix' *to make* pōauau W.286 'mistaken, confused']
narrator *noun* wahapū [waha W.473 'voice' wahapū W.473 'eloquent']
nasal bone *noun* wheua ihu [wheua W.496 'bone' ihu W.75 'nose']
nasal passage *noun* awa hau [awa W.23 'channel, river' hau W.38 'breath'], pongāihu [W.292 'nostril']
nasopharynx *noun* awa ihu [awa W.23 'channel, river' ihu W.75 'nose']
national anthem *noun* ngaringari a te motu [ngaringari W.230 'song to make people pull together' motu W.211 'island']
natural gas *noun* hau manawa [hau TM 'gas' manawa W.174 'bowels of the earth'], kapuni [name of gas field]
natural number *noun* tau tatau [tau TM 'number', tatau W.395 'count']
natural resource *noun* rawa taiao [rawa W.331 'goods property' taiao TM 'environment']
natural selection *noun* whiringa taiao [whiriwhiri W.497 'select, choose' taiao TM 'environment']
nature *noun* ao tūroa [ao W.11 'world' tūroa W.460 'established, of long standing']
nature *noun* (*essential quality*) iho [W.75 'heart, inside, kernel, pitch, umbilical cord']

naval ship *noun* wakatauā [waka common usage 'boat' tauā W.397 'hostile expedition, army']
navigator *transitive verb* urungi [W.470 'rudder, steering paddle, steer']
navy *noun* tauā moana [tauā W.397 'hostile expedition, army' moana W.204 'sea, lake']
nearly *adverb* kainamu [W.88 'be within a little of'] *e.g. Kei te aha te tāima? Kua kainamu ki te whā. 'What's the time? It's nearly four.'*
near-post *noun* poutata [pou W.297 'pole, post' tata W.393 'near']
nebulous *adjective* hāraurau [W.37 'see or hear indistinctly' hārau 'feel for with the hand, grope for']
necrophilia *noun* kaipirau [W.89 'dishonour after death, dishonour applied to a dead body']
necrophiliac *noun* kaipirau [W.89 'dishonour after death, dishonour applied to a dead body']
needle *noun* (*sewing*) mātuhi [W.195 'a small bone needle with eye']
negative *adjective* (*number*) tōraro [tō W.428 'that of' raro W.327 'the bottom, the underside']
negative charge *noun* tāhiko [tā TM 'negative end' hiko common usage 'electricity']
negative end *noun* (*electricity*) pito-tā [pito W.284 'end, extremity' tā common usage used to indicate indefinite locality]
negotiate *intransitive verb* whakawhiti whakaaro [whakawhiti W.497 'exchange' whakaaro W.16 'thought, opinion']
neighbour *noun* kiritata [kiri W.119 'person, skin' tata W.393 'close']

neologism noun kupu hou [kupu W.157 'word' hou W.62 'new']

neon noun (gas) haukura [hau TM 'gas' kura W.157 'red, glowing, precious']

neon light noun rama haukura [rama W.322 'torch or other artificial light' haukura TM 'neon']

nerve, optic noun io whatu [io W.78 'nerve' whatu W.492 'eye']

nerve cells noun pūtau io [pūtau TM 'cell' io W.78 'nerve']

nervous condition noun mate ioio [mate W.192 'sickness' io W.78 'nerve']

nervous system noun io tōpū [io W.78 'nerve' tōpū W.437 'assembled, in a body']

net noun (sport) mātiratira [W.194 'a net attached to stakes in the tideway']

net adjective (finances) more [W.209 'bare, plain, without appendages']

net noun (geometry) raumata [W.330 'mesh of a net']

net aerial noun (sport) pūhihi mātiratira [pūhihi W.304 'antennae' mātiratira TM 'net']

net ball noun (tennis) tukurua [tukurua W.452 'repeat an operation, do a second time' tuku TM 'serve']

netball noun poi tarawhiti [poi TM 'ball' tarawhiti W.390 'hoop, ring']

network noun kōtuitui [kōtui W.150 'fasten by lacing, interlace, interlaced']

neuralgia noun iotārūrū [io TM 'nerve' tārūrū W.392 'painful, acute']

neurotic adjective mānuka rau [mānuka W.177 'troubled, anxious, sad, having the emotions stirred' mānukanuka 'anxiety, misgiving, apprehension' rau W.328 'multitude, number, embarrassed, entangled, confused']

neutral, remain (dispute) whakaraupapa [W.330 'remain tranquil']

neutralise transitive verb (chemistry) whakapāhare [whaka- W.486 'causative prefix' to make pāhare TM 'salt']

neutron noun (physics) iramoe [ira TM 'particle' moe W.204 'sleep, repose']

newton noun (physics) wae taipana [wae TM 'unit' taipana TM 'force']

nib noun (pen) kīra [W.119 'quill']

nichrome noun kitakōreko [konukita TM 'chromium' konukōreko TM 'nickel']

nickel noun konukōreko [konu- TM 'prefix denoting natural metal' kōreko W.141 'white, dazzled']

nickname noun ingoa kārangaranga [ingoa W.78 'name' kārangaranga W.98 'call frequently']

nicotine noun parawaro [para W.262 'impurity, waste' waro TM 'carbon']

nitrate noun pākawa ota [pākawa TM '-ate' hauota TM 'nitrogen']

nitrite noun pākati ota [pākati TM '-ite' hauota TM 'nitrogen']

nitrogen noun hauota [hau TM 'gas' ota W.242 'vegetation']

nitrous oxide noun hāora ota-rua [hāora TM 'oxygen' hauota TM 'nitrogen' rua W.349 'two']

no admittance phrase kaua e kuhu mai [kaua W.105 'do not' kuhu W.154 'introduce oneself into']

no ball phrase (cricket) tuku hē [tuku W.451 'send' hē W.43 'wrong']

no exit phrase kaua e puta mā konei [kaua W.105 'do not' puta W.315 'pass through or out' konei W.133 'this place']

nocturnal adjective huna [W.69 'concealed, unnoticed']

nominate transitive verb kōhari [W.124 'select, pick out']

nomination noun kōharinga [kōhari TM 'nominate']

non-biodegradable adjective pōpopo-kore [pōpopo W.292 'rotten, decayed, worm-eaten' kore W.140 'no, not']

nonconformist noun korokē [W.144 'extraordinary, strange, out of the common']

non-fiction adjective pono [W.291 'true, genuine']

non-Māori adjective tauiwi [W.398 'strange, tribe, foreign race']

non-molestation order noun whakatau ārai mamae [whakatau TM 'ruling' ārai W.14 'keep off, ward off' mamae W.162 'feel pain or distress of body or mind']

non-standard adjective (mathematics) aronga kē [aro W.16 'face, turn towards, be inclined, be disposed' kē W.111 'different, of another kind']

non-standard unit of measurement waeine aronga kē [waeine TM 'unit of measurement' aronga kē TM 'non-standard']

non-stick *adjective* (*kitchenware*) pirikore [piri W.283 'stick, adhere, cling' kore W.140 'no, not']

nontane *noun* (*science*) īwaro [iwa W.80 'nine' waro TM 'alkane']

noodle *noun* kihu parāoa [kihukihu W.117 'thrum' parāoa < Eng. 'flour']

normal distribution *noun* tītari māori [tītari TM 'distribution' māori W.179 'normal']

northwards *adverb* whakararo [whaka- W.485 'towards, in the direction of' raro W.327 'north, the north']

not negotiable *phrase* (*cheque*) kaua i tua atu i te ingoa e mau nei [kaua W.105 'do not' tua W.444 'on the farther side' i W.73 'from' ingoa W.78 'name' mau W.196 'fixed']

note *noun* (*music*) orotahi [oro W.242 'sound' tahi W.359 'one, single']

notebook *noun* pukatuhi [pukapuka W.306 'book' tuhi W.448 'write']

note-taking *noun* tuhi tīpoka [tuhi W.448 'write' tīpokapoka W.422 'taking some and leaving some']

notice *noun* pānui [W.257 'publish, proclaim']

nought *noun* kore [korenga W.141 'non-existence, non-occurrence']

noun *noun* kupu ingoa [kupu W.157 'word' ingoa W.78 'name']

noun, abstract *noun* kupu ingoa kurehu [kupu ingoa TM 'noun' kurehu W.158 'indistinctly seen']

noun, concrete *noun* kupu ingoa uka [kupu ingoa TM 'noun' uka W.466 'hard, firm']

nuclear *adjective* (*physics*) karihi [W.101 'stone of a fruit, kernel']

nuclear bomb *noun* pahū karihi [pahū TM 'bomb' karihi TM 'nuclear']

nuclear energy *noun* pūngao karihi [pūngao TM 'energy' karihi TM 'nuclear']

nuclear family *noun* whānau whaiaro [whānau W.487 'family' whaiaro W.485 'self, person']

nuclear fission *noun* whakangotangota [whaka- W.486 'causative prefix' *to make* ngota W.235 'fragment, particle' TM 'atom' ngotangota W.235 'smashed to atoms']

nuclear warfare *noun* umu pongipongi [W.292 'an incantation and rite to cause death']

nuclear-armed ship *noun* wakatauā karihi [wakatauā TM 'naval ship' karihi TM 'nuclear']

nuclear-powered ship *noun* kaipuke pūngao-karihi [kaipuke W.89 'ship' pūngao TM 'energy' karihi TM 'nuclear']

nucleus *noun* karihi [W.101 'stone of a fruit, kernel']

nuisance *noun* pōrearea [W.293 'tiresome, importunate']

number *noun* tau [W.395 'count, repeat one by one']

number, binary *noun* tau kaupapa-rua [tau TM 'number' kaupapa-ā-tau TM 'number base' rua W.349 'two']

number, cardinal *noun* tau maha [tau TM 'number' maha W.162 'many, number']

number, counting *noun* tau tatau [tau TM 'number' tatau W.395 'count']

number, decimal *noun* tau-ā-ira [tau TM 'number' ā W.1 'after the manner of' ira TM 'decimal'], tau ngahuru [tau TM 'number' ngahuru W.227 'ten']

number, even *noun* taurua [tau TM 'number' rua W.349 'two']

number, irrational *noun* tau tatū kore [tau TM 'number' tatū W.395 'reach the bottom, be at ease' kore W.140 'no, not']

number, natural *noun* tau tatau [TM 'counting number']

number, negative *noun* tau tōraro [tau TM 'number' tōraro TM 'negative']

number, octal *noun* tau kaupapa-waru [tau TM 'number' kaupapa-ā-tau TM 'number base' waru W.480 'eight']

number, odd *noun* taukehe [tau TM 'number' kehe W.112 'an odd number in counting']

number, positive *noun* tau tōrunga [tau TM 'number' tōrunga TM 'positive']

number, prime *noun* punga [W.310 'odd number, anchor']

number, rational *noun* tau hautau [tau TM 'number' hautau TM 'fraction']

number, real *noun* tau tūturu [tau TM 'number' tūturu W.460 'fixed, permanent']

number, whole *noun* tau oti [tau TM 'number' oti W.424 'finished'], tau poha [tau TM 'number' poha W.286 'full']

number base *noun* kaupapa-ā-tau [kaupapa W.107 'stage, platform' ā W.1 'after the manner of' tau TM 'number']

number eight *noun* (*rugby*) poumuri [pou W.297 'support' muri W.214 'the rear']

number line *noun* rārangi tau [rārangi W.324 'line, row' tau TM 'number']

number plate *noun* tauwaka [tau TM 'number' waka common usage 'vehicle']

number story *noun* (*mathematics*) pakitau [paki W.253 'tales, subject of talk' tau TM 'number']

number system *noun* pūnaha tau [pūnaha TM 'system' tau TM 'number']

number table *noun* papatau [papa W.259 'anything broad, flat and hard' tau TM 'number']

numeral tohutau [tohu W.431 'mark, sign' tau TM 'number']

numerator *noun* taurunga [tau TM 'number' runga W.352 'the top, the upper part']

nun *noun* ngoi atua [tore atua W.438 'a woman with an atua as husband' ngoi W.234 'strength, energy' atua 'god']

nurse *noun* tapuhi [W.385 'nurse, carry in the arms, tend in sickness or distress']

nurse, charge *noun* tapuhi matua [tapuhi TM 'nurse' matua W.195 'main, chief']

nurse, staff *noun* tapuhi mātāmuri [tapuhi TM 'nurse' mātāmuri W.188 'last, latter']

nursery *noun* kōhanga [whare kōhanga W.124 'the place to which the mother and new-born child were removed']

nut *noun* (*machinery*) peru [W.278 'head, as of a nail, etc.']

nylon *noun, adjective* ngaiaku [ngai W.227 'dried leaves of raupō, flax, etc., used for walls or thatch of a house' akuaku W.7 'firm strong']

nylon cord *noun* here ngaiaku [here W.46 'string or cord to tie with' ngaiaku TM 'nylon']

nylon rope *noun* taura ngaiaku [taura W.402 'rope, cable' ngaiaku TM 'nylon']

nylon thread *noun* miro ngaiaku [miro W.203 'thread, twisted cord' ngaiaku TM 'nylon']

O

oath *noun* kupu taurangi [kupu W.157 'word, anything said' kī taurangi W.402 'promise, pledge']
object *noun* (*grammar*) pūnga [pū W.300 'origin, source']
objective *noun* whāinga [whai W.484 'follow, pursue, aim at']
objective, long-term *noun* whāinga roa [whāinga TM 'objective' roa W.344 'long']
objective, short-term *noun* whāinga poto [whāinga TM 'objective' poto W.297 'short']
objective lens *noun* (*microscope*) arotahi whakarahi [arotahi TM 'lens' whakarahi TM 'enlarge']
oboe *noun* pūtōiri [pū W.300 'tube' tōiri W.432 'tingle, vibrate, resound']
observation *noun* mātakitaki [W.188 'look at, inspect, watch, peer, pry']
obsessed koromaki [W.144 'be fully intent upon an object, pursue with all one's mind']
occupational safety *noun* ārai hauata mahi [ārai W.14 'keep off, ward off' hauata W.40 'accident' mahi W.163 'work']
octagon *noun* tapawaru [tapa W.381 'margin, edge' waru W.480 'eight']
octane *noun* wāwaro [waru W.480 'eight' waro TM 'alkane']
octave *noun* waruoro [waru W.480 'eight' orotahi TM 'note']
odds *noun* (*probability*) tūponotanga [tūpono W.457 'chance to hit']
odometer *noun* ine hauroa [ine TM 'meter' hauroa W.41 'length, long']
oesophagus *noun* pū kai [pū W.300 'tube' kai W.86 'food']
off-break *noun* (*cricket*) epa ātea [epa TM 'bowl' ātea TM 'off-side']

offence *noun* (*sport*) hara [W.36 'sin, offence']
offence *noun* (*sport, vs. defence*) huaki [W.65 'assault, charge, attack']
officer *noun* kiriārahi [kiri W.119 'person' ārahi W.14 'lead, conduct, escort']
official *noun* kiriāwhina [kiri W119 'person' āwhina W.25 'assist, benefit, befriend']
official *noun* atoato [W.19 'marshal, regulate the formation of a corps on the march']
off-ramp *noun* pekaputa [peka W.275 'branch of a tree, river, etc.' puta W.315 'pass out']
off-side *adjective* (*cricket*) ātea [W.19 'clear, free from obstruction, out of the way']
offside *adjective* (*sport*) takamua *intransitive verb* [takamua W.368 'fore, front' taka W.366 'range, roam at large, veer']
off-spinner *noun* epa tāwhiro ātea [epa TM 'bowl' tāwhirowhiro W.409 'whirl, spin' ātea TM 'off-side']
oil, crude *noun* hinumata [hinu W.51 'oil' mata W.185 'raw, uncooked, fresh, as water']
oil, olive *noun* noni tākou [noni TM 'vegetable oil' tākou W.374 'a tree similar to the olive']
oil, vegetable *noun* noni [noni W.224 'oil']
oil spill *noun* rukenga hinu [ruke W.351 'pour forth, discharge, vent' hinu W.51 'oil']
oil gland *noun* (*botany*) repenoni [repe W.336 'gland' noni W.224 'oil']
ointment *noun* pūreke [W.313 'a decoction of bark and ashes used for certain skin complaints']
olfactory nerve *noun* io ihu [io W.78 'nerve' ihu W.75 'nose']
-ologist *suffix* kaimātai [kai W.86 'a prefix

to transitive verbs to form nouns denoting an agent' mātai W.187 'inspect, examine']
-ology *suffix* mātai [TM 'study']
Olympic Games *noun* Taumāhekeheke o te Ao [taumāhekeheke W.399 'compete with one another in friendly rivalry for the possession of the same object' ao W.11 'world']
on edge *adjective* (*colloquial*) tūtakarerewa [W.462 'alert, unsettled, apprehensive']
on loan *phrase* taurewa *adjective* [W.402 'not paid for']
oncology *noun* mātai mate pukupuku [mātai TM 'study' mate pukupuku TM 'cancer']
one-on-one (*basketball*) kura horahora [W.158 'spread out, extend, applied to a war party']
one-way *adjective* (*traffic*) ahutahi [ahu W.3 'move in a certain direction' tahi W.359 'one, single']
on-ramp *noun* pekauru [peka W.275 'branch of a tree, river, etc.' uru W.469 'enter']
opal *noun* ōpure [W.240 'varied with patches of colour']
opening ceremony *noun* whakatuwheratanga [whakatuwhera W.464 'open, set open']
open-side *adjective* takiraha [W.372 'wide, extended, open space']
open-side *noun* taha takiraha [taha W.357 'side' takiraha W.372 'wide, extended, open space']
opera *noun* whakaari pūoru [whakaari TM 'drama' pūoru TM 'music']
operate *intransitive verb* (*perform surgery*) tapahi [W.382 'cut, chop']
operation *noun* (*general*) mahi [W.163 'work, occupation, do, perform']
operation *noun* (*mathematics*) paheko [W.247 'join, combine']
operation, binary *noun* paheko tōrua [paheko TM 'operation' tōrua W.441 'twofold']
operation, inverse *noun* paheko kōaro [paheko TM 'operation' kōaro TM 'inverse']
opponent *noun* hoariri [W.54 'foe, enemy']
optic *adjective* whatu [W.492 'eye, pupil of the eye']

optical *adjective* whatu [W.492 'eye, pupil of the eye']
optician *noun* kaimātai whatu [kai W.86 'a prefix to transitive verbs to form nouns denoting an agent' mātai W.187 'inspect, examine' whatu W.492 'eye, pupil of the eye']
orang-utan *noun* tuahuru [W.445 'hairy, shaggy, rough']
orange *adjective* karaka [W.98 'corynocarpus laevigata, a tree, and fruit of same']
orange, dark *adjective* pākākā [W.250 'scorched, red or brown']
orange-red *adjective* whero [W.495 'red, orange']
orbit *noun* āmionga [amio W.8 'circle round']
orchestra *noun* tira pūoru [tira W.422 'file of men, row, company of travellers, choir' pūoru TM 'music']
order *transitive verb* (*sequence*) whakaraupapa [whaka- W.486 'causative prefix' *to make* raupapa W.330 'put in order, ordered, completed']
order *noun* (*sequence*) raupapa [W.330 'put in order, ordered, completed']
order *noun* (*biology*) pūtoi [W.317 'tribe, family']
Order of St. John *noun* Kāhui o Hoani [kāhui W.885 'assemblage' Hoani < Eng. 'John']
order of symmetry tau hangarite [tau TM 'number' hangarite TM 'symmetry']
ore *noun* tokahuke [toka W.433 'stone, rock' huke W.68 'dig up, expose by removing the earth, excavate']
organ *noun* (*music*) pūkeru [pū W.300 'tube' pūkeru W.308 'blow']
organ, internal *noun* (*generic*) whēkau [W.493 'internal organs of the body, entrails']
organ, reproductive *noun* taihemahema [W.363 'genitals of either sex']
organ donation *noun* tuku whēkau [tuku W.451 'give up, present, offer' whēkau TM 'organ']
organic *adjective* paraumu [W.265 'black soil, humus']
organic compound *noun* (*carbon*) matūwaro [matū TM 'matter, chemical' waro TM 'carbon']

organisation *noun* (*institution*) whakahaere [W.30 'conduct any business, execute']
organiser *noun* kaiwhakahaere [kai W.86 'a prefix to transitive verbs to form nouns denoting an agent' whakahaere W.30 'conduct any business, execute']
organism *noun* kaiao [W.86 'alive, living']
orgasm *noun* tokomauri [W.434 'excite one's affections, enamour, hiccough']
orienteering *noun* awhe-ararau [awhe W.24 'go, travel' ara W.13 'path' rau W.328 'hundred, number']
origami *noun* whētuitui [W.496 'fold, double, a garment etc.']
ornamental *adjective* nekoneko [W.221 'fancy border of a cloak']
ornithologist *noun* kaimātai aotea [kaimātai TM '-ologist' aotea W.12 'bird']
ornithology *noun* mātai aotea [mātai TM 'study' aotea W.12 'bird']
orogenesis *noun* (*geology*) orokohanga paemaunga [orokohanga TM 'creation' pae W.244 'horizontal ridges of hills' maunga W.197 maunga 'mountain']
orthodontics *noun* whakatika niho tāpiki [whakatika W.417 'straighten, correct' niho W.221 'tooth' tāpiki W.384 'be entangled, doubled over' niho tāpiki 'a tooth overriding another']
orthodontist *noun* rata niho tāpiki [rata W.327 'doctor' niho W.221 'tooth' tāpiki W.384 'be entangled, doubled over' niho tāpiki 'a tooth overriding another']
osmosis *noun* rerewai [rere W.337 'flow' wai W.474 'water, liquid']
out *adverb* (*sport*) kua puta [puta W.315 'pass out']
out *adverb* (*tennis*) kei waho [waho W.474 'the outside']
out for a duck *phrase* (*cricket*) e waru pū [W.480 'not at all, by no means']
out of play *phrase* kua puta [puta W.315 'pass out']
out on the full *phrase* (*sport*) kotahi atu ki waho [idiom kotahi W.147 'one' atu W.20 'to indicate a direction or motion onwards or away from the speaker' waho W.474 'the outside']
outcome *noun* pata [W.269 'advantage, fruit'], hua [W.64 'product' huanga W.64 'benefit']
outfield *noun* (*sport*) whaitua [W.485 'region, space']

outfield, left *noun* whaitua mauī [whaitua W.485 'region, space' mauī W.196 'left, on the left hand']
outfield, right *noun* whaitua matau [W.485 'region, space' matau W.192 'right, on the right hand']
outlier *noun* (*mathematics*) mōwaho [W.212 'on the outside']
outline *noun* hua [W.64 'outline, leading lines of a pattern in carving']
outpatient *noun* tūroro noho kāinga [tūroro W.460 'sick person' noho W.223 'remain, stay' kāinga W.81 'place of abode']
outpost *adjective, noun* taupuni tawhiti [taupuni W.401 'temporary encampment, place of assignation' tawhiti W.409 'distant, widely separated']
outside centre *noun* (*sport*) pūwaho [pū W.300 'heart, centre' waho W.474 'the outside']
outswinger *noun* epa tataha whakawaho [epa TM 'bowl' tataha W.357 'swerve' whakawaho TM 'outwards']
out-tray *noun* (*office equipment*) pae reta atu [pae W.246 'dish' reta < Eng. 'letter' atu W.20 'indicate a direction away from speaker']
outwards *adverb* whakawaho [whaka- W.485 'towards, in the direction of' waho W.474 'the outside']
ovary *noun* kiato kākano [kiato W.117 'receptacle for holding certain sacred things' kākano TM 'ovum']
oven *noun* umu [W.467 'earth oven']
oven cloth *noun* pareumu [pare W.266 'protection' umu TM 'oven']
oven-light *noun* rama umu [rama W.322 'torch or other artificial light' umu TM 'oven']
oven-timer *noun* pūoho umu [pūoho TM 'alarm' umu TM 'oven']
oven-tray *noun* pae umu [paepae W.245 'dish, open, shallow vessel' umu TM 'oven']
oven-window *noun* kotopihi umu [kotopihi W.150 'window' umu TM 'oven']
over *noun* (*cricket*) paiepa [paiere W.249 'bind together on bundles, bundle' epa TM 'bowl']
over rate *noun* (*cricket*) pāpātanga paiepa [pāpātanga TM 'rate' paiepa TM 'over']

overcrowding noun noho apiapi [noho W.223 'sit, dwell' apiapi W.12 'crowded, dense']

overdose noun kai inati [kai W.85 'eat' inati W.77 'excessive, trouble, bane, disaster, omen, portent, generally bad']

overhead projector OHP noun rauata [rau W.328 'number, multitude' ata W.18 'reflected image']

overloaded adjective (weight) tōpāparu [W.437 'deeply laden']

overlocker noun paretoki [W.267 'a method of fastening the fringe to the bottom of a garment']

overpopulated adjective apiapi [W.12 'crowded, dense']

overthrow noun (sport) pahemo [W.247 'pass by, pass on one side, miss']

overview noun tirohanga whānui [tirohanga W.424 'view, sight, aspect' whānui W.487 'broad, wide'], tiro whānui [tiro W.424 'look, survey, view' whānui W.487 'broad, wide']

overweight adjective (traffic loading) tōpāparu [W.437 'deeply laden']

oviduct noun pūkākano [pū W.300 'tube' kākano TM 'ovum']

ovulate intransitive verb tuku kākano [tuku W.451 'send' kākano TM 'ovum']

ovulation noun tuku kākano [TM 'ovulate']

ovum noun kākano [W.94 'seed, stock, descent']

own goal noun (soccer) paneke ninipa [paneke TM 'goal' ninipa W.322 'awkward, unfortunate, unskilful']

oxidant noun piti hāora [piti W.284 'add' hāora TM 'oxygen'], tango irahiko [tango W.380 'take away, remove' irahiko TM 'electron']

oxidise transitive verb piti hāora [TM 'oxidant'], tango irahiko [TM 'oxidant']

oxygen noun hāora [hā W.29 'breath, breathe' ora W.241 'alive']

ozone noun pekerangi [W.276 'screen, barrier, the outermost palisade of a complete stockade']

ozone layer noun pekerangi [W.276 'screen, barrier, the outermost palisade of a complete stockade']

P

pacify *transitive verb* whakamahuru [W.165 'appease, soothe']

pack *noun* (*tramping*) peketua [W.276 'supplementary load carried on the back']

package *noun* mōkī [W.207 'bundle, parcel, packet'], mōkihi [W.207 'bundle, parcel, packet']

packaging *noun* tākai [tākai W.367 'wrap up, wrap round, wind round']

padding *noun* (*sport*) parekiri [pare W.266 'turn aside, ward off' parepare W.266 'protection' kiri W.119 'skin, person, self']

paddy *noun* (*rice cultivation*) māra raihi [māra W.180 'plot of ground under cultivation' raihi < Eng. 'rice']

page break *noun* (*word-processing*) wehe whārangi [wehe W.481 'detach, divide' whārangi W.489 'page of a book']

page view *noun* (*word-processing*) tiro whārangi [tiro W.424 'look' whārangi W.489 'page of a book']

pager *noun* pūoho [W.311 'start, take alarm']

paginate *transitive verb* whakawhārangi [whaka- W.486 'causative prefix' *to make* whārangi W.489 'page of a book']

painting *noun* (*art*) kōwaiwai [W.151 'an ancient style of painting, for adorning the person and dwellings']

palaeontologist *noun* kaimātai roke kanae [kaimātai TM '-ologist' roke kanae TM 'fossil']

palaeontology *noun* mātai roke kanae [mātai TM 'study' roke kanae TM 'fossil']

palate, hard *noun* ngao mārō [ngao W.229 'palate' mārō W.183 'hard']

palate, soft *noun* ngao ngohe [ngao W.229 'palate' ngohe W.234 'supple, soft']

palindrome *noun* kōaro rite [kōaro W.122 'upside down' rite W.343 'alike, corresponding']

pallid *adjective* kōmā [W.131 'pale, whitish']

pamphlet *noun* pānui whakamārama [pānui W.257 'publish, advertise publicly' whakamārama W.180 'illuminate, explain']

panacea *noun* titikura [W.425 'charm to restore to health, sick or wounded people']

pancake *noun* pāraharaha [W.263 'flat']

pancreas *noun* repe taiaki huka [repe W.336 'gland' taiaki huka TM 'insulin']

panelbeater *noun* takapapa [W.368 'flatten out']

panelbeating *noun* takapapa [W.368 'flatten out']

panther *noun* pānihi [ninihi W.221 'move stealthily']

pantry *noun* pātaka [W.270 'storehouse raised upon posts, elevated stage for storing food']

paper dart *noun* tekapepa [teka W.410 'dart thrown for amusement' pepa < Eng. 'paper']

paper towel *noun* ūkui pepa [ūkui W.466 'scour, rub, wipe' pepa < Eng. 'paper']

paper-clip *noun* kini pepa [kini W.118 'nip, pinch' pepa < Eng. 'paper']

paper-folding *noun* (*origami*) whētuitui [W.496 'fold, double, a garment etc.']

paper-shredder *noun* whakangaku pepa [whaka- W.486 'causative prefix' *to make* ngakungaku W.228 'reduced to shreds' pepa < Eng. 'paper']

paper-towel rack *noun* tārawa ūkui pepa [tārawa W.389 'line or rail on which anything is hung' ūkui pepa TM 'paper towel']

par the course *phrase* (*golf*) eke pai [W.27 'get aground, come to land' pai W.249 'suitable, satisfactory']

par the hole *phrase* (*golf*) eke pai [W.27 'get aground, come to land' pai W.249 'suitable, satisfactory']

parabola *noun* unahi [W.467 'scale of fish etc.']

parachute *noun, intransitive verb* hekerangi [heke W.44 'descend' rangi W.323 'sky']

parachuting *noun* hekerangi [heke W.44 'descend' rangi W.323 'sky']

paraffin *noun* hinu mewaro [hinu W.51 'oil, fat' mewaro TM 'methane']

paragraph *noun* kōwae [W. 151 'divide, part, set apart']

parallel *adjective* whakarara [W.326 'mark in parallel lines']

parallel bars *noun* tāuhu whakarara [tāuhu TM 'bar' whakarara TM 'parallel']

parallelogram *noun* tapawhā whakarara [tapawhā TM 'quadrilateral' whakarara TM 'parallel']

paralysis *noun* iokerewai [io W.78 'nerve' kēkerewai W.114 'numb']

paramedic *noun* manapou [W.173 'anything to support life']

parameter *noun* tawhā [tapawhā W.381 'four-sided']

paraplegic *adjective, noun* kātete-hauā [kātete W.103 'leg, the whole leg from the thigh downwards' hauā W.39 'crippled']

parasailing *noun* reretō [rere W.337 'fly' tō W.428 'drag, haul']

parasite *noun* pirinoa [W.284 'semi-parasitic plants' piri W.283 'stick, cling']

parasitic *adjective* pirinoa [TM 'parasite']

park, angle *noun* tūnga tāhapa [tūnga waka TM 'carpark' tāhapa W.358 'at an acute angle']

park, double *noun* tū upane [tū W.443 'remain' upane W.468 'abreast, in even rank']

parka *noun* wairaka [W.476 'a kind of rough rain cloak']

parking meter *noun* ine tūwaka [ine W.78 'measure' tū W.443 'stand, remain' waka common usage 'vehicle']

parking warden *noun* atoato waka [atoato TM 'marshal' waka common usage 'vehicle']

Parkinson's disease *noun* mate paiori [mate W.192 'sickness' paiori W.250 'emaciated']

parole *noun* tuku whakamātau [tuku W.451 'let go, allow' whakamātau W.192 'make trial of, test']

parsnip *noun* uhitea [uhi W.471 'root crops' tea W.410 'white, light in colour']

particle *noun* (*chemistry*) matūriki [matū TM 'matter' riki W.340 'small']

particle *noun* (*language*) pakuriki [W.256 'particle, vestige']

particle *noun* (*physics*) ira [W.79 'freckle, mole']

partition *noun* pātaki [pātakitaki W.270 'divisions or containing barriers in a store pit, screen of brush, boundary, division']

part-time *adjective* harangotengote [W.37 'do piecemeal or by instalments']

pass *transitive verb* (*hockey, soccer*) tuku [W.451 'send, give up']

pass *transitive verb* (*with hands, sport*) maka [W.168 'throw, cast']

pass *transitive verb* (*with hands, sport*) panga [W.257 'throw']

pass off *noun* (*netball*) huripi [W.71 'start off']

pass the blame *phrase* uapare *transitive verb* [W.465 'attribute to another what is charged to oneself']

passing-lane *noun* arahipa [ara W.13 'path' hipa W.52 'pass, go by']

passive *noun* (*grammar*) huriaro [W.71 'turn right round']

passive smoking *noun* mina-auahi [minamina W.202 'affected by' auahi 'smoke']

passive suffix *noun* kuhimuri huriaro [kuhimuri TM 'suffix' huriaro TM 'passive']

passive verb *noun* kupumahi huriaro [kupumahi TM 'verb' huriaro TM 'passive']

passport *noun* uruwhenua [uru W.469 'enter, reach a place, arrive' whenua W.494 'land, country']

pasta *noun* parāoa rimurapa [parāoa < Eng. 'flour' rimurapa W.341 'bull kelp']

paste *noun* (*food*) kukū [W.153 'firm, stiff, not watery']

pastel *noun* (*colour*) kanotea [kano W.94 'colour' tea W.410 'pale']

pastel *noun* (*crayon*) piakano [pia W.279 'gum of tree' kano W.94 'colour']

pastry *noun* pōhā [W.286 'a cake of hīnau meal']

pastry, filo *noun* raupōhā [rau W.349 'leaf' pōhā TM 'pastry']

pastry, flaky *noun* pōhā aparau [pōhā TM 'pastry' apa W.12 'layer' rau W.328 'hundred, multitude']

patchwork *noun* kānihinihi [kānihi W.94 'patch a garment']

pate *noun* (*food*) panihā [pani W.257 'spread' hāhā W.29 'savoury']

patient *noun* tūroro [W.460 'sick person']

patio *noun* rueke [W.350 'verandah, porch']

pavilion *noun* wharau [W.489 'temporary shed or booth']

pawn *noun* (*chess*) kurumetometo [W.159 'person of no account, of small stature']

pay *transitive verb*, *noun* utu [W.471 'return for anything, price']

pedal *noun* taumanu [W.399 'projecting foot piece of a kō']

pedestrian *noun* kaiwaewae [kai W.86 'fulfil its proper function' waewae W.472 'leg, foot']

pedestrian crossing *noun* rewarangi [whakarewarangi W.339 'a floor mat made with alternate strips of black and yellow flax']

peduncle *noun* (*botany*) tāpua [tā W.354 'stalk, stem' pua W.301 'flower']

peephole *noun* huhu [W.66 'window']

peer group *noun* aropā [W.17 'clump of one species of tree']

pellet *noun* (*ammunition*) hāmoamoa [W.33 'small spherical stones which were used as bullets']

penal programme *noun* kaupapa whiu [kaupapa TM 'programme' whiu TM 'penalty']

penalise *transitive verb* whiu [W.498 'whip, chastise']

penalised, to be *passive verb* (*sport*) hara tautuku [hara W.36 'sin, offence' tautuku W.405 'stoop, bend down; so give way']

penalty *noun* tautuku [W.405 'stoop, bend down; so give way']

penalty area *noun* āpure tautuku [āpure W.13 'patch, circumscribed area' tautuku W.405 'stoop, bend down; so give way']

penalty bully *noun* hakehakeā tautuku [hakehakeā TM 'bully off' tautuku W.405 'stoop, bend down; so give way']

penalty corner *noun* koko tautuku [koko W.130 'corner' tautuku W.405 'stoop, bend down; so give way']

penalty kick *noun* whana tautuku [whana W.486 'kick' tautuku W.405 'stoop, bend down; so give way']

penalty pass *noun* maka tautuku [maka TM 'pass' tautuku W.405 'stoop, bend down; so give way']

penalty shot *noun* (*netball*) tītere tautuku [tītereTM 'shoot' tautuku W.405 'stoop, bend down; so give way']

penalty spot *noun* maru tautuku [maru W.184 'mark, sign' tautuku W.405 'stoop, bend down; so give way']

penalty stroke *noun* hahau tautuku [hahau W.39 'strike, smite, deal blows to' tautuku TM 'penalty']

penalty try *noun* paneke tautuku [paneke TM 'try' tautuku TM 'penalty']

pencil *noun* pene rākau [pene < Eng. 'pen' rākau W.321 'wooden']

pencil-holder *noun* ipupene [ipu W.79 'vessel for holding anything' pene < Eng. 'pen']

pencil-sharpener *noun* whakakoi pene [whaka- W.486 'causative prefix' *to make* koi W.127 'sharp' pene < Eng. 'pen']

pendulum *noun* tārere [W.391 'swing with the legs off the ground, holding on to a rope']

penicillin *noun* rongoā paturopi [rongoā W.346 'remedy, medicine' paturopi TM 'antibody']

peninsula *noun* kūrae [W.158 'project, be prominent, headland'], koutu [W.151 'promontory, point of land']

penny-farthing *noun* (*bicycle*) kapa-whārangi [kapa common usage 'penny' whārangi < Eng. 'farthing']

pension, war *noun* penihana pakanga [penihana TM 'pension' pakanga W.250 'war']

pentagon, regular *noun* taparima rite [tapa W.381 'edge' rima W.340 'five' rite W.343 'alike']

pentane *noun* pēwaro [pē < Eng. 'pen-' waro TM 'alkane']

pentanol *noun* waihā pēwaro [waihā TM 'hydroxide' pēwaro TM 'pentane']

pentathlete *noun* kaipara rima [kaipara TM 'athlete' rima W.340 'five']

pentathlon *noun* kaipara rima [kaipara TM 'athletics' rima W.340 'five']
peppercorn *noun* huakini [hua W.64 'fruit' kikini W.118 'pungent']
percent *noun* ōrau [ō W.237 'of, belonging to' rau W.328 'hundred']
percentage *noun* ōrau [ō W.237 'of, belonging to' rau W.328 'hundred']
percolate *transitive verb* komama [W.131 'run or fall through a small aperture']
percolator *noun* komama [TM 'percolate']
perfume *noun* rautangi [W.331 'a preparation of scented oils']
period *noun* (*time*) wā [W.472 'time']
period *noun* (*punctuation*) kopi [TM 'full stop']
periodical *noun* (*publication*) hautaka [hau W.39 'be published abroad, report' taka W.366 'come round, as a date or period of time etc.']
periodic detention *noun* whakarau harangotengote [whakarau W.328 'take captive' harangotengote W.37 'do piecemeal or by instalments']
periosteum *noun* (*anatomy*) kiriuhi wheua [kiriuhi TM 'membrane' wheua W.496 'bone']
permanent disability *noun* hauāuki [hauā TM 'disabled' āuki W.22 'old, of long standing' ukiuki W.466 'lasting, continuous']
permutation *noun* kōwhiringa whai raupapa [kōwhiri W.153 'select' whai W.484 'possessing' raupapa TM 'sequence']
perpendicular *adjective* tūtika [W.462 'upright']
personal *adjective* whaiaro [W.485 'self, person']
personal computer *noun* rorohiko whaiaro [rorohiko TM 'computer' whaiaro TM 'personal']
personal effects *noun* taputapu whaiaro [taputapu W.385 'goods, property' whaiaro TM 'personal']
personal foul *noun* hara tinana [hara TM 'foul' tinana W.419 'body, trunk, person']
pessary *noun* (*suppository*) kuhi taiawa [kuhi W.154 'thrust in, insert' taiawa W.363 'vagina']
pessimistic *adjective* kārangirangi [W.98 'doubtful' kārangi W.98 'restless, unsettled']

pest *noun* (*nuisance*) pōrearea [W.293 'tiresome, importunate']
pest *noun* (*destructive organism*) riha [W.340 'nit, bad']
pesticide *noun* paturiha [patu W.272 'kill' riha TM 'pest']
petal *noun* raupua [rau W.328 'leaf' pua W.301 'flower']
petiole *noun* tātārau [tātā W.354 'stem, stalk' rau W.328 'leaf']
petrol gauge *noun* ine hinu [ine TM 'gauge' kōhinu TM 'petrol']
petroleum *noun* hinumata [hinu common usage 'petrol' mata W.185 'raw, uncooked, fresh, as water']
petty cash *noun* ō manapou [ō manapou W.237 'light provisions' manapou W.173 'anything to support life']
phagocyte *noun* (*anatomy*) ngenimomi [ngeni W.233 'something small, particle' momi W.208 'swallow up']
pharmacist *noun* taka rongoā [taka W.366 'prepare' rongoā W.346 'remedy, medicine']
pharmacy *noun* (*dispensary*) whakaipurangi rongoā [whakaipurangi W.79 'a small storehouse on a single post, head or source of a stream' rongoā W.346 'remedy, medicine']
pharmacy *noun* (*study*) mātauranga taka rongoā [mātauranga common usage 'knowledge' taka rongoā TM 'pharmacist']
pharynx *noun* pūhoromi [pū W.300 'tube' horomi W.61 'swallow']
phenomenal *adjective* (*extraordinary occurrence*) whakaharahara [W.36 'extraordinary, marvellous']
phloem *noun* (*botany*) tarikai [tari W.391 'carry, bring' kai W.86 'food']
phobia *noun* mae [W.162 'paralysed with fear']
phoneme *noun* oro [W.242 'rumble, sound']
phonetic spelling *noun* tuhi-ā-whakahua [tuhi W.448 'write' ā W.1 'after the manner of' whakahua W.64 'pronounce']
phonetics mātauranga whakahua [mātauranga common usage 'knowledge' whakahua W.64 'pronounce']
phoney *adjective* hāwatewate [W.43 'false, untrue']

phonology *noun* weteoro [wete W.483 'untie, unravel' oro TM 'phoneme']

phosphate *noun* pākawa tūtae-whetū [pākawa TM '-ate' pūtūtae-whetū TM 'phosphorus']

phosphite *noun* pākati tūtae-whetū [pākawa TM '-ite' pūtūtae-whetū TM 'phosphorus']

phosphorescent *adjective* pūtūtae-whetū [Biggs 140 'phosphorescent substance']

phosphorus *noun* pūtūtae-whetū [Biggs 140 'phosphorescent substance']

photocopier *noun* pūrere whakaahua [pūrere TM 'machine' whakaahua W.4 'acquire form']

photocopy *transitive verb* whakaahua [W.4 'acquire form']

photograph *noun* whakaahua [W.4 'acquire form']

photographer *noun* kaiwhakaahua [kai W.86 'a prefix to transitive verbs to form nouns denoting an agent' whakaahua W.4 'acquire form']

photosynthesis *noun* pātātoko [pātā W.269 'prepare food' toko W.434 'ray of light']

phrase *noun* kīanga [W.116 'act of speaking, saying']

phyllode *noun* (*botany*) tātārau [tātā W.354 'stalk, stem' rau W.328 'leaf']

phylum *noun* (*biology*) pori [W.294 'tribe']

physical contact *noun* (*sport*) whakapā tinana [whakapā W.243 'cause to touch, touch' tinana W.419 'body']

physicist *noun* mata ahupūngao [mata W.185 'eye, face' ahupūngao TM 'physics']

physics *noun* ahupūngao [ahu W.3 'move, point in a certain direction' pūngao TM 'energy']

physiological *adjective* whaiaroaro [TM 'physiology']

physiology *noun* whaiaroaro [W.485 'self, person']

physiotherapist *noun* kairomiromi [kai W.86 'a prefix to transitive verbs to form nouns denoting an agent' romiromi W.346 'press, squeeze']

pi *noun* (*mathematics*) pī [W.279 'origin']

piccolo *noun* pōrutu [W.295 'a sort of flute played by blowing into or across the end']

picket fence *noun* takitaki [Best *Māori Agriculture* 40-1 'fence consisting of upright stakes'], raihe [Best *Māori Agriculture* 40-1 'fence consisting of upright stakes']

picture *noun* whakaahua [W.4 'acquire form']

piecemeal *adjective* kōhikohiko [W.125 'do irregularly, a bit here and a bit there']

pig-headed *adjective* ūpoko mārō [idiom ūpoko W.468 'head' mārō W.183 'unyielding, headstrong'], kakī mārō [idiom kakī W.92 'neck' mārō W.183 'unyielding, headstrong']

pigment *noun* tae [W.356 'dye, stain, colour']

pigsty *noun* pākoro [pākorokoro W.255 'encircle, hem in, a rude form of hut' pākoro 'small fenced enclosure']

pike *noun* (*diving*) tūpou [W.457 'bow the head, stoop down, fall or throw oneself headlong, dive']

pikelet *noun* paraha [W.263 'flat, broad' cf. pancake TM 'pāraharaha']

pile *noun* (*house*) poutoka [pou W.297 'support, post' toka W.433 'firm, solid, rock']

piles *noun* (*haemorrhoids*) tero puta [tero W.413 'rectum, anus' puta W.315 'blister, come out']

pilot light *noun* (*oven*) hana [W.33 'shine, glow, flame']

pin *noun* tāpine [tā W.355 'prefix having causative force similar to that of whaka-' pine W.281 'close together']

pinchbar *noun* whiti [W.497 'prise, as with a lever']

pinch-hitter *noun* (*softball*) hai [W.30 'the name of the principal stone in the game of ruru']

ping-pong *noun* poikōpiko [poi TM 'ball' kōpiko W.137 'go alternately in opposite directions']

pink *adjective* mākurakura [W.171 'light red, glowing, reddish (as sunrise)']

pink, pale *adjective* mākuratea [mākura TM 'pink' tea W.410 'white, light in colour']

pinnacle *noun* taumata [W.399 'brow of a hill']

pinnate *adjective* (*botany*) mata raukura [mata W.185 'surface' raukura W.329 'feather, plume']

pinniped *noun, adjective* whānau ā tākaru [whānau W.487 'offspring, family group' tākaru ā W.1 'after the manner of' W.369 'splash about, flounder']

pinpoint *transitive verb* tautuhi [W.405 'indicate, define']

pipedream *noun* waitara [W.477 'project or scheme of a fanciful or difficult nature']

pipette *noun* ngongoiti [ngongo W.234 'suck, suck out' iti W.80 'small']

pistil *noun* (*botany*) puapua [W.301 'pudenda muliebria' pua W.301 'flower']

pistol *noun* ngutu pārera [ngutu W.236 'lip' pārera W.267 'duck']

piston *noun* kōkeke [W.129 'wind about, move backwards and forwards']

piston-ring *noun* tarawhiti kōkeke [tarawhiti W.390 'hoop, ring' kōkeke TM 'piston']

piston-rod *noun* tāuhu kōkeke [tāuhu W.360 'rod used as a stiffener' kōkeke TM 'piston']

pita bread *noun* pāpaki [pāpaki W.253 'sew two kete mouth to mouth to hold maize etc.' pakipaki W.253 'wallet with a flap to cover the opening']

pitch *noun* (*softball*) epa [W.28, 'throw, cast, pelt']

pitch *noun* (*tone*) tangi [W.379 'sound, resound']

pitch, illegal *noun* epa hē [epa TM 'pitch' hē TM 'illegal']

pitcher *noun* (*softball*) kaiepa [kai W.86 'a prefix to transitive verbs to form nouns denoting an agent' epa TM 'pitch']

pitcher's plate *noun* tāpora kaiepa [tāpora W.384 'a coarse floor mat' kaiepa TM 'pitcher']

pituitary gland *noun* repe whakatupu [repe W.336 'gland' whakatupu W.458 'cause to grow']

pivot *intransitive verb* kaurori [W.108 'swing, turn on a pivot']

pizza *noun* parehe [W.266 'flat cake of meal from fern root']

place *noun* (*sport*) toanga mātāmuri [toa W.428 'brave, victorious' mātāmuri W.188 'latter']

place-judge *noun* kaiwhakatau toanga mātāmuri [kai W.86 'a prefix to transitive verbs to form nouns denoting an agent' whakatau TM 'decide' toanga mātāmuri TM 'place']

plague *noun* urutā [W.470 'epidemic']

plain *noun* (*computer style*) tōkau [W.433 'plain, devoid of ornament']

plaintiff *noun* kaiwhakapā hē [kai W.86 'a prefix to transitive verbs to form nouns denoting an agent' whakapā hē W.243 'accuse, bring a charge of wrongdoing against anyone']

plan *noun* mahere [W.163 'plan']

plane *noun* (*mathematics*) papa [W.259 'anything broad, flat and hard']

planet *noun* aorangi [ao W.11 'world' rangi W.323 'sky, heaven, upper regions']

planetarium *noun* (*building*) kōpae aorangi [kōpae W.135 'circular house' aorangi TM 'planet']

planetarium *noun* (*device*) whakaata aorangi [whakaata W.18 'reflect, simulate by gesture, pretend' aorangi TM 'planet']

plank *noun* papa [W.259 'slab, board']

plant *noun* (*industry*) rawa whakanao [rawa W.331 'goods, property' whakanao TM 'manufacture']

plant *noun* (*biology*) tipu [W.457 'shoot, bud, grow']

plant, medicinal *noun* rongoā [W.346 'remedy, preservative against sickness, medicine']

plasma *noun* (*medicine*) wētoto [wē W.481 'water, liquid' toto W.441 'blood']

plaster *noun* (*medicine*) tāpiri [tāpi W.383 'apply dressing to wound' piri W.283 'stick, adhere to']

plaster cast *noun* pāpāuku [pāpākiri Biggs 184 'splint made of bark' uku W.466 'white clay']

plastic *noun, adjective* kirihou [kiri W.119 'skin' hou W.62 'new']

plastic bag *noun* kopa kirihou [kopa W.135 'wallet, satchel' kopa whakawiri tītoki 'bag for squeezing the oil from tītoki berries' kirihou TM 'plastic']

plastic surgery *noun* whakamōhou kiri [whakamōhou W.206 'renew' mohou 'fresh, new' kiri W.119 'skin']

plasticine *noun* kerepeti [W.114 'clay worked and pressed']

plate *noun* (*weightlifting*) pōria [W.294 'load with a weight, ring of bone or stone on the leg of a captive bird']

plate umpire *noun* kaiwawao tāpora [kaiwawao TM 'umpire' tāpora TM 'plate']

platelet *noun* mōtepe [mōtete W.211 'small piece, fragment' tepe W.412 'congeal, coagulate, clot']

platter *noun* pātua [W.272 'a receptacle for food']

platyhelminth *noun* (*zoology*) ngunu papatahi [ngunu W.236 'worm' papatahi W.261 'flat']

play *noun* (*theatre*) whakaari [W.15 'show, expose to view']

play dough *noun* poikere [poi W.288 'make into a ball, knead, work up' kere W.114 'clay, earth']

play off *noun* whiringa toa [whiriwhiri W.497 'select, choose' toa W.429 'victorious']

player *noun* kaitākaro [kai W.86 'a prefix to transitive verbs to form nouns denoting an agent' tākaro W.369 'play, sport']

plaza, shopping *noun* papa hokohoko [papa W.259 'site' hokohoko W.57 'merchandise, traffic, trade, exchange']

pleat *noun* rererua [W.338 'double, in two thicknesses or folds']

pleura *noun* kiripūkahu [kiriuhi TM 'membrane' pūkahukahu W.306 'lungs']

pleurisy *noun* kiripūkahu kakā [kiripūkahu TM 'pleura' kakā TM 'inflammation']

plug-hole *noun* putanga wai [puta W.315 'opening, hole, pass out' wai W.474 'water']

plumber *noun* mataaro kōrere [mataaro TM 'master' kōrere W.141 'gutter, tap, anything to guide the passage of liquids']

plural *adjective* kikorua [W.118 'twofold, double, having descent through more than one line of ancestry']

pluralize *transitive verb* whakakikorua [whaka- W.486 'causative prefix' *to make* kikorua TM 'plural']

plywood *noun* papa tāpatu [papa W.259 'anything broad, flat and hard, board' tāpatupatu W.383 'place in layers, lay one on another']

pneumonia *noun* pūkahu kakā [pūkahukahu W.306 'lungs' kakā TM 'inflammation']

poach *transitive verb* (*hunting*) kaihaumi *intransitive verb* [W.40 'person who wanders over other people's land and takes birds etc.']

poacher *noun* kaihaumi [W.40 'person who wanders over other people's land and takes birds etc.']

pocket-knife *noun* pīauau pūkoro [pīauau W.279 'knife, cutting instrument' pūkoro W.308 'pocket']

podium *noun* tūāpapa [W.446 'platform, foundation']

poem *noun* mōteatea [W.211 'lament']

poem *noun* (*light-hearted*) ruri [W.352 'song, ditty']

point, to score *phrase* (*sport*) paneke [W.257 'move forwards']

point size *noun* (*printing*) rahi [W.320 'size']

poison *noun* tāoke [tā- W.355 'prefix, having a causative force similar to that of whaka-' oke W.239 'ill, ailing, sick person']

poisonous *adjective* tāoke [TM 'poison']

poker *noun* (*fire*) pīnohi [W.281 'sticks used for handling hot stones']

poker machine *noun* whakatūaho [W.444 'deceive, beguile']

pole *noun* (*physics*) pito [W.284 'end, extremity']

pole *noun* (*points on earth's axis*) tōpito o te ao [W.437 'end, extremity' ao W.11 'world']

pole, north *noun* tōpito whakararo [tōpito TM 'pole' W.437 'end, extremity' whakararo TM 'northwards']

pole, south *noun* tōpito whakarunga [tōpito TM 'pole' W.437 'end, extremity' whakarunga TM 'southwards']

pole vault *noun* (*sport*) tūtoko [Best *Games and Pastimes* 20]

pole vaulter *noun* kaitūtoko [kai W.86 'a prefix to transitive verbs to form nouns denoting an agent' tūtoko TM 'pole vault']

policy *noun* kaupapa [W.107 'level surface, platform, raft, groundwork to which feathers were attached in making a cloak']

policy, accounting *noun* kaupapa kaute [kaupapa TM 'policy' mahi kaute TM 'accounting']

poliomyelitis *noun* whakamemeke [W.200 'wasting, shrivelling of the limbs']

political *adjective* tōrangapū [TM 'politics']

political science *noun* mātauranga tōrangapū [mātauranga common usage 'knowledge' tōrangapū TM 'politics']

politician *noun* kaitōrangapū [kai W.86 'a prefix to transitive verbs to form nouns

denoting an agent' tōrangapū TM 'politics']
politics *noun* tōrangapū [tō W.428 'drag, haul' rangapū W.323 'company']
pollination *noun* ruinga hae [rui W.350 'scatter, sow, cause to fall in drops' hae W.29 'pollen of flowers']
pollutant *noun* parakino [para W.262 'sediment, impurity, refuse, waste' kino W.118 'evil, bad']
pollution *noun* parahanga [W.262 'rubbish, litter']
polyester *noun* pareaku [pare < Eng. 'poly' aku W.7 'firm, strong']
polygon *noun* taparau [tapa W.381 'margin, edge' rau W.328 'multitude, number']
polygon, regular *noun* taparau rite [taparau TM 'polygon' rite W.343 'alike']
polyhedron *noun* matarau [mata W.185 'face, surface' rau W.328 'multitude, number']
polymer *noun* (*chemistry*) waerau [wae TM 'unit' rau W.328 'multitude, number']
polymeric *adjective* waerau [wae TM 'unit' rau W.328 'multitude, number']
polynomial *noun* pūrau [pū TM 'power' rau W.328 'multitude, number']
polysaccharide *noun* hukarau [huka < Eng. 'sugar' rau W.328 'multitude, number']
polysaturated *adjective* pūhake-rau [pūhake W.303 'full to overflowing' rau W.328 'multitude, number']
polystyrene *noun* kōmāmā [W.131 'light in weight, soft' mā W.161 'white']
polyunsaturated *adjective* hamanga-rau [hamanga W.33 'not full' rau W.328 'multitude, many']
pommel *noun* pūrori [W.314 'knob, as on a huata spear or handle of a mere']
pommel horse *noun* (*gymnastics*) hōiho pūrori [hōiho < Eng. 'horse' pūrori TM 'pommel']
pompous *adjective* aweawe [W.24 'distant, out of reach']
popcorn *noun* kānga pāhūhū [W.248 'popped corn']
population *noun* taupori [tau TM 'number' W.396 'alight, come to rest' pori W.294 'people, tribe']
pornographic *adjective* karihika [W.101 'lewd, immoral, copulation']
pornographic picture *noun* whakaahua karihika [whakaahua TM 'picture' karihika W.101 'lewd, immoral, copulation']
pornography *noun* karihika [W.101 'lewd, immoral, copulation']
port *noun* (*computer*) kapiti hiko [kapiti W.96 'cleft, crevice, joined, brought together' hiko common usage 'electric']
portable *adjective* hikawe [W.49 'carry a burden']
porter *noun* (*doorkeeper*) rōpā [W.346 'slave, servant']
position *noun* (*sport*) wāhi tū [wāhi W.474 'place, locality' tū W.443 'stand']
positional error *noun* (*sport*) hapa tū [hapa TM 'fault' tū W.443 'stand']
positive *adjective* (*number*) tōrunga [tō W.428 'that of' runga W.352 'the top, the upper part']
positive end *noun* (*electricity*) pito-tī [pito W.284 'end, extremity' tī common usage used to indicate indefinite locality]
postage *noun* utu karere [utu W.471 'price' karere W.100 'messenger']
postage stamp *noun* pane kuīni [pane W.257 'head' kuīni < Eng. 'queen']
postal code *noun* tohu karere [tohu W.431 'mark, sign, direct, guide' karere W.100 'messenger']
poster *noun* pānui whakaahua [pānui W.257 'advertise publicly' whakaahua TM 'picture']
postgraduate student *noun* tāura [W.402 'the second order of learners being initiated in esoteric lore']
postmortem *noun* tirotiro tūpāpaku [tirotiro W.424 'investigate' tūpāpaku W.456 'corpse']
postpone *transitive verb* pāuhu [W.273 'put off, adjourn']
postscript *noun* kupu āpiti [kupu W.157 'message, word' āpiti W.12 'supplement anything deficient']
potassium *noun* konurehu [konu- TM 'prefix denoting natural metal' rehu W.334 'spray, fine dust']
potassium permanganate *noun* patuero poroporo [patuero TM 'antiseptic' poroporo TM 'deep purple']
potato masher *noun* pehu rīwai [pehu W.275 'mash, pound' rīwai W.344 'potato']

potato masher *noun* penu taewa [penupenu W.277 'mashed' taewa W.357 'potato']

potato peeler *noun* tahi rīwai [tahi W.359 'scrape' rīwai W.344 'potato']

potato peeler *noun* tahi taewa [tahi W.359 'scrape' taewa W.357 'potato']

pot-belly stove *noun* porohatete [porokawa W.295 'round in shape' hatete W.38 'fire']

potential *noun* pūmanawa nohopuku [pūmanawa W.309 'natural talents, intuitive cleverness' nohopuku W.223 'be silent, be still']

potential *adjective* torohū [W.440 'latent']

pot-mitt *noun* rari [W.327 'wash, scour']

potter *noun* ringa kerepeti [ringa W.341 'hand' kerepeti W.114 'clay worked and pressed']

pottery *noun* kerepeti [W.114 'clay worked and pressed']

pottery *noun* matapaia [W.189 'clay which when baked hard was used as stone for cooking']

powder bowl *noun* oko paura [oko W.239 'wooden bowl' paura < Eng. 'powder']

power *noun* (*mathematics*) pū [W.300 'originate, source']

power *noun* (*electricity*) hiko [common usage 'electricity']

power cord *noun* taura hiko [taura W.402 'cable, cord' hiko common usage 'electricity']

power cut *noun* koti hiko [koti W.149 'interrupt, cut off, so cut across the path' hiko common usage 'electricity']

power pole *noun* pouhiko [pou W.297 'post, pole' hiko common usage 'electricity']

power supply *noun* punahiko [puna W.309 'spring of water' hiko common usage 'electricity']

power-walking *noun* tairakaraka [tai- W.362 'prefix sometimes with a qualifying force' raka W.321 'agile, go' whakaraka W.321 'walk, step out']

practical *noun, adjective* taha wheako [taha W.357 'side' wheako W.493 'experience intimate acquaintance or knowledge']

practice *noun* (*training*) whakawaiwai [W.475 'practise the use of weapons']

practise *intransitive verb, transitive verb* (*training*) whakawai [W.474 'practise the use of weapons']

preamble *noun* kupu whakamahuki [kupu W.157 'word, message' whakamahuki W.165 'explain']

precept *noun* ture [W.459 'law']

precipitate *intransitive verb* (*chemistry*) tīwharawhara [W.427 'be split, be separated']

precipitate *transitive verb* (*chemistry*) whakatīwhara [whaka- W.486 'causative prefix' *to make* tīwharawhara TM 'precipitate']

precis *noun, transitive verb* tīpoka [tīpokapoka W.422 'taking some and leaving some']

predator *noun* konihi [W.134 'attack by stealth, a small marauding party moving stealthily']

predict *transitive verb* matapae [matakite W.188 'one who foresees an event, practise divination' whakapae TM 'contend']

prediction *noun* matapae [matapae TM 'predict']

preference *noun* (*choice*) tino hiahia [tino W.420 'exact, veritable, very' hiahia W.47 'desire, wish, impulse, thought']

prefix *noun* kuhimua [kuhi W.154 'insert' mua W.213 'front']

pregnancy, ectopic *noun* kikiri mōwaho [kikiri W.119 'begin to grow, as a child in the womb' mōwaho W.212 'outside, on the outside']

prejudge *transitive verb* (*justice*) whakatoihara [W.432 'disparage']

prejudice *noun* (*justice*) whakatoihara [W.432 'disparage']

preoccupation *noun* tāuteute [W.404 'be engrossed, be occupied, be absorbed in occupation']

preoccupied *adjective* tāuteute [W.404 'be engrossed, be occupied, be absorbed in occupation']

prepay *transitive verb* utu tōmua [utu TM 'pay' tōmua W.435 'early']

prepayment *noun* utu tōmua [utu TM 'pay' tōmua W.435 'early']

preposition *noun* uhono [W.466 'connected, join']

prerequisite *noun* (*education*) akoranga tōmua [akoranga TM 'course' tōmua W.435 'previous']

presbyopia *noun* mate whēkaro [mate 192 'damaged, sickness' whēkaro W.493 'be dimly visible']

press conference *noun* hui pāpāho [hui W.66 'congregate, come together' pāpāho TM 'broadcast']

press release *noun* pānui pāpāho [pānui W.257 'advertise publicly, proclaim' pāpāho TM 'broadcast']

press statement *noun* pānui pāpāho [pānui W.257 'advertise publicly, proclaim' pāpāho TM 'broadcast']

press-stud *noun* paruru [W.269 'place close together, compact']

press-up *noun, adjective (exercise)* whakamārō poho [whakamārō W.183 'extend, stretch' mārōrō W.183 'strong, sturdy' poho W.287 'chest']

pressure *noun (exertion of force)* kaha [W.82 'strength']

prima facie *noun* tūmatanui [W.453 'open, public, without disguise']

primary *adjective (first importance)* mātāmua [W.188 'first, fore'], matua [W.195 'main, chief, important']

prime number *noun* punga [W.310 'odd number, anchor']

primer *noun (sealing substance)* kiriwai [W.119 'inner skin']

principle *noun (maxim)* mātāpono [mātāpuna W.190 'source of a river' pono W.291 'true']

print *transitive verb (lettering)* āta tuhi [āta W.17 'slowly, clearly' tuhi W.448 'write']

print *transitive verb (written material)* tā [W.354 'tattoo, paint']

print preview *(word-processing)* tiro tānga [tiro W.424 'look' tānga TM 'hard copy']

printer *noun (machine)* pūreretā [pūrere TM 'machine' tā TM 'print']

prism *noun* poro [W.294 'block, piece of anything cut or broken off short']

private *adjective* tūmataiti [tūmatanui W.453 'open, public, without disguise' iti W.80 'small']

private *adjective* motuhake [W.212 'separated']

Private Bag *noun* Pouaka Motuhake [pouwaka W.299 'post surmounted by a small receptacle for valued possessions' motuhake W.212 'separated' TM 'private']

probability *noun (statistics)* tūponotanga [tūpono W.457 'chance to hit']

probation *noun* tuku matakana [tuku W.451 'let go, allow' matakana W.187 'wary, watchful, on the lookout']

probation officer *noun* matakana [W.187 'wary, watchful, on the lookout']

probationer *noun* tangatanga [whaketangatanga W.378 'loosen, release from restraint, endeavour to loosen or disengage']

problem *noun (education)* panga [W.257 'riddle, game of guessing']

problem *noun (mathematics)* rapanga [rapa W.325 'seek, look for' panga W.257 'riddle, game of guessing']

procedure *noun* huarahi [W.65 'road, highway']

process *noun* hātepe [W.38 'proceed in an orderly manner, follow in regular sequence']

procrastinate *intransitive verb* waiho mō raurangi [waiho W.475 'let be' raurangi W.330 'another time, another day']

produce *transitive verb* whakanao [W.218 'make, manipulate, operate on']

product *noun (mathematics)* otinga [oti W.242 'finished'], hua [W.64 'fruit, product']

professional *noun* ngaio [W.227 'expert, clever, deliberate, thorough']

professional *noun, adjective* whaiutu [whai W.484 'possessing, equipped with' utu TM 'pay']

professor *noun* ahorangi [W.3 'teacher of high standing in the school of learning']

proficient *adjective* tohunga [W.431 'skilled person']

prognosis *noun* waitohu [W.477 'prognosticate']

programme *noun* kaupapa [W.107 'stage, platform, groundwork']

programme, television *noun* whakaaturanga [whakaatu W.20 'point out, show, call attention to']

progress *noun, intransitive verb* kauneke [W.107 'move forward']

project *noun* pūtere [W.317 'raft, go in a body']

projectile *noun, adjective* tītere [W.425 'throw, cast']

prominent *adjective* kōhure [W.127 'outstanding, conspicuous']

prone *adjective* tāpapa [W.382 'lie flat, face down']

proof *noun* tohu [W.431 'mark, sign, proof']

prop *noun* (*rugby*) poumua [pou W.297 'support' mua W.213 'the front']

propane *noun* pōwaro [pō < Eng. 'pro-' waro TM 'alkane']

propanoic acid *noun* waikawa pōwaro [waikawa TM 'acid' pōwaro TM 'propane']

propanol *noun* waihā pōwaro [waihā TM 'hydroxide' pōwaro TM 'propane']

propel *transitive verb* tītoko [W.426 'propel with a pole']

propeller *noun* uruuru [W.469 'blade of a weapon, urge, hasten']

proper noun *noun* kupu ingoa tangata [kupu W.157 'word' ingoa W.78 'name' tangata W.379 'human being']

property *noun* (*characteristic*) āhuatanga [W.4 'likeness']

property, physical *noun* āhuatanga rongo [āhuatanga TM 'property' rongo W.346 'apprehend by the senses']

proportion *noun* ōwehe [ō W.237 'of, belonging to' wehe W.481 'detach, divide']

proportional representation *noun* whakawhiwhi-ā-ōrau [whakawhiwhi TM 'award' ā W.1 'after the manner of' ōrau TM 'percentage']

pros and cons *phrase* huapai, huakino [hua W.64 'fruit, product' pai W.249 'good, suitable, satisfactory' kino W.118 'evil, bad']

prosecutor *noun* kaiwhakapā hē [kai W.86 'a prefix to transitive verbs to form nouns denoting an agent' whakapā hē W.243 'accuse, bring a charge of wrongdoing against anyone']

prostate *noun* repe tātea [repe W.336 'gland' tātea W.394 'semen']

protective gear *noun* (*sport*) parekiri [pare W.266 'turn aside, ward off' parepare 'protection' kiri W.119 'skin, person, self']

protein *noun* pūmua [pū W.300 'origin, source' pūhui TM 'compound' mua W.213 'the fore']

protest *intransitive verb* mautohe [W.198 'oppose persistently']

protestor *noun* waha mautohe [waha W.473 'voice, raise up, carry on the back' mautohe W.198 'oppose persistently']

protista *noun* pūtau-tahi [pūtau TM 'cell' tahi W.359 'one, single']

proton *noun* iraoho [ira 'particle' TM 'dot' oho W.238 'be awake']

protophyta *noun* tipu pūtau-tahi [tipu TM 'plant' pūtau-tahi TM 'single-celled']

protozoa *noun* hātare pūtau-tahi [hātaretare TM 'invertebrate' pūtau-tahi TM 'single-celled']

protractor *noun* inekoki [ine W.78 'measure' koki W.129 'angle']

provocative *adjective* taunanawe [W.400 'excite, provoke']

prune *transitive verb* kaikawau [W.88 'lop, cut the tips off anything']

pseudo *adjective* kikoika [whakakikoika W.118 'feign']

psyche *noun* awe wairua [Best *Spiritual and Mental Concepts* 16]

psychedelic *adjective* (*colour*) kita takawhīwhiwhi [kita W.120 'intensely, brightly, of colours' W.370 takawhīwhiwhi 'entangled, interlaced']

psychiatric disorder *noun* mate hinengaro [mate W.192 'sickness' hinengaro W.51 'seat of the thoughts and emotions']

psychiatrist *noun* rata mate hinengaro [rata W.327 'doctor' mate hinengaro TM 'psychiatric disorder']

psychiatry *noun* mātauranga mate hinengaro [mātauranga common usage 'knowledge' mate hinengaro TM 'psychiatric disorder']

psychic *adjective* kauwaka [W.109 'human medium of an atua or spirit']

psychological *adjective* hinengaro [W.51 'seat of the thoughts and emotions']

psychologist *noun* kaimātai hinengaro [kaimātai TM '-ologist' hinengaro TM 'psychological']

psychology *noun* mātai hinengaro [mātai TM 'study' hinengaro W.51 'seat of the thoughts and emotions']

psychotherapist *noun* kaiwhakaora hinengaro [kai W.86 'a prefix to transitive verbs to form nouns denoting an agent' whakaora W.241 'restore to health' hinengaro W.51 'seat of the thoughts and emotions']

pterosaur *noun* pōrewakohu [W.294 'some fabulous bird']

puberty *noun* puke huruhuru *intransitive verb* [puke W.307 'pubes, mons veneris' huruhuru W.72 'coarse hair, bristles'], mātātahi [W.191 'young people']

pubis *noun* wheua puke huruhuru [wheua W.496 'bone' puke W.307 'pubes, mons veneris' huruhuru W.72 'coarse hair, bristles']

public *adjective* tūmatanui [W.453 'open, public, without disguise']

publish *transitive verb* whakaputa [W.316 'cause to come forth']

publisher *noun* kaiwhakaputa pukapuka [kai W.86 'a prefix to transitive verbs to form nouns denoting an agent' whakaputa TM 'publish' pukapuka W.306 'book']

pulley *noun* tauru [W.403 'roller for moving a canoe']

pulmonary artery *noun* ia pūkahu toto ruhi [iatoto TM 'blood vessel' pūkahukahu W.306 'lungs' toto W.441 'blood' ruhi W.350 'exhausted, spent']

pulmonary vein *noun* ia pūkahu kawe hāora [iatoto TM 'blood vessel' pūkahukahu W.306 'lungs' kawe W.111 'carry, convey' hāora TM 'oxygen']

pulse *noun* mokowhiti [W.208 'beat, palpitate'], manawa [W.174 'heart']

pulse, carotid *noun* manawa kakī [manawa W.174 'heart' kakī W.92 'neck'], mokowhiti kakī [mokowhiti W.208 'beat, palpitate' kakī W.92 'neck']

pulse, wrist *noun* manawa ringa [manawa W.174 'heart' ringa W.341 'hand'], mokowhiti ringa [mokowhiti W.208 'beat, palpitate' ringa W.341 'hand']

punctual *adjective* ū ki te haora i whakaritea [ū W.464 'be firm, be fixed' haora < Eng. 'hour' whakaritea W.343 'arrange']

punctuation *noun* tohutuhi [tohu W.431 'mark, sign' tuhi W.448 'write']

puncture *noun, transitive verb* poka [W.288 'make a hole in, pierce']

puncture-repair-kit *noun* kānihi poka [kānihi W.94 'patch a garment' poka TM 'puncture']

pure competition *noun* (*economics*) mua kai kai [Brougham and Reed 29]

purple *adjective* tawa [after colour of fruit of tawa tree]

purple, deep *adjective* poroporo [W.294 'solanium nigrum and solanum aviculare, plants']

purpose *noun* whāinga [whai W.484 'follow, pursue, aim at']

push in *noun* (*hockey*) tuku paetaha [tuku W.451 'send' paetaha TM 'sideline']

putt *noun, intransitive verb* tīpao [tī W.414 'sticks about 18 inches long' pao W.258 'strike']

putter *noun* tīpao [tī W.414 'sticks about 18 inches long' pao W.258 'strike']

putting green *noun* āpure tīpao [āpure W.13 'patch, circumscribed area' tīpao TM 'putt, putter']

pyramid *noun* koeko tarawhā [koeko W.123 'tapering to a point' tara W.387 'side wall of a house' whā W.484 'four']

pyromania *noun* kaikora [TM 'pyromaniac']

pyromaniac *noun* kaikora [kora W.139 'spark, fire, fuel' kaikora W.88 'person of no account, vagabond']

Q

quadrilateral *noun* tapawhā [tapa W.381 'edge' whā W.484 'four']

quadriplegic *adjective, noun* hauā-pekewhā [hauā W.39 'crippled' peke W.276 'limb, generally' whā W.484 'four']

quadruped *noun* pekewhā [haere pekewhā W.276 'go on all fours']

qualification *noun* tohu mātauranga [tohu W.431 'mark, sign, proof' mātauranga common usage 'knowledge']

qualify *intransitive verb* uru [W.469 'enter, participate in']

qualitative *adjective* ine (i te) kounga [ine W.78 'measure, compare' kou W.151 'good']

quality *noun* pai [W.249 'suitability'], kounga [kou W.151 'good']

quality, high *adjective* kairangi [W.89 'anything held in high estimation, finest vareity of greenstone']

quantitative *adjective* ine (i te) nui [ine W.78 'measure, compare' nui W.224 'size, greatness']

quantity surveyor *noun* kaiwhakatau utu hanga whare [kai W.86 'a prefix to transitive verbs to form nouns denoting an agent' whakatau TM 'determine' utu W.471 'price' hanga W.34 'make, build' whare W.489 'house, habitation']

quarry *noun, transitive verb* tākongakonga [tā- W.355 'prefix having a causative force similar to that of whaka-' kongakonga W.134 'crumbled into fragments']

quarter *noun* hauwhā [hautau TM 'fraction' whā W.484 'four']

quarter final *noun* (*contest*) taumātakirua [taumātakitahi W.400 'select a champion for each side in fighting' TM 'semi-final' rua W.349 'two']

quaver *noun* orohaurua [orotahi W.242 'crotchet' haurua TM 'half']

queen bee *noun* pī huauri [pī < Eng. 'bee' huauri W.66 'having offspring']

queen wasp *noun* katipō huauri [katipō W.103 'wasp' huauri W.66 'having offspring']

question, leading *noun* mākoi [W.171 'pointed question']

question mark *noun* tohu pātai [tohu W.431 'mark, sign' pātai W.269 'question, inquire']

questionnaire *noun* rārangi pātai [rārangi W.324 'line, rank row' pātai W.269 'question, inquire']

quilt *noun* papangarua [W.259 'twofold, of fabric']

quit *transitive verb* whakamutu [W.215 'leave off, cause to cease']

quiz *noun* kai roro [kai Best *Games and Pastimes* 'generic term for guessing games' roro W.347 'brains'], kai hinengaro [kai Best *Games and Pastimes* 'generic term for guessing games' hinengaro W.51 'seat of the thoughs and emotions']

quorum *noun* tokamatua [W.433 'body of persons']

quota *noun* motunga [motumotu W.212 'divided into isolated portions']

quotation mark, double *noun* kokorukī [koru W.147 'a bulbed motif in carving and scroll painting' kī W.15 'say, speak, utter']

quotation mark, single *noun* korukī [koru W.147 'a bulbed motif in carving and scroll painting' kī W.15 'say, speak, utter']

quotient *noun* huawehe [hua W.64 'fruit, product' wehe W.481 'divide']

R

race noun (*foot race*) tauomaoma [tau- W.397 'prefix denoting reciprocal action' oma W.239 'run'], (*competition event*) tauwhāinga [W.405 'contend, vie']
raceme noun (*botany*) pūhui roa [pūhui TM 'compound' roa W.344 'long']
racism noun whakatoihara iwi [whakatoihara W.432 'disparage' iwi W.80 'nation, people'], aukati iwi [aukati TM 'discrimination' iwi W.80 'nation, people']
radar noun hihiani [hihi W.48 'ray' ani W.9 'resounding, echoing']
radar beam noun hihi [W.48 'ray']
radar detector noun pūoko hihiani [pūoko TM 'detector' hihiani TM 'radar']
radar screen noun pātū hihiani [pātū W.272 'screen, wall' hihiani TM 'radar']
radiation noun iraruke [ira rukeruke TM 'radioactive']
radiator noun (*cooling device*) whakapongi [whaka- W.486 'causative prefix' *to make* pongi W.292 'cool']
radiator noun (*heating device*) whakamahana [W.162 'warm']
radical adjective wāwāhi tikanga [wāwāhi W.473 'break, split, break open' tikanga W.416 'anything normal or usual, rule, plan']
radio frequency noun aratuku [ara W.13 'way, path' tuku W.451 'send']
radio telescope noun pūoko irirangi [pūoko TM 'detector' irirangi TM 'radio wave']
radio wave noun irirangi [W.80 'having a supernatural sound' reo irirangi W.80 'radio']
radioactive adjective ira rukeruke [ira TM 'particle' rukeruke W.351 'throw about' ruke W.351 'throw, cast forth, discharge']
radioactive decay noun horo iraruke [horo W.60 'fall in fragments, crumble down' ira rukeruke TM 'radioactive']
radioactive waste noun para iraruke [para W.262 'impurity, refuse, waste' ira rukeruke TM 'radioactive']
radioactivity noun ira rukeruke [TM 'radioactive']
radiology noun rongoā iraruke [rongoā W.346 'remedy, preservative against sickness or death' ira rukeruke TM 'radioactive']
radiotherapy noun haumanu iraruke [haumanu W.40 'revive, restore to health' iraruke TM 'radiation']
radish noun uhikura [uhi W.471 'root crops' kura W.157 'red, glowing']
radium noun konuruke [konu- TM 'prefix denoting natural metal' ira rukeruke TM 'radioactive']
radius noun pūtoro [pū W.300 'centre' toro W.438 'stretch forth, extend']
raffia noun munga [W.214 'palm']
raincoat noun uarua [W.465 'cloak with a cape to it']
rally noun (*tennis etc*) taupatupatu [W.401 'compete or vie with one another']
ramification noun rara [W.326 'effect, repercussion']
ramrod noun toromoka [W.440 'probe, thrust, with any long instrument']
random adjective matapōkere [W.189 'blindly, at random, in the dark']
range noun (*mathematics*) huinga hua [huinga TM 'set' hua TM 'result']
range noun whānui [W.487 'broad, wide']
range noun (*practice area*) whaitua whakawai [whaitua W.485 'region, space' whakawai TM 'practise']
ranking noun waitohu [W.477 'mark, signify, indicate']

rare *adjective* (*meat*) mangungu [W.178 'uncooked, underdone']

rate *noun* pāpātanga [pā W.243 'be connected with, touch, strike']

rate *noun* auau [W.21 'frequently repeated, again and again, frequently']

rates *noun* (*land etc.*) tāke kaunihera [tāke < Eng. 'tax' kaunihera < Eng. 'council']

ratio taupāpātanga [tau W.397 'prefix denoting reciprocal action' pā W.243 'touch, reach, strike, be connected with']

rationale *noun* pūtake [W.316 'base, root, reason, cause'], pūnga [W.300 'reason, cause, origin']

ray (*mathematics*) hihi [W.48 'ray of sun']

rayon *noun* reiaku [rei- < Eng. 'ray-' kakaaku TM 'textile fibre']

reach up *intransitive verb* hītamo [W.53 'reach or stretch up at full length']

react *intransitive verb* (*chemistry*) hohe [whakahohe W.55 'invigorate, energise']

reactant *noun* (*chemistry*) matū hohe [matū TM 'substance' hohe TM 'react']

reaction *noun* (*chemistry*) hohenga [hohe TM 'react']

reactivity *noun* (*chemistry*) kaha hohenga [kaha W.82 'strength' hohenga TM 'reaction']

reafforest *transitive verb* whakawao [whaka- W.486 'causative prefix' *to make* wao W.479 'forest']

realise *intransitive verb* huatau [W.66 'thought, think']

rear light *noun* (*vehicle*) ramamuri [rama W.322 'torch or other artificial light' muri W.214 'the rear']

rear mirror *noun* whakaata muri [whakaata TM 'mirror' muri W.214 'the rear']

rearrange *transitive verb* (*mathematics*) whakataurite [whaka- W.486 'causative prefix' *to make* taurite W.403 'opposite, alike, matching']

rebellion *noun* whana [W.486 'revolt, rebel']

receipt *noun* puka whakamana utu [puka TM 'form' whaka- W.486 'causative prefix' *to make* mana W.172 'authority' utu W.471 'price']

receiver *noun* (*tennis*) kaiwhakahoki [kai W.86 'a prefix to transitive verbs to form nouns denoting an agent' whakahoki W.57 'cause to return, give back']

reception area *noun* taupaepae [W.400 'meet and escort visitors in as they arrive']

receptionist *noun* kiripaepae [kiri W.119 'person' taupaepae W.400 'meet and escort visitors in as they arrive']

receptive language *noun* reo torohū [reo W.336 'language' torohū TM 'potential'], reo nohopuku [reo W.336 'language' nohopuku TM 'potential']

recessive gene iramoe [ira TM 'gene' moe W.204 'sleep, repose']

recidivism *noun* kai ruaki [kai W.85 'consume, eat' ruaki W.350 'vomit']

recidivist *noun* kai ruaki [kai W.85 'consume, eat' ruaki W.350 'vomit']

recipe *noun* tohutaka [tohutohu W.431 'direct, guide, instruct, advise' taka W.366 'prepare']

recipient *noun* kaiwhiwhi [kai W.86 'a prefix to transitive verbs to form nouns denoting an agent' whiwhi W.499 'possesed of, having acquired']

reciprocal number *noun* (*mathematics*) tau taupoki [tau TM 'number', taupoki W.401 'turn over']

recommend *transitive verb* taunaki [W.400 'support, reinforce']

record *noun* (*music*) kōpae puoru [kōpae TM 'disc' pūoru TM 'music']

record *noun* (*document*) kōrero [W.141 'tell, say, narrative, discussion']

recorder *noun* (*audio*) hopureo [hopu W.59 'catch, seize, catch up' reo W.336 'voice'], whakauenuku [W.465 'keep, retain']

recorder *noun* (*musical instrument*) rehu [W.334 'flute, play the flute']

recreation *noun* hākinakina [W.32 'sport, enjoy oneself']

recruit *transitive verb* kimi tangata [kimi W.118 'seek, look for' tangata W.379 'human being']

rectangular prism *noun* poro mataono [poro W.294 'block' mata W.185 'race, surface' ono W.240 'six']

recurrent *adjective* auau [W.21 'frequently repeated, again and again']

recurring *adjective* auau [W.21 'frequently repeated, again and again']

recurved *adjective* makau [W.169 'bent, curved']

recycle *transitive verb* hangarua [hanga W.34 'make, build, fashion' rua W.349 'two, second']

red, basic *adjective* kura [W.157 'red']
red, dark *adjective* kurauri [kura W.157 'red' uri W.469 'dark, deep in colour']
red, light *adjective* kuratea [kura W.157 'red' teatea W.410 'white, light in colour']
red admiral butterfly pēpepe mōrea [pēpepe W.277 'moth, butterfly' mōrea W.210 'red']
red cabbage *noun* nīko whero [nīko W.222 'wild cabbage' whero 'red']
reddish-brown *adjective* ura [W.468 'red, brown, glowing'], kōkōwai [W.131 'earth from which red ochre is procured by burning red ochre']
reductant *noun* (*chemistry*) tango hāora [tango W.380 'take away, remove' hāora TM 'oxygen']
redundancy payment *noun* utu whakamutu mahi [utu W.471 'reward, price' whakamutu W.215 'leave off, cause to cease' mahi W.163 'work']
redundant *adjective* (*language*) tāwere [W.407 'having an odd number or excess' tāwerewere 'hanging freely, suspended']
reduplicate *transitive verb* rererua [W.338 'double, in two thicknesses or folds']
reduplication *noun* rererua [W.338 'double, in two thicknesses or folds']
refer *intransitive verb* (*person*) whakapā [W.243 'cause to touch']
refer *intransitive verb* (*written material*) titiro [W.424 'look into, examine']
refer *transitive verb* (*direct*) whakamōhio [whaka- to make mōhio W.205 'know, recognise']
referee *noun* kaiwawao [kai W.86 'a prefix to transitive verbs to form nouns denoting an agent' wawao W.479 'part combatants']
reference *noun* (*office administration*) tau kōnae [tau TM 'number' kōnae TM 'file']
reference *noun* (*authority source*) tohutoro [tohu W.431 'mark, point out, show' toro W.439 'explore, discover, enquire into by divination']
reference catalogue *noun* rārangi tohutoro [rārangi TM 'list' tohutoro TM 'reference']
reference section *noun* (*library*) papatara [W.261 'storehouse, stage for food' whakatara W.386 'invoke, consult'], pūranga kōrero [pūranga W.312 'heap, lie in a heap' puri W.314 'retain possession of, keep' kōrero W.141 'speak talk, address, story, narrative']
reflect *transitive verb* (*mathematics*) whakaata [W.18 'reflect, as water']
reflection *noun* (*mathematics*) whakaata [W.18 'reflection']
reflection symmetry *noun* hangarite whakaata [hangarite TM 'symmetry' whakaata TM 'reflect']
reflex *noun* pūmanawa karo mate [pūmanawa TM 'skill' karo W.101 'avoid a blow' mate W.192 'injury, wound']
reflex action *noun* whetau [W.495 'move quickly to avoid a blow']
refraction *noun* ata tāhapa [ata W.18 'form, shape, reflected image' tāhapa W.358 'at an acute angle']
refrigerator *noun* whata mātao [whata W.490 'elevated stage for storing food, be laid, rest' mātao W.189 'cold']
refuge *noun* punanga [W.310 'any place used as a refuge for non-combatants in troubled days']
refugee *noun* rerenga [W.337 'person who has escaped, fugitive, survivor']
regional *adjective* ā-rohe [ā W.1 'after the manner of' rohe W.344 'boundary']
registrar *noun* pouroki [pou W.297 'expert, support' rokiroki kōrero TM 'registry']
registry *noun* rokiroki kōrero [rokiroki W.345 'store, collection of articles, preserve' kōrero TM 'record']
regulation *noun* ture ārahi [ture W.459 'law' ārahi W.14 'lead, conduct']
rehabilitate *transitive verb* whakaauraki [whaka- W.486 'causative prefix' *to make* auraki W.22 'turn aside, return']
rehabilitation *noun* whakaauraki [TM 'rehabilitate']
rehearse *intransitive verb* whakaharatau [W.37 'practise, acquire dexterity']
reheat *transitive verb* tāmahana [W.375 'cook a second time, warm up cooked food']
relation *noun* (*mathematics*) pānga [pā W.243 'be connected with']
relationship *noun* (*mathematics, science etc.*) pānga [pā W.243 'be connected with']
relay *noun* tānga [W.378 'division, company, relay']

relay race *noun* tauoma tānga [tauomaoma TM 'race' tānga W.378 'division, company, relay']
relevant *adjective* hāngai [W.34 'opposite, confronting, at right angles']
reliable *adjective* (*data etc.*) tika [W.416 'just, right, correct']
relinquish *transitive verb* tuku [W.451 'let go, give up']
remainder *noun* toenga [W.429 'remnant'], tāwerenga [tāwere W.407 'having an odd number or excess' tāwerewere W.407 'hanging free']
remission *noun* (*medicine*) tangatanga [W.378 'free from pain, easy, comfortable']
remote control device *noun* rou mamao [rou W.348 'a long stick used to reach anything, reach or procure by means of a pole' mamao W.178 'distant, far away']
remote sensor *noun* pūoko mamao [pūoko TM 'sensor' mamao W.178 'distant, far away']
remuneration *noun* taiutu [tai- W.362 'prefix, sometimes with a qualifying force' utu TM 'pay']
renal *adjective* tākihi [W.372 'kidney']
renal dialysis *noun* tātari tākihi [tātari TM 'filter' tākihi TM 'renal']
renal disease *noun* mate tākihi [mate W.192 'sickness' tākihi TM 'renal']
renew *noun* whakahou [whaka- W.486 'causative prefix' to make hou W.62 'new, recent, fresh']
reparation *noun* paremata [W266 'payment, return']
repeat *transitive verb* whakahoki [W.57 'turn back, cause to return']
repeating pattern *noun* (*mathematics*) tauira tāruarua [tauira TM 'pattern' tārua W.392 'repeat any process']
repel *transitive verb* whakahoe [W.55 'wave the hand in token of refusal, etc., reject']
repiler *noun* (*building*) kaiwhakahou poutoka [kai W.86 'a prefix to transitive verbs to form nouns denoting an agent' whakahou TM 'renew' poutoka TM 'pile']
replayed ball *noun* (*netball*) hopurua [hopu W.59 'catch, seize' rua W.349 'two, second']
replicate *transitive verb* tukurua [W.452 'repeat an operation, do a second time']

report *noun* pūrongo [pūrongorongo W.314 'tell news, report']
reporter *noun* wahapū [W.473 'eloquent']
representative *noun* (*group*) māngai [W.177 'mouth']
reproduce *intransitive verb* (*biology*) whakaputa uri [whakaputa W.316 'cause to come forth' uri W.469 'offspring']
reproduction *noun* (*biology*) whakaputa uri [TM 'reproduce']
reproductive organ *noun* taihemahema [W.363 'genitals of either sex']
reproductive organ, female *noun* taihema kouwha [taihemahema W.363 'genitals of either sex' kouwha W.151 'female of animals and trees']
reproductive organ, male *noun* taihema toa [taihemahema W.363 'genitals of either sex' toa W.428 'male of animals']
rescue breathing *noun* hā whakaora [hā W.29 'breath' whakaora W.241 'save alive, restore to health']
research *noun, transitive verb* rangahau [W.323 'seek, search out, pursue']
researcher *noun* kairangahau [kai W.86 'a prefix to transitive verbs to form nouns denoting an agent' rangahau TM 'research']
reserve *noun* (*sport*) whakahirihiri [W.53 'assist, relieve'], piki [W.280 'second, support in a duel']
reservoir *noun* hikuwai [W.50 'source of a stream']
resist *transitive verb* papare [pare W.266 'ward off, turn aside, avoid, abstain from']
resistance *noun* (*force*) parenga [pare W.266 'turn aside, ward off']
resistance *noun* (*capacity to resist*) kaha papare [kaha W.82 'strong, able, strength' papare W.266 'turn aside, ward off']
resource *noun* rawa [W.331 'goods, property']
resource *noun* (*education*) rauemi [rau W.328 'multitude, number' emi W.27 'be assembled, be gathered together']
resource, natural *noun* rawa taiao [rawa W.331 'goods, property' taiao W.362 'world, country, district']
resource centre *noun* whakaipurangi [W.79 'head or source of a stream, small storehouse on a single post']
resource management *noun* penapena rawa [penapena W.277 'take care of, tend,

husband, preserve knowledge' rawa W.331 'goods, property, advantage, benefit']

respiration *noun* hanga pūngao [hanga W.34 'make, build' pūngao TM 'energy']

respiratory disease *noun* mate romahā [mate W.192 'sickness' romahā TM 'respiratory system'], matehā [mate W.192 'sickness' hā W.29 'breath, breathe']

respiratory system *noun* (*biology*) romahā [roma W.346 'channel' hā W.29 'breath']

respire *intransitive verb* whakahā [W.29 'breathe, emit breath']

respondent *noun* (*justice*) tangata e whakapaetia ana [tangata W.379 'human being' whakapae W.245 'accuse, make an accusation']

rest *noun* (*music*) ngū [W.235 'silent, dumb, speechless']

rest home *noun* tuohunga [W.455 'dwelling place, house']

restraint, child *noun* whakatina tamariki [whakatina W.419 'fasten, fix, confine, put under restraint' tamariki W.376 'child']

result *noun* (*mathematics*) otinga [oti W.242 'finished']

result *noun* hua [W.64 'product' huanga W.64 'benefit']

resuscitate *noun* whakaora [W.241 'save alive']

retina *noun* (*eye*) mata tuaroa [mata W.185 'eye, face, surface' tuaroa W.447 'back part of a house']

retire *intransitive verb* (*work*) whakangāriro [W.225 'take breath' riro W.343 'intensive']

retire *intransitive verb* (*sport*) unu [W.467 'slip out of a crowd']

retort *noun* (*chemistry*) puoto kakīroa [puoto W.311 'vessel' kakī W.92 'neck' roa W.344 'long']

retort stand *noun* (*chemistry*) tūnga puoto kakīroa [tūnga W.443 'time, circumstance etc. of standing' puoto kakīroa TM 'retort']

returns desk *noun* (*library*) wāhi whakahoki [wāhi W.474 'place, locality' whakahoki W.57 'cause to return, give back']

review *transitive verb* arotake [TM 'evaluate']

revise *transitive verb* whakapai ake [whakapai W.249 'make good, set in order' ake W.6 'intensifying the force']

revolution *noun* (*overthrow*) pāhoro [W.248 'take by assault, storm a fortress, fall, capture of a fortress']

revolution *noun* (*rotation*) huringa [huri W.71 'turn round, revolve']

revolving door *noun* kūaha kōtiri [kūaha W.154 'gateway, entrance' kōtiri W.149 'come or go one at a time']

rheumatoid arthritis *noun* kaikōiwi [W.88 'rheumatism']

rhizome *noun* akakōare [akakōareare W.6 'edible rhizome of raupō']

rhombus *noun* tapawhā rite tītaha [tapawhā rite TM 'square' tītaha W.424 'lean to one side, slant']

rhyme *noun* huarite [whakahua W.64 'pronounce' rite W.343 'alike, corresponding']

rhythm *noun* (*sound*) manawataki [manawa W.174 'mind, spirit, heart' taki W.371 'tow with a line, lead, bring along' taki TM 'beat']

rhythmic *adjective* (*sound*) manawataki [manawa W.174 'mind, spirit, heart' taki W.371 'tow with a line, lead, bring along' taki TM 'beat']

rice bubbles *noun* puarere [pua W.301 'seed' rere W.337 'flow']

rider *noun* (*person*) kaieke [kai W.86 'a prefix to transitive verbs to form nouns denoting an agent' eke W.27 'mount']

right-angled *adjective* hāngai [W.34 'at right angles']

right-angled triangle *noun* tapatoru hāngai [tapatoru TM 'triangle' hāngai TM 'right-angled']

ring *noun* (*boxing*) tūāpapa mekemeke [tūāpapa W.446 'terrace, platform' meke W.200 'strike with the fist, blow with the fist']

ring *noun* tarawhiti [W.390 'hoop, ring']

ring binder *noun* ruruku [W.351 'draw together with a cord, bind together, enfold, enwrap, band, girdle, bond']

rise *noun* (*softball*) epa piki [epa TM 'pitch' piki W.280 'ascend']

rising intonation *noun* piki [W.280 'climb, ascend']

road block *noun* aukati [W.22 'stop one's way, prevent one from passing, line which one may not pass']

road sign *noun* tohu haere ara [tohu W.431 'mark, sign' haere W.30 'come, go' ara W.13 'way, path']

roast *noun* parahunu [parahunuhunu W.263 'roast']

roasting dish *noun* paehunu [paepae W.245 'dish, open shallow vessel' parahunuhunu W.263 'roast']

robot *noun* karetao [W.100 'a toy carved in human form, with arms moved by pulling a string']

rock, igneous *noun* toka ngiha [toka W.433 'stone, rock' ngiha TM 'igneous']

rock, metamorphic *noun* toka kāhuarau [toka W.433 'stone, rock' kāhuarau TM 'metamorphic']

rock, sedimentary *noun* toka parataiao [toka W.433 'stone, rock' para W.262 'sediment, impurity' taiao TM 'environment']

rock-climbing *noun* piki toka [piki W.280 'climb, ascend' toka W.433 'stone, rock']

rocketry *noun* mātauranga waka tuarangi [mātauranga common usage 'knowledge' waka tuarangi TM 'spacecraft']

role-play *noun, intransitive verb* whakatau [W.396 'imitate, make believe, simulate']

roll *transitive verb (dice)* pīrori [W.284 'roll along, as a ball']

rollerblades *noun* koneke [W.133 'slide along']

roller-coaster *noun* rōnakinaki [rōnaki W.346 'sloping, slanting, gliding easily, steady, continuous' naki W.217 'glide, move with an even motion']

rolling pin *noun* takapapa [W.368 'flatten out' taka W.366 'prepare' papa W.259 'flat']

room *noun* taiwhanga [W.365 'place, locality]

root *noun (mathematics)* pūtake [W.316 'base, root']

root canal *noun (tooth)* awa pūtake [awa W.23 'channel' pūtake W.316 'root']

rope ladder *noun* mekameka [W.200 'a form of ladder']

rotation *noun (mathematics)* hurihanga [huri W.71 'revolve']

rotation, centre of *noun* pū hurihanga [pū W.300 'centre' hurihanga TM 'rotation']

rotational symmetry *noun* hangarite hurihanga [hangarite TM 'symmetry' hurihanga TM 'rotation']

rote count *intransitive verb* tatau ā-kākā [tatau W.395 'count' ā W.1 'after the manner of' kākā W.81 'native parrot']

rough *noun (golf)* ururua [W.470 'overgrown with bushes, fresh growth, brushwood']

round *noun (boxing)* tūāmeke [tūāmoe W.446 'spell of unbroken sleep' tūāoma W.446 'stage of a journey' mekemeke TM 'boxing']

round *noun (sport)* whiringa [whiriwhiri W.497 'select, choose']

round *transitive verb (mathematics)* whakaawhiwhi [whaka- W.486 'causative prefix' *to make* āwhiwhi W.25 'near, approximate']

round, preliminary *noun (race)* whiringa taumātakitahi [whiriwhiri W.497 'select, choose' taumātakitahi W.400 'select a champion for each side in fighting']

round, qualifying *noun* whiringa uru [whiriwhiri W.497 'select, choose' uru TM 'qualify']

roundabout *noun* takaāwhio [W.367 'go round about']

routine *noun (gymnastics)* hātepe [W.38 'proceed in an orderly manner, follow in regular sequence']

royalty *noun (payment)* tiringa [tiri W.423 'throw a present before one, share, portion']

rubber *noun (eraser)* muku [W.213 'wipe, rub, smear']

rubber *noun (substance)* taherapa [tahe W.358 'sap of a tree, exude' rapa < Eng. 'rubber']

rubber band *noun* hererapa [here W.46 'tie, tie up, fasten with cords' rapa < Eng. 'rubber']

rubber scraper *noun (cooking)* akuaku [W.7 'scrape out, cleanse']

rubber stamp *noun* pourapa [pou W.297 'plunge in, fix' rapa < Eng. 'rubber']

rubbish bag *noun* pōtete para [pōtete W.296 'a bag or receptacle tied up at the mouth' para W.262 'impurity, refuse, waste']

rubbish bin *noun* ipupara [ipu W.79 'vessel

for holding anything' para W.262 'impurity, refuse, waste']

rubbish dump *noun* ruapara [rua W.349 'pit, hole' para W.262 'impurity, refuse, waste'], maunga para [maunga W.197 'mountain' para W.262 'refuse, waste']

rubella *noun* kōpukupuku [W.138 'rash on the skin']

ruck *transitive verb* hōkari [W.56 'move anything by stretching out the legs']

ruler *noun* (*instrument*) tauine [taura ine W.78 'measuring line']

ruling *noun* (*decision*) whakatau [whaka- W.486 'causative prefix' *to make* W.396 'come to rest']

run out (*cricket*) kūrapa [W.158 'unsuccessful in fishing or acquiring property']

run rate *noun* (*cricket*) auau oma [auau TM 'frequency' oma W.239 'run']

run-up *noun* (*gymnastics*) whakatata [W.393 'approach']

rung *noun* kaupae [W.107 'step or support for the foot in a ladder']

runner *noun* (*person*) waetea [W.473 'good runner, one strong of foot']

runner-up *noun* tuarua [tua W.444 'prefix used with numerals to form ordinals' rua W.349 'two']

rural delivery *noun* karere tuawhenua [karere W.100 'messenger' tuawhenua W.448 'mainland, interior']

S

sabre *noun* hoari piko [hoari < Eng. 'sword' piko W.281 'bent, curved']
saccharine *noun* āwenewene [W.24 'very sweet']
saddle *noun* (*horse-riding*) tārua [W.392 'hollow, saddle in ridge']
safe *noun* (*valuables*) kiato [W.117 'receptacle used for holding certain sacred things, compact']
safe *adjective* haumaru [whakahau W.39 'shelter' maru W.184 'shelter, shield, safeguard'], (*softball*) oraiti [W.241 'escaping with difficulty']
safety, occupational *noun* ārai hauata mahi [ārai W.14 'keep off, ward off' hauata W.40 'accident' mahi W.163 'work']
safety zone *noun* āpure punanga [āpure W.13 patch, circumscribed area' punanga W.310 'any place used as a refuge for non-combatants in troubled days']
safety-belt *noun* whakatina [W.419 'fasten, fix, confine, put under restraint']
safety-pin *noun* autui [W.23 'a cloak pin of whalebone or boar's tusk']
safety-rail *noun* whakatonu [W.436 'cautious, careful']
sailor *noun* kaumoana [W.106 'mariner, one of a crew of a canoe']
salad, green *noun* huamata [hua W.64 'fruit' mata W.185 'raw, uncooked']
salad bowl *noun* oko huamata [oko W.239 'wooden bowl, or other open vessel' hua W.64 'fruit' mata W.185 'raw, uncooked']
salad dressing *noun* wairanu huamata [wairanu TM 'sauce' huamata TM 'green salad']
salmon pink *adjective* (*colour*) para-karaka [W.263 'an orange-red stone']
saloon *noun* (*hotel*) whaitua inuinu [whaitua W.485 'space' inuinu W.78 'drink frequently']
salt *noun* (*chemistry*) pāhare [W.247 'bitter']
salted *adjective* (*food*) mina-tote [minamina W.202 'affected by' minamina auahi W.202 'tasting of smoke' tote < Eng. 'salt']
sample *noun* tauira [W.398 'pattern, copy']
sample *noun* (*statistics*) tīpako [W.421 'pick out, select']
sample *noun* hukihuki [W.68 'unfinished, incomplete, as of a sample']
sanctuary *noun* punanga [W.310 'any place used as a refuge for non-combatants in troubled days']
sand *transitive verb* (*wood etc.*) whakamahine [W.164 'make smooth, polish']
sand dune *noun* tāhuahua [W.360 'sandhills, in lumps or hillocks']
sandpaper *noun* hōanga [W.55 'a kind of sandstone used in the process of cutting and grinding stone implements']
sandpaper, coarse *noun* hōanga matanui [W.55 'coarse sandstone used in grinding implements']
sandpaper, fine *noun* hōanga matarehu [W.55 'fine sandstone used in grinding implements']
sane *adjective* ngākau ora [ngākau W.227 'seat of affections or feelings, mind, inclination, desire, spirit' ora W.240 'well, in health, safe']
sanitary pad *noun* kope [W.136 'a woman's girdle of soft mosses used for health purposes, soft masses used as wrappers or absorbents']
sanity *noun* ngākau ora [ngākau W.227 'seat of affections or feelings, mind,

inclination, desire, spirit' ora W.240 'well, in health, safe']

saprophyte noun (*biology*) hamupirau [hamuhamu W.33 'eat scraps of food' pirau W.283 'rotten, decay, death']

satellite noun amiorangi [amio W.8 'go round about, circle round' rangi W.323 'sky, heaven, upper regions']

satin noun papamōhinu [papanga TM 'fabric' mōhinuhinu W.205 'shiny, glistening, glossy']

satire noun pūhohe [W.305 'mocking, laughing']

satirical adjective pūhohe [TM 'satire']

saturated adjective kueo [W.154 'soaked']

sauce noun wairanu [W.476 'gravy, juice']

sauna noun koromāhu [W.144 'steam']

save transitive verb (*computer*) pupuri [W.305 'retain possession of, keep, keep in memory']

saxophone noun pūtohe [pū W.300 'flute, pipe, tube' tohe W.430 'vibrating reed of a pūkaea trumpet']

scale noun (*measurement*) tauine [taura ine W.78 'measuring line']

scale, point on noun tongari [W.436 'notch, nick']

scale factor noun taurahi [tau TM 'number' rahi W.320 'size']

scalene noun hikuwaru [W.50 'crooked, asymmetrical']

scalene triangle noun tapatoru hikuwaru [tapatoru TM 'triangle' hikuwaru TM 'scalene']

scales noun (*weighing*) whārite [W.343 'compare, liken, balance by an equivalent']

scanner noun matawai [W.192 'look closely']

scarlet adjective hīwera [W.54 'gleaming red']

scarper intransitive verb (*slang*) karapetapeta [W.99 'move quickly']

scavenge intransitive verb hamuhamu [W.33 'eat scraps of food']

scavenger noun hamu [hamuhamu TM 'scavenge']

scene noun (*drama*) kāpeka [W.96 'branch of a tree or river']

scheme noun (*employment*) kaupapa [W.107 'stage, platform, groundwork']

schizophrenia noun wairua tuakoi [wairua W.477 'spirit, insubstantial image, shadow' tuakoi W.445 'divide, separate, misconceive, imagine, be deceived']

schizophrenic noun, adjective wairua tuakoi [TM 'schizophrenia']

scholar noun ngore [W.235 'pupil in sacred lore, etc.']

scholarship noun tahua ngore [tahua W.360 'fund, some of money' ngore TM 'scholar']

school, composite noun kura hiato [kura < Eng. 'school' hiato TM 'composite']

science noun pūtaiao [pū W.300 'source, origin' taiao TM 'environment']

scientist noun kaimātai pūtaiao [kai W.86 'a prefix to transitive verbs to form nouns denoting an agent' mātai W.187 'inspect, examine' pūtaiao TM 'science']

scissors noun (*synchronised swimming*) kapekapetau [W.96 'move quickly to and fro']

sclera noun (*anatomy*) teatea [W.410 'white in colour' whakatea 'show the whites of the eyes']

sclerosis, arterial noun ia toto mārō [ia toto TM 'blood vessel' mārō W.183 'hard, unyielding']

scone noun takakau [taka W.366 'prepare' kau W.104 'alone, per se' parāoa takakau common usage 'bread prepared by one who lives alone']

score intransitive verb (*sport*) paneke [TM 'goal, point']

score noun (*sport*) tapeke [W.383 'total']

score, final noun tapeke [W.3883 'total']

scoreboard noun papa tapeke [papa W.259 'anything broad, flat, hard' tapeke TM 'score']

scorer noun (*person who scores goal*) kaipaneke [kai W.86 'a prefix to transitive verbs to form nouns denoting an agent' paneke TM 'goal, point']

scorer noun (*score-keeper*) kaiāmiki [TM 'scribe, minute-taker']

scorpion noun hikutimo [hiku W.50 'tail of a fish or reptile' timo W.418 'prick, strike with a pointed instrument']

scourer noun rari [W.327 'wash, scour']

scrabble noun ketukupu [ketuketu W.115 'scratch up, move leaves in looking for anything' kupu W.157 'word']

screen noun (*computer*) mata [W.15 'face, surface']

screen print *noun* kōwaiwai papanga [kōwaiwai W.151 'an ancient style of painting for adorning the person and dwellings' papanga TM 'fabric']

screw *transitive verb* (*rugby*) takahuri [W.367 'roll, turn' takahurihuri W.367 'keep on turning round']

screw *noun* (*building*) tīwiri [tīrau W.423 'peg, stick' wiri W.483 'bore twist' TM 'screwdriver']

screwdriver *noun* wiri [W.483 'bore, twist, gimlet']

scribe *noun* kaituhi [kai W.86 'a prefix to transitive verbs to form nouns denoting an agent' tuhi W.448 'write, delineate'], kaiāmiki [kai W.86 'a prefix to transitive verbs to form nouns denoting an agent' āmiki W.8 'tell a story without omitting any particular']

scrotum *noun* pūkoro raho [pūkoro W.308 'sheath, case, pocket' raho W.320 'testicle']

scrubbing-brush *noun* kauoro [W.107 'grind by rubbing']

scrum *noun* taupurupuru [W.402 'support a person by putting the arm around him']

scrum, collapsed taupuru hinga [taupurupuru TM 'scrum' hinga W.51 'fall from an erect position']

scrumptious *adjective* mōwaiwai [W.212 'making the mouth water']

scurvy *noun* kōpaka huaora C [kōpaka W.135 'be short of a thing, be in want' huaora C TM 'vitamin C']

seaplane *noun* wakareretai [waka rererangi common usage 'aeroplane' tai W.361 'the sea']

search party *noun* ohu-rapa [ohu W.238 'company of volunteer workers' rapa W.325 'seek, seek for']

searchlight *noun* rama haurapa [rama W.322 'torch or other artificial light' haurapa W.41 'search diligently for']

second *noun* (*time*) kimonga [kimo W.118 'blink']

second five-eighth *noun* toparua [topatahi TM 'first five-eighth' rua W.349 'two']

second half *noun* wāhanga tuarua [wāhanga TM 'division' tua W.444 'prefix used with numerals to form ordinals' rua W.349 'two']

second row *noun* kaparua [kapa W.95 'rank, row' rua W.349 'two']

seconder *noun* (*meeting*) kaitautoko [kai W.86 'a prefix to transitive verbs to form nouns denoting an agent' tautoko W.404 'prop up, support']

secret *noun* kōrero tārehu [kōrero W.141 'tell, say' tārehu W.390 'cover, seal, be indistinctly seen']

secret agent *noun* mata hunahuna [mataara W.186 'witness, observe' hunahuna W.69 'concealed, seldom seen' mata hunahuna W.69 'a charm to effect concealment from a foe']

secrete *transitive verb* (*medicine*) pipī [W.279 'ooze, soak in']

secretion *noun* pipīnga [pipī W.279 'ooze, soak in']

section *noun* wāhanga [wāhi W.474 'part, portion']

section, longitudinal *noun* haratua [W.37 'dress timber longitudinally, cut, gash']

sector *noun* (*mathematics*) wāhanga [wāhi 'break, split, part, portion']

sector *noun* (*population*) rāngai [rāngai W.323 'flock, shoal, company']

sector, private *noun* rāngai tūmataiti [rāngai W.323 'flock, shoal, company' tūmataiti TM 'private']

sector, public *noun* rāngai tūmatanui [rāngai W.323 'flock, shoal, company' tūmatanui TM 'public']

security guard *noun* kaupare māhie [kaupare W.107 'avert' māhie W.164 'crime, evil']

sediment *noun* (*geology*) parataiao [para W.262 'sediment, impurity' taiao TM 'environment']

sedimentary *adjective* parataiao [TM 'sediment']

sedimentary layer *noun* kahupapa parataiao [kahupapa W.5 'layer, matted mass' parataiao TM 'sedimentary']

seed-bed *noun* pārekereke [W.266 'seedling bed']

seedless *adjective* patakore [pata W.269 'seed, grain' kore W.140 'no, not']

segment *noun* wāhi [W.474 'part, portion']

segregate *transitive verb* whakatāuke [whaka- W.486 'causative prefix' *to make* tāuke W.399 'apart, separate']

segregation *noun* whakatāuke [TM 'segregate']

seismograph *noun* kauwhata rū [kauwhata TM 'graph' rū W.349 'earthquake']

seismometer *noun* ine rū [ine TM 'meter' rū W.349 'earthquake']

selection, artificial *noun* whiringa tangata [whiriwhiri W.497 'select, choose' tangata W.379 'man, human being']

selection, natural *noun* whiringa taiao [whiriwhiri W.497 'select, choose' taiao TM 'environment']

self defence *noun* parahau whaiaro [parahau W.263 'protection, defence' whaiaro W.485 'self, person']

self-disciplined *adjective* urupū [W.470 'diligent, persevering']

seller *noun* kaihoko [kai W.86 'a prefix to transitive verbs to form nouns denoting an agent' hoko W.57 'sell']

sellotape *noun* hāpiapia [W.36 'sticky, clammy']

semi-breve *noun* orowhā [oro W.242 'sound' whā W.484 'four']

semicircle *noun* (*mathematics*) porohita wherua [porohita W.295 'circle' wherua W.41 'divided']

semicircle *noun* ruawhetū [W.350 'a semicircular depression']

semi-colon *noun* kopi-piko [kopi TM 'full stop' piko TM 'comma']

semi-detached *adjective* motupiri [motu W.211 'severed, anything isolated' piri W.283 'be attached, be fastened']

semifinal *noun* taumātakitahi [W.400 'select a champion for each side in fighting']

semi-gloss *adjective* tākarokaro [W.369 'shine dimly']

seminar *noun* hui [W.66 'congregate, come together']

semi-permeable membrane *noun* kiriuhi hītari [kiriuhi TM 'membrane' hītari W.53 'sieve']

semi-quaver *noun* orohauwhā [oro W.242 'sound' hauwhā TM 'quarter']

semi-skilled *adjective* ihupuku [W.75 'inexperienced, hesitating, scrupulous, industrious, eager']

senate *noun* kāhui hanga ture [kāhui W.85 'assemblage' hanga W.34 'make, fashion' ture W.459 'law']

send off *transitive verb* (*sport*) pana [W.256 'expel']

senses *noun* rongo me te kite [rongo W.346 'apprehend by the senses, except sight' kite W.120 'see, perceive']

sensitive *adjective* (*skin*) rauangi [W.329 'thin, fine, tender, finely divided strands of flax for making nets']

sensor *noun* pūoko [pūrere TM 'machine' oko W.239 'hear']

sentence *noun* (*language*) rerenga [W.337 'small branches, offshoots of a family']

sentence *noun, transitive verb* (*justice*) whiu [W.498 'whip, chastise']

separated *adjective* (*marital status*) mahue [W.165 'forsaken, deserted, given up'], wehe [W.481 'detach, divide']

separation order *noun* whakamana wehenga [whakamana W.172 'give effect to, make effective' wehe TM 'separated']

septic *adjective* ero [W.28 'putrid']

septum *noun* pātaki [TM 'partition']

sequel *noun* whakahiku [W.50 'to follow on']

sequence *noun* raupapa [W.330 'put in order, ordered, completed']

sequin *noun* kora [W.139 'small fragment, speck, spark, gleam']

series *noun* raupapa [TM 'sequence']

serrated *adjective* mimira [W.202 'a saw-like cutting instrument made by lashing strips of obsidian or shark's teeth']

serve *noun, transitive verb* (*tennis etc.*) tuku [tuku W.451 'send']

server *noun* kaituku [kai W.86 'a prefix to transitive verbs to form nouns denoting an agent' tuku TM 'serve']

servery *noun* tīmanga [W.418 'elevated stage on which food is kept']

service *noun* (*public sector*) ratonga [rato W.327 'be served or provided']

service *noun* (*tennis etc.*) tuku [TM 'serve']

service area *noun* rohe tuku [rohe W.344 'boundary' tuku TM 'serve']

service court, left *noun* rohetuku mauī [rohe tuku TM 'service area' mauī W.196 'left, on the left hand']

service court, right *noun* rohetuku matau [rohe tuku TM 'service area' matau W.192 'right, on the right hand']

service judge *noun* (*tennis*) kaiwhakawā tuku [kaiwhakawā W.472 'judge' tuku TM 'service']

serviette *noun* parehūhare [pare W.266 'turn aside, ward off' parahūhare W.263 'spittle or scraps of food adhering to lips']

serving fork *noun* mārau toha [mārau W.181 'fork' toha W.429 'distribute']

serving plate *noun* pereti toha [pereti < Eng. 'plate' toha W.429 'distribute']
serving spoon *noun* kokotoha [koko W.130 'spoon' toha W.429 'distribute']
session *noun* wāhanga [TM 'division']
set *noun* (*mathematics*) huinga [hui W.66 'come together, congregate']
set *noun, transitive verb* (*volleyball*) whakamohiki [whaka- W.486 'causative prefix' *to make* mohiki W.205 'raised up, lifted up']
set *noun* (*tennis etc.*) tūākari [tūāoma W.446 'stage of a journey' kakari W.101 'fight, battle, general engagement']
set *noun* (*theatre*) whakarākei [W.321 'adorn, decorate']
set, complement of *noun* huinga rāwāhi [huinga TM 'set' rāwāhi W.332 'the other side of a sea, river, etc.']
set, empty *noun* huinga piako [huinga TM 'set' piako W.279 'hollow, empty']
set, universal *noun* huinga ao [huinga TM 'set' ao W.7 'world']
sets, disjoint *noun* huinga ritua [huinga TM 'set' ritua W.343 'be divided, be separated']
set of six *phrase* (*rugby league*) paihere [W.249 'bundle, bring into close quarters']
set point *noun* (*tennis etc.*) tata tūākari [tata W.393 'near' tūākari TM 'set']
sets, intersection of *phrase* pūruatanga [W.315 'junction of two streams']
sets, union of *noun* hononga [hono W.58 'splice, join']
settee *noun* (*furniture*) hāneanea [W.33 'pleasant, comfortable']
severance pay *noun* utu whakamutu mahi [utu W.471 'reward, price' whakamutu W.215 'leave off, cause to cease' mahi W.163 'work']
sewage *noun* parakaingaki [W.263 'filth, excrement']
sewer *noun* pininga parakaingaki [pininga W.281 'applied to a stream which disappears underground' parakaingaki W.263 'filth, excrement' TM 'sewage']
sewing-machine *noun* pūrere tuitui [pūrere TM 'machine' tuitui W.449 'sew']
sexual abuse *noun* taitōkai [tai W.361 'anger, rage, violence' W.362 'prefix, sometimes with a qualifying force' tōkai W.433 'copulate']
sexual violation *noun* koeretanga [W.123 'strip off, tear apart' see W.314 pūrikoriko for example]
sexuality *noun* hōkakatanga [hōkaka W.56 'desire']
sexually transmitted disease *noun* mate paipai [mate W.192 'sickness'] paipai W.249 'venereal disease'], pakiwhara [W.254 'venereal disease']
shandy *noun* (*beverage*) piarēmana [pia < Eng. 'beer' rēmana < Eng. 'lemon']
shank *noun, transitive verb* (*golf*) hau arenga [hau W.39 'strike, smite' arenga W.14 'point of a weapon']
shanty *noun* (*song*) ruritai [ruri W.352 'song, ditty' tai W.361 'sea']
shanty *noun* (*dwelling*) kuha kāinga [W.154 'a scrap of a dwelling place']
shanty town *noun* kuha papa kāinga [kuha kāinga TM 'shanty' papa W.259 'earth floor or site']
shape *noun* hanga [W.34 'build, fashion']
sharp *adjective* (*music*) piki [W.280 'climb, ascend']
shawl *noun* hikurere [W.50 'a small garment for the shoulders']
shear *transitive verb* (*mathematics*) whakatītaha [whaka- W.486 'causative prefix' *to make* tītaha TM 'shear']
shear *noun* (*mathematics*) tītaha [W.424 'lean to one side, slant']
sheet *noun* (*stationery*) puka [pukapuka W.306 'book, paper'], whārangi [W.489 'leaf or page of a book']
sheet metal *noun* piharoa [W.279 'iron']
shelf *noun* pae [W.244 'any transverse beam, perch, rest']
shelf-life *noun* houanga [W.63 'an interval of time, definite or indefinite' hou W.62 'recent, new, fresh']
shelterbelt *noun* pāhauhau [W.247 'wind screen for crops']
shepherd *transitive verb* (*rugby*) taupā [W.400 'obstruct, prevent']
shepherding *noun* (*rugby*) taupā [W.400 'obstruct, prevent']
shift the blame *phrase* (*justice*) uapare *transitive verb* [W.465 'attribute to another what is charged to oneself']
shift work *noun* mahi tīpako [mahi W.163 'work, work at, occupation' tīpakopako W.421 'in detached parties, not in one body, at odd times']
shift worker *noun* kaimahi tīpakopako [kai

W.86 'a prefix to transitive verbs to form nouns denoting an agent' mahi W.163 'work, work at, occupation' tīpakopako W.421 'in detached parties, not in one body, at odd times']

shin-pad noun paretā [pare W.266 'turn aside, ward off' tā W.354 'shin, lower joint of the leg']

shoot intransitive verb (netball) tītere [W.425 'throw, cast']

shooting noun (sport) puhipuhi [pū W.300 'gun']

shooting circle noun rohe tītere [rohe W.344 'boundary' tītere TM 'shoot']

shoplifter noun kaiā [W.86 'steal, thief, stealthy']

shopping centre noun papa hokohoko [papa W.259 'site' hokohoko W.57 'merchandise, traffic, trade, exchange']

short pass noun (netball) maka uri [maka TM 'pass' uriuri W.469 'short in time or distance']

short wave noun aratuku poto [aratuku TM 'radio frequency' poto W.297 'short']

shortage noun kōpaka [W.135 'be short of a thing, be in want']

short-sighted adjective kanohi kākāpō [kanohi W.94 'eye' kākāpō W.91 'ground parrot' kāpō W.96 'blind']

shortstop noun (softball) tukupoto [W.452 'hasten, short, the short side of a pā']

shot noun (shotput) matā [W.185 'lead']

shot noun (attempted goal) tītere [W.425 'throw, cast']

shot noun (photography) whakaahua [TM 'picture']

shot noun (lawn bowls) paneke [TM 'goal, point']

shotput noun panga matā [panga W.257 'throw, lay, place' matā TM 'shot']

shotputter noun kaipanga matā [kai W.86 'a prefix to transitive verbs to form nouns denoting an agent' panga matā TM 'shotput']

shower noun (bathroom) hīrere [W.53 'gush, waterfall, torrent']

shrub noun (generic) mauwha [W.198 'small bushes, brushwood']

shut down transitive verb (machine) whakaweto [whaka- W.486 'causative prefix' to make weto W.483 'be extinguished']

shut down intransitive verb (terminated) kore [W.141 'cease to be, be destroyed']

shuttle noun (vehicle) waka kōpiko [waka common usage 'vehicle' kōpiko W.137 'go alternately in opposite directions']

shuttle, space noun waka kōpiko tuarangi [waka kōpiko TM 'shuttle' tuarangi TM 'outer space']

shuttlecock noun pūkura [pūtoi W.317 'bunch' kura W.157 'ornamented with feathers']

sickbay noun taiwhanga paruhi [taiwhanga TM 'room' paruhi W.269 'listless, languid']

side noun (polygon) tapa [W.381 'margin, edge']

sideline noun paetaha [pae W.245 'margin, boundary' taha W.357 'side, margin, edge'], tapa [W.381 'margin, edge']

sideline, doubles noun paetaha tokowhā [paetaha TM 'sideline' tokowhā TM 'doubles']

sideline, singles noun paetaha tokorua [paetaha TM 'sideline' tokorua TM 'singles']

sideline umpire noun kaiwawao paetaha [kaiwawao TM 'umpire' paetaha TM 'sideline']

sideshow noun mataraharaha [W.190 'freedom from care']

sidestroke noun kau tāhoe [Best Games and Pastimes 40 'sidestroke']

siesta noun moe ahiahi [moe W.204 'sleep, repose, close the eyes' ahiahi common usage 'afternoon']

sifter noun tātari [W.391 'strainer, sift']

sightscreen noun pūrangiaho [W.312 'seeing clearly']

sightseeing noun hōpara [W.59 'go about, explore, cover, traverse']

sightseer noun wae hōpara [wae W.472 'foot, leg' hōpara TM 'sightseeing']

sign intransitive verb (use sign language) rotarota [W.348 'sign with the hands, without speaking']

sign language noun reo rotarota [reo W.336 'language' rotarota W.348 'sign with the hands, without speaking']

signature noun waitohu [W.477 'mark, signify, indicate']

significant adjective tāpua [W.385 'stand out, be prominent']

significant figure noun (*mathematics*) mati tāpua [mati TM 'figure' tāpua TM 'significant']
silage noun karapēpē [W.99 'fermenting']
silicon noun takawai [W.370 'quartz']
silicon chip noun pāra takawai [pāra W.261 'a flake of stone' takawai TM 'silicon']
silk noun papamāene [papanga TM 'fabric' māeneene W.162 'soft to the touch']
silo noun kōpapa [W.136 'storehouse for food, concave']
silver noun, adjective kawata [W.110 'glisten, shine, gleam']
silvery adjective kawata [W.110 'glisten, shine, gleam']
silviculture noun pokapoka rākau [pokapoka W.288 'plant in holes, begin to plant' rākau W.321 'tree']
simile noun kupu whakarite [kupu W.157 'word, saying' whakarite W.343 'make like, liken']
simplify transitive verb whakamahuki [whakamahuki W.165 'explain' mahuki 'clear, plain']
simplify transitive verb (*mathematics*) rūnā [W.352 'reduce, pare down']
simulate transitive verb whaihanga [W.485 'make, construct, busy oneself with, manipulate']
simulation noun whaihanga [TM 'simulate']
sin-bin noun (*rugby league*) pae whiu [pae W.244 'perch, rest' whiu W.498 'chastise, put, place']
sine noun (*mathematics*) aho [W.13 'string, line']
single-celled adjective pūtau-tahi [pūtau TM 'cell' tahi W.359 'one, single']
singles adjective (*tennis, etc.*) tokorua [toko W.434 'prefix used with adjectives of number' rua W.349 'two']
singular adjective (*language*) kikotahi [kikorua W.118 'twofold, double, having descent through more than one line of ancestry' TM 'plural' tahi W.359 'one']
sink noun (*basin*) kāraha [W.97 'calabash with wide mouth, bowl, basin']
sinus noun pakohu [W.255 'rent, cleft, chasm, cavity']
sinusitis noun pakohu kakā [pakohu W.255 'rent, cleft, chasm, cavity' kakā TM 'inflammation']

siphon noun, transitive verb ngongo [W.234 'tube, suck out']
situation noun (*circumstance*) tūāhua [tū W.442 'manner, sort of' āhua W.4 'form, appearance']
six-yard box noun (*sport*) tapawhā [W.381 'four-sided']
skate intransitive verb reti [W.338 'toboggan board, convey, carry'], noun kopareti [kopa W.135 'sandal' reti TM 'skate']
skeet noun puarere [W.302 'decoy bird, of small birds only']
sketch noun, transitive verb huahua [W.65 'sketch out a pattern before carving']
sketch noun (*theatre*) whakaari paki [whakaari TM 'play' paki W.253 'tales']
ski noun retihuka [reti W.338 'toboggan board, convey, carry' huka W.67 'frost, snow']
skiff noun tāwai [W.406 'a canoe without its attached sides']
skiing noun retihuka [reti W.338 'toboggan board, convey, carry' huka W.67 'frost, snow']
skill noun tautōhito [W.404 'adept, person of experience'], pūkenga [W.307 'skilled in, versed in']
skim transitive verb (*reading*) kaperua [W.96 'glance quickly']
skin-deep adjective kirimoko [W.119 'skin']
skin-diving noun ruruku [ruku W.351 'sink, dive']
skip noun (*rubbish container*) taiaroa para [taiaroa W.362 'basket, receptacle' para W.262 'impurity, refuse, waste']
skip-pass noun (*sport*) maka tīpoka [maka TM 'pass' tīpoka W.422 'skip over, pass by, omit']
skittle noun, transitive verb pātuki [W.272 'strike, knock']
skunk noun pūhonga [W.305 'stinking, offensive, stink, stench']
skydiver noun tiripou [W.423 'swoop down']
skyscraper noun whare tīkoke [whare W.489 'house, habitation' tīkoke W.418 'high up in the heavens']
slamdunk noun kuru [W.159 'pelt, thump, throw']
slang noun (*kupu*) mātāhae [kupu W.157 'anything said' mātāhae W.186 'divergent stream from the main channel of a river']

slash noun (*punctuation*) rītaha [W.343 'lean on one side, incline']

slasher noun tāwai [W.406 'cut or clear undergrowth, etc.']

sleeping bag noun pūngene [pūngenengene W.311 'muffled up']

slice noun, transitive verb (*golf*) kōripi whakawaho [kōripi W.142 'slice, turn sideways' whakawaho TM 'outwards']

slide noun (*film*) kiriata [kiriata TM 'film']

slide-projector noun pūrere kiriata [pūrere TM 'machine' kiriata TM 'film']

slip noun (*cricket*) kōripi [W.142 'cut, slice, turn sideways']

slum noun puni tuakoka [puni W.310 'place of encampment' tuakoka W.445 'poverty-stricken']

small claims court noun whare whakawā take namunamu [whare whakawā TM 'court' take TM 'matter, claim' namunamu W.217 'small, diminutive']

smallbore rifle noun kūpara iti [kūpara TM 'calibre' iti W.80 'small']

smash noun, transitive verb (*sport*) haukere [hau W.39 'strike, smite' kere W.114 'intensive, used with words of breaking'], peke pakihiwi [W.276 'effective in action, striking direct powerful blows']

smirk intransitive verb tāpahi [W.382 'grin, distort the countenance']

smog noun kōtuhi [W.150 'hazy, smoky appearance of atmosphere, discoloured']

smoke alarm noun pūoho auahi [pūoho TM 'alarm' auahi W.21 'smoke']

smoked adjective mina-auahi [minamina W.202 'affected by' minamina auahi 'tasting of smoke']

smoko noun henga [W.46 'food for a working party']

smuggle transitive verb toropuku [W.440 'secret, stealthy']

smut noun houhou [W.63 'disagreeable, unpleasant']

snack noun paramanawa [W.264 'refreshment']

snap noun (*card-game*) taupaki [W.400 'pat, slap']

snatch noun, intransitive verb (*weightlifting*) pōike [W.288 'place aloft']

snorkel noun ngongohā [ngongo W.234 'tube, suck' hā W.29 'breath, breathe']

snorkelling noun rukuruku [W.351 'dive, dip frequently']

snowfield noun papahuka [papa W.259 'anything broad, flat and hard' huka W.67 'frost, snow']

sober adjective nguengue [W.235 'quiet, silent, reserved']

soccer noun poikiri [poi TM 'ball' kiri W.119 'skin'], hōkarikari [W.56 'stretch out one's legs, move anything by stretching out the legs']

soccer ball noun poikiri [poikiri TM 'soccer']

social adjective hapori [W.36 'section of a tribe, family']

social services noun tauwhiro hapori [tauwhiro W.405 'tend, care for, be alert, be on one's guard' hapori TM 'social'], tauwhiro tangata [tauwhiro W.405 'tend, care for, be alert, be on one's guard' tangata W.379 'human being']

social studies noun mātauranga noho hapori [mātauranga common usage 'knowledge' noho W.223 'settle, dwell, live' hapori TM 'social']

social work noun tauwhiro hapori [W.405 'tend, care for, be alert, be on one's guard' hapori TM 'social']

social worker noun tauwhiro [W.405 'tend, care for, be alert, be on one's guard']

socialism noun mana hapori [mana W.172 'power, control, authority' hapori TM 'social, community']

socialist noun kaikōkiri mana hapori [kai W.86 'a prefix to transitive verbs to form nouns denoting an agent' kōkiri TM 'champion' mana hapori TM 'socialism']

society noun hapori whānui [hapori TM 'community, social' whānui W.487 'broad, wide']

sociologist noun kaimātai hapori [kaimātai TM '-ologist' hapori TM 'social']

sociology noun mātauranga hapori [mātauranga common usage 'knowledge' hapori TM 'social']

socket noun (*electricity*) kapiti hiko [kapiti W.96 'cleft, crevice, joined, brought together' hiko common usage 'electricity']

Socratic adjective (*method of instruction*) tīwhiri [W.428 'means of discovering or disclosing something lost or hidden']

sodium noun konutai [konu- TM 'prefix denoting natural metal' tai W.361 'the sea']

softball *noun* poiuka [poi TM 'ball' uka W.466 'hard, firm']

software *noun* (*computer*) pūmanawa rorohiko [pūmanawa W.309 'natural talents, intuitive cleverness' rorohiko TM 'computer']

solar *adjective* kōmaru [W.131 'sun']

solar energy *noun* pūngao kōmaru [pūngao TM 'energy' kōmaru TM 'solar']

solar panel *noun* papa kōmaru [papa W.259 'anything broad, flat and hard' kōmaru TM 'solar']

solar system *noun* rerenga o Tama-nui-te-rā [rerenga W.337 'voyage, journey, setting or rising of the sun' Tama-nui-te-rā common usage 'personification of the sun']

solder *noun, transitive verb* tūhoto [W.449 'join']

solidify *intransitive verb* totoka [W.433 'become solid, set'], *transitive verb* whakatoka [W.433 'make solid']

solstice, summer *noun* ihu o Hineraumati [ihu W.75 'nose, bow of a canoe, etc. Hineraumati Best *Astronomical Knowledge* 18]

solstice, winter *noun* ihu o Hinetakurua [ihu W.75 'nose, bow of a canoe, etc. Hinetakurua Best *Astronomical Knowledge* 18]

solute *noun* rewanga [rewa W.339 'be or become liquid, melt']

solution *noun* (*to problem*) rongoā [W.346 'remedy']

solution *noun* wairewa [wai W.474 'water, liquid' rewa W.339 'be or become liquid, melt']

solution *noun* (*mathematics*) otinga [W.242 'finished'], hua [TM 'result']

solution, dilute *noun* wairewa meha [wairewa TM 'solution' memeha W.200 'weak, pass away']

solve *transitive verb* (*mathematics*) whakaoti [W.242 'finish'], (*problem*) whakamatara [W.190 'unravel, loosen, undo']

solvent *noun* whakarewa [whaka- W.486 'causative prefix' *to make* rewa W.339 'be or become liquid']

somersault *noun* pōtēteke [W.296 'turning over and over']

sonic *adjective* pāorooro [W.258 'resounding']

sonic boom *noun* papārangi [papā W.244 'burst, explode' rangi W.323 'sky']

soprano *noun* reo tōiri [reo W.336 'voice, tone' tōiri W.432 'tingle, vibrate, resound']

sorry, I am *phrase* taku hē [taku W.374 'my' hē W.43 'error, mistake, fault']

sort *transitive verb* kōmaka [W.131 'sort out']

S.O.S. *abbreviation* tono rauora [tono W.436 'bid, command' rauora W.330 'save alive']

souffle *noun* kerehunga [W.114 'fluff']

sound *noun* (*geography*) kūiti moana [kūiti W.154 'narrow, confined' moana W.204 'sea, lake']

sound effects *noun* (*music, etc.*) orotaunaki [oro W.242 'rumble, sound' taunaki W.400 'support, reinforce']

soup *noun* waihāro [W.38 'a sort of soup made by mixing meal of hīnau berries with water and boiling same']

soup bowl *noun* oko waihāro [oko W.239 'wooden bowl, or other open vessel' waihāro TM 'soup']

soup ladle *noun* kōtutu [W.150 'ladle for liquids']

soup-spoon *noun* koko waihāro [koko W.130 'spoon' waihāro TM 'soup']

source *noun* matatiki [W.191 'spring of water']

southwards *adverb* whakarunga [whaka- W.485 'towards, in the direction of' runga W.352 'the south, the southern parts']

spa *noun* wai koropupū [wai W.474 'water' koropupū W.145 'bubble up']

space *noun* (*punctuation*) mokowā [W.208 'space, interval']

space, outer *noun* tuarangi [tua W.444 'the farther side of' rangi W.323 'heaven, upper regions']

space bar *noun* (*keyboard*) pātuhi mokowā [pātuhi TM 'key' mokowā TM 'space']

space probe *noun* (*astronomy*) pōkai ātea [pōkai W.289 'travel about' ātea TM 'space']

spacecraft *noun* waka tuarangi [waka rererangi common usage 'aeroplane' tuarangi TM 'outer space']

spaghetti *noun* kihu parāoa [kihukihu W.117 'thrum' parāoa < Eng. 'flour']

spanner *noun* wāwāhi [W.473 'split, lay open']

spark-plug *noun* puru kora [puru W.314 'plug, bung' kora W.139 'spark, fire, fuel']

spastic *adjective* mate hukihuki [mate W.185 'sickness' hukihuki W.68 'convulsive twitching or contraction of the nerves or muscles, spasm, convulsions']

spatial *adjective* mokowā [W.208 'space, interval']

spatula *noun* rapa [W.325 'anything broad, flat and hard, blade of a paddle, etc.']

speaker *noun* (*electronic audio system*) tukuoro [tuku W.451 'send, let go' oro W.242 'sound']

spear tackle *noun* (*sport*) rutu kōpeo [rutu TM 'tackle' kōpeo W.136 'spear']

special *adjective* motuhake [W.212 'separated']

special *adjective* tino pai [tino W.420 'very, quite, veritable' pai W.249 'good, excellent']

specialisation *noun* whakawhāititanga [whakawhāiti W.485 'put into small space, compress']

specialist *noun* mātanga [W.188 'knowing, experienced person']

species *noun* momo [W.208 'offspring, descendant, race, breed, blood']

species, introduced *noun* momo rāwaho [momo TM 'species' rāwaho W.332 'outside']

specimen *noun* (*example*) tauira [TM 'sample']

specimen *noun* (*sample*) tīpakonga [TM 'sample']

spectator *noun* karumātaki [karu W.102 'eye, look at' mātaki W.188 'look at, watch']

spectroscope *noun* wete hihi [wete W.483 'untie, unravel' hihi W.48 'ray']

spectrum *noun* (*electromagnetic*) hihinga [hihi W.48 'ray of the sun']

spectrum, *noun* (*colour*) tūāwhiorangi [W.448 'rainbow, or perhaps a personification thereof']

speech therapist *noun* kaiwhakatika reo kōrero [kai W.86 'a prefix to transitive verbs to form nouns denoting an agent' whakatika W.417 'straighten, correct' reo W.336 'speech' kōrero W.141 'talk']

speedometer *noun* ine rere [ine TM 'meter' rere W.337 'fly, rush, run']

spell *transitive verb* tātaki [taki W.371 'recite, lead, bring along']

speller *noun* (*computer*) pūmanawa tātaki kupu [pūmanawa rorohiko TM 'software' tātaki kupu TM 'spelling']

spelling *noun* tātaki kupu [tātaki TM 'spell' kupu W.157 'word']

sperm *noun* wai tātea [W.394 'semen']

spermatic canal *noun* awa tātea [awa W.23 'channel' tātea TM 'sperm']

spermatic cord *noun* aho tātea [aho W.3 'string, line' tātea TM 'sperm']

spermatozoon *noun* tātea [W.394 'semen']

spermicide *noun* patu tātea [patu W.272 'kill' wai tātea 'sperm']

sphere *noun* tīrake [tīrakerake Biggs 22 'full moon']

spherical *adjective* tīrake [tīrakerake Biggs 22 'full moon']

spice *noun* namunamuā [W.217 'flavour imparted to food by something with which it has been in contact']

spike *noun, transitive verb* (*volleyball*) haukuru [W.40 'smash']

spina bifida *noun* ritua tuaiwi [ritua W.343 'be divided, be separated' tuaiwi TM 'spine']

spinach *noun* rengamutu [W.336 'New Zealand spinach']

spinal canal *noun* awa tuaiwi [awa W.23 'channel' tuaiwi TM 'spine']

spinal cord *noun* aho tuaiwi [aho W.33 'string, line' tuaiwi TM 'spine']

spine *noun* tuaiwi [W.445 'backbone']

spinner (*fishing tackle*) pā [W.244 'fish hook made with pāua shell in lieu of bait']

spinneret *noun* pūwenu [pū W.300 'origin, source' wenu W.494 'twist or spin a strand of cord']

spire *noun* koinga [koi W.127 'sharp, spike']

splint *noun* pāpā-kiri [Biggs 184 'splint made of bark' W.260 'bark']

split *noun* (*exercise*) tūwhanga [tūwhangawhanga W.463 'diverging wide apart']

split ends *noun* (*hair*) tatarakina *intransitive verb* [Biggs 88 'hair split at ends']

spool *noun* pōkai [W.289 'ball of string, roll']

spore noun pua atua [pua W.301 'seed' puarere W.302 'run to seed, pappus of thistles' whare atua W.489 'mushroom'], tihenga atua [tihe W.415 'sneeze' whare atua W.489 'mushroom']

spot check noun, transitive verb (test) hihira matapōkere [hihira TM 'check' matapōkere TM 'random']

spotlight noun tīwhiri [W.428 'torch, means of discovering or disclosing something lost or hidden']

spreadeagle transitive verb whakaineine [W.78 'extend']

spreadsheet noun ripanga [ripa W.341 'row, rank, line']

spreadsheet, accounting noun ripanga kaute [ripanga TM 'spreadsheet' kaute TM 'accounting']

sprig noun (shoe) maihao [W167 'finger, toe']

spring noun (device) whana [W.486 'spring of a trap, recoil']

spring balance noun whārite whana [whārite TM 'balance' whana TM 'spring']

spring onion noun rikiriki [riki common usage 'onion']

springboard noun hūpana [W.70 'fly up or fly back, as a spring']

sprint noun, intransitive verb kōpere [W.137 'rush']

sprinter noun wae kōpere [wae W.472 'leg, foot' kōpere TM 'sprint']

sprocket noun tara [W.386 'tooth of a comb']

sprocket-wheel noun kōpaetara [kōpae W.135 'circular' tara TM 'cog']

squadron noun matua [W.195 'division of an army, company']

squadron, airforce noun matua tauārangi [matua TM 'squadron' tauārangi TM 'airforce']

squadron, naval noun matua tauā moana [matua TM 'squadron' tauā moana TM 'navy']

square noun tapawhā rite [tapawhā TM 'quadrilateral' rite W.343 'alike, corresponding']

square root noun (mathematics) pūtakerua [pūtake W.316 'base, root' rua W.349 'two']

squash noun (game) poipātū [poi TM 'ball' pātū W.272 'screen, wall']

squash noun (food) kamokamo [W.92 'fruit of the gourd, possibly from cucumber, and restricted to imported gourds']

squat down intransitive verb noho hītengi [noho hītengitengi W.53 'squat with the toes only on the ground']

stable adjective (physics, chemistry) upa [W.468 'fixed, settled, at rest']

stadium noun taiwhanga hākinakina [taiwhanga W.365 'place, locality' hākinakina TM 'sport']

staff noun kaimahi [kai W.86 'a prefix to transitive verbs to form nouns denoting an agent' mahi W.163 'work, work at, occupation']

staff recruitment noun kimi kaimahi [kimi W.118 'seek, look for' kaimahi TM 'staff']

stain noun, transitive verb (impart colour) tawau [W.407 'milky juice of plants, stain therefrom']

stained adjective (discoloration) poapoa [W.286 'stain, discoloration']

stained-glass window noun mataaho ōpure [mataaho W.186 'window' ōpurepure TM 'multi-coloured']

stake noun, intransitive verb (gambling) takiari [W.372 'omen of a certain class, good or bad']

stalactite noun keo iri [keo W.114 'frost' keokeo 'peaked, pointed' iri W.79 'hang, be suspended']

stalagmite noun keo tū [keo W.114 'frost' keokeo 'peaked, pointed' tū W.443 'stand, be erect']

stale adjective (food) kōwhau [W.153 'dry and tasteless']

stamen noun pūtawa [W.317 'testicle']

stamp-pad noun hautai [W.42 'sponge']

stand down transitive verb whakawātea [whaka- W.486 'causative prefix' to make W.480 'clear, free']

standard noun (level of excellence) pai [W.249 'suitability']

standard adjective (norm) aro whānui [aro W.16 'turn towards, be inclined, favour' whānui W.487 'broad, wide']

standard deviation noun (mathematics) ine mahora [ine W.78 'measure' mahora W.164 'spread out, scattered']

standard form noun (mathematics) tānga ngahuru [tā TM 'print' ngahuru W.227 'ten']

standard unit of measurement *phrase* waeine aro whānui [waeine TM 'unit of measurement' aro W.16 'turn towards, be inclined, favour' whānui W.487 'broad, wide']

standing order *noun* ture ārahi [ture W.459 'law' ārahi W.14 'lead, conduct']

standoff *noun* (*rugby*) topatahi [whakatopatopa W.437 'give commands' topa 'dart, swoop' tahi W.359 'one']

staple *noun, transitive verb* makatiti [W.169 'fasten with a peg or pin, pierce']

staple remover *noun* tango makatiti [tango W.380 'remove' makatiti TM 'staple']

stapler *noun* makatiti [W.169 'fasten with a peg or pin, pierce']

starch *noun* (*science*) māngaro [W.177 'mealy']

start up *transitive verb* (*computer*) whakaoho [W.238 'startle, rouse']

starting-block *noun* (*athletics*) tia ngapu [tia W.414 'peg' ngapu W.229 'stretch forwards ready to run']

starting-gate *noun* ngapunga [ngapu W.229 'stretch forwards ready to run']

starting-line *noun* wī ngapunga ['Best Games and Pastimes 165 'a circle marked on the ground around which players stand' ngapunga TM 'starting-gate']

starting-pistol *noun* pū tīmata [pū W.300 'gun' tīmata W.418 'begin']

static *adjective* (*inactivity*) pateko [W.271 'motionless, idle']

station *noun* (*depot, place etc.*) taupuni [W.401 'place of assignation']

stationary *adjective* whakapahoho [W.248 'remain listless and inactive']

stationery *noun* pānga tuhituhi [pā W.243 'be connected with' tuhituhi W.448 'write']

statistic *noun* tatauranga [tatau W.395 'count, tie with a cord, thread on a string']

statistics *noun* tatauranga [tatau W.395 'count, tie with a cord, thread on a string']

statute *noun* ture [W.459 'law']

stave *noun* (*music*) ahoaho [aho W.3 'woof, cross threads of a mat']

STD clinic *noun* pouāwhina mate paipai [pou W.297 'support' āwhina W.25 'assist' mate W.192 'sickness' paipai W.249 'venereal disease']

steak *noun* motū [W.211 'piece of flesh, or fat, titbit']

steak knife *noun* māripi motū [māripi W.182 'knife' motū TM 'steak']

steal a base *phrase* (*softball*) oma whānako [oma W.239 'run' whānako W.487 'steal, thieve']

steeplechase *noun* oma tauārai [oma W.239 'run' tauārai W.397 'screen, barrier, obstruction']

steeplechaser *noun* wae tauārai [wae W.472 'leg, foot' oma tauārai TM 'steeplechase']

stegosaurus *noun* mokotuapaka [moko W.207 'a general term for lizards, huge mythical creature of lizard-like shape' tuapaka W.446 'hard, and so applied to steel']

stem and leaf graph *noun* kauwhata rautō [kauwhata TM 'graph' rau W.328 'leaf' tō W.428 'stem']

step *noun* (*procedure*) upane [W.468 'terrace of a hill']

stepping-stone *noun* pūreirei [W.313 'isolated rock, patch of anything']

stereo *noun, adjective* tīwharawhara [W.427 'penetrating, be split, be separated']

sterilisation *noun* (*medicine*) kokoti-uru [W.131 'rite intended to prevent conception']

steroid *noun* pūtaiaki [pūhui TM 'compound' taiaki TM 'hormone']

stethoscope *noun* pūoko whakaroto [pūoko TM 'detector, sensor' whakaroto TM 'inwards']

stew *noun* tatao [W.381 'remain a long time in the process of cooking']

stick figure *noun* tuahiwi [tuahiwi W.444 'skeleton']

sticking-plaster *noun* tāpi [W.383 'apply, as dressings to a wound']

stiff-arm *noun* (*rugby, etc.*) ringa mārō [ringa W.341 'hand, arm' mārō W.183 'stretched out, stiff']

stigma *noun* (*botany*) tauhae [tau W.396 'alight, come to rest' hae W.29 'pollen']

stir-fry *noun, transitive verb* kapekape [W.96 'stick to rake out embers or food']

stirrup *noun* tōeke [W.429 'loop of cord put loosely around the feet to enable them to grasp a tree in climbing']

stoat *noun* toriura [tori W.438 'energetic, busy, bustling' ura W.468 'brown']

stock noun (food) wairenga [W.477 'gravy or broth from cooked meat']

stock car noun waka tukituki [waka common usage 'vehicle' tukituki W.450 'demolish, knock to pieces, batter, dash']

stone-fruit noun hua karihi [hua W.64 'fruit' karihi W.101 'stone of a fruit, kernel']

stop watch noun wati tumu [wati < Eng. 'watch' tumu W.454 'halt suddenly']

stopcock noun katiwai [kati W.103 'prevent, close up' wai W.474 'water']

storage noun rokiroki [W.345 'store, collection of articles, tied up, secured']

storey noun papa [W.259 'anything broad, flat and hard, site']

storytelling noun kōrero paki [kōrero W.142 'story, tell' pakipaki W.253 'tales']

stove noun umu [W.467 'earth oven']

strainer noun (fencing) tānekaha [W.373 'an implement for tightening the lashings of a canoe by twisting, taut, tight']

strap noun (cycling) tōeke [W.429 'loop of cord put loosely around the feet to enable them to grasp a tree in climbing']

strategic adjective rautaki [rauhanga W.329 'cunning, resourceful' taki W.371 'lead, bring along']

strategy noun rautaki [rauhanga W.329 'cunning, resourceful' taki W.371 'lead, bring along']

stratosphere noun kōhaupapa [kōpaki W.135 'envelop, envelope' hau TM 'gas' papa W.259 'layer']

stratus noun kupenga a Tara-mainuku [W.157 'clouds in strata']

straw noun (liquids) ngongo [W.234 'tube, suck out']

street kid noun tamaiti ihongaro [tamaiti W.375 'child' iho W.75 'that wherein consists the strength of a thing' ngaro W.230 'distressed, oppressed, at a loss']

street sign noun tohuara [tohu W.431 'mark, sign' ara W.13 'way, path']

stress noun (emotional, mental) kōhukihuki [W.126 'be pressing, make itself felt' kōhuki 'anguish, distress of mind']

stress, emotional noun ngākau kōhuki [ngākau W.227 'seat of affections or feelings, mind' kōhukihuki TM 'stress']

stress, mental noun wairua kōhuki [wairua W.477 'spirit' kōhukihuki TM 'stress']

stress, primary noun (language) haukeri [hau W.38 'wind, air, breath' keri W.114 'rush along violently, as the wind']

stress, secondary noun (language) haumatapū [hau W.38 'air, wind, breath' matapū W.190 'a wind']

stress, tertiary noun (language) haumuri [hau W.38 'air, wind, breath' muri W.214 'breeze, afterwards']

stress, weak noun (language) haukiore [hau W.38 'wind, air, breath' manawa-kiore W.174 'the last faint breath of a dying man']

stressed out adjective (colloquial) pōkaikaha [W.289 'confused, at a loss, in doubt']

stretch noun, intransitive verb (exercise) matiti [W.194 'stretched out as of limbs']

stretch fabric noun papa kūtoro [papanga TM 'fabric' kūtoro W.160 'stretched at full length, a closely woven fabric']

stretcher noun (hospital equipment) kauamo [W.105 'litter, bed arranged between two poles to carry sick person']

strike noun (industrial) auporo [W.22 'cut short, stop']

strike noun (softball, good ball) poitika [poi TM 'ball' tika W.416 'straight, direct, correct']

strike noun (softball, connect with ball) haukuru [TM 'hit']

strike, hunger noun whakapuango [W.302 'starve']

strike-out noun (softball) poi mīere [poi TM 'ball' mīere W.201 'become powerless, be exhausted']

striker noun (soccer) tairere [taitai W.362 'dash, strike' rere W.337 'be carried on the wind, fly']

strike-zone noun (softball) rohe haukuru [rohe W.344 'boundary' haukuru TM 'hit']

striking circle noun (sport) rohe taitai [rohe W.344 'boundary' taitai W.362 'dash, strike']

string noun (musical instrument) kū [W.153 'one string instrument, make a low inarticulate sound, grating sound']

stroke noun (medicine) roro ikura [roro W.347 'brains' ikura W.76 'haemorrhage']

stroke noun (swimming) tāhoe [W.359 'swim, stretch out the arms alternately in swimming']

stroke *noun* (*golf*) hahau [W.39 'strike, smite']

stroke play *noun* (*golf*) tapeke hahau [tapeke TM 'total, score' hahau TM 'stroke']

structure *noun* anga [W.10 'shell, skeleton']

student allowance *noun* tahua tauira [tahua W.360 'fund, some of money' tauira common usage 'student']

studio *noun* papamahi [papa W.259 'anything broad, flat and hard' mahi W.163 'work, work at'], taupuni mahi taupuni [W.401 'place of assignation' mahi W.163 'work, occupation']

study *transitive verb* (*investigate*) mātai [W.187 'inspect, examine']

study *transitive verb* (*learn*) whai mātauranga [whai W.484 'follow, pursue, go in search of' mātauranga common usage 'knowledge']

stump *noun* (*cricket*) tumu [W.453 'stump, stake, field of battle']

stumped, to be *intransitive verb* taka [W.366 'fall away, fail of fulfilment']

stuntperson *noun* manawa kai tūtae [W.174 'daring, undaunted']

style *noun* (*botany*) awahae [awa W.23 'channel, river' hae W.29 'pollen']

subatomic particle *noun* ngotangota [W.235 'fragment, particle, smashed to atoms']

subconscious *adjective* mauri pōtere [mauri W.197 'life principle, thymos of man' pōteretere W.296 'drift about, backwards and forwards']

subcutaneous *noun* tua-o-kiri [tua W.444 'on the farther side' kiri W.119 'skin']

sub-directory *noun* (*computer*) rārangi kōnae [rārangi W.324 'rank, row' kōnae TM 'file']

subject *noun* (*education*) marau [W.181 'subject of talk']

subject *noun* (*grammar*) marau [W.181 'subject of talk']

subject *noun* (*topic*) kaupapa [TM 'topic']

sub-machine-gun *noun* taiparapara [taipara W.364 'fire a volley at']

submarine *noun* (*vessel*) waka whakatakere [waka common usage 'boat' whakatakere W.371 'bottom of a channel or of deep water, bed of a river']

submarine *adjective* whakatakere [W.371 'bottom of a channel or of deep water, bed of a river']

submarine warship *noun* wakatauā whakatakere [wakatauā TM 'frigate' whakatakere W.371 'bottom of a channel or of deep water, bed of a river']

submission *noun* tāpaetanga kōrero [tāpae W.382 'place before a person, present' kōrero W.141 'tell, speak, talk']

submit *transitive verb* (*reports etc.*) whakatakoto [whaka- W.486 'causative prefix' *to make* takoto W.374 'lay down']

subscript *adjective* hauraro [W.31 'low down, pendent'], *noun* pū hauraro [pū TM 'character' hauraro W.31 'low down, pendent']

subset *noun* huinga roto [huinga TM 'set' roto W.348 'the inside']

subsidy *noun* pūtea tāpiri [pūtea TM 'fund' tāpiri W.384 'add, supplement']

substance *noun* (*chemistry*) matū [W.195 'gist, kernel, fat']

sub-standard *adjective* (*manufactured products*) pakatiti [W.251 'defective in food']

substitute *transitive verb* (*mathematics*) whakauru atu [whaka- W.486 'causative prefix' *to make* uru W.469 'join, insert' atu W.20 'to indicate a direction away from speaker']

substitute *noun* (*basketball*) whakahirihiri [W.53 'assist, relieve'], (*contest*) piki [W.280 'second, support in a duel']

subtle *adjective* mata hunahuna [W.69 'a charm to effect concealment from a foe' hunahuna 'concealed, seldom seen']

subtlety *noun* mata hunahuna [TM 'subtle']

subtract *transitive verb* tango [W.380 'take away, remove']

subtraction *noun* tangohanga [tango TM 'subtract']

successful *adjective* angitu [W.11 'luck, success']

succulent *adjective* tuawhiti [W.448 'thick, fleshy, fat, of good quality']

sucrose *noun* huka [huka < Eng. 'sugar']

suds *noun* huhuka [W.67 'foaming']

sue *transitive verb* whakapahuhu [W.248 'use charms to induce shame in an ill-doer']

suede *noun* perehunga [W.278 'nap']

suet *noun* aro [W.16 'fat covering the kidneys']

suffix *noun* hiku [W.50 'tail of a fish or reptile, rear of an army']

suffix, passive *noun* hiku huriaro [hiku TM 'suffix' huriaro TM 'passive']

suffragette movement *noun* wāhine kōkiri mana pōti [wāhine W.474 'women' kōkiri W.130 'rush forward, charge' mana W.172 'authority, control' pōti < Eng. 'vote']

suggestion box *noun* pae huatau [pae W.245 'open, shallow vessel' huatau W.66 'thought, think']

sulphate *noun* pākawa pungatara [pākawa TM '-ate' pungatara TM 'sulphur']

sulphite *noun* pākati pungatara [pākati TM '-ite' pungatara TM 'sulphur']

sulphur *noun* pungatara [W.311 'native sulphur']

sum *noun* tapeke [W.383 'total']

summarise *transitive verb* tīpoka [tīpokapoka W.422 'taking some and leaving some']

summary *noun* tīpoka [tīpokapoka W.422 'taking some and leaving some']

summary jurisdiction *noun* mana whakatau inamata [mana W.172 'power, authority' whakatau TM 'decide' inamata W.77 'immediately']

sump oil *noun* hinu pūkaha [hinu TM 'oil' pūkaha TM 'engine']

sunblock *noun* pare tīkākā [pare W.266 'turn aside, ward off, protection' tīkākā TM 'sunburn']

sunburn *noun* tīkākā [W.416 'burnt by the sun']

sunburnt *adjective* tīkākā [TM 'sunburn']

suntanned *adjective* rauwhero [W.331 'ruddy, brown']

superficial *adjective* kirimoko [W.119 'skin']

superlative *noun* kupu tawhiti [kupu W.157 'word' kei tawhiti W.409 'matchless, unrivalled']

superscript *adjective* ripa [W.341 'the upper side, top'], *noun* pū ripa [pū TM 'character' ripa W.341 'the upper side, top']

superset *noun* huinga nui [huinga TM 'set' nui W.224 'large']

supersonic *adjective* paorangi [W.258 'resounding']

superstition *noun* ohiti [W.238 'cautious, on one's guard']

superstitious *adjective* manawa hopo [manawa W.174 'heart, mind, spirit' hopo W.59 'fearful, apprehensive, overawed']

suppository *noun* kuhitou [kuhi W.154 'insert, introduce' tou W.442 'anus']

Supreme Court *noun* Kōti Matua [kōti < Eng. 'court' matua W.195 'main, chief']

surfboard *noun* kōpapa [Best *Games and Pastimes* 42 'surfboard']

surf life-saver *noun* kauhauora [W.106 'a charm to secure safety' kau W.104 'swim' hauora W.41 'healthy']

surf life-saving *noun* kauhauora [W.106 'a charm to secure safety' kau W.104 'swim' hauora W.41 'healthy']

surf-casting *noun* māngoingoi [W.178 'fish with a line from the shore']

surgeon *noun* mātanga [W.188 'knowing, experienced person']

surgery *noun* (*place*) taiwhanga rata [taiwhanga TM 'room' rata W.327 'doctor']

surgery, to perform *intransitive verb* hāparapara *transitive verb* [W.35 'cut, sever']

surgical *adjective* hāparapara [W.35 'cut, sever']

surgical block *noun* whaitua hāparapara [whaitua TM 'block' hāparapara TM 'to perform surgery']

surgically *adverb* hāparapara [W.35 'cut, sever']

survey *transitive verb, noun* (*overview*) tiro whānui [tiro W.424 'look, survey, view' whānui W.487 'broad, wide'], (*statistics*) rangahau [W.323 'seek, search out, pursue']

suspect *noun* tangata e whakapaetia ana [tangata W.379 'human being' whakapae W.245 'accuse, make an accusation']

suspect *transitive verb* whakapae [W.245 'accuse, make an accusation']

suture *noun* tuinga [tui W.449 'sew']

sweat gland *noun* repe werawera [repe W.336 'gland' werawera W.482 'sweat'], repe tōtā [repe W.336 'gland' tōtā W.441 'sweat']

swede *noun* pōwhata [W.287 'wild turnip']

sweeper *noun* (*cricket*) tārake [W.387 'clear off, sweep away, standing out in the open']

swimmer *noun* kaikauhoe [kai W.86 'a

prefix to transitive verbs to form nouns denoting an agent' kauhoe W.106 'swim']

swimming costume *noun* kahu kakau [kahu W.84 'garment' kakau W.104 'swim']

swing *noun* (*golf*) hahau [W.39 'strike, smite']

switch *noun* (*electrical*) whakakā [whaka- W.486 'causative prefix' *to make* kā W.81 'take fire, be lighted, burn']

switch off *transitive verb* whakaweto [whaka- W.486 'causative prefix' *to make* weto W.483 'be extinguished'], tinei [W.419 'put out, quench, extinguish']

switch on *transitive verb* whakakā [whaka- W.486 'causative prefix' *to make* kā W.81 'take fire, be lighted, burn']

switchboard *noun* (*electricity*) papahiko [papa W.259 'anything broad, flat and hard' hiko TM 'electricity'], (*telephone*) papawaea [papa W.259 'anything broad, flat and hard' waea < Eng. 'wire']

syllable *noun* kū [W.153 'make a low inarticulate sound, grating sound']

syllabus *noun* marautanga [marau TM 'subject']

symbiosis *noun* taupuhipuhi [W.401 'lean one on another, support a person by placing the arm around him']

symbiotic *adjective* taupuhipuhi [TM 'symbiosis']

symbol *noun* tohu [W431 'mark, sign, point out']

symmetrical *adjective* hangarite [hanga W.34 TM 'shape' rite W.343 'alike, corresponding']

symmetry *noun* hangarite [hanga W.34 TM 'shape' rite W.343 'alike, corresponding']

symmetry, line *noun* hangarite rārangi [hangarite TM 'symmetry' rārangi W.324 'line']

symmetry, rotational *noun* hangarite huri [hangarite TM 'symmetry' huri TM 'rotate']

symphysis *noun* (*anatomy*) hononga [hono W.58 'splice, join']

symptom *noun* tohumate [tohu W.431 'mark, sign, mate W.192 'sickness']

synchronised *adjective* tukutahi [W.452 'together, simultaneous']

synchronised swimming *noun* kauhoe tukutahi [kauhoe W.106 'swim' tukutahi TM 'synchronised']

synopsis *noun* whakarāpopoto [whaka- W.486 'causative prefix' *to make* rāpopoto W.326 'be assembled' whakarāpopoto common usage 'summarise']

syntax *noun* wetereo [TM 'grammar']

synthesis *noun* kōtuitanga [kōtui W.150 'lace, fasten via lacing, interlace']

synthesise *transitive verb* kōtuitui [kōtui W.150 'lace, fasten via lacing, interlace']

synthesiser *noun* (*music*) whakatukutahi [whaka- W.486 'causative prefix' *to make* tukutahi W.452 'together, simultaneous']

synthetic *adjective* waihanga [TM 'artificial, man-made']

syringe *noun* pūwero [pū W.300 'tube' wero W.482 'pierce, spear']

system *noun* pūnaha [pū W.300 'base, foundation' nahanaha W.216 'well arranged, in good order']

system, economic *noun* pūnaha ōhanga [pūnaha TM 'system' ōhanga TM 'economics']

systematic *adjective* nahanaha [W.216 'well arranged, in good order']

T

table *noun* (*data*) ripanga [TM 'spreadsheet']

table tennis *noun* poikōpiko [poi TM 'ball' kōpiko W.137 'go alternately in opposite directions']

tablecloth *noun* takapapa [W.368 'mat on which to spread cooked food']

tablespoon *noun* kokotoha [koko W.130 'spoon' toha W.429 'distribute']

tabulate *transitive verb* whakaripa [whaka- W.486 'causative prefix' *to make* ripa W.341 'row, rank, line, furrow']

tabulation *noun* whakaripanga [whaka- W.486 'causative prefix' *to make* ripa W.341 'row, rank, line, furrow']

tackle *noun* (*contact sport*) rutu [W.353 'dash down, fell, overcome']

tackle, body *noun* rutu tinana [rutu TM 'tackle tinana W.419 'body, trunk']

tackle, dangerous *noun* tairutu [tai W.361 'anger, violence' rutu TM 'tackle']

tackle, fifth *noun* rutu tuarima [rutu TM 'tackle' tua W.444 'prefix used with numerals to form ordinals' rima W.340 'five']

tackle, flying *noun* rutu rere [rutu TM 'tackle' rere W.337 'fly']

tackle, head-high *noun* upokotaua [W.468 'surprise attack']

tackle, illegal *noun* rutu hē [rutu TM 'tackle' hē TM 'illegal']

tackle, late *noun* rutu tōmuri [rutu TM 'tackle tōmuri W.435 'late']

tackle, low *noun* rutu hakahaka [rutu TM 'tackle' hakahaka W.31 'low']

tactic *noun* rauhanga [W.329 'cunning, resourceful']

tactical *adjective* rauhanga [W.329 'cunning, resourceful']

tag *transitive verb* (*touch*) pā [W.243 'touch']

tag *noun* (*game*) tauwhaiwhai [W.405 'fly, hasten' whaiwhai W.485 'chase, hunt']

tail bone *noun* timu [W.419 'end, tail']

tail light *noun* ramamuri [rama W.322 'torch or other artificial light' muri W.213 'the rear']

takeaways ō rangaranga [ō W.237 'provision for a journey' rangaranga W.322 'take up, lift up, move']

take-off board *noun* (*athletics*) hūpana [W.70 'fly up or fly back, as a spring']

talcum powder *noun* papaurangi [W.261 'a plant used as scent for oil']

tally chart *noun* tūtohi tatau [tūtohi W.462 'sign, indication' tatau W.395 'count']

tambourine *noun* tatangi [W.379 'jingle, rattle']

tampon *noun* puru taiawa [puru W.314 'plug, cork, bung' taiawa W.363 'vagina']

tandem *adjective* taupiri [taupiripiri Best *Games and Pastimes* 19, 31 'style of foot race in which competitors run in pairs holding each other round the neck' W.401 'clinging close, maintaining attachment']

tangent *noun* (*mathematics*) pātapa [pā W.243 'touch', strike' tapa W.381 'edge']

tap *noun, transitive verb* (*sport*) papaki [W.253 'slap, pat']

tap *noun* (*water*) katiwai [kati W.103 'prevent, close up' wai W.474 'water']

tape recorder *noun* whakauenuku [W.465 'keep, retain'], hopureo [hopu W.59 'catch, seize, catch up' reo W.336 'voice']

tape-measure *noun* tīeke [taura tīeke W.415 'line for measuring the diagonals of a house']

tar *noun* kauri tawhiti [W.108 'a

bituminous substance found on the beach, soot from burnt kauri gum or resinous wood']

target *noun* (*shooting*) pārure [W.269 'prey']

target, moving *noun* (*shooting*) pārure tīrore [pārure TM 'target' tīrore W.424 'decoy kākā']

target, static *noun* (*shooting*) pārure pateko [pārure TM 'target' pateko W.271 'motionless, idle']

tariff *noun* (*tax*) tāke hoko tāwāhi [tāke < Eng. 'tax' hoko W.57 'buy, sell' tāwāhi W.406 'the other side of the sea']

tarmac *noun* whātika rererangi [whātika W.417 'way, path, set out on journey' waka rererangi common usage 'aeroplane']

tarsus *noun* wheua punga [wheua W.496 'bone' punga W.311 'ankle']

task, difficult *noun* waitara [W.477 'project or scheme of a fanciful or difficult nature']

taste bud *noun* tāwara [W.406 'flavour, taste, sweet, pleasant to the taste']

tax, provisional *noun* tāke tārewa [tāke < Eng. 'tax' tārewa W.391 'hanging, unsettled']

tax return *noun* (*form*) puka tāke [puka TM 'form' tāke < Eng. 'tax']

taxi *noun* wakatono [waka common usage 'vehicle' tono W.436 'bid, command']

taxi rank *noun* tūnga wakatono [tūnga W.443 'circumstance, time etc. of standing' wakatono TM 'taxi']

taxonomy *noun* tātai hono [tātai W.393 'recite genealogies' hono W.58 'join']

tea break *noun* henga [W.46 'food for a working party']

tea-bag *noun* tīraurau [tī TM 'tea' rau W.328 'gather into a basket etc.']

tea-cosy *noun* uhi tīpāta [uhi W.471 'cover, covering' tīpāta < Eng. 'teapot']

tea-leaves *noun* tīraurau [tī < Eng. 'tea' rau W.328 'leaf' raurau 'foliage']

team *noun* kapa [W.95 'rank, row, play sport']

team event *noun* tauwhāinga-ā-kapa [tauwhāinga TM 'event' ā W.1 'after the manner of' kapa TM 'team']

team pursuit *noun* whaiwhai-ā-kapa [whaiwhai W.484 'chase, hunt' ā W.1 'after the manner of' kapa TM 'team']

teargas *noun* kōpani [W.136 'an incantation to blind the eyes of a pursuer']

teaspoon *noun* kokoiti [koko W.130 'spoon' iti W.80 'small']

technologist *noun* ringa hangarau [ringa W.341 'hand' hangarau TM 'technology']

technology *noun* hangarau [hanga W.34 'make, fashion, work, business' rau W.328 'multitude, number']

tee *noun* (*golf, area*) tīhoka [W.416 'stick in, thrust in']

tee *noun* (*golf equipment*) tī [tīrau W.423 'peg, stick']

tee off *intransitive verb* tītere [W.425 'throw, cast']

telegram *noun* karere waea [karere TM 'message' waea < Eng. 'wire']

telephone directory *noun* pukapuka tau waea [pukapuka W.306 'book' tau waea TM 'telephone number']

telephone number *noun* tau waea [tau TM 'number' waea common usage 'telephone']

telescope *noun* karu whakatata [karu W.102 'eye, look at' whaka- W.486 'causative prefix' *to make* tata W.393 'near']

teletext *noun* pānui whakaata [pānui W.257 'advertise publicly, public notice' pouaka whakaata common usage 'television']

telex *noun* waea tuhi [waea < Eng. 'wire' tuhi W.448 'write']

temperature *noun* mahana [W.162 'warm']

template *noun* tauira [W.398 'pattern, copy']

temporal bone *noun* wheua rahirahinga [wheua W.496 'bone' rahirahinga W.320 'temple of the head']

temporary *adjective* rangitahi [W.324 'ephemeral, transient']

temporary staff *noun* kaimahi rangitahi [kaimahi TM 'staff' rangitahi TM 'temporary']

tender *transitive verb* (*submit*) tāpae [W.382 'place before a person, present']

tender *noun* (*contract*) tono [W.436 'bid, command']

tendon *noun* iohere [io W.78 'sinew, muscle, strand of rope' here W.46 'tie, fasten with cords']

tendon, Achilles *noun* io punga [iohere TM 'tendon' punga W.311 'ankle']

tennis serve *noun* (*volleyball*) tuku tēnehi [tuku TM 'serve' tēnehi < Eng. 'tennis']

tenor noun reo iere [reo W.336 'voice, tone' iere W.74 'singing, sing']

tension noun (*mental*) maniore [W.175 'anxiety']

tension noun (*tightness*) renarena [W.336 'taut' rena W.335 'stretch out']

tent noun pūroku [whare pūrokuroku W.314 'temporary shelter, hut' pūrokuroku 'wrinkled, rolled up clumsily']

tepid adjective aromahana [W.17 'lukewarm']

terminal noun (*public transport*) tauranga [W.396 'resting place, anchorage']

terminal illness noun mate tuamatangi [mate W.192 'sickness' tuamatangi W.446 'last respiration before death, dying gasp']

terylene noun tereaku [tere < Eng. 'tery' akuaku W.7 'firm, strong']

tessellation noun rōpinepine [rōpine W.347 'place close together']

test, fair noun (*science*) whakamātau tika [whakamātautau W.192 'test' tika W.417 'correct, straight, right']

testimonial noun kupu tautoko [kupu W.157 'word, speak, anything said' tautoko W.404 'prop up, support']

testimonial noun (*personal*) taunaki pūmanawa [taunaki W.400 'support, reinforce' pūmanawa W.309 'natural talents, intuitive cleverness']

tetanus noun kauae-timu [kauae W.105 'jaw' timu W.419 'involuntary contraction of muscles']

text noun tuhinga [tuhi W.448 'write']

textbook noun pukapuka matua [pukapuka W.306 'book' matua W.195 'main, chief']

textile fibre noun kaka-aku [kaka W.91 'fibre' akuaku W.7 'firm, strong']

theatre noun whare tapere [W.383 'house in which the members of the hapū met for amusement']

theatre, operating noun taiwhanga hāparapara [TM 'surgery']

theme noun kaupapa [W.107 'stage, platform, groundwork']

theory noun ariā [W.15 'notion, idea, feeling, be seen indistinctly']

therapeutic adjective haumanu [W.40 'revive, restore to health']

therapy noun haumanu [W.40 'revive, restore to health']

thermometer noun ine mahana [ine TM 'meter' mahana W.162 'warm']

thermoplastic noun kirihou rerehū [kirihou TM 'plastic' rerehū W.338 'be heated']

thermos noun takawai [W.370 'calabash used as a water bottle']

thermosphere noun kōhau āhuru [kōpaki W.135 'envelop, envelope' hau TM 'gas' āhuru W.4 'warm']

thermostat noun whakaū mahana [whakaū W.464 'make firm' mahana W.162 'warm']

thesaurus noun punakupu [puna W.309 'spring of water' kupu W.157 'word']

thicken transitive verb (*cooking*) takaete [taka W.366 'prepare' ete W.28 'thicken']

thimble noun huhimati [huhi W.66 'cover' mati W.193 'finger']

thoracic noun rei [W.335 'breast, chest']

thoughtlessly adverb pokerenoa [W.290 'wilful, reckless']

three-dimensional adjective ahu-tengi [ahu W.3 'move in a certain direction' tengi W.412 'three']

throttle noun (*mechanical*) katihinu [katirere TM 'tap' hinu common usage 'petrol']

throw transitive verb whiu [W.498 'a certain throw in wrestling, fling, toss']

throw, torpedo noun epa tōkiri [epa W.28 'throw, cast' tōkiri W.434 'thrust lengthwise']

throw-in noun (*sport*) tōkiri [W.434 'thrust lengthwise']

throwing arc noun (*athletics*) wī tuatuku [wī TM 'line' tuatuku W.447 'let go']

throwing area noun (*athletics*) pūihi tuatuku [pūihi W.305 'division in a kūmara field' tuatuku W.447 'let go']

throwing circle noun (*athletics*) tuatuku [W.447 'let go']

throw-up noun (*netball*) tauhone [tauhonehone W.398 'snatch or pull from one another']

thyroid gland noun repe tenga [repe W.336 'gland' tenga W.412 'goitre, crop of a bird']

tidal zone noun ara o Hinekirikiri [ara W.13 'way, path' hine W.51 'girl, chiefly used in addressing a girl or young woman' kirikiri W.119 'gravel' common usage 'sandy']

tie *noun* (*draw*) haupārua [TM 'draw']
tie-breaker *noun* tuku mātātahi [W.191 'fight a duel']
tighthead *noun* (*rugby, ball-play*) whānako taupuru [whānako W.487 'steal' taupurupuru TM 'scrum']
tighthead prop *noun* (*rugby*) poumua matau [pou W.297 'support' matau W.192 'right']
tights *noun* (*clothing*) kiri kātete [kiri W.119 'skin' kātete W.103 'the whole leg from the thigh downwards']
tile, floor *noun* tangariki [W.379 'inferior kind of floor mat']
tile, roof *noun* tāpatu [W.383 'thatch, cover in a roof' tāpatupatu 'place in layers, lay one on another']
time out for injury *phrase* taupua whara [taupua W.401 'take breath, subside' whara W.489 'be struck, be hit accidentally']
time signature *noun* (*music*) tohu rere [tohu W.431 'mark, sign' rere W.337 'fly']
timekeeper *noun* mata wati [mata W.185 'eye, face' wati < Eng. 'watch']
time-out *noun* taupua [W.401 'take breath, subside']
time-series data *noun* raraunga houanga [raraunga TM 'data' houanga W.63 'an interval of time']
time-sheet *noun* puka hāora mahi [puka TM 'form' hāora < Eng. 'hour' mahi W.163 'work']
timetable *noun* wātaka [wā W.472 'time' taka W.366 'come round, as a date or period of time']
tin *noun* (*container*) puoto [W.311 'vessel']
tin-opener *noun* tīwara [W.427 'cleave in twain, split']
tinsel *noun* kohiko [W.125 'flash, twinkle']
tissue paper *noun* rauangiangi [rauangi W.329 'thin, fine, tender, finely divided strands of flax for making nets']
titrate *transitive verb* (*chemistry*) ine kukū [ine TM 'measure' kukū TM 'concentration']
toast-rack *noun* tītara [W.424 'a framework of sticks for supporting bundles of fern root']
toaster *noun* tāina [W.364 'singe']
tobacco *noun* tōrori [W.440 'native-grown tobacco']
toddler *noun* pangore [W.258 'children, immature']
toilet bowl *noun* putanga hamuti [putanga W.315 'escape' hamuti W.33 'human excrement']
toilet seat *noun* pae hamuti [W.245 'horizontal beam of latrine']
tolerance *noun* (*people etc.*) manawa nui [W.174 'patient, forbearing']
tolerance *noun* (*pain*) manawa toa [manawa nui W.174 'stout-hearted, patient, forbearing' toa W.428 'brave']
tolerant *adjective* (*people etc.*) manawa nui [W.174 'patient, forbearing']
toll-call *noun* waea ki tawhiti [waea < Eng. 'wire' ki W.116 'to' tawhiti W.409 'a distant locality']
tomentum *noun* (*botany*) mōnehu [W.209 'the fine rusty pubescence on the unexpanded fronds of bracken and other ferns']
tongs *noun* (*kitchenware*) pīnohi [W.281 'sticks used for handling hot stones, tongs']
tonic *noun* (*medicine*) rongoā [W.346 'remedy, preservative against sickness or death']
tonsil *noun* miramira [W.202 'uvula']
tonsillitis *noun* miramira kakā [W.202 'uvula' kakā TM 'inflammation']
tool *noun* pāraha [pāraharaha W.263 'tool made of thin iron, hoop iron, or anything similar']
tooth, canine *noun* niho kata [niho W.221 'tooth' kata W.102 'laugh']
tooth, canine *noun* niho rei [niho W.221 'tooth' rei W.334 'tusk']
tooth, molar *noun* niho kōhari [niho W.221 'tooth' kōhari W.124 'mash, crush']
tooth, premolar *noun* niho pūrākau [niho W.221 'tooth' pūrākau W.312 'double, of teeth']
toothpaste *noun* paniaku [pani W.257 'smear, spread anything upon something else' akuaku W.7 'scrape out, cleanse']
topic *noun* kaupapa [W.107 'stage, platform, groundwork']
torque *noun* taipana takahuri [taipana TM 'force' takahurihuri W.367 'keep on turning round, roll over and over']
toss *noun* (*coin*) tutukai [Best *Games and Pastimes* W.117]

toss-up *noun* (*coin*) tutukai [Best *Games and Pastimes* W.117]

toupee *noun* uru tiwha [uru W.469 'hair of the head' tiwha W.427 'patch, spot, applied to a bald patch on the head']

tourism *noun* tāpoi [W.384 'be travelled round']

tourist *noun* wae tāpoi [wae W.472 'leg, foot' tāpoi TM 'tourism']

tournament *noun* whakataetae [W.356 'try strength, contend']

tourniquet *noun* pāpuni [W.261 'stanch, check the flow of blood']

towbar *noun* pongare [W.292 'knobbed, ending in a knob']

towel-rack *noun* tārawa [W.389 'line or rail on which anything is hung']

toxic *adjective* tāoke [tā- W.355 'prefix having a causative force' oke W.239 'ill, ailing, sick person']

toxic algal bloom pūkohu ngaruru tāoke [pūkohu ngaruru TM 'algal bloom' tāoke TM 'toxic']

toxin *noun* tāoke [tā- W.355 'prefix having a causative force' oke W.239 'ill, ailing, sick person']

toy, mechanical *noun* takawairore [W.370 'a toy consisting of an irregular disc having two slightly excentric holes through which strings were passed']

toy, soft *noun* newanewa [W.221 'smooth, soft']

trace element *noun* kikini [W.118 'pinch off']

trachea *noun* pūkorokoro [W.308 'windpipe']

track *noun* (*course*) ara tauoma [ara W.13 'way, path' tauomaoma TM 'race'], (*athletics*) ara amio [ara W.13 'way, path' amio W.8 'circle round'], ara kaipara [ara W.13 'way, path' kaipara TM 'athletics']

track event *noun* tauomaoma [TM 'foot race']

tract *noun* (*anatomy*) roma [W.346 'channel']

trade *noun* mahi [W.163 'work, work at, occupation']

tradesperson *noun* ringarehe [ringa W.341 'hand' rehe W.333 'expert, deft person']

traffic, heavy *noun* mātotorutanga o te waka [mātotoru W.194 'thick' waka 'vehicle']

traffic island *noun* motuara [motu W.211 'island' ara W.13 'way, path']

traffic jam *noun* inaki waka [inaki W.77 'overlap, crowd one upon another, pack closely' waka common usage 'vehicle']

trailer *noun* tauaru [W.397 'follow']

train *noun* rerewhenua [rere W.337 'flow, fly, rush' whenua W.494 'land, country, ground']

train *transitive verb* (*teach*) whakangungu [W.236 'defend, protect, parry, shield']

trainer *noun* kaiwhakangungu [kai W.86 'a prefix to transitive verbs to form nouns denoting an agent' whakangungu TM 'train']

training whakangungu [W.236 'defend, protect, parry, shield']

training scheme *noun* kaupapa whakangungu [kaupapa TM 'scheme' whakangungu TM 'training']

tramper *noun* kaihōpara [W.59 'go about, explore, cover, traverse']

trampoline *noun* tūraparapa [turapa W.458 'spring, rebound, recoil, spring up']

transfer *transitive verb* whakawhiti [W.497 'convey across, exchange']

transformation *noun* huringa [huri W.71 'turn to, set about']

transformation *noun* (*mathematics*) panoni [W.257 'change']

transformation geometry *noun* āhuahanga panoni [āhuahanga TM 'geometry' panoni TM 'transformation']

transfusion, blood *noun* whāngai toto [whāngai W.488 'feed' toto W.441 'blood']

transition *noun* tauwhiro [tauwhirowhiro TM 'transitional']

transitional *adjective* tauwhirowhiro [W.405 'be near the change (of the moon)']

transitive verb *noun* kupumahi whaihoa [kupumahi TM 'verb' whai W.484 'possessing, equipped with' hoa W.54 'companion, mate']

translate *transitive verb* whakamāori [W.179 'explain, elucidate'] *e.g. whakamāori(hia) ki te reo Wīwī* 'translate into French'

translation *noun* (*mathematics*) nekehanga [W.220 'move']

transmitter *noun* tare [W.390 'send']

transparency *noun* puata [W.303 'clear, transparent']
transpiration *noun* puhawai [TM 'transpire']
transpire *intransitive verb* (*biology*) puhawai [puha W.303 'make a faint emission of the breath' wai W.474 'water, liquid']
transplant *transitive verb* whakatō [W.428 'plant, introduce, insert']
trapezium *noun* taparara [tapawhā TM 'quadrilateral' whakarara TM 'parallel']
trash *noun* para [W.262 'refuse, waste']
trash *transitive verb* (*computer*) porowhiu [W.295 'throw']
tray *noun* paepae [W.245 'dish, open shallow vessel']
tread *noun* tapore [W.384 'footprints, depression as in soft ground']
treadmill *noun* tīkeikei [tīkei W.417 'extend, stretch out, as the legs in stepping over an object']
treatment *noun* (*medicine*) rongoā [W.346 'take care of, apply medicines to']
tree diagram *noun* (*mathematics*) hoahoa rākau [hoahoa TM 'diagram' rākau W.321 'tree']
trend *noun* ia [W.74 'current, rushing stream']
trespass *intransitive verb* kaihaumi [TM 'trespasser']
trespasser *noun* kaihaumi [W.40 'person who wanders over lands of other people where he has no rights']
triangle *noun* tapatoru [tapa W.381 'margin, edge' toru W.441 'three']
triangle, equilateral *noun* tapatoru rite [tapatoru TM 'triangle' rite W.343 'alike, corresponding']
triangle, isoceles *noun* tapatoru waerite [tapatoru TM 'triangle' wae W.472 'leg' rite W.343 'alike, corresponding']
triangle, right-angled *noun* tapatoru hāngai [tapatoru TM 'triangle' hāngai TM 'right angle']
triangle, scalene *noun* tapatoru hikuwaru [tapatoru TM 'triangle' hikuwaru W.50 'crooked, asymmetrical']
triangular prism *noun* porotoru [poro W.294 'block' toru W.441 'three']
triceps *noun* uatoru [ua TM 'muscle' toru W.441 'three']
trifoliate *noun* tawhera-toru [tawhera W.408 'leaf' toru W.441 'three']

trim *transitive verb* kaikawau [W.88 'lop, cut the tips off anything']
trio *adjective* matengi [W.193 'three']
triphthong *noun* (*language*) orotoru [oro W.242 'sound' toru W.441 'three']
triple *adjective* tōtoru [W.442 'threefold']
triple jump *noun* (*athletics*) peke tōtoru [peke W.276 'spring, leap, jump' tōtoru TM 'triple']
triple jumper *noun* peke tōtoru [TM 'triple jump']
tripod *noun* waetoru [wae W.472 'leg' toru W.441 'three']
tripping *transitive verb* (*soccer*) hīrau [W.52 'entangle, trip up']
trolley *noun* tōneke [tō W.428 'drag, haul' kōneke W.133 'sledge']
trombone *noun* pūhōkai [pū W.300 'tube, flute, blow' hōkaikai W.56 'extended and retract alternately']
trophy *noun* tohutoa [TM 'medal']
tropical rain forest *noun* ngāoreore [ngāherehere W.226 'forest' ngaore W.229 'succulent, tender, soft']
troposphere *noun* (*atmosphere*) kōhauhuri [kōpaki W.135 'envelop, envelope' hau TM 'gas' huri W.71 'turn, turn round']
trough *noun* (*physics*) hārua [W.38 'depression, valley']
trowel *noun* pāpako [W.254 'loosen the soil around plants']
trumpet *noun* (*music*) pūawanui [pū W.300 'tube, pipe, blow' awanui W.23 'a trumpet shell']
trustee *noun* matapopore [W.189 'watchful over, careful of, husband, prize']
try *noun* (*rugby, etc.*) paneke [TM 'goal']
try, pushover *noun* paneke taiari [paneke TM 'try' taiari W.362 'beat, drive back, smash, crush']
tuba *noun* pūnguru [pū W.300 'pipe, tube, blow' nguru W.236 'utter a suppressed groan, murmur, rumble']
tube *noun* (*tyre*) pukuhau [puku W.308 'abdomen, stomach, swelling' hau W.38 'air']
tuck *noun* (*diving*) hūmene [W.69 'gathered up into small compass, folded up']
tuft *adjective* weku [wekuweku W.481 'tufted, in tufts']
tugboat *noun* wakatō [waka W.478 'canoe in general' tō W.428 'drag, haul']

tunnel *noun* arapoka [ara W.13 'way, path' poka W.288 'bore, dig out'], anaroa [ana W.9 'cave' roa W.344 'long']

turbine, water *noun* kapowai [kapo W.96 'catch at, snatch, lightning' wai W.474 'water']

turbine, wind *noun* kapohau [kapo W.96 'catch at, snatch, lightning' hau W.38 'wind, air']

turbine blade *noun* uruuru [W.469 'blade of a weapon' uru 'enter, reach a place']

turbo *noun* matangirua [W.189 'to use both sail and paddles in a canoe']

turn off *transitive verb (machinery etc.)* whakaweto [TM 'switch off'], tinei [TM 'switch off']

turn on *transitive verb (machinery etc.)* whakakā [TM 'switch on']

turned-on *adjective (emotions)* tōiriiri [W.432 'tingle, vibrate']

turning judge *noun (swimming)* kaiwhakawā huringa [kaiwhakawā W.472 'judge' huri W.71 'turn round']

turning line *noun (swimming)* tohu huringa [tohu W.431 'mark, sign' huri W.71 'turn round']

turnip *noun* kotami [W.148 'wild turnip']

turret *noun* huki [W.68 'a round house with conical roof']

tweezers *noun* kukuweu [kuku W.155 'pincers, tweezers' weu W.483 'single hair']

twist *noun, intransitive verb (diving)* takahiri [W.367 'turn, twist']

two-dimensional *adjective* ahu-rua [ahu W.3 'move in a certain direction' rua W.349 'two']

type *transitive verb, intransitive verb (text)* patopato [patō W.271 'emit a sharp sudden sound, crack, snap'], paopao [pao W.258 'strike, crack, break']

typesetter *noun* whakarauwaka tuhinga [whakarauwaka W.331 'lay off in beds or divisions' tuhinga TM 'text']

typewriter *noun* pae patopato [pae W.245 'any transverse beam' patopato TM 'type']

tyrannosaurus *noun* moko-ngarengare [moko W.207 'a general term for lizards, huge mythical creature of lizard-like shape' ngarengare W.230 'tyrannous, overbearing']

tyre *noun* rapa [W.325 'anything broad and flat, united by a membrane, webbed']

U

ulna *noun* (*bone*) pūkaka ringa [pūkaka W.306 'long bones of the arm or leg' ringa W341 'arm']

ultra-violet ray *noun* hihi katikati [hihi W.48 'ray of the sun' katikati W.103 'bite frequently, of action of the sun']

umbel *noun* (*botany*) pirara [W.283 'separated, divided, gaping, branching']

umpire *noun* kaiwawao [kai W.86 'a prefix to transitive verbs to form nouns denoting an agent' wawao W.479 'part combatants']

unanimous *noun* oropapa [W.242 'all alike, without exception']

unattractive *adjective* tukuperu [W.452 'person of uninviting appearance']

unconscious *adjective* mauri moe [mauri W.197 'life principle, thymos of man' moe W.204 'sleep, dream']

under par *phrase* (*golf*) eke panuku [eke W.27 'get aground, come to land' panuku W.257 'move on after']

underarm serve *noun* tuku kaku [tuku TM 'serve' kaku W.92 'scoop up']

undercarriage *noun* kōhiwi [W.125 'body of a canoe without attached parts, skeleton, trunk of a tree, heartwood']

undercover agent *noun* mata hunahuna [mataara W.186 'witness, observe' hunahuna W.69 'concealed, seldom seen' mata hunahuna W.69 'a charm to effect concealment from a foe']

undercut *transitive verb* kaikape [W.88 'outrun, steal']

undergraduate student *noun* pia [W.279 'the first order of learners being initiated in esoteric lore']

underline *transitive verb* tāraro [tā W.354 'tattoo, paint' raro W.327 'the underside' tāraro W.389 'adorned, ornamented']

understudy *noun* piki [W.280 'second, support in a duel']

undertaker *noun* whakatakataka tūpāpaku [whakatakataka W.366 'set anyone on his way, send forth' takataka 'make ready' tūpāpaku W.456 'corpse']

underwear *noun* kōpū [W.138 'an inner garment']

undo *transitive verb* (*computer*) whakakore [W.141 'cause not to be']

unearth *transitive verb* houhou [W.63 'dig up, obtain by digging']

unethical *adjective* makihuhunu [W.170 'take an unfair advantage of' maki W.170 'prefix indicating an action is done for one's own benefit' huhunu W.70 'plunder, maltreat']

unethical practice *noun* makihuhunu [W.170 'take an unfair advantage of' maki W.170 'prefix indicating an action is done for one's own benefit' huhunu W.70 'plunder, maltreat']

unfeasible *adjective* kāore e whaihua [kāore W.95 'not' whaihua TM 'beneficial, worthwhile']

unicellular *adjective* pūtau-tahi [pūtau TM 'cell' tahi W.359 'one, single']

unicorn *noun* pihi makaurangi [pihi common usage 'horn' makaurangi W.169 'spiral lines, adorn with spirals']

union *noun* (*sets*) hononga [W.58 'splice, join, marry']

unique *adjective* ahurei [W.4 'chief, prominent, unique']

unit *noun* wae [W.472 'divide, part, portion']

unit of measurement *noun* waeine [wae W.472 'divide, part, portion' ine W.78 'measure']

universe *noun* ao tukupū [ao W.11 'world' tukupū W.452 'coming down on all sides, covering completely, spread over']

unorthodox *adjective* korokē [W.144 'extraordinary, strange, out of the common']

unreliable *adjective* hārakiraki [W.36 'inconstancy, erratic disposition']

unskilled *adjective* ninipa [W.222 'awkward, unfortunate, unskilful'], tahangoi [W.357 'hesitating, awkward, unaccustomed']

unstable *adjective* (*chemistry*) katote [W.104 'not fixed, displaced']

upper *adjective* whakarunga [whaka- W.485 'towards, in the direction of' runga W.352 'the top, the upper part']

upper bar *noun* (*gymnastics*) tāuhu whakarunga [tāuhu TM 'bar' whakarunga TM 'upper']

upper case *noun* pūmatua [pū TM 'letter, character' matua W.195 'main, chief, important']

upright *noun* pou [W.297 'post, pole, support']

upwards whakarunga *adverb* [whaka- W.485 'towards, in the direction of' runga W.352 'the top, the upper part']

uranium *noun* konuruke [konu- TM 'prefix denoting natural metal' ira rukeruke TM 'radioactive']

urban *adjective* tāone [tāone < Eng. 'town']

urban-based *adjective* noho tāone [noho W.223 'dwell, live, be located' tāone < Eng. 'town']

urea *noun* tiomimi [tio TM 'crystal' mimi W.202 'urine']

ureter *noun* (*anatomy*) awa mimi [awa W.23 'channel, river' mimi W.202 'urine']

urethra *noun* (*anatomy*) taiawa mimi [taiawa W.363 'channel' mimi W.202 'urine']

urgent *adjective* whāwhai [W.484 'be in haste, be hurried, exert oneself'] e.g. *E whāwhaitia ana tō whakautu* 'your response is urgently needed'

urinary tract *noun* roma mimi [roma W.346 'current, stream, channel' mimi W.202 'urine']

urinary tract infection *noun* mate roma mimi [mate W.192 'sickness' roma mimi TM 'urinary tract']

urology *noun* mātai roma mimi, taihemahema [mātai TM 'study' roma mimi TM 'urinary tract' taihemahema TM 'reproductive organs']

used *adjective* (*second-hand*) nguture [W.236 'worn with use']

useful *adjective* whaihua [whai W.484 'possessing, equipped with' huanga W.64 'advantage, benefit']

utensil *noun* taputapu [W.385 'goods, property, appliances']

uterus *noun* kōpū [W.138 'belly, womb']

U-turn *noun* kōnumi [W.134 'take a backward course']

V

vaccine *noun* kano ārai mate [kano W.94 'seed' ārai W.14 'screen, ward off' mate W.192 'sickness']

vacuole *noun* (*biology*) miru [mirumiru Biggs 23 'bubble']

vacuum *noun* mārua [W.184 'hollow, void']

vacuum cleaner *noun* hororē [horohororē W.61 'to eat greedily']

vain *adjective* whakatāupe [W.401 'regard oneself with admiration, i.e. bend over the wai whakaata']

valid *adjective* whaitake [whai W.484 'possessing, equipped with' take W.370 'well founded, firm lasting'], (*law*) whaimana [whai W.484 'possessing, equipped with' mana W.172 'authority, power, influence'], (*statistics*) pono [W.291 'true']

valuable *adjective* tino taonga [tino W.420 'veritable, very' taonga W.381 'anything highly prized'] *e.g. He tino taonga ana kōrero. 'Her comments were most valuable.'*

value *noun* (*mathematics*) uara [W.465 'value']

value, absolute *noun* (*mathematics*) uara pū [uara TM 'value' pū W.300 'base, foundation']

value, face *noun* (*mathematics*) uara mata [uara TM 'value' mata W.185 'face']

value, place *noun* uara tū [uara TM 'value' tū W.443 'stand']

valve *noun* takirere [taki W.371 'lead, bring along' rere W.337 'flow']

valve *noun* katirere [kati W.103 'block up, close in' rere W.337 'flow']

van *noun* kōporo [waka kōporo W.138 'a square-sterned canoe']

vanity *noun* whakatāupe [W.401 'regard oneself with admiration, i.e. bend over the wai whakaata']

vapour trail *noun* tākohu [W.373 'vapour']

variable *noun* (*mathematics*) taurangi [W.402 'unsettled, changing, changeable']

variable *noun* (*science*) tāupe [W.401 'variable']

variable, control *noun* (*science*) tāupe whakaū [tāupe TM 'variable' whakaū W.465 'make firm, establish']

varicose vein *noun* tīponapona [tīpona W.422 'form a swelling or knot']

varicotomy *noun* tango tīponapona [tango W.380 'take away, remove' tīponapona TM 'varicose vein']

varnish *transitive verb* whakamōhinu [whaka- W.486 'causative prefix' *to make* mōhinuhinu W.205 'shiny, glistening, glossy'], *noun* mōhinuhinu [W.205 'shiny, glistening, glossy']

vas deferens *noun* ara tātea [ara W.13 'way, means of conveyance' tātea W.394 'semen']

vascular *adjective* iaia toto [iaia W.74 'veins' toto W.441 'blood']

vault *noun, intransitive verb* (*gymnastics*) kōkiri [kōkirikiri W.130 'leap, fly headlong' kōkiri Best *Games and Pastimes* 46 'water jump']

vault *noun* (*storage*) pūwhenua [W.319 'cave used as a dwelling place']

vaulting-horse *noun* hōiho [< Eng. 'horse']

vector (*mathematics*) pere [W.278 'arrow, dart']

vegemite *noun* īhipani [īhi TM 'yeast' pani W.257 'spread']

vegetable-crisper *noun* pātengitengi [W.271 'a storehouse or pit for kūmara']

vein *noun* ia auraki [iaia W.74 'veins' auraki W.22 'return']
velcro *noun* piripiri [W.283 'a creeping burr' piri 'stick, adhere, cling']
velocity *noun* tere [W.412 'swift, move quickly, flow']
velodrome *noun* āmikumiku [W.8 'make a circuit round']
velvet *noun* mōnehu [W.209 'the fine rusty pubescence on the unexpanded fronds of bracken and other ferns']
velvety *adjective* mōnehunehu [mōnehu W.209 'the fine rusty pubescence on the unexpanded fronds of bracken and other ferns']
veneer *noun* papaangi [papa W.259 'anything broad, flat and hard' angiangi W.11 'thin']
Venn diagram *noun* whakaahua huinga [whakaahua TM 'picture' huinga TM 'set'], hoahoa huinga [hoahoa TM 'diagram' huinga TM 'set']
vent *noun* aumanga [W.22 'a hollowed-out space, on the underside of the ridge-pole immediately over the front wall of a house, designed as a smoke vent']
ventricle *noun* (*brain*) ana roro [ana W.9 'cave' roro W.347 'brains']
ventricle *noun* (*heart*) mānawanawa [W.174 mānawanawa 'space' manawa 'heart']
ventriloquist *noun* motatau [W.211 'talk to oneself']
verb *noun* kupumahi [kupu W.157 'word' mahi W.163 'do, perform, function']
verb, active *noun* kupumahi ngoi [kupumahi TM 'verb' ngoi W.234 'strength, energy']
verb, di-transitive *noun* kupumahi punarua [kupumahi TM 'verb' punarua W.310 'having two wives']
verb, intransitive *noun* kupumahi takakau [kupumahi TM 'verb' takakau W.368 'free from the marriage tie, at leisure']
verb, transitive *noun* kupumahi whaihoa [kupumahi TM 'verb' whai W.484 'possessing, equipped with' hoa W.54 'companion, mate']
verbalist *noun* hinengaro whakairo kupu [hinengaro W.51 'seat of the thoughts and emotions' whakairo W.80 'ornament with a pattern, used of carving, tatooing, painting, weaving' kupu W.157 'anything said, word, talk']
verify *transitive verb* tautoko [W.404 'prop up, support'], whakatūturu [whaka- W.486 'causative prefix' *to make* tūturu W.460 'fixed, permanent']
versatile *adjective* ringa raka [ringa W.341 'hand' raka W.321 'agile, adept']
vertex *noun* akitū [W.7 'point, end, summit']
vesicle *noun* pakohu [W.255 'cleft, chasm, cavity']
vessel, blood *noun* ia toto [ia W.74 'current' toto W.441 'blood']
vessels, blood *noun* iaia toto [ia W.74 'current' toto W.441 'blood']
vestibule *noun* mahau [W.163 'porch, verandah']
veterinarian *noun* rata kararehe [rata W.327 'doctor' kararehe W.99 'quadruped']
veterinary science *noun* mātauranga hauora kararehe [mātauranga common usage 'knowledge' hauora W.41 'healthy, well, lively' kararehe W.99 'quadruped']
vibration *noun* ngateri [W.231 'vibrate, shake']
vice-president *noun* tumuaki tuarua [tumuaki W.454 'head, president' tua W.444 'prefix used with numerals to form ordinals' rua W.349 'two']
victim *noun* pārurenga [W.269 'a person subjected to violence or ill treatment'], mārurenga [W.185 'one who has suffered plunder and ill treatment']
video *adjective* ataata [ata W.18 'reflected image']
video cassette *noun* rīpene ataata [rīpene < Eng. 'ribbon' ataata TM 'video']
video cassette recorder *noun* pūrere ataata [pūrere TM 'machine ataata TM 'video']
video game *noun* tākaro ataata [tākaro W.369 'play, sport' ataata TM 'video']
video programme *noun* whakaari ataata [whakaari W.15 'show, expose to view' ataata TM 'video']
vinyl *noun* tapeha [W.383 'rind, bark, skin']
viola *noun* (*music*) tiora [W.420 'shrill']
violate sexually *transitive verb* koere [W.123 'strip off, tear apart' see W.314 pūrikoriko for example]
violin *noun* tōiri [W.432 'tingle, vibrate, resound']

viral *adjective* wheori [W.494 'diseased, ill']
virus *noun* wheori [W.494 'diseased, ill']
visa *noun* (*passport*) kōkota [W.147 'a mark made at cross-roads to show which road has been taken']
visiting hours *noun* hāora toro [hāora < Eng. 'hour' toro W.439 'go to see, visit']
vitamin *noun* huaora [hua W.64 'fruit' huanga 'advantage, benefit' ora W.240 'well, in health, alive']
vitamin C *noun* huaora C [hua W.64 'fruit' huanga 'advantage, benefit' ora W.240 'well, in health, alive']
vitreous humour *noun* (*anatomy*) piakamo [piapia W.279 'glairy, viscid' kamo W.92 'eye']
vocal cords *noun* kūrua [kū W.153 'a one-string instrument, make a low inarticulate sound' kukū 'make a grating sound' rua W.349 'two']
volatile *adjective* (*chemistry*) tākohukohu [tākohu W.373 'mist, vapour']
volcano *noun* ahi tipua [Best *Tūhoe, Children of the Mist* 977]
volley *noun* (*sport*) haupatu [W.41 'strike, dash, assault']

volleyball *noun* poirewa [poi TM 'ball' rewa W.339 'be elevated, be high up']
volt *noun* wae ngaohiko [wae TM 'unit' ngao W.229 'energy' hiko common usage 'electricity']
voltage *noun* ngaohiko [ngao W.229 'strength, energy' hiko common usage 'electricity']
voltmeter *noun* ine ngaohiko [ine TM 'meter' ngaohiko TM 'voltage']
volume *noun* rōrahi [rō W.344 'roto' W.348 'the inside' rahi W.320 'size' rōraha W.347 'spreading, extended']
volume *noun* (*sound*) kaha [W.82 'strength'] *e.g. Whakaitihia te kaha. 'Turn down the volume.' Whakakahahia ake te kaha. 'Turn up the volume.'*
voluntary *adjective* tūao [TM 'volunteer']
volunteer *noun* tūao [W.446 'work for a time or as a volunteer']
volunteer services abroad *phrase* tūao tāwāhi [tūao TM 'volunteer, voluntary' tāwāhi W.406 'the other side of the sea']
vowel *noun* pūare [pū TM 'letter, character' are W.14 'open']

W

waiting room *noun* taiwhanga [W.365 'place, locality, wait for']
walking frame *noun* tautītī [W.404 'support an invalid in walking']
walkman *noun* (*radio*) pokotaringa [W.290 'ear']
wall *noun* (*soccer*) pātū [W.272 'screen, wall']
waltz *noun* tengitengi [hītengi W.53 'hop on one foot' tengi W.412 'three']
ward *noun* (*hospital*) mātūtū [W.195 'convalescent, not quite healed or cured']
ward of court *noun* mataporenga [matapore TM 'guardian' matapore W.189 'watchful over, careful over']
warm down *intransitive verb* (*exercise*) whakamakaka [W.168 'bend the body and stretch oneself to relieve the muscles when weary']
warm up *intransitive verb* (*exercise*) kōiriiri [kōiri W.12 'bend the body, sway, move to and fro']
warming-drawer *noun* (*stove*) kōnao [W.133 'earth oven for which the stones are heated in a fire beside the pit, not in the pit']
warrant *noun* whakamana [W.172 'give effect to, make effective']
warrant, committal *noun* whakamana mau herehere [whakamana TM 'warrant' mau herehere TM 'imprison']
warrant, search *noun* whakamana haurapa [whakamana TM warrant' haurapa W.41 'search diligently for']
warrant of fitness *noun* whakamana waka [whakamana TM 'warrant' waka TM 'vehicle']
warrant to seize property *noun* whakamana herepū rawa [whakamana TM 'warrant' herepū W.46 'seize, catch and hold firmly' rawa W.331 'goods, property']
warship *noun* wakatauā [waka W.478 'canoe in general' tauā W.397 'hostile expedition, army']
washer *noun* (*plumbing*) mōria [W.210 'ring for the leg of a captive kākā']
washing-machine *noun* pūrere horoi [pūrere TM 'machine' horoi W.61 'cleanse, wash']
waste, biodegradable *noun* kapurangi [W.97 'rubbish, weeds, a kind of woody fungus']
waste-disposal unit *noun* horomiti pakopako [horomiti W.61 'eat ravenously, devour' pakopako W.255 'gleanings, scraps of food']
water *transitive verb* (*plants etc.*) hāwaiwai [whā W.484 'causative prefix' wai W.474 'water']
water conservation *noun* whāomo wai [whāomoomo W.239 'tend, use sparingly, husband' wai W.474 'water']
water hazard *noun* (*golf*) hāpua whakatara [hāpua W.36 'pool, lagoon' whakatara W.386 'challenge, put on one's mettle']
water tank *noun* kōpapa wai [kōpapa W.136 'storehouse for food' wai W.474 'water']
water-heater *noun* whakawera wai [whaka- W.486 'causative prefix' *to make* wera W.482 'heated, hot' wai W.474 'water']
water-jump *noun* (*steeplechase*) hāpua whakatara [TM 'water hazard']
water-jump *noun* (*water-skiing*) kōkiri [Best Games and Pastimes 46 'springless springboard']
water-ski *noun* retiwai [TM 'waterskiing']
waterskiing *noun* retiwai [reti W.338

140

'convey, carry, as a boat' wai W.474 'water']

water-slide *noun* awa peopeo [awa W.23 'channel, river' peopeo W.277 'slippery']

waterway *noun* arawai [ara W.13 'way, path' wai W.474 'water']

water-wings *noun* (*buoyancy aid*) pōito [Best *Games and Pastimes* 42 'floats fastened to a child learning to swim']

wave jumper *noun* peke ngaru [peke W.276 'spring, leap, jump' ngaru W.230 'wave']

wavelength *noun* (*radio*) roa o te ngaru [roa W.344 'long' ngaru W.230 'wave']

wax gland *noun* repe tāturi [repe TM 'gland' tāturi W.395 'wax in the ear']

way out *noun* araputa [ara W.13 'way, path' puta W.315 'come, come forth, come out']

weasel *noun* tori uaroa [tori W.438 'energetic, busy, bustling' ua W.465 'neck, back of the neck' roa W.344 'long']

weather *noun* huarere [paihuarere W.250 'perfect of weather']

weather forecast *noun* tohu huarere [tohu W.431 'point out, show' huarere TM 'weather']

weather forecaster *noun* matapae huarere [matapae TM 'forecaster' huarere TM 'weather']

weatherboard *noun* koropū [W.145 'built with wrought timber']

weatherboard house *noun* whare koropū [whare W.489 'house' koropū W.145 'built with wrought timber']

weathered *adjective* pūnguru [W.311 'worn down, worn away, blunt']

week *noun* rāwhitu [rā W.319 'day' whitu W.498 'seven']

weekend *noun* paunga rāwhitu [pau W.273 'consumed, exhausted' rāwhitu TM 'week']

weigh *transitive verb* ine taumaha [ine W.78 'measure' taumaha W.399 'heavy']

weight *noun* taumaha [W.399 'heavy']

weight *noun* (*weightlifting*) mōtū [W.211 'a heavy kind of stone used for making sinkers for nets and fishing lines']

weightlifter *noun* kaimōhiki [kai W.86 'a prefix to transitive verbs to form nouns denoting an agent' mōhiki W.205 'raised up, lifted up']

weightlifting *noun* mōhiki [W.205 'raised up, lifted up']

wetsuit *noun* kirirua [W.119 'a black thick-skinned species of eel']

wheel *noun* porotiti [W.295 'disc, teetotum, revolving']

wheel brace *noun* tauteka [W.404 'brace, tighten by twisting, piece of wood used to twist up the lashing of anything in order to tighten it']

wheelchair *noun* kōrea [W.141 'small canoe']

whey *noun* waikuruwhatu [wai W.474 'water, liquid' kurukuruwhatu W.159 'curdled, as milk']

whiff *noun* hīrea [W.53 'faint odour, pleasant or unpleasant']

whisk *noun* kōrori [W.145 'stir round']

whisky *noun* (*golf*) nape [W.218 'make a false stroke with the paddle']

whiteboard *noun* papamā [papa W.259 'anything broad, flat and hard' mā W.161 'white']

whitewater rafting *noun* eke kohuka [eke W.27 'place oneself or be placed upon another object' kohuka W.126 'froth, foam']

wicket *noun* (*strip of ground*) tumu [W.453 'field of battle'], (*stump*) tumutumu [tumu W.453 'stump, stake, field of battle']

wicket-keeper *noun* tautopenga [whakatautopenga W.404 'rearguard']

width *noun* whānui [W.487 'broad, wide']

wig *noun* uru whakapīwari [uru W.469 'hair of the head' whakapīwari W.285 'bedeck, ornament']

win *intransitive verb* toa [W.428 'victorious'], eke panuku [eke panuku 'to hit home' eke W.27 'come to land, reach a summit etc.' panuku W.257 'move on after']

wind dispersal *noun* (*biology*) puananī [W.302 'wind-dispersed seeds']

windbreak *noun* pāhauhau [W.247 'wind screen for crops']

wind-chimes *noun* iere [W.74 'sound of voices, singing']

windscreen *noun* mataaho waka [mataaho W.186 'window' waka TM 'vehicle']

wind-sock *noun* pīwari kai hau [pīwari W.285 'wave in the wind' kai W.85 'eat' hau W.38 'wind, air']

windsurfing *noun* mirihau [haumiri W.41 'hug, sail along the shore']

windsurfing board *noun* mirihau [haumiri W.41 'hug, sail along the shore']

wind-vane *noun* matahau [mata W.185 'face, edge, point' hau W.38 'wind']

wing *noun* (*sport*) paihau [W.249 'wing, side']

wing, left *noun* (*sport*) paihau mauī [paihau W.249 'wing, side' mauī W.196 'left, on the left side']

wing, right *noun* (*sport*) paihau matau [paihau W.249 'wing, side' matau W.192 'right, on the right hand']

wing attack *noun* paihau tuki [paihau W.249 'wing' tuki W.450 'attack']

wing defence *noun* paihau pare [paihau W.249 'wing' pare W.266 'ward off']

winger *noun* (*sport*) paihau [W.249 'wing, side']

winger, left *noun* (*sport*) paihau mauī [paihau W.249 'wing, side' mauī W.196 'left, on the left side']

winger, right *noun* (*sport*) paihau matau [paihau W.249 'wing, side' matau W.192 'right, on the right hand']

winner *noun* toa [W.428 'brave, victorious']

withdrawal slip *noun* tango pūtea [tango W.380 'take away, remove' pūtea TM 'fund']

witness *noun* mataara [W.186 'witness, observe']

wok *noun* pararaha [W.264 'a shallow vessel made by cutting a slice from a gourd, wide and shallow, of a vessel']

women's refuge *noun* whare punanga [whare W.489 'house' punanga W.310 'any place used as a refuge for noncombatants in troubled days. Hence kāinga punanga, whare punanga, pā punanga']

wood *noun* (*golf*) rākau [W.321 'weapon, wooden']

wooden spoon *noun* kape [W.96 'stick for moving or stirring anything']

woodwork *noun* raweke rākau [raweke W.333 'prepare, dress, manipulate, fashion' rākau W.321 'wood, timber']

woody *adjective* (*vegetables*) kākoa [W.92 'full of hard fibres']

word processor *noun* punenga kupu [punenga W.310 'clever, intelligent, always seeking and acquiring useful knowledge' kupu W.157 'word']

work gang *noun* (*of workers*) tokomatua [W.434 'company, band of persons']

workbench *noun* poutaka [W.299 'platform erected on one post']

workbook *noun* pukapuka tuhi [pukapuka W.306 'book' tuhi W.449 'write, draw']

working party *noun* (*committee*) awheawhe [W.24 'work in a body on anything']

workshop *noun* (*seminar*) awheawhe [W.24 'work in a body on anything']

workstation *noun* taupuni mahi [taupuni W.401 'place of assignation' mahi W.163 'work, occupation']

worthwhile *adjective* whaihua [whai W.484 'possessing, equipped with' huanga W.64 'advantage, benefit']

wrench *noun* wāwāhi [W.473 'break, split']

wrestling (*sport*) mamau [W.196 'grasp, grab, wrestle with']

write *transitive verb* (*lettering*) tuhi rere [tuhi W.448 'write' rere W.337 'flow']

writing pad *noun* tuataka tuhi [tuataka W.447 'heap, lying in a heap' tuhi W.449 'write']

written *adjective* ā-tuhi [ā W.1 'after the manner of' tuhi W.448 'write']

written consent *noun* whakaae-ā-tuhi [whakaae W.2 'consent' ā-tuhi TM 'written']

X

x-axis tuaka pae [tuaka W.445 'midrib of leaf' pae W.244 'any transverse beam']

x-ray *noun, transitive verb* whakaata roto [whakaata W.18 'reflect, look, peer into' roto W.348 'the inside']

xylem *noun* (*botany*) tariwai [tari W.391 'carry, bring' wai W.474 'water']

xylophone *noun* pakakau [W.251 'two sticks with which a sort of tune is played']

Y

yacht *noun* pere rua [W.278 'a canoe with two sails']

yachting *noun* pere rua [W.278 'a canoe with two sails']

yarn, to spin a *phrase* (*story-telling*) kōrero ahiahi [W.142 'idle tales']

y-axis tuaka pou [tuaka W.445 'midrib of leaf', poupou W.297 'steep, perpendicular, upright']

yeast *noun* īhi [ī W.73 'ferment, turn sour' hī W.47 'rise']

yellow, golden *adjective* pīngao [W.281 'a plant, the leaves of which dry a bright orange colour']

yoghurt *noun* waipupuru [waiū pupuru W.315 'curdled milk' pupuru 'thick, stiff, semi-solid']

yoke bone *noun* (*anatomy*) wheua pāpāringa [wheua W.496 'bone' pāpāringa W.260 'cheek']

zero *noun* kore [korenga W.141 'non-existence, non-occurrence']

zilch *noun* kore [korenga W.141 'non-existence, non-occurrence']

zinc konutea [konu- TM 'prefix denoting natural metal' tea W.410 'white, clear']

zip *noun* puoto whakawera wai [puoto W.311 'vessel' whaka- W.486 'causative prefix' *to make* wera W.482 'heated, hot' wai W.474 'water']

zodiac *noun* poutiriao [Best *Māori Mythology and Religion* 106 'supernormal beings as guardians and controllers of the different realms of the earth, the heavens, and the oceans']

zoologist *noun* kaimātai kararehe [kaimātai TM '-ologist' kararehe W.99 'quadruped' common usage 'animal']

zoology *noun* mātauranga kararehe [mātauranga common usage 'knowledge' kararehe W.99 'quadruped' common usage 'animal']

zoom lens *noun* arotahi topa [arotahi TM 'lens' topa W.436 'fly, soar, swoop']

Reo Māori – Reo Pākehā
Māori – English

A

aeha *noun* (*golf*) bogey [W.2 'interjection denoting vexation']

ahi tipua *noun* volcano [Best *Tūhoe, Children of the Mist* 977]

aho *noun* (*mathematics*) sine [W.3 'string, line]

aho *noun* (*mathematics*) chord [W.3 'string, line']

aho tātea *noun* spermatic cord [aho W.3 'string, line' tātea TM 'sperm']

aho tuaiwi *noun* spinal cord [aho W.33 'string, line' tuaiwi TM 'spine']

ahoaho *noun* (*music*) stave [aho W.3 'woof, cross threads of a mat']

ahopae *noun* latitude [aho W.3 'string, line, cross threads of a mat' pae W.244 'horizontal ridges, circumference']

ahopou *noun* longitude [aho W.3 'line' poupou W.297 'perpendicular, upright'] *adjective* longitudinal [TM 'longitude']

ahorangi *noun* professor [W.3 'teacher of high standing in the school of learning']

āhua *noun* (*geometric shape*) figure [W.4 'form, appearance']

āhuahanga *noun* geometry [āhua TM 'figure' hanga W.34 'make, build, property']

āhuahanga panoni *noun* transformation geometry [āhuahanga TM 'geometry' panoni TM 'transformation']

āhuatanga *noun* characteristic, property, aspect, feature [W.4 'character, likeness']

āhuatanga matū *noun* chemical property [āhuatanga TM 'property' matū TM 'chemical']

āhuatanga pūmau *noun* invariant property [āhuatanga TM 'characteristic' pūmau TM 'invariant']

āhuatanga rongo *noun* physical property [āhuatanga TM 'property' rongo W.346 'apprehend by the senses']

āhuatanga tinana *noun* (*biology*) physical feature [āhuatanga TM 'feature' tinana W.419 'body']

āhuatanga urutau *noun* adaptive features [āhuatanga TM 'feature' urutau TM 'adapt']

ahumahi *noun* industry [ahu W.3 'tend, foster, fashion' mahi W.163 'work, work at']

ahumahi *adjective* industrial [ahu W.3 'tend, foster, fashion' mahi W.163 'work, work at']

ahumoana *noun* fish farming [ahuwhenua common usage 'agriculture' ahu W.3 'tend, foster' moana W.204 'sea, lake']

ahunga *noun* bearing [ahu W.3 'move in a certain direction']

ahuone *noun* horticulture [ahu W.3 'tend, foster' oneone W.240 'earth, soil, land']

ahuone *adjective* horticultural [ahu W.3 'tend, foster' oneone W.240 'earth, soil, land']

ahupūngao *noun* physics [ahu W.3 'move, point in a certain direction' pūngao TM 'energy']

ahurei *adjective* unique [W.4 'chief, prominent']

ahu-rua *adjective* two-dimensional [ahu W.3 'move in a certain direction' rua W.349 'two']

ahutahi *adjective* (*traffic*) one-way [ahu W.3 'move in a certain direction' tahi W.359 'one, single']

ahu-tengi *adjective* three-dimensional [ahu W.3 'move in a certain direction' tengi W.412 'three']

ahuwhenua *adjective* agricultural [ahuwhenua W.3 'cultivate the soil']

ākahukahu *adjective* abstruse [W.6 'indistinct, scarcely visible']

akakōare *noun* rhizome [akakōareare W.6 'edible rhizome of raupō']

ākau roa *noun* detour [W.6 'circuitous route']

akiaki paturopi *noun* antigen [akiaki W.7 'urge on' paturopi TM 'antibody']

akitū *noun* vertex [W.7 'point, end, summit']

akoranga *noun* lesson [ako W.7 'learn, teach']

akoranga *noun* educational course [W.7 'circumstance of learning']

akoranga me mātua tutuki *noun* (*education*) compulsory course [akoranga TM 'course' mātua W.195 'first' tutuki W.450 'be completed']

akoranga tautokorua *noun* (*education*) co-requisite [akoranga TM 'educational course' tautokorua W.404 'simultaneous, both together']

akoranga tōmua *noun* (*education*) pre-requisite [akoranga TM 'educational course' tōmua W.435 'previous']

akuaku *noun* (*cooking*) rubber scraper [W.7 'scrape out, cleanse']

amiami *noun* herb [W.8 'sweet smelling shrub']

āmiki *noun* (*meeting*) minute-taking [W.8 'tell a story without omitting any particular']

amikuka *noun* dried herbs [amiami TM 'herb' kuka W.155 'dry leaves']

āmikumiku *noun* velodrome [W.8 'make a circuit round']

āmionga *noun* orbit [amio W.8 'circle round']

amiorangi *noun* satellite [amio W.8 'go round about, circle round' rangi W.323 'sky, heaven, upper regions']

ana pākeho *noun* limestone cave [ana W.9 'cave' pākeho W.252 'limestone']

ana roro *noun* (*brain*) ventricle [ana W.9 'cave' roro W.347 'brains']

anaroa *noun* tunnel [ana W.9 'cave' roa W.344 'long']

ānau kati *noun* closed curve [ānau W.9 'curve' kati W.103 'closed']

anuanu *noun* aversion [W.10 'offensive, disgusting']

anga *noun* structure [W.10 'shell, skeleton']

angaroto *noun, adjective* chordate [anga W.10 'skeleton' roto W.348 'inside']

angawaho *noun* arthropod [anga W.10 'skeleton, shell' waho W.474 'the outside']

angitu *adjective* successful [W.11 'luck, success']

angitu *noun* (*success*) coup [W.11 'luck, success']

ao koiora *noun* biosphere [ao W.11 'world' koiora TM 'biology']

ao ōhanga *noun* economy [ao W.11 'world' ōhanga TM 'economics']

ao tukupū *noun* universe [ao W.11 'world' tukupū W.452 'coming down on all sides, covering completely, spread over']

ao tūroa *noun* nature [ao W.11 'world' tūroa W.460 'established, of long standing']

aonanī *noun* Brussels sprouts [ao W.11 'bud' nanī W.218 'wild cabbage']

aorangi *noun* planet [ao W.11 'world' rangi W.323 'sky, heaven, upper regions']

aorangi iti *noun* asteroid [aorangi TM 'planet' iti W.80 'small']

apataki *noun* customer base [W.12 'retinue, following']

apataki *noun* client base [W.12 'retinue, following']

apatono *noun* delegation [apārangi W.12 'company of persons, especially distinguished persons' tono W.436 'demand']

apiapi *adjective* overpopulated [W.12 'crowded, dense']

āpiti poto *noun* (*rugby*) short lineout [āpititū TM 'lineout' poto W.297 'short']

āpititū *noun* (*rugby*) lineout [āpititū W.13 'fight at close quarters'

āpure *noun* (*data-processing*) field [W.13 'patch, circumscribed area']

āpure ika *noun* local non-commercial fishing zone [āpure W.13 'patch, circumscribed area' ika W.76 'fish']

āpure moana *noun* marine reserve [āpure W.13 'patch, circumscribed area' moana W.204 'sea, lake']

āpure punanga *noun* safety zone [āpure W.13 patch, circumscribed area' punanga W.310 'any place used as a refuge for non-combatants in troubled days']

āpure tautuku *noun* penalty area [āpure W.13 'patch, circumscribed area' tautuku W.405 'stoop, bend down; so give way']

āpure tīpao *noun* putting green [āpure W.13 'patch, circumscribed area' tīpao TM 'putt, putter']

āputa *noun* (*punctuation*) dash [W.13 'causing a gap']

ara amio *noun* (*cycling, horse-racing*) circuit [ara W.13 'way, path' amio W.8 'circle round']

ara amio *noun* (*athletics*) track [ara W.13 'way, path' amio W.8 'circle round']

ara iahiko *noun* (*electricity*) circuit [ara W.13 'way, path' iahiko TM 'electric current']

ara (iahiko) hātepe *noun* series circuit [ara iahiko TM 'circuit' hātepe W.38 'follow in regular sequence']

ara (iahiko) whakarara *noun* parallel circuit [ara iahiko TM 'circuit' whakarara TM 'parallel']

ara kaipara *noun* (*athletics*) track [ara W.13 'way, path' kaipara TM 'athletics']

ara maiangi *noun* escalator [ara W.13 'means of conveyance' maiangi W.166 'rise up']

ara nekeneke *noun* conveyor belt [ara W.13 'means of conveyance' nekeneke W.220 'move gradually']

ara o Hinekirikiri *noun* tidal zone [ara W.13 'way, path' Hinekirikiri personification hine W.51 'girl, chiefly used in addressing a girl or young woman' kirikiri W.119 'gravel' common usage 'sandy']

ara tātea *noun* vas deferens [ara W.13 'way, means of conveyance' tātea W.394 'semen']

ara tauoma *noun* (*course*) track [ara W.13 'way, path' tauomaoma TM 'race']

ara tautika *noun* equal opportunities [ara W.13 'path' tautika W.404 'even, level, straight']

arahāmoa *noun* (*gun*) barrel [ara W.13 'means of conveyance' hāmoamoa TM 'bullet']

arahipa *noun* passing-lane [ara W.13 'path' hipa W.52 'pass, go by']

ārai hapū *noun* contraceptive [ārai W.14 'ward off' hapū W.36 'pregnant']

ārai hauata mahi *noun* occupational safety [ārai W.14 'keep off, ward off' hauata W.40 'accident' mahi W.163 'work']

ārai mate *noun* immunity [ārai W.14 'ward off, obstruct' mate W.192 'sickness']

ārai tinana *noun* body protection [ārai W.14 'ward off' tinana W.419 'body']

ārai whara *noun* injury prevention [ārai W.14 'ward off' whara W.489 'be struck, be hit accidentally']

ārai-ā-ngaoaho *noun* (*science*) light-dependent resistor [ārai W.14 'ward off' ā W.1 'after the manner of' ngao W.229 'strength, energy' aho W.3 'radiant light']

aramatā *noun* (*gun*) barrel [ara W.13 'means of conveyance' matā W.185 'bullet']

arapoka *noun* tunnel [ara W.13 'way, path' poka W.288 'bore, dig out']

araputa *noun* way out [ara W.13 'way, path' puta W.315 'come, come forth, come out']

ararewa *noun* elevator [ara W.13 'means of conveyance' rewa W.339 'be elevated, be high up']

ararewa *noun* (*elevator*) lift [ara W.13 'means of conveyance' rewa W.339 'be elevated']

aratohu *noun* guideline [ara W.13 'way, path' tohu W.431 'show']

aratuku *noun* (*radio*) air waves [ara W.13 'way, path, means of conveyance' tuku W.451 'send']

aratuku *noun* radio frequency [ara W.13 'way, path' tuku W.451 'send']

aratuku poto *noun* short wave [aratuku TM 'radio frequency' poto W.297 'short']

aratuku roa *noun, adjective* (*radio*) long wave [aratuku TM 'radio frequency' roa W.344 'long']

ārau *noun, transitive verb* (*volleyball*) block [W.14 'gather, entangle']

ārau hē *noun* (*volleyball*) illegal block [ārau TM 'block' hē W.43 'wrong, error']

arawai *noun* waterway [ara W.13 'way, path' wai W.474 'water']

arawhiti *noun* bridge [ara W.13 'way, path' whiti W.497 'cross over, reach the opposite side']

arawhiti rangitahi *noun* bailey bridge [arawhiti TM 'bridge' rangitahi W.324 'ephemeral, transient']

ariā *noun* theory [W.15 'notion, idea, feeling, be seen indistinctly']

aro *noun* suet [W.16 'fat covering the kidneys']

aro mahana *noun* warm front [aro W.16 'front' mahana W.162 'warm']

aro mātao *noun* cold front [aro W.16 'front' mātao W.189 'cold']

aro pahoho *noun* stationary front [aro W.16 'front' pahoho W.248 'still, immovable, quiet']

aro whānui *adjective* (*norm*) standard [aro W.16 'turn towards, be inclined, favour' whānui W.487 'broad, wide']

ā-rohe *adjective* local, regional [ā W.1 'after the manner of' rohe W.344 'boundary']

aromahana *adjective* tepid [W.17 'lukewarm']

aromātai *transitive verb* evaluate [aro W.16 'consider, think' mātai W.187 'inspect, examine'], *noun* evaluation [TM 'evaluate']

aromatawai *transitive verb* assess [aro W.16 'turn towards' matawai W.192 'look closely']

aromatawai *noun* assessment [TM 'assess']

aronga kē *adjective* (*mathematics*) non-standard [aro W.16 'face, turn towards, be inclined, be disposed' kē W.111 'different, of another kind']

aropā *noun* cohort [W.17 'clump of one species of tree']

aropā *noun* peer group [W.17 'clump of one species of tree']

arotahi *transitive verb* take aim [W.17 'look in one direction, look steadily']

arotahi *noun, transitive verb* focus [W.17 'look in one direction, look steadily']

arotahi *noun* lens [W.17 'look in one direction, look steadily']

arotahi hakoko *noun* concave lens [arotahi TM 'lens' hakoko W.32 'concave']

arotahi takarepa *noun* (*vision*) astigmatism [arotahi TM 'lens' takarepa W.369 'deficient, imperfect']

arotahi topa *noun* zoom lens [arotahi TM 'lens' topa W.436 'fly, soar, swoop']

arotahi whakarahi *noun* (*microscope*) objective lens [arotahi TM 'lens' whakarahi TM 'enlarge']

arotake *transitive verb* assess, evaluate, review [aro W.16 'consider, think' take W.370 'base, cause, reason']

arotake *noun* assessment [TM 'assess']

arotake pukapuka *noun* book review [arotake TM 'review' pukapuka W.306 'book']

arotakenga *noun* evaluation [arotake TM 'evaluate']

aroturuki *transitive verb* monitor [aro W.16 'consider, think' turuki W.461 'come as a supplement, follow, reinforce']

aruaru *intransitive verb* interject [W.17 'interrupt']

arumoni *adjective* commercial [aru W.17 'follow, pursue' moni < Eng. 'money']

ata *noun* (*computer*) icon [W.18 'form, shape, semblance']

ata tāhapa *noun* refraction [ata W.18 'form, shape, reflected image' tāhapa W.358 'at an acute angle']

āta tuhi *transitive verb* (*lettering*) print [āta W.17 'slowly, clearly' tuhi W.448 'write']

ataata *adjective* video [ata W.18 'reflected image']

ataata-rongo *adjective* audio-visual [ataata TM 'video' rongo W.346 'hear']

atarua *noun* blurred vision [W.18 'dim-sighted']

ā-tau *adjective* annual [ā W.1 'after the manner of' tau W.395 'year']

ate *adjective* hepatic [W.19 'liver']

ate kakā *noun* hepatitis [ate W.19 'liver' kakā TM 'inflammation']

ate ūtonga *noun* liver cirrhosis [ate W.19 'liver' ūtonga W.471 'hard, hardened']

ātea *adjective* (*cricket*) off-side [W.19 'clear, free from obstruction, out of the way']

ateate *noun* gastrocnemius muscle [W.19 'calf of the leg']

atoato *noun* marshal [W.19 'marshal, regulate the formation of a corps on the march']

atoato *noun* official [W.19 'marshal, regulate the formation of a corps on the march']

atoato waka *noun* parking warden [atoato TM 'marshal' waka common usage 'vehicle']

atorua *noun* marquee [W.20 'a long temporary house used for a feast']

ā-tuhi *adjective* written [ā W.1 'after the manner of' tuhi W.448 'write']

auaha *adjective* creative [W.21 'leap, throb, create, form, fashion']

auahatanga *noun* creativeness [auaha TM 'creative']

auau *noun* frequency [auau W.21 'frequently, again and again']

auau 150

auau *adjective* recurring [W.21 'frequently repeated, again and again']
auau *noun* rate [W.21 'frequently repeated, again and again, frequently']
auau oma *noun* (*cricket*) run rate [auau TM 'frequency' oma W.239 'run']
aukati *adjective* (*language*) exclusive [W.22 'line which one may not pass']
aukati *noun* roadblock [W.22 'stop one's way, prevent one from passing, line which one may not pass']
aukati *transitive verb* (*justice*) discriminate [W.22 'stop one's way, prevent one from passing, line which one may not pass']
aukati *noun* (*justice*) discrimination [W.22 'stop one's way, prevent one from passing, line which one may not pass']
aukati iwi *noun* racism [aukati TM 'discrimination' iwi W.80 'nation, people']
aukume *noun* magnet [au W.20 'current' kume W.155 'pull, drag']
aukume *adjective* magnetic [TM 'magnet']
aukume *noun* magnetic force [TM 'magnet']
aukume-ā-hiko *noun* electromagnet [au W.20 'current, whirlpool' kume W.155 'drag, pull' ā W.1 'after the manner of' hiko common usage 'electricity']
aumanga *noun* vent [W.22 'a hollowed-out space, on the underside of the ridge-pole immediately over the front wall of a house, designed as a smoke vent']
aumoana *adjective* blue-grey [W.22 'blue clay, open sea']
aunoa *adjective* automatic [au W.20 'current, whirlpool' noa W.222 'spontaneously']
auporo *noun* (*industrial*) strike [W.22 'cut short, stop']
aupuru koko *noun* (*boxing*) corner pad [aupuru W.22 'cushion or pad under a load to prevent chafing' koko W.130 'corner']
autaki *noun* detour [W.23 'roundabout, circuitous']
autangi *noun* string instrument [au W.20 'string, cord' tangi W.379 'sound, give forth a sound']
autaua *noun* commentator [W.23 'one who announces the approach of a fighting party']

autui *noun* safety-pin [W.23 'a cloak pin of whalebone or boar's tusk']
awa *noun* canal [W.23 'channel, river, gorge']
awa hau *noun* nasal passage [awa W.23 'channel, river' hau W.38 'breath']
awa ihu *noun* nasopharynx [awa W.23 'channel, river' ihu W.75 'nose']
awa kōpaka *noun* glacier [awa W.23 'river, gully, gorge' kōpaka W.135 'ice, frost']
awa mimi *noun* (*anatomy*) urethra [awa W.23 'channel, river' mimi W.202 'urine']
awa o te atua *noun* menstrual cycle [awa W.23 'river' atua W.20 'menses']
awa peopeo *noun* water-slide [awa W.23 'channel, river' peopeo W.277 'slippery']
awa pūtake *noun* (*tooth*) root canal [awa W.23 'channel' pūtake W.316 'root']
awa taringa *noun* ear canal [awa W.23 'channel' taringa W.391 'ear']
awa tātea *noun* spermatic canal [awa W.23 'channel' tātea TM 'sperm']
awa tuaiwi *noun* spinal canal [awa W.23 'channel' tuaiwi TM 'spine']
awa wahine *noun* menstrual cycle [awa W.23 'river' wahine W.474 'woman']
awahae *noun* (*botany*) style [awa W.23 'channel, river' hae W.29 'pollen']
awahuke *noun* lode [awa W.23 'furrow, channel' huke W.68 'dig up, expose by removing the earth, excavate']
awatea *adjective* diurnal [W.24 'broad daylight']
awe wairua *noun* psyche [Best *Spiritual and Mental Concepts* 16]
aweawe *adjective* pompous [W.24 'distant, out of reach']
āwenewene *noun* saccharine [W.24 'very sweet']
āwenewene *noun* artificial sweetener [W.24 'very sweet']
awhe *transitive verb* box in [W.24 'hem in, surround']
awhe hua *noun* egg-ring [awhe W.24 'hem in, encircle' hua W.64 'egg of a bird']
awhe-ararau *noun* orienteering [awhe W.24 'go, travel' ara W.13 'path' rau W.328 'hundred, number']
awheawhe *noun* (*committee*) working party [W.24 'work in a body on anything']
awheawhe *noun* (*seminar*) workshop [W.24 'work in a body on anything']

E

e waru pū *phrase* (*cricket*) out for a duck [W.480 'not at all, by no means']

eke kohuka *noun* whitewater rafting [eke W.27 'place oneself or be placed upon another object' kohuka W.126 'froth, foam']

eke ngaru *noun* boogie-boarding [eke W.27 'generally place oneself or be placed upon another object' ngaru W.230 'wave']

eke pai *phrase* (*golf*) par the course, par the hole [W.27 'get aground, come to land' pai W.249 'suitable, satisfactory']

eke panuku *intransitive verb* win [eke panuku common usage 'to hit home' eke W.27 'come to land, reach a summit etc.' panuku W.257 'move on after']

eke panuku *phrase* (*sport*) to win match, (*golf*) under par, (*netball, soccer etc.*) to win game [eke W.27 'come to land' panuku W.257 'move on after']

eke tangaroa *phrase* to win championship, to win a final [eke W.27 'come to land' eke tangaroa common usage 'strike home' tangaroa common usage 'God of the sea']

epa *noun, transitive verb* (*cricket*) bowl [W.28 'throw, cast']

epa *noun* (*softball*) pitch [W.28, 'throw, cast, pelt']

epa ātea *noun* (*cricket*) off-break [epa TM 'bowl' ātea TM 'off-side']

epa akitō *noun* slow bowl [epa TM 'bowl' akitō W.7 'be slow, lengthened out']

epa hē *noun* illegal pitch [epa TM 'pitch' hē TM 'illegal']

epa māminga *noun* (*softball*) change up [epa TM 'pitch' māminga W.172 'use anything for the purposes of deception, feign']

epa maurua *noun* seam bowl [epa TM 'bowl' maurua W.198 'seam between two widths of floor mat']

epa piki *noun* (*softball*) rise [epa TM 'pitch' piki W.280 'ascend']

epa rere *noun* fast bowl [epa TM 'bowl' rere W.337 'rush, hasten']

epa taka *noun* (*softball pitch*) drop [epa TM 'pitch' taka W.366 'fall away']

epa tataha whakaroto *noun* inswinger [epa TM 'bowl' tataha W.357 'swerve' whakaroto TM 'inwards']

epa tataha whakawaho *noun* outswinger [epa TM 'bowl' tataha W.357 'swerve' whakawaho TM 'outwards']

epa tāwhiro ātea *noun* off-spinner [epa TM 'bowl' tāwhirowhiro W.409 'whirl, spin' ātea TM 'off-side']

epa tāwhiro wae *noun* leg-spinner [epa TM 'bowl' tāwhirowhiro W.409 'turn, whirl, spin' wae W.472 'leg']

epa tāwhirowhiro *noun* spin bowl [epa TM 'bowl' tāwhirowhiro W.409 'whirl spin']

epa tōkiri *noun* torpedo throw [epa W.28 'throw, cast' tōkiri W.434 'thrust lengthwise']

epa tūpana *noun* bouncer [epa TM 'bowl' tūpana W.456 'spring up, recoil']

epa wī *noun* (*cricket*) blockholer [epa W.28 'throw, cast' wī TM 'crease']

ero *adjective* septic [W.28 'putrid']

ewaro *noun* ethane [e < Eng. 'e-' waro TM 'alkane']

H

hā whakaora *noun* rescue breathing [hā W.29 'breath' whakaora W.241 'save alive, restore to health']

haepapa *noun* (*equity*) justice [W.30 'straight, correct']

haere pakituri *intransitive verb* hitch-hike [W.254 'to go on foot']

hahau *noun* (*golf*) stroke [W.39 'strike, smite']

hahau *noun* (*golf*) swing [W.39 'strike, smite']

hahau *noun* chemotherapy [W.39 'a charm for curing tumours']

hahau tautuku *noun* penalty stroke [hahau W.39 'strike, smite, deal blows to' tautuku TM 'penalty']

hahaupōro *noun* golf [hahau W.39 'strike, smite' pōro < Eng. 'ball']

hāheke *noun* falling intonation [hā W.29 'sound, tone of voice' heke W.44 'descend']

hai *noun* (*softball*) pinch-hitter [W.30 'the name of the principal stone in the game of ruru']

haitutu *adjective* muggy [W.31 'close, oppressive, of atmosphere']

hake *noun* hockey [W.31 'humped, crooked']

hake ukauka *noun* cash register [hake W.31 'a wooden bowl or trough' ukauka TM 'cash']

hakehakeā *noun* (*hockey*) bully off [W.31 'facing one, opposite' hake TM 'hockey']

hakehakeā tautuku *noun* penalty bully [hakehakeā TM 'bully off' tautuku W.405 'stoop, bend down; so give way']

haki kairota *noun* linesman's flag [haki common usage 'flag' kairota TM 'linesman']

hākinakina *noun* recreation [W.32 'sport, enjoy oneself']

hākinakina tauwhāinga *noun* competition sport [hākinakina TM 'sport' tauwhāinga W.405 'contend, vie']

hākinakina whakataetae *noun* competition sport [hākinakina TM 'sport' whakataetae W.356 'try strength, contend']

hako *noun* clown [whakahako W.32 'bedeck oneself']

hakune *adjective* methodical [W.32 'be deliberate, be careful']

hamanga-rau *adjective* polyunsaturated [hamanga W.33 'not full' rau W.328 'multitude, many']

hāmene whakaea nama *noun* default summons [hāmene < Eng. 'summons' whakaea W.26 'pay for' nama common usage 'debt']

hāmoamoa *noun* (*ammunition*) pellet, bullet [W.33 'small spherical stones which were used as bullets']

hamu *noun* scavenger [hamuhamu TM 'scavenge']

hamuhamu *intransitive verb* scavenge [W.33 'eat scraps of food']

hamupirau *noun* (*biology*) saprophyte [hamuhamu W.33 'eat scraps of food' pirau W.283 'rotten, decay, death']

hana *noun* (*oven*) pilot light [W.33 'shine, glow, flame']

hānea *noun* armchair [hāneanea W.33 'pleasant, comfortable']

hāneanea *noun* (*furniture*) settee, lounge suite [W.33 'pleasant, comfortable']

hānene *intransitive verb* breathe gently [W.33 'blowing gently' hā W.29 'breath, breathe']

hanumi *transitive verb (computer)* merge [W.34 'be merged or swallowed up']

hanumi *adjective* homogenised [W.34 'be merged, swallowed up, be mixed']

hanga *noun* shape [W.34 'build, fashion']

hanga metarahi *noun* civil engineer [hanga W.34 'make, build, fashion, thing' metarahi W.201 'great']

hanga pūngao *noun* respiration [hanga W.34 'make, build' pūngao TM 'energy']

hāngai *adjective* relevant [W.34 'opposite, confronting, at right angles']

hāngai *adjective* right-angled [W.34 'at right angles']

hangarau *noun* technology [hanga W.34 'make, fashion, work, business' rau W.328 'multitude, number']

hangarau kai *noun* food technology [hangarau TM 'technology' kai W.85 'food']

hangarau-koiora *noun* biotechnology [hangarau TM 'technology' mātauranga koiora TM 'biology']

hangarite *noun* symmetry, *adjective* symmetrical [hanga TM 'shape' rite W.343 'alike, corresponding']

hangarite huri *noun* rotational symmetry [hangarite TM 'symmetry' huri TM 'rotate']

hangarite hurihanga *noun* rotational symmetry [hangarite TM 'symmetry' hurihanga TM 'rotation']

hangarite rārangi *noun* line symmetry [hangarite TM 'symmetry' rārangi W.324 'line']

hangarite whakaata *noun* reflection symmetry [hangarite TM 'symmetry' whakaata TM 'reflect']

hangarua *transitive verb* recycle [hanga W.34 'make, build, fashion' rua W.349 'two, second']

hāora *noun* oxygen [hā W.29 'breath, breathe' ora W.241 'alive']

hāora ota-rua *noun* nitrous oxide [hāora TM 'oxygen' hauota TM 'nitrogen' rua W.349 'two']

hāora toro *noun* visiting hours [hāora < Eng. 'hour' toro W.439 'go to see, visit']

hapa *noun (error)* fault [W.35 'crooked, be in need of anything']

hapa pokerenoa *noun* intentional foul [hapa TM 'fault' pokerenoa W.290 'wilful, reckless']

hapa tū *noun (sport)* positional error [hapa TM 'fault' tū W.443 'stand']

hapa-ā-ringa *phrase (volleyball)* hand-over-net [hapa TM 'fault' ā W.1 'after the manner of' ringa W.341 'hand']

hapa-ā-ringa *noun (soccer)* handball [hapa TM 'fault' ā W.1 'after the manner of' ringa W.341 'hand']

hāparapara *transitive verb* to perform surgery, *adjective* surgical, *adverb* surgically [W.35 'cut, sever']

haparua *noun* double fault [hapa TM 'fault' rua W.349 'two']

hapawae *noun* foot-fault [hapa TM 'fault' wae W.472 'foot']

hapawene *noun* multiple foul [hapa TM 'foul' wene W.482 'many, numerous']

hāpiapia *adjective* gelatinous [W.36 'sticky, clammy' pia W.279 'gum of trees or any similar exudation']

hāpiapia *noun* sellotape [W.36 'sticky, clammy']

hapori *noun* community, *adjective* social [W.36 'section of a tribe, family']

hapori whānui *noun* society [hapori TM 'community, social' whānui W.487 'broad, wide']

hāpua ruku *noun* diving pool [hāpua W.36 'pool, lagoon' ruku W.351 'dive']

hāpua whakatara *noun (steeplechase)* water-jump [TM 'water hazard']

hāpua whakatara *noun (golf)* water hazard [hāpua W.36 'pool, lagoon' whakatara W.386 'challenge, put on one's mettle']

hara *noun* infringement, *(sport)* offence, foul [W.36 'sin, offence']

hara kaikoka *noun* violent crime [taihara TM 'crime' kaikoka W.88 'violent']

hara kōti matua *noun* indictable offence [hara W.36 'offence' Kōti Matua TM 'supreme court']

hara namunamu *noun* minor offence [hara W.36 'sin, offence' namunamu W.217 'small, diminutive']

hara tautuku *phrase (sport)* to be penalised [hara W.36 'sin, offence' tautuku W.405 'stoop, bend down; so give way']

hara tinana *noun* personal foul [hara TM 'foul' tinana W.419 'body, trunk, person']

hārakiraki *adjective* unreliable [W.36 'inconstancy, erratic disposition']

harangotengote *adjective* part-time [W.37 'do piecemeal or by instalments']

hararua *noun* double foul [hara TM 'foul' rua W.349 'two']

haratau *noun* craft [W.37 'dexterous, suitable, approved']

haratau *noun* craftsperson [haratau W.37 'dexterous, suitable, approved']

haratua *noun* longitudinal section [W.37 'dress timber longitudinally, cut, gash']

hāraurau *adjective* nebulous [W.37 'see or hear indistinctly' hārau 'feel for with the hand, grope for']

hārua *noun (physics)* trough [W.38 'depression, valley']

hātare pūtau-tahi *noun* protozoa [hātaretare TM 'invertebrate' pūtau-tahi TM 'single-celled']

hātaretare *noun, adjective* invertebrate [W.38 'slug or snail']

hātepe *noun* process [W.38 'proceed in an orderly manner, follow in regular sequence']

hātepe *noun* algorithm [W.38 'proceed in an orderly manner, follow a sequence']

hātepe *noun (gymnastics)* routine [W.38 'proceed in an orderly manner, follow in regular sequence']

hātepe ture *noun* legal process [hātepe TM 'process' ture TM 'legal']

hatete *noun* burner [W.38 'fire']

hatete *noun (appliance)* heater [W.38 'fire']

hau *noun* gas [W.38 'wind, air']

hau arenga *noun, transitive verb (golf)* shank [hau W.39 'strike, smite' arenga W.14 'point of a weapon']

hau kōwhai *noun* fluorine [hau TM 'gas' kōwhai common usage 'yellow']

hau māota *noun* chlorine [hau TM 'gas' māota W.179 'green']

hau manawa *noun* natural gas [hau TM 'gas' manawa W.174 'bowels of the earth']

hau rite *noun* equivalent fraction [hautau TM 'fraction' [hautau TM 'fraction' taurite TM 'equivalent']

hau rūnā *noun* simplest form of fraction [hautau TM 'fraction' rūnā W.352 'reduce, pare down']

hau taurite *noun* equivalent fraction [hau TM 'fraction' taurite TM 'equivalent']

hauā *adjective* disabled [W.39 'cripple, crippled']

hauā-pekewhā *adjective, noun* quadriplegic [hauā W.39 'crippled' peke W.276 'limb, generally' whā W.484 'four']

hauāuki *noun* permanent disability [hauā TM 'disabled' āuki W.22 'old, of long standing' ukiuki W.466 'lasting, continuous']

hauhā *noun* carbon dioxide [hau TM 'gas' whakahā W.29 'emit breath']

hauhauaitu *noun* hypothermia [W.39 'pinched with cold, listless, weak']

haukere *noun, transitive verb (sport)* smash [hau W.39 'strike, smite' kere W.114 'intensive, used with words of breaking']

haukeri *noun (language)* primary stress [hau W.38 'wind, air, breath' keri W.114 'rush along violently, as the wind']

haukini *noun* ammonia [hau TM 'gas' kini W.118 'acrid, pungent']

haukino *noun* carbon monoxide [hau TM 'gas' kino W.118 'bad']

haukiore *noun (language)* weak stress [hau W.38 'wind, air, breath' manawa-kiore W.174 'the last faint breath of a dying man']

haukiri *noun* autobiography [hau W.39 'resound, be published abroad' kiri W.119 'person, self']

haukore *adjective (tyre)* flat [hau W.38 'air' kore W.140 'no, not']

haukori *noun* aerobics [W.40 'move briskly']

haukoti *noun (mathematics)* intercept [W.40 'intercept, cut off']

haukura *noun (gas)* neon [hau TM 'gas' kura W.157 'red, glowing, precious']

haukuru *noun (basketball)* jam [W.40 'smash' kuru W.159 'strike with the fist, thump']

haukuru *noun, transitive verb (volleyball)* spike [W.40 'smash']

haukuru *transitive verb, noun (cricket, etc.)* hit, *(softball)* hit, strike, *(golf)* drive [W.40 'smash']

haumāmā *noun* helium [hau TM 'gas' māmā W.161 'light, not heavy']

haumano *(prefix)* milli- [hautau TM 'fraction' mano W.176 'thousand']

haumanu *noun* therapy [W.40 'revive, restore to health']

haumanu *adjective* therapeutic [W.40 'revive, restore to health']

haumanu iraruke *noun* radiotherapy [haumanu W.40 'revive, restore to health' iraruke TM 'radiation']

haumaru *adjective* safe [whakahau W.39 'shelter' maru W.184 'shelter, shield, safeguard']

haumatapū *noun (language)* secondary stress [hau W.38 'air, wind, breath' matapū W.190 'a wind']

haumi *intransitive verb (finance)* invest [W.40 'reserve, lay aside, lengthen by addition']

haumi *noun (finance)* investment [W.40 'reserve, lay aside, lengthen by addition']

haumi popoto *noun (finance)* short-term investment [haumi TM 'investment' poto W.297 'short']

haumi roroa *noun (finance)* long-term investment [haumi TM 'investment' roa W.344 'long']

haumura *noun* flammable gas [hau TM 'gas' mura W.214 'blaze, flame']

haumuri *noun (language)* tertiary stress [hau W.38 'air, wind, breath' muri W.214 'breeze, afterwards']

hauora hinengaro *noun* mental health [hauora W.41 'health, vigour' hinengaro W.51 'seat of the thoughts and emotions']

hauota *noun* nitrogen [hau TM 'gas' ota W.242 'vegetation']

haupara *noun (vehicle)* exhaust [hau TM 'gas' para W.262 'impurity, waste']

haupārua *noun (sport, result)* draw, tie, *(tennis)* deuce [W.41 'fight with loss on both sides']

haupatu *noun (sport)* volley [W.41 'strike, dash, assault']

haupōro *noun (sport)* golf club [hahau W.39 'strike, smite' pōro < Eng. 'ball']

haupū rawa *noun (accounting)* capital [haupū W.41 'heap, mound, lie in a heap' rawa W.331 'goods, property']

hāura *adjective* basic brown [W.41 'brown']

hāura pango *adjective* black-brown [hāura W.41 'brown' pango W.258 'black']

hauraro *noun, adjective* subscript [W.31 'low down, pendent']

hauraro *adjective (clothing)* full-length [W.41 'low, pendent']

hāuratea *adjective* pale brown [hāura W.41 'brown' tea W.410 'light in colour']

hāurauri *adjective* dark brown [hāura W.41 'brown' uri W.469 'dark, deep in colour']

haurewa *noun, transitive verb (golf)* chip [hau W.39 'strike, smite' rewa W.339 'float, be high up']

hauroki *noun, adjective* diagonal [hauroki W.41 'the diagonals in measuring the ground plan of a house']

haurongo *noun* biography [hau W.39 'resound, be published abroad' rongo W.346 'tidings, report, fame']

hautai *noun* stamp pad, ink pad [W.42 'sponge']

hautaka *noun (publication)* journal, a periodical [hau W.39 'be published abroad, report' taka W.366 'come round, as a date or period of time etc.']

hautau *noun* fraction, fractional number [hau W.39 'excess parts, fraction over any complete measurement' tau TM 'number']

hautau ngahuru *noun* decimal fraction [hautau TM 'fraction' ngahuru TM 'decimal']

hautau-ā-ira *noun* decimal fraction [hautau TM 'fraction' tau-ā-ira TM 'decimal']

hautō *noun (furniture)* drawer [W.42 'draw, drag']

hauwai *noun* hydrogen [hau TM 'gas' wai W.474 'water']

hauwhā *noun* quarter [hautau TM 'fraction' whā W.484 'four']

hauwhiti *noun* croquet [hau W.39 'strike, smite' whiti W.498 'pass through, hoop']

hāwaiwai *noun* irrigate [whā W.484 'causative prefix' wai W.474 'water']

hāwaiwai *transitive verb (plants etc.)* water [whā W.484 'causative prefix' wai W.474 'water']

hāwatewate *adjective* phoney [W.43 'false, untrue']

hē *adjective* incorrect [W.43 'wrong, erring, mistaken']

hē ā-ture *adjective* illegal [hē W.43 'wrong, erring, fault' ā W.1 'after the manner of' ture W.459 'law']

he momo *phrase* heredity [W.208 'blood, breed, offspring']

he tikanga, he pononga *noun* affidavit [W.291 'an expression of emphatic assent, approval or affirmation']

he tikanga, he pononga *adjective* axiomatic [W.291 'an expression of emphatic assent, approval or affirmation']

hēhē *noun* false start [W.43 'wrong, not fulfilling requirements']

heipū *transitive verb* chance on [W.44 'coming or going straight towards, hitting exactly']

heipūtanga *noun* chance [heipū W.44 'hitting exactly']

heitara *transitive verb* defame [W.44 'accusation, charge, scandal']

heitara *noun* defamation [W.44 'accusation, charge, scandal']

hekenga uara *noun* depreciation [heke W.44 'descend, ebb' uara TM 'value']

hekerangi *noun, intransitive verb* parachute [heke W.44 'descend' rangi W.323 'sky']

hekerangi *noun* parachuting [heke W.44 'descend' rangi W.323 'sky']

hemarehe *adjective* left-handed [hema W.45 'left hand' rehe W.333 'expert, neat-handed, deft person']

hemi *noun* (*cricket, score*) extra [hemihemi W.45 'excess over a definite number']

henga *noun* tea break, smoko [W.46 'food for a working party']

here *noun* lien [W.46 'tie, tie up']

here *noun* (*restriction*) condition [W.46 'tie up, fasten with cords']

here *noun* (*restriction*) limit [W.46 'tie up, fasten with cords']

here ngaiaku *noun* nylon cord [here W.46 'string or cord to tie with' ngaiaku TM 'nylon']

herekore *adjective* (*mathematics*) associative [here W.46 'tie, tie up' kore W.140 'no, not']

herenga waka *noun* marina [here W.46 'tie, tie up, fasten with cords' waka common usage 'boat']

herepū *noun* (*seize goods etc.*) embargo [W.46 'seize, catch and hold firmly']

hererapa *noun* rubber band [here W.46 'tie, tie up, fasten with cords' rapa < Eng. 'rubber']

hereumu *noun* bakery [W.46 'cooking shed, kitchen']

hewaro *noun* (*chemistry*) heptane [he < Eng. 'hep-' waro TM 'alkane']

hiato *adjective* composite [W.48 'be gathered together']

hiatonga *noun* aggregate [hiato W.48 'be gathered together']

hīeweewe *noun* chromatography [W.48 'separated, disengaged, divided']

hihi *noun* (*mathematics*) ray [W.48 'ray of sun']

hihi *noun* radar beam [W.48 'ray']

hihi irirangi *noun* aerial [hihi W.48 'long plume, feelers of crayfish, long slender appendages' reo irirangi W.80 'radio']

hihi katikati *noun* ultra-violet ray [hihi W.48 'ray of the sun' katikati W.103 'bite frequently, of action of the sun']

hihi pōkākā *noun* infra-red rays [hihi W.48 'ray' pōkākā W.289 'heat']

hihi taiaho *noun* laser beam [hihi W.49 'ray of the sun' taiaho TM 'laser']

hihiani *noun* radar [hihi W.48 'ray' ani W.9 'resounding, echoing']

hihinga *noun* (*electromagnetic*) spectrum [hihi W.48 'ray of the sun']

hihira *transitive verb* (*inspect*) check [W.52 'go over carefully']

hihira matapōkere *noun, transitive verb* (*test*) spot check [hihira TM 'check' matapōkere TM 'random']

hīkaro *transitive verb* infer [W.49 'extract, pick out']

hīkaro *noun* inference [TM 'infer']

hikawe *adjective* portable [W.49 'carry a burden']

hīkawekawe *noun* (*goods*) deliveries [hikawe W.49 'carry a burden']

hīkeikei *noun* hopscotch [W.49 'hop']

hiki *transitive verb* adjourn [W.49 'lift up']

hiki *adjective* adjourned [TM 'adjourn']

hikituri *noun* (*aerobics*) doggy lifts [hiki W.49 'lift up, raise' turi W.459 'knee']

hikiwaka *noun* (*vehicle*) jack [hiki W.49 'lift up, raise' waka common usage 'vehicle']

hiko *noun* electric shock [common usage 'electricity']

hiko *noun* (*electricity*) power [common usage 'electricity']

hiko *adjective* electronic [common usage 'electricity']

hiku *noun* (*word-processing*) footer [W.50 'tail of fish, rear of army etc.']

hiku *noun* fullback [W.50 'rear of an army on march']

hiku *noun* suffix [W.50 'tail of a fish or reptile, rear of an army']

hiku huriaro *noun* passive suffix [hiku TM 'suffix' huriaro TM 'passive']

hiku whēkau *noun* (*anatomy*) appendix [hiku W.50 'tail, rear, tip' whēkau W.493 'entrails']

hiku whēkau kakā *noun* appendicitis [hiku whēkau TM 'appendix' kakā TM 'inflammation']

hikumahi *noun adverb* [hiku W.50 'tail of a fish or reptile, rear of an army' kupumahi TM 'verb']

hikupeke *noun* miniskirt [W.50 'hanging down a short distance']

hikurere *noun* shawl [W.50 'a small garment for the shoulders']

hikuroa *noun* entourage [W.68 'train, retinue']

hikutimo *noun* scorpion [hiku W.50 'tail of a fish or reptile' timo W.418 'prick, strike with a pointed instrument']

hikuwai *noun* reservoir [W.50 'source of a stream']

hikuwaru *adjective (shape)* irregular [W.50 'crooked, asymmetrical']

hikuwaru *noun* scalene [W.50 'crooked, asymmetrical']

hīmoemoe *adjective* acidic [hīmoemoe W.50 'acid, sour' moemoe W.205 'sour, acid, i.e., causing one to close the eyes']

hinengaro *adjective* psychological [W.51 'seat of the thoughts and emotions']

hinengaro hauā *adjective* intellectually handicapped [hinengaro W.51 'seat of the thoughts and emotions' hauā W.39 'lame, crippled']

hinengaro makere *adjective* absent-minded [hinengaro W.51 'seat of the thoughts and emotions' makere W.169 'be lost, abandoned, fail, cease']

hinengaro taihara *noun* criminal mind [hinengaro W.51 'seat of the thoughts and emotions' taihara TM 'crime']

hinengaro whakairo kupu *noun* verbalist [hinengaro W.51 'seat of the thoughts and emotions' whakairo W.80 'ornament with a pattern, used of carving, tatooing, painting, weaving' kupu W.157 'anything said, word, talk']

hinonga *noun* enterprise [W.51 'doing, undertaking']

hinonga Kāwanatanga *noun* State-owned enterprise [hinonga TM 'enterprise' Kāwanatanga < Eng. 'Government']

hinu makawe *noun* hair cream [hinu W.51 'oil' makawe W.169 'hair']

hinu mewaro *noun* paraffin [hinu W.51 'oil, fat' mewaro TM 'methane']

hinu pūkaha *noun* sump oil [hinu W.51 'oil' pūkaha TM 'engine']

hinu urutapu *noun* crude oil [hinu W.51 'oil' urutapu W.470 'untouched, in a state of nature, chaste, pure']

hinumata *noun* petroleum [hinu common usage 'petrol' mata W.185 'raw, uncooked, fresh, as water']

hinga *intransitive verb* lose, *noun* loss, *phrase (cricket)* bowled [W. 52 'be outdone in a contest']

hinganga kaipatu *phrase* fall of wicket [hinga W.52 'be outdone in a contest' kaipatu TM 'batsman']

hingarua *noun (softball)* double play [hinga W.52 'be outdone in a contest' rua W.349 'two']

hipora *noun* jute [W.52 'a coarsely made mat, a rough basket, a rough flax cape']

hīrangi *noun* heatwave [W.52 'quivering of atmosphere, from heat']

hīrau *transitive verb (soccer)* tripping [W.52 'entangle, trip up']

hīrea *noun* whiff [W.53 'faint odour, pleasant or unpleasant']

hīrere *noun (bathroom)* shower [W.53 'gush, waterfall, torrent']

hirikakā *noun* chilli [hiri W.53 'brisk, requiring exertion' kakā W.81 'red-hot, glow']

hiringa *noun* inspiration [W.53 'energy, determination']

hiringa mahara *noun (idea)* conception [hiri W.53 'spring up, rise up, of thoughts' mahara W.163 'thought']

hītamo *intransitive verb* reach up [W.53 'reach or stretch up at full length']

hītokitoki *noun* hopscotch [W.54 'hop on one foot']

hīwera *adjective* scarlet [W.54 'gleaming red']

hoa moe māori *noun* de facto partner [hoa W.54 'spouse, husband, wife' moe W.205 'sleep together' māori W.179 'freely, without ceremony']

hoahoa *noun, transitive verb* design [W.54 'layout, plan, arrange']

hoahoa *noun* diagram, figure [W.54 'plan of a house']

hoahoa *noun (diagram)* figure [TM 'diagram']

hoahoa papa *noun* floor plan [hoahoa W.54 'plan of a house' papa W.259 'earth floor or site of a native house']

hoahoa pere *noun* arrow diagram [hoahoa W.54 'lay out, plan' pere W.278 'dart']

hoahoa pūweru *noun* fashion design [hoahoa TM 'design' pūweru W.318 'clothing, garment']

hoahoa rākau *noun* (*mathematics*) tree diagram [hoahoa TM 'diagram' rākau W.321 'tree']

hoahoa taurahi *noun* scale diagram [hoahoa TM 'diagram' taurahi TM 'scale']

hoahoa huinga Venn diagram [hoahoa TM 'diagram' huinga TM 'set']

hoahoanga *noun* architecture [hoahoa W.54 'plan of a house']

hoamahi *noun* colleague [hoa W.54 'friend' mahi W.163 'work']

hōanga *noun* sandpaper [W.55 'a kind of sandstone used in the process of cutting and grinding stone implements']

hōanga matanui *noun* coarse sandpaper [W.55 'coarse sandstone used in grinding implements']

hōanga matarehu *noun* fine sandpaper [W.55 'fine sandstone used in grinding implements']

hoapori *noun* dependent partner [hoa W.54 'spouse' pori W.294 'dependants']

hoari piko *noun* sabre [hoari < Eng. 'sword' piko W.281 'bent, curved']

hoariri *noun* opponent [W.54 'foe, enemy']

hoatu taurewa *transitive verb* (*used by person giving*) lend [hoatu W.55 'give, away from speaker' taurewa W.402 'not paid for, unrequited']

hohe *intransitive verb* (*chemistry*) react [whakahohe W.55 'invigorate, energise']

hohenga *noun* (*chemistry*) reaction [hohe TM 'react']

hohoko *adjective* alternating [W.57 'alternate']

hōiho *noun* vaulting-horse [< Eng. 'horse']

hōiho pūrori *noun* (*gymnastics*) pommel horse [hōiho < Eng. 'horse' pūrori TM 'pommel']

hōkaikai *noun* goosestep [W.56 'extend and retract alternately, as the legs in swimming']

hōkakatanga *noun* sexuality [hōkaka W.56 'desire']

hōkari *transitive verb* ruck [W.56 'move anything by stretching out the legs']

hōkarikari *noun* soccer, (*aerobics*) hoedown [W.56 'stretch out one's legs, move anything by stretching out the legs']

hoki whakamuri *intransitive verb* backspace [hoki W.57 'return' whakamuri W.214 'backwards']

hoko harangotengote *noun* hire purchase [hoko W.57 'buy' harangotengote W.37 'do piecemeal or by instalments']

hoko ki tai *noun, transitive verb* export [hoko W.57 'barter, buy, sell' ki W.116 'to' tai W.361 'the sea, the other side']

hoko ki uta *noun, transitive verb* import [hoko W.57 'barter, buy, sell' ki W.116 'to' uta W.470 'the land, the interior']

hoko tāpui *noun* (*commerce*) lay-by [hoko W.57 'buy' tāpui W.385 'set aside, bespeak, reserve']

hōnea kore *noun* (*astronomy*) black hole [hōnea W.58 'escape' kore W.140 'no']

hono *transitive verb* fuse, *noun* fusion, (*law*) joinder [W.58 'splice, join']

hononga *noun* union of sets [hono W.58 'splice, join']

hononga *noun* (*anatomy*) symphysis [hono W.58 'splice join']

hononga *noun* (*sets*) union [W.58 'splice, join, marry']

hononga hiko *noun* electrical connection [hononga W.58 'splice, join' hiko common usage 'electricity']

hongere (pouaka whakaata) *noun* television channel [hongere W.58 'channel' pouaka whakaata common usage 'television']

hongi kāpia *noun* glue-sniffing [hongi W.58 'sniff' kāpia TM 'glue']

hongi wairou *noun* solvent abuse [hongi W.58 'sniff' wai W.474 'liquid, oil etc.' rou W.349 'intoxicated']

hōpara *noun* sightseeing [W.59 'go about, explore, cover, traverse']

hopu kōrero *noun* dictaphone [hopu W.59 'catch, snatch' kōrero W.141 'speak, talk']

hopuoro *noun* microphone [hopu W.59 'catch' oro W.242 'rumble, sound']

hopureo *noun* (*audio*) recorder, tape recorder [hopu W.59 'catch, seize, catch up' reo W.336 'voice']

hopurua *noun* (*netball*) replayed ball [hopu W.59 'catch, seize' rua W.349 'two, second']

horahanga *noun* (*mathematics*) area [hora W.59 'spread out']

hōreke *noun* (*event*) javelin [hōreke W.60 'throw a spear']

hōrete *noun* (*tool*) drill [W.60 'native drill']

hori *intransitive verb* misfire [W.60 'mistake, misjudge']

hōripi *noun, transitive verb* (*food*) fillet [W.60 'cut, lacerate, slit']

horo iraruke *noun* radioactive decay [horo W.60 'fall in fragments, crumble down' ira rukeruke TM 'radioactive']

horo whenua *noun* erosion [horo W.60 'fall in fragments, crumble down' whenua W.494 'land, ground']

horomiti pakopako *noun* waste-disposal unit [horomiti W.61 'eat ravenously, devour' pakopako W.255 'gleanings, scraps of food']

horopaki *noun* context [W.61 'surround']

horopeta *noun* dosage, dose [W.61 'bolt, swallow without chewing']

hororē *noun* vacuum cleaner [horohororē W.61 'to eat greedily']

horotete *noun* knock-out [W.62 'exhausted, prostrated']

hoto *noun* link [W.62 'join']

houanga *noun* shelf-life [W.63 'an interval of time, definite or indefinite' hou W.62 'recent, new, fresh']

houanga memeha *noun* (*science*) half-life [houanga W.63 'an interval of time, definite or indefinite' hou W.62 'recent, new, fresh' memeha W.200 'decaying, weak, be dissolved, pass away']

houhou *noun* smut [W.63 'disagreeable, unpleasant']

houhou *transitive verb* unearth [W.63 'dig up, obtain by digging']

hū *intransitive verb* (*volcano*) erupt [W.64 'hiss, bubble up, any explosive sound']

hua *noun* asset [W.64 'fruit, product' huanga 'advantage, benefit']

hua *noun* outlines, contour line [W.64 'outline, leading lines of a pattern in carving']

hua *noun* (*conclusion*) finding, result, outcome [W.64 'fruit, product']

hua *noun* (*education*) answer [W.64 'fruit, product']

hua *noun* (*mathematics*) product, solution [W.64 'fruit, product']

hua karihi *noun* stone-fruit [hua W.64 'fruit' karihi W.101 'stone of a fruit, kernel']

hua nganga *noun* drupe [hua W.64 'fruit' nganga W.228 'stone of fruit']

hua pūmau *noun* fixed asset [hua TM 'asset' pūmau W.309 'fixed']

hua wātea *noun* current asset [hua TM 'asset' wātea W.480 'free']

hua whakawhiti *noun* cross product [hua TM 'result, product', whakawhiti W.497 'cross over']

huahae *noun* catkin [hua W.64 'product, progeny' hae W.29 'pollen']

huahua *noun, transitive verb* sketch [W.65 'sketch out a pattern before carving']

huahuka *noun* fructose [hua W.64 'fruit' huka < Eng. 'sugar']

huaki *noun* (*sport, vs. defence*) offence [W.65 'assault, charge, attack']

huaki reta *noun* letter-opener [huaki W.65 'open' reta < Eng. 'letter']

huakini *noun* peppercorn [hua W.64 'fruit' kikini W.118 'pungent']

huakiwi *noun* kiwifruit [hua W.64 'fruit' kiwi < Eng. 'kiwi (fruit)']

huamata *noun* green salad [hua W.64 'fruit' mata W.185 'raw, uncooked']

huamoni *noun* interest [hua W.64 'fruit' huanga W.64 'advantage, benefit' moni < Eng. 'money']

huanui *noun* (*mathematics*) locus [W.65 'path, pathway']

huanui rererangi *noun* flight path [huanui W.65 'road, highway, pathway' waka rererangi common usage 'aeroplane']

huānga *noun* (*mathematics*) element, member [W.65 'relative, member of same hapū']

huaora *noun* vitamin [hua W.64 'fruit' huanga 'advantage, benefit' ora W.240 'well, in health, alive']

huaora C *noun* vitamin C [hua W.64 'fruit' huanga 'advantage, benefit' ora W.240 'well, in health, alive']

huaota *adjective* botanical [hua W.64 'bear fruit or flowers, abundance' otaota W.242 'herbs in general, vegetation']

huapai, huakino *phrase* pros and cons [hua W.64 'fruit, product' pai W.249 'good, suitable, satisfactory' kino W.118 'evil, bad']

huarahi *noun* method, procedure [W.65 'road, highway']

huarākau haemata *noun* fruit salad [huarākau common usage 'fruit' haemata W.29 'cut up in an uncooked state']

huarere *noun* weather [paihuarere W.250 'perfect of weather']

huarewa *noun* gallery, mezzanine [W.65 'raised aloft']

huarite *noun* rhyme [whakahua W.64 'pronounce' rite W.343 'alike, corresponding']

huatango *noun* (*arithmetic*) difference [hua TM 'result, outcome' tango TM 'subtract']

huatau *intransitive verb* realise [W.66 'thought, think']

huawehe *noun* quotient [hua W.64 'fruit, product' wehe W.481 'divide']

huhimati *noun* thimble [huhi W.66 'cover' mati W.193 'finger']

huhu *noun* peephole [W.66 'window']

huhuka *noun* suds [W.67 'foaming']

hūhunu *noun, transitive verb* barbecue [W.70 'be charred, scorched']

hui *noun* seminar [W.66 'congregate, come together']

hui pāpāho *noun* press conference [hui W.66 'congregate, come together' pāpāho TM 'broadcast']

huinga *noun* (*mathematics*) set [hui W.66 'come together, congregate']

huinga ao *noun* universal set [huinga TM 'set' ao W.7 'world']

huinga hua *noun* (*mathematics*) range [huinga TM 'set' hua TM 'result']

huinga mutu-hengahenga *noun* finite set [huinga TM 'set' mutu-hengahenga TM 'finite']

huinga nui *noun* superset [huinga TM 'set' nui W.224 'large']

huinga piako *noun* (*mathematics*) empty set [huinga TM 'set' piako W.279 'hollow, empty']

huinga pū *noun* (*mathematics*) domain [huinga TM 'set' pū W.300 'origin, source, base']

huinga rāwāhi *noun* complement of set [huinga TM 'set' rāwāhi W.332 'the other side of a sea, river, etc.']

huinga rāwaho *noun* (*mathematics*) complement (of set) [huinga 'set' rāwaho 'from outside']

huinga ritua *noun* disjoint sets [huinga TM 'set' ritua W.343 'be divided, be separated']

huinga roto *noun* subset [huinga TM 'set' roto W.348 'the inside']

huinga taurite equivalent set [huinga TM 'set' taurite TM 'equivalent']

huinga whāioio *noun* infinite set [huinga TM 'set' tau whāioio TM 'infinite number']

huirapa *noun* flippers [W.67 'having the toes united by a membrane, webbed']

huka *noun* sucrose [huka < Eng. 'sugar']

huka kairākau *noun* blizzard [W.89 'a very severe front']

huka makawe *noun* (hair) mousse [huka W.67 'foam, froth' makawe W.169 'hair']

huka-one *noun* castor sugar [huka < Eng. 'sugar' one W.239 'sand']

hukarau *noun* polysaccharide [huka < Eng. 'sugar' rau W.328 'multitude, number']

hukarua *noun* disaccharide [huka < Eng. 'sugar' rua W.349 'two']

hukatahi *noun* monosaccharide [huka < Eng. 'sugar' tahi W.359 'one']

huke *transitive verb* mine [W.68 'dig up, expose by removing the earth, excavate']

huke waro coal mine [huke W.68 'dig up, expose by removing the earth, excavate' waro W.480 'charcoal, deep hole or pit']

huki *noun* turret [W.68 'a round house with conical roof']

hukihuki *noun* (*preliminary outline*) draft [W.68 'unfinished, incomplete']

hukihuki *noun* sample [W.68 'unfinished, incomplete, as of a sample']

hūmene *noun* (*diving*) tuck [W.69 'gathered up into small compass, folded up']

humenga uta *noun* land anemone [humenga W.69 'sea anemone' uta W.470 'the land, the interior']

huna *adjective* nocturnal [W.69 'concealed, unnoticed']

hūnga *noun* (*volcano*) eruption [W.64 'hiss, bubble up, any explosive sound']

hunga mahi *noun* labour force [hunga W.70 'company of persons, people' mahi W.163 'work, work at']

hunga pāpāho *noun* media [hunga W.70 'company of persons, people' pāpāho TM 'broadcast']

hunga whakawā *noun* jury [hunga W.70 'company of persons' whakawā W.472 'adjudicate on']

hūpana *noun* springboard [W.70 'fly up or fly back, as a spring']

hūpana *noun* (*athletics*) take-off board [W.70 'fly up or fly back, as a spring']

huri *transitive verb* convert [W.71 'turn round']

huriaro *noun* homing device [W.71 'turn right round']

huriaro *noun* (*grammar*) passive [W.71 'turn right round']

hurihanga *noun* (*computer*) conversion [huri W.71 'turn round']

hurihanga *noun* (*mathematics*) rotation [huri W.71 'revolve']

huringa *noun* transformation [huri W.71 'turn to, set about']

huringa *noun* (*rotation*) revolution [huri W.71 'turn round, revolve']

huringa pūngao *noun* energy transformation [huringa TM 'transformation' pūngao TM 'energy']

huripi *noun* (*netball*) pass off [W.71 'start off']

huripi *intransitive verb* (*golf*) tee off [W.71 'start off']

huruhuru *noun* fur [W.72 'coarse hair, bristles']

huruhuru *adjective* furry [W.72 'coarse hair, bristles']

hutihiki *noun* (*weightlifting*) clean and jerk [huti W.72 'hoist, haul up' hiki W.49 'lift up, raise']

# I

ia *noun* trend [W.74 'current, rushing stream']

ia auraki *noun* vein [iaia W.74 'veins' auraki W.22 'return']

ia kawe hāora *noun* artery [ia W.74 'current' kawe W.111 'carry, convey' hāora TM 'oxygen']

ia pūkahu kawe hāora *noun* pulmonary vein [iatoto TM 'blood vessel' pūkahukahu W.306 'lungs' kawe W.111 'carry, convey' hāora TM 'oxygen']

ia pūkahu toto ruhi *noun* pulmonary artery [iatoto TM 'blood vessel' pūkahukahu W.306 'lungs' toto W.441 'blood' ruhi W.350 'exhausted, spent']

ia tōiti *noun* (*anatomical*) capillary [iatuku TM 'artery' tōiti W.432 'little finger or toe']

ia toto *noun* blood vessel [ia W.74 'current' iaia 'veins' toto W.441 'blood']

ia toto mārō *noun* arterial sclerosis [ia toto TM 'blood vessel' mārō W.183 'hard, unyielding']

iaia toto *adjective* vascular [iaia W.74 'veins' toto W.441 'blood']

iaia toto *noun* blood vessels [ia W.74 'current' toto W.441 'blood']

iaia-manawa *adjective* cardiovascular [iaia TM 'blood vessels' manawa W.174 'heart']

iaia-roro *adjective* cerebrovascular [iaia TM 'blood vessels' roro W.347 'brains']

iahiko *noun* electrical current [ia W.74 'current' hiko common usage 'electricity']

iakawe *noun* convection current [ia W.74 'current' kawe W.111 'convey' mahana W.162 'warm']

iatuku *noun* artery [ia W.74 'current' tuku W.451 'send']

iatuku roro *noun* cerebral artery [iatuku TM 'artery' roro W.347 'brains']

iere *noun* wind-chimes [W.74 'sound of voices, singing']

iheu *transitive verb* distil [iheuheu W.74 'separate']

iheunga *noun* distillation [iheuheu W.74 'separate']

īhi *noun* yeast [ī W.73 'ferment, turn sour' hī W.47 'rise']

īhipani *noun* marmite [īhi TM 'yeast' pani W.257 'spread']

īhipani *noun* vegemite [īhi TM 'yeast' pani W.257 'spread']

iho *noun* (*essential quality*) nature [W.75 'heart, inside, kernel, pitch, umbilical cord']

ihu o Hineraumati *noun* summer solstice [ihu W.75 'nose, bow of a canoe, etc.' Hineraumati personification Best *Astronomical Knowledge* 18]

ihu o Hinetakurua *noun* winter solstice [ihu W.75 'nose, bow of a canoe, etc.' Hinetakurua personification Best *Astronomical Knowledge* 18]

ihu oneone *noun* horticulturalist [W.75 'soiled face, one who works hard']

ihumanea *adjective* intuitive [W.466 'knowing, clever']

ihupuku *adjective* conscientious [W.75 'hesitating, scrupulous, industrious, eager']

ihupuku *adjective* semi-skilled [W.75 'inexperienced, hesitating, scrupulous, industrious, eager']

ihupuku *noun* achiever [W.75 'hesitating, scrupulous, industrious, eager']

ika kaiepa *phrase* caught and bowled [ika W.76 'victim' kaiepa TM 'bowler']

ika oneone *noun* amphibian [ika W.76 'fish' oneone W.240 'land']

ikarangi *noun* galaxy [W.76 'cluster' te ika o te rangi, ika-roa, ika a Māui W.76 'Milky Way' rangi W.323 'sky, upper regions, heaven']

ikura roro *noun* cerebral haemorrhage [ikura W.76 'haemorrhage' roro W.347 'brains']

inaki waka *noun* traffic jam [inaki W.77 'overlap, crowd one upon another, pack closely' waka common usage 'vehicle']

inanga *noun* bamboo [W.77 'grass tree']

ine *noun, transitive verb* gauge [W.78 'measure']

ine *noun* meter [W.78 'measure']

ine hauroa *noun* odometer [ine TM 'meter' hauroa W.41 'length, long']

ine hiko-manawa *noun* electrocardiograph [ine W.78 'measure' iahiko TM 'electrical current' manawa W.174 'heart']

ine hinu *noun* petrol gauge [ine TM 'gauge' kōhinu TM 'petrol']

ine iahiko *noun* ammeter [ine W.78 'measure' ia W.74 'current' hiko W.50 'flash, as lightning']

ine kiato wai *noun* hydrometer [ine TM 'meter' kiato TM 'density' wai W.474 'water']

ine (i te) kounga *adjective* qualitative [ine W.78 'measure, compare' kou W.151 'good']

ine kukū *transitive verb* (*chemistry*) titrate [ine TM 'measure' kukū TM 'concentration']

ine kume-ā-papa *noun* (*science*) gravimeter [ine TM 'meter' kume W.155 'pull, drag' ā W1 'after the manner of' papa W.259 'earth']

ine kurahau *noun* barometer [ine TM 'meter' kurahau awatea TM 'cyclone' kurahaupō TM 'anticyclone']

ine mahana *noun* thermometer [ine TM 'meter' mahana W.162 'warm']

ine mahora *noun* (*mathematics*) standard deviation [ine W.78 'measure' mahora W.164 'spread out, scattered']

ine (i te) nui *noun* quantitative [ine W.78 'measure, compare' nui W.224 'size, greatness']

ine ngaohiko *noun* voltmeter [ine TM 'meter' ngaohiko TM 'voltage']

ine rere *noun* speedometer [ine TM 'meter' rere W.337 'fly, rush, run']

ine rū *noun* seismometer [ine TM 'meter' rū W.349 'earthquake']

ine taumaha *transitive verb* weigh [ine W.78 'measure' taumaha W.399 'heavy']

ine tūwaka *noun* parking meter [ine W.78 'measure' tū W.443 'stand, remain' waka common usage 'vehicle']

inekoki *noun* protractor [ine W.78 'measure' koki W.129 'angle']

inenga *noun* measurement [ine W.78 'measure']

ingoa kārangaranga *noun* nickname [ingoa W.78 'name' kārangaranga W.98 'call frequently']

io ihu *noun* olfactory nerve [io W.78 'nerve' ihu W.75 'nose']

io punga *noun* Achilles tendon [iohere TM 'tendon' punga W.311 'ankle']

io tōpū *noun* nervous system [io W.78 'nerve' tōpū W.437 'assembled, in a body']

io whatu *noun* optic nerve [io W.78 'nerve' whatu W.492 'eye']

iohere *noun* tendon [io W.78 'sinew, muscle, strand of rope' here W.46 'tie, fasten with cords']

iohere kātete *noun* hamstring [iohere TM 'tendon' kātete W.103 'leg, the whole leg from the thigh downwards']

iokerewai *noun* paralysis [io W.78 'nerve' kēkerewai W.114 'numb']

iorongo *noun* auditory nerve [io W.78 'nerve' rongo W.346 'hear']

iotārūrū *noun* neuralgia [io TM 'nerve' tārūrū W.392 'painful, acute']

ipuhua *noun* egg-cup [ipu W.79 'vessel for holding anything' hua W.64 'egg of a bird']

ipupara *noun* rubbish bin [ipu W.79 'vessel for holding anything' para W.262 'impurity, refuse, waste']

ipupene *noun* pencil-holder [ipu W.79 'vessel for holding anything' pene < Eng. 'pen']

ipurangi *noun* (*computer*) internet [whakaipurangi W.79 'head or source of a stream, a small storehouse on a single post' ipu W.79 'vessel for holding anything' rangi W.324 'heaven, upper regions, abode of supernatural beings']

ipurau *noun* beaker [ipu W.79 'calabash with narrow mouth, vessel for carrying anything' rau W.328 'lay hold of, handle']

ira *noun* decimal point [TM 'dot']

ira *noun* gene [W.79 'life principle']
ira *noun* dot [W.79 'mole, freckle']
ira *noun* (*physics*) particle [W.79 'freckle, mole']
ira ngahuru *noun* decimal point [ira TM 'dot' ngahuru TM 'decimal']
ira rukeruke *adjective* radioactive [ira TM 'particle' rukeruke W.351 'throw about' ruke W.351 'throw, cast forth, discharge']
ira rukeruke *noun* radioactivity [TM 'radioactive']
irahiko *noun* electron [ira TM 'particle' hiko common usage 'electricity']
iraira *adjective* dotted [ira TM 'dot']
iramoe *noun* (*physics*) neutron [ira TM 'particle' moe W.204 'sleep, repose']

iramoe recessive gene [ira TM 'gene' moe W.204 'sleep, repose']
iranoi *transitive verb, intransitive verb* mutate [ira TM 'gene' nonoi W.223 'disfigured']
iranoi *noun* mutation [TM 'mutate']
iraoho *noun* proton [ira TM 'particle' oho W.238 'be awake']
iraruke *noun* radiation [ira rukeruke TM 'radioactive']
irirangi *noun* radio wave [W.80 'having a supernatural sound' reo irirangi W.80 'radio']
iroriki *noun* germ [iro W.80 'maggot, threadworm, vermin' riki W.340 'small']
iti *noun* minimum [W.80 'small']
īwaro *noun* (*science*) nontane [iwa W.80 'nine' waro TM 'alkane']

K

ka whaihua *adjective* feasible [whaihua TM 'beneficial, worthwhile']

kaha *noun* (*exertion of force*) pressure [W.82 'strength']

kaha *noun* (*sound*) volume [W.82 'strength'] e.g. *Whakaitihia te kaha. 'Turn down the volume.' Whakakahahia ake te kaha. 'Turn up the volume.'*

kaha hohenga *noun* (*chemistry*) reactivity [kaha W.82 'strength' hohenga TM 'reaction']

kaha papare *noun* (*capacity to resist*) resistance [kaha W.82 'strong, able, strength' papare W.266 'turn aside, ward off']

kaha tīwera *noun* amplitude [kaha W.82 'strength' tīwera TM 'amplify']

kahakawe iahiko *noun* (*electricity*) conductivity [kaha W. 82 'strength' kawe W.111 'convey' iahiko TM 'electrical current']

kahapupuri *noun* capacity [kaha W.82 'strength' pupuri W.314 'hold, retain possession of']

kahika *noun* mayor [W.83 'chief']

kahika *noun* mayoress [W.83 'chief']

kaho *noun* crossbar [W.83 'batten laid horizontally']

kahotea *adjective* (*colour*) cream [kaho W.84 'anything light-coloured' kahotea W.84 'variety of greenstone having light-coloured streaks in it; nearly white']

kahu *noun* albumen [W.84 'white of an egg']

kahu *noun* amniotic sac [W.84 'membrane enveloping foetus']

kahu kakau *noun* swimming costume [kahu W.84 'garment' kakau W.104 'swim']

kāhuarau *noun* metamorphosis [kāhua W.85 'form, appearance' rau W.328 'number']

kāhuarau *adjective* metamorphic [kāhua W.85 'form, appearance' rau W.328 'number']

kāhui hanga ture *noun* senate [kāhui W.85 'assemblage' hanga W.34 'make, fashion' ture W.459 'law']

Kāhui o Hoani *noun* Order of St. John [kāhui W.885 'assemblage' Hoani < Eng. 'John']

kahupapa *noun* gib-board [W.85 'layer, matted mass']

kahupapa parataiao *noun* sedimentary layer [kahupapa W.5 'layer, matted mass' parataiao TM 'sedimentary']

kahupeka *noun* bullet-proof vest [W.85 'stiff, closely woven mat of flax worn as protection in war, strapped on like the tātua']

kahupiri *noun* leotard [kahu W.84 'garment' piri W.283 'stick, adhere, cling']

kahurangi *noun* (*title*) dame [W.85 'honourable, distinguished, prized']

kai *intransitive verb* feed [W.85 'eat']

kai hinengaro *noun* quiz [kai Best *Games and Pastimes* 'generic term for guessing games' hinengaro W.51 'seat of the thoughs and emotions']

kai inati *noun* overdose [kai W.85 'eat' inati W.77 'excessive, trouble, bane, disaster, omen, portent, generally bad']

kai konu-okehu *noun* barium meal [kai W.85 'eat' konu-okehu TM 'barium']

kai mahara *noun* guessing game [kai Best *Games and Pastimes* 116 'generic term for guessing games' mahara W.163 'memory, bear in mind, remember']

kai roro *noun* quiz [kai Best *Games and Pastimes* 'generic term for guessing games' roro W.347 'brains']

kai ruaki *noun* recidivism [kai W.85 'consume, eat' ruaki W.350 'vomit']

kai ruaki *noun* recidivist [kai W.85 'consume, eat' ruaki W.350 'vomit']

kaiā *noun* shoplifter [W.86 'steal, thief, stealthy']

kaiahuwhenua *noun* farmer [kai W.86 'a prefix to transitive verbs to form nouns denoting an agent' ahuwhenua W.3 'cultivate the soil']

kaiahuwhenua *noun* agriculturalist [kai W.86 'a prefix to transitive verbs to form nouns denoting an agent' ahuwhenua W.3 'cultivate the soil']

kaiaka *adjective* competent [W.86 'forward in attainments, adept, proficient']

kaiaka *noun* knight [W.86 'forward in attainments, adept, proficient, man, adult']

kaiāmiki *noun* (*score-keeper*) scorer [TM 'scribe, minute-taker']

kaiāmiki *noun* (*meeting*) minute-taker [kai W.86 'a prefix to transitive verbs to form nouns denoting an agent' āmiki TM 'minute-taking']

kaiāmiki *noun* scribe [kai W.86 'a prefix to transitive verbs to form nouns denoting an agent' āmiki W.8 'tell a story without omitting any particular']

kaiao *noun* organism [W.86 'alive, living']

kaiārai *noun* (*sport*) guard [kai W.86 'a prefix to transitive verbs to form nouns denoting an agent' ārai W.14 'keep off, ward off']

kaiāwhina *noun* assistant [kai W.86 'a prefix to transitive verbs to form nouns denoting an agent' āwhina W.25 'assist, benefit']

kaieke *noun* (*person*) rider [kai W.86 'a prefix to transitive verbs to form nouns denoting an agent' eke W.27 'mount']

kaieke pahikara *noun* cyclist [kai W.86 'a prefix to transitive verbs to form nouns denoting an agent' eke W.27 'place oneself upon another object' pahikara < Eng. 'bicycle']

kaiepa *noun* (*cricket*) bowler [kai W.86 'a prefix to transitive verbs to form nouns denoting an agent' epa TM 'bowl']

kaiepa *noun* (*softball*) pitcher [kai W.86 'a prefix to transitive verbs to form nouns denoting an agent' epa TM 'pitch']

kaihahau *noun* (*sport*) batter [kai W.86 'a prefix to transitive verbs to form nouns denoting an agent' hahau W.39 'strike, smite']

kaihau *noun, adjective* bankrupt [W.87 'acquire property without payment or return made']

kaihau *noun* bankruptcy [W.87 'acquire property without payment or return made']

kaihaumi *intransitive verb* trespass, poach [W.40 'person who wanders over other people's land and takes birds etc.']

kaihaumi *noun* trespasser, poacher [W.40 'person who wanders over other people's land and takes birds etc.']

kaihiki *noun* (*weightlifting*) lifter [kai W.86 'a prefix to transitive verbs to form nouns denoting an agent' hiki W.49 'lift up, raise']

kaihoahoa *noun* architect [kai W.86 'a prefix to transitive verbs to form nouns denoting an agent' hoahoa W.54 'plan of a house']

kaihoahoa pūweru *noun* fashion designer [kai W.86 'a prefix to transitive verbs to form nouns denoting an agent' hoahoa pūweru TM 'fashion design']

kaihoko *noun* seller [kai W.86 'a prefix to transitive verbs to form nouns denoting an agent' hoko W.57 'sell']

kaihoko *noun* buyer [kai W.86 'a prefix to transitive verbs to form nouns denoting an agent' hoko W.57 'buy']

kaihōpara *noun* explorer [kai W.86 'a prefix to transitive verbs to form nouns denoting an agent' hōpara W.59 'go about, explore, cover, traverse']

kaihōpara *noun* tramper [kai W.86 'a prefix to transitive verbs to form nouns denoting an agent' hōpara W.59 'go about, explore, cover, traverse']

kaihopu tuatahi *noun* first receiver [kai W.86 'a prefix to transitive verbs to form nouns denoting an agent' hopu W.59 'catch' tua W.444 'prefix used with numerals to form ordinals' tahi W.359 'one']

kaihōreke *noun* javelin thrower [kai W.86 'a prefix to transitive verbs to form nouns denoting an agent' hōreke W.60 'throw a spear']

kaikape *transitive verb* undercut [W.88 'outrun, steal']

kaikape *noun* (*tennis etc.*) game [W.88 'outrun']

kaikauhoe *noun* swimmer [kai W.86 'a prefix to transitive verbs to form nouns denoting an agent' kauhoe W.106 'swim']

kaikawau *transitive verb* trim, prune [W.88 'lop, cut the tips off anything']

kaikawe poi *noun* ball carrier [kai W.86 'a prefix to transitive verbs to form nouns denoting an agent' kawe W.111 'carry, convey' poi TM 'ball']

kaikiko *adjective* carnivorous [kai W.85 'eat' kiko W.117 'flesh']

kaikiri *noun* irreconcilable breakdown [W.88 'cherish hostile feelings, quarrel']

kaikōiwi *noun* rheumatoid arthritis [W.88 'rheumatism']

kaikōkiri mana hapori *noun* socialist [kai W.86 'a prefix to transitive verbs to form nouns denoting an agent' kōkiri TM 'champion' mana hapori TM 'socialism']

kaikōkiri mana wahine *noun* feminist [kai W.86 'a prefix to transitive verbs to form nouns denoting an agent' kōkiri TM 'champion' mana W.172 'influence, power, control' wahine W.474 'woman']

kaikora *noun* pyromania [TM 'pyromaniac']

kaikora *noun* pyromaniac [kora W.139 'spark, fire, fuel' kaikora W.88 'person of no account, vagabond']

kaikorohiti *noun* chiropractor [kai W.86 'a prefix to transitive verbs to form nouns denoting an agent' korohiti W.147 'jerk, give a sudden impulse to']

kaikōtaha *noun* (*athletics*) hammer-thrower [kai W.86 'a prefix to transitive verbs to form nouns denoting an agent' kōtaha kurutai W.147 'a stone weapon attached to a cord by which it was recovered after having been thrown at the enemy']

kaimahi *noun* clerk [kai W.86 'a prefix to transitive verbs to form nouns denoting an agent' mahi W.163 'work, work at, occupation']

kaimahi *noun* staff [kai W.86 'a prefix to transitive verbs to form nouns denoting an agent' mahi W.163 'work, work at, occupation']

kaimahi kāwananatanga *noun* civil servant [kaimahi TM 'staff' kāwanatanga < Eng. 'government']

kaimahi kōhikohiko *noun* casual worker [kai W.86 'a prefix to transitive verbs to form nouns denoting an agent' mahi W.163 'work, work at' kōhikohiko W.125 'do irregularly, a bit here and a bit there']

kaimahi rangitahi *noun* temporary staff [kaimahi TM 'staff' rangitahi TM 'temporary']

kaimahi tīpakopako *noun* shift worker [kai W.86 'a prefix to transitive verbs to form nouns denoting an agent' mahi W.163 'work, work at, occupation' tīpakopako W.421 'in detached parties, not in one body, at odd times']

kaimahi waimori *noun* casual worker [kai W.86 'a prefix to transitive verbs to form nouns denoting an agent' mahi W.163 'work' waimori W.476 'working intermittently']

kaimātai *noun* -ologist [kai W.86 'a prefix to transitive verbs to form nouns denoting an agent' mātai W.187 'inspect, examine']

kaimātai aotea *noun* ornithologist [kaimātai TM '-ologist' aotea W.12 'bird']

kaimātai hapori *noun* sociologist [kaimātai TM '-ologist' hapori TM 'social']

kaimātai hinengaro *noun* psychologist [kaimātai TM '-ologist' hinengaro TM 'psychological']

kaimātai huaota *noun* botanist [kai W.86 'a prefix to transitive verbs to form nouns denoting an agent' mātai W.187 'inspect, examine' huaota TM 'botany']

kaimātai kararehe *noun* zoologist [kaimātai TM '-ologist' kararehe W.99 'quadruped' common usage 'animal']

kaimātai koiora *noun* biologist [kaimātai TM '-ologist' koiora TM 'biology']

kaimātai matawhenua *noun* geographer [kai W.86 'a prefix to transitive verbs to form nouns denoting an agent' mātai W.187 'inspect, examine' matawhenua TM 'geography']

kaimātai momo tangata *noun* ethnologist [kaimātai TM '-ologist' mātauranga momo tangata TM 'ethnology']

kaimātai pūtaiao *noun* scientist [kai W.86 'a prefix to transitive verbs to form nouns denoting an agent' mātai W.187 'inspect, examine' pūtaiao TM 'science']

kaimātai roke kanae *noun* palaeontologist [kaimātai TM '-ologist' roke kanae TM 'fossil']

kaimātai tikanga tangata *noun* anthropologist [kaimātai TM '-ologist' mātauranga tikanga tangata TM 'anthropology']

kaimātai whatu *noun* optician [kai W.86 'a prefix to transitive verbs to form nouns denoting an agent' mātai W.187 'inspect, examine' whatu W.492 'eye, pupil of the eye']

kaimōhiki *noun* weightlifter [kai W.86 'a prefix to transitive verbs to form nouns denoting an agent' mōhiki W.205 'raised up, lifted up']

kainamu *adverb* almost, nearly [W.88 'be within a little of'] *e.g. Kei te aha te tāima? Kua kainamu ki te whā. 'What's the time? It's almost four.'*

kainonoke *noun* judoist [kai W.86 'a prefix to transitive verbs to form nouns denoting an agent' nonoke TM 'judo']

kāinga *noun* habitat [W.81 'place of abode']

kāinga māngai kāwanatanga *noun* embassy [kāinga W.81 'place of abode' māngai TM 'representative' kāwanatanga < Eng. 'government']

Kāinga Māngai Kāwanatanga *noun* High Commission [kāinga W.81 'place of abode' māngai TM 'representative' kāwanatanga < Eng. 'government']

kāinga taupua *noun* hostel [W.401 'temporary abode']

kaipakihi *noun* businessman [W.89 'business, affairs, concerns']

kaipakihi *noun* businesswoman [W.89 'business, affairs, concerns']

kaipaneke *noun* (*person who scores goal*) scorer [kai W.86 'a prefix to transitive verbs to form nouns denoting an agent' paneke TM 'goal, point']

kaipanga matā *noun* shotputter [kai W.86 'a prefix to transitive verbs to form nouns denoting an agent' panga matā TM 'shotput']

kaipara *noun* athlete [Best *Games and Pastimes* 23 'athletics']

kaipara *noun* athletics [Best *Games and Pastimes* 23 'athletics']

kaipara ngahuru *noun* decathlete [kaipara TM 'athlete' ngahuru W.227 'ten']

kaipara ngahuru *noun* decathlon [kaipara TM 'athletics' ngahuru W.227 'ten']

kaipara rima *noun* pentathlete [kaipara TM 'athlete' rima W.340 'five']

kaipara rima *noun* pentathlon [kaipara TM 'athletics' rima W.340 'five']

kaipara whitu *noun* heptathlete [kaipara TM 'athlete' whitu W.498 'seven']

kaipara whitu *noun* heptathlon [kaipara TM 'athletics' whitu W.498 'seven']

kaipare *noun* (*sport*) defender [kai W.86 'a prefix to transitive verbs to form nouns denoting an agent' pare W.266 "ward off"]

kaipatapatai *noun* interviewer [kai W.86 'a prefix to transitive verbs to form nouns denoting an agent' patapatai W.269 'question, inquire']

kaipatu *noun* batsman [kai W.86 'a prefix to transitive verbs to form nouns denoting an agent' patu W.272 'strike, beat']

kaipatu pūkura *noun* badminton player [kai W.86 'a prefix to transitive verbs to form nouns denoting an agent' patu W.272 'strike, beat' pūkura TM 'badminton']

kaipeke tāepa *noun* hurdler [kai W.86 'a prefix to transitive verbs to form nouns denoting an agent' peke W.276 'leap, jump' tāepa TM 'hurdle']

kaipirau *noun* necrophilia [W.89 'dishonour after death, dishonour applied to a dead body']

kaipirau *noun* necrophiliac [W.89 'dishonour after death, dishonour applied to a dead body']

kaipīrori maita *noun* (*lawn bowls*) bowler [kai W.86 'a prefix to transitive verbs to form nouns denoting an agent' pīrori W.284 'roll along, as a ball etc.' maita TM 'lawn bowls']

kaipītaka *noun* gymnast [kai W.86 'a prefix to transitive verbs to form nouns denoting an agent' pītakataka TM 'gymnastics']

kaipōkai tuarangi *noun* astronaut [kai W.86 'a prefix to transitive verbs to form nouns denoting an agent' pōkai W.289 'travel about' tuarangi TM 'outer space']

kaiponapona *noun* arthritis [kaikōiwi W.88 'rheumatism' ponapona W.291 'joint in the arm or leg']

kaipuke pūngao-karihi *noun* nuclear-powered ship [kaipuke W.89 'ship' pūngao TM 'energy' karihi TM 'nuclear']

kairanaki *noun* avenger [kai W.86 'a prefix to transitive verbs to form nouns denoting an agent' ranaki W.322 'avenge']

kairangahau *noun* researcher [kai W.86 'a prefix to transitive verbs to form nouns denoting an agent' rangahau TM 'research']

kairangi *adjective* high quality [W.89 'anything held in high estimation, finest variety of greenstone']

kairapu *adjective* contestable [W.89 'contend for']

kairarau matū *noun* (*science*) chemist [kai W.86 'a prefix to transitive verbs to form nouns denoting an agent' rarau W.328 'lay hold of, grasp, handle' matū TM 'chemistry']

kairauhī *noun* consul [kai W.86 'a prefix to transitive verbs to form nouns denoting an agent' rauhī W.329 'take care of, foster, protect']

kairauhī *noun* guardian [kai W.86 'a prefix to transitive verbs to form nouns denoting an agent' rauhī W.329 'take care of, tend, foster, protect']

kairauhī matua *noun* consul general [kai W.86 'a prefix to transitive verbs to form nouns denoting an agent' rauhī W.329 'take care of, foster, protect' matua W.195 'main, chief']

kairaupī *noun* bee-keeper [kai W.86 'a prefix to transitive verbs to form nouns denoting an agent' raupī W.330 'take care of, cover up' rau W.328 'gather into a basket etc.' pī' < Eng. bee']

kairaupī *noun* apiarist [kai W.86 'a prefix to transitive verbs to form nouns denoting an agent' raupī W.330 'take care of, cover up' rau W.328 'gather into a basket etc.' pī < Eng. 'bee']

kairehu *noun* anaesthetist [kai W.86 'a prefix to transitive verbs to form nouns denoting an agent' rehu W.334 'render drowsy or unconscious']

kairērere *noun* (*sport*) long-jump [Best *Games and Pastimes* 30]

kairērere *noun* (*sport*) long-jumper [kairērere TM 'long-jump']

kairomiromi *noun* physiotherapist [kai W.86 'a prefix to transitive verbs to form nouns denoting an agent' romiromi W.346 'press, squeeze']

kairota *noun* linesman [kai W.86 'a prefix to transitive verbs to form nouns denoting an agent' rotarota W.348 'sign with the hands']

kairuruku *noun* coordinator [kai W.86 'a prefix to transitive verbs to form nouns denoting an agent' ruruku W.351 'draw together with a cord']

kaitākaro *noun* player [kai W.86 'a prefix to transitive verbs to form nouns denoting an agent' tākaro W.369 'play, sport']

kaitaki kiriata *noun* film producer [kai W.86 'a prefix to transitive verbs to form nouns denoting an agent' taki W.371 'lead, bring along' kiriata TM 'film']

kaitango *noun* buyer [kai W.86 'a prefix to transitive verbs to form nouns denoting an agent' tango W.380 'take possession of, acquire']

kaitātai aro whenua *noun* geologist [kai W.86 'a prefix to transitive verbs to form nouns denoting an agent' tātai aro whenua TM 'geology']

kaitātari kaute *noun* auditor [kai W.86 'a prefix to transitive verbs to form nouns denoting an agent' tātari kaute TM 'audit']

kaitatau moni *noun* bank teller [kai W.86 'a prefix to transitive verbs to form nouns denoting an agent' tatau W.395 'count' moni < Eng. 'money']

kaitaunaki *noun* attesting witness [kai W.86 'a prefix to transitive verbs to form nouns denoting an agent' taunaki W.400 'support, reinforce']

kaitaunaki *noun* advocate [kai W.86 'a prefix to transitive verbs to form nouns denoting an agent' taunaki W.400 'support, reinforce']

kaitautoko *noun* (*meeting*) seconder [kai W.86 'a prefix to transitive verbs to form nouns denoting an agent' tautoko W.404 'prop up, support']

kaitautoko *noun* advocate [kai W.86 'a prefix to transitive verbs to form nouns denoting an agent' tautoko W.404 'support']

kaitipu *noun* herbivore [kai W.85 'eat' tipu TM 'plant']

kaitirotiro matewhawhati *noun* coroner [kai W.86 'a prefix to transitive verbs to form nouns denoting an agent' tirotiro W.424 'investigate' matewhawhati TM 'unexpected death']

kaitono *noun* applicant [kai W.86 'a prefix to transitive verbs to form nouns denoting an agent' tono W.436 'bid']

kaitono

kaitono *noun (applicant)* candidate [kai W.86 'a prefix to transitive verbs to form nouns denoting an agent' tono TM 'apply' kaitono TM 'applicant']

kaitono *noun* claimant [kai W.86 'a prefix to transitive verbs to form nouns denoting an agent' tono W.436 'bid, demand']

kaitōrangapū *noun* politician [kai W.86 'a prefix to transitive verbs to form nouns denoting an agent' tōrangapū TM 'politics']

kaituhi *noun (bowls)* marker [TM 'scribe']

kaituhi *noun* scribe [kai W.86 'a prefix to transitive verbs to form nouns denoting an agent' tuhi W.448 'write, delineate']

kaituhi huringa *noun* lap scorer [kaituhi TM 'scribe' huringa TM 'revolution']

kaituki *noun* cox [W.90 'the man who gives the time to the paddlers in a canoe']

kaituku *noun* donor [kai W.86 'a prefix to transitive verbs to form nouns denoting an agent' tuku W.451 'present, offer']

kaituku *noun* server [kai W.86 'a prefix to transitive verbs to form nouns denoting an agent' tuku TM 'serve']

kaituku hāmene *noun* bailiff [kai W.86 'a prefix to transitive verbs to form nouns denoting an agent' tuku W.451 'send' hāmene < Eng. 'summons']

kaitūpeke *noun* high jumper [kai W.86 'a prefix to transitive verbs to form nouns denoting an agent' tūpeke TM 'high jump']

kaitūtoko *noun* pole vaulter [kai W.86 'a prefix to transitive verbs to form nouns denoting an agent' tūtoko TM 'pole vault']

kaiurungi *noun* captain [kai W.86 'a prefix to transitive verbs to form nouns denoting an agent' urungi W.470 'steer, rudder']

kaiwaewae *noun* pedestrian [kai W.86 'fulfil its proper function' waewae W.472 'leg, foot']

kaiwawao *noun* referee, umpire [kai W.86 'a prefix to transitive verbs to form nouns denoting an agent' wawao W.479 'part combatants']

kaiwawao paetaha *noun* sideline umpire [kaiwawao TM 'umpire' paetaha TM 'sideline']

kaiwawao pūrei *noun* base umpire [kaiwawao TM 'umpire' pūrei TM 'base']

kaiwawao tāpora *noun* plate umpire [kaiwawao TM 'umpire' tāpora TM 'plate']

kaiwetereo *noun* grammarian [kai W.86 'a prefix to transitive verbs to form nouns denoting an agent' wetereo TM 'grammar']

kaiwhakaahua *noun* camera person, photographer [kai W.86 'a prefix to transitive verbs to form nouns denoting an agent' whakaahua TM 'photograph']

kaiwhakaako *noun* coach, educator [kai W.86 'a prefix to transitive verbs to form nouns denoting an agent' whakaako W.7 'teach']

kaiwhakahaere *noun* organiser, manager [kai W.86 'a prefix to transitive verbs to form nouns denoting an agent' whakahaere W.30 'conduct any business, execute']

kaiwhakahaere tapuhi *noun* matron [kaiwhakahaere TM 'manager' tapuhi TM 'nurse']

kaiwhakahoki *noun (tennis)* receiver [kai W.86 'a prefix to transitive verbs to form nouns denoting an agent' whakahoki W.57 'cause to return, give back']

kaiwhakahou poutoka *noun (house)* repiler [kai W.86 'a prefix to transitive verbs to form nouns denoting an agent' whakahou TM 'renew' poutoka TM 'pile']

kaiwhakamahiri pirihi *noun* curate [kai W.86 'a prefix to transitive verbs to form nouns denoting an agent' whakamahiri W.164 'assist' pirihi < Eng. 'priest']

kaiwhakangungu *noun* trainer [kai W.86 'a prefix to transitive verbs to form nouns denoting an agent' whakangungu TM 'train']

kaiwhakaora hinengaro *noun* psychotherapist [kai W.86 'a prefix to transitive verbs to form nouns denoting an agent' whakaora W.241 'restore to health' hinengaro W.51 'seat of the thoughts and emotions']

kaiwhakapā hē *noun* plaintiff, prosecutor [kai W.86 'a prefix to transitive verbs to form nouns denoting an agent' whakapā hē W.243 'accuse, bring a charge of wrongdoing against anyone']

kaiwhakapae *noun* complainant [kai W.86 'a prefix to transitive verbs to form nouns denoting an agent' whakapae W.245 'accuse']

kaiwhakaputa pukapuka *noun* publisher [kai W.86 'a prefix to transitive verbs to form nouns denoting an agent' whakaputa TM 'publish' pukapuka W.306 'book']

kaiwhakataetae *noun* contestant [kai W.86 'a prefix to transitive verbs to form nouns denoting an agent' whakataetae W.356 'try strength, contend']

kaiwhakatāhei tohutoa *noun* medal presenter [kai W.86 'a prefix to transitive verbs to form nouns denoting an agent' whakatāhei tohutoa TM 'medal presentation']

kaiwhakatau toanga mātāmuri *noun* place-judge [kai W.86 'a prefix to transitive verbs to form nouns denoting an agent' whakatau TM 'decide' toanga mātāmuri TM 'place']

kaiwhakatau utu hanga whare *noun* quantity surveyor [kai W.86 'a prefix to transitive verbs to form nouns denoting an agent' whakatau TM 'determine' utu W.471 'price' hanga W.34 'make, build' whare W.489 'house, habitation']

kaiwhakatika reo kōrero *noun* speech therapist [kai W.86 'a prefix to transitive verbs to form nouns denoting an agent' whakatika W.417 'straighten, correct' reo W.336 'speech' kōrero W.141 'talk']

kaiwhakatika tuhinga *noun* editor [kai W.86 'a prefix to transitive verbs to form nouns denoting an agent' whakatika W.417 'correct' tuhinga TM 'text']

kaiwhakatikatika pūkaha *noun* mechanic [kai W.86 'a prefix to transitive verbs to form nouns denoting an agent' whakatika TM 'fix' pūkaha TM 'engine']

kaiwhakawā huringa *noun* (*swimming*) turning judge [kaiwhakawā W.472 'judge' huri W.71 'turn round']

Kaiwhakawā Matua *noun* Chief Judge [kaiwhakawā W.472 'judge' matua W.195 'main, chief']

kaiwhakawā tuku *noun* (*tennis*) service judge [kaiwhakawā W.472 'judge' tuku TM 'service']

Kaiwhakawā Tūmatanui *noun* Justice of the Peace [kaiwhakawā W.472 'judge' tūmatanui TM 'public']

kaiwhakawaiwai *noun* coach [kai W.86 'a prefix to transitive verbs to form nouns denoting an agent' whakawaiwai W.475 'practise the use of weapons']

kaiwhakawhiwhi mahi *noun* employer [kai W.86 'a prefix to transitive verbs to form nouns denoting an agent' whakawhiwhi W.499 'present' mahi W.163 'work']

kaiwhāki *noun* informant [kai W.86 'a prefix to transitive verbs to form nouns denoting an agent' whāki W.486 'reveal, disclose']

kaiwhao *noun* mollusc [W.90 'a mollusc']

kaiwhītiki *noun* (*rugby*) lock [kai W.86 'a prefix to transitive verbs to form nouns denoting an agent' whītiki W.498 'tie, bind, gird']

kaiwhiwhi *noun* recipient [kai W.86 'a prefix to transitive verbs to form nouns denoting an agent' whiwhi W.499 'possessed of, having acquired']

kaiwhiwhi takuhe *noun* (*Government*) beneficiary [kaiwhiwhi TM 'recipient' takuhe TM 'benefit']

kakā *noun* inflammation, *adjective* inflamed [W.81 'red-hot, glow']

kaka *noun* (*synthetic filament*) fibre [W.91 'fibre, single hair']

kaka kīrehe *noun* animal fibre [kaka W.91 'fibre' kīrehe W.119 'quadruped']

kaka kōata *noun* fibreglass [kaka W.91 'fibre' matakōata TM 'glass']

kaka tipu *noun* plant fibre [kaka W.91 'fibre' tipu TM 'plant']

kaka waihanga *noun* man-made fibre [kaka W.91 'fibre' waihanga W.485 'make, build, construct']

kaka-aku *noun* textile fibre [kaka W.91 'fibre' akuaku W.7 'firm, strong']

kākahu taumau *noun* bridal wear [kākahu W.84 'garment' taumau W.400 'be betrothed']

kākano *noun* (*human*) egg [W.94 'seed, stock, descent']

kākano *noun* ovum [W.94 'seed, stock, descent']

kākano whakauru *noun* bicultural person [W.94 'variegated, also applied to a person sprung from two tribes']

kākano whakauru *noun* hybrid [W.94 'variegated, also applied to a person sprung from two tribes']

kakape *noun* chopstick [kape W.96 'pick out, move with the point of a stick']

kākāriki *adjective* bright glossy green [W.91 'small green parrot, parakeet']

kakawaea *noun* filament [kaka TM 'fibre' waea < Eng. 'wire']

kakawe iahiko *noun* (*electrical*) conductor [kawe iahiko TM 'conduction']

kakī mārō *adjective* pig-headed [idiom kakī W.92 'neck' mārō 'W.183 'unyielding, headstrong']

kākoa *adjective* fibroid [W.92 'full of hard fibres']

kākoa *adjective* (*vegetables*) woody [W.92 'full of hard fibres']

kākoa *adjective* fibrous [W.92 'full of hard fibres']

kaku *noun* (*tennis*) half volley [W.92 'scrape up, scoop up']

kamo *noun* (*microscope*) eyepiece [W.92 'eye']

kamokamo *noun* (*food*) squash [W.92 'fruit of the gourd, possibly from cucumber, and restricted to imported gourds']

kamoriki *noun* gherkin [kamo W.92 'fruit of the gourd, possibly from cucumber, and restricted to imported gourds' riki W.340 'small']

kāmuri *noun* cafeteria [W.93 'cooking shed']

kāmuri *noun* canteen [W.93 'cooking shed']

kānapanapa *adjective* blue-green [W.93 'dark green, as deep water']

kānapanapa *adjective* sea green [W.93 'dark green, as deep water']

kanekane *adjective* garlic [W.93 'pungent']

kānihi poka *noun* puncture-repair-kit [kānihi W.94 'patch a garment' poka TM 'puncture']

kānihinihi *noun* patchwork [kānihi W.94 'patch a garment']

kanikani keretao *noun* break-dancing [kanikani W.93 'dance' keretao W.114 'a grotesque figure with arms moved by a string']

kano ārai mate *noun* vaccine [kano W.94 'seed' ārai W.14 'screen, ward off' mate W.192 'sickness']

kanohi hōmiromiro *adjective* keen-sighted [W.58 'said of one who has sharp sight for very small objects']

kanohi kāhu *adjective* long-sighted [kanohi W.94 'eye' kāhu W.84 'hawk']

kanohi kākāpō *adjective* short-sighted [kanohi W.94 'eye' kākāpō W.91 'ground parrot' kāpō W.96 'blind']

kanohi wera *noun* kitchen hand [kanohi W.94 'face' wera W.482 'hot']

kanokawhe *noun* coffee bean [kano W.94 'seed' kawhe < Eng. 'coffee']

kanokore *adjective* colourless [kano W.94 'colour' kore W.140 'no, not']

kanopīni *noun* broad beans [kano W.94 'seed' pīni < Eng. 'bean']

kanorau *noun* diversity [kano W.94 'colour, sort, kind, seed, texture' rau W.328 'multitude']

kanorau *adjective* diverse [kano W.94 'colour, sort, kind, seed, texture' rau W.328 'multitude']

kanotea *noun* (*colour*) pastel [kano W.94 'colour' tea W.410 'pale']

kānga pāhūhū *noun* popcorn [W.248 'popped corn']

kānga rere *noun* cornflakes [kānga < Eng. 'corn' rere W.337 'flow, fall, of rain']

kao *noun* fritter [W.94 'a preparation of kūmara, grated, cooked, and dried in the sun']

kāore e whaihua *adjective* unfeasible [kāore W.95 'not' whaihua TM 'beneficial, worthwhile']

kāore e whaihua not feasible [kāore W.95 'not' whaihua TM 'beneficial, worthwhile']

kapa *noun* team [W.95 'rank, row, play sport']

kapa manawa *noun* heartbeat [kakapa W.95 'throb, palpitate' manawa W.174 'heart, breath']

kapamua *noun* front-line players [kapa W.95 'stand in a row or rank' mua W.213 'the front']

kapamuri *noun* back line players [kapa W.95 'stand in a row or rank' muri W.214 'rear, hind part']

kaparua *noun* second row [kapa W.95 'rank, row' rua W.349 'two']

kapa-whārangi *noun* (*bicycle*) penny-farthing [kapa common usage 'penny' whārangi < Eng. 'farthing']

kape *noun* wooden spoon [W.96 'stick for moving or stirring anything']

kāpeka *noun (drama)* scene [W.96 'branch of a tree or river']

kāpeka rorohiko *noun* computer terminal [kāpeka W.96 'branch of a tree or river' rorohiko TM 'computer']

kapekape *noun, transitive verb* stir-fry [W.96 'stick to rake out embers or food']

kapekapetau *noun (synchronised swimming)* scissors [W.96 'move quickly to and fro']

kaperua *transitive verb (reading)* skim [W.96 'glance quickly']

kapewhiti *noun* cash flow [W.96 'come and go frequently']

kāpia *noun* cellulose adhesive [W.96 'kauri gum, resin']

kāpia *noun* glue [W.96 'kauri gum, resin']

kapiti hiko *noun (electricity)* socket [kapiti W.96 'cleft, crevice, joined, brought together' hiko common usage 'electricity']

kapiti hiko *noun (computer)* port [kapiti W.96 'cleft, crevice, joined, brought together' hiko common usage 'electric']

kapohau *noun* wind turbine [kapo W.96 'catch at, snatch, lightning' hau W.38 'wind, air']

kapowai *noun* water turbine [kapo W.96 'catch at, snatch, lightning' wai W.474 'water']

kapua whakapipi *noun* cumulus [kapua W.97 'cloud, bank of clouds' whakapipi W.282 'heap, pile, pile one upon another']

kapuni *noun* natural gas [name of gas field]

kapunipuni *noun* (CNG) compressed natural gas [kapuni TM 'natural gas' puni W.310 'stopped up, blocked']

kapurangi *noun* biodegradable waste [W.97 'rubbish, weeds, a kind of woody fungus']

kaputino *noun* cappucino [< Eng. 'cappucino']

kapuwae *noun* instep [kapu W.97 'sole of the foot, hollow of the hand' wae W.472 'foot']

kāraha *noun (basin)* sink [W.97 'calabash with wide mouth, bowl, basin']

kāraha *noun* handbasin [W.97 'wide and shallow, calabash with a wide mouth, bowl, basin']

karahā *noun* mouth freshener [kakara W.97 'scent, smell, flavour' hā W.29 'breath, taste, flavour']

karahā *noun* breath freshener [kakara W.97 'scent, smell, flavour' hā W.29 'breath, taste, flavour']

karaka *adjective* orange [W.98 'corynocarpus laevigata, a tree, and fruit of same']

kārangirangi *adjective* pessimistic [W.98 'doubtful' kārangi W.98 'restless, unsettled']

karapēpē *noun* silage [W.99 'fermenting']

karapetapeta *intransitive verb (slang)* scarper [W.99 'move quickly']

karapitipiti *noun* grandstand [W.99 'put or fasten together side by side']

kārau *noun* grappling-iron [W.99 'dredge for shellfish, grapnel']

kare-ā-roto *noun* emotions [W.100 'object of passionate affection']

kārearea *noun (golf)* eagle [W.100 'hawk']

karera *adjective* pale green [W.100 'light green']

karere *noun* message [W.100 'messenger']

karere rorohiko *noun* electronic mail [karere TM 'message' rorohiko TM 'computer']

karere tuawhenua *noun* rural delivery [karere W.100 'messenger' tuawhenua W.448 'mainland, interior']

karere waea *noun* telegram [karere TM 'message' waea < Eng. 'wire']

karetao *noun* robot [W.100 'a toy carved in human form, with arms moved by pulling a string']

karihi *noun* nucleus [W.101 'stone of a fruit, kernel']

karihi *adjective (physics)* nuclear [W.101 'stone of a fruit, kernel']

karihika *noun* pornography [W.101 'lewd, immoral, copulation']

karihika *adjective* crude, pornographic [W.101 'lewd, immoral, copulation']

kāriki *adjective* basic green [kākāriki W.91 'green']

kārikitea *adjective* light green [kāriki TM 'green' tea W.410 'light in colour']

kārikiuri *adjective* dark green [kāriki TM 'green' uri W469 'dark, green in colour']

kāripēke *noun* bank card [kāri < Eng. 'card' pēke < Eng. 'bank']

karo *intransitive verb* duck [W.101 'parry, avoid a blow']

karo *transitive verb* evade [W.101 'parry, avoid a blow']

karo aituā waka *noun* defensive driving [karo W.123 'parry, avoid' aituā W.5 'misfortune, trouble, disaster, accident' waka TM 'vehicle']

karu *noun* eyeball [W.102 'eye']

karu whakarahi *noun* magnifying glass, microscope [karu W.102 'eye' whakarahi TM 'enlarge']

karu whakatata *noun* telescope [karu W.102 'eye, look at' whaka- W.486 'causative prefix' to make tata W.393 'near']

karumātaki *noun* spectator [karu W.102 'eye, look at' mātaki W.188 'look at, watch']

karurua whakarahi *noun* binocular microscope [karu W.102 'eye' rua W.349 'two' whakarahi TM 'enlarge']

karurua whakatata *noun* binoculars [karu W.102 'eye' rua W.349 'two' whakatata W.393 'approach']

katete *noun* extension cord [W.103 'lengthen by adding a piece']

kātete-hauā *adjective, noun* paraplegic [kātete W.103 'leg, the whole leg from the thigh downwards' hauā W.39 'crippled']

kati *noun* (*weightlifting*) collar [W.103 'closed, close up']

kati *noun* (*computer*) close [W.103 'close up, shut']

kati kōtuhi *noun* greenhouse effect [kati W.103 'close in, barrier, trap' kōtuhi W.150 'hazy, smoky appearance of atmosphere, discoloured']

katihinu *noun* (*mechanical*) throttle [katirere TM 'tap' hinu common usage 'petrol']

katipō huauri *noun* queen wasp [katipō W.103 'wasp' huauri W.66 'having offspring']

katirere *noun* valve [kati W.103 'block up, close in' rere W.337 'flow']

katiwai *noun* stopcock [kati W.103 'prevent, close up' wai W.474 'water']

katiwai *noun* (*water*) tap [kati W.103 'prevent, close up' wai W.474 'water']

kātoretore *intransitive verb* glow dimly [W.104 'glimmering, dimly luminous']

katote *adjective* (*chemistry*) unstable [W.104 'not fixed, displaced']

kau aihe *noun* (*style of swimming*) butterfly [kau W.104 'swim' aihe W.5 'dolphin']

kau āpuru *noun* breaststroke [Best *Games and Pastimes* 40 'breaststroke']

kau kiore *noun* backstroke [Best *Games and Pastimes* 40 'swimming on the back']

kau tāhoe *noun* sidestroke [Best *Games and Pastimes* 40 'sidestroke']

kau tāhoe *noun* lifesaving stroke [Best *Games and Pastimes* 40 'sidestroke']

kau tāwhai *noun* (*swimming*) freestyle [W.407 'swim, stretching the arms alternately']

kaua e kuhu mai *phrase* no admittance [kaua W.105 'do not' kuhu W.154 'introduce oneself into']

kaua e puta mā konei *phrase* no exit [kaua W.105 'do not' puta W.315 'pass through or out' konei W.133 'this place']

kaua i tua atu i te ingoa e mau nei *phrase* (*cheque*) not negotiable [kaua W.105 'do not' tua W.444 'on the farther side' i W.73 'from' ingoa W.78 'name' mau W.196 'fixed']

kauae *noun* alveolar bone [kauae W.105 'jaw']

kauae-timu *noun* tetanus [kauae W.105 'jaw' timu W.419 'involuntary contraction of muscles']

kauamo *noun* (*hospital equipment*) stretcher [W.105 'litter, bed arranged between two poles to carry sick person']

kauhauora *noun* surf life-saving [W.106 'a charm to secure safety' kau W.104 'swim' hauora W.41 'healthy']

kauhauora *noun* surf life-saver [W.106 'a charm to secure safety' kau W.104 'swim' hauora W.41 'healthy']

kauhoe tukutahi *noun* synchronised swimming [kauhoe W.106 'swim' tukutahi TM 'synchronised']

kauhuri *noun* hinge [W.106 'swing on a pivot, as a door']

kauhuri *transitive verb* flip [W.106 'turn bottom upwards, turn over the soil']

kauhuri hua *noun* egg-slice [kauhuri TM 'flip' hua W.64 'egg of a bird']

kauhuri ika *noun* fish-slice [kauhuri TM 'flip' ika W.76 'fish']

kaui *noun* (*decoration*) mobile [W.106 'cord or stick on which articles are strung']

kaumoana *noun* sailor [W.106 'mariner, one of a crew of a canoe']

kauneke *noun, intransitive verb* progress [W.107 'move forward']

kaunuku *transitive verb, intransitive verb, noun (rugby)* maul [W,107 'centre of an army when formed for a rush, move steadily, large splitting wedge']

kaunukunuku *noun* rolling maul [kaunuku TM 'maul' nuku W.225 'move, extend']

kauoro *noun* scrubbing-brush [W.107 'grind by rubbing']

kaupae *noun* rung [W.107 'step or support for the foot in a ladder']

kaupane *noun (computer)* monitor [W.107 'head, upper end']

kaupapa *noun* policy [W.107 'level surface, platform, raft, groundwork to which feathers were attached in making a cloak']

kaupapa *noun (employment)* scheme [W.107 'stage, platform, groundwork']

kaupapa *noun* programme [W.107 'stage, platform, groundwork']

kaupapa *noun (topic)* subject [TM 'topic']

kaupapa *noun* topic [W.107 'stage, platform, groundwork']

kaupapa *noun* theme [W.107 'stage, platform, groundwork']

kaupapa kaute *noun* accounting policy [kaupapa TM 'policy' mahi kaute TM 'accounting']

kaupapa whakangungu *noun* training scheme [kaupapa TM 'scheme' whakangungu TM 'training']

kaupapa whakawhiwhi mahi *noun* job scheme [kaupapa TM 'scheme' whaka- W.486 'causative prefix' to make whiwhi W.499 'possessed of, having acquired' mahi W.163 'work']

kaupapa whiu *noun* penal programme [kaupapa TM 'programme' whiu TM 'penalty']

kaupapa-ā-rua *adjective (number)* binary [kaupapa W.107 'platform, layer' ā W.1 'after the manner of' rua W.349 'two']

kaupapa-ā-tau *noun* number base [kaupapa W.107 'stage, platform' ā W.1 'after the manner of' tau TM 'number']

kaupare hoariri *noun* defence [kaupare W.107 'turn in a different direction, avert' hoariri W.54 'enemy, foe']

kaupare māhie *noun* security guard [kaupare W.107 'avert' māhie W.164 'crime, evil']

kauri tawhiti *noun* tar [W.108 'a bituminous substance found on the beach, soot from burnt kauri gum or resinous wood']

kaurori *intransitive verb* pivot [W.108 'swing, turn on a pivot']

kaurori *noun* fulcrum [W.108 'swing, turn on a pivot, as a door']

kaurori *noun* hinge [W.108 'swing, turn on a pivot']

kauruku *transitive verb* colour in [W.108 'slightly shaded with colour']

kaute *noun (statement of expenditure)* account [< Eng. 'account']

kaute tahua *noun* accrual accounting [mahi kaute TM 'accounting' tahua TM 'accumulated funds']

kauwae *noun* mandible [W.105 'jaw']

kauwae whakarunga *noun (anatomy)* maxilla [kauwae W.105 'jaw' whakarunga TM 'upper']

kauwaka *adjective* psychic [W.109 'human medium of an atua or spirit]

kauwhata *noun* graph [W.109 'stage or frame for fish etc.']

kauwhata io *noun* bar graph [kauwhata TM 'graph' io W.78 'warp, vertical threads in weaving']

kauwhata ira *noun (mathematics)* dot plot [kauwhata TM 'graph' ira TM 'dot']

kauwhata kauamo *noun* box and whisker graph [kauwhata TM 'graph' kauamo W.105 'pole of ladder']

kauwhata pere *noun* arrow diagram [kauwhata TM 'graph' pere W.278 'dart']

kauwhata porohita *noun* pie graph [kauwhata TM 'graph' porohita W.295 'circle']

kauwhata pou *noun* bar graph [kauwhata TM 'graph' pou W.297 'upright' poupou W.297 'upright slabs forming the solid framework of the walls of a whare']

kauwhata pou hiato *noun* composite bar graph [kauwhata pou TM 'bar graph' hiato W.48 'be gathered together']

kauwhata rārangi *noun (mathematics)* line graph [kauwhata TM 'graph' rārangi W.324 'line']

kauwhata rautō *noun* stem and leaf graph [kauwhata TM 'graph' rau W.328 'leaf' tō W.428 'stem']

kauwhata rū *noun* seismograph [kauwhata TM 'graph' rū W.349 'earthquake']

kauwhata toro *noun* line graph [kauwhata TM 'graph' toro W.438 'stretch forth, creep, extend']

kawata *noun, adjective* silver [W.110 'glisten, shine, gleam']

kawata *adjective* silvery [W.110 'glisten, shine, gleam']

kawau moeroa *noun* driftnet [W.110 'term applied to eel pots and such nets as are allowed to remain in the water']

kawau moeroa *noun* driftnet fishing [W.110 'term applied to eel pots and such nets as are allowed to remain in the water']

kawe *transitive verb* (*transmit heat, energy*) conduct [kawe W.111 'convey, carry']

kawe rererangi *noun* aircraft carrier [kawe W.111 'carry, convey' waka rererangi common usage 'aeroplane']

kawe iahiko *noun* (*electricity*) conduction [kawe W.111 'convey, carry' iahiko TM 'electrical current']

kawekawe *noun* cartage [kawe W.111 'carry, convey']

kawhe kutē *noun* espresso [kutētē W.167 'squeeze fluid out of anything; applied to milking']

kei waho *phrase* (*tennis*) out [waho W.474 'the outside']

keka *adjective* temporarily deranged [W.113 'mentally deranged, beside oneself with grief']

keka *adjective* hysterical [W.113 'mentally deranged, beside oneself with grief']

keo iri *noun* stalactite [keo W.114 'frost' keokeo 'peaked, pointed' iri W.79 'hang, be suspended']

keo tū *noun* stalagmite [keo W.114 'frost' keokeo 'peaked, pointed' tū W.443 'stand, be erect']

kerehunga *noun* souffle [W.114 'fluff']

kerepeti *noun* plasticine [W.114 'clay worked and pressed']

kerematua *noun* pottery [W.114 stiff clay']

ketehae *noun* (*flower*) anther [kete W.115 'basket' hae W.29 'pollen']

ketukupu *noun* scrabble [ketuketu W.115 'scratch up, move leaves in looking for anything' kupu W.157 'word']

ki te ingoa e mau nei *phrase* account payee only [ki W.116 'to' ingoa W.78 'name' mau W.196 'fixed']

kīaka *noun* litre [W.116 'calabash' kī W.115 'full']

kīaka haumano *noun* millilitre [kīaka TM 'litre' haumano TM 'milli-']

kīanga *noun* (*mathematics*) expression [kī W.115 'saying, word']

kīanga *noun* phrase [W.116 'act of speaking, saying']

kiato *noun* density [W.116 'compact']

kiato *noun* (*valuables*) safe [W.117 'receptacle used for holding certain sacred things, compact']

kiato kākano *noun* ovary [kiato W.117 'receptacle for holding certain sacred things' kākano TM 'ovum']

kihu parāoa *noun* noodle, spaghetti [kihukihu W.117 'thrum' parāoa < Eng. 'flour']

kikini *noun* trace element [W.118 'pinch off']

kikiri *noun* embryo [W.119 'begin to grow, as a child in the womb']

kikiri mōwaho *noun* ectopic pregnancy [kikiri W.119 'begin to grow, as a child in the womb' mōwaho W.212 'outside, on the outside']

kikoika *adjective* pseudo [whakakikoika W.118 'feign']

kikorua *adjective* plural [W.118 'twofold, double, having descent through more than one line of ancestry']

kikotahi *adjective* (*language*) singular [kikorua W.118 'twofold, double, having descent through more than one line of ancestry' TM 'plural' tahi W.359 'one']

kimi kaimahi *noun* staff recruitment [kimi W.118 'seek, look for' kaimahi TM 'staff']

kimi tangata *transitive verb* recruit [kimi W.118 'seek, look for' tangata W.379 'human being']

kimonga *noun* (*time*) second [kimo W.118 'blink']

kini pepa *noun* paper-clip [kini W.118 nip, pinch' pepa < Eng. 'paper']

kīra *noun* (*pen*) nib [W.119 'quill']

kīrehu *noun* (*local usage*) idiom [kī W.115 'saying' rehu W.334 'dimly seen, obscure']

kiri *noun* dermis [W.119 'skin']

kiri kātete *noun* (*clothing*) tights [kiri W.119 'skin' kātete W.103 'the whole leg from the thigh downwards']

kiri whakatara *noun* (*golf*) hazard [kirikiri W.119 'gravel' whakatara W.386 'challenge, put on one's mettle']

kiriārahi *noun* officer [kiri W.119 'person' ārahi W.14 'lead, conduct, escort']

kiriāwhina *noun* official [kiri W119 'person' āwhina W.25 'assist, benefit, befriend']

kiriaku *noun, adjective* acrylic [kiri W.119 'skin' akuaku W.7 'firm, strong']

kiriata *noun* film, slide [kiri W.119 'skin' ata W.18 'shape, semblance, reflected image']

kiriata mōkito *noun* microfilm [kiriata TM 'film' mōkitokito W.207 'minute, small']

kiriata mororiki *noun* microfiche [kiriata TM 'film' mororiki W.210 'small']

kirihou *noun, adjective* plastic [kiri W.119 'skin' hou W.62 'new']

kirihou rerehū *noun* thermoplastic [kirihou TM 'plastic' rerehū W.338 'be heated']

kirihuna *noun* camouflage [kiri W.119 'skin' huna W.69 'conceal']

kirikamo *noun* conjunctiva [kiri W.119 'skin' kamo W.92 'eye']

kirikamo kakā *noun* conjunctivitis [kirikamo TM 'conjunctiva' kakā TM 'inflammation']

kirimana *noun* (*binding agreement*) contract [kiri W.119 'skin, bark' mana W.172 'effectual, binding' authoritative']

kirimata *noun* foreskin [kiri W.119 'skin' matamata W.185 'extremity']

kirimōhinu *noun* (*pottery*) glaze [kiri W.119 'skin' mōhinuhinu W.205 'shiny, glistening, glossy']

kirimoko *adjective* skin-deep, superficial [W.119 'skin']

kirimōwaho *noun* (*eye*) cornea [kiriuhi TM 'membrane' mōwaho W.212 'outward, on the outside']

kirinuku *noun* (*geology*) crust [kiri W.119 'skin' nuku W.225 'the earth']

kiripaepae *noun* receptionist [kiri W.119 'person' taupaepae W.400 'meet and escort visitors in as they arrive']

kiripūkahu *noun* pleura [kiriuhi TM 'membrane' pūkahukahu W.306 'lungs']

kiripūkahu kakā *noun* pleurisy [kiripūkahu TM 'pleura' kakā TM 'inflammation']

kirirarau *noun* citizen [kiri W.119 'person,' rarau W.328 'settle down, remain, take root']

kiriroto *noun* endoderm [kiri W.119 'skin' roto W.348 'inside']

kirirua *noun* wetsuit [W.119 'a black thick-skinned species of eel']

kirirua *noun* bodysuit [W.119 'a black thick-skinned species of eel']

kiritaki *noun* client, customer [kiri W.119 'person' apataki W.12 'retinue, following']

kiritara *noun* echinoderm [kiri W.119 'skin' tara W.386 'point, spike']

kiritata *noun* neighbour [kiri W.119 'person, skin' tata W.393 'close']

kiritautohe *noun* antagonist [kiri W.119 'person' tautohe W.404 'contend, persist, contest, quarrel']

kiriuhi *noun* membrane [kiri W.119 'skin' uhi W.471 'cover']

kiriuhi hītari *noun* semi-permeable membrane [kiriuhi TM 'membrane' hītari W.53 'sieve']

kiriuhi pūtau *noun* cell membrane [kiriuhi TM 'membrane' pūtau TM 'cell']

kiriuhi ua *noun* meninx [kiriuhi TM 'membrane' ua W.465 'backbone, neck, back of the neck']

kiriuhi ua kakā *noun* meningitis [kiriuhi TM 'membrane' ua W.465 'backbone, neck, back of the neck' kakā TM 'inflammation']

kiriuhi wheua *noun* (*anatomy*) periosteum [kiriuhi TM 'membrane' wheua W.496 'bone']

kiriwaho *noun* epidermis [kiri W.119 'skin' waho W.474 'outside']

kiriwai *noun* (*sealing substance*) primer [W.119 'inner skin']

kiriwai *noun* mesoderm [W.119 'inner skin']

kiriwara *noun* addict [kiri W.119 'person' waranga TM 'addiction']

kita takawhīwhiwhi *adjective* (*colour*) psychedelic [kita W.120 'intensely, brightly, of colours' takawhīwhiwhi W.370 'entangled, interlaced']

kitakita *noun* bacteria [W.120 'anything very small']

kitakōreko *noun* nichrome [konukita TM 'chromium' konukōreko TM 'nickel']

kīwaha *noun* colloquialism [kī W.115 'saying' waha W.473 'mouth']

kiwi *adjective* basic grey [kiwikiwi W.120 'grey']

kiwitea *adjective* pale grey [kiwi TM 'grey' tea W.410 'light in colour']

kōaka *noun* hemp [W.121 'coarse mat made of flax leaves']

kōaro *noun, adjective (mathematics)* inverse [W.122 'inverted, turned right round, upside down']

kōaro rite *noun* palindrome [kōaro W.122 'upside down' rite W.343 'alike, corresponding']

kōata *noun (material)* glass [kōataata W.122 'transparent']

kōata *noun (drinking vessel)* glass [kōataata W.122 'transparent']

kōataata *noun, adjective (type of glass)* crystal [W.122 'transparent']

kōawa *noun* canal [W.122 'watercourse, narrow gully']

kōawa taringa *noun* ear canal [kōawa TM 'canal' taringa 'ear']

koeko *noun* cone [W.123 'tapering to a point']

koeko *adjective* conical [W.123 'tapering to a point']

koeko porohita *noun (geometry)* cone [koeko W.123 'tapering to a point' porohita W.295 'circular']

koeko tarawhā *noun* pyramid [koeko W.123 'tapering to a point' tara W.387 'side wall of a house' whā W.484 'four']

koere *noun* corset [W.123 'woven belt or girdle']

koere *transitive verb* violate sexually [W.123 'strip off, tear apart' see W.314 pūrikoriko for example]

koeretanga *noun* sexual violation [W.123 'strip off, tear apart' see W.314 pūrikoriko for example]

koero *noun* menopause [W.123 'sickness, particularly later stage of menstruation']

kōetoeto *noun* kindling [W.123 'dry twigs']

kōhanga *noun* nursery [whare kōhanga W.124 'the place to which the mother and new-born child were removed']

kōhari *transitive verb* nominate [W.124 'select, pick out']

kōharinga *noun* nomination [kōhari TM 'nominate']

kōhau āhuru *noun* thermosphere [kōpaki W.135 'envelop, envelope' hau TM 'gas' āhuru W.4 'warm']

kōhauhau *noun* atmosphere [kōpaki W.135 'envelop' hau TM 'gas']

kōhauhuri *noun (atmosphere)* troposphere [kōpaki W.135 'envelop, envelope' hau TM 'gas' huri W.71 'turn, turn round']

kōhaukura *noun* chromosphere [kōpaki W.135 'envelop' hau TM 'gas' kura W.157 'red']

kōhaupapa *noun* stratosphere [kōpaki W.135 'envelop, envelope' hau TM 'gas' papa W.259 'layer']

kōhauwaenga *noun (science)* mesosphere [kōpaki W.135 'envelop' hau TM 'gas' waenga W.472 'the middle, the midst']

kōheri *noun* egg-beater [W.125 'buffet, whisk']

kohiko *noun* tinsel [W.125 'flash, twinkle']

kohikohiko *adjective* piecemeal [W.125 'do irregularly, a bit here and a bit there']

kōhine *noun* female adolescent [W.125 'girl']

kōhiwi *noun* undercarriage [W.125 'body of a canoe without attached parts, skeleton, trunk of a tree, heartwood']

kōhukihuki *noun (emotional, mental)* stress [W.126 'be pressing, make itself felt' kōhuki 'anguish, distress of mind']

kōhukihuki *adjective* frustrated [W.126 'be pressing, make itself felt' kōhuki 'anguish, distress of mind']

kōhure *adjective* distinctive [W.127 'outstanding, conspicuous']

kōhure *adjective* prominent [W.127 'outstanding, conspicuous']

koinga *noun* spire [koi W.127 'sharp, spike']

kōiriiri *intransitive verb (exercise)* warm up [kōiri W.12 'bend the body, sway, move to and fro']

kōkau *adjective* informal [W.129 'unadorned, without usual preparations']

kōkeke *noun* piston [W.129 'wind about, move backwards and forwards']

koki hāngai *adjective* right angle [koki W.129 'angle' W.34 'at right angles']

koki hāpūpū *noun* obtuse angle [koki W.129 'angle' hāpūpū W.36 'blunt']

koki hōtiu *noun* oblique angle [koki W.129 'angle' hōtiu W.62 'oblique, inclined']

koki mōwaho *noun* reflex angle [koki W.129 'angle' mōwaho W.212 'on the outside']

koki rewa *noun* angle of elevation [koki W.129 'angle' rewa W.339 'be elevated, be high up']

koki tāhapa *noun* acute angle [koki W.129 'angle' tāhapa W.358 'at an acute angle']

koki tauaro vertically opposite angle [koki W.129 'angle' tauaro W.397 'facing towards one, opposite']

koki tauroto co-interior angle [koki W.129 'angle', tau W.396 'come to anchor, lie to' roto W.348 'the inside']

koki tūrite *noun* corresponding angle [koki W.129 'angle' tūnga W.443 'place of standing' rite W.343 'alike, corresponding']

koki whakahāngai *noun* complementary angle [koki W.129 'angle' whaka- W.486 'causative prefix' to make hāngai TM 'right-angle']

koki whakarārangi *noun* supplementary angle [koki W.129 'angle' whaka- W.486 'causative prefix' to make rārangi W.324 'line']

koki whakaroto *noun* interior angle [koki W.129 'angle' whakaroto TM 'inwards']

kokinga waru *noun* fodder [W.129 'food of indifferent quality, such as is eaten in time of scarcity']

kōkiri *intransitive verb* (*rugby*) drive [W.130 'body of men rushing forward']

kōkiri *noun, intransitive verb* (*gymnastics*) vault [kōkirikiri W.130 'leap, fly headlong' kōkiri Best *Games and Pastimes* 46 'water jump']

kōkiri *noun* diving board [Best *Games and Pastimes* 46 'springboard']

kōkiri *noun* (*water-skiing*) water-jump [Best *Games and Pastimes* 46 'springless springboard']

kōkiri *transitive verb* (*support*) champion [W.130 'rush forward, charge, body of men rushing forward']

kōkiri mana wahine *noun* feminism [kōkiri TM 'champion' mana W.172 'influence, power, control' wahine W.474 'woman']

kōkiri tiketike *noun* (*diving*) high board [kōkiri TM 'diving board' tiketike W.417 'lofty, high']

kōkiri tūringa *noun* handstand vault [kōkiri TM 'vault' tūringa TM 'handstand']

koko purini *noun* dessert spoon [koko W.130 'spoon' purini < Eng. 'pudding']

koko tautuku *noun* penalty corner [koko W.130 'corner' tautuku W.405 'stoop, bend down; so give way']

koko waihāro *noun* soup-spoon [koko W.130 'spoon' waihāro TM 'soup']

kōkōhiko *noun* electric fan [kōkō W.121 'wind' hiko common usage 'electric']

kōkōwai *adjective* reddish-brown [W.131 'earth from which red ochre is procured by burning red ochre']

kokoine *noun* measuring spoon [koko W.130 'spoon' ine W.130 'measure']

kokoiti *noun* teaspoon [koko W.130 'spoon' iti W.80 'small']

kokorukī *noun* double quotation mark [koru W.147 'a bulbed motif in carving and scroll painting' kī W.15 'say, speak, utter']

kōkota *noun* (*passport*) visa [W.147 'a mark made at cross-roads to show which road has been taken']

kokoti-uru *noun* (*medicine*) sterilisation [W.131 'rite intended to prevent conception']

kokotoha *noun* serving spoon [koko W.130 'spoon' toha W.429 'distribute']

kokotoha *noun* tablespoon [koko W.130 'spoon' toha W.429 'distribute']

kōmā *adjective* pallid [W.131 'pale, whitish']

koma *noun* gram [W.131 'a kind of stone']

koma haumano *noun* milligram [koma TM 'gram' haumano TM 'milli-']

koma-mano *noun* kilogram [koma TM 'gram' mano W.176 'thousand']

kōmaka *transitive verb* sort, classify [W.131 'sort out']

kōmāmā *noun* polystyrene [W.131 'light in weight, soft' mā W.161 'white']

komama *transitive verb* percolate, *noun* percolator [W.131 'run or fall through a small aperture']

kōmanawa *noun* hydrant [W.131 'spring of water']

kōmaoa wae, waha *noun* foot-and-mouth disease [komāoa W.131 'ulcerated' wae W.472 'foot' waha W.473 'mouth']

kōmaru *adjective* solar [W.131 'sun']

kōmiringa kōpaki *noun* mailroom [kōmiri W.132 'sort out' kōpaki W.135 'envelope, wrap, envelop']

kōmitimiti *intransitive verb* integrate [W.132 'mingle' te komititanga o ngā wai W.132 'the junction of the waters']

komoringa *noun* glove, mitt [komo W.132 'put in, insert' ringa W.341 'hand']

komonga hahau *noun* batting glove [komonga TM 'glove' kaihahau TM 'batter']

komonga mekemeke *noun* boxing glove [komonga TM 'glove' mekemeke TM 'boxing']

komoringa umu *noun* oven glove [komoringa TM 'glove' umu TM 'oven']

kōmutu *noun* (*kitchenware*) lid [W.133 'calabash with top cut off and used as a lid']

kōnae *noun* (*document*) file [W.133 'small basket woven from strips of flax']

kōnakonako *noun* halogen lamp [W.133 'dazzling light, glare']

kōnao *noun* (*stove*) warming-drawer [W.133 'earth oven for which the stones are heated in a fire beside the pit, not in the pit']

koneke *noun* rollerblades [W.133 'slide along']

koneke ngaru *noun* boogie board [koneke W.133 'slide along' ngaru W.230 'wave']

konekone *noun* aversion [W.133 'repugnance']

konihi *noun* predator [W.134 'attack by stealth, a small marauding party moving stealthily']

konu- (*used as prefix*) natural metal [kongakonga W.134 'fragment, chip' nuku W.225 'the earth']

konu-okehu *noun* barium [konu- TM 'prefix denoting natural metal' okehu W.239 'soft white stone']

konukita *noun* chromium [konu- TM 'prefix denoting natural metal' kitakita W.120 'intensely, brightly, of colours']

konukōreko *noun* nickel [konu- TM 'prefix denoting natural metal' kōreko W.141 'white, dazzled']

konukura *noun* (*metal*) copper [konu- TM 'prefix denoting natural metal' kura W.157 'red ochre']

kōnumi *noun* U-turn [W.134 'take a backward course']

konumohe *noun* aluminium [konu- TM 'prefix denoting natural metal' mohe W.205 'soft, yielding']

konuoi *noun* mercury [konu- TM 'prefix denoting natural metal' oi W.238 'move continuously']

konupora *noun* magnesium [konu- TM 'prefix denoting natural metal' pora W.293 'a white stone']

konupūmā *noun* calcium [konu- TM 'prefix denoting natural metal' pūmā W.309 'whitish grey']

konurehu *noun* potassium [konu- TM 'prefix denoting natural metal' rehu W.334 'spray, fine dust']

konukarihi *noun* uranium [konu- TM 'prefix denoting natural metal' karihi TM 'nuclear']

konuruke *noun* radium [konu- TM 'prefix denoting natural metal' ira rukeruke TM 'radioactive']

konutai *noun* sodium [konu- TM 'prefix denoting natural metal' tai W.361 'the sea']

konutai waihā *noun* (*sodium hydroxide*) caustic soda [konutai TM 'sodium' waihā TM 'hydroxide']

konutea zinc [konu- TM 'prefix denoting natural metal' tea W.410 'white, clear']

konuuku *noun* beryllium [konu- TM 'prefix denoting natural metal' uku W.466 'white clay']

konga kouawai *noun* gallstone [konga W.134 'fragment, chip' kouawai W.151 'gall bladder']

konganuku *noun* natural metal [kongakonga W.134 'fragment, chip' nuku W.225 'the earth']

konganuku taumaha *noun* (*chemistry*) heavy metal [konganuku TM 'metal' taumaha W.399 'heavy']

kōngohe *adjective* ductile [konu- TM 'prefix denoting natural metal' ngohe W.234 'supple, soft']

kopa kirihou *noun* plastic bag [kopa W.135 'wallet, satchel' kopa whakawiri tītoki 'bag for squeezing the oil from tītoki berries' kirihou TM 'plastic']

kōpae *noun* (*computer*) disk [kōpaepae W.135 'plaited circular band for lining an oven']

kōpae aorangi *noun* (*building*) planetarium [kōpae W.135 'circular house' aorangi TM 'planet']

kōpae matua *noun* hard disk [kōpae TM 'disk' matua W.195 'main']

kōpae pīngore *noun* floppy disk [kōpae TM 'disk' pīngore W.282 'flexible, bending']

kōpae pūoru *noun* (*music*) record [kōpae TM 'disc' pūoru TM 'music']

kōpaepae *noun* diskette [W.135 'plaited circular band for lining an oven']

kōpaepae pūoru *noun* (*music*) compact disc [W.135 'plaited circular band for lining an oven' pūoru TM 'music']

kōpaetara *noun* cogwheel, sprocket-wheel [kōpae W.135 'circular' tara TM 'cog']

kōpaka *noun* shortage [W.135 'be short of a thing, be in want']

kōpaka huaora C *noun* scurvy [kōpaka W.135 'be short of a thing, be in want' huaora C TM 'vitamin C']

kōpaki *noun* (*stationery*) folder [W.135 'wrap, envelop, enfold']

kōpaki *noun* mail [W.135 'envelope, wrap, envelop']

kōpaki rangi *noun, adjective* air-mail [kōpaki TM 'mail' rangi W.323 'sky, heaven']

kopamārō *noun* briefcase [kopa W.135 'wallet, satchel' mārō W.183 'hard, unyielding']

kōpani *noun* epiglottis [W.136 'lid of box, etc., shut up, close up']

kōpani *noun* teargas [W.136 'an incantation to blind the eyes of a pursuer']

kōpapa *noun* silo [W.136 'storehouse for food, concave']

kōpapa *noun* surfboard [Best *Games and Pastimes* 42 'surfboard']

kōpapa wai *noun* water tank [kōpapa W.136 'storehouse for food' wai W.474 'water']

kōpapa whakawera wai *noun* hot-water cylinder [kōpapa wai TM 'water tank' whaka- W.486 'causative prefix' to make wera W.482 'heated, hot']

kōpare *noun* face-mask [W.135 'shade or veil the eyes']

kopareti *noun* skate [kopa W.135 'sandal' reti TM 'skate']

kopatio *noun* freezer bag [kopa kirihou TM 'plastic bag' whakatio TM 'freeze']

kope *noun* sanitary pad [W.136 'a woman's girdle of soft mosses used for health purposes, soft masses used as wrappers or absorbents']

kope *noun* nappy [W.136 'soft mosses used as wrappers or absorbents']

kōpere *noun, intransitive verb* sprint [W.137 'rush']

kopi *noun* (*punctuation*) full stop, period [W.137 'shut, closed, completed']

kopi-piko *noun* semi-colon [kopi TM 'full stop' piko TM 'comma']

kōpiro *noun* (*anatomy*) colon [W.137 'intestines']

kōpiro *noun* large intestine [W.137 'intestines']

kōpiro koromeke *noun* small intestine [kōpiro W.284 'intestines' koromeke W.144 'in loops, coils, or kinks']

kōpiro pae *noun* (*anatomy*) transverse colon [kōpiro TM 'colon' pae W.245 'transverse beam']

kōpiro whakahume *noun* (*anatomy*) sigmoid colon [kōpiro TM 'colon' whakahume W.69 'be drawn between the legs (of the tail of a dog)']

kopirua *noun* (*punctuation*) colon [kopi TM 'full stop' rua W.349 'two']

kōporo *noun* van [waka kōporo W.138 'a square-sterned canoe']

kopou *transitive verb* appoint [W.138 'appoint']

kopounga *noun* (*employment*) appointment [kopou TM 'appoint']

kopounga *noun* successful candidate [kopou W.138 'appoint']

kōpū *noun* underwear [W.138 'an inner garment']

kōpū *noun* uterus [W.138 'belly, womb']

kōpuha *noun* cabin [W.138 'small house']

kōpukupuku *noun* German measles, rubella [W.138 'rash on the skin']

kōpurawhetū *noun* (*generic term*) fungi [W.139 'a fungus']

kora *noun* sequin [W.139 'small fragment, speck, spark, gleam']

kora mātātoka *noun* fossil fuel [kora W.139 'fuel' mātātoka TM 'fossilised']

koraha *noun* desert [W.139 'open country']

kōrahirahi *noun* enamel [W.139 'thin, somewhat transparent']

koranu *noun* metal alloy [konu- TM 'prefix for natural metals' ranu W.322 'mix']

korare *noun* beet [W.140 'greens, leaves of edible vegetables']

kore *noun* zero, zilch, nought [korenga W.141 'non-existence, non-occurrence']

kore *intransitive verb* (*terminated*) shut down [W.141 'cease to be, be destroyed']

kōrea *noun* wheelchair [W.141 'small canoe']

kōrekoreko *adjective* fluorescent [W.141 'dazzled']

kōrero *noun* discourse [W.141 'speak, conversation']

kōrero *noun* (*document*) record [W.141 'tell, say, narrative, discussion']

kōrero *noun* information [W.142 'news, narrative, discussion']

kōrero ahiahi *noun* (*story-telling*) to spin a yarn [W.142 'idle tales']

kōrero nehe *noun* ancient history [kōrero W.141 'tell, say, story, narrative' nehe W.220 'ancient times']

kōrero o mua *noun* history [kōrero W.141 'tell, say, story, narrative' mua W.213 'before, formerly']

kōrero paki *noun* storytelling [kōrero W.142 'story, tell' pakipaki W.253 'tales']

kōrero tārehu *noun* secret [kōrero W.141 'tell, say' tārehu W.390 'cover, seal, be indistinctly seen']

kōrero tinana *noun* body language [kōrero W.141 'tell, say' tinana W.419 'body']

kōreti *noun* kayak [W.142 'a small canoe']

kōrinorino *noun* dreadlocks [W.142 'twist, hank, curl']

kōripi *noun* (*cricket*) slip [W.142 'cut, slice, turn sideways']

kōripi wae *noun* (*cricket*) leg slip [kōripi W.142 'cut, slice, turn sideways' wae W.472 'leg']

kōripi whakaroto *noun, transitive verb* (*golf*) hook [koripi W.142 'slice, turn sideways' whakaroto TM 'inwards']

kōripi whakawaho *noun, transitive verb* (*golf*) slice [kōripi W.142 'slice, turn sideways' whakawaho TM 'outwards']

koroī *noun* conifer, gymnosperm [W.144 'fruit of white pine, the tree itself']

koroī *noun* (*fruit of tree*) cone [W.144 'fruit of white pine']

korokē *adjective* ironic [W.144 'extraordinary, strange, out of the common']

korokē *noun* nonconformist, unorthodox, eccentric [W.144 'extraordinary, strange, out of the common']

koromāhu *noun* sauna [W.144 'steam']

koromaki obsessed [W.144 'be fully intent upon an object, pursue with all one's mind]

koroputa hei *noun* chicken pox [koroputaputa W.145 'smallpox' heihei W.44 'barnyard fowl']

koroputa kau *noun* cowpox [koroputaputa W.145 'smallpox' kau < Eng. 'cow']

koropū *noun* weatherboard [W.145 'built with wrought timber']

kororā *adjective* blue-grey [W.145 'blue penguin, grey']

kōrori *noun* whisk [W.145 'stir round']

koru *noun* (*intestine*) coil [W.147 'folded, coiled, looped']

korukī *noun* single quotation mark [koru W.147 'a bulbed motif in carving and scroll painting' kī W.15 'say, speak, utter']

kōrure-kore *adjective* (*mathematics*) commutative [kōrure W.147 'change' kore W.140 'no, not']

kōtaha kurutai *noun* (*athletics event*) hammer-throwing [W.147 'a stone weapon attached to a cord by which it was recovered after having been thrown at the enemy']

kotahi atu, āe *phrase* (*golf*) hole in one [idiom kotahi W.147 'one' atu W.20 'to indicate a direction or motion onwards or away from the speaker' āe W.1 'yes']

kotahi atu ki uta *noun* (*softball*) home run [idiom kotahi W.147 'one' atu W.20 'to indicate a direction or motion onwards or away from the speaker' uta TM 'home base']

kotahi atu ki waho *phrase* (*sport*) out on the full [idiom kotahi W.147 'one' atu W.20 'to indicate a direction or motion onwards or away from the speaker' waho W.474 'the outside']

kotakota rīwai *noun* (*potato*) chippies [kotakota W.147 'chips, shavings' rīwai W.344 'potato']

kotami *noun* turnip [W.148 'wild turnip']

kotē kanekane *noun* garlic crusher [kotē W.148 'squeeze out, crush, mash' kanekane TM 'garlic']

kotē rēmana *noun* lemon-squeezer [kotē W.148 'squeeze out' rēmana < Eng. 'lemon']

koti hiko *noun* power cut [koti W.149 'interrupt, cut off, so cut across the path' hiko common usage 'electricity']

koti kamo *noun* choroid membrane [koti W.148 'divide' kamo W.92 'eye']

Kōti Matua *noun* Supreme Court [Kōti < Eng 'court' matua W.195 'main, chief']

kotimutu *noun* flask [W.149 'calabash with small end cut off so as to form a bottle']

kotiti *intransitive verb* (*swimming*) break lanes [kōtītiti W.149 'wander about, be irregular']

kotiti *noun* deviance [W.146 'be distorted or displaced']

kotiti margin of error [W.149 'be distorted or displaced']

kotopihi umu *noun* oven-window [kotopihi W.150 'window' umu TM 'oven']

kōtuhi *noun* smog [W.150 'hazy, smoky appearance of atmosphere, discoloured']

kōtui *noun* (*rugby*) bind [W.150 'fasten by lacing']

kōtuitanga *noun* synthesis [kōtui W.150 'lace, fasten via lacing, interlace']

kōtuitui *noun* network [kōtui W.150 'fasten by lacing, interlace, interlaced']

kōtuitui *transitive verb* synthesise [kōtui W.150 'lace, fasten via lacing, interlace']

kōtutu *noun* souplade [W.150 'ladle for liquids']

kou whakangahu rauiti *noun* (*microscope*) fine focusing knob [kou W.150 'knob, end, protuberance' whaka- W.486 'causative prefix' to make ngahu TM 'in focus' rauiti W.329 'small, fine, thin']

kou whakangahu raunui *noun* (*microscope*) coarse focusing knob [kou W.150 'knob, end, protuberance' whaka- W.486 'causative prefix' to make ngahu TM 'in focus' raunui W.330 'broad']

kounga *noun* quality [kou W.151 'good']

kōurapaka *noun* crustacean [kōura W.151 'crayfish' pāpaka W.250 'crab']

koutata *noun* antelope [W.151 'smooth, sleek']

koutu *noun* peninsula [W.151 'promontory, point of land']

kōwae *noun* (*unit*) module [W.151 'divide, part']

kōwae *noun* paragraph [W. 151 'divide, part, set apart']

kōwaiwai *noun* (*art*) painting, visual art [W.151 'an ancient style of painting, for adorning the person and dwellings']

kōwaiwai papanga *noun* screen print [kōwaiwai W.151 'an ancient style of painting for adorning the person and dwellings' papanga TM 'fabric']

kōwaiwai-haratau *noun* art and craft [kōwaiwai W.151 'an ancient style of painting for adorning the person and dwellings' haratau W.37 'dexterous, suitable, approved']

kōwakawaka *adjective* corrugated [W.152 'grooved, fluted']

kōwao puaheiri *noun* abominable snowman [kōwao W.152 'living in the woods, wild' puaheiri W.301 'snow']

kōwhau *adjective* (*food*) stale [W.153 'dry and tasteless']

kōwhiringa *noun* combination [kōwhiri W.153 'select']

kōwhiringa whai raupapa *noun* permutation [kōwhiri W.153 'select' whai W.484 'possessing' raupapa TM 'sequence']

kū *noun* syllable [W.153 'make a low inarticulate sound, grating sound']

kū *noun* (*musical instrument*) string [W.153 'one string instrument, make a low inarticulate sound, grating sound']

kua puta *adverb* (*sport*) out, out of play [puta W.315 'pass out']

kūaha kōtiri *noun* revolving door [kūaha W.154 'gateway, entrance' kōtiri W.149 'come or go one at a time']

kūaha matua *noun* main entrance [kūaha W.154 'entrance' matua W.195 'main']

kueo *adjective* saturated [W.154 'soaked']

kuha kāinga *noun* (*dwelling*) shanty [W.154 'a scrap of a dwelling place']

kuha papa kāinga *noun* shanty town [kuha kāinga TM 'shanty' papa W.259 'earth floor or site']

kuhi *noun* (*language*) affix [W.154 'insert']

kuhi *noun* implant [W.154 'insert']

kuhi taiawa *noun* (*suppository*) pessary [kuhi W.154 'thrust in, insert' taiawa W.363 'vagina']

kuhimua *noun* prefix [kuhi W.154 'insert' mua W.213 'front']

kuhimuri huriaro *noun* passive suffix [kuhimuri TM 'suffix' huriaro TM 'passive']

kuhitou *noun* enema [kuhi W.154 'insert, introduce' tou W.442 'anus']

kuhitou *noun* suppository [kuhi W.154 'insert, introduce' tou W.442 'anus']

kuhitou konu-okehu *noun* barium enema [kuhi W.154 'insert, introduce' tou W.442 'anus' konu-okehu TM 'barium']

kuhiwē *noun* infix [kuhi W.154 'insert' wē W.481 'the middle']

kūiti *adjective* (*rugby*) blind-side [W.154 'narrow, confined']

kūiti moana *noun* (*geography*) sound [kūiti W.154 'narrow, confined' moana W.204 'sea, lake']

kūititanga *noun* isthmus [W154 'narrow, confined']

kūkamo *noun* cucumber [kū- < Eng 'cu-' kamokamo W.92 'fruit of a gourd, possibly from cucumber']

kukarou *noun* cocaine [kuka W.155 'dry leaves' rou W.349 'intoxicated, as with tutu juice']

kukū *noun* (*food*) paste [W.153 'firm, stiff, not watery']

kukū *noun* (*substance*) concentrate, concentration [W.153 'thickened, thick liquid']

kukume *transitive verb* (*physics*) attract [kumekume W.156 ' draw, attract']

kukune *noun* foetus [W.156 'swell, as pregnancy advances']

kukuweu *noun* tweezers [kuku W.155 'pincers, tweezers' weu W.483 'single hair']

kumamatanga *noun* appetiser [W.155 'something to tempt the appetite']

kume-ā-papa *noun* gravity [kume W.155 'pull, drag' ā W1 'after the manner of' papa W.259 'earth']

kūmete *noun* serving bowl [W.156 'wooden bowl or trough']

kumi ihupoto *noun* alligator [kumi W.156 'a huge fabulous reptile' ihu W.75 'nose' poto W.297 'short']

kumi ihuroa *noun* crocodile [kumi W.156 'a huge fabulous reptile' ihu W.75 'nose' roa W.344 'long']

kūnāwheke *adjective* insidious [whakakūnāwheke W.156 'nag, gnaw, work, of suppressed ill-feeling']

kunenga mai *noun* evolution [kune W.156 'swell as pregnancy advances, spring, grow' mai W.166 'indicating a relation or aspect towards the speaker']

kūoro *noun* mouli [W.156 'grind, rub down, grate']

kuoro tīhi *noun* cheese grater [kuoro W.156 'grate' tīhi < Eng. 'cheese']

kūpara *noun* calibre [W.157 'size, extent']

kūpara iti *noun* smallbore rifle [kūpara TM 'calibre' iti W.80 'small']

kupenga a Tara-mainuku *noun* stratus [W.157 'clouds in strata']

kupu āhua *noun* adjective [kupu W.157 'word' āhua W.4 'character, appearance']

kupu āhua whakataurite *noun* comparative adjective [kupu āhua TM 'adjective' whakataurite TM 'compare']

kupu āpiti *noun* postscript [kupu W.157 'message, word' āpiti W.12 'supplement anything deficient']

kupu hou *noun* neologism [kupu W.157 'word' hou W.62 'new']

kupu ingoa *noun* noun [kupu W.157 'word' ingoa W.78 'name']

kupu ingoa kurehu *noun* abstract noun [kupu ingoa TM 'noun' kurehu W.158 'indistinctly seen']

kupu ingoa tangata *noun* proper noun [kupu W.157 'word' ingoa W.78 'name' tangata W.379 'human being']

kupu ingoa uka *noun* concrete noun [kupu ingoa TM 'noun' uka W.466 'hard, firm']

kupu ingoa wāhi *noun* locative noun [kupu ingoa TM 'noun' wāhi W.474 'place, locality']

(kupu) mātāhae *noun* slang [kupu W.157 'anything said' mātāhae W.186 'divergent stream from the main channel of a river']

kupu pono *noun* axiom [kupu W.157 'saying' pono W.291 'true']

kupu tāpiri *noun* footnote [kupu W.157 'word, talk' tāpiri W.384 'add, append, supplement']

kupu taurangi *noun* guarantee [kupu W.157 'anything said, word' kī taurangi W.402 'promise, pledge']

kupu taurangi *noun* oath [kupu W.157 'word, anything said' kī taurangi W.402 'promise, pledge']

kupu tautoko *noun* testimonial [kupu W.157 'word, speak, anything said' tautoko W.404 'prop up, support']

kupu tawhiti *noun* superlative [kupu W.157 'word' kei tawhiti W.409 'matchless, unrivalled']

kupu whakamahuki *noun* preamble [kupu W.157 'word, message' whakamahuki W.165 'explain']

kupu whakarite *noun* metaphor [kupu W.157 'word, saying' whakarite W.343 'make like, liken']

kupu whakarite *noun* simile [kupu W.157 'word, saying' whakarite W.343 'make like, liken']

kupuhoto *noun* (*language*) conjunction,

connective [kupu W.157 'word' hoto W.62 'join']

kupumahi *noun* verb [kupu W.157 'word' mahi W.163 'do, perform, function']

kupumahi auau *noun* frequentative verb [kupumahi TM 'verb' auau W.21 'frequently repeated, again and again']

kupumahi huriaro *noun* passive verb [kupumahi TM 'verb' huriaro TM 'passive']

kupumahi ngoi *noun* active verb [kupumahi TM 'verb' ngoi W.234 'strength, energy']

kupumahi punarua *noun* di-transitive verb [kupumahi TM 'verb' punarua W.310 'having two wives']

kupumahi takakau *noun* intransitive verb [kupumahi TM 'verb' takakau W.368 'free from the marriage tie, at leisure']

kupumahi whaihoa *noun* transitive verb [kupumahi TM 'verb' whai W.484 'possessing, equipped with' hoa W.54 'companion, mate']

kuputohu *noun* (*syntax*) article [kupu W.157 'word' tohu W.431 'show, point out, look towards']

kuputohu *noun* (*book etc.*) index [kupu W.157 'word' tohu W.431 'guide, direct']

kura *adjective* basic red [W.157 'red']

kura hiato *noun* composite school [kura < Eng. 'school' hiato TM 'composite']

kura horahora (*basketball*) man to man, full court press, one-on-one [W.158 'spread out, extend, applied to a war party']

kura pūhou *noun* kindergarten [kura < Eng. 'school' pūhou W.305 'young']

kura rata *noun* medical school [kura common usage 'school' rata W.327 'doctor']

kūrae *noun* peninsula [W.158 'project, be prominent, headland']

kurahau-awatea *noun* (*meteorological*) cyclone, depression [Best *Astronomical Knowledge* 19 'sign of bad weather']

kurahauao *noun* (*solar system*) corona [kurahaupō W.158 'lunar rainbow' ao W.11 'bright']

kurahaupō *noun* anticyclone [Best *Astronomical Knowledge* 19 'sign of good weather']

kuranoho *noun* boarding school [kura < Eng. 'school' noho W.223 'remain, dwell']

kūrapa (*cricket*) run out [W.158 'unsuccessful in fishing or acquiring property']

kuratea *adjective* light red [kura W.157 'red' teatea W.410 'white, light in colour']

kuratea *noun* brass [konukura TM 'copper' konutea TM 'zinc']

kurauri *adjective* dark red [kura W.157 'red' uri W.469 'dark, deep in colour']

kuru *noun* slamdunk [W.159 'pelt, thump, throw']

kūrua *noun* vocal cords [kū W.153 'a one-string instrument, make a low inarticulate sound' kukū 'make a grating sound' rua W.349 'two']

kurumetometo *noun* (*chess*) pawn [W.159 'person of no account, of small stature']

kurutai *noun* (*athletics*) hammer [kōtaha kurutai W.147 'a stone weapon attached to a cord by which it was recovered after having been thrown at the enemy' kurutai W.159 'a hard, dark-coloured stone used for making weapons']

kurutangi *noun* (*ear*) anvil [W.159 'stone beater']

kutētē *noun* espresso machine [kawhe kutē TM 'espresso']

kutētē *transitive verb* (*liquid*) express [kutētē W.167 'squeeze fluid out of anything; applied to milking']

Kūwatawata *noun* Charon [Smith *The Lore of the Whare Wānanga* 184]

M

mae *noun* phobia [W.162 'paralysed with fear']
mae ahoaho *noun* agoraphobia [mae W.162 'paralysed with fear' ahoaho W.3 'open space']
mae apiapi *noun* claustrophobia [mae TM 'phobia' apiapi W.12 'confined, constricted']
māhaki *adjective* humble [W.162 'mild, meek']
mahana *noun* temperature [W.162 'warm']
mahau *noun* vestibule [W.163 'porch, verandah']
māhauhau *noun* bivouac [W.163 'a temporary shelter shed']
mahere *noun* chart [W.163 'plan']
mahere *noun* plan [W.163 'plan']
mahere ariā *noun* concept map [mahere TM 'map' ariā W.15 'notion, idea']
mahere huānga *noun* (*mathematics*) array [mahere W.163 'plan' huānga W.65 'relative, member of same clan']
mahere hura *noun* flip chart [mahere TM 'chart' hura W.70 'uncover, expose']
mahere rangatōpū *noun* corporate plan [mahere TM 'plan' rangatōpū TM 'corporate']
mahere ripo *noun* flow chart [mahere TM 'chart' ripo W.342 'whirlpool, eddy']
mahere whai whakamārama *noun* annotated diagram [mahere W.163 'plan' whai W.484 'possessing, equipped with' whakamārama W.180 'explain, illuminate']
mahere whenua *noun* map [mahere W.163 'plan' whenua W.494 'land, country']
maheu tātari kaute *noun* audit trail [maheu W.163 'trail or track through fern or scrub' tātari kaute TM 'audit']

mahi *noun* (*general*) operation [W.163 'work, occupation, do, perform']
mahi *noun* trade [W.163 'work, work at, occupation']
mahi kaute *noun* (*audit*) accounting [mahi W.163 'work, be occupied with' kaute common usage 'account']
mahi kōhikohiko *noun* casual job [mahi W.163 'work, work at' kōhikohiko W.125 'do irregularly, a bit here and a bit there']
mahi mātātoa *noun* adventure [mahi W.163 'occupation, do, perform' mātātoa W.191 'fearless, active, vigorous, energetic']
mahi ngātahi *intransitive verb* cooperate, *noun* cooperation [mahi W.163 'work, work at' ngātahi W.231 'together']
mahi ngātahi *noun* industrial relations [mahi W.163 'work, work at' ngātahi W.231 'together']
mahi tārake *noun* fieldwork [mahi W.163 'work, work at' tārake W.387 'isolated, standing in the open']
mahi taurangi *noun* algebra [mahi W.163 'perform, work at' taurangi TM 'variable']
mahi tīpako *noun* shift work [mahi W.163 'work, work at, occupation' tīpakopako W.421 'in detached parties, not in one body, at odd times']
mahi toi *noun* art [mahi W.163 'work, occupation' toi W.431 'art']
mahi waimori *noun* casual job [mahi W.163 'work' waimori W.476 'working intermittently']
mahue *adjective* (*marital status*) separated [W.165 'forsaken, deserted, given up']
mahuki *adjective* comprehensible [W.165 'clear, plain']

māhuri *adjective* (*level*) intermediate [W.165 'young tree, sapling']
māia *noun* competitor [W.166 'brave warrior, fellow, bold, capable']
maihao *noun* (*shoe*) sprig [W.167 'finger, toe']
maika *noun* banana [< Hawai'i 'banana']
maiki *noun* incident [W.167 'misfortune']
maita *noun* (*lawn bowls*) bowl [< Hawai'i 'bowls' Best *Games and Pastimes* 173]
maita *noun* (*sport*) bowls [< Hawai'i 'bowls']
maita mā *noun* (*lawn bowls*) jack [maita TM 'bowl' mā W.161 'white']
maka *transitive verb* (*with hands, sport*) pass [W.168 'throw, cast']
maka hara *noun* (*soccer*) foul throw [maka W.168 'throw' hara TM 'foul']
maka māminga *noun* (*rugby*) dummy [maka TM 'pass' māminga W.172 'pretend, feign']
maka pātea *noun* free throw [maka W.168 'throw' pātea TM 'free']
maka tautuku *noun* penalty pass [maka TM 'pass' tautuku W.405 'stoop, bend down; so give way']
maka tīpoka *noun* (*sport*) skip-pass [maka TM 'pass' tīpoka W.422 'skip over, pass by, omit']
maka tūpana *noun* bounce pass [maka W.168 'throw' tūpana TM 'bounce']
maka uri *noun* (*netball*) short pass [maka TM 'pass' uriuri W.469 'short in time or distance']
maka whakamua *noun* forward pass [maka TM 'pass' whakamua 'forwards']
makatiti *noun, transitive verb* staple [W.169 'fasten with a peg or pin, pierce']
makatiti *noun* stapler [W.169 'fasten with a peg or pin, pierce']
makau *adjective* recurved [W.169 'bent, curved']
makawe o Raukatauri *noun* (*generic term*) fern [W.169 'a fern']
makihuhunu *noun* unethical practice, *adjective* immoral, unethical [W.170 'take an unfair advantage of' maki W.170 'prefix indicating an action is done for one's own benefit' huhunu W.70 'plunder, maltreat']
mākiri *transitive verb* (*remove bones*) bone [W.170 'take the bones out of pigeons, etc.']

mākoi *noun* leading question [W.171 'pointed question']
mākōwaro *noun* chlorofluorocarbon [hau māota TM 'chlorine' hau kōwhai TM 'fluorine' waro TM 'carbon']
mākurakura *adjective* pink [W.171 'light red, glowing, reddish (as sunrise)']
mākuratea *adjective* pale pink [mākura TM 'pink' tea W.410 'white, light in colour']
mamau *noun* (*judo*) hold [W.196 'grasp, grab, wrestle with']
mamau (*sport*) wrestling [W.196 'grasp, grab, wrestle with']
mana *noun* jurisdiction [W.172 'authority, control']
mana hapori *noun* socialism [mana W.172 'power, control, authority' hapori TM 'social, community']
mana kōkiri *noun* mandate [mana W.172 'authority, control' kōkiri W.130 'rush forward, charge']
mana pupuri tamariki *noun* (*children*) custody [mana W.172 'authority, control' pupuri W.314 'retain possession of' tamariki W.376 'children']
mana tangata *noun* human rights [mana W.172 'control, power' tangata W379 'human being']
mana tangata whenua *noun* indigenous rights [mana W.172 'control', having power' tangata whenua W.494 'natives']
mana tokitoki *noun* monopoly [mana W.172 'power, control, authority, influence' tokitoki W.434 'altogether, without exception']
mana whakairo hinengaro *noun* intellectual property rights [mana W.172 'authority, control' whakairo W.80 'ornament with a pattern, used of carving, tatooing, painting, weaving' hinengaro W.51 'seat of the thoughts and emotions']
mana whakaputa whakaaro *phrase* freedom of speech [mana W.172 'power, control' whakaputa W.316 'cause to come forth' whakaaro W.16 'thought, opinion']
mana whakatau inamata *noun* summary jurisdiction [mana W.172 'power, authority' whakatau TM 'decide' inamata W.77 'immediately']
mana whakauru *phrase* freedom of association [mana W.172 'power, control' whakauru W.465 'ally oneself to, join']

mana-ā-rohe *noun* local authority [mana W.172 'authority, control' ā W.1 'after the manner of' rohe W.344 'boundary']
manapori *noun* democracy [mana W.172 'power, control' pori W.294 'people, tribe']
manapori *adjective* democratic [mana W.172 'power, control' pori W.294 'people, tribe']
manapou *noun* paramedic [W.173 'anything to support life']
manapou hiko *noun* (*medicine*) life-support system [W.173 'anything to support life' hiko common usage 'electric']
manatārua *noun* copyright [mana W.172 'authority, power' tārua TM 'copy']
manatōpū *noun* incorporated society [mana W.172 'authority' tōpū W.437 'assembled, in a body']
manatunga *noun* memento [W.173 'keepsake']
manawa *noun* pulse [W.174 'heart']
manawa hopo *adjective* superstitious [manawa W.174 'heart, mind, spirit' hopo W.59 'fearful, apprehensive, overawed']
manawa kai tūtae *noun* daredevil [W.174 'daring, undaunted']
manawa kai tūtae *noun* stuntperson [W.174 'daring, undaunted']
manawa kakī *noun* carotid pulse [manawa W.174 'heart' kakī W.92 'neck']
manawa nui *adjective* (*people etc.*) tolerant [W.174 'patient, forbearing']
manawa nui *noun* (*people etc.*) tolerance [W.174 'patient, forbearing']
manawa ringa *noun* wrist pulse [manawa W.174 'heart' ringa W.341 'hand']
manawa toa *noun* (*pain*) tolerance [manawa nui W.174 'stout-hearted, patient, forbearing' toa W.428 'brave']
manawa tōrōkiri *phrase* hole in the heart [manawa W.174 'heart' tōrōkiri W.440 'defect, flaw in timber due to injury to the growing tree']
manawa toto pūroto *noun* ischaemic heart disease [manawa W.174 'heart' toto W.441 'blood' pūroto W.314 'sluggish, of a stream']
manawa wawaro *noun* heart murmur [manawa W.174 'heart' wawaro W.480 'indistinct sound of voices, murmur']
manawa whenua *noun* mineral [W.174 'from the bowels of the earth']

manawa-hē *noun* heart attack, cardiac arrest [manawa W.174 'heart' hē W.43 'in trouble or difficulty, fail']
manawataki *noun* (*sound*) rhythm [manawa W.174 'mind, spirit, heart' taki W.371 'tow with a line, lead, bring along' taki TM 'beat']
manawataki *adjective* (*sound*) rhythmic [manawa W.174 'mind, spirit, heart' taki W.371 'tow with a line, lead, bring along' taki TM 'beat']
mānawanawa *noun* (*heart*) atrium [W.174 mānawanawa 'space' manawa W.174 'heart']
mānawanawa *noun* (*heart*) ventricle [W.174 mānawanawa 'space' manawa 'heart']
manene *noun* immigrant [W.175 'stranger, one living in a strange country']
maninirau *noun* circus [manini W.175 'pleasant, agreeable' rau W.328 'hundred, multitude']
maniore *noun* (*mental*) tension [W.175 'anxiety']
mānuka rau *adjective* neurotic [mānuka W.177 'troubled, anxious, sad, having the emotions stirred' mānukanuka 'anxiety, misgiving, apprehension' rau W.328 'multitude, number, embarrassed, entangled, confused']
manutaki *noun* dean [W.176 'a bird acting as sentry for a flock']
manuware *adjective* farcical [W.177 'foolish, foolishness']
manga *noun* (*university*) faculty [W.177 'branch of a river, tree etc.']
manga *noun* (*theatre*) act [W.177 'branch of a tree']
māngai *noun* (*one who acts on behalf of someone else*) agent, commissary, representative, delegate [W.177 'mouth']
māngai kāwanatanga *noun* ambassador [māngai W.177 'mouth' kāwanatanga < Eng. 'government']
Māngai Kāwanatanga *noun* High Commissioner [māngai TM 'representative' kāwanatanga < Eng. 'government']
māngaro *noun* (*science*) starch [W.177 'mealy']
māngohe *adjective* malleable [W.178 'soft']
māngoingoi *noun* surf-casting [W.178 'fish with a line from the shore']

mangungu *adjective* (*meat*) rare [W.178 'uncooked, underdone']
māori *noun* aborigine [W.179 'person of the native race']
māota *noun* chlorophyll [W.179 'green, fresh-grown']
māotaota *adjective* evergreen [maota W.179 'fresh-grown, green']
māpara *noun* maraca [W.179 'pieces of wood used as castanets']
māra kūmara a Ngātoro-i-rangi *noun* cirrocumulus [W.180 'a mackerel sky']
māra raihi *noun* (*rice cultivation*) paddy [māra W.180 'plot of ground under cultivation' raihi < Eng. 'rice']
marae o pī *noun* beehive [marae W.180 'village common' pī < Eng. 'bee']
maramara *noun* miscellaneous *adjective* [W.180 'piece, bit, portion']
maramataka *noun* calendar [marama W.180 'month' taka W.366 'come round, as a date or period of time']
mārau *noun* carving fork [W.181 'fork']
mārau *noun* (*cutlery*) fork [W.181 'fork, pronged stick for catching eels']
marau *noun* (*education*) subject [W.181 'subject of talk']
marau *noun* (*grammar*) subject [W.181 'subject of talk']
mārau purini *noun* dessert fork [mārau TM 'fork' purini < Eng. 'pudding']
mārau toha *noun* serving fork [mārau W.181 'fork' toha W.429 'distribute']
marautanga *noun* curriculum [marau W.181 'subject of talk']
marautanga *noun* syllabus [marau TM 'subject']
mārehe *noun* meticulous [W.181 'painstaking, deft']
maremaretai *noun* agar [W.181 'jellyfish']
maremaretai *noun* (*biology, nutrient substance*) culture [TM 'agar']
māripi *noun* carving knife [W.182 'cutting instrument, knife']
māripi motū *noun* steak knife [māripi W.182 'knife' motū TM 'steak']
maru tautuku *noun* penalty spot [maru W.184 'mark, sign' tautuku W.405 'stoop, bend down; so give way']
mārua *noun* vacuum [W.184 'hollow, void']
mārurenga *noun* victim [W.185 'one who has suffered plunder and ill treatment']

matā *noun* (*shotput*) shot [W.185 'lead']
mata *noun* (*computer*) screen [W.15 'face, surface']
mata ahupūngao *noun* physicist [mata W.185 'eye, face' ahupūngao TM 'physics']
mata hunahuna *adjective* subtle [W.69 'a charm to effect concealment from a foe' hunahuna 'concealed, seldom seen']
mata hunahuna *noun* subtlety [TM 'subtle']
mata hunahuna *noun* secret agent, undercover agent [mataara W.186 'witness, observe' hunahuna W.69 'concealed, seldom seen' mata hunahuna W.69 'a charm to effect concealment from a foe']
mata kōata *noun* sheet of glass [mata W.185 'surface, face' kōata TM 'glass']
mata raukura *adjective* (*botany*) pinnate [mata W.185 'surface' raukura W.329 'feather, plume']
mata rorohiko *noun* computer screen [mata W.185 'face, surface' rorohiko TM 'computer']
mata tuaroa *noun* (*eye*) retina [mata W.185 'eye, face, surface' tuaroa W.447 'back part of a house']
mata wati *noun* timekeeper [mata W.185 'eye, face' wati < Eng. 'watch']
mataaho ōpure *noun* stained-glass window [mataaho W.186 'window' ōpurepure TM 'multi-coloured']
mataaho waka *noun* windscreen [mataaho W.186 'window' waka TM 'vehicle']
mataara *noun* witness [W.186 'witness, observe']
mataaro *noun* (*trade*) master [mata W.185 'eye, face' aro W.16 'be inclined, be disposed']
mataaro hiko *noun* electrician [mataaro TM 'master' hiko common usage 'electricity']
mataaro hiko matua *noun* (*film*) gaffer [mataaro hiko TM 'electrician' matua W.195 'main, chief']
mataaro kōrere *noun* plumber [mataaro TM 'master' kōrere W.141 'gutter, tap, anything to guide the passage of liquids']
mataaro pūkaha *noun* mechanical engineer [mataaro TM 'master' pūkaha TM 'engine']

mata-ā-ruru *noun* (*eye*) iris [W.185 'eye, rings of pāua shell inserted in carved work']

matahau *noun* wind-vane [mata W.185 'face, edge, point' hau W.38 'wind']

matahua *adjective* egg-shaped [mata W.185 'surface, face' hua W.64 'egg of a bird']

matahuarere *noun* meteorologist [mata W.185 'eye, face' huarere TM 'weather']

mataine *noun* dial [mata W.183 'face, surface' ine W.78 'measure']

mātāira *noun* gene pool [mātā W.185 'heap, layer', receptacle' ira TM 'gene']

mātai *transitive verb* (*investigate*) study [W.187 'inspect, examine']

mātai āhuatanga wahine *noun* gynaecology [mātai TM 'study' āhuatanga TM 'aspect' wahine W.474 'woman']

mātai aotea *noun* ornithology [mātai TM 'study' aotea W.12 'bird']

mātai hinengaro *noun* psychology [mātai TM 'study' hinengaro W.51 'seat of the thoughts and emotions']

mātai huarere *noun* meteorology [mātai TM 'study' huarere TM 'weather']

mātai kōpiro *noun* gastroenterology [mātai TM 'study' kōpiro TM 'intestines']

mātai matawhenua *noun* geography [mātai TM 'study' mata W.185 'surface' whenua W.494 'land, ground']

mātai mate pukupuku *noun* oncology [mātai TM 'study' mate pukupuku TM 'cancer']

mātai repe *noun* endocrinology [mātai TM 'study' repe W.336 'gland']

mātai roke kanae *noun* palaeontology [mātai TM 'study' roke kanae TM 'fossil']

mātai roma mimi, taihemahema *noun* urology [mātai TM 'study' roma mimi TM 'urinary tract' taihemahema TM 'reproductive organs']

mātai tahumaero *noun* epidemiology [mātai W.187 'inspect, examine' W.361 'sickness, disease']

mātai whaipara tangata *noun* archaeology [mātai W.187 'inspect, examine' whaipara W.485 'remains' tangata W.379 'human being']

matakana *noun* probation officer [W.187 'wary, watchful, on the lookout']

mātakitaki *noun* observation [W.188 'look at, inspect, watch, peer, pry']

mātāmua *adjective* (*first importance*) primary [W.188 'first, fore']

mātāmuatanga *noun* (*biology*) kingdom [mātāmua W.188 'first']

mātanga *noun* specialist [W.188 'knowing, experienced person']

mātanga *noun* surgeon [W.188 'knowing, experienced person']

matangirua *noun* turbo [W.189 'to use both sail and paddles in a canoe']

matangurunguru *adjective* dissenting [W.189 'discontented, disappointed']

mataono *noun* (*non-technical*) cube [mata W.185 'surface' ono W.240 'six']

mataono *adjective* cuboid [mata W.185 'surface' ono W.240 'six']

mataono rite *noun* (*mathematical*) cube [mata W.185 'surface' ono W.240 'six' rite W.343 'alike']

mataora *noun* life cycle [W189 'living, alive']

matapae *transitive verb* predict, forecast [matakite W.188 'one who foresees an event, practise divination' whakapae TM 'contend']

matapae *noun* prediction [matapae TM 'predict']

matapae *noun* fortune-teller [matakite W.188 'seer, one who foresees an event' whakapae TM 'contend']

matapae huarere *noun* weather forecaster [matapae TM 'forecaster' huarere TM 'weather']

matapaia *noun* earthenware, pottery [W.189 'clay which when baked hard was used as stone for cooking']

matapakinga *noun* discussion [matapaki W.189 'make the subject of talk, discuss']

matapakinga ahumahi *noun* industrial relations negotiations [matapaki W.189 'make the subject of talk, discuss' ahumahi TM 'industry']

matapipi *noun* doorstop [W.189 'small entering wedge for splitting timber']

matapōkere *adjective* random [W.189 'blindly, at random, in the dark']

mātāpono *noun* (*maxim*) principle [mātāpuna W.190 'source of a river' pono W.291 'true']

mātāpono *noun* maxim [mātāpuna W.190 'source of a river' pono W.291 'true']

mātāpono koiora *noun* biological principles [mātāpono TM 'principle' koiora TM 'biology']

matapōuri *noun, adjective* melancholy [W.189 'sad, gloomy']

matapopore *noun* trustee [W.189 'watchful over, careful of, husband, prize']

matapopore *noun* guardian [W.189 'watchful over, careful of, husband, prize']

mataporenga *noun* ward of court [matapore TM 'guardian' matapore W.189 'watchful over, careful over']

mātāpunenga *noun* encyclopedia [mātā W.185 'receptacle, packed with' punenga W.310 'clever, intelligent, always seeking and acquiring useful knowledge']

mataraharaha *noun (show)* fair, sideshow [W.190 'freedom from care']

matarau *noun* polyhedron [mata W.185 'face, surface' rau W.328 'multitude, number']

matareka *adjective* affable [W.190 'pleasant, like, be fond of']

matarere *noun* bayonet [W.190 'a detachable spear point']

mātātahi *noun* puberty [W.191 'young people']

matatākihi *adjective* kidney-shaped [mata W.185 'face, surface' tākihi W.372 'kidney']

matatapu *adjective* confidential [matanui W.188 'open, aboveboard' tapu W.385 'inaccessible']

matatika *noun* ethics, *adjective* moral, ethical [W.191 'right, straight' mata W.185 'face, eye']

matatiki *noun* source [W.191 'spring of water']

mātātoa *adjective* adventurous [W.191 'fearless, active, vigorous, energetic']

mātātoka *adjective* fossilised [mātā W.185 'heap, layer, deep swamp' mātāniho W.188 'print or mark of teeth' toka W.433 'stone, rock']

mātauranga auroa *noun* continuing education [mātauranga common usage 'education' auroa W.22 'prolonged, extended']

mātauranga hapori *noun* sociology [mātauranga common usage 'knowledge' hapori TM 'social']

mātauranga hauora kararehe *noun* veterinary science [mātauranga common usage 'knowledge' hauora W.41 'healthy, well, lively' kararehe W.99 'quadruped']

mātauranga huaota *noun* botany [mātauranga common usage 'knowledge' hua W.64 'bear fruit or flowers, abundance' otaota W.242 'herbs in general, vegetation']

mātauranga kararehe *noun* zoology [mātauranga common usage 'knowledge' kararehe W.99 'quadruped' common usage 'animal']

mātauranga koiora *noun* biology [mātauranga common usage 'knowledge' koiora W.128 'life']

mātauranga koiora mororiki *noun* microbiology [mātauranga common usage 'knowledge' koiora TM 'biology' mororiki TM 'microbe']

mātauranga mate hinengaro *noun* psychiatry [mātauranga common usage 'knowledge' mate hinengaro TM 'psychiatric disorder']

mātauranga matū *noun* chemistry [mātauranga common usage 'knowledge' matū TM 'chemical']

mātauranga matūwaro *noun* organic chemistry [mātauranga common usage 'knowledge' matū TM 'chemical' waro TM 'carbon']

mātauranga momo tangata *noun* ethnology [mātauranga common usage 'knowledge' momo W.208 'race, breed, blood' tangata W.379 'human being']

mātauranga momo whakaheke *noun (study)* genetics [mātauranga common usage 'knowledge' momo whakaheke TM 'inherited characteristics']

mātauranga noho hapori *noun* social studies [mātauranga common usage 'knowledge' noho W.223 'settle, dwell, live' hapori TM 'social']

mātauranga ōhanga *noun (study)* economics [mātauranga common usage 'knowledge' ō W.237 'provision for a journey' hanga W.34 'make, build, fashion, business, practice, etc.']

mātauranga taihara *noun* criminology [mātauranga common usage 'knowledge' taihara TM 'crime']

mātauranga taka rongoā *noun (study)* pharmacy [mātauranga common usage 'knowledge' taka rongoā TM 'pharmacist']

mātauranga taupuhi kaiao *noun* (*study*) ecology [mātauranga common usage 'knowledge' taupuhi kaiao TM 'ecology']

mātauranga tikanga tangata *noun* anthropology [mātauranga common usage 'knowledge' tikanga 'custom, practice' tangata W.379 'human being']

mātauranga tioata *noun* crystallography [mātauranga common usage 'knowledge' tioata TM 'crystal']

mātauranga tōrangapū *noun* political science [mātauranga common usage 'knowledge' tōrangapū TM 'politics']

mātauranga waka tuarangi *noun* rocketry [mātauranga common usage 'knowledge' waka tuarangi TM 'spacecraft']

mātauranga wetereo *noun* linguistics [mātauranga common usage 'knowledge' wete W.483 'untie, unravel' reo W.336 'language']

mātauranga whakahua phonetics [mātauranga common usage 'knowledge' whakahua W.64 'pronounce']

matawaenga *adjective* crucial [W.192 'left in a dilemma']

matawai *noun* inspector [W.192 'look closely' mata W.185 'eye, face']

matawai *noun* scanner [W.192 'look closely']

matawai roro *noun* brain scanner, CT Scanner [matawai W.192 'look closely' roro W.347 'brains']

matawai ū *noun* mammography [matawai W.192 'look closely' ū W.464 'breast']

Mate Ārai Kore (*acronym*) AIDS [mate W.192 'sickness' ārai W.14 'ward off, screen' kore W.140 'no, not']

mate arotahi *noun* cataract [mate W.192 'sickness' arotahi TM 'lens']

mate hinengaro *noun* psychiatric disorder [mate W.192 'sickness' hinengaro W.51 'seat of the thoughts and emotions']

mate horokiwa *noun* muscular dystrophy [mate W.192 'sickness' horokiwa W.61 'wasting away of the body in disease']

mate hukihuki *adjective* spastic [mate W.185 'sickness' hukihuki W.68 'convulsive twitching or contraction of the nerves or muscles, spasm, convulsions']

mate hūkiki *noun* epilepsy [mate W.192 'sickness' hūkiki W.68 'shiver violently']

mate iaia-manawa *noun* cardiovascular disease [mate W.192 'sickness' iaiamanawa TM 'cardio-vascular']

mate iaia-roro *noun* cerebrovascular disease [mate W.192 'sickness' iaia-roro TM 'cerebro-vascular']

mate ioio *noun* nervous condition [mate W.192 'sickness' io W.78 'nerve']

mate kiripaka *noun* asbestosis [mate W.192 'sickness' papa kiripaka TM 'asbestos']

mate miru pupuhi *noun* emphysema [mate W.192 'sickness' miru TM 'alveolus' pupuhi W.304 'swell']

mate ohorere *noun* sudden death [mate W.192 'death' ohorere W.238 'start suddenly']

mate paiori *noun* Parkinson's disease [mate W.192 'sickness' paiori W.250 'emaciated']

mate paipai *noun* sexually transmitted disease [mate W.192 'sickness' paipai W.249 'venereal disease']

mate pāwera *noun* allergy [mate W.192 'sickness' pāwera W.273 'sore, tender to the touch, affected']

mate pouraka *noun* cot death [mate W.192 'dead' pouraka W.298 'rude form of cradle for infants']

mate pukupuku *noun* cancer [mate W.192 'sickness' puku W.308 'swelling, tumour, knob']

mate pukupuku o te kiri *noun* carcinoma [mate pukupuku TM 'cancer' kiri W.119 'skin']

mate pukupuku o te waha whare tangata *noun* cervical cancer [mate pukupuku TM 'cancer' waha whare tangata TM 'cervix']

mate pūira kehe *noun* Down's syndrome [mate W.192 'sickness' pūira TM 'chromosome' kehe W.122 'an odd number']

mate ringarau *noun* kleptomania [mate W.192 'sickness, disease' ringa 'W.341 'hand' rau W.328 'hundred' rarau W.328 'lay hold of, grasp']

mate roma mimi *noun* urinary tract infection [mate W.192 'sickness' roma mimi TM 'urinary tract']

mate romahā *noun* respiratory disease [mate W.192 'sickness' romahā TM 'respiratory system']

mate roro *noun* brain damage [mate W.192 'sickness, injury, wound' roro W.347 'brains']

mate ruru toto noun leukaemia [mate W.192 'sickness' ruru W.352 'attack invade' toto W.441 'blood']

mate tākihi noun kidney disease, renal disease [mate W.192 'sickness' tākihi W.372 'kidney']

mate tuamatangi noun terminal illness [mate W.192 'sickness' tuamatangi W.446 'last respiration before death, dying gasp']

mate wairoro noun hydrocephalus [mate W.192 'sickness' wai W.474 'water' roro W.347 'brains' wairoro W.477 'brains']

(mate) whakaataata noun narcissism [mate W.192 'sickness' whakaata W.18 'look at one's reflected image, in water or in mirror']

mate whakatiki noun anorexia [mate W.192 'sickness' whakatiki W.418 'keep short of food']

mate whakatīmohea noun cerebral palsy [mate W.192 'sickness' whaka- W.486 'causative prefix' to make tīmohea W.419 'weak, flaccid']

mate whawhati tata noun emergency [mate W.192 'danger, calamity' whawhati tata W.491 'happen suddenly']

mate whēkaro noun presbyopia [mate 192 'damaged, sickness' whēkaro W.493 'be dimly visible']

matehā noun respiratory disease [mate W.192 'sickness' hā W.29 'breath, breathe']

matehuka noun diabetes [mate W.192 'sickness' huka < Eng. 'sugar']

matehuka noun diabetic [mate W.192 'sickness' huka < Eng. 'sugar']

matengi adjective trio [W.193 'three']

matewhawhati noun unexpected death [mate W.192 'death' matawhawhati W.192 'sudden, unexpected']

mati noun (mathematics) digit [W.193 'finger']

mati noun (mathematics, digit) figure [W.193 'finger']

mati tāpua noun (mathematics) significant figure [mati TM 'figure' tāpua TM 'significant']

matihao noun cleats [W.193 'claw']

matira noun fishing rod [W.194 'fish with a rod, tilt up, point upwards']

matire noun baton [W.194 'wand, rod']

mātiratira noun (sport) net [W.194 'a net attached to stakes in the tideway']

matiti noun, intransitive verb (exercise) stretch [W.194 'stretched out as of limbs']

mātiti rerewai noun dish-rack [mātiti W.194 'wooden rack or grid on which birds were placed for roasting' rere W.337 'escape' wai W.474 'water']

mātotorutanga o te waka noun heavy traffic [mātotoru W.194 'thick' waka 'vehicle']

matū noun matter [W.195 'gist, kernel, of a matter']

matū noun (chemistry) chemical, substance [W.195 'gist, kernel, fat']

matū hohe noun (chemistry) reactant [matū TM 'substance' hohe TM 'react']

mātua auxiliary verb must [W.195 'first'] e.g. me mātua haere 'must go'

matua noun squadron [W.195 'division of an army, company']

matua adjective (first importance) primary [W.195 'main, chief, important']

matua tauā moana noun naval squadron [matua TM 'squadron' tauā moana TM 'navy']

matua tauārangi noun airforce squadron [matua TM 'squadron' tauārangi TM 'airforce']

mātuhi noun (sewing) needle [W.195 'a small bone needle with eye']

matūniho noun dentine [matū W.195 'fat, gist, kernel' niho W.221 'tooth']

matūora noun biochemistry [matū TM 'matter' ora W.241 'alive']

matūriaka noun metabolism [matū TM 'matter' riaka W.339 'put forth strength, energy']

matūriki noun (chemistry) particle [matū TM 'matter' riki W.340 'small']

matūriki ārepa noun alpha particle [matūriki TM 'particle' ārepa < Eng. 'alpha']

matūriki kama noun gamma particle [matūriki TM 'particle' kama < Eng. 'gamma']

matūriki peta noun beta particle [matūriki TM 'particle' peta < Gk. 'beta"]

mātutū intransitive verb convalesce [W.195 'convalescent, not quite healed']

mātutū noun (hospital) ward [W.195 'convalescent, not quite healed or cured']

matūwaro *noun* (*carbon*) organic compound [matū TM 'matter, chemical' waro TM 'carbon']

mau *intransitive verb* (*sport*) field [W.196 'caught seized, captured, overtaken']

mau herehere *transitive verb* imprison [mau W.196 'confined, constrained' whare herehere W.46 'prison']

mau tangetange *adjective* proven guilty [mau W.196 'caught, seized captured' tangetange W.379 'forthwith']

maunga para *noun* rubbish dump [maunga 197 'mountain' para W.262 'refuse, waste']

mauri moe *adjective* unconscious [mauri W.197 'life principle, thymos of man' moe W.204 'sleep, dream']

mauri ngaro *intransitive verb* coma *noun* [mauri W.197 'life principle, thymos of man' ngaro W.230 'absent, disappeared']

mauri ngaro *adjective* comatosed [mauri W.197 'life principle, thymos of man' ngaro W.230 'absent, disappeared']

mauri ora *adjective* (*awake*) conscious [mauri W.197 'life principle, thymos of man' ora W.240 'well, in health']

mauri pōtere *adjective* subconscious [mauri W.197 'life principle, thymos of man' pōteretere W.296 'drift about, backwards and forwards']

mauroa *phrase* held ball [mau W.196 'lay hold of' roa W.344 'long, of time']

mautohe *intransitive verb* protest [W.198 'oppose persistently']

mauwha *noun* (*generic*) shrub [W.198 'small bushes, brushwood']

me mātua oma *phrase* (*softball*) force play [me W.199 'mild imperative' mātua TM 'must' oma W.239 'run']

meka *noun* fact [W.200 'true']

meka *adjective* factual [TM 'fact']

meka matua *noun* basic facts [meka TM 'fact' 'true', matua W.195 'main, important']

mekameka *noun* rope ladder [W.200 'a form of ladder']

mekemeke *noun* (*sport*) boxing [meke W.200 'strike with the fist, blow with the fist']

memeka *adjective* (*chemistry*) aliphatic [mekameka W.200 'chain']

mewaro *noun* methane [me < Eng. 'me-' waro TM 'alkane']

mīere *intransitive verb* (*softball*) strike out [W.201 'become powerless, be exhausted']

mīere *intransitive verb* lose [W.201 'become powerless, be exhausted']

mihiwai *noun* gemstone [W.202 'a kind of stone']

mimira *adjective* serrated [W.202 'a saw-like cutting instrument made by lashing strips of obsidian or shark's teeth']

mina-auahi *adjective* smoked [minamina W.202 'affected by' minamina auahi 'tasting of smoke']

mina-auahi *noun* passive smoking [minamina W.202 'affected by' auahi W.21 'smoke']

mina-tote *adjective* (*food*) salted [minamina W.202 'affected by' tote < Eng. 'salt']

mina-tote *adjective* (*food*) corned [minamina W.202 'affected by' tote < Eng. 'salt']

mino *noun* borrow [minono W.202 'beg']

mira *noun* serrated edge knife [mira W.202 'a sawlike cutting instrument lashed to a wooden handle']

mira maitai *noun* hacksaw [mira W.202 'a saw-like cutting instrument made by lashing strips of obsidian or shark's teeth to a wooden handle' maitai < Eng. 'metal']

mira parāoa *noun* bread knife [mira W.202 'a sawlike cutting instrument lashed to a wooden handle' parāoa < Eng. 'bread']

miramira *transitive verb* highlight *noun* highlighter [W.202 'give prominence to']

miramira *noun* tonsil [W.202 'uvula']

miramira *adjective* (*printing*) bold [W.202 'give prominence to']

miramira kakā *noun* tonsillitis [W.202 'uvula' kakā TM 'inflammation']

miri *noun* hypnotherapy [W.203 'assuage, tranquillize, a karakia, with rites, for soothing pain, grief etc.']

mirihau *noun* windsurfing [haumiri W.41 'hug, sail along the shore']

mirihau *noun* windsurfing board [haumiri W.41 'hug, sail along the shore']

miro *noun* cotton thread [W.203 'thread']

miro ngaiaku *noun* nylon thread [miro W.203 'thread, twisted cord' ngaiaku TM 'nylon']

miru *noun* alveolus [mirumiru Biggs 23 'bubble']

miru *noun* (*biology*) vacuole [mirumiru Biggs 23 'bubble']

mita pūtoru *noun* cubic metre [mita < Eng. 'metre' pūtoru TM 'cubed']

moanarua *transitive verb* darn [W.204 'repair a garment by weaving a fresh piece']

moanarua *noun* darning [W.204 'repair a garment by weaving a fresh piece']

moari *noun* maypole [Best *Games and Pastimes* 48 'swing']

moe ahiahi *noun* siesta [moe W.204 'sleep, repose, close the eyes' ahiahi common usage 'afternoon']

moe hōtoke *intransitive verb* hibernate [moe W.204 'sleep' hōtoke W.62 'winter, cold']

moe māori *noun* de facto marriage [moe W.204 'marry, sleep together' māori W.179 'freely, without ceremony']

moke *noun* monk [W.207 'solitary person']

moko tuauri *noun* dinosaur [moko W.207 'a general term for lizards, huge mythical creature of lizard-like shape' tuauri W.448 'ancient, ancient times']

mokoā taipana *noun* forcefield [mokoā W.208 'space, interval' taipana TM 'force']

mokoā wēanga *noun* (*softball*) centre outfield [mokoā W.208 'space' wēanga TM 'centre']

mokokairau *noun* brontosaurus [moko W.207 'lizard' kai W.85 'eat' rau W.328 'leaf']

mokomakiki *noun* ankylosaurus [moko W.207 'a general term for lizards, huge mythical creature of lizard-like shape' makiki W.170 'stiff']

moko-ngarengare *noun* tyrannosaurus [moko W.207 'a general term for lizards, huge mythical creature of lizard-like shape' ngarengare W.230 'tyrannous, overbearing']

mokoone *noun* beach skink [moko W.207 'a general term for lizards' one W.239 'beach']

mokori anō *phrase* fortunately [W.208 'it is well']

mokotai *noun* mosasaur [moko W.207 'a general term for lizards, huge mythical creature of lizard-like shape' tai W.361 'the sea']

mokotuapaka *noun* stegosaurus [moko W.207 'a general term for lizards, huge mythical creature of lizard-like shape' tuapaka W.446 'hard, and so applied to steel']

mokowā *adjective* spatial [W.208 'space, interval']

mokowā *noun* (*punctuation*) space [W.208 'space, interval']

mokowā aukume *noun* magnetic field [mokowā W.208 'space' aukume TM 'magnet']

mokowhiti *noun* heartbeat, pulse [W.208 'beat, palpitate']

mokowhiti kakī *noun* carotid pulse [mokowhiti W.208 'beat, palpitate' kakī W.92 'neck']

mokowhiti ringa *noun* wrist pulse [mokowhiti W.208 'beat palpitate' ringa W.341 'hand']

momihau *noun* extractor fan [momi W.208 'suck, suck up, swallow up' hau W.38 'air']

momo *noun* species [W.208 'offspring, descendant, race, breed, blood']

momo, he *phrase* hereditary [W.208 'blood, breed, offspring'] e.g. *He momo tērā. 'That's a hereditary trait.'*

momo rāwaho *noun* introduced species [momo TM 'species' rāwaho W.332 'outside']

momo whakaheke inherited characteristic [momo W.208 'blood, breed, offspring' heke W.44 'descend']

momotuhi *noun* (*computer*) font [momo W.208 'race, breed' tuhi W.448 'write']

momotunga whenua *noun* continental drift [momotu W.212 'sever, separate' whenua W.494 'land']

moni *noun* cash [< Eng. 'money']

moni tāpui *noun* deposit, down payment [moni < Eng. 'money' tāpui W.385 'set aside, bespeak, reserve']

moni whiwhi *noun* (*revenue*) income [moni < Eng. 'money' whiwhi W.499 'possessed of, having acquired']

moni whiwhi tōmua *noun* prepaid income [moni whiwhi TM 'income' tōmua W.435 'early']

mōhanihani *noun* matt finish [W.205 'smooth']

mōhiki *noun* weightlifting [W.205 'raised up, lifted up']

mōhinuhinu *transitive verb, noun* (*food*) glaze [W.205 'shiny, glistening, glossy']

mōhinuhinu *noun* varnish *adjective* high-gloss [W.205 'shiny, glistening, glossy']

mōkī *noun* package [W.207 'bundle, parcel, packet']

mōkihi *noun* package [W.207 'bundle, parcel, packet']

mōkitokito *adjective* microscopic [W.207 'minute, small']

mōnehu *noun* (*botany*) tomentum [W.209 'the fine rusty pubescence on the unexpanded fronds of bracken and other ferns']

mōnehu *noun* velvet [W.209 'the fine rusty pubescence on the unexpanded fronds of bracken and other ferns']

mōnehunehu *adjective* velvety [mōnehu W.209 'the fine rusty pubescence on the unexpanded fronds of bracken and other ferns']

more *adjective* (*finances*) net [W.209 'bare, plain, without appendages']

mōrea *phrase* at risk [mōrearea W.210 'exposed to danger']

mōrearea *noun* danger [W.210 'exposed to great danger']

mōria *noun* (*plumbing*) washer [W.210 'ring for the leg of a captive kākā']

mōriroriro *transitive verb* become alienated [W.210 'become estranged']

moromoroiti *noun* micro-organism [moroiti W.210 'small']

mororiki *noun* microbe [W.210 'small']

motatau *noun* ventriloquist [W.211 'talk to oneself']

mōteatea *noun* poem [W.211 'lament']

mōtepe *noun* platelet [mōtete W.211 'small piece, fragment' tepe W.412 'congeal, coagulate, clot']

moto *noun* (*boxing etc.*) blow [W.211 'strike with the fist']

mōtū *noun* (*weightlifting*) weight [W.211 'a heavy kind of stone used for making sinkers for nets and fishing lines']

motuara *noun* traffic island [motu W.211 'island' ara W.13 'way, path']

motuhake *adjective* special [W.212 'separated']

motuhake *adjective* private [W.212 'separated']

motuhenga *noun* documentary [W.212 'straight, true, genuine']

motukore *adjective* (*mathematics*) continuous [motu W.211 'broken off, separated, anything isolated' kore W.140 'no, not']

motunga *noun* quota [motumotu W.212 'divided into isolated portions']

motunga koeko *noun* conic section [motu W.212 'severed, isolated' koeko W.123 'tapering to a point']

motupiri *adjective* semi-detached [motu W.211 'severed, anything isolated' piri W.283 'be attached, be fastened']

motū *noun* steak [W.211 'piece of flesh, or fat, titbit']

motu whakawhānau *noun* Caesarian section [motu W.211 'severed, cut, wound' whaka- W.486 'causative prefix' to make whānau W.487 'be born']

moutī *noun* (*shooting*) dead target [W.212 'decoy kākā']

mōwaho *adjective* ectopic [W.212 'outside, on the outside']

mōwaho *noun* (*mathematics*) outlier [W.212 'on the outside']

mōwaiwai *adjective* scrumptious [W.212 'making the mouth water']

mōwhiti *noun* goggles [karu mōwhiti W.213 'spectacles']

mū *noun* (*board game*) draughts [Best Games and Pastimes 180 'draughts']

mua kai kai *phrase* (*economics*) pure competition [Brougham and Reed 29]

mua kai kai *phrase* (*electoral system*) first-past-the-post ['mua kai kai, muri kai huare' Brougham and Reed 29 'the early ones get the best, the late ones get the spittle']

muku *noun* dishcloth [W.213 'wipe, rub']

muku *noun* (*eraser*) rubber [W.213 'wipe, rub, smear']

munga *noun* raffia [W.214 'palm']

muratahi *noun* bunsen burner [mura W.214 'blaze, flame' tahi W.359 'single']

mure *noun* extortion [W.214 'endeavour to obtain by unfair means']

mutu-hengahenga *adjective* finite [mutu W.215 'brought to an end' hengahenga W.46 'intensive quite']

N

nahanaha *adjective* systematic [W.216 'well arranged, in good order']

nakunaku *noun, transitive verb* mince [W.217 'reduce to fragments, broken in pieces, crushed']

nakunaku *transitive verb* digest [W.217 'reduced to fragments, broken in pieces, crushed']

nakunaku *noun* digestion [W.217 'reduced to fragments, broken in pieces, crushed']

nama *noun* invoice [common usage 'account']

nama kāore i utua *noun* bad debt [nama common usage 'debt' kāore W.95 'no, not' utu W.471 'return for anything']

namunamuā *noun* spice [W.217 'flavour imparted to food by something with which it has been in contact']

nanati *noun* (*wrestling, judo etc.*) lock [W.219 'pinched, constricted']

nanī *noun* cabbage [W.218 'wild cabbage']

nape *noun* ligament [W.218 'ligament of a bivalve']

nape *noun* (*golf*) whisky [W.218 'make a false stroke with the paddle']

nape *noun* (*golf*) airshot [W.218 'make a false stroke with the paddle']

natihau *noun* (*vehicle*) choke [nati W.219 'pinch, contract' W.39 hau 'air']

nehu-tōkau *noun* eco-funeral [nehu W.220 'bury' tōkau W.433 'plain, devoid of ornament']

nekehanga *noun* (*mathematics*) translation [W.220 'move']

nekeneke *noun* manoeuvre [W.220 'move gradually']

nekeneke *adjective* mobile [neke W.220 'move']

nekoneko *adjective* ornamental [W.221 'fancy border of a cloak']

newanewa *noun* soft toy [W.221 'smooth, soft']

niho kata *noun* canine tooth [niho W.221 'tooth' kata W.102 'laugh']

niho kōhari *noun* molar tooth [niho W.221 'tooth' kōhari W.124 'mash, crush']

niho more *noun* dentures [niho W.221 'tooth' more W.209 'toothless']

niho pūrākau *noun* premolar tooth [niho W.221 'tooth' pūrākau W.312 'double, of teeth']

niho rei *noun* canine tooth [niho W.221 'tooth' rei W.334 'tusk']

nihowhiti *noun* (*machinery*) gear [niho W.221 'tooth' whiti W.497 'change, cross over' W.498 'hoop']

nihowhiti *noun* gearwheel [TM 'gear']

nīko *noun* cabbage [W.222 'wild cabbage']

niko tātea *noun* (*testicle*) epididymis [niko W.222 'form into a bight or coil, go round about' semen W.394 'semen']

nīko whero *noun* red cabbage [nīko W.222 'wild cabbage' whero W.222 'red']

ninipa *phrase* (*cricket*) hit wicket [W.222 'awkward, unfortunate, unskilful']

ninipa *adjective* unskilled [W.222 'awkward, unfortunate, unskilful']

noho apiapi *noun* overcrowding [noho W.223 'sit, dwell' apiapi W.12 'crowded, dense']

noho hītengi *intransitive verb* squat down [noho hītengitengi W.53 'squat with the toes only on the ground']

noho matatapu *noun* confidentiality [noho W.223 'stay, remain, lie' matatapu TM 'confidential']

noho tāone *adjective* urban-based [noho W.223 'dwell, live, be located' tāone < Eng. 'town']

noho tapu *intransitive verb (prohibited access)* embargo [noho W.223 'remain' tapu W.385 'inaccessible']

nohoanga kaiwhakaako *noun* coaches' box [nohoanga W.223 'seat' kaiwhakaako TM 'coach']

nohopuku *intransitive verb, noun* diet [W.223 'fast']

nohopuku *noun (science)* inertia [W.223 'be silent, be still']

nohopuku *adjective (science)* inert [W.223 'be silent, be still']

noni *noun* vegetable oil [noni W.224 'oil']

noni tākou *noun* olive oil [noni TM 'vegetable oil' tākou W.374 'a tree similar to the olive']

nonoke *noun* judo [W.223 'struggle together, wrestle']

nuku *noun (printing)* indent [W.225 'move']

nuku matau *noun* indent right [nuku TM 'move' matau W.192 'right']

nuku mauī *noun* indent left [nuku TM 'indent' mauī W.196 'left']

Ng

ngahi hapori *noun (justice)* community service [ngahi W.232 'suffer penalty, be punished' hapori TM 'community']

ngahi whakatikatika *noun* corrective training [ngahi W.232 'suffer penalty, be punished' whakatika W.417 'straighten, correct']

ngahuru *adjective* decimal [W.227 'ten']

ngahuru auau *noun* recurring decimal [ngahuru TM 'decimal' auau TM 'recurring']

ngahuru whāioio *noun* infinite decimal [ngahuru TM 'decimal' tau whāioio TM 'infinite number']

ngaiaku *noun, adjective* nylon [ngai W.227 'dried leaves of raupō, flax, etc., used for walls or thatch of a house' akuaku W.7 'firm strong']

ngaio *noun* professional [W.227 'expert, clever, deliberate, thorough']

ngākau kawa *noun* bad attitude [ngākau W.227 'heart, seat of affections or feelings' kawa W.109 'unpleasant to the taste, bitter, sour']

ngākau kōhuki *noun* emotional stress [ngākau W.227 'seat of affections or feelings, mind' kōhukihuki TM 'stress']

ngākau kōnatunatu *noun* dilemma [ngākau W.227 'seat of feelings' kōnatunatu W.133 'heart distressed by conflicting emotions']

ngākau ora *noun* sanity, *adjective* sane [ngākau W.227 'seat of affections or feelings, mind, inclination, desire, spirit' ora W.240 'well, in health, safe']

ngākau reka *noun* good attitude [ngākau W.227 'heart, seat of affections or feelings' reka W.335 'pleasant, agreeable']

ngākau tahi *adjective* confident [ngākau W.227 'inclination, spirit']

ngākau titikaha *adjective* confident [ngākau W.227 'inclination, spirit' titikaha W.425 'steadfast']

ngākau-kore *noun* apathy, *adjective* apathetic [W.227 'disinclined, having no heart for anything, dispirited']

ngako *noun (chemistry)* fats [W.228 'fat']

ngakototo *noun* cholesterol [ngako W.228 'fat' toto W.441 'blood']

ngangahu *adjective* in focus [W.226 'sharply cut, clearly seen']

ngao mārō *noun* hard palate [ngao W.229 'palate' mārō W.183 'hard']

ngao ngohe *noun* soft palate [ngao W.229 'palate' ngohe W.234 'supple, soft']

ngaohiko *noun* voltage [ngao W.229 'strength, energy' hiko common usage 'electricity']

ngāoreore *noun* tropical rain forest [ngāherehere W.226 'forest' ngaore W.229 'succulent, tender, soft']

ngapunga *noun* starting-gate [ngapu W.229 'stretch forwards ready to run']

ngaringari *noun* choral [W.230 'song to make people pull together']

ngaringari a te motu *noun* national anthem [ngaringari W.230 'song to make people pull together' motu W.211 'island']

ngaruiti *noun (kitchenware)* microwave [ngaru W.230 'wave' iti W.80 'small']

ngateri *noun* vibration [W.231 'vibrate, shake']

ngawaro *noun* dectane [ngahuru W.227 'ten' waro TM 'alkane']

ngāwhā *adjective* geothermal [W.232 'boiling spring or other volcanic activity']

ngehi pata *noun* butter conditioner [ngehi W.233 'reduced to a state of softness' pata < Eng. 'butter']

ngeni waitinana *noun* lymphocyte [ngeni W.233 'something small, particle' waitinana TM 'lymph']

ngenimā *noun (anatomy)* leucocyte [ngeni W.233 'something small, particle' mā W.161 'white']

ngenimomi *noun (anatomy)* phagocyte [ngeni W.233 'something small, particle' momi W.208 'swallow up']

ngeniwhero *noun (anatomy)* erythrocyte [ngeni W.233 'something small, particle' whero W.495 'red']

ngiha *adjective* igneous [ngiha W.233 'fire, burn']

ngingiha *noun* combustion [W.233 'burn']

ngō *noun* aphid [ngongo W.234 'juice of flowers etc., suck']

ngoi atua *noun* nun [ngoi W.234 'strength, energy' atua 'god' tore atua W.438 'a woman with an atua as husband']

ngoikura *noun* ladybird [ngoi W.234 'creep, crawl' kura W.157 'red, precious']

ngongō *noun* inhaler [ngongo W.234 'suck' huangō W.65 'difficulty of breathing, asthma']

ngongo *noun, transitive verb* siphon [W.234 'tube, suck out']

ngongo *noun (liquids)* straw [W.234 'tube, suck out']

ngongohā *noun* snorkel [ngongo W.234 'tube, suck' hā W.29 'breath, breathe']

ngongoiti *noun* pipette [ngongo W.234 'suck, suck out' iti W.80 'small']

ngore *noun* scholar [W.235 'pupil in sacred lore, etc.']

ngota *noun* atom [ngotangota W.235 'smashed to atoms']

ngota katote *noun* ion [ngota TM 'atom' katote W.104 'not fixed, displaced, quake, shake']

ngotangota *noun* subatomic particle [W.235 'fragment, particle, smashed to atoms']

ngoto *noun* glottal stop [ngotongoto W.235 'make a clicking noise with the tongue' whakangoto 'impress, mark']

ngū *noun (music)* rest [W.235 'silent, dumb, speechless']

nguengue *noun* introvert, *adjective* introverted [W.235 'quiet, silent, reserved']

nguengue *adjective* sober [W.235 'quiet, silent, reserved']

ngunu *noun, transitive verb* grill [W.236 'singe, roast food on glowing embers']

ngunu *noun (biology)* annelid [W.236 'worm']

ngunu papatahi *noun (zoology)* platyhelminth [ngunu W.236 'worm' papatahi W.261 'flat']

ngutu pārera *noun* pistol [ngutu W.236 'lip' pārera W.267 'duck']

nguture *adjective (second-hand)* used [W.236 'worn with use']

O

ō manapou *noun* petty cash [ō manapou W.237 'light provisions' manapou W.173 'anything to support life']

ō rangaranga takeaways [ō W.237 'provision for a journey' rangaranga W.322 'take up, lift up, move']

ōhanga *noun* economics [ō W.237 'provision for a journey' hanga W.34 'make, build, fashion, business, practice, etc.']

ōhia manomano *noun* brainstorm [ōhia W.238 'think on the spur of the moment' manomano W.176 'innumerable, hoard, swarm']

ōhia manomano *noun* brainstorming [TM 'brainstorm']

ohiti *noun* superstition [W.238 'cautious, on one's guard']

ohorangi *noun* christening [Best *Spiritual and Mental Concepts* 31]

ohu *noun* (*venture*) cooperative [W.239 'do by aid of a company of volunteer workers']

ohu-rapa *noun* search party [ohu W.238 'company of volunteer workers' rapa W.325 'seek, seek for']

okewa *noun* fate [toitoi okewa TM 'tempt fate']

okewa whakapipi *noun* cumulo-nimbus [okewa W.239 'nimbus, rain cloud' whakapipi W.282 'heap, pile, pile one upon another']

oko *noun* (*crockery*) bowl [W.239 'wooden bowl or other open vessel']

oko huamata *noun* salad bowl [oko W.239 'wooden bowl, or other open vessel' hua W.64 'fruit' mata W.185 'raw, uncooked']

oko koikara *noun* finger bowl [oko TM 'bowl' koikara W.128 'finger']

oko paura *noun* powder bowl [oko W.239 'wooden bowl' paura < Eng. 'powder']

oko waihāro *noun* soup bowl [oko W.239 'wooden bowl, or other open vessel' waihāro TM 'soup']

oko purini *noun* dessert bowl [oko W.239 'wooden bowl or other open vessel' purini < Eng. 'pudding']

okopoke *noun* mixing bowl [oko W.239 'wooden bowl or other open vessel' pokepoke W.289 'mix up with water or other fluid']

okoi waha whare tangata *noun* cervical smear [okoi W.239 'scrape' waha W.473 'mouth, entrance' whare tangata common usage 'womb']

okotahi *noun* exception [W.239 'solitary, few']

okouku *noun* crockery [oko W.239 'wooden bowl or other open vessel' uku W.466 'white clay']

oma hauroa *noun* marathon [oma W.239 'run' hauroa W.4 'long']

oma taitua *noun* middle-distance run [oma W.239 'run' taitua W.365 'distant']

oma tauārai *noun* steeplechase [oma W.239 'run' tauārai W.397 'screen, barrier, obstruction']

oma taumano *noun* long-distance run [oma W.239 'run' taumano W.399 'long, for a long time']

oma whānako *phrase* (*softball*) steal a base [oma W.239 'run' whānako W.487 'steal, thieve']

ope *noun* brigade [W.240 'troop']

ōpure *noun* opal [W.240 'varied with patches of colour']

ōpurepure *adjective* multicoloured [W.240 'varied with patches of colour']

oraiti *adjective* (*softball*) safe [W.241 'escaping with difficulty']

oranga taihema *noun* (*sexual & reproductive health*) family planning [ora W.240 'well, in health, safe' oranga W.241 'welfare' taihemahema W.363 'genitals of either sex']

ōrangi *adjective* basic blue [ō W.237 'of' te kahu o te rangi W.84 'blue sky']

ōrangitea *adjective* light blue [ōrangi TM 'basic blue' teatea W.410 'light in colour']

ōrau *noun* percent [ō W.237 'of, belonging to' rau W.328 'hundred']

ōrau *noun* percentage [ō W.237 'of, belonging to' rau W.328 'hundred']

ori hīteki *noun* ballet [ori W.241 'sway, move about' hītekiteki W.53 'walk on tiptoe']

oro *noun* phoneme [W.242 'rumble, sound']

orohaurua *noun* quaver [orotahi W.242 'crotchet' haurua TM 'half']

orohauwhā *noun* semi-quaver [oro W.242 'sound' hauwhā TM 'quarter']

orokohanga *noun* (*formation*) establishment [oroko W.242 'for the first time' hanga W.34 'build, fashion']

orokohanga *noun* creation [oroko W.242 'for the first time' hanga W.34 'build, fashion']

orokohanga paemaunga *noun* (*geology*) orogenesis [orokohanga TM 'creation' pae W.244 'horizontal ridges of hills' maunga W.197 maunga 'mountain']

orooro *noun* (*music*) key [oro W.242 'clump, sound']

oropapa *noun* unanimous [W.242 'all alike, without exception']

ororua *noun* diphthong [oro W.242 'sound' rua W.349 'two']

orotahi *noun* crotchet [oro W.242 'sound' tahi W.359 'one']

orotahi *noun* (*music*) note [oro W.242 'sound' tahi W.359 'one, single']

orotaunaki *noun* (*music, etc.*) sound effects [oro W.242 'rumble, sound' taunaki W.400 'support, reinforce']

orotoru *noun* (*language*) triphthong [oro W.242 'sound' toru W.441 'three']

orowaru *noun* breve [oro W.242 'sound' waru W.480 'eight']

orowhā *noun* semi-breve [oro W.242 'sound' whā W.484 'four']

ōrua *noun* (*music*) harmony [W.242 'coincide, coincide with']

otinga *noun* (*mathematics*) answer, result, solution, product [W.242 'finished']

otinga *noun* (*geometry*) image [oti W.242 'used ... to denote the operation is finished']

owaro *noun* hextane [ono W.240 'six' waro TM 'alkane']

ōwehe *noun* proportion [ō W.237 'of, belonging to' wehe W.481 'detach, divide']

P

pā *transitive verb (touch)* tag [W.243 'touch']
pā *(fishing tackle)* spinner [W.244 'fish hook made with pāua shell in lieu of bait') object']
pā whakarere *adjective (sudden, of illness, etc.)* acute [pā W.244 'be struck, overcome' whakarere W.338 'suddenly']
pae *noun* shelf [W.244 'any transverse beam, perch, rest']
pae hamuti *noun* toilet seat [W.245 'horizontal beam of latrine']
pae huatau *noun* suggestion box [pae W.245 'open, shallow vessel' huatau W.66 'thought, think']
pae hūtoto *noun (sport)* blood bin [pae W.244 'perch, rest' hūtoto W.73 'bloody']
pae hūtoto *noun (rugby league)* headbin [pae W.244 'perch, rest' hūtoto W.73 'bloody']
pae kaneke *noun* advantage line [pae W.245 'margin, boundary' kaneke W.93 'progress']
pae paneke *noun* goal line [pae W.245 'margin, boundary' paneke TM 'goal']
pae patopato *noun* typewriter [pae W.245 'any transverse beam' patopato TM 'type']
pae poihemo *noun (sport)* dead ball line [pae W.245 'margin, boundary' poi TM 'ball' hemo W.45 'miss a mark, die']
pae reta atu *noun (office equipment)* out-tray [pae W.246 'dish' reta < Eng. 'letter' atu W.20 'indicate a direction away from speaker']
pae reta mai *noun (office equipment)* in-tray [pae W.246 'dish' reta < Eng. 'letter' mai W.166 'indicating a relation or aspect towards']
pae tuki *noun (sport)* attack line [pae W.245 'margin, boundary' tuki W.450 'attack, ram']

pae umu *noun* oven-tray [paepae W.245 'dish, open, shallow vessel' umu TM 'oven']
pae whakahirihiri *noun (sport)* interchange bench [pae W.244 'perch, rest' whakahirihiri TM 'reserve, substitute']
pae whiu *noun (rugby league)* sin-bin [pae W.244 'perch, rest' whiu W.498 'chastise, put, place']
paearu *noun* criterion [paepae W.245 'beam, bar' aru W.17 'follow, pursue']
paehunu *noun* roasting dish [paepae W.245 'dish, open shallow vessel' parahunuhunu W.263 'roast']
pāeke *noun* innings [Salmond *Hui* 153 'order of speaking where all the speakers of the local side are followed by the visitors']
pāeke whakararo *noun (softball)* bottom of innings [pāeke TM 'innings' whakararo TM 'lower']
pāeke whakarunga *noun (softball)* top of innings [pāeke TM 'innings' whakarunga TM 'upper']
paekura *noun* lost property bin [W.246 'lost property']
paekuru *noun* anvil [pae W.244 'transverse beam' kuru W.159 'strike, pound']
paengao *noun* alveolar [pae W.244 'gum, border, edge' ngao W.229 'palate']
paepae *noun* tray [W.245 'dish, open shallow vessel']
paepae porotio *noun* ice-cube tray [paepae W.245 'open, shallow vessel' porotio TM 'ice-cube']
paepae whakaheke *noun* long-drop [W.245 'horizontal beam of a latrine']
paetaha *noun* sideline [pae W.245 'margin, boundary' taha W.357 'side, margin, edge']

203

paetaha tokorua *noun* singles sideline [paetaha TM 'sideline' tokorua TM 'singles']

paetaha tokowhā *noun* doubles sideline [paetaha TM 'sideline' tokowhā TM 'doubles']

paetopī *noun* baking tray [pae W.245 'open shallow vessel' topī W.437 'cook in a small oven']

pāhare *noun* (*chemistry*) salt [W.247 'bitter']

pāhare *noun* (*chemistry*) ester [W.247 'bitter']

pāhauhau *noun* shelterbelt, windbreak [W.247 'wind screen for crops']

paheko *noun* (*mathematics*) operation [W.247 'join, combine']

paheko kōaro *noun* inverse operation [paheko TM 'operation' kōaro TM 'inverse']

paheko matū *noun* chemical change [pakeho W.247 'combine, co-operate' matū TM 'chemical, substance']

paheko tōrua *noun* binary operation [paheko TM 'operation' tōrua W.441 'twofold']

paheko-rua *adjective* binary operation [paheko W.247 'join, combine' rua W.349 'two']

pāhekoheko *noun* medley [pāhekoheko W.247 'join, combine']

pahemo *noun* (*sport*) overthrow [W.247 'pass by, pass on one side, miss']

pāhīhī *noun* fountain pen [W.247 'flow in driblets']

pahore o Rehua *noun* equinox [Best *Tūhoe, Children of the Mist* 819, 820]

pāhoro *noun* (*overthrow*) revolution [W.248 'take by assault, storm a fortress, fall, capture of a fortress']

pāhotanga *noun* broadcasting [pāho W.248 'be noised abroad']

pahū *noun* bomb [W.248 'burst, explode']

pahū *noun* drum [W.248 'explode, alarum beaten like a gong']

pahū *noun* explosive [W.248 'burst, explode']

pahū *noun* explosion [W.248 'burst, explode']

pahū karihi *noun* nuclear bomb [pahū TM 'bomb' karihi TM 'nuclear']

pāhuki *noun* hedge [W.248 'screen of brushwood']

pāhūhū *noun* bombardment [pahū TM 'bomb']

pai *noun* (*level of excellence*) quality, standard [W.249 'suitability']

pai haere *intransitive verb* improve [pai W.249 'good' haere W.30 'become']

paiepa *noun* (*cricket*) over [paiere W.249 'bind together on bundles, bundle' epa TM 'bowl']

paiepa omakore *noun* maiden over [paiepa TM 'over' oma W.239 'run' kore W.140 'no']

paihau *noun* (*sport*) wing, winger [W.249 'wing, side']

paihau matau *noun* (*sport*) right wing, right winger [paihau W.249 'wing, side' matau W.192 'right, on the right hand']

paihau mauī *noun* (*sport*) left wing, left winger [paihau W.249 'wing, side' mauī W.196 'left, on the left side']

paihau pare *noun* wing defence [paihau W.249 'wing' pare W.266 'ward off']

paihau tuki *noun* wing attack [paihau W.249 'wing' tuki W.450 'attack']

paihere *phrase* (*rugby league*) set of six [W.249 'bundle, bring into close quarters']

pairi *noun* (*building*) lining [pairi ponga W.250 'slabs of tree-fern trunks used in building of huts and for lining store pits']

pāitiiti *transitive verb* decelerate [W.250 'decrease, subside']

pāitiiti *noun* deceleration [TM 'decelerate']

paitu kanekane *noun* (*food*) ginger [paitu W.250 'fern root with coarse fibres' kanekane W.93 'pungent']

pākai raho *noun* (*sport, protection*) box [pākai W.251 'shield, screen' raho W.320 'testicle']

pākaituki *noun* (*vehicle*) bumper [pākai W.251 'shield, screen' tūtuki W.450 'strike against another']

pākākā *adjective* dark orange [W.250 'scorched, red or brown']

pākaka raima *noun* (*building*) boxing [pākaka W.251 'surround, hem in, small enclosure' raima common usage 'concrete']

pakakau *noun* xylophone [W.251 'two sticks with which a sort of tune is played']

pakakē *noun* bitumen [W.251 'a black bituminous substance found on beaches']

pakakū *noun* asphalt [W.251 'a bituminous substance found on the beaches']

pakakū *noun* banjo [W.251 'make a harsh grating sound' kū W.153 'said to have been a one string instrument played by tapping with a stick']

pākati *(chemistry, salt or ester of '-ous' acid)* -ite [pāhare TM 'salt, ester' kakati W.103 'sting, bite']

pākati ota *noun* nitrite [pākati TM '-ite' hauota TM 'nitrogen']

pākati pungatara *noun* sulphite [pākati TM '-ite' pungatara TM 'sulphur']

pākati tūtae-whetū *noun* phosphite [pākawa TM '-ite' pūtūtae-whetū TM 'phosphorus']

pakatiti *adjective (manufactured products)* sub-standard [W.251 'defective in food']

pakaua *adjective* leathery [W.252 'muscular, brawny, sinewy, wiry']

pākawa *(chemistry, salt or ester of -ic acid')* -ate [pāhare TM 'salt, ester' waikawa TM 'acid']

pākawa konukita *noun* chromate [pākawa TM '-ate' konukita TM 'chromium']

pākawa kura pungawera *noun* copper sulphate [pākawa TM '-ate' konukura TM 'copper' pungawera W.311 'sulphur']

pākawa ota *noun* nitrate [pākawa TM '-ate' hauota TM 'nitrogen']

pākawa pungatara *noun* sulphate [pākawa TM '-ate' pungatara TM 'sulphur']

pākawa tūtae-whetū *noun* phosphate [pākawa TM '-ate' pūtūtae-whetū TM 'phosphorus']

pākawa waro *noun* carbonate [pākawa TM '-ate' waro TM 'carbon']

pākawarua konukita *noun* dichromate [pākawa TM '-ate' rua W.349 'two' konukita TM 'chromium']

pākī *noun* hamburger [parāoa < Eng. 'bread' kīnaki W.118 'food which is eaten along with other food' kī W.115 'full']

pakihi *noun (enterprise)* business [kaipakihi W.89 'business, affairs, concerns']

pakini *noun* apostrophe [W.254 'nick, notch']

pakitau *noun (mathematics)* number story [paki W.253 'tales, subject of talk' tau TM 'number']

pakitau whakatairite *noun* comparative number story [pakitau TM 'number story' whakatairite whaka- W.486 'causative prefix' *to make* tairite W.365 'like, on a level with']

pakiwaituhi *noun* cartoon [pakiwaitara W.254 'fiction, folklore' tuhi W.448 'draw, adorn with painting']

pakiwhara *noun* sexually transmitted disease [W.254 'venereal disease']

pakohe *adjective* dark grey [W.255 'a dark grey stone']

pakohu *noun (anatomy)* chamber [W.255 'cavity']

pakohu *noun* sinus [W.255 'rent, cleft, chasm, cavity']

pakohu *noun* vesicle [W.255 'rent, cleft, chasm, cavity']

pakohu kakā *noun* sinusitis [pakohu W.255 'rent, cleft, chasm, cavity' kakā TM 'inflammation']

pakohu roro *noun* cranium [pakohu W.255 'cavity' roro W.347 'brains']

pakoire *transitive verb* imitate, mimic [W.255 'imitate the cry of a bird']

pakoire *noun* mimicry [W.255 'imitate the cry of a bird']

pākoro *noun* pigsty [pākorokoro W.255 'encircle, hem in, a rude form of hut' pākoro 'small fenced enclosure']

pakuriki *noun (language)* particle [W.256 'particle, vestige']

pana *transitive verb* dismiss [W.256 'expel']

pana *transitive verb (sport)* send off [W.256 'expel']

pane *noun (document)* header [W.257 'head']

paneke *noun (basketball, point)* basket [TM 'goal, point']

paneke *phrase (sport)* to score point [W.257 'move forwards']

paneke *noun (rugby, etc.)* try [TM 'goal']

paneke *noun (score)* goal [W.257 'move forwards']

paneke *intransitive verb (sport)* score [TM 'goal, point']

paneke *noun (lawn bowls)* shot [TM 'goal, point']

paneke ninipa *noun (soccer)* own goal [paneke TM 'goal' ninipa W.322 'awkward, unfortunate, unskilful']

paneke taiari *noun* pushover try [paneke TM 'try' taiari W.362 'beat, drive back, smash, crush']

paneke tautuku *noun* penalty try [paneke TM 'try' tautuku TM 'penalty']

panekoti hauraro *noun* ankle-length skirt [panekoti common usage 'skirt' hauraro W.41 'low down, pendent']

pane kuīni *noun* postage stamp [pane W.257 'head' kuīni < Eng. 'queen']

pani ngutu *noun* lipstick [pani W.257 'paint, besmear' ngutu W.236 'lip']

paniaku *noun* toothpaste [pani W.257 'smear, spread anything upon something else' akuaku W.7 'scrape out, cleanse']

panihā *noun* (*food*) pate [pani W.257 'spread' hāhā W.29 'savoury']

pānihi *noun* panther [ninihi W.221 'move stealthily']

panikakā *noun* mustard [pani W.257 'smear, spread' kakā W.81 'red-hot']

panoni *noun* (*mathematics*) transformation [W.257 'change']

panoni tinana *noun* (*biology*) physical change [panoni W.257 'change' tinana W.419 'body']

pānui *transitive verb* dictate [W.257 'read or speak aloud']

pānui *noun* notice [W.257 'publish, proclaim']

pānui *noun* advertisement [pānui W.257 'advertise publicly, publish, public notice']

pānui hara *noun* infringement notice [pānui TM 'notice' hara TM 'infringement']

pānui pāpāho *noun* press release [pānui W.257 'advertise publicly, proclaim' pāpāho TM 'broadcast']

pānui pāpāho *noun* press statement [pānui W.257 'advertise publicly, proclaim' pāpāho TM 'broadcast']

pānui whakaahua *noun* poster [pānui W.257 'advertise publicly' whakaahua TM 'picture']

pānui whakaata *noun* teletext [pānui W.257 'advertise publicly, public notice' pouaka whakaata common usage 'television']

pānui whakamārama *noun* pamphlet [pānui W.257 'publish, advertise publicly' whakamārama W.180 'illuminate, explain']

pānui-ā-waha *noun* dictation [pānui W.257 'read or speak aloud' ā W.1 'after the manner of' waha W.473 'voice, mouth']

pānuitanga *noun* advertising [pānui W.257 'advertise publicly, publish, public notice']

pānga *noun* (*mathematics*) relation [pā W.243 'be connected with']

pānga *noun* dividend [pā W.243 'be connected with']

pānga *noun* effect [pā W.243 'touch, strike']

pānga *noun* (*mathematics*) function [pā W.243 'be connected with, operate on']

pānga *noun* apparatus [pā W.243 'be connected with']

pānga *noun* (*mathematics, science etc.*) relationship [pā W.243 'be connected with']

panga *noun* (*education*) problem [W.257 'riddle, game of guessing']

panga *transitive verb* (*with hands, sport*) pass [W.257 'throw']

panga matā *noun* shotput [panga W.257 'throw, lay, place' matā TM 'shot']

pānga rārangi *noun* linear function [pānga TM 'function' rārangi W.324 'line']

pānga tuhituhi *noun* stationery [pā W.243 'be connected with' tuhituhi W.448 'write']

pānga tuku iho *noun* (*property of deceased person*) estate [pā W.243 'be connected with' tuku W.451 'present, offer' iho W.75 'downwards']

pangakupu *noun* crossword [panga W.257 'riddle, game of guessing' kupu W.157 'word']

pāngarau *noun* mathematics [pā W.243 'touch, be connected with' rau W.328 'hundred, multitude']

pangore *noun* toddler [W.258 'children, immature']

panguru *noun* (*instrument*) bass [W.258 'bass, gruff']

pāngurunguru *noun* double bass [panguru W.258 'bass, gruff' TM 'bass (instrument)']

pao *noun* (*popular song*) hit [W.258 'sing, strike, as with a hammer']

pao taka *noun* (*tennis*) drop shot [pao W.258 'strike, pound' taka W.366 'fall off, fall away']

paoka *noun* (*cutlery*) fork [W.258 'pointed stick, stab, pierce']

pāokaoka *noun* cutlery [paoka W.258 'pointed stick, skewer, used for picking up food']

paopao *transitive verb, intransitive verb (text)* type [pao W.258 'strike, crack, break']

paorangi *adjective* supersonic [W.258 'resounding']

pāorooro *adjective* sonic [W.258 'resounding']

papa *noun* (*mathematics*) plane [W.259 'anything broad, flat and hard']

papa *noun* storey [W.259 'anything broad, flat and hard, site']

papa *noun* plank [W.259 'slab, board']

papa ahumahi *noun* industrial land [papa W.259 'earth floor, site' ahumahi TM 'industry']

papa hākinakina *noun* (*sport*) field [papa W.259 'site' hākinakina TM 'sport']

papa hokohoko *noun* shopping centre, shopping plaza [papa W.259 'site, traffic' hokohoko W.57 'merchandise, trade, exchange']

papa kiripaka *noun* asbestos [papa W.259 'anything broad, flat and hard' kiripaka W.119 'flint, quartz']

papa kōmaru *noun* solar panel [papa W.259 'anything broad, flat and hard' kōmaru TM 'solar']

papa kotikoti *noun* chopping board [papa W.259 'anything broad, flat and hard' kotikoti W.149 'cut to pieces']

papa kūtoro *noun* stretch fabric [papanga TM 'fabric' kōtoro W.160 'stretched at full length, a closely woven fabric']

papa maita *noun* (*lawn bowls*) green [papa TM 'field' maita TM 'lawn bowls']

papa maramara *noun* chipboard [papa W.259 'anything broad, flat and hard' maramara W.180 'chip, splinter']

papa pānui rorohiko *noun* electronic bulletin board [papa W.259 'anything broad, flat and hard' pānui W.257 'advertise publicly' rorohiko TM 'computer']

papa parāoa *noun* breadboard [papa W.259 'anything broad, flat and hard' parāoa common usage 'bread']

papa pātuhi *noun* computer keyboard [papa W.259 'anything broad, flat and hard' pātuhi TM 'key']

papa pātuhi *noun* keyboard [papa W.259 'anything broad, flat and hard' pātuhi TM 'key']

papa pūkura *noun* badminton court [papa tākaro TM 'court' pūkura TM 'badminton']

papa rererangi *noun* airport [papa W.259 'earth floor or site' waka rererangi common usage 'aeroplane']

papa tākaro *noun* adventure playground [papa W.259 'earth floor or site' pukutākaro W.309 'playful, sportive']

papa tākaro *noun* court [papa W.259 'site' tākaro W.369 'play, sport']

papa tākaro *noun* (*sport*) field [papa W.259 'site' tākaro W.369 'play, sport']

papa tāpatu *noun* plywood [papa W.259 'anything broad, flat and hard, board' tāpatupatu W.383 'place in layers, lay one on another']

papa tapeke *noun* scoreboard [papa W.259 'anything broad, flat, and hard' tapeke TM 'score']

papa tāuru *noun* top floor [papa W.259 'earth floor or site' tāuru W.403 'top of a tree etc.']

papa tuatahi *noun* first floor [papa W.259 'earth floor or site' tua W.444 'prefix used with numerals to form ordinals' tahi W.359 'one']

papa whenua *noun* ground floor [papa W.259 'earth floor or site' whenua W.494 'ground']

papaangi *noun* veneer [papa W.259 'anything broad, flat and hard' angiangi W.11 'thin']

papahamo *noun* (*bed*) headboard [papa W.259 'board' hamo W.33 'back of head']

papahewa *noun* glaucoma [W.260 'diseased in the eyes']

papahiko *noun* (*electricity*) switchboard [papa W.259 'anything broad, flat and hard' hiko common usage 'electrcity']

pāpāho *intransitive verb, transitive verb* broadcast [pāho W.248 'be noised abroad']

pāpāhua *noun* alkali [W.248 'plunder']

papahuka *noun* snowfield [papa W.259 'anything broad, flat and hard' huka W.67 'frost, snow']

papahune *noun* cotton fabric [papanga TM 'cloth' hune W.69 'down, of birds etc., pappus of seeds of raupō']

pāpaki *noun* pita bread [pāpaki W.253 'sew two kete mouth to mouth to hold maize etc.' pakipaki W.253 'wallet with a flap to cover the opening']

papaki *noun, transitive verb* (*sport*) tap [W.253 'slap, pat']

pāpā-kiri *noun* splint [Biggs 184 'splint made of bark' W.260 'bark']

pāpako *noun* trowel [W.254 'loosen the soil around plants']

papakupu *noun* dictionary, glossary [papa W.259 'box, chest' kupu W.157 'word']

papamā *noun* whiteboard [papa W.259 'anything broad, flat and hard' mā W.161 'white']

papamāene *noun* silk [papanga TM 'fabric' māeneene W.162 'soft to the touch']

papamahi *noun* studio [papa W.259 'anything broad, flat and hard' mahi W.163 'work, work at']

papamārō *noun* hardboard [papa W.259 'anything broad, flat and hard' mārō W.183 'hard, solid, unyielding']

papamōhinu *noun* satin [papanga TM 'fabric' mōhinuhinu W.205 'shiny, glistening, glossy']

papamuka *noun* linen [papanga TM 'fabric, textile' muka W.213 'prepared fibre of flax']

papamuri *noun* backboard [papa W.259 'anything broad, flat and hard' muri W.214 'rear, back']

papanga *noun* fabric, material, cloth [papanga rua W.259 'twofold, of fabric']

papangarua *noun* duvet, quilt [W.259 'twofold, of fabric']

pāpapa *noun* bran [W.259 'husk, such as bran chaff etc.']

pāpapa *noun* eggshell [W.259 'shell of an egg, crayfish, etc.']

paparahua *noun* dining-room table [W.260 'kind of table from which food was eaten']

paparahua *noun* kitchen table [W.260 'kind of table from which food was eaten']

paparai *noun* corduroy [papanga TM 'cloth' rarai W.321 'ribbed, furrowed']

papārangi *noun* sonic boom [papā W.244 'burst, explode' rangi W.323 'sky']

paparawhi *noun* clipboard [papa W.259 'anything broad, flat and hard' rawhi TM 'clip']

papare *transitive verb* resist [pare W.266 'ward off, turn aside, avoid, abstain from']

papare māhunga *noun* (*sport*) headgear [pare W.266 'protection' māhunga W.165 'head']

papatai *noun* reclaimed land [papa W.259 'earth' tai W.361 'the sea, the coast']

pāpātanga *noun* rate [pā W.243 'be connected with, touch, strike']

pāpātanga paiepa *noun* (*cricket*) over rate [pāpātanga TM 'rate' paiepa TM 'over']

papatara *noun* kitchen cupboard [W.261 'storehouse, stage for food']

papatara *noun* (*library*) reference section [W.261 'storehouse, stage for food' whakatara W.386 'invoke, consult']

papatau *noun* number table [papa W.259 'anything broad, flat and hard' tau TM 'number']

papatīhi *noun* cheeseboard [papa W.259 'anything broad, flat and hard' tīhi < Eng. 'cheese']

papatipu *noun* (*science*) mass [W.261 'solid mass']

papatohu *noun* dashboard [papa W.259 'anything broad, flat and hard' tohu W.431 'mark, sign, show, point out']

papatohu *noun* directory board [papa W.259 'anything broad, flat and hard' tohutohu W.431 'show, direct, guide']

papatohu *noun* (*control desk*) console [papa W.259 'anything broad, flat and hard' tohu W.431 'mark, sign, show, point out']

pāpāuku *noun* plaster cast [pāpākiri Biggs 184 'splint made of bark' uku W.466 'white clay']

papaurangi *noun* talcum powder [W.261 'a plant used as scent for oil']

papawaea *noun* (*telephone*) switchboard [papa W.259 'anything broad, flat and hard' waea < Eng. 'wire']

papawaka *noun* carpark [papa W.259 'site' waka common usage 'vehicle']

papī *transitive verb* excrete [W.261 'ooze, leak']

papī *noun* excretion [W.261 'ooze, leak']

pāpono *noun* (*statistics*) event [pā W.243 'reach, strike' tūpono W.457 'light upon accidentally, chance to hit']

pāpuni *noun* tourniquet [W.261 'stanch, check the flow of blood']

para *noun* trash [W.262 'refuse, waste']

para iraruke *noun* radioactive waste [para W.262 'impurity, refuse, waste' ira rukeruke TM 'radioactive']

pāra takawai *noun* silicon chip [pāra W.261 'a flake of stone' takawai TM 'silicon']

pāraha *noun* tool [pāraharaha W.263 'tool made of thin iron, hoop iron, or anything similar']

paraha *noun* pikelet [W.263 'flat, broad' cf. pancake TM 'pāraharaha']

pāraharaha *noun* pancake [W.263 'flat']

parahanga *noun* pollution [W.262 'rubbish, litter']

parahau whaiaro *noun* self defence [parahau W.263 'protection, defence' whaiaro W.485 'self, person']

parahunu *noun* roast [parahunuhunu W.263 'roast']

parai rumaki *noun* deep-fryer [parai < Eng. 'fry' rumaki W.351 'immerse' rumaki W.352 'basket of seed potatoes']

parakaingaki *noun* sewage [W.263 'filth, excrement']

para-karaka *adjective* (*colour*) salmon pink [W.263 'an orange-red stone']

parakete *noun* loot [W.263 'booty']

parakino *noun* pollutant [para W.262 'sediment, impurity, refuse, waste' kino W.118 'evil, bad']

paramanawa *noun* morning tea [W.264 'refreshment']

paramanawa *noun* snack [W.264 'refreshment']

paramanawa *noun* afternoon tea [W.264 'refreshment']

parāoa rimurapa *noun* pasta [parāoa < Eng. 'flour' rimurapa W.341 'bull kelp']

pararaha *noun* wok [W.264 'a shallow vessel made by cutting a slice from a gourd, wide and shallow, of a vessel']

pararahi *noun* flan [W.264 'flat']

parataiao *adjective* sedimentary [TM 'sediment']

parataiao *noun* (*geology*) sediment [para W.262 'sediment, impurity' taiao TM 'environment']

paraumu *adjective* organic [W.265 'black soil, humus']

parawaro *noun* nicotine [para W.262 'impurity, waste' waro TM 'carbon']

pare tīkākā *noun* sunblock [pare W.266 'turn aside, ward off, protection' tīkākā TM 'sunburn']

pareaku *noun* polyester [pare < Eng. 'poly' aku W.7 'firm, strong']

parehe *noun* pizza [W.266 'flat cake of meal from fern root']

parehua *noun* balcony [W.266 'terrace, ridge']

parehūhare *noun* serviette [pare W.266 'turn aside, ward off' parahūhare W.263 'spittle or scraps of food adhering to lips']

pārekereke *noun* seed-bed [W.266 'seedling bed']

parekiri *noun* (*sport*) padding [pare W.266 'turn aside, ward off' parepare W.266 'protection' kiri W.119 'skin, person, self']

parekiri *noun* (*sport*) protective gear [pare W.266 'turn aside, ward off' parepare W.266 'protection' kiri W.119 'skin, person, self']

paremata *transitive verb* compensate [W.266 'payment, return']

paremata *noun* reparation [W266 'payment, return']

paremata *noun* compensation [W.266 'payment, return']

parenga *noun* (*force*) resistance [pare W.266 'turn aside, ward off']

paretā *noun* shin-pad [pare W.266 'turn aside, ward off' tā W.354 'shin, lower joint of the leg']

paretoki *noun* overlocker [W.267 'a method of fastening the fringe to the bottom of a garment']

paretua *noun* cushion [W.267 'pad under a load to protect the back']

pareumu *noun* oven cloth [pare W.266 'protection' umu TM 'oven']

pari hūhare *noun* usage bib (food) [pari common usage 'bodice' parahūhare W.33 'scraps of food']

pari tākaro *noun* (*netball*) bib [pari common usage 'bodice' tākaro W.369 'play, sport']

pārōnaki (*mathematics*) derivative [pānga TM 'function' rōnaki TM 'gradient']

pārongo *noun* information [pā W.243 'reach, strike, be connected with' rongo W.346 'tidings, report']

paruhi *noun* godchild [W.269 'favourite, darling']

pārure *noun* (*shooting*) target [W.269 'prey']

pārure pateko *noun* (*shooting*) static target [pārure TM 'target' pateko W.271 'motionless, idle']

pārure tīrore *noun* (*shooting*) moving target [pārure TM 'target' tīrore W.424 'decoy kākā']

pārurenga *noun* victim [W.269 'a person subjected to violence or ill treatment']

paruru *noun* press-stud [W.269 'place close together, compact']

pata *noun* outcome [W.269 'advantage, fruit']

pata pūngao *noun* (*biology*) mitochondrian [pata W.269 'seed, grain, numerous' pūngao TM 'energy']

pātahi *adjective* (*mathematics*) common [pā W.243 'touch, affect' tahi W.359 'together']

patahua *noun* muesli [pata W.269 'seed, grain' hua W.64 'fruit']

pātaka *noun* pantry, larder [W.270 'storehouse raised upon posts, elevated stage for storing food']

pātaki *noun* septum [TM 'partition']

pātaki *noun* partition [pātakitaki W.270 'divisions or containing barriers in a store pit, screen of brush, boundary, division']

patakakā *noun* mustard seed [pata W.269 'seed, grain' kakā W.81 'red-hot']

patakore *adjective* seedless [pata W.269 'seed, grain' kore W.140 'no, not']

pātapa *noun* (*mathematics*) tangent [pā W.243 'touch, strike' tapa W.381 'edge']

patapatai *noun, transitive verb* interview [W.269 'question, inquire']

pātata *adjective* adjacent [W.270 'near']

pātātea *noun* (*contraceptive*) diaphragm [pā W.243 'block up, obstruct' tātea W.394 'semen']

patatini *noun* berry [pata W.260 'seed' tini W.419 'very many']

pātātoko *noun* photosynthesis [pātā W.269 'prepare food' toko W.434 'ray of light']

pātea *adjective* (*sport*) free [W.270 'unencumbered, freed from burdens']

pateko *adjective* (*inactivity*) static [W.271 'motionless, idle']

pātengi raraunga *noun* database [pātengi W.271 'storehouse or pit for kūmara' raraunga TM 'data']

pātengitengi *noun* vegetable-crisper [W.271 'a storehouse or pit for kūmara']

patete *intransitive verb* accelerate [W.271 'move along']

pātoi *transitive verb* (*rugby*) draw [W.272 'lure, entice']

patopato *transitive verb, intransitive verb* (*text*) type [patō W.271 'emit a sharp sudden sound, crack, snap']

pātū *noun* (*soccer*) wall [W.272 'screen, wall']

patu ā-iraruke *transitive verb* irradiate [patu W.272 'kill' ā W.1 'after the manner of' irarukeTM 'radiation']

pātū hihiani *noun* radar screen [pātū W.272 'screen, wall' hihiani TM 'radar']

patu hiaruaki *noun* anti-emetic [patu W.272 'subdue' hia W.47 'wish, impulse' ruaki W.350 'vomit']

pātū kanohi *noun* face-guard [pātū W.272 'screen, wall' kanohi W.94 'face']

patu kitakita *transitive verb* disinfect [patu W.272 'kill' kitakita TM 'bacteria']

patu kitakita *noun* disinfectant [patu W.272 'kill' kitakita TM 'bacteria']

patu koko *noun* (*hockey*) corner hit [patu W.272 'hit' koko W.130 'corner']

patu mōrūruru *noun* deodorant, antiperspirant [patu W.272 'strike, subdue' mōrūruru W.210 'odour of human sweat']

patu tarutaru *noun* herbicide [patu W.272 'kill' tarutaru W.392 'herbage, small vegetation, grass']

patu tātea *noun* spermicide [patu W.272 'kill' wai tātea 'sperm']

patu tokopā *noun* antacid [patu 272 'subdue' tokopā W.435 'heartburn, indigestion, belch']

pātua *noun* platter [W.272 'a receptacle for food']

patuero *noun, adjective* antiseptic [W.272 'subdue, beat' ero W.28 'putrid']

patuero poroporo *noun* potassium permanganate [patuero TM 'antiseptic' poroporo TM 'deep purple']

pātuhi *noun* (*computer*) key [pā W.243 'touch' tuhi W.448 'write']

pātuhi mokowā *noun* (*keyboard*) space bar [pātuhi TM 'key' mokowā TM 'space']

patui whatu *noun* knitting-needle [patui W.272 'needle of bone or wood' whatu W.492 'weave garments']

pātuki *noun, transitive verb* skittle [W.272 'strike, knock']

patungārara *noun* insecticide [patu W.272 'kill' ngārara W.229 'insect']

pātūpoho *noun* (*anatomy*) diaphragm [pātū W.272 'screen, wall' poho W.287 'chest, stomach']

paturiha *noun* pesticide [patu W.272 'kill' riha TM 'pest']

paturopi *noun* antibody [patu W.272 'kill' ropi W.347 'body']

paturua *noun* double hit [patu TM 'hit' rua W.349 'two']

patu-tāoke *noun* antitoxin [patu W.272 'subdue, beat' tāoke TM 'toxin']

pāuhu *transitive verb* postpone [W.273 'put off, adjourn']

paunga rāwhitu *noun* weekend [pau W.273 'consumed, exhausted' rāwhitu TM 'week']

pawapawa *noun* incense [W.273 'strongly scented' pawa 'smoke']

pāwera *adjective* allergic [W.273 'sore, tender to the touch, affected'] *e.g. Pāwera katoa au i te hae. 'I am allergic to pollen'*

pāwhatiwhati *noun* maze [ara pāwhati W.274 'track marked by breaking branches']

pāwhiri *transitive verb* (*computer*) click on [pā W.243 'touch' kōwhiri W.153 'select']

pehu *noun* (*computer*) cursor [W.275 'dart, spear']

pehu rīwai *noun* potato masher [pehu W.275 'mash, pound' rīwai W.344 'potato']

pehukawhe *noun* coffee-grinder [pehu W.275 'pound' kanokawhe TM 'coffee bean']

pehutapa *noun* (*computer*) chooser [pehu W.275 'dart, spear' tapa W.381 'command, give the word for']

pekanga *noun* (*telephone*) extension [peka W.275 'branch of a tree, river etc.']

pekanga mātauranga *noun* (*field of study*) discipline [pekanga W.275 'branch, road' mātauranga common usage 'knowledge']

pekaputa *noun* off-ramp [peka W.275 'branch of a tree, river, etc.' puta W.315 'pass out']

pekauru *noun* on-ramp [peka W.275 'branch of a tree, river, etc.' uru W.469 'enter']

peke *adjective* (*finance*) gross [W.276 'be all included']

peke katoa *adjective* inclusive [W.276 'be all included']

peke ngaru *noun* wave jumper [peke W.276 'spring, leap, jump' ngaru W.230 'wave']

peke pakihiwi *noun, transitive verb* (*sport*) smash [W.276 'effective in action, striking direct powerful blows']

peke tōtoru *noun* (*athletics*) triple jump [peke W.276 'spring, leap, jump' tōtoru TM 'triple']

peke tōtoru *noun* triple jumper [TM 'triple jump']

pekekiwi *noun, transitive verb* (*golf*) duff [W.276 'strike at random, without effect']

pekerangi *noun* ozone, ozone layer [W.276 'screen, barrier, the outermost palisade of a complete stockade']

pekerangi *noun* disco, disco-dancing [W.276 'a dance accompanied by song, perform such a dance']

peketua *noun* backpack, pack [W.276 'supplementary load carried on the back']

pekewhā *noun* quadruped [haere pekewhā W.276 'go on all fours']

penapena rawa *noun* resource management [penapena W.277 'take care of, tend, husband, preserve knowledge' rawa W.331 'goods, property, advantage, benefit']

pene rākau *noun* pencil [pene < Eng. 'pen' rākau W.321 'wooden']

pene whītau *noun* felt pen [pene < Eng. 'pen' whītau TM 'felt']

penihana pakanga *noun* war pension [penihana TM 'pension' pakanga W.250 'war']

penu taewa *noun* potato masher [penupenu W.277 'mashed' taewa W.357 'potato']

pepamingo *noun* crepe paper [pepa < Eng. 'paper' mingo W.202 'curly, wrinkled']

pēpepe mōrea red admiral butterfly [pēpepe W.277 'moth, butterfly' mōrea W.210 'red']

pere (*mathematics*) vector [W.278 'arrow, dart']

pere rua *noun* yacht [W.278 'a canoe with two sails']

pere rua *noun* yachting [W.278 'a canoe with two sails']

perehunga *noun* suede [W.278 'nap']

pereti toha *noun* serving plate [pereti < Eng. 'plate' toha W.429 'distribute']

peru *noun* (*machinery*) nut [W.278 'head, as of a nail, etc.']

petapeta *adverb* collectively [W.278 'all at once']

pewa *noun* arc [W.278 'anything bow-shaped']

pēwaro *noun* pentane [pē < Eng. 'pen-' waro TM 'alkane']

pī *noun* (*mathematics*) pi [W.279 'origin']

pī huauri *noun* queen bee [pī < Eng. 'bee' huauri W.66 'having offspring']

pia *noun* apprentice [W.279 'the first order of learners being initiated in esoteric lore']

pia *noun* undergraduate student [W.279 'the first order of learners being initiated in esoteric lore']

pia makawe *noun* hair gel [pia W.279 'gum of trees or any similar exudation' makawe W.169 'hair']

piakamo *noun* (*anatomy*) vitreous humour [piapia W.279 'glairy, viscid' kamo W.92 'eye']

piakano *noun* (*crayon*) pastel [pia W.279 'gum of tree' kano W.94 'colour']

piapahū *noun* gelignite [pahū TM 'explosive' hāpiapia TM 'gelatinous']

piarēmana *noun* (*beverage*) shandy [pia < Eng. 'beer' rēmana < Eng. 'lemon']

pīari *noun* abnormality [W.279 'deformed, stunted person']

pīauau *noun* paring knife [W.279 'cutting instrument, knife']

pīauau pūkoro *noun* pocket-knife [pīauau W.279 'knife, cutting instrument' pūkoro W.308 'pocket']

piere *noun* aperture [W.279 'cleft, crack, chink']

pīhangaiti *noun* honeycomb [W.279 'be gathered together, compact']

pīhaonga *noun* apiary [pīhao W.279 'surround' pī < Eng. 'bee' hao W.35 'catch, enclose']

piharoa *noun* sheet metal [W.279 'iron']

piharoa *noun* long-run roofing [W.279 'iron']

piharoa kōwakawaka *noun* corrugated iron [piharoa W.279 'iron' TM 'sheet metal' kōwakawaka TM 'corrugated']

pīhau *noun* inflatable dinghy [W.280 'some form of canoe']

pihi *noun* antler [W.280 'shoot, sprout']

pihi makaurangi *noun* unicorn [pihi common usage 'horn' makaurangi W.169 'spiral lines, adorn with spirals']

pihi pīni *noun* bean sprout [pihi W.280 'shoot, sprout' pīni < Eng. 'bean']

pihinga *noun* beginners' course [pihi W.280 'spring up, begin to grow']

pihiringa *noun* moose [pihi W.280 'shoot, sprout' ringa W.341 'hand(-like)']

piki *noun* deputy [W.280 'second, support in a duel, assistant']

piki *noun* (*sport, contest*) reserve, substitute [W.280 'second, support in a duel']

piki *noun* understudy [W.280 'second, support in a duel']

piki *noun* rising intonation [W.280 'climb, ascend']

piki *adjective* (*music*) sharp [W.280 'climb, ascend']

piki toka *noun* rock-climbing [piki W.280 'climb, ascend' toka W.433 'stone, rock']

piko *noun* comma [W.281 'curve, curved']

pīkoikoi *intransitive verb* of female masturbate [atua pīkoikoi W.281 'clitoris']

pikopewa *noun* hook and eye [piko W.281 'bent, curved, curve' pewa W.278 'anything bowed shaped']

pine *noun* (*machinery*) bolt [W.281 'close together']

pīnekeneke *noun* compression [pineke W.281 'close together, compressed']

pininga parakaingaki *noun* sewer [pininga W.281 'applied to a stream which disappears underground' parakaingaki W.263 'filth, excrement' TM 'sewage']

pīnohi *noun* (*fire*) poker [W.281 'sticks used for handling hot stones']

pīnohi *noun* (*kitchenware*) tongs [W.281 'sticks used for handling hot stones, tongs']

pīngao *adjective* golden yellow [W.281 'a plant, the leaves of which dry a bright orange colour']

pipī *transitive verb* (*medicine*) secrete [W.279 'ooze, soak in']

pipīnga *noun* secretion [pipī W.279 'ooze, soak in']

pirara *noun* (*botany*) umbel [W.283 'separated, divided, gaping, branching']

piri-ki-tata bumper to bumper [piri W.283 'come close, keep close' tata W.393 'near']

pirikore *noun* mystery [piri W.283 'stick, adhere, cling' piringa 'hiding place' koko W.130 'corner, recess']

pirikore *adjective* (*kitchenware etc.*) non-stick [piri W.283 'stick, adhere, cling' kore W.140 'no, not']

pirinoa *noun* parasite [W.284 'semi-parasitic plants' piri W.283 'stick, cling']

pirinoa *adjective* parasitic [TM 'parasite']

piripiri *noun* velcro [W.283 'a creeping burr']

pīrori *transitive verb* (*dice*) roll [W.284 'roll along, as a ball']

pīrorohū *noun* bumble-bee [pī < Eng. 'bee' rorohū W.348 'buzz, buzz about']

pītakataka *noun* gymnastics [W.284 'tumble about, be constantly on the move, waggle']

pītau pīni *noun* green beans [pītau W.284 'young succulent shoot of a plant' pīni < Eng. 'bean']

pītau-ira *noun* deoxyribonucleic acid DNA [pītau W.284 'perforated spiral carving, young succulent shoot of a plant, circinate frond of a fern' ira TM 'gene']

pītawitawi *adjective* floppy [W.284 'bending, sagging']

piti hāora *transitive verb* oxidise *noun* oxidant [piti W.284 'add' hāora TM 'oxygen']

pito *noun* (*physics*) pole [W.284 'end, extremity']

pito-tā *noun* (*electricity*) anode, negative end [pito W.284 'end, extremity' tā common usage used to indicate indefinite locality]

pito-tī *noun* (*electricity*) cathode, positive end [pito W.284 'end, extremity' tī common usage used to indicate indefinite locality]

pīwari *noun* flag [W.285 'wave in the wind']

pīwari kai hau *noun* wind sock [pīwari W.285 'wave in the wind' kai W.85 'eat' hau W.38 'wind, air']

pīwari koko *noun* (*sport*) corner flag [pīwari TM 'flag' koko W.130 'corner']

poapoa *adjective* (*discoloration*) stained [W.286 'stain, discoloration']

poautinitini *noun* apocalypse, holocaust [W.286 'tribulation, evil, death']

pōhā *noun* pastry [W.286 'a cake of hīnau meal']

pōhā aparau *noun* flaky pastry [pōhā TM 'pastry' apa W.12 'layer' rau W.328 'hundred, multitude']

pohokore *noun* malnutrition [W.287 'starved, emaciated']

pohokore *adjective* malnourished [W.287 'starved, emaciated']

poi *noun* (*sport*) ball [W.288 'ball, lump']

poi tarawhiti *noun* netball [poi TM 'ball' tarawhiti W.390 'hoop, ring']

poi teitei *noun* (*sport*) high ball [poi TM 'ball' teitei W.410 'high, lofty']

poihemo *noun* (*sport*) dead ball [poi TM 'ball' hemo W.45 'miss a mark, die']

pōike *noun, intransitive verb* (*weightlifting*) snatch [W.288 'place aloft']

poikere *noun* play dough [poi W.288 'make into a ball, knead, work up' kere W.114 'clay, earth']

poikiri *noun* soccer [poi TM 'ball' kiri W.119 'skin']

poikiri *noun* soccer ball [poikiri TM 'soccer']

poikōpiko *noun* ping-pong [poi TM 'ball' kōpiko W.137 'go alternately in opposiite directions']

poikōpiko *noun* table tennis [poi TM 'ball' kōpiko W.137 'go alternately in opposite directions']

poikurukuru *noun* (*golf*) divot [W.288 'lump, clod']

poipātū *noun* (*game*) squash [poi TM 'ball' pātū W.272 'screen, wall']

poirewa *noun* volleyball [poi TM 'ball' rewa W.339 'be elevated, be high up']

poirewa one *noun* beach volleyball [poirewa TM 'volleyball' one W.239 'beach']

poitika *noun* (*softball*) strike [poi TM 'ball' tika W.416 'straight, direct, correct']

pōito *noun* (*buoyancy aid*) water wings [Best *Games and Pastimes* 42 'floats fastened to a child learning to swim']

poitūkohu *noun* basketball [poi TM 'ball' tūkohu TM 'basket']

poiuka *noun* softball [poi TM 'ball' uka W.466 'hard, firm']

poka *noun, transitive verb* puncture [W.288 'make a hole in, pierce']

poka kirimata *noun* male circumcision [W.288 'cut out' kiri W.119 'skin' mata W.185 'point, extremity']

poka (raho) *transitive verb* castrate [poka W.288 'cut out' raho W.320 'testicles']

pokapoka rākau *noun* silviculture [pokapoka W.288 'plant in holes, begin to plant' rākau W.321 'tree']

pokapū *noun* centre, agency [W.289 'middle, centre']

pokapū *noun* (*soccer*) centre spot [W.289 'middle, centre']

pokepoke *noun* (*solid*) mixture [W.289 'mix up with water or other fluid']

pokerehū by mistake [W.290 'unintentional']

pokerenoa *adverb* thoughtlessly [W.290 'wilful, reckless']

pokewai *noun* (*food*) batter [pokepoke W.289 'mix up with water of other liquid' waiwai W.474 'watery']

pokiwaka *noun* (*vehicle*) bonnet [poki W.290 'cover over' waka common usage 'vehicle']

pokorua *noun* larynx [W.290 'pit, hollow']

pokotaringa *noun* (*radio*) walkman [W.290 'ear']

pono *adjective* non-fiction [W.291 'true, genuine']

pono *adjective* (*statistics*) valid [W.291 'true']

pongāihu *noun* nasal passage [W.292 'nostril']

pongare *noun* towbar [W.292 'knobbed, ending in a knob']

pōkākā *noun* heat capacity [W.289 'hot, heat']

pōkai *noun* spool [W.289 'ball of string, roll']

pōkai ātea *noun* (*astronomy*) space probe [pōkai W.289 'travel about' ātea TM 'space']

pōkai waea *noun* cable drum [pōkai W.289 'coil, roll up' waea < Eng. 'wire']

pōkaikaha *adjective* frustrated [W.289 'confused, at a loss, in doubt']

pōkaikaha *adjective* (*colloquial*) stressed out [W.289 'confused, at a loss, in doubt']

pōkaimiro *noun* cotton reel [pōkai W.289 'ball of string' miro W.203 'thread']

pōpopo *adjective* biodegradable [W.292 'rotten, decayed, worm-eaten']

pōpopo-kore *adjective* non-biodegradable [pōpopo W.292 'rotten, decayed, worm-eaten' kore W.140 'no, not']

porapora *noun* duffel coat [W.293 'a coarse, shaggy cloak']

pōreāreā *noun* interruption [W.293 'tiresome, importunate']

pōreārea *noun* nuisance, pest [W.293 'tiresome, importunate']

pōrewakohu *noun* pterosaur [W.294 'some fabulous bird']

pori *noun* (*biology*) phylum [W.294 'tribe']

pōria *noun* (*weightlifting*) plate [W.294 'load with a weight, ring of bone or stone on the leg of a captive bird']

poro *noun* prism [W.294 'block, piece of anything cut or broken off short']

poro mataono *noun* rectangular prism [poro W.294 'block' mata W.185 'race, surface' ono W.240 'six']

poroāwhio *noun* discus [porohita W.295 'circle, wheel, ring' āwhio W.25 'go round about' āwhiowhio W.25 'whirlwind']

porohatete *noun* pot-belly stove [porokawa W.295 'round in shape' hatete W.38 'fire']

porohaurangi *noun* drunkard [poro W.294 'dazed, half stunned' haurangi W.41 'drunken']

porohita *noun* (*netball*) centre circle [W.295 'ring, circle']

porohita weherua *noun* (*mathematics*) semicircle [porohita W.295 'circle' weherua W.41 'divided']

porokakī *noun* head-high tackle [porokakī W.295 'neck' poro W.294 'strike down']

porokere *noun* brick [poro W.294 'block' kere W.114 'clay, earth']

poropango *adjective* indigo black [poroporo TM 'deep purple' pango W.258 'black']

poroporo *adjective* deep purple [W.294 'solanum nigram and solanum avicuare, plants']

pororangi *adjective* indigo blue [poroporo TM 'deep purple' ōrangi TM 'blue']

pororere *noun*, *transitive verb* guillotine [W.295 'lopped off, cut off']

pororere *transitive verb* amputate [W.295 'cut off, lopped off']

porotea *adjective* mauve [poroporo TM 'deep purple' teatea W.410 'light in colour']

porotio *noun* ice cube [poro W.294 'block' tio W.420 'ice']

porotiti *noun* wheel [W.295 'disc, teetotum, revolving']

porotoru *noun* triangular prism [poro W.294 'block' toru W.441 'three']

porowhiu *transitive verb* (*computer*) trash [W.295 'throw']

pōrutu *noun* piccolo [W.295 'a sort of flute played by blowing into or across the end']

pōtae kauhoe *noun* swimming cap [pōtae W.296 'cap, hat' kauhoe W.106 'swim']

pōtae mārō *noun* helmet [pōtae W.296 'hat' mārō W.183 'hard, strong, sturdy']

pōtae pūāhuru *noun* balaclava [pōtae W.296 'covering for the head' pūāhuru

W.302 'close, warm' pū W.300 'source' āhuru W.4 'warm']

pōtarotaro *noun* lawnmower [W.296 'cut close, cropped']

pōtātaka *noun* cartwheel [pōtēteke W.296 'turning over and over' tātaka W.366 'turn or roll from side to side' cf. TM pōtēteke]

pōtete *noun* frill [W.296 'curly, crinkled, puckered up']

pōtete para *noun* rubbish bag [pōtete W.296 'a bag or receptacle tied up at the mouth' para W.262 'impurity, refuse, waste']

pōtēteke *noun* somersault [W.296 'turning over and over']

pōtēteke rua *noun* double somersault [pōtēteke TM 'somersault' rua W.349 'two']

pōtēteke whakamuri *noun* back somersault [pōtēteke W.296 'turning over and over' whakamuri TM 'backwards']

pōtētete *adjective* frilly [pōtete W.296 'curly, crinkled, puckered up']

pou *noun* upright [W.297 'post, pole, support']

pou koko *noun* corner post [pou W.297 'post' koko W.130 'corner']

pou pīwari *noun* flagpole [pou W.297 'pole' pīwari TM 'flag']

pou tarāwaho *noun* framework [W.297 'boundary marks']

pou tarāwaho *noun* frame of reference [W.297 'boundary marks']

pouāwhina mate paipai *noun* STD clinic [pou W.297 'support' āwhina W.25 'assist' mate W.192 'sickness' paipai W.249 'venereal disease']

pouāwhina oranga taihema *noun* family planning clinic [pou W.297 'support, sustenance' āwhina W.25 'assist' oranga taihema TM 'family planning']

Pouaka Motuhake *noun* Private Bag [pouwaka W.299 'post surmounted by a small receptacle for valued possessions' motuhake W.212 'separated' TM 'private']

pouhiko *noun* power pole [pou W.297 'post, pole' hiko common usage 'electricity']

poumao *noun* (*sport*) far post [pou W.297 'post, pole' mamao W.178 'distant, far away']

poumua *noun* (*rugby*) prop [pou W.297 'support' mua W.213 'the front']

poumua matau *noun* (*rugby*) tighthead prop [pou W.297 'support' matau W.192 'right']

poumua maui *noun* (*rugby*) loosehead prop [poumua TM 'prop' maui W.196 'on the left hand']

poumuri *noun* (*rugby*) number eight [pou W.297 'support' muri W.214 'the rear']

poupare *noun* goal defence [pou W.297 'support' poutūmārō TM 'goal' pare W.266 'ward off']

pouraka *noun* bassinet [W.298 'rude form of cradle for infants']

pouraka *noun* (*bassinet*) cot [W.298 'rude form of cradle for infants']

pourama *noun* lamp-post [pou W.297 'post, pole' rama TM 'lamp']

pourangi *noun* date stamp [pou W.297 'fix' rangi W.324 'day']

pourapa *noun* rubber stamp [pou W.297 'plunge in, fix' rapa < Eng. 'rubber']

pouroki *noun* registrar [pou W.297 'expert, support' rokiroki kōrero TM 'registry']

poutaha *noun* flanker [pou W.297 'support, post' taha W.357 'side, edge']

poutaha *noun* (*rugby*) breakaway [pou W.297 'support, post' taha W.357 'side, edge']

poutaha kūiti *noun* blind-side flanker [poutaha TM 'flanker' kūiti W.154 'narrow, confined']

poutaha takiraha *noun* open-side flanker [poutaha TM 'flanker' takiraha W.372 'wide, extended, open space']

poutaka *noun* workbench [W.299 'platform erected on one post']

poutaka *noun* loose forward [pou W.297 'support, post' taka W.366 'range, roam at large, undergo change in direction']

poutata *noun* nearpost [pou W.297 'pole, post' tata W.393 'near']

poutiriao *noun* zodiac [Best *Māori Mythology and Religion* 106 'supernormal beings as guardians and controllers of the different realms of the earth, the heavens, and the oceans']

poutoka *noun* (*house*) pile [pou W.297 'support, post' toka W.433 'firm, solid, rock']

poutoko *noun* halfback [poutokomanawa W.297 'post supporting ridge-pole of meeting house']

poutoko ture *noun* barrister, lawyer [pou W.297 'expert' toko W.434 'support, prop up' ture W.459 'law']

poutoko ture karauna *noun* crown prosecutor [poutoko ture TM 'lawyer' karauna < Eng. 'crown']

poutuki *noun* goal attack [pou W.297 'support' poutūmārō TM 'goal' tuki W.450 'attack']

poutūmārō *noun* goalpost [pou W.297 'pole, post' tū W.443 'be erect' mārō W.183 'unyielding, hard' poutūmārō W.299 'high, on the meridian']

poutūmārō *noun* (*sport, structure*) goal [pou W.297 'pole, post' tū W.443 'be erect' mārō W.183 'unyielding, hard' poutūmārō W.299 'high, on the meridian']

pōwaka nihowhiti *noun* gearbox [pōwaka W.299 'wooden chest' nihowhiti TM 'gear']

pōwaro *noun* propane [pō < Eng. 'pro-' waro TM 'alkane']

pōwhata *noun* swede [W.287 'wild turnip']

pū *noun* (*geometry*) centre [W.300 'heart, centre']

pū *noun* (*printing*) character [pū TM 'letter of alphabet']

pū *noun* (*alphabet*) letter [W.300 'main stock, origin, source']

pū *noun* (*mathematics*) power [W.300 'originate, source']

pū hauraro *noun* subscript [pū TM 'character' hauraro W.31 'low down, pendent']

pū hurihanga *noun* centre of rotation [pū W.300 'centre' hurihanga TM 'rotation']

pū kai *noun* oesophagus [pū W.300 'tube' kai W.86 'food']

pū kākano *noun* oviduct [pū W.300 'tube' kākano TM 'ovum']

pū kākano *noun* Fallopian tube [pū W.300 'tube' kākano TM 'ovum']

pū kaunuku *noun* (*soccer*) centre half [pū W.300 'centre' kaunuku W.107 'centre of any army when formed for a rush, move steadily']

pū kume-ā-papa *noun* centre of gravity [pū W.300 'centre' kume-ā-papa TM 'gravity']

pū kurutē *noun* air gun [pū W.300 'gun' kurutē W.159 'compress (air)']

pū matau *noun* inside right [pū W.300 'centre' matau W.192 'right']

pū mauī *noun* inside left [pū W.300 'centre' left W.196 'left']

pū ripa *noun* superscript [pū TM 'character' ripa W.341 'the upper side, top']

pū taringa *noun* Eustachian tube [pū W.300 'tube' taringa W.391 'ear']

pū tautuhi *noun* definite article [pūtohu TM 'article' tautuhi W.405 'indicate, define']

pū tīmata *noun* starting-pistol [pū W.300 'gun' tīmata W.418 'begin']

pū tiripapā *noun* machine-gun [pū W.300 'gun' tiripapā W.423 'explode in succession']

pū tōngāmimi *noun* urinary catheter [pū W.300 'tube' tōngāmimi W.436 'bladder']

pū whakarahi *noun* centre of enlargement [pū W.300 'centre' whakarahi TM 'enlarge']

pū whakarahi *noun* microscope tube [pū W.300 'tube' whakarahi TM 'enlarge']

pua atua *noun* spore [pua W.301 'seed' puarere W.302 'run to seed, pappus of thistles' whare atua W.489 'mushroom']

pūahi *noun* cigarette lighter [pū W.300 'source, tube' ahi W.2 'fire']

pūaho *noun* (*electricity*) bulb [pū W.300 'source, origin' aho W.3 'radiant light, shine']

pūāhuru ringa *noun* mitten [pūāhuru W.302 'close, warm' pū W.300 'source' āhuru W.4 'warm' ringa W.341 'hand']

pūāhuru taringa *noun* earmuff [pūāhuru W.302 'close, warm' pū W.300 'source' āhuru W.4 'warm' taringa W.391 'ear']

puananī *noun* (*biology*) wind dispersal [W.302 'wind-dispersed seeds']

pūangi *noun* balloon [pū W.300 'tube' angi W.11 'move freely, to float']

puapua *noun* (*botany*) pistil [W.301 'pudenda muliebria' pua W.301 'flower']

pūare *noun* vowel [pū TM 'letter, character' are W.14 'open']

puarere *noun* rice bubbles [pua W.301 'seed' rere W.337 'flow']

puarere *noun* skeet [W.302 'decoy bird, of small birds only']

pūarero tātari *noun* filter funnel [pūarero

W.302 'funnel entrance to eel-pot' tātari TM 'filter']

puata *noun* transparency [W.303 'clear, transparent']

pūawanui *noun* (*music*) trumpet [pū W.300 'tube, pipe, blow' awanui W.23 'a trumpet shell']

puehu huka *noun* icing sugar [puehu W.303 'dust' huka < Eng. 'sugar']

pūhahana *noun* cayenne pepper [W.304 'hot to the taste']

pūhake-rau *adjective* polysaturated [pūhake W.303 'full to overflowing' rau W.328 'multitude, number']

pūhau māota *noun* chloride [pūhui TM 'compound' hau māota TM 'chlorine']

puhawai *intransitive verb* (*biology*) transpire [puha W.303 'make a faint emission of the breath' wai W.474 'water, liquid']

puhawai *noun* transpiration [TM 'transpire']

pūhihi *noun* (*aerial*) antenna [pūhihi W.304 'antennae of insect']

pūhihi *noun* aerial [pūhihi W.304 'antennae of insect']

pūhihi mātiratira *noun* (*sport*) net aerial [pūhihi W.304 'antennae' mātiratira TM 'net']

pūhiko *noun* (*electrical*) battery [pū W.300 'source, cause' hiko common usage 'electricity']

pūhiko *noun* electrical cell [pū W.300 'source' hiko common usage 'electricity']

puhipuhi *noun* (*sport*) shooting [pū W.300 'gun']

pūhohe *noun* satire [W.305 'mocking, laughing']

pūhohe *adjective* satirical [TM 'satire']

pūhōkai *noun* trombone [pū W.300 'tube, flute, blow' hōkaikai W.56 'extended and retract alternately']

pūhonga *noun* skunk [W.305 'stinking, offensive, stink, stench']

pūhoromi *noun* pharynx [pū W.300 'tube' horomi W.61 'swallow']

pūhouhou *adjective* juvenile [W.305 'young, youthful']

pūhui *noun* (*chemistry*) compound [pū W.300 'origin, source' hui W.66 'come together, double up']

pūhui konganuku *noun* alloy [pūhui TM 'compound' konganuku TM 'natural metal']

pūhui roa *noun* (*botany*) raceme [pūhui TM 'compound' roa W.344 'long']

pūihi tuatuku *noun* (*athletics*) throwing area [pūihi W.305 'division in a kūmara field' tuatuku W.447 'let go']

pūira *noun* chromosome [pū W.300 'tube' ira TM 'gene']

puka *noun* (*stationery*) card [pukapuka W.306 'book, paper']

puka *noun* (*stationery*) form [pukapuka W.306 'book, paper, letter']

puka *noun* (*stationery*) sheet [pukapuka W.306 'book, paper']

puka hāora mahi *noun* time-sheet [puka TM 'form' hāora < Eng. 'hour' mahi W.163 'work']

puka maheni *noun* (*book*) magazine [pukapuka W.306 'book' maheni W.163 'smooth, sleek']

puka tāke *noun* (*form*) tax return [puka TM 'form' tāke < Eng. 'tax']

puka whakamana utu *noun* receipt [puka TM 'form' whaka- W.486 'causative prefix' *to make* mana W.172 'authority' utu W.471 'price']

puka whakauru *noun* enrolment form [puka TM 'form' whakauru TM 'enrol']

pūkaha *noun* engine [pū W.300 'source, origin' kaha W.82 'strength']

pūkahu kakā *noun* pneumonia [pūkahukahu W.306 'lungs' kakā TM 'inflammation']

pūkaka *noun* femur [W.306 'long bones of the arm or leg']

pūkaka ringa *noun* (*bone*) ulna [pūkaka W.306 'long bones of the arm or leg' ringa W341 'arm']

pūkane *noun* bromine [pūhui TM 'chemical compound' kanekane W.93 'pungent']

pukapuka kaute *noun* account book [pukapuka W.306 'book' kaute common usage 'accounting']

pukapuka mahere whenua *noun* atlas [pukapuka W.306 'book' mahere TM 'plan' whenua W.494 'land, country']

pukapuka matua *noun* textbook [pukapuka W.306 'book' matua W.195 'main, chief']

pukapuka tao *noun* cookery book [pukapuka W.306 'book' tao W.381 'cook in a native oven']

pukapuka tau waea *noun* telephone directory [pukapuka W.306 'book' tau waea TM 'telephone number']

pukapuka tuhi *noun* workbook [pukapuka W.306 'book' tuhi W.449 'write, draw']

pūkarakara *transitive verb* marinate [W.307 'fragrant, well flavoured']

pūkati *noun* consonant [pū TM 'letter, character' kati W.103 'shut, closed, of a passage']

pukatono *noun* application form [puka TM 'form' tono TM 'apply']

pukatuhi *noun* notebook [pukapuka W.306 'book' tuhi W.448 'write']

pūkawa raurarahi *noun* continental shelf [pūkawa W.307 'reef' raurarahi W.330 'broad, expansive']

pūkawe hāora *noun* bronchus [pū W.300 'tube' kawe W.111 'carry, convey' hāora TM 'oxygen']

pūkawe kakā *noun* bronchitis [pūkawe hāora TM 'bronchus' kakā TM 'inflamed']

puke huruhuru *intransitive verb* puberty [puke W.307 'pubes, mons veneris' huruhuru W.72 'coarse hair, bristles']

pūkenga *noun* lecturer [W.307 'skilled in, versed in, repository']

pūkenga *noun* skill [W.307 'skilled in, versed in']

pūkenga kawe-ā-riri *noun* military strategist [pūkenga W.307 'skilled in, versed in, repository' kawe-ā-riri W.111 'warfare, battle']

pukepoto *adjective* dark blue [W.307 'a dark-blue earth used as a pigment']

pūkeru *noun* (*music*) organ [pū W.300 'tube' pūkeru W.308 'blow']

pūkohu ngaruru *noun* algal bloom [pūkohu W.308 'moss, mossy' ngaruru W.231 'strong in growth, flourishing']

pūkohu ngaruru tāoke toxic algal bloom [pūkohu ngaruru TM 'algal bloom' tāoke TM 'toxic']

pūkohu wai *noun* algae [pūkohu W.308 'moss' wai W.474 'water']

pūkoro haupōro *noun* golf bag [pūkoro W.308 'a long, bag-shaped net for eels' haupōro TM 'golf-club']

pūkoro raho *noun* scrotum [pūkoro W.308 'sheath, case, pocket' raho W.320 'testicle']

pūkoro ure *noun* condom [pūkoro W.308 'sheath, pocket' ure W.468 'membrum virile']

pūkorokoro *noun* trachea [W.308 'windpipe']

puku *noun* (*netball*) centre third [W.308 'stomach']

puku hamuti *noun* (*anatomy*) bowels [puku W.308 'stomach, entrails' hamuti W.33 'human excrement']

puku rorohiko *noun* disk-drive unit [puku W.308 'memory, abdomen, stomach' rorohiko TM 'computer']

pukuhau *noun* (*tyre*) tube [puku W.308 'abdomen, stomach, swelling' hau W.38 'air']

pukuhiko *noun* (*electrical*) generator [puku W.308 'stomach' hiko common usage 'electricity']

pukuhohe *noun* good sense of humour [pukukata W.309 'laughing, hilarious' hohehohe W.55 'wrinkled with laughter']

pukuhohe *noun* comedian, comic [pukukata W.309 'laughing, hilarious' hohehohe W.55 'wrinkled with laughter']

pukuhohe *adjective* comic, humorous [pukukata W.309 'laughing, hilarious' hohehohe W.55 'wrinkled with laughter']

pukumaire *noun* defence [W.309 'a term applied to a line of fortifications']

pūkura *noun* badminton [TM 'shuttlecock']

pūkura *noun* shuttlecock [pūtoi W.317 'bunch' kura W.157 'ornamented with feathers']

pukuruaki *noun* bulimia [puku W.309 'stomach, secretly' ruaki W.350 'vomit']

pūmā *adjective* whitish grey [W.309 'whitish, grey']

pūmahara *noun* (*computer*) memory [W.309 'memories']

pūmanawa karo mate *noun* reflex [pūmanawa TM 'skill' karo W.101 'avoid a blow' mate W.192 'injury, wound']

pūmanawa nohopuku *noun* potential [pūmanawa W.309 'natural talents, intuitive cleverness' nohopuku W.223 'be silent, be still']

pūmanawa rorohiko *noun* (*computer*) software [pūmanawa W.309 'natural talents, intuitive cleverness' rorohiko TM 'computer']

pūmanawa tangata *noun* human resources [pūmanawa W.309 'natural talents, intuitive cleverness' tangata W.379 'human being']

pūmanawa tātaki kupu *noun (computer)* speller [pūmanawa rorohiko TM 'software' tātaki kupu TM 'spelling']

pūmanawa whai mahere whenua *noun* mapping skills [pūmanawa TM 'skill' whai W.484 'follow' mahere whenua TM 'map']

pūmāota *noun* chloroplast [pū W.300 'tube, origin' māota TM 'chlorophyll']

pūmate *noun* hazard [pū W.300 'source, origin' mate W.192 'injury, danger, calamity']

pūmatua *noun* capital letter, upper case [pū TM 'letter of alphabet' matua W.195 'parent, main']

pūmau *adjective* invariant [W.309 'fixed, constant']

pūmau pūira *noun (biology)* mitosis [pūmau W.309 'fixed, constant' pūira TM 'chromosome']

pūmotu *noun (chemistry)* element [pū W.300 'origin, source' motu W.211 'anything isolated']

pūmua *noun* protein [pū W.300 'origin, source' pūhui TM 'compound' mua W.213 'the fore']

pūmua kuruwhatu *noun* casein [pūmua TM 'protein' kurukuruwhatu W.159 'curdled, as milk']

pūmua whākōkī *noun* enzyme [pūmua TM 'protein' whākōkī TM 'catalyst']

pūmuri *noun (soccer)* centre back [pū W.300 'centre' muri W.214 'the rear']

puna manawa *noun* mineral water [W.174 'a spring from the heart of the earth']

pūnaha *noun* system [pū W.300 'base, foundation' nahanaha W.216 'well arranged, in good order']

pūnaha ngahuru *noun* decimal system [pūnaha TM 'system' ngahuru TM 'decimal']

pūnaha ōhanga *noun* economic system [pūnaha TM 'system' ōhanga TM 'economics']

pūnaha rau *noun* metric system [pūnaha TM 'system' rau W.328 'hundred']

pūnaha tau *noun* number system [pūnaha TM 'system' tau TM 'number']

pūnaha tau-ā-ira *noun* decimal system [pūnaha TM 'system' tau-ā-ira TM 'decimal']

pūnaha tuke *noun* metric system [pūnaha TM 'system' tuke TM 'metre']

pūnaha ture taihara *noun* criminal justice system [pūnaha TM 'system' ture 'law' taihara TM 'crime']

punahiko *noun* power supply [puna W.309 'spring of water' hiko common usage 'electricity']

punakupu *noun* thesaurus [puna W.309 'spring of water' kupu W.157 'word']

punanga *noun* refuge, sanctuary [W.310 'any place used as a refuge for non-combatants in troubled days']

punatoto *noun* bloodbank [puna W.309 'spring of water' toto W.441 'blood']

punenga kupu *noun* word processor [punenga W.310 'clever, intelligent, always seeking and acquiring useful knowledge' kupu W.157 'word']

puni kaiao *noun* ecological niche [puni W.310 'place of encampment' kaiao TM 'organism']

puni tuakoka *noun* slum [puni W.310 'place of encampment' tuakoka W.445 'poverty-stricken']

puninga *noun* genus [W.310 'tribe, family']

pūnoa *noun* indefinite article [pūtohu TM 'article' noa W.222 'indefinite']

pūnotinoti *transitive verb (mend)* cobble [W.310 'stitch roughly, patch up roughly']

pūnga *noun (grammar)* object [pū W.300 'origin, source']

pūnga *noun* rationale [W.300 'reason, cause, origin']

punga *noun* prime number [W.310 'odd number, anchor']

pūngao *noun* energy [pū W.300 'source' ngao W.229 'strength, sprout, shoot']

pūngao hiko *noun* electrical energy [pūngao TM 'energy' hiko common usage 'electricity']

pūngao karihi *noun* nuclear energy [pūngao TM 'energy' karihi TM 'nuclear']

pūngao konikoni *noun* kinetic energy [pūngao TM 'energy' konikoni W.134 'move, alter one's position']

pūngao kōmaru *noun* solar energy [pūngao TM 'energy' kōmaru TM 'solar']

pūngao matū *noun* chemical energy [pūngao TM 'energy' matū TM 'chemical']

pūngao pōkākā *noun* heat energy [pūngao TM 'energy' pōkākā W.289 'hot, heat']

pungatara *noun* sulphur [W.311 'native sulphur']

pūngawī *noun* bagpipes [pū W.300 'pipe, tube' ngawī W.232 'squeal, howl']

pūngene *noun* sleeping bag [pūngenengene W.311 'muffled up']

pūngoi *noun* calorie [pū W.300 'source, origin' ngoi W.234 'energy']

pūnguru *noun* tuba [pū W.300 'pipe, tube, blow' nguru W.236 'utter a suppressed groan, murmur, rumble']

pūnguru *adjective* weathered [W.311 'worn down, worn away, blunt']

pūoho *noun* alarm [pūoho W.311 'start, take alarm']

pūoho *noun* pager [W.311 'start, take alarm']

pūoho *noun* beeper [W.311 'start, take alarm']

pūoho auahi *noun* smoke alarm [pūoho TM 'alarm' auahi W.21 'smoke']

pūoho umu *noun* oven-timer [pūoho TM 'alarm' umu TM 'oven']

pūoko *noun* detector [pūrere TM 'machine' oko W.239 'hear']

pūoko *noun* sensor [pūrere TM 'machine' oko W.239 'hear']

pūoko aho *noun* light sensor [pūoko TM 'detector' aho W.3 'radiant light']

pūoko hihiani *noun* radar detector [pūoko TM 'detector' hihiani TM 'radar']

pūoko irirangi *noun* radio telescope [pūoko TM 'detector' irirangi TM 'radio wave']

pūoko maitai *noun* metal detector [pūoko TM 'sensor, detector' maitai < Eng. 'metal']

pūoko mamao *noun* remote sensor [pūoko TM 'sensor' mamao W.178 'distant, far away']

pūoko pōkākā *noun* heat sensor [pūoko TM 'sensor' pōkākā W.289 'heat']

pūoko whakaroto *noun* stethoscope [pūoko TM 'detector, sensor' whakaroto TM 'inwards']

pūoru *noun* music [W.311 'sound']

puoto *noun* (*container*) cylinder [W.311 'vessel']

puoto *noun* (*container*) can, tin [W.311 'vessel']

puoto hāora *noun* aqualung [puoto W.311 'vessel' hāora TM 'oxygen']

puoto kakīroa *noun* (*chemistry*) retort [puoto W.311 'vessel' kakī W.92 'neck' roa W.344 'long']

puoto kapuni *noun* gas cylinder [puoto TM 'cylinder' kapuni TM 'natural gas']

puoto katirere *noun* burette [puoto W.311 'vessel' katirere TM 'tap']

puoto whakawera *noun* (*science*) crucible [puoto W.311 'vessel' whaka- W.486 'causative prefix' *to make* wera W.482 'heated, hot']

puoto whakawera wai *noun* zip [puoto W.311 'vessel' whaka- W.486 'causative prefix' *to make* wera W.482 'heated, hot' wai W.474 'water']

pūpoho kōnae *noun* filing cabinet [pūpoho W.311 'wooden trough for holding huahua' kōnae TM 'file']

pupuha *transitive verb* emit [W.303 'blow, spout']

pupuri *transitive verb* (*computer*) save [W.305 'retain possession of, keep, keep in memory']

puraku *noun* body bag [W.312 'coffin or wrap']

pūranga *noun* archive [pū W.300 'source, base' pūranga W.312 'lie in a heap']

pūranga *noun* (*cards*) deck [pū W.300 'source, base' pūranga W.312 'lie in a heap']

pūranga iahiko *noun* capacitor [pūranga W.312 'lie in a heap' iahiko TM 'electric charge']

pūranga kōrero *noun* (*library*) reference section [pūranga W.312 'heap, lie in a heap' puri W.314 'retain possession of, keep' kōrero W.141 'speak talk, address, story, narrative']

pūrangiaho *noun* sightscreen [W.312 'seeing clearly']

pūrangiaho *noun* big screen [W.312 'seeing clearly']

pūrau *noun* polynomial [pū TM 'power' rau W.328 'multitude, number']

pūrei *noun* (*softball etc.*) base [W.313 'isolated rock, patch of anything']

pūrei kapi *noun* (*softball*) loaded bases [pūrei TM 'base' kapi W.96 'be covered, be occupied']

pūreirei *noun* stepping-stone [W.313 'isolated rock, patch of anything']

pūrei rua *noun* (*softball etc.*) second base [pūrei TM 'base' rua W.349 'two']

pūrei tahi *noun* (*softball etc.*) first base [pūrei TM 'base' tahi W.359 'one']

pūrei toru noun (*softball etc.*) third base [pūrei TM 'base' toru W.441 'three']

pūreke noun ointment [W.313 'a decoction of bark and ashes used for certain skin complaints']

pūrere noun appliance [pūrere TM 'machine']

pūrere noun device [pū W.300 'source, base' rere W.337 'fly, flow']

pūrere noun machine [pū W.300 'source, foundation, base' rere W.373 'flow, fly']

pūrere ataata noun video cassette recorder [pūrere TM 'machine ataata TM 'video']

pūrere horoi noun washing-machine [pūrere TM 'machine' horoi W.61 'cleanse, wash']

pūrere horoi maitai noun (*machine*) dishwasher [pūrere TM 'machine' horoi W.61 'clean, wash, scour' maitai < Eng. 'metal' common usage 'dishes']

pūrere kawhe noun coffee-maker [pūrere TM 'machine' kawhe < Eng. 'coffee']

pūrere kiriata noun slide-projector [pūrere TM 'machine' kiriata TM 'film']

pūrere pahū noun drum machine [pūrere TM 'machine' pahū TM 'drum']

pūrere tāpane noun franking machine [pūrere TM 'machine' tāpene TM 'frank']

pūrere tuitui noun sewing-machine [pūrere TM 'machine' tuitui W.449 'sew']

pūrere tuitui noun (*book*) binding machine [pūrere TM 'machine' tui W.449 'sew, fasten by passing a cord through holes']

pūrere whakaahua noun photocopier [pūrere TM 'machine' whakaahua W.4 'acquire form']

pūreretā noun (*machine*) printer [pūrere TM 'machine' tā TM 'print']

puretumu noun decontamination [W.313 'perform rites to obtain satisfaction for a disaster']

pūriki noun lowercase letter [pū TM 'letter of alphabet' riki W.340 'small']

puringa noun (*weight-training*) grip [puri W.314 'hold in the hand']

pūroku noun tent [whare pūrokuroku W.314 'temporary shelter, hut' pūrokuroku 'wrinkled, rolled up clumsily']

pūrongo noun report [pūrongorongo W.314 'tell news, report']

pūrongo pēke noun bank statement [pūrongo TM 'report' pēke < Eng. 'bank']

pūrongo pūtea noun financial statement [pūrongo TM 'report' pūtea TM 'financial']

pūrori noun pommel [W.314 'knob, as on a huata spear or handle of a mere']

pūrori noun gazebo [W.314 'small circular hut']

pūroro noun brain stem [W.300 'foot, base' roro W.347 'brains']

pūroto noun (*sport*) inside centre [pū W.300 'heart, centre' roto W.348 'the inside']

puru kora noun spark-plug [puru W.314 'plug, bung' kora W.139 'spark, fire, fuel']

puru taiawa noun tampon [puru W.314 'plug, cork, bung' taiawa W.363 'vagina']

pūrua noun (*linguistics*) digraph [pū TM 'letter' rua W.349 'two']

pūruatanga phrase intersection of sets [W.315 'junction of two streams']

puta intransitive verb exit [W.315 'pass through or out']

puta noun (*anatomy*) foramen [W.315 'hole']

puta aunoa noun (*computer*) default [puta 315 'come, come forth, come out' aunoa TM 'automatic']

pūtahi noun agency [W.316 'join, meet, as two paths or streams running one into the other']

pūtahi noun institute [W.316 'join, meet, as two paths or streams running one into the other']

pūtahi noun (*agency*) centre [W.316 'join, meet, as two paths or streams running one into the other']

pūtahitanga noun (*mathematics*) intersection [pūtahi W.316 'join, meet']

pūtahoro noun clarinet [W.316 'a long wooden trumpet']

pūtaiaki noun steroid [pūhui TM 'compound' taiaki TM 'hormone']

pūtaiao noun science [pū W.300 'source, origin' taiao TM 'environment']

pūtake noun rationale [W.316 'base, root, reason, cause']

pūtake noun (*mathematics*) root [W.316 'base, root']

pūtakerua noun (*mathematics*) square root [pūtake W.316 'base, root' rua W.349 'two']

putanga noun exit [puta W.315 'pass through or out']

putanga *noun* (*publication*) issue [puta W.315 'come forth, come out']

putanga *noun* edition [puta W.315 'come forth, come out']

putanga hamuti *noun* toilet bowl [putanga W.315 'escape' hamuti W.33 'human excrement']

putanga papawaka *noun* carpark exit [puta W.315 'pass out of, escape' papawaka 'carpark']

putanga wai *noun* plug-hole [puta W.315 'opening, hole, pass out' wai W.474 'water']

pūtangi *noun* (*music*) horn [pū W.300 'tube' tangi W.379 'sound']

pūtangitangi *noun* harmonica [pū W.300 'flute, blow gently' tangi W.379 'sound, give forth a sound']

pūtau *noun* cell [pū W.300 'origin, source' tau W.396 'be able']

pūtau io *noun* nerve cells [pūtau TM 'cell' io W.78 'nerve']

pūtau-tahi *noun* protista [pūtau TM 'cell' tahi W.359 'one, single']

pūtau-tahi *adjective* single-celled [pūtau TM 'cell' tahi W.359 'one, single']

pūtau-tahi *adjective* unicellular [pūtau TM 'cell' tahi W.359 'one, single']

pūtawa *noun* stamen [W.317 'testicle']

pūtea *noun* finance [TM 'fund']

pūtea *adjective* financial [TM 'fund']

pūtea *noun* bank account [W.317 'bag or basket of fine woven flax']

pūtea *noun* fund [W.317 'bag or basket of fine woven flax']

pūtea haki *noun* cheque account [pūtea TM 'account' haki < Eng. 'cheque']

pūtea kāwanatanga *noun* government grant [pūtea TM 'fund' kāwanatanga < Eng. 'government']

pūtea penapena *noun* savings account [pūtea TM 'account' penapena W.277 'take care of, tend, husband']

pūtea penapoto *noun* short-term deposit [pūtea TM 'account' pena W.277 'take care of, tend, husband' poto W.297 'short']

pūtea penaroa *noun* long-term deposit [pūtea TM 'account' pena W.277 'take care of, tend, husband' roa W.344 'long']

pūtea penihana kāwanatanga *noun* government superannuation fund [pūtea TM 'fund' penihana < Eng. 'pension' kāwanatanga < Eng. 'government']

pūtea tāpiri *noun* subsidy [pūtea TM 'fund' tāpiri W.384 'add, supplement']

pūtea tangonoa *noun* autocall account [pūtea TM 'fund' tango W.380 'remove' noa W.222 'without restraint']

pūtea taurewa *noun* (*financial*) loan [pūtea TM 'fund' taurewa W.402 'not paid for']

pūtea tukutahi *noun* joint account [pūtea TM 'account' tukutahi W.452 'together, simultaneous']

pūtepe *noun* (*anatomy*) fibrin [pūmua TM 'protein' tepe W.412 'clot, coagulate']

pūtere *noun* project [W.317 'raft, go in a body']

pūtiwha *noun* boron [pūhui TM 'compound' tiwha W.427 'gleam']

pūtohe *noun* saxophone [pū W.300 'flute, pipe, tube' tohe W.430 'vibrating reed of a pūkaea trumpet']

pūtohu *noun* (*grammar*) article [pū W.300 'source, base' tohu W.431 'point at, show']

pūtoi *noun* (*biology*) order [W.317 'tribe, family']

pūtōiri *noun* oboe [pū W.300 'tube' tōiri W.432 'tingle, vibrate, resound']

pūtoro *noun* radius [pū W.300 'centre' toro W.438 'stretch forth, extend']

pūtororē *noun* (*vehicle*) exhaust [W.317 'jet of gas from burning wood']

pūtoru *adjective* (*mathematics*) cubed [pū TM 'power' toru W.441 'three']

pūtoru *adjective* (*mathematics*) cubic [pū TM 'power' toru W.441 'three']

pūtoto *noun* haemoglobin [pūmua TM 'protein' toto W.441 'blood']

putu *noun* (*mathematics, unit of angle*) degree [W.317 'lie one upon another']

putuputu *phrase* in dribs and drabs [W.317 'frequent, at short intervals']

pūtūtae-whetū *noun* phosphorus [Biggs 140 'phosphorescent substance']

pūtūtae-whetū *adjective* phosphorescent [Biggs 140 'phosphorescent substance']

pūwaha *noun* delta [W.317 'mouth of a river etc.']

pūwaho *noun* (*sport*) outside centre [pū W.300 'heart, centre' waho W.474 'the outside']

pūwaro *noun* butane [pū < Eng. 'bu-' waro TM 'alkane']

pūwenu *noun* spinneret [pū W.300 'origin, source' wenu W.494 'twist or spin a strand of cord']

pūwere *noun* arachnid [pūwerewere W.318 'spider']

pūwero *noun* syringe [pū W.300 'tube' wero W.482 'pierce, spear']

pūweru ruarangi *noun* kaftan [pūweru W.318 'clothing generally, garment' ruarangi W.350 'large']

pūwētoto *noun* (*anatomy*) fibrinogen [pūmua TM 'protein' wētoto TM 'blood plasma']

pūwhenua *noun* (*storage*) vault [W.319 'cave used as a dwelling place']

pūwhenua *noun* basement [W.319 'cave used as a dwelling place' pū W.300 'base, foundation' whenua W.494 'ground']

R

rahi *noun (printing)* point size [W.320 'size']

rāhui haere pō *noun* curfew [rāhui W.321 'protect by a rāhui' haere W.30 'go' pō W.285 'night']

raihe *noun* picket fence [Best *Māori Agriculture* 40-41 'fence consisting of upright stakes']

rakahinonga *noun* entrepreneur [raka W.321 'agile, adept, go, spread abroad' hinonga TM 'enterprise']

rākau *noun (sport)* bat [W.321 'weapon']

rākau *noun (golf)* wood [W.321 'weapon, wooden']

rākau hake *noun* hockey-stick [rākau W.321 'stick' hake TM 'hockey']

rama *noun* lamp [W.322 'torch or other artificial light']

rama haukura *noun* neon light [rama W.322 'torch or other artificial light' haukura TM 'neon']

rama haurapa *noun* searchlight [rama W.322 'torch or other artificial light' haurapa W.41 'search diligently for']

rama huri *noun* indicator light [rama W.322 'torch or other artificial light' huri W.71 'turn']

rama tumu *noun* brake lights [rama W.322 'torch or other artificial light' tumu W.454 'halt suddenly']

rama umu *noun* oven-light [rama W.322 'torch or other artificial light' umu TM 'oven']

ramamua *noun (vehicle)* headlight [rama W.322 'torch or other artificial light' mua W.213 'the front']

ramamuri *noun (vehicle)* tail light [rama W.322 'torch or other artificial light' muri W.213 'the rear']

ramamuri *noun (vehicle)* rear light [rama W.322 'torch or other artificial light' muri W.214 'the rear']

ramarama *intransitive verb* glow brightly [W.322 'gleam']

rangahau *noun, transitive verb* research [W.323 'seek, search out, pursue']

rangahau *noun (statistics)* survey [W.323 'seek, search out, pursue']

rāngai *noun (population)* sector [rāngai W.323 'flock, shoal, company']

rāngai tūmataiti *noun* private sector [rāngai W.323 'flock, shoal, company' tūmataiti TM 'private']

rāngai tūmatanui *noun* public sector [rāngai W.323 'flock, shoal, company' tūmatanui TM 'public']

rangatira *noun* landlord [W.323 'chief, master or mistress']

rangatira *noun* employer [W.323 'master or mistress']

rangatōpū *noun* body corporate [ranga W.322 'company of persons' tōpū W.437 'in a body, assembled']

rangatōpū *noun* corporate body [ranga W.322 'company of persons' tōpū W.437 'in a body, assembled']

rangatōpū *adjective* corporate [ranga W.322 'company of persons' tōpū W.437 'in a body, assembled']

rangitahi *adjective* temporary [W.324 'ephemeral, transient']

rango *noun (mathematics)* cylinder [W.324 'roller upon which a heavy body is dragged']

raorao *noun (golf)* fairway [W.325 'level or undulating country']

rapa *noun* spatula [W.325 'anything broad, flat and hard, blade of a paddle, etc.']

rapa *noun* tyre [W.325 'anything broad,

flat and hard, united by a membrane, webbed']
rapanga *noun* (*mathematics*) problem [rapa W.325 'seek, look for' panga W.257 'riddle, game of guessing']
rāpoi ngota *noun* molecule [rāpoi W.326 'cluster' ngota TM 'atom']
rārā *noun* branchlet [W.319 'twig, small branch']
rara *noun* ramification [W.326 'effect, repercussion']
rara *noun* implication [W.326 'effect, repercussion']
rarai *adjective* corrugated [W.321 'ribbed, furrowed']
raranu *noun* (*liquid*) mixture [ranu W.322 'mix' whakaranu W.322 'gravy, juice of anything']
rārangi *noun* catalogue, list [W.324 'line, rank, row']
rārangi hangarite *phrase* (*mathematics*) line of symmetry [rārangi W.324 'line' hangarite TM 'symmetry']
rārangi hangarite *noun* (*mathematics*) mirror line [rārangi W.324 'line' hangarite TM 'symmetry']
rārangi kai *noun* menu [rārangi W.324 'line, rank, row' kai W.86 'food']
rārangi kōnae *noun* file list [rārangi W.324 'line, rank, row' kōnae TM 'file']
rārangi kōnae *noun* (*computer*) sub-directory [rārangi W.324 'rank, row' kōnae TM 'file']
rārangi kōpaki *noun* (*computer*) directory [rārangi W.324 'rank, row' kōpaki TM 'folder']
rārangi pātai *noun* questionnaire [rārangi W.324 'line, rank row' pātai W.269 'question, inquire']
rārangi ringarehe *noun* trade directory [rārangi W.324 'line, rank, row' ringarehe TM 'tradesperson']
rārangi take *noun* agenda [rārangi W.324 'line, rank, row' take TM 'matter']
rārangi taputapu *noun* (*equipment etc.*) inventory [rārangi TM 'list' taputapu W.385 'goods, property, appliances']
rārangi tau *noun* (*mathematics*) number line [rārangi W.324 'line, row' tau TM 'number']
rārangi tau waea *noun* telephone directory [W.324 'line, rank, row' tau waea TM 'telephone number']

rārangi tohutoro *noun* reference catalogue [rārangi TM 'list' tohutoro TM 'reference']
rārangi tono *noun* (*computer*) menu [rārangi W.324 'line, rank, row' tono W.436 'bid, command']
rārangi weherua *noun* bisector [rārangi W.324 'line' weherua W.481 'divided']
raraunga *noun* citizenship [rarau W.328 'settle down, remain, take root']
raraunga *noun* data [rarau W.328 'lay hold of, receptacle']
raraunga houanga *noun* time-series data [raraunga TM 'data' houanga W.63 'an interval of time']
raraunga motukore *noun* continuous data [raraunga TM 'data' motu W.211 'broken off, separated, anything isolated' kore W.140 'no, not']
raraunga motumotu *noun* discrete data [raraunga TM 'data' motumotu W.212 'divided into isolated portions']
rarawe *noun* (*science apparatus*) boss [W.333 'clasp tightly']
rari *noun* scourer [W.327 'wash, scour']
rari *noun* pot-mitt [W.327 'wash, scour']
rata kararehe *noun* veterinarian [rata W.327 'doctor' kararehe W.99 'quadruped']
rata mate hinengaro *noun* psychiatrist [rata W.327 'doctor' mate hinengaro TM 'psychiatric disorder']
rata niho tāpiki *noun* orthodontist [rata W.327 'doctor' niho W.221 'tooth' tāpiki W.384 'be entangled, doubled over' niho tāpiki 'a tooth overriding another']
rātaka *noun* diary [rā W.319 'day' taka W.366 'come round, as a date or period of time']
ratonga *noun* (*public sector*) service [rato W.327 'be served or provided']
ratonga ahi *noun* fire service [ratonga TM 'service' ahi W.2 'fire']
ratonga hapori *noun* (*organisation*) community service [ratonga TM 'service' hapori TM 'community']
ratonga haumanu *noun* clinical services [ratonga TM 'service' haumanu W.40 'revive, restore to health']
ratonga matehuka, matehā *noun* diabetic and respiratory services [ratonga TM 'services' matehuka TM 'diabetes' matehā TM 'respiratory disease']

ratonga mate whawhati tata *noun* emergency service [ratonga TM 'service' mate whatati tata TM 'emergency']

ratonga rangatōpū *noun* corporate service [ratonga TM 'service' rangatōpū TM 'corporate']

rau matatiki *noun* artesian bore [W.191 'strong gushing spring of water']

rau pūtea *noun* deposit slip [rau W.328 'gather into a basket etc.' pūtea TM 'account']

rauamiami *noun* mixed herbs [rau W.328 'leaf, number' amiami W.8 'a sweet-smelling shrub']

rauangi *adjective (skin)* sensitive [W.329 'thin, fine, tender, finely divided strands of flax for making nets']

rauangiangi *noun* tissue paper [rauangi W.329 'thin, fine, tender, finely divided strands of flax for making nets']

rauata *noun* overhead projector OHP [rau W.328 'number, multitude' ata W.18 'reflected image']

rauemi *noun (education)* resource [rau W.328 'multitude, number' emi W.27 'be assembled, be gathered together']

rauemi ako *noun (teaching)* material [rauemi TM 'resource' ako W.7 'teach, instruct, advise']

rauemi tuhi *noun (textual)* material [rauemi TM 'resource' tuhi W.448 'delineate, draw']

rauhanga *noun* tactic [W.329 'cunning, resourceful']

rauhanga *adjective* tactical [W.329 'cunning, resourceful']

rauhītanga *noun* guardianship [rauhī W.329 'take care of, tend, foster, protect']

raumanga *noun* kitchen bench [W.330 'platform for storing food']

raumata *noun (geometry)* net [W.330 'mesh of a net']

raupapa *noun* series, sequence [W.330 'put in order, ordered, completed']

raupapa *noun (sequence)* order [W.330 'put in order, ordered, completed']

raupapa paheko *(abbreviation, mathematics)* BEDMAS [raupapa TM 'order, sequence' paheko TM 'operation']

raupāpapa *noun* bran flakes [rau W.328 'leaf, multitude' pāpapa W.259 'husk, such as bran chaff etc.']

raupōhā *noun* filo pastry [rau W.349 'leaf' pōhā TM 'pastry']

raupua *noun* petal [rau W.328 'leaf' pua W.301 'flower']

rautaki *noun* strategy [rauhanga W.329 'cunning, resourceful' taki W.371 'lead, bring along']

rautaki *adjective* strategic [rauhanga W.329 'cunning, resourceful' taki W.371 'lead, bring along']

rautangi *noun* perfume [W.331 'a preparation of scented oils']

rauwiringa kaiao *noun* ecosystem [rauwiri W.331 'interlace with twigs' kaiao TM 'organism']

rauwhero *adjective* suntanned [W.331 'ruddy, brown']

rauwhero *adjective (skin-colour)* bronze [W.331 'ruddy, brown']

rawa *noun* chattel [W.331 'goods, property']

rawa *noun* resource [W.331 'goods, property']

rawa mārena *noun* matrimonial property [rawa W.332 'goods, property' mārena < Eng. 'marriage']

rawa taiao *noun* natural resource [rawa W.331 'goods, property' taiao W.362 'world, country, district']

rawa whakanao *noun (industry)* plant [rawa W.331 'goods, property' whakanao TM 'manufacture']

raweke ira *noun* genetic engineering [raweke W.333 'manipulate, meddle with, disturb' ira TM 'gene']

raweke pūtea *noun* embezzlement [raweke W.333 'meddle with, disturb, interfere with' pūtea TM 'fund, finance']

raweke rākau *noun* woodwork [raweke W.333 'prepare, dress, manipulate, fashion' rākau W.321 'wood, timber']

rawhi *noun* clip [W.333 'grasp, hold firmly']

rawhipuka *noun (documents)* bulldog clip [rawhi W.333 'grasp, hold firmly' pukapuka W.306 'book, paper, letter']

rāwhitu *noun* week [rā W.319 'day' whitu W.498 'seven']

reho *noun* misconduct [W.334 'bad']

rehu *noun (musical instrument)* recorder [W.334 'flute, play the flute']

rehu makawe *noun* hairspray [rehu W.334 'spray' makawe W.169 'hair']

rehu matūriki *noun* aerosol [rehu W.344 'spray, fine dust' matūriki TM 'particle']

rehu tokitoki *noun* general anaesthetic [rehu W.334 'render drowsy or unconscious' tokitoki W.434 'altogether, without exception']

rehukakā *noun* mustard powder [rehu W.334 'fine dust' kakā W.81 'red-hot']

rehunga *noun* anaesthesia [rehu W.334 'render drowsy or unconscious']

rei *noun* thoracic [W.335 'breast, chest']

reiaku *noun* rayon [rei- < Eng. 'ray-' kaka-aku TM 'textile fibre']

reihuka *noun* lactose [rei W.335 'breast, chest' huka < Eng. 'sugar']

remu *noun* hem [W.335 'lower end of anything']

renarena *noun* (*tightness*) tension [W.336 'taut' rena W.335 'stretch out']

rengakura *noun* beetroot [renga W.336 'mealy fern-root' kura W.157 'red']

rengamutu *noun* spinach [W.336 'New Zealand spinach']

reo iere *noun* tenor [reo W.336 'voice, tone' iere W.74 'singing, sing']

reo kē *noun* foreign language [reo W.336 'language, dialect' kē W.111 'different, of another kind, of non-identity']

reo mārū *noun* baritone [reo W.336 'voice, tone' mārū W.184 'low in tone']

reo nohopuku *noun* receptive language [reo W.336 'language' nohopuku TM 'potential']

reo nguru *noun* (*choral singing*) bass [reo W.336 'voice, tone' tanguru W.258 'bass, gruff']

reo pekerangi *noun* alto [reo W.336 'voice, tone' pekerangi W.276 'a voice pitched above the rest in singing']

reo rotarota *noun* sign language [reo W.336 'language' rotarota W.348 'sign with the hands, without speaking']

reo tauiwi *noun* foreign language [reo W.336 'language, dialect' tauiwi W.398 'strange tribe, foreign race']

reo tōiri *noun* soprano [reo W.336 'voice, tone' tōiri W.432 'tingle, vibrate, resound']

reo torohū *noun* receptive language [reo W.336 'language' torohū TM 'potential']

reorua *adjective* bilingual [reo W.336 'language' rua W.349 'two']

reohori falsetto [reo W.336 'voice, tone' hori W.60 'false']

repe hūare *noun* parotid gland [repe W.336 'gland' hūare W.65 'spittle']

repe hūare pupuhi *noun* mumps [repe W.336 'gland' hūare W.65 'spittle' pupuhi W.304 'swell']

repe roimata *noun* lachrymal gland [repe W.336 'gland' roimata W.345 'tears']

repe tātea *noun* prostate [repe W.336 'gland' tātea W.394 'semen']

repe tāturi *noun* (*ear*) wax gland [repe W.336 'gland' tāturi W.395 'wax in the ear']

repe taiaki huka *noun* pancreas [repe W.336 'gland' taiaki huka TM 'insulin']

repe tenga *noun* thyroid gland [repe W.336 'gland' tenga W.412 'goitre']

repe tōtā *noun* sweat gland [repe W.336 'gland' tōtā W.441 'sweat']

repe tupu *noun* pituitary gland [repe W.336 'gland' tupu W.457 'grow']

repe ure *noun* prostate gland [repe W.336 'gland' ure W.468 'membrum virile']

repe werawera *noun* sweat-gland [repe W.336 'gland' werawera W.482 'sweat']

repe whakatupu *noun* pituitary gland [repe W.336 'gland' whakatupu W.458 'cause to grow']

repenoni *noun* oil gland [repe W.336 'gland' noni W.224 'oil']

rere o te awa atua *noun* menstruation [rere W.337 'flow' awa W.23 'river' atua W.20 'menses']

rere o te toto *noun* (*blood*) circulation [rere W.337 'flow' toto W.441 'blood']

rere o te toto *noun* blood pressure [rere W.337 'flow' toto W.441 'blood']

rere pūangi *noun* ballooning [rere W.337 'be carried on the wind' pūangi TM 'balloon']

rere pūroto *noun* (*blood*) bad circulation [rere W.337 'flow' pūroto W.314 'sluggish, of a stream']

rere pūroto *adjective* ischaemic [rere W.337 'flow' pūroto W.314 'sluggish, of a stream']

rere rōnaki *noun* (*blood*) good circulation [rere W.337 'flow' rōnaki W.346 'gliding easily']

rere whakamua *intransitive verb* (*cycling*) break away [rere W.337 'rush, hasten, flee' whakamua TM 'forwards']

rereangi *noun* hang-gliding [rere W.337 'fly' angi W.11 'move freely, float']

rerehua *adjective* artistic [W.338 'pleasant to the sight, beauty']

rerehua *adjective* aesthetically pleasing [W.338 'pleasant to the sight, beauty']

rerenga *noun* refugee [W.337 'person who has escaped, fugitive, survivor']

rerenga *noun (language)* sentence [W.337 'small branches, offshoots of a family']

rerenga ahi *noun* fire escape [rerenga W.337 'place of escaping' ahi W.2 'fire']

rerenga ahi *noun* fire exit [rerenga W.337 'place of escaping' ahi W.2 'fire']

rerenga awa wahine *noun* menstruation [rere W.337 'flow' awa W.23 'river' wahine W.474 'woman']

rerenga o Tama-nui-te-rā *noun* solar system [rerenga W.337 'voyage, journey, setting or rising of the sun' Tama-nui-te-rā common usage 'personification of the sun']

rererua *transitive verb* reduplicate [W.338 'double, in two thicknesses or folds']

rererua *noun* reduplication [W.338 'double, in two thicknesses or folds']

rererua *noun* pleat [W.338 'double, in two thicknesses or folds']

reretō *noun* parasailing [rere W.337 'fly' tō W.428 'drag, haul']

rerewai *noun* osmosis [rere W.337 'flow' wai W.474 'water, liquid']

rerewhenua *noun* train [rere W.337 'flow, fly, rush' whenua W.494 'land, country, ground']

reti *intransitive verb* skate [W.338 'toboggan board, convey, carry']

reti kōpaka *noun* ice-skating [reti TM 'skate' kōpaka W.135 'ice, frost, hail']

retihuka *noun* skiing [reti W.338 'toboggan board, convey, carry' huka W.67 'frost, snow']

retihuka *noun* ski [reti W.338 'toboggan board, convey, carry' huka W.67 'frost, snow']

retiwai *noun* waterskiing [reti W.338 'convey, carry, as a boat' wai W.474 'water']

retiwai *noun* water-ski [TM 'waterskiing']

rewa *intransitive verb* defrost [rewa W.339 'melt, be or become liquid']

rewanga *noun* solute [rewa W.339 'be or become liquid, melt']

rewarangi *noun* pedestrian crossing [whakarewarangi W.339 'a floor mat made with alternate strips of black and yellow flax']

rewarewa *noun* native honeysuckle [JB *Māori Plant Names* 20]

rīanga *noun* insurance [rī W.339 'bond, screen, protect' rīanga W.339 'screen']

rīanga tangata *noun* life insurance [rīanga TM 'insurance' tangata W.379 'human being']

rīanga waka *noun* car insurance [rīanga TM 'insurance' waka common usage 'vehicle']

rīanga whare *noun* house insurance [rīanga TM 'insurance' whare W.489 'house']

riha *noun (destructive organism)* pest [W.340 'nit, bad']

rikiriki *noun* spring onion [riki common usage 'onion']

rikiroa *noun* leek [riki common usage 'onion' roa W.344 'long, tall']

rino haupōro *noun (golf)* iron [rino W.341 'iron' haupōro TM 'golf club']

rinokita *noun* chrome steel [rino W.341 'iron' konukita TM 'chromium']

ringa *noun* handlebar [W.341 'hand']

ringa hangarau *noun* technologist [ringa W.341 'hand' hangarau TM 'technology']

ringa kerepeti *noun* potter [ringa W.341 'hand' kerepeti W.114 'clay worked and pressed']

ringa mārō *noun (rugby, etc.)* stiff-arm [ringa W.341 'hand, arm' mārō W.183 'stretched out, stiff']

ringa pīau *noun* blacksmith [ringa W.341 'hand' pīau W.279 'iron']

ringa raka *adjective* versatile [ringa W.341 'hand' raka W.321 'agile, adept']

ringa tārake *noun (sport)* fielder [ringa W.341 'hand' tārake W.387 'standing out in the open']

ringa tītere *noun* goal shoot [ringa W.341 'hand' tītere TM 'shoot']

ringahopi *noun* laundry-hand [ringa W.341 'hand' hopi < Eng. 'soap']

ringakuti *noun* fist [ringa W.341 'hand' kuti W.160 'close the hand']

ringarapa *noun (unskilled person)* amateur [ringa W.341 rapa W.325 'awkward, unskilful, inexpert']

ringarau *noun* kleptomaniac [mate ringarau TM 'kleptomania']

ringarehe *noun* tradesperson [ringa W.341 'hand' rehe W.333 'expert, deft person']

ringawera *noun* kitchen hand [ringa W.341 'hand' wera W.482 'hot']

ripa *noun* (*text*) line [W.341 'row, rank, line, furrow']

ripa *adjective* superscript [W.341 'the upper side, top']

ripanga *noun* spreadsheet [ripa W.341 'row, rank, line']

ripanga *noun* (*data*) table [TM 'spreadsheet']

ripanga kaute *noun* balance sheet [ripanga TM 'spreadsheet' kaute TM 'account']

ripanga kaute *noun* accounting spreadsheet [ripanga TM 'spreadsheet' kaute TM 'accounting']

rīpene ataata *noun* video cassette [rīpene < Eng. 'ribbon' ataata TM 'video']

ripi *noun* frisbee [W.341 'small discs of bark thrown by children into the air in some game']

ripiripi pīni *noun* bean slicer [ripi W.341 'cutting implement, slice off, cut' pīni < Eng. 'bean']

ripiwae *noun* leg-bye [ripi W.341 'glance off' wae W.472 'leg']

ripoinga *noun* memoirs [W.342 'haunts' ripoi 'go, travel']

rīrapa *adjective* (*biology*) divaricating [W.342 'matted, in close tangled masses']

riri tara-ā-whare *noun* infighting [W.342 'quarrel between sections of the same hapū, civil war']

rīroa *noun* mainstream [W.323 'main pathway in a pā']

rītaha *noun* (*punctuation*) slash [W.343 'lean on one side, incline']

rītaha *adjective* biased [W.343 'lean to one side, incline']

rite pū *phrase* identically equal to [rite W.343 'like, alike' pū W.300 'very, precise, exactly']

rito *noun* (*phrase*) head [W.343 'centre shoot or heart of monocotyledonous plant']

ritua *adjective* disjoint [W.343 'be divided, be separated']

ritua tuaiwi *noun* spina bifida [ritua W.343 'be divided, be separated' tuaiwi TM 'spine']

roa o te ngaru *noun* (*radio*) wavelength [roa W.344 'long' ngaru W.230 'wave']

rōau *noun* handrail [W.344 'rail in a fence']

rohe āta haere *phrase* limited speed zone [rohe W.344 'boundary' āta W.17 'slowly' haere W.30 'go']

rohe haukuru *noun* (*softball*) strike zone [rohe W.344 'boundary' haukuru TM 'hit']

rohe taitai *noun* (*sport*) striking circle [rohe W.344 'boundary' taitai W.362 'dash, strike']

rohe tītere *noun* (*basketball*) keyhole [rohe W.344 'boundary' tītere TM 'shoot']

rohe tītere *noun* shooting circle [rohe W.344 'boundary' tītere TM 'shoot']

rohe tītere *noun* (*netball*) goal circle [rohe W.344 'boundary' tītere TM 'shoot']

rohe tuku *noun* service area [rohe W.344 'boundary' tuku TM 'serve']

roherohe *noun* (*golf course*) hole [W.344 'mark off by boundaries, separate']

rohetuku matau *noun* right service court [rohe tuku TM 'service area' matau W.192 'right, on the right hand']

rohetuku maui *noun* left service court [rohe tuku TM 'service area' maui W.196 'left, on the left hand']

roi huamata *noun* coleslaw [roi W.345 'grated kūmara' huawhenua common usage 'vegetable' huarākau common usage 'fruit' mata W.185 'raw, uncooked']

rōkara *noun* clove [rōhutu W.345 'myrtus obcordata' kakara W.97 'scent, smell, flavour']

roke kanae *noun* fossil [W.345 'a belemnite fossil shell']

roke kanae *noun* coral [W.345 'a belemnite fossil shell']

rokiroki *noun* storage [W.345 'store, collection of articles, tied up, secured']

rokiroki kōrero *noun* registry [rokiroki W.345 'store, collection of articles, preserve' kōrero TM 'record']

rokiroki mātao *noun* coolstore [rokiroki W.345 'store, collection of articles, preserve' mātao W.189 'cold']

rokohanga *phrase* be happened upon [W.345 'be found, be come upon']

roma *noun* (*anatomy*) tract [W.346 'channel']

roma mimi *noun* urinary tract [roma W.346 'current, stream, channel' mimi W.202 'urine']

roma nakunaku *noun* digestive tract [roma TM 'tract' nakunaku TM 'digest']

romahā *noun* (*biology*) respiratory system [roma W.346 'channel' hā W.29 'breath']

rōnaki *noun* gradient [W.346 'sloping, slanting']

rōnakinaki *noun* roller-coaster [rōnaki W.346 'sloping, slanting, gliding easily, steady, continuous' naki W.217 'glide, move with an even motion']

rongo me te kite *noun* senses [rongo W.346 'apprehend by the senses, except sight' kite W.120 'see, perceive']

rongoā *noun* (*medicine*) treatment [W.346 'take care of, apply medicines to']

rongoā *noun* solution (*to problem*) [W.346 'remedy']

rongoā *noun* medicinal plant [W.346 'remedy, preservative against sickness, medicine']

rongoā *noun* (*medicine*) tonic [W.346 'remedy, preservative against sickness or death']

rongoā *noun* medication [W.346 'drugs, medicine']

rongoā iraruke *noun* radiology [rongoā W.346 'remedy, preservative against sickness or death' iraruke TM 'radioactive']

rongoā patu mamae *noun* analgesic [rongoā W.346 'remedy' patu W.272 'subdue' mamae W.162 'pain']

rongoā paturopi *noun* antibiotic [rongoā W.346 'medicine' paturopi TM 'antibody']

rongoā paturopi *noun* penicillin [rongoā W.346 'remedy, medicine' paturopi TM 'antibody']

rōpā *noun* (*doorkeeper*) porter [W.346 'slave, servant']

ropi pūeru *noun* mannequin [ropi W.347 'body, figure' pūeru W.318 'clothing generally, garment']

rōpinepine *noun* tessilation [rōpine W.347 'place close together']

rōrahi *noun* volume [rō W.344 'roto' W.348 'the inside' rahi W.320 'size' rōraha W.347 'spreading, extended']

rore ārai hapū *noun* intra-uterine device [rore W.347 'ensnare, impede' ārai hapū TM 'contraceptive']

roro *noun* foyer [W.347 'front end of a whare']

roro *noun* (*building*) lobby [W.347 'front end of a whare']

roro ararewa *noun* lift lobby [roro W.347 'front end of a whare' ararewa TM 'lift']

roro ikura *noun* (*medicine*) stroke [roro W.347 'brains' ikura W.76 'haemorrhage']

roro matua *noun* main foyer [roro TM 'foyer' matua W.195 'main']

roro tapepe *noun* multiple sclerosis [roro W.347 'brains, marrow' tapepe W.383 'stumble, make a mistake, speak inarticulately']

roro tuarongo *noun* (*brain*) cerebellum [roro W.347 'brains' tuarongo W.447 'back of the interior of a house']

roroha *adjective*, *noun* elastic [roha W.344 'spread out, expanded']

rorohiko *noun* computer [roro W.347 'brains' hiko common usage 'electric']

rorohiko matua *noun* (*computer*) mainframe [rorohiko TM 'computer' matua W.195 'main, chief']

rorohiko mōkito *noun* microcomputer [rorohiko TM 'computer' mōkitokito W.207 'minute, small']

rorohiko pōnaho *noun* (*computer*) laptop [rorohiko TM 'computer' pōnaho W.291 'diminutive, small']

rorohiko whaiaro *noun* personal computer [rorohiko TM 'computer' whaiaro TM 'personal']

rorotu *transitive verb* hypnotise [rotu TM 'hypnosis']

rotarota *intransitive verb* (*use sign language*) sign [W.348 'sign with the hands, without speaking']

rotu *noun* hypnosis [W.348 'a spell for putting persons in a deep sleep']

rou mamao *noun* remote control device [rou W.348 'a long stick used to reach anything, reach or procure by means of a pole' mamao W.178 'distant, far away']

rōwai *adjective* aquatic [rō W.344 roto W.348 'in' wai W.474 'water']

rua *noun* (*golf*) hole [W.349 'hole']

rua tāra *noun* two dollar coin [rua W.349 'two' tara < Eng. 'dollar']

ruahuru *noun* hair follicle [W.349 'pit, hole' huru W.72 'hair']

ruakākano *noun* (*ovary*) follicle [rua W.349 'pit, hole' kākano TM 'egg']

ruapara *noun* rubbish dump [rua W.349

'pit, hole' para W.262 'impurity, refuse, waste']

ruawhetū *noun* semicircle [W.350 'a semicircular depression']

ruawhetū *adjective* semicircular [W.350 'a semicircular depression']

rueke *noun* decking [W.350 'verandah, porch']

rueke *noun* patio [W.350 'verandah, porch']

ruinga hae *noun* pollination [rui W.350 'scatter, sow, cause to fall in drops' hae W.29 'pollen of flowers']

rukenga hinu *noun* oil spill [ruke W.351 'pour forth, discharge, vent' hinu W.51 'oil']

ruku porotēteke *noun* armstand dive [ruku W.351 'dive' porotēteke W.295 'turned right over']

ruku whakamuri *noun* backward dive [ruku W.351 'dive' whakamuri TM 'backwards']

rukuruku *noun* snorkelling [W.351 'dive, dip frequently']

rumaki parai *transitive verb* deep-fry [rumaki W.351 'immerse' rumaki W.352 'basket of seed potatoes' parai < Eng. 'fry']

rumaki parai taewa *noun* (*cooking*) chip basket [rumaki W.351 'immerse' W.352 'basket of seed potatoes' parai < Eng. 'fry' taewa W.357 'potato']

rūnā *transitive verb* (*mathematics*) simplify [W.352 'reduce, pare down']

rūnā pūira *noun* (*biology*) meiosis [rūnā W.352 'reduce, pare down' pūira TM 'chromosome']

runaruna *noun* hobby [W.352 'pastime']

rūnanga *noun* boardroom [W.352 'public meeting house']

ruri *noun* (*light-hearted*) poem [W.352 'song, ditty']

ruritai *noun* (*song*) shanty [ruri W.352 'song, ditty' tai W.361 'sea']

ruruku *transitive verb* coordinate [W.351 'draw together with a cord']

ruruku *noun* ring-binder [W.351 'draw together with a cord, bind together, enfold, enwrap, band, girdle, bond']

ruruku *noun* skin-diving [ruku W.351 'sink, dive']

rutu *noun* (*contact sport*) tackle [W.353 'dash down, fell, overcome']

rutu hakahaka *noun* low tackle [rutu TM 'tackle' hakahaka W.31 'low']

rutu hē *noun* illegal tackle [rutu TM 'tackle' hē TM 'illegal']

rutu kātete *noun* low tackle [rutu TM 'tackle' kātete W.103 'the whole leg from the thigh downwards']

rutu kōpeo *noun* (*sport*) spear tackle [rutu TM 'tackle' kōpeo W.136 'spear']

rutu rere *noun* flying tackle [rutu TM 'tackle rere W.337 'fly']

rutu tinana *noun* body tackle [rutu TM 'tackle' tinana W.419 'body, trunk']

rutu tōmuri *noun* late tackle [rutu TM 'tackle' tōmuri W.435 'late']

rutu tuarima *noun* fifth tackle [rutu TM 'tackle' tua W.444 'prefix used with numerals to form ordinals' rima W.340 'five']

T

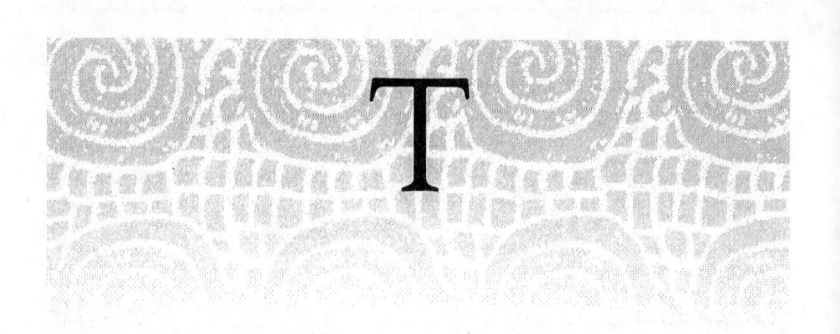

tā *transitive verb* (*written material*) print [W.354 'tattoo, paint']

tā taiaho *noun* laser printer [pūreretā TM 'printer' taiaho TM 'laser']

tae *noun* pigment [W356 'dye, stain, colour']

tāepa *noun* (*athletics*) hurdle [W.363 'fence, wall']

taera rua *adjective* bisexual [taera W.356 'sexual desire' rua W.349 'two']

taero *noun* bureaucracy [W.356 'obstruction, hindrance']

taha kūiti *noun* (*rugby*) blind side [taha W.357 'side' kūiti W.154 'narrow, confined']

taha rerehua *noun* aesthetics [taha W.357 'side' rerehua W.338 'pleasant to the sight, beauty']

taha takiraha *noun* open-side [taha W.357 'side' takiraha W.372 'wide, extended, open space']

taha wae *noun, adjective* leg-side [taha W.357 'side, edge' wae W.472 'leg']

taha wheako *noun, adjective* practical [taha W.357 'side' wheako W.493 'experience intimate acquaintance or knowledge']

tahaahi *noun* hearth [W.357 'stones set in the floor of a whare to mark the fireplace']

tahangoi *adjective* unskilled [W.357 'hesitating, awkward, unaccustomed']

taherapa *noun* (*substance*) rubber [tahe W.358 'sap of a tree, exude' rapa < Eng. 'rubber']

tahi rīwai *noun* potato peeler [tahi W.359 'scrape' rīwai W.344 'potato']

tahi taewa *noun* potato peeler [tahi W.359 'scrape' taewa W.357 'potato']

tāhiko *noun* negative charge [tā TM 'negative end' hiko common usage 'electricity']

tāhoe *noun* (*swimming*) stroke [W.359 'swim, stretch out the arms alternately in swimming']

tahora *noun* grasslands [W.360 'uncultivated open country']

tāhū *noun* (*cricket*) bail [W.360 'horizontal rod']

tahu tūpāpaku *transitive verb* cremate, *noun* cremation [tahu W.360 'set on fire, burn' tūpāpaku W.456 'corpse']

tahua *noun* accumulated funds [W.360 'heap of food, sum of money']

tahua ngore *noun* scholarship [tahua W.360 'fund, some of money' ngore TM 'scholar']

tahua tauira *noun* student allowance [tahua W.360 'fund, sum of money' tauira common usage 'student']

tahua tauira tāpiri *noun* bursary [tahua W.360 'fund, sum of money' tauira common usage 'student' tāpiri W.384 'supplement, anything added or appended']

tāhuahua *noun* sand dune [W.360 'sandhills, in lumps or hillocks']

tāhuhu tangata *noun* curriculum vitae [tāhuhu W.360 'ridgepole of a house, direct line of ancestry, any rod used as stiffener' tangata W.379 'human being']

tāhuhu whakapeto *noun* food chain [tāhuhu W.360 'continuous, running in an unbroken line' whakapeto TM 'consumer']

tahumaero *adjective* epidemiological [W.361 'sickness, disease']

tāhuna *noun* dune [W.361 'sandbank, seaside, beach']

tai matapari *noun* fiord [tai W.361 'sea' matapari W.189 'cliff']

taiaho *noun* laser [taiahoaho W.362 'very bright']

taiaki *noun* hormone [tai W.362 'prefix, sometimes with a qualifying force' akiaki W.7 'urge on']

taiaki huka *noun* insulin [taiaki TM 'hormone' huka < Eng. 'sugar']

taiaki whakatupu *noun* growth hormone [taiaki TM 'hormone' whakatupu W.458 'cause to grow']

taiao *noun* environment [W.362 'world, country' taitaiao 'dawn']

taiapa *noun* (*printing*) bracket [W.363 'fence, wall']

taiaroa para *noun* mini-bin [taiaroa W.362 'basket, receptacle' para W.262 'impurity, refuse, waste']

taiaroa para *noun* (*rubbish container*) skip [taiaroa W.362 'basket, receptacle' para W.262 'impurity, refuse, waste']

taiawa mimi *noun* (*anatomy*) urethra [taiawa W.363 'channel' mimi W.202 'urine']

taihara *noun* crime [tai- W.362 'prefix having no apparent effect on the meaning' hara W.36 'sin, offence']

taihara *adjective, noun* criminal [taihara TM 'crime']

taihara rupe *noun* dangerous criminal [taihara TM 'criminal' rupe W.352 'treat with violence']

taihemahema *noun* reproductive organ [W.363 'genitals of either sex']

taihema kouwha *noun* female reproductive organ [taihemahema W.363 'genitals of either sex' kouwha W.151 'female of animals and trees']

taihema toa *noun* male reproductive organ [taihemahema W.363 'genitals of either sex' toa W.428 'male of animals']

taihema-kore *adjective* (*organism*) asexual [taihema W.363 'genitals of either sex' kore W.140 'no, not']

taimiri *noun* heroin [tai 362 'prefix, sometimes with a qualifying force' miri W.203 'assuage, tranquillise']

tāina *noun* toaster [W.364 'singe']

taiohinga *noun* adolescence [W.364 'young, youthful']

taioma *intransitive verb* gallop [taioma W.364 'run' tai W.362 'prefix with a qualifying force' oma W.239 'move quickly, run']

taiopenga *noun* carnival, festival [taiope W.364 'gather together']

taipahū *noun* dynamite [tai W.362 'prefix, sometimes with a qualifying force' pahū TM 'explosive']

taipana *noun* (*physics*) force [tai- W.362 'prefix sometimes with a qualifying force' pana W.256 'thrust, drive away, cause to come or go forth in any way']

taipana takahuri *noun* torque [taipana TM 'force' takahurihuri W.367 'keep on turning round, roll over and over']

taipana tō *noun* pull force [taipana TM 'force' tō W.428 'drag, haul']

taipana ue *noun* push force [taipana TM 'force' ue W.465 'push, shove']

taiparapara *noun* sub-machine-gun [taipara W.364 'fire a volley at']

tairakaraka *noun* power-walking [tai- W.362 'prefix sometimes with a qualifying force' raka W.321 'agile, go' whakaraka W.321 'walk, step out']

tairere *noun* (*soccer*) striker [taitai W.362 'dash, strike' rere W.337 'be carried on the wind, fly']

tairite *adjective* congruent [W.365 'like, on a level with']

tairutu *noun* dangerous tackle [tai W.361 'anger, violence' rutu TM 'tackle']

taitai *noun* dishwashing brush [taitai W.362 'brush']

taitai pounamu *noun* (*kitchenware*) bottle-brush [taitai W.362 'brush' pounamu W.298 'bottle']

taitama *noun* male adolescent [W.365 'young man']

taitamāhine *noun* female adolescent [W.365 'young woman']

taitōkai *noun* sexual abuse [tai W.361 'anger, rage, violence' W.362 'prefix, sometimes with a qualifying force' tōkai W.433 'copulate']

taituarā *noun* (*finance*) collateral [W.365 'support']

taiutu *noun* remuneration [tai- W.362 'prefix, sometimes with a qualifying force' utu TM 'pay']

taiwhanga *noun* (*building*) chamber, room [W.365 'place, locality']

taiwhanga *noun* waiting room [W.365 'place, locality, wait for']

taiwhanga hākinakina *noun* stadium [taiwhanga W.365 'place, locality' hākinakina TM 'sport']

taiwhanga hāparapara *noun* operating theatre [TM 'surgery']

taiwhanga mate whawhati tata *noun* accident and emergency unit [taiwhanga TM 'room' mate whawhati tata TM 'emergency']

taiwhanga paruhi *noun* sick bay [taiwhanga TM 'room' paruhi W.269 'listless, languid']

taiwhanga pūtaiao *noun* laboratory [taiwhanga TM 'room' pūtaiao TM 'science']

taiwhanga rata *noun* (*place*) surgery [taiwhanga TM 'room' rata W.327 'doctor']

taiwhanga rorohiko *noun* computer room [taiwhanga TM 'room' rorohiko TM 'computer']

taiwhanga taputapu *noun* equipment room [taiwhanga TM 'room' taputapu TM 'equipment']

taiwhanga whakaatu *noun* (*exhibition*) gallery [taiwhanga TM 'room' whakaatu TM 'exhibit']

taka *intransitive verb* drop [W.366 'fall off, fall away']

taka *intransitive verb* to be stumped [W.366 'fall away, fail of fulfilment']

taka *adjective* (*music, key*) flat [W.366 'fall away, fall off']

taka mā muri *intransitive verb* double around [taka W.366 'undergo change in direction, veer, go around' mā W.161 'by way of' muri W.214 'rear']

taka rongoā *noun* pharmacist [taka W.366 'prepare' rongoā W.346 'remedy, medicine']

taka whakamua *noun* (*rugby*) knock-on [taka W.366 'fall off, fail of fulfilment' whakamua TM 'forwards']

takaaku *noun* dacron [taka- < Eng. 'dac-' kaka-aku TM 'textile fibre']

takaāwhio *noun* roundabout [W.367 'go round about']

takaete *transitive verb* (*cooking*) thicken [taka W.366 'prepare' ete W.28 'thicken']

tākai *noun, transitive verb* bandage [W.367 'wrap up, wind round']

tākai *noun* packaging [tākai W.367 'wrap up, wrap round, wind round']

tākai kōataata *noun* cellophane [tākai W.367 'wrap up, wrap round' kōataata W.122 'transparent']

tākai-koha *noun* gift-wrapping [tākai W.367 'wrap up, wrap round' koha W.123 'present, gift']

takahi *transitive verb* contravene [W.367 'disobey, violate']

takahi i te ture *phrase* to commit a crime [takahi W.367 'disobey, violate' ture W.459 'law']

takahiri *noun, intransitive verb* (*diving*) twist [W.367 'turn, twist']

takahuri *transitive verb* (*rugby*) screw [W.367 'roll, turn' takahurihuri W.367 'keep on turning round']

takakau *noun* scone [taka W.366 'prepare' kau W.104 'alone, per se' parāoa takakau common usage 'bread prepared by one who lives alone']

takamua *noun* (*sport*) forward [W.368 'fore, front']

takamua *intransitive verb* (*sport*) offside [takamua W.368 'fore, front' taka W.366 'range, roam at large, veer']

takapapa *noun* panelbeater [W.368 'flatten out']

takapapa *noun* rolling pin [W.368 'flatten out' taka W.366 'prepare' papa W.259 'flat']

takapapa *noun* panelbeating [W.368 'flatten out']

takapapa *noun* tablecloth [W.368 'mat on which to spread cooked food']

takāpui *adjective* homosexual, gay [takatāpui W.369 'intimate companion of the same sex']

tākaro ataata *noun* video game [tākaro W.369 'play, sport' ataata TM 'video']

tākarokaro *adjective* semi-gloss [W.369 'shine dimly']

takarepa *adjective* flawed [W.369 'deficient, imperfect, mutilated']

takarepa-kore *adjective* flawless [takarepa W.369 'deficient, imperfect, mutilated' kore W.140 'no, not']

takatā *noun* editor [taka W.366 'prepare' tā TM 'print']

takatātai *noun* abacus [taka W.366 'drop down' tātai TM 'calculate']

takawaenga *intransitive verb* liaise *noun* liaison [W.370 'go-between, mediator']

takawaenga kāwanatanga noun diplomat [takawaenga W.366 'go, pass round' waenga W.472 'the middle, the midst' kāwanatanga < Eng. 'government']
takawai noun silicon [W.370 'quartz']
takawai noun thermos [W.370 'calabash used as a water bottle']
takawai noun jug [W.370 'calabash used as a water bottle']
takawairore noun mechanical toy [W.370 'a toy consisting of an irregular disc having two slightly excentric holes through which strings were passed']
takawiri haurua noun (*synchronised swimming*) half-twist [takawiri W.370 'twisted' haurua TM 'half']
takawhetanga nā te ngutu phrase subject of gossip [W.370 'something to set the lips moving, subject of free conversation']
takawhita adjective hyperactive [W.370 'thrown into disorder, anxious, eager']
takawhīwhiwhi noun kaleidoscope [W.370 'entangled, interlaced']
take noun (*polygon*) base [W.370 'base of a hill etc.']
take noun (*issue*) matter [W.370 'subject of an argument etc.']
take noun (*concern*) issue [W.370 'subject of an argument etc.']
take noun (*issue*) concern [W.370 'subject of an argument etc.']
take noun claim [W.370 'subject of an argument etc.']
take atu anō noun hidden agenda [take W.370 'subject of an argument etc.' atu W.20 'other' anō W.10 'again, also']
tāke hoko tāwāhi noun (*tax*) tariff [tāke < Eng. 'tax' hoko W.57 'buy, sell' tāwāhi W.406 'the other side of the sea']
Tāke Hokohoko noun Goods & Services Tax [tāke < Eng. 'tax' hoko W.57 'buy, sell']
take huna noun hidden agenda [take W.370 'subject of an argument etc.' huna W.69 'concealed']
tāke kaunihera noun (*land etc.*) rates [tāke < Eng. 'tax' kaunihera < Eng. 'council']
tāke tārewa noun provisional tax [tāke < Eng. 'tax' tārewa W.391 'hanging, unsettled']
take tāwāhi noun international affairs [take TM 'issue, matter' tāwāhi W.406 'the other side of the sea']

taki noun (*music*) beat [W.371 'tow with a line, lead, bring along' takitaki 'song']
takiari noun, intransitive verb (*gambling*) stake [W.372 'omen of a certain class, good or bad']
takiari noun, intransitive verb (*gambling*) bet [W.372 'omen of a certain class, good or bad']
tākihi adjective renal [W.372 'kidney']
takiraha noun (*sport*) outfield [W.372 'wide, flat, extended, open space']
takirere noun valve [taki W.371 'lead, bring along' rere W.337 'flow']
takitahi noun linoleum [W.373 'an inferior kind of floor mat']
takitaki noun picket fence [Best *Māori Agriculture* 40-1 'fence consisting of upright stakes']
tākohu noun vapour trail [W.373 'vapour']
tākohukohu adjective (*chemistry*) volatile [tākohu W.373 'mist, vapour']
tākongakonga noun, transitive verb quarry [tā- W.355 'prefix having a causative force similar to that of whaka-' kongakonga W.134 'crumbled into fragments']
takoto noun layout [W.373 'lie, be in a position']
taku hē phrase I am sorry, I apologise [taku W.374 'my' hē W.43 'error, mistake, fault']
takuahi noun (*soccer*) half [W.374 'centre of line of battle as opposed to paihau']
takuahi noun midfielder [W.374 'centre of line of battle as opposed to the paihau']
takuahi noun (*netball*) centre [W.374 'centre of line of battle as opposed to the paihau']
takuahi noun fireguard [W.374 'stones let into the floor of a house as a fender for fire']
takuahi matau noun (*soccer*) right half [takuahi TM 'half' matau W.192 'right, on the right hand']
takuahi maui noun (*soccer*) left half [takuahi TM 'half' maui W.196 'left, on the left hand']
takuhe noun (*Government*) benefit [takoha W.373 'pledge, token, gift']
takuhe noun (*finance*) grant [W.374 'secure, without apprehension']
takuhe hāura noun invalid benefit [takuhe TM 'benefit' hāura W.41 'sick person, invalid']

takuhe koremahi *noun* unemployment benefit [takuhe TM 'benefit' kore W.140 'no' mahi W.163 'work']

takuhe matua kotahi *noun* domestic purposes benefit [takuhe TM 'benefit' matua W.195 'parent' kotahi W.147 'one']

takuhe matua tōtahi *noun* domestic purposes benefit [takuhe TM 'benefit' matua W.195 'parent' tōtahi W.441 'single']

takuhe pani *noun* orphan's benefit [takuhe TM 'benefit' pani W.257 'orphan']

takuhe pouaru *noun* widow's benefit [takuhe TM 'benefit' pouaru W.298 'widow, widower']

takuhe ratonga tāpiri *noun* supplementary services benefit [takuhe TM 'benefit' ratonga TM 'service' tāpiri W.384 'supplement']

takuhe tahumaero *noun* sickness benefit [takuhe TM 'benefit' tahumaero W.361 'sickness, disease']

takuhe tamaiti atawhai-kore *noun* unsupported child's benefit [takuhe 'benefit' tamaiti W.375 'child' atawhai W.19 'foster' kore W.140 'no']

takuhe ukauka *noun* maintenance benefit [takuhe TM 'benefit' ukauka W.466 'bear, support, sustain']

takuhe whānau *noun* family support [takuhe TM 'benefit' whānau W.487 'offspring, family group']

Takuhe Whakangā Pūmau *noun* Guaranteed Retirement Income [takuhe TM 'benefit' whakangā riro TM 'retire' pūmau W.309 'permanent']

tāmahana *transitive verb* reheat [W.375 'cook a second time, warm up cooked food']

tāmahana *noun* bubble and squeak [W.375 'cook a second time, warm up cooked food']

tamaiti ihongaro *noun* street kid [tamaiti W.375 'child' iho W.75 'that wherein consists the strength of a thing' ngaro W.230 'distressed, oppressed, at a loss']

tāmua *noun* forehand [tātā W.354 'strike, beat with a stick' mua W.213 'front']

tāmuri *noun* backhand [tā W.354 'aim a blow at' muri W.214 'backwards']

tāne *noun* male gender [W.377 'male']

tāne moe tāne *noun* homosexual man [tāne W.377 'male' moe W.205 'sleep together' tāne W.377 'male']

tāne moe wahine *noun* heterosexual man [tāne W.377 'male' moe W.205 'sleep together' wahine W.474 'woman, female']

tāne takāpui *noun* homosexual man [tāne W.377 'male' takāpui TM 'homosexual']

tānekaha *noun* (*fencing*) strainer [W.373 'an implement for tightening the lashings of a canoe by twisting, taut, tight']

tānga *noun* (*word-processing*) hard copy [tā TM 'print']

tānga *noun* relay [W.378 'division, company, relay']

tānga ngahuru *noun* (*mathematics*) standard form [tā TM 'print' ngahuru W.227 'ten']

tānga whenua *noun* local community [W.378 'people of the place']

tānga whenua *noun* community [W.378 'people of the place']

tangariki *noun* floor tile [W.379 'inferior kind of floor mat']

tangata e whakapaetia ana *noun* (*justice*) respondent [tangata W.379 'human being' whakapae W.245 'accuse, make an accusation']

tangata e whakapaetia ana *noun* suspect [tangata W.379 'human being' whakapae W.245 'accuse, make an accusation']

tangata nohoutu *noun* boarder [tangata 'person' noho W.223 'dwell, live' utu W.471 'price']

tangatanga *noun* (*medicine*) remission [W.378 'free from pain, easy, comfortable']

tangatanga *noun* probationer [whakatangatanga W.378 'loosen, release from restraint, endeavour to loosen or disengage']

tangi *noun* intonation [W.379 'sound, cry of things animate or inanimate']

tangi *noun* (*tone*) pitch [W.379 'sound, resound']

tango *transitive verb* subtract [W.380 'take away, remove']

tango hāora *noun* (*chemistry*) reductant [tango W.380 'take away, remove' hāora TM 'oxygen']

tango irahiko *transitive verb* oxidise *noun* oxidant [tango W.380 'take away, remove' irahiko TM 'electron']

tango makatiti *noun* staple remover [tango W.380 'remove' makatiti TM 'staple']

tango pūtea *noun* withdrawal slip [tango W.380 'take away, remove' pūtea TM 'fund']

tango tīponapona *noun* varicotomy [tango W.380 'take away, remove' tīponapona TM 'varicose vein']

tangohanga *noun* subtraction [tango TM 'subtract']

tangotāoke *transitive verb* detoxify [tango W.380 'take away, remove' tāoke TM 'toxin, poison']

tangotāoke *noun* detoxification [tango W.380 'take away, remove' tāoke TM 'toxin, poison']

tao *noun* (*equipment*) javelin [W.380 'spear']

tāoke *noun* poison, toxin *adjective* poisonous, toxic [tā- W.355 'prefix having a causative force' oke W.239 'ill, ailing, sick person']

tāone *adjective* urban [tāone < Eng. 'town']

taonga ake *noun* personal effects [taonga W.385 'goods, property' ake W.6 'self']

taonga pūoru *noun* musical instrument [taonga W.381 'property, anything highly prized' pūoro TM 'music']

taonga tauhokohoko *noun* medium of exchange [taonga W.381 'property, anything highly prized' tauhokohoko TM 'commerce']

tapa *noun* (*polygon*) side [W.381 'margin, edge']

tapa *noun* sideline [W.381 'margin, edge']

tāpae *transitive verb* (*submit*) tender [W.382 'place before a person, present']

tāpae tuhinga whakapae *transitive verb* indict [tāpae W.382 'place before a person, present' tuhinga TM 'document' whakapae TM 'accusation']

tāpaepae *noun* jigsaw puzzle [tāpae W.382 'transverse, lay across' kaiwhakatāpaepae W.90 'the name of a game']

tāpaetanga kōrero *noun* submission [tāpae W.382 'place before a person, present' kōrero W.141 'tell, speak, talk']

tāpahi *intransitive verb* smirk [W.382 'grin, distort the countenance']

tapahi *intransitive verb* (*perform surgery*) operate [W.382 'cut, chop']

tāpane *transitive verb* (*stamp*) frank [tā- W.355 'prefix, having apparently a causative force similar to that of whaka' tā TM 'print' pane 'stamp']

tapanga *noun* label [tapa W.381 'call, name']

tapaono *noun* hexagon [tapa TM 'side' ono W.240 'six']

tāpapa *adjective* prone [W.382 'lie flat, face down']

taparara *noun* trapezium [tapawhā TM 'quadrilateral' whakarara TM 'parallel']

taparau *noun* polygon [tapa W.381 'margin, edge' rau W.328 'multitude, number']

taparau rite *noun* regular polygon [taparau TM 'polygon' rite W.343 'alike']

tāpare *noun, transitive verb* (*picture*) frame [tāparepare W.383 'be bounded, be enclosed']

taparima rite *noun* regular pentagon [tapa W.381 'edge' rima W.340 'five' rite W.343 'alike']

taparua keke *noun* cake tin [taparua W.383 'a square receptacle for kūmara' keke < Eng. 'cake']

taparua parāoa *noun* breadbin [taparua W.383 'square receptacle for kūmara' parāoa common usage 'bread']

tapatoru *noun* triangle [tapa W.381 'margin, edge' toru W.441 'three']

tapatoru hāngai *noun* right-angled triangle [tapatoru TM 'triangle' hāngai TM 'right angle']

tapatoru hikuwaru *noun* scalene triangle [tapatoru TM 'triangle' hikuwaru W.50 'crooked, asymmetrical']

tapatoru rite *noun* equilateral triangle [tapatoru TM 'triangle' rite W.343 'alike, corresponding']

tapatoru waerite *noun* isosceles triangle [tapatoru TM 'triangle' waerite TM 'isosceles']

tāpatu *noun* roof tile [W.383 'thatch, cover in a roof' tāpatupatu 'place in layers, lay one on another']

tapawaru *noun* octagon [tapa W.381 'margin, edge' waru W.480 'eight']

tapawhā *noun* quadrilateral [tapa W.381 'edge' whā W.484 'four']

tapawhā *noun* (*sport*) six-yard box [W.381 'four-sided']

tapawhā rite *noun* square [tapawhā TM 'quadrilateral' rite W.343 'alike, corresponding']

tapawhā rite tītaha *noun* rhombus [tapawhā rite TM 'square' tītaha W.424 'lean to one side, slant']

tapawhā whakarara *noun* parallelogram [tapawhā TM 'quadrilateral' whakarara TM 'parallel']

tapeha *noun* vinyl [W.383 'rind, bark, skin']

tapeke *noun* (*sport*) score, final score [W.383 'total']

tapeke *noun* sum [tapeke W.383 'total']

tapeke hahau *noun* (*golf*) stroke play [tapeke TM 'total, score' hahau TM 'stroke']

tāpi *noun* (*medicine*) dressing [W. 383 'apply, as dressings to a wound']

tāpi *noun* sticking-plaster [W. 383 'apply, as dressings to a wound']

tāpine *noun* pin [tā W.355 'prefix having causative force similar to that of whaka-' pine W.281 'close together']

tāpine *noun* buckle [tā W.355 prefix having a causative force similar to that of whaka' pine W.281 'close together']

tāpīpī *noun* crockpot [W.384 'small earth oven']

tāpiri *transitive verb* (*mathematics*) add [W.384 'add']

tāpiri *noun* (*medicine*) plaster [tāpi W.383 'apply dressing to wound' piri W.283 'stick, adhere to']

tāpiri irahiko *noun* antioxidant [tāpiri W.384 'add' irahiko TM 'electron']

tāpiritanga *noun* (*mathematics*) addition [tāpiri W.384 'add']

tāpiritanga *noun* (*written material*) appendix [tāpiri W.384 'append, supplement']

tāpoi *noun* tourism [W.384 'be travelled round']

tāpora *noun* hessian [W.384 'a coarse floor mat']

tāpora kaiepa *noun* pitcher's plate [tāpora W.384 'a coarse floor mat' kaiepa TM 'pitcher']

tapore *noun* tread [W.384 'footprints, depression as in soft ground']

tāpua *noun* (*botany*) peduncle [tā W.354 'stalk, stem' pua W.301 'flower']

tāpua *adjective* significant [W.385 'stand out, be prominent']

tapuhi *noun* nurse [W.385 'nurse, carry in the arms, tend in sickness or distress']

tapuhi mātāmuri *noun* staff nurse [tapuhi TM 'nurse' mātāmuri W.188 'last, latter']

tapuhi matua *noun* charge nurse [tapuhi TM 'nurse' matua W.195 'main, chief']

tāpui *transitive verb* earmark [tāpui W.385 'set aside, bespeak, reserve']

tapukara *noun* fingerprint [tapuwae W.386 'footprint' koikara W.128 'finger']

taputapu *noun* apparatus, equipment, gear [W.385 'goods, property, appliances']

taputapu *noun* equipment, gear [W.385 'goods, property, appliances']

taputapu *noun* utensil [W.385 'goods, property, appliances']

taputapu rorohiko *noun* (*computer*) hardware [taputapu TM 'equipment' rorohiko TM 'computer']

taputapu tākaro *noun* sports equipment [taputapu TM 'equipment' tākaro W.369 'sport']

taputapu whaiaro *noun* personal effects [taputapu W.385 'goods, property' whaiaro TM 'personal']

tāra *noun* dollar coin [< Eng. 'dollar']

tara *noun* sprocket [W.386 'tooth of a comb']

tara *noun* (*individual tooth*) cog [W.386 'tooth of a comb']

tārahu *noun* (*cooking*) element, hotplate [W.387 'native oven, heat a native oven']

tārahu umu *noun* (*oven*) element [tārahu W.387 'heat a native oven' umu TM 'oven']

tārake *noun* (*cricket*) sweeper [W.387 'clear off, sweep away, standing out in the open']

tāraro *transitive verb* underline [tā W.354 'tattoo, paint' raro W.327 'the underside' tāraro W.389 'adorned, ornamented']

tarau turipona *noun* knickerbockers [tarau common usage 'trousers' turipona W.459 'knee joint']

taraupiri *noun* (*tights*) leggings [tarau < Eng. 'trousers' piri W.283 'stick, adhere, cling']

tārawa *noun* towel-rack [W.389 'line or rail on which anything is hung']

tārawa ūkui pepa *noun* paper-towel rack [tārawa W.389 'line or rail on which anything is hung' ūkui pepa TM 'paper towel']

tarawhiti *noun* ring [W.390 'hoop, ring']

tarawhiti kōkeke *noun* piston-ring

[tarawhiti W.390 'hoop, ring' kōkeke TM 'piston']

tare *noun* transmitter [W.390 'send']

tārere *noun* pendulum [W.391 'swing with the legs off the ground, holding on to a rope']

tārewa *adjective* inconclusive [W.391 'unsettled, hanging']

tarikai *noun* (*botany*) phloem [tari W.391 'carry, bring' kai W.86 'food']

taringa kurī *noun* flapjack [W.391 'jew's ear fungus']

taringa roto *noun* inner ear [taringa W.391 'ear' roto W.348 'inside']

taringa waenga *noun* middle ear [taringa W.391 'ear' waenga W.472 'the midst']

taringa waho *noun* outer ear [taringa W.391 'ear' waho W.474 'outside']

tariwai *noun* (*botany*) xylem [tari W.391 'carry, bring' wai W.474 'water']

tāroa *noun* hypotenuse [W.392 'long']

tārua *noun, transitive verb* (*computer*) backup [tārua W.392 'repeat any process' tā TM 'print']

tārua *noun* (*horse-riding*) saddle [W.392 'hollow, saddle in ridge']

tārua *transitive verb, noun* (*document*) copy [tā TM 'print' tārua W.392 'repeat any process']

tārua *transitive verb, noun* duplicate [taruarua W.392 'repeated']

tata kaikape *noun* (*tennis*) advantage [tata W.393 'near' kaikape TM 'game']

tata kaikape *noun* (*tennis etc.*) game point [tata W.393 'near' kaikape TM 'game']

tata piro *noun* match point [tata W.393 'near' piro W.284 'victory in a game']

tata toa *noun* match point [tata W.393 'near' toa W.428 'victorious']

tata tūākari *noun* (*tennis etc.*) set point [tata W.393 'near' tūākari TM 'set']

tata wharengaro *adjective* (*species*) endangered [tata W.393 'near' wharengaro W.489 'a line or family which has become extinct']

tātai *transitive verb* calculate, compute [W.393 'arrange, set in order, measure, be ranged in order']

tātai aro whenua *noun* geology [tātai W.393 'arrange, set in order' tātai aro rangi W.393 'study the heavens for guidance in navigation' whenua W.494 'ground']

tātai arorangi *noun* astronomy [W.393 'study the heavens for guidance in navigation etc.']

tātai hono *noun* taxonomy [tātai W.393 'recite genealogies' hono W.58 'join']

tātaitai *noun* calculator [tātai TM 'calculate']

tātaitanga *noun* calculation [tātai TM 'calculate']

tātaitanga *noun* computing [tātai TM 'calculate']

tātaka ruku *noun* diving beetle [tātaka W.394 'brown beetle' ruku W.351 'dive']

tātāki *transitive verb* (*sport*) disqualify [W.371 'take to one side, take out of the way']

tātaki *transitive verb* spell [taki W.371 'recite, lead, bring along']

tātaki kupu *noun* spelling [tātaki TM 'spell' kupu W.157 'word']

tatangi *noun* tambourine [W.379 'jingle, rattle']

tatao *noun* stew [W.381 'remain a long time in the process of cooking']

tatarakina *intransitive verb* (*hair*) split ends [Biggs 88 'hair split at ends']

tātārau *noun* petiole [tātā W.354 'stem, stalk' rau W.328 'leaf']

tātārau *noun* (*botany*) phyllode [tātā W.354 'stalk, stem' rau W.328 'leaf']

tātaretare *noun* chainsaw [tātare W.395 'a saw-like weapon made from teeth of a shark']

tātari *transitive verb* analyse [W.391 'sift, sieve']

tātari *noun, transitive verb* filter [W.391 'strain, sift']

tātari *noun* sifter [W.391 'strainer, sift']

tātari kaute *noun, transitive verb* audit [tātari TM 'analyse' kaute TM 'account']

tātari tākihi *noun* renal dialysis [tātari TM 'filter' tākihi TM 'renal']

tātari toto *noun* haemodialysis [tātari TM 'analyse' toto W.441 'blood']

tātari whanonga *noun* behaviour analysis [tātari TM 'analyse' whanonga W.487 'behaviour, conduct']

tātari-kume-ā-papa *noun* gravimetric analysis [tātari TM 'analyse' kume-ā-papa TM 'gravity']

tātaritanga *noun* analysis [tātari TM 'analyse']

tatau ā-kākā *intransitive verb* rote count [tatau W.395 'count' ā W.1 'after the manner of' kākā W.81 'native parrot']

tatau waikauere *noun* (*boxing*) count-out [tatau TM 'number' waikauere W.475 'without energy, subdued']

tatauranga *noun* statistic [tatau W.395 'count, tie with a cord, thread on a string']

tatauranga *noun* statistics [tatau W.395 'count, tie with a cord, thread on a string']

tatauranga taupori *noun* demography [tatauranga TM 'statistics' tau W.395 'count, alight, come to rest' pori W.294 'people, tribe']

tātea *noun* spermatozoon [W.394 'semen']

tātua pūpara *noun* bum-bag [W.395 'girdle in which valuables were carried']

tātua raho *noun* jockstrap [tātua W.395 'girdle' raho W.320 'testicle']

tau *noun* number [W.395 'count, repeat one by one']

tau hautau *noun* rational number [tau TM 'number' hautau TM 'fraction']

tau hanumi *noun* mixed number [tau TM 'number' hanumi W.34 'be mixed']

tau hangarite order of symmetry [tau TM 'number' hangarite TM 'symmetry']

tau kaupapa-rua *noun* binary number [tau TM 'number' kaupapa-ā-tau TM 'number base' rua W.349 'two']

tau kaupapa-waru *noun* octal number [tau TM 'number' kaupapa-ā-tau TM 'number base' waru W.480 'eight']

tau kiato *noun* compact numeral [tau TM 'number' kiato W.116 'compact, in small compass']

tau kōnae *noun* (*office administration*) reference [tau TM 'number' kōnae TM 'file']

tau maha *noun* cardinal number [tau TM 'number' maha W.162 'many, number']

tau ngahuru *noun* decimal number [tau TM 'number' ngahuru W.227 'ten']

tau oti *noun* whole number [tau TM 'number' oti W.424 'finished']

tau papatipu *noun* mass number [tau TM 'number' papatipu W.261 'solid mass']

tau poha *noun* whole number [tau TM 'number' poha W.286 'full']

tau pūmau *noun* (*mathematics*) constant [tau TM 'number' pūmau W.309 'constant']

tau roha *noun* expanded numeral [tau TM 'number' roha W.344 'spread out, expanded']

tau tāke *noun* IRD number [tau TM 'number' tāke < Eng. 'tax']

tau tapa *noun* (*tennis*) line ball [tau W.396 'alight, come to rest' tapa W.381 'margin, edge']

tau tatau *noun* counting number [tau TM 'number' tatau W.395 'count']

tau tatau *noun* natural number [TM 'counting number']

tau tatū kore *noun* irrational number [tau TM 'number' tatū W.395 'reach the bottom, be at ease' kore W.140 'no, not']

tau taupoki *noun* (*mathematics*) reciprocal number [tau TM 'number' taupoki W.401 'turn over']

tau toharite *noun* (*mean*) average [tau TM 'number' toha W.429 'distribute' rite W.343 'alike']

tau toharite *noun* (*average*) arithmetic mean [tau TM 'number' tohatoha 429 'distribute' rite W.343 'alike']

tau tōpū *noun* integer [tau TM 'number' tōpū W.437 'assembled, in a body']

tau tōraro *noun* negative number [tau TM 'number' tōraro TM 'negative']

tau tōrunga *noun* positive number [tau TM 'number' tōrunga TM 'positive']

tau tūturu *noun* real number [tau TM 'number' tūturu W.460 'fixed, permanent']

tau waea *noun* telephone number [tau TM 'number' waea common usage 'telephone']

tau waenga *noun* (*statistics*) median [tau TM 'number' waenga W.472 'dividing line']

tau whāioio *adjective* infinite number [tau TM 'number' whāioio W.485 'very, numerous']

tau whakarahi *noun* scale factor of enlargement [tau TM 'number' whakarahi TM 'enlarge']

tau whakarea *noun* coefficient [tau TM 'number' whakarea TM 'multiply']

tau whakawehe *noun* divisor [tau TM 'number' whakawehe TM 'divide']

tau-ā-ira *noun* decimal number [tau TM 'number' ā W.1 'after the manner of' ira TM 'decimal']

tau-ā-ira *adjective* decimal [tau TM

'number' ā W.1 'after the manner of' ira TM 'dot']

tau-ā-ira auau *noun* recurring decimal [tau-ā-ira TM 'decimal' auau TM 'recurring']

tau-ā-ira whāioio *noun* infinite decimal [tau-ā-ira TM 'decimal number' tau whāioio TM 'infinite number']

tauā moana *noun* navy [tauā W.397 'hostile expedition, army' moana W.204 'sea, lake']

tauārai *transitive verb* insulate [W.397 'screen, barrier']

tauārai *noun* insulator [W.397 'screen, barrier']

tauārai *noun* insulation [W.397 'screen, barrier']

tauārangi *noun* airforce [taua W.397 'hostile expedition, army' rangi W.323 'sky']

tauaro *adverb* directly [W.397 'straight, direct']

tauaru *noun* trailer [W.397 'follow']

tauhae *noun* (*botany*) stigma [tau W.396 'alight, come to rest' hae W.29 'pollen']

tauhanga *noun* arithmetic [tau TM 'number' hanga W.34 'make, practice']

tauhena *adjective* miniature [W.405 'dwarfish, of small stature']

tauhena rākau *noun* bonsai tree [rākau W.321 'tree' W.405 'dwarfish, of small stature']

tauhokohoko *noun* commerce [tau- W.397 'prefix denoting reciprocal action' hokohoko W.57 'trade, exchange']

tauhone *noun* (*netball*) throw-up [tauhonehone W.398 'snatch or pull from one another']

tauhonehone *noun* (*basketball*) jump ball [W.398 'snatch or pull from one another']

tāuhu *noun* horizontal bar [W.360 'ridge-pole of a house, any horizontal rod used as a stiffener']

tāuhu karawhiti *noun* asymmetric bars [tāuhu W.360 'horizontal bar' karawhiti W.99 'uneven, irregular']

tāuhu kōkeke *noun* piston-rod [tāuhu W.360 'rod used as a stiffener' kōkeke TM 'piston']

tāuhu whakarara *noun* parallel bars [tāuhu TM 'bar' whakarara TM 'parallel']

tāuhu whakararo *noun* (*gymnastics*) lower bar [tāuhu TM 'bar' whakararo TM 'lower']

tāuhu whakarunga *noun* (*gymnastics*) upper bar [tāuhu TM 'bar' whakarunga TM 'upper']

tauine *noun* (*instrument*) ruler [taura ine W.78 'measuring line']

tauine *noun* (*measurement*) scale [taura ine W.78 'measuring line']

tauira *noun* (*model*) draft [W.398 'pattern']

tauira *noun* formula [W.398 'pattern']

tauira *noun* (*example*) illustration [W.398 'pattern, copy']

tauira *noun* model [W.398 'pattern, copy']

tauira *noun* sample [W.398 'pattern, copy']

tauira *noun* (*example*) specimen [TM 'sample']

tauira *noun* template [W.398 'pattern, copy']

tauira *noun* example [W.398 'pattern, copy']

tauira tāruarua *noun* (*mathematics*) repeating pattern [tauira TM 'pattern' tārua W.392 'repeat any process']

tauiwi *adjective* non-Māori [W.398 'strange, tribe, foreign race']

tāuke *adjective* (*statistics*) exclusive [W.399 'apart, separate']

taukehe *noun* odd number [tau TM 'number' kehe W.112 'an odd number in counting']

taumaha *noun* weight [W.399 'heavy']

Taumāhekeheke o te Ao *noun* Olympic Games [taumāhekeheke W.399 'compete with one another in friendly rivalry for the possession of the same object' ao W.11 'world']

taumanu *transitive verb* (*justice*) impound [W.399 'take possession of another's goods']

taumanu *transitive verb* (*vehicle licence*) disqualify [W.399 'take possession of another's goods']

taumanu *noun* pedal [W.399 'projecting foot piece of a kō']

taumata *noun* level [W.399 'brow of a hill']

taumata *noun* (*education*) grade [W.399 'brow of a hill']

taumata *noun* pinnacle [W.399 'brow of a hill']

taumātakirua *noun* (*contest*) quarter final [taumātakitahi W.400 'select a champion for each side in fighting' TM 'semi-final' rua W.349 'two']

taumātakitahi *noun* semifinal [W.400 'select a champion for each side in fighting']

taunaha *noun* liability [W.400 'bespeak']

taunaha tāpui limited liability [taunaha TM 'liability' tāpui W.385 'set aside, reserve']

taunahatanga *noun* financial liability [W.400 'bespeak']

taunaki *transitive verb* recommend, advocate [W.400 'support, reinforce']

taunaki pūmanawa *noun* (*personal*) testimonial [taunaki W.400 'support, reinforce' pūmanawa W.309 'natural talents, intuitive cleverness']

taunaki whanonga *noun* character reference [taunaki W.400 'support, reinforce' whanonga W.487 'behaviour, conduct']

taunakitanga *noun* evidence [taunaki W.400 'support, reinforce']

taunanawe *adjective* provocative [W.400 'excite, provoke']

taunga (*mathematics*) coordinates [taunga W.396 'resting place, anchorage']

taunga rererangi *noun* airport [taunga W.396 'resting place, anchorage' waka rererangi common usage 'aeroplane']

taunga waka āwhiowhio *noun* heliport [taunga W.396 'resting place, anchorage' waka āwhiowhio TM 'helicopter']

taungota *noun* atomic number [tau TM 'number' ngota TM 'atom']

tauoma tānga *noun* relay race [tauomaoma TM 'race' tānga W.378 'division, company, relay']

tauomaoma *noun* (*foot race*) race [tau- W.397 'prefix denoting reciprocal action' oma W.239 'run']

tauomaoma *noun* track event [TM 'foot race']

taupā *noun* double contact [W.400 'obstruct, prevent' tau W.397 'prefix denoting reciprocal action' pā W.243 'touch, strike']

taupā *transitive verb* (*rugby*) shepherd [W.400 'obstruct, prevent']

taupā *noun* (*rugby*) shepherding [W.400 'obstruct, prevent']

taupaepae *noun* reception area [W.400 'meet and escort visitors in as they arrive']

taupaki *noun* (*card-game*) snap [W.400 'pat, slap']

taupāpātanga ratio [tau W.397 'prefix denoting reciprocal action' pā W.243 'touch, reach, strike, be connected with']

taupatupatu *noun* (*tennis etc.*) rally [W.401 'compete or vie with one another']

tāupe *noun* (*science*) variable [W.401 'variable']

tāupe whakaū *noun* (*science*) control variable [tāupe TM 'variable' whakaū W.465 'make firm, establish']

tāupeupe *adjective* conditional [tāupe W.401 'bending, not rigid, variable']

taupiri *adjective* tandem [taupiripiri Best *Games and Pastimes* 19, 31 'style of foot race in which competitors run in pairs holding each other round the neck' W.401 'clinging close, maintaining attachment']

taupori *noun* population [tau TM 'number' W.396 'alight, come to rest' pori W.294 'people, tribe']

taupori *adjective* demographical [tau W.395 'count' W.396 'alight, come to rest' pori W.294 'people, tribe']

tauporo *transitive verb* curtail [W.401 'bring to an end, cut short']

taupū *noun* (*mathematics*) exponent [tau TM 'number' pū TM 'power']

taupū *noun* index [tau TM 'number' pū 'power']

taupū kōaro *noun* logarithm [taupū TM 'exponent' kōaro W.122 'inverted']

taupua *noun* time-out [W.401 'take breath, subside']

taupua whara *phrase* time out for injury [taupua W.401 'take breath, subside' whara W.489 'be struck, be hit accidentally']

taupuhi kaiao *noun* (*organism*) ecology [taupuhi W.401 'lean one on another' kaiao TM 'organism']

taupuhipuhi *noun* interdependence [W.401 'lean on one another, support a person by placing the arm around him']

taupuhipuhi *noun* symbiosis [W.401 'lean one on another, support a person by placing the arm around him']

taupuhipuhi *adjective* symbiotic [TM 'symbiosis']

taupuni *noun* (*depot, place etc.*) station [W.401 'place of assignation']

taupuni *noun* depot [W.401 'place of assignation']

taupuni mahi *noun* workstation [taupuni W.401 'place of assignation' mahi W.163 'work, occupation']

taupuni mahi *noun* studio [taupuni W.401 'place of assignation' mahi W.163 'work, occupation']

taupuni tawhiti *adjective, noun* outpost [taupuni W.401 'temporary encampment, place of assignation' tawhiti W.409 'distant, widely separated']

taupuru hinga *noun* collapsed scrum [taupurupuru TM 'scrum' hinga W.51 'fall from an erect position']

taupuru mua *noun* front row [taupurupuru W.402 'support a person by putting the arm around him' mua W.213 'front']

taupuru muri *noun* (*rugby*) back row [taupurupuru W.402 'support a person by putting the arm around him' muri W.214 'rear, hind part']

taupuru whānako *noun* (*rugby, ball-play*) tighthead [whānako W.487 'steal' taupurupuru TM 'scrum']

taupurupuru *noun* scrum [W.402 'support a person by putting the arm around him']

tauputu *noun* (*vehicle*) boot [W.402 'lie in a heap']

tauputu *noun* (*mathematics*) mode [tau TM 'number' putu W.317 'lie in a heap' pūputu 'frequent']

tāura *noun* postgraduate student [W.402 'the second order of learners being initiated in esoteric lore']

taura hiko *noun* electrical cord [taura W.402 'cable, cord' hiko common usage 'electricity']

taura hiko *noun* power cord [taura W.402 'cable, cord' hiko common usage 'electricity']

taura katete *noun* extension cord [taura W.402 'cord' katete W.103 'lengthen by adding a piece']

taura ngaiaku *noun* nylon rope [taura W.402 'rope, cable' ngaiaku TM 'nylon']

taura rere *noun* flying fox [taura W.402 'cable' rere W.337 'fly']

taura tīeke *noun* measuring tape [W.415 'line for measuring the diagonals of a house']

taurahi *noun* scale factor [tau TM 'number' rahi W.320 'size']

tauraki *noun* dehydrator [W.402 'dry by exposure to the sun, dried']

tauranga *noun* landing pad [W.396 'resting place, anchorage']

tauranga *noun* (*public transport*) terminal [W.396 'resting place, anchorage']

taurangi *noun* (*mathematics*) variable [W.402 'unsettled, changing, changeable']

taurangi *adjective* algebraic [taurangi TM 'variable']

tauraro *noun* denominator [tau TM 'number' raro W.359 'together']

tauraro pātahi *noun* common denominator [tauraro TM 'denominator' pātahi TM 'common']

taurea *noun* multiple [tau TM 'number' whakarea TM 'multiply']

taurea pātahi *noun* common multiple [taurea TM 'multiple' pātahi TM 'common']

taurewa *adjective* on loan [W.402 'not paid for']

taurite *adjective* equivalent [W.403 'alike, matching']

tauru *noun* pulley [W.403 'roller for moving a canoe']

taurua *noun* even number [tau TM 'number' rua W.349 'two']

taurunga *noun* numerator [tau TM 'number' runga W.352 'the top, the upper part']

tautapa *transitive verb* delegate [W.403 'nominate, designate']

tautara *noun* (*equipment*) accessory [W.403 'fasten affix']

tautara *noun* (*building*) fixture [W.403 'fasten, affix']

tautara *noun* appendage [W.403 'fasten, affix']

tautara *noun* fishing rod [W.403 'rod to support a line when fishing from a canoe or when fishing for eels']

tauteka *noun* (*weight training*) bar [W.404 'pole on which a weight is carried between two persons']

tauteka *noun* wheel brace [W.404 'brace, tighten by twisting, piece of wood used to twist up the lashing of anything in order to tighten it']

tauteka *noun* (*weight training*) barbell [W.404 'pole on which a weight is carried between two persons']

tauteka pukapuka *noun* book end [tauteka W.404 'brace, prop' pukapuka W.306 'book']

tāuteute *adjective* preoccupied [W.404 'be engrossed, be occupied, be absorbed in occupation']

tāuteute *noun* preoccupation [W.404 'be engrossed, be occupied, be absorbed in occupation']

tautītī *noun* walking frame [W.404 'support an invalid in walking']

tautō *adjective* articulated [W.404 'trail, drag']

tautōhito *noun* skill [W.404 'adept, person of experience']

tautoko *transitive verb* verify [W.404 'prop up, support']

tautoko *transitive verb* advocate [W.404 'prop up, support']

tautokorua *adjective* concurrent [W.404 'simultaneous, both together']

tautokorua *adjective (combined)* joint [W.404 'simultaneous, both together']

tautopenga *noun* backstop, catcher, goalkeep, goalkeeper, wicket-keeper [whakatautopenga W.404 'rearguard']

tautuhi *transitive verb* identify [W.405 'indicate, define']

tautuhi *transitive verb* pinpoint [W.405 'indicate, define']

tautuku *intransitive verb (traffic)* give way [W.405 'stoop, bend down; so give way']

tautuku *intransitive verb, transitive verb* cede, default [W.405 'stoop, bend down; so give way']

tautuku *noun* penalty [W.405 'stoop, bend down; so give way']

tauwaka *noun* number plate [tau TM 'number' waka common usage/'vehicle']

tauwehe *noun (mathematics)* factor [tau TM 'number' wehe W.481 'divide']

tauwehe pātahi *noun* common factor [tauwehe TM 'factor' pātahi TM 'common']

tauwhāinga *noun (sport)* event [W.405 'contend, vie']

tauwhāinga *noun (competition event)* race [W.405 'contend, vie']

tauwhāinga-ā-kapa *noun* team event [tauwhāinga TM 'event' ā W.1 'after the manner of' kapa TM 'team']

tauwhaiwhai *noun (cycling)* individual pursuit [tau W.396 'prefix denoting reciprocal action' whaiwhai W.485 'chase, hunt']

tauwhaiwhai *noun (game)* tag [W.405 'fly, hasten' whaiwhai W.485 'chase, hunt']

tauwhaiwhai ā-kapa *noun* individual team trial [tauwhaiwhai TM 'individual pursuit' ā W.1 'after the manner of' kapa W.95 'rank, row']

tauwhiro *noun* social worker [W.405 'tend, care for, be alert, be on one's guard']

tauwhiro *noun* transition [tauwhirowhiro TM 'transitional']

tauwhiro hapori *noun* social work [W.405 'tend, care for, be alert, be on one's guard' hapori TM 'social']

tauwhiro hapori *noun* social services [tauwhiro W.405 'tend, care for, be alert, be on one's guard' hapori TM 'social']

tauwhiro tangata *noun* social services [tauwhiro W.405 'tend, care for, be alert, be on one's guard' tangata W.379 'human being']

tauwhirowhiro *adjective* transitional [W.405 'be near the change (of the moon)']

tawā *noun (music)* fret [W.405 'ridge']

tawa *adjective* purple [after colour of fruit of tawa tree]

tāwai *noun* slasher [W.406 'cut or clear undergrowth, etc.']

tāwai *noun* skiff [W.406 'a canoe without its attached sides']

tāwakawaka *noun (music)* keyboard [tāwakawaka W.406 'striped, banded, a cloak of dressed flax made in black and white stripes']

tāwara *noun* taste bud [W.406 'flavour, taste, sweet, pleasant to the taste']

tāwari *noun* counterclaim [W.406 'oppose a claim to land etc.']

tawau *noun, transitive verb (impart colour)* stain [W.407 'milky juice of plants, stain therefrom']

tawau *noun* latex [W.407 'milky juice of plants']

tawau rapa *noun (rubber)* latex [W.407 'milky juice of plants']

tāwere *adjective (language)* redundant [W.407 'having an odd number or excess' tāwerewere 'hanging freely, suspended']

tāwerenga *noun* remainder [tāwere W.407 'having an odd number or excess' tāwerewere W.407 'hanging free']

tawhā *noun* boundary [tapawhā W.381 'four-sided']

tawhā *noun* boundary line [tapawhā W.381 'four-sided']

tawhā *noun* parameter [tapawhā W.381 'four-sided']

tawhā tītere *noun* goal third [tapawhā W.381 'four-sided' tītere TM 'shoot']

tawhā waengapū *noun* (*lawn bowls*) centre [tawhā TM 'boundary' waengapū W.473 'the midst']

tawhera *noun* compound leaf [W.408 'leaf']

tawhera whakarahi *noun* microscope slide [tawhera W.408 'leaf' whakarahi TM 'enlarge']

tawheraiti *noun* (*biology*) leaflet [tawhera W.408 'leaf' iti W.80 'small']

tawherarima *adjective, noun* 5-foliate [tawhera W.408 'leaf' rima W.340 'five']

tawhera-toru *noun* trifoliate [tawhera W.408 'leaf' toru W.441 'three']

tawherawhitu *adjective, noun* 7-foliate [tawhera W.408 'leaf' whitu W.498 'seven']

tāwhiri *noun* air freshener [W.409 'gum of pittosporum, used as a scent']

tāwhirowhiro *noun* kitchen whizz [W.409 'whirl, whizz']

tāwhiti *noun* mousetrap [W.409 'snare, trap']

tē aro *adjective* incomprehensible [tē W.409 'not' aro W.16 'know, understand'] *e.g. Tē aro i a au tana reta.*

teatea *noun* (*anatomy*) sclera [W.410 'white in colour' whakatea 'show the whites of the eyes']

teitei *noun* altitude [W.410 'high, lofty']
teitei *noun* (*sport*) clearance [W.410 'high']
teitei *noun* (*gymnastics*) lift [W.410 'high, lofty']

tekapepa *noun* paper dart [teka W.410 'dart thrown for amusement' pepa < Eng. 'paper']

tengitengi *noun* waltz [hītengi W.53 'hop on one foot' tengi W.412 'three']

teo *noun* (*golf*) birdie [W.412 'small, of birds']

teraku *noun* (*board game*) draughts [Best Games and Pastimes 181 'draughts']

tere *noun* velocity [W.412 'swift, move quickly, flow']

tereaku *noun* terylene [tere < Eng. 'tery' akuaku W.7 'firm, strong']

terehuka *noun* dextrose [tere- < Eng. 'dex' tere W.412 'swift, active' huka < Eng. 'sugar']

tero puta *noun* haemorrhoids, piles [tero W.413 'rectum, anus' puta W.315 'blister, come out']

tī *noun* (*golf equipment*) tee [tīrau W.423 'peg, stick']

tia *noun* drawing pin [W.414 'stick, peg, drive in peg']

tia *noun* (*furniture*) hook [W.414 'peg, stake' ara tiatia W.414 'a series of pegs stuck in to assist in climbing a steep ascent']

tia ngapu *noun* (*athletics*) starting-block [tia W.414 'peg' ngapu W.229 'stretch forwards ready to run']

tīanga *noun* groundsheet [W.414 'mat to lie on']

tīare *noun* (*music*) clave [tīare W.414 'hollow, empty, void' tītī W.414 'sticks thrown from one player to another in the game of tī rākau']

tīeke *noun* tape-measure [taura tīeke W.415 'line for measuring the diagonals of a house']

tīere *noun* air freshener [W.414 'scent']

tīhake *noun* casserole dish [W.415 'pot, vessel']

tihenga atua *noun* spore [tihe W.415 'sneeze' whare atua W.489 'mushroom']

tīhoka *noun* (*golf, area*) tee [W.416 'stick in, thrust in']

tika *adjective* (*data etc.*) reliable [W.416 'just, right, correct']

tīkākā *noun* sunburn [W.416 'burnt by the sun']

tīkākā *adjective* sunburnt [TM 'sunburn']

tikanga ōhanga *noun* principles of economics [tikanga W.417 'rule, plan, method' ōhanga TM 'economics']

tikanga reorua *noun* bilingualism [tikanga W.416 'plan method' reorua TM 'bilingual']

tikanga ture *noun* legal system [tikanga W.416 'rule, method, plan' ture TM 'legal']

tikanga whakakonekone *noun* aversion therapy [tikanga W.416 'method' whaka- W.486 'causative prefix' *to make* konekone W.133 'repugnance']

tikanga whakawhenumi *noun* assimilation policy [tikanga W.416 'rule, plan' whakawhenumi W.494 'mix up one thing with another']

tikanga-rua *noun* biculturalism [TM 'bicultural']

tikanga-rua *adjective* (*politics*) bicultural [tikanga W.416 'custom, habit' rua W.349 'two']

tīkape pounamu *noun* bottle-opener [tīkapekape W.417 'move or stir with the point of a stick' pounamu W.298 'bottle']

tīkeikei *noun* treadmill [tīkei W.417 'extend, stretch out, as the legs in stepping over an object']

tīkera (hiko) *noun* electric jug [tīkera 'kettle' hiko common usage 'electric']

tīkohu parāoa *noun* macaroni [tīkohu W.418 'hollowed out, bent, curved' parāoa < Eng. 'flour']

tīkoke *noun* (*rugby*) bomb [W.418 'high up in the heavens']

tīkoke *noun, transitive verb* lob [W.418 'high up in the heavens']

tima *noun* hoe [Best *Māori Agriculture* 46 'a form of grubber']

tīmanga *noun* servery [W.418 'elevated stage on which food is kept']

tīmata *noun* kickoff [W.418 'begin']

tīmori *noun* clay pigeon [W.419 'decoy bird']

timu *noun* tail bone, coccyx [W.419 'end, tail']

tinei *transitive verb* (*machinery etc.*) turn off [TM 'switch off']

tinei *transitive verb* switch off [W.419 'put out, quench, extinguish']

tino hiahia *noun* (*choice*) preference [tino W.420 'exact, veritable, very' hiahia W.47 'desire, wish, impulse, thought']

tino pai *adjective* special [tino W.420 'very, quite, veritable' pai W.249 'good, excellent']

tino taonga *adjective* valuable [tino W.420 'veritable, very' taonga W.381 'anything highly prized'] e.g. *He tino taonga ana kōrero. 'Her comments were most valuable.'*

tino taonga *adjective* indispensable [tino W.420 'veritable, very' taonga W.381 'anything highly prized'] *He tino taonga taua wahine. 'That woman is indispensable.'*

tino taonga *adjective* invaluable [tino W.420 'veritable, very' taonga W.381 'anything highly prized'] *He tino taonga tana āwhina mai. 'His assistance was invaluable.'*

tioata *noun* (*science*) crystal [tio W.420 'ice' kōataata W.122 'transparent']

tioata *adjective* crystalline [tio W.420 'ice' kōataata W.122 'transparent']

tiomimi *noun* urea [tio TM 'crystal' mimi W.202 'urine']

tiora *noun* (*music*) viola [W.420 'shrill']

tīpae rongoā *noun* medicine cabinet [tīpae W.421 'small basket' rongoā W.436 'medicine']

tīpae whawhati tata *noun* first-aid kit [tīpae W.421 'small basket' matewhawhati tata TM 'emergency']

tīpako *transitive verb* (*word-processing, text*) highlight [W.421 'pick out, select']

tīpako *noun* (*statistics*) sample [W.421 'pick out, select']

tīpako rītaha *noun* biased sample [tīpako TM 'sample' rītaha TM 'biased']

tīpakonga *noun* (*sample*) specimen [TM 'sample']

tīpao *noun, intransitive verb* putt [tī W.414 'sticks about 18 inches long' pao W.258 'strike']

tīpao *noun* putter [tī W.414 'sticks about 18 inches long' pao W.258 'strike']

tīpaopao kupu *noun* dyslexia [tīpaopao W.421 'put out of proper sequence' kupu W.157 'word']

tipihori *adjective* (*shape*) irregular [W.422 'askew, placed irregularly']

tīpoka *transitive verb* summarise, precis *noun* summary, precis [tīpokapoka W.422 'taking some and leaving some']

tīpona waitinana *noun* lymph node [tīpona W.422 'form a swelling or knot' waitinana TM 'lymph']

tīponapona *noun* varicose vein [tīpona W.422 'form a swelling or knot']

tipu *noun* (*biology*) plant [W.457 'shoot, bud, grow']

tipu pūtau-tahi *noun* protophyta [tipu TM 'plant' pūtau-tahi TM 'single-celled']

tira pūoru *noun* orchestra [tira W.422 'file of men, row, company of travellers, choir' pūoru TM 'music']

tīrake *noun* sphere [tīrakerake Biggs 22 'full moon']

tīrake *adjective* spherical [tīrakerake Biggs 22 'full moon']

tīramaroa *noun* lighthouse [W.423 'a term applied to some light, like a torch, seen on mountain tops']

tīrari *noun* (*vehicle*) distributor [W.425 'distribute']

tīraurau *noun* tea-bag [tī < Eng. 'tea' rau W.328 'gather into a basket etc.']

tīraurau *noun* tea-leaves [tī < Eng. 'tea' rau W.328 'leaf' raurau 'foliage']

tīrepa *noun* (*building*) insulation [W.423 'line with reeds the roof of a native house']

tīrewa *noun* jungle gym [W.423 'scaffolding or raised frame for hanging things upon']

tiri porokere *noun* bricklayer [tiri W.423 'place one on another, stack, place one by one' porokere TM 'brick']

tirikohu waehere *noun* bungy-jumping [tirikohu 'dive' wae W.472 'leg, foot' here W.46 'fasten with cord']

tirikohu whakamua *noun* forward dive [tirikohu common usage 'dive' whaka- W.485 'in the direction of' mua W.213 'the front']

tiringa *noun* (*payment*) royalty [tiri W.423 'throw a present before one, share, portion']

tiripou *noun* skydiver [W.423 'swoop down']

tiriwae *noun* (*aerobics*) grapevine [tiriwā W.424 'plant at wide intervals' wae W.472 'foot']

tiro tānga (*word-processing*) print preview [tiro W.424 'look' tānga TM 'hard copy']

tiro whānui *noun, transitive verb* (*overview*) survey [tiro W.424 'look, survey, view' whānui W.487 'broad, wide']

tiro whānui *noun* overview [tiro W.424 'look, survey, view' whānui W.487 'broad, wide']

tiro whārangi *noun* (*word-processing*) page view [tiro W.424 'look' whārangi W.489 'page of a book']

tirohanga whānui *noun* overview [tirohanga W.424 'view, sight, aspect' whānui W.487 'broad, wide']

tīrongo *noun* bin-liner [W.424 'slabs of stem of tree fern used for lining a kūmara pit']

tirotiro tūpāpaku *noun* autopsy, postmortem [tirotiro W.424 'investigate' tūpāpaku W.456 'corpse']

tītaha *noun* (*mathematics*) shear [W.424 'lean to one side, slant']

tītaha *adjective* italic [W.424 'slant, be on one side']

tītaha *intransitive verb* lunge [W.424 'lean to one side']

tītara *noun* toast-rack [W.424 'a framework of sticks for supporting bundles of fern root']

tītari māori *noun* normal distribution [tītari TM 'distribution' māori W.179 'normal']

tītaringa *noun* (*statistics*) distribution [tītari W.425 'scatter about, disperse, distribute']

tītere *intransitive verb* (*netball*) shoot [W.425 'throw, cast']

tītere *noun* (*attempted goal*) shot [W.425 'throw, cast']

tītere *noun, adjective* projectile [W.425 'throw, cast']

tītere tautuku *noun* (*netball*) penalty shot [tītere TM 'shoot' tautuku W.405 'stoop, bend down; so give way']

titikura *noun* panacea [W.425 'charm to restore to health, sick or wounded people']

titiro *intransitive verb* (*written material*) refer [W.424 'look into, examine']

tītipu mōkito *noun* (*biology, microorganism*) culture [tipu W.457 'grow' mōkitokito W.207 'minute, small']

tītohu *noun* diploma [W.426 'show, display' tohu mātauranga TM 'qualification']

tītoi *intransitive verb* of male masturbate [W.426 'retract the prepuce']

tītoko *transitive verb* propel [W.426 'propel with a pole']

tīwani *noun* curette [W.427 'strip, make bare, stripped bare']

tīwara *noun* tin-opener, can-opener [W.427 'cleave in twain, split']

tīwera *transitive verb* amplify [tīwerawera W.427 'loud, intense']

tīwerawera *noun* amplifier [W.427 'loud, intense']

tīwēwē *noun* cymbal [W.427 'scream, unrestrained, uncontrolled']

tīwiri *noun* (*building*) screw [tīrau W.423 'peg, stick' wiri W.483 'bore twist' TM 'screwdriver']

tiwha *noun* (*eye*) iris [W.427 'rings of pāua shell inserted in carved work, generally as eyes, spot' titiwha W.427 'show out, gleam']

tīwharawhara *noun, adjective* stereo [W.427 'penetrating, be split, be separated']

tīwharawhara *intransitive verb (chemistry)* precipitate [W.427 'be split, be separated']

tīwhiri *noun* spotlight [W.428 'torch, means of discovering or disclosing something lost or hidden']

tīwhiri *adjective (method of instruction)* Socratic [W.428 'means of discovering or disclosing something lost or hidden']

toa *intransitive verb* win [W.428 'victorious']

toa *noun* winner, medallist [W.428 'brave, victorious']

toa mātāmua *noun* gold medallist [toa W.428 'victorious, brave' mātāmua W.188 'first']

toa mātāmuri *noun* bronze medallist [toa W.428 'victorious, brave' mātāmuri W.188 'last, latter']

toa mātāwaenga *noun* silver medallist [toa W.428 'victorious, brave' waenga W.472 'the middle, the midst']

toa rongoā *noun (shop)* chemist [toa < Eng. 'shop' rongoā W.346 'remedy, medicine']

toanga mātāmuri *noun (sport)* place [toa W.428 'brave, victorious' mātāmuri W.188 'latter']

tōeke *noun* stirrup [W.429 'loop of cord put loosely around the feet to enable them to grasp a tree in climbing']

tōeke *noun (cycling)* strap [W.429 'loop of cord put loosely around the feet to enable them to grasp a tree in climbing']

toenga *noun* remainder [W.429 'remnant']

tohanga *noun (document)* handout [tohatoha W.429 'distribute, disperse']

tohipa *phrase* miss a target [W.430 'pass on one side']

tohitū waka rererangi *noun* hangar [whare tohitū W.430 'a house with a door at the end' waka rererangi common usage 'aeroplane']

tohitū whakanao *noun* factory [whare tohitū W.430 'a house with a door at the end' whakanao TM 'produce']

tohu *noun* symbol [W431 'mark, sign, point out']

tohu *noun (music)* clef [W.431 'mark, sign']

tohu *noun* proof [W.431 'mark, sign, proof']

tohu haere ara *noun* road sign [tohu W.431 'mark, sign' haere W.30 'come, go' ara W.13 'way, path']

tohu huarere *noun* weather forecast [tohu W.431 'point out, show' huarere TM 'weather']

tohu huringa *noun (swimming)* turning line [tohu W.431 'mark, sign' huri W.71 'turn round']

tohu kairangi *noun* doctorate [tohu mātauranga TM 'qualification' kairangi W.89 'finest variety of greenstone, anything held in high estimation']

tohu karere *noun* postal code [tohu W.431 'mark, sign, direct, guide' karere W.100 'messenger']

tohu mātauranga *noun* qualification [tohu W.431 'mark, sign, proof' mātauranga common usage 'knowledge']

tohu orooro *noun (music)* key signature [tohu W.431 'mark sign' oro W.242 'clump, sound']

tohu pātai *noun* question mark [tohu W.431 'mark, sign' pātai W.269 'question, inquire']

tohu paerua *noun* post-graduate degree [tohu mātauranga TM 'degree' pae W.245 'transverse beam' rua W.349 'two']

tohu paetahi *noun* baccalaureate [tohu mātauranga TM 'qualification' pae W.244 'step, bar' tahi W.359 'one, first']

tohu paetahi *noun* undergraduate degree [tohu mātauranga TM 'qualification' pae W.244 'step, bar' tahi W.359 'one, first']

tohu rere *noun (music)* time signature [tohu W.431 'mark, sign' rere W.337 'fly']

tohu tiorea *noun (printing)* circumflex [tohu W.431 'mark' tohutio TM 'acute' tohurea TM 'grave']

tohu waikawa *noun* litmus [tohu W.431 'mark, proof' waikawa TM 'acid']

tohu whakahua kupu *noun (mark indicating correct pronunciation)* accent [tohu W.431 'mark' whakahua W.64 'pronounce' kupu W.157 'word']

tohu-ā-kupu *transitive verb (publication)* index [tohu W.431 'guide, direct' ā W.1 'after the manner of' kupu W.157 'word']

tohuara *noun* street sign [tohu W.431 'mark, sign' ara W.13 'way, path']

tohuhā *noun* exclamation mark [tohu W.431 'mark, sign' hā W.29 'interjection What!']

tohumate *noun* symptom [tohu W.431 'mark, sign' mate W.192 'sickness']

tohunga *noun* expert, *adjective* proficient [W.431 'skilled person']

tohunga huaota noun botanist [tohunga TM 'expert' huaota TM 'botany']

tohunga tikanga tangata noun anthropologist [tohunga TM 'expert' mātauranga tikanga tangata TM 'anthropology']

tohunga wetereo noun linguist [tohunga W.431 'skilled person' wete W.483 'untie, unravel' reo W.336 'language']

tohungarua transitive verb (give out) administer [W.431 'dole out']

tohungatanga noun competence [tohunga W.431 'skilled person']

tohurea noun (punctuation) grave [tohu W.431 'mark' rea W.333 'make a low sound']

tohurehe noun (golf) handicap [tohu W.431 'mark, sign' rehe W.333 'expert, deft person']

tohutaka noun recipe [tohutohu W.431 'direct, guide, instruct, advise' taka W.366 'prepare']

tohutau numeral [tohu W.431 'mark, sign' tau TM 'number']

tohutio noun (punctuation) acute [tohu W.431 'mark' tio W.420 'cry']

tohutoa noun trophy [TM 'medal']

tohutoa noun medal [tohu W.431 'mark, sign, proof' toa W.428 'victorious, brave']

tohutō noun macron [tohu W.431 'mark, sign' tō W.428 'drag']

tohutoro noun (authority source) reference [tohu W.431 'mark, point out, show' toro W.439 'explore, discover, enquire into by divination']

tohutuhi noun punctuation [tohu W.431 'mark, sign' tuhi W.448 'write']

tohutuku noun accreditation [tohu W.431 'mark, sign, proof' tuku W.451 'present']

tohuwehe noun hyphen [tohu W.431 'mark, sign' wehe W.481 'divide']

tōiri noun violin [W.432 'tingle, vibrate, resound']

tōiriiri adjective (emotions) turned-on [W.432 'tingle, vibrate']

tōiriiri adjective excited [W.432 'tingle, vibrate']

toitoi intransitive verb jog [W.432 'move quickly, trot']

toitoi manawa transitive verb motivate [toitoi W.432 'encourage, incite' manawa W.174 'mind, spirit']

toitoi okewa phrase tempt fate [toitoiokewa W.432 'speak beforehand of game etc., one is going to catch, thereby incurring pūhore' pūhore W.305 'unsuccessful in fishing, an omen of ill success in fishing or fowling']

toka kāhuarau noun metamorphic rock [toka W.433 'stone, rock' kāhuarau TM 'metamorphic']

toka ngiha noun igneous rock [toka W.433 'stone, rock' ngiha TM 'igneous']

toka parataiao noun sedimentary rock [toka W.433 'stone, rock' para W.262 'sediment, impurity' taiao TM 'environment']

tokahuke noun ore [toka W.433 'stone, rock' huke W.68 'dig up, expose by removing the earth, excavate']

tōkai-kore adjective (reproduction) asexual [tōkai W.433 'copulate' kore W.140 'no, not']

tokamatua noun quorum [W.433 'body of persons']

tokanga noun (picnic basket) hamper [W.433 'large basket for food']

tokanga mātao noun chilly-bin [tokanga W.433 'large basket for food' mātao W.189 'cold']

tokapū noun corporation [toka W.433 'firm, solid' pū W.300 'root, foundation, base']

tōkarikari transitive verb calibrate [whakatōkarikari W.443 'cut in notches' tōkari TM 'point on scale']

tōkarikari noun calibration [whakatōkarikari W.443 'cut in notches' tōkari TM 'point on scale']

tōkau noun (computer style) plain [W.433 'plain, devoid of ornament']

tōkeke adjective equitable [W.433 'just, impartial']

tokerauhoro adjective deciduous [tokerau W.433 'autumn' rau W.328 'leaf' horo W.60 'drop off']

tōkiri noun (sport) throw-in [W.434 'thrust lengthwise']

tokoiti noun, adjective (group) minority [toko W.434 'prefix used with adjectives of number' iti W.80 'small']

tokomatua noun (workers) gang, workgang [W.434 'company, band of persons']

tokomauri noun orgasm [W.434 'excite one's affections, enamour']

tokorau transitive verb divorce [W.435 'separate, divorce']

tokorau moe *noun* dissolution of marriage [toko rau W.435 'separate, divorce' moe W.204 'marry']

tokorua *adjective (tennis, etc.)* singles [toko W.434 'prefix used with adjectives of number' rua W.349 'two']

tokowhā *adjective (tennis, etc.)* doubles [toko W.434 'prefix used with adjectives of number' whā W.484 'four']

tokowhā tāne, wahine *noun* combined doubles, mixed doubles [tokowhā TM 'doubles' tāne W.377 'male' wahine W.474 'woman']

tomokanga papawaka *noun* carpark entrance [tomokanga W.435 'entrance, gateway' papawaka TM 'carpark']

tonapuku *noun* melanoma [tona W.435 'excrescence, wart, corn, etc.' puku W.308 'swelling, tumour']

tōneke *noun* trolley [tō W.428 'drag, haul' kōneke W.133 'sledge']

tono *intransitive verb (submit application)* apply [W.436 'bid']

tono *noun* claim [W.436 'bid, demand']

tono *noun (contract)* tender [W.436 'bid, command']

tono *noun* application [W.436 'bid']

tono kia uru mai *transitive verb* co-opt [tono W.436 'bid, command' uru W.469 'participate in']

tono rauora *(abbreviation)* S.O.S. [tono W.436 'bid, command' rauora W.330 'save alive']

tongako *noun* eczema [tongako W.436 'be scabbed, fester']

tōngāmimi kakā *noun* cystitis [tōngāmimi W.436 'bladder' kakā TM 'inflammation']

tongari *noun* point on scale [W.436 'notch, nick']

tongi *noun* Braille dot [W.436 'point, speck']

tongi *noun* macula [W.436 'speck']

topa pū *noun (rugby)* centre [topa W.436 'soar, swoop' pū W.300 'centre']

tōpāparu *adjective (traffic loading)* overloaded, overweight [W.437 'deeply laden']

toparua *noun* second five-eighth [topatahi TM 'first five-eighth' rua W.349 'two']

toparua *noun (rugby)* inside centre [topatahi TM 'first five-eighth' rua W.349 'two']

topatahi *noun* first five-eighth [whaka-topatopa W.437 'give commands' topa 'dart, swoop' tahi W.359 'one']

topatahi *noun (rugby)* standoff [whaka-topatopa W.437 'give commands' topa 'dart, swoop' tahi W.359 'one']

topenga *noun* cross-section [tope W.437 'cut, fell' topetope 'cut up, slice, divide']

tōpīpī *noun* baking [W.437 'small native earth oven, cook in a small oven']

tōpito o te ao *noun (points on earth's axis)* pole [W.437 'end, extremity' ao W.11 'world']

tōpito whakararo *noun* north pole [tōpito TM 'pole' W.437 'end, extremity' whakararo TM 'northwards']

tōpito whakarunga *noun* south pole [tōpito TM 'pole' W.437 'end, extremity' whakarunga TM 'southwards']

tōrangapū *noun* politics [tō W.428 'drag, haul' rangapū W.323 'company']

tōrangapū *adjective* political [TM 'politics']

tōraro *adjective (number)* negative [tō W.428 'that of' raro W.327 'the bottom, the underside']

tori hura *noun* ferret [tori W.438 'energetic, busy, bustling' hura W.70 'discover, hunt out']

tori uaroa *noun* weasel [tori W.438 'energetic, busy, bustling' ua W.465 'neck, back of the neck' roa W.344 'long']

tōrino *noun* helix [W.438 'twisted spiral']

toritea *noun* ermine [tori W.438 'energetic, busy, bustling' teatea W.410 'white or light in colour']

toriura *noun* stoat [tori W.438 'energetic, busy, bustling' ura W.468 'brown']

toro teka *noun (game)* dart-throwing [Best Games and Pastimes 62 'dart-throwing']

toroa *noun (golf)* albatross [W.439 'albatross']

torohaki *noun* momentum [W.439 'impel, push, thrust']

torohū *adjective* potential [W.440 'latent']

tōrōkiri *noun* defect, flaw [W.440 'defect, flaw in timber, due to injury to the growing tree']

toromoka *noun* ramrod [W.440 'probe, thrust, with any long instrument']

toropuku *transitive verb* smuggle [W.440 'secret, stealthy']

tōrori *noun* tobacco [W.440 'native-grown tobacco']

tororua *noun (rugby)* double movement

[toro W.438 'stretch forth, extend' rua W.349 'two']

tōrua *noun* duet [W.441 'twofold']

tōrua *adjective* dual [W.441 'twofold']

tōrunga *adjective* (*number*) positive [tō W.428 'that of' runga W.352 'the top, the upper part']

tote *noun* common salt [tote < Eng. 'salt']

toto pōrutu *noun* high blood pressure [toto W.441 'blood' pōrutu W.295 'dashing, surging, of the sea']

toto pūroto *noun* low blood pressure [toto W.441 'blood' pūroto W.314 'sluggish, of a stream']

toto rōnaki *noun* normal blood pressure [toto rōnaki W.346 'steady, gliding easily']

toto tepekore *noun* haemophilia [toto W.441 'blood' tepe W.412 'coagulate' kore W.140 'no, not']

tōtōā *adjective* irresponsible [W.441 'wasteful, use carelessly, disrespectful']

totoka *intransitive verb* solidify [W.433 'become solid, set']

tōtoru *adjective* triple [W.442 'threefold']

toutou kawhe *noun* coffee bag [toutou W.442 'dip into a liquid' kawhe < Eng. 'coffee']

touwhero *noun* baboon [tou W.442 'posterior' whero W.495 'red']

tū upane *noun* double park [tū W.443 'remain' upane W.468 'abreast, in even rank']

tua whāioio *noun* infinity [tua W.444 'the future, the past' whāioia W.485 'very numerous']

tuahiwi *noun* stick figure [tuahiwi W.444 'skeleton']

tūāhua *noun* (*circumstance*) situation [tū W.442 'manner, sort of' āhua W.4 'form, appearance']

tuahuru *noun* orang-utan [W.445 'hairy, shaggy, rough']

tuaiwi *noun* spine [W.445 'backbone']

tuaka *noun* axis [W.445 'midrib of leaf']

tuaka hangarite *noun* axis of symmetry [tuaka TM 'axis' hangarite TM 'symmetry']

tuaka pae x-axis [tuaka W.445 'midrib of leaf' pae W.244 'any transverse beam']

tuaka pou y-axis [tuaka W.445 'midrib of leaf', poupou W.297 'steep, perpendicular, upright']

tūākari *noun* (*tennis etc.*) set [tūāoma W.446 'stage of a journey' kakari W.101 'fight, battle, general engagement']

tuaki *transitive verb* dissect [W.445 'disembowel fish or birds']

tuakiri *noun* (*personal*) identity [W.445 'person, personality']

tuakitanga *noun* dissection [tuaki W.445 'disembowel fish or birds']

tuakoi *noun* hemisphere [W.445 'boundary, division']

tuakoi raki *noun* northern hemisphere [tuakoi W.445 'boundary, division' raki W.322 'north']

tuakoi tonga *noun* southern hemisphere [tuakoi W.445 'boundary, division' tonga W.436 'south']

tuakoi uru *noun* western hemisphere [tuakoi W.445 'boundary, division' uru W.469 'west']

tuakoi whiti *noun* eastern hemisphere [tuakoi W.445 'boundary, division' whiti W.497 'east']

tūāmeke *noun* (*boxing*) round [tūāmoe W.446 'spell of unbroken sleep' tūāoma W.446 'stage of a journey' mekemeke TM 'boxing']

tuanaki *noun* calculus [W.446 'move with an even motion']

tūao *noun* volunteer [W.446 'work for a time or as a volunteer']

tūao *adjective* voluntary [TM 'volunteer']

tua-o-kiri *noun* subcutaneous [tua W.444 'on the farther side' kiri W.119 'skin']

tūao tāwāhi *phrase* volunteer services abroad [tūao TM 'volunteer, voluntary' tāwāhi W.406 'the other side of the sea']

tūāoma *noun* (*athletics*) leg [W.446 'stage of a journey']

tūāpapa *noun* dais, podium [W.446 'platform, foundation']

tūāpapa mekemeke *noun* (*boxing*) ring [tūāpapa W.446 'terrace, platform' meke W.200 'strike with the fist, blow with the fist']

tuarā *noun* (*rugby*) back [tuarā W.226 'back, support, ally']

tuarā matau *noun* (*rugby*) right back [tuarā TM 'back' matau W.192 'right, on the right hand']

tuarā maui *noun* (*rugby*) left back [tuarā TM 'back' maui W.196 'left, on the left hand']

tuarā tumuaki *noun* assistant director [tuarā W.446 'assist, ally, support, back' tumuaki W.454 'head, president']

tuarangi *noun* outer space [tua W.444 'the farther side of' rangi W.323 'heaven, upper regions']

tuari tihirua *noun* bimodal distribution [tuari common usage 'distribute' tihi W.416 'peak' rua W.349 'two']

tuarua *noun* runner-up [tua W.444 'prefix used with numerals to form ordinals' rua W.349 'two']

tuataka tuhi *noun* writing pad [tuataka W.447 'heap, lying in a heap' tuhi W.449 'write']

tuatete *noun* hedgehog [W.447 'furnished with spines']

tuatuku *noun (athletics)* throwing circle [W.447 'let go']

tūāwhiorangi *noun usage (colour)* spectrum [W.448 'rainbow, or perhaps a personification thereof']

tuawhiti *adjective* succulent [W.448 'thick, fleshy, fat, of good quality']

tuha *intransitive verb* ejaculate [W.463 'spit, spit out']

tuhi matapō *noun* Braille [tuhi W.448 'write' matapō W.189 'blind']

tuhi rere *transitive verb (lettering)* write [tuhi W.448 'write' rere W.337 'flow']

tuhi tīpoka *noun* note-taking [tuhi W.448 'write' tīpokapoka W.422 'taking some and leaving some']

tuhi-ā-whakahua *noun* phonetic spelling [tuhi W.448 'write' ā W.1 'after the manner of' whakahua W.64 'pronounce']

tuhinga *noun* document [tuhi W.448 'write']

tuhinga *noun* text [tuhi W.448 'write']

tuhinga whakapā hē *noun (justice)* charge sheet [tuhinga TM 'document' whakapā hē TM 'charge']

tuhinga whakapae *noun* indictment [tuhinga TM 'document' whakapae TM 'accusation']

tūhiti *transitive verb* extradite [W.464 'expel, banish']

tūhoto *noun, transitive verb* solder [W.449 'join']

tui *transitive verb (book)* bind [W.449 'sew, fasten by passing a cord through holes']

tuimāwhai *transitive verb* crochet [tui W.449 'lace, fasten by passing a cord through holes' māwhaiwhai W.198 'spider web']

tuimāwhai *noun* crocheting [tui W.449 'lace, fasten by passing a cord through holes' māwhaiwhai W.198 'spider web']

tuinga *noun (book)* binding [W.449 'sew, fasten by passing a cord through holes']

tuinga *noun* suture [tui W.449 'sew']

tuke *noun* metre [W.450 'a measure of length from one elbow to the fingers of the other extended arm']

tuke haumano *noun* millimetre [tuke TM 'metre' haumano TM 'milli-']

tuke pūtoru *noun* cubic metre [tuke TM 'metre' pūtoru TM 'cubed']

tuki *noun, transitive verb (softball)* bunt [W.450 'butt, knock']

tuki *noun (rugby, league)* hit [W.450 'ram, knock, pound']

tūkino *noun* abuse [W.450 'ill-treat, use with violence, distressed, in trouble']

tukipoto *noun* guerilla warfare [W.450 'sudden attack by a taua']

tukipoto *noun (overthrow)* coup [W.450 'sudden attack by a taua']

tukirae *noun (sport)* header [tuki W.450 'ram, knock' rae W.320 'forehead']

tukirae *noun, transitive verb* headbutt [tuki W.450 'ram, knock' rae W.320 'forehead']

tūkohu *noun (basketball, structure)* basket [W.451 'cylindrical basket']

tuku *transitive verb* relinquish, release, discharge [W.451 'let go, give up']

tuku *transitive verb (hockey, soccer)* pass [W.451 'send, give up']

tuku *transitive verb (lawn bowls)* bowl [W.451 'let go, send']

tuku *noun, transitive verb (rugby, league)* handover [W.451 'let go, give up']

tuku *noun, transitive verb (tennis etc.)* serve [tuku W.451 'send']

tuku *noun (tennis etc.)* service [TM 'serve']

tuku hē *phrase (cricket)* no ball [tuku W.451 'send' hē W.43 'wrong']

tuku kākano *intransitive verb* ovulate *noun* ovulation [tuku W.451 'send' kākano TM 'ovum']

tuku kaku *noun* underarm serve [tuku TM 'serve' kaku W.92 'scoop up']

tuku kōrero ā-kaka *noun* fibre optics [tuku W.451 'send' kōrero 'information' ā W.1 'after the manner of' kaka TM 'fibre']

tuku mātātahi *noun* tie-breaker [W.191 'fight a duel']

tuku mātātahi *noun (contest)* final [W.191 'fight a duel']

tuku mana whakahaere *noun* devolution [tuku W.451 'allow, let, let go, give up' mana W.172 'authority, power' whakahaere TM 'control, manage']

tuku matakana *noun* probation [tuku W.451 'let go, allow' matakana W.187 'wary, watchful, on the lookout']

tuku paetaha *noun (hockey)* push in [tuku W.451 'send' paetaha TM 'sideline']

tuku tēnehi *noun (volleyball)* tennis serve [tuku TM 'serve' tēnehi < Eng. 'tennis']

tuku whakamātau *noun* parole [tuku W.451 'let go, allow' whakamātau W.192 'make trial of, test']

tuku whakarunga *noun* hook serve [tuku TM 'serve' whaka- W.485 'in the direction of' runga W.352 'the top, upwards']

tuku whēkau *noun* organ donation [tuku W.451 'give up, present, offer' whēkau TM 'organ']

tukuata *noun* film projector [tuku W.451 'send' kiriata TM 'film']

tukuoro *noun (electronic audio system)* speaker [tuku W.451 'send, let go' oro W.242 'sound']

tukuperu *adjective* unattractive [W.452 'person of uninviting appearance']

tukupoto *noun (softball)* shortstop [W.452 'hasten, short, the short side of a pā']

tukurua *transitive verb* replicate [W.452 'repeat an operation, do a second time']

tukurua *noun (squash, tennis etc.)* let [W.452 'repeat an operation, do a second time']

tukurua *noun (tennis)* net ball [tukurua W.452 'repeat an operation, do a second time' tuku TM 'serve']

tukutahi *adjective* synchronised [W.452 'together, simultaneous']

tukutahi *adjective (combined)* joint [W.452 'together, simultaneous']

tuma pahū *noun* bomb threat [tuma W.452 'challenge' pahū TM 'bomb']

tūmataiti *adjective* private [tūmatanui W.453 'open, public, without disguise' iti W.80 'small']

tūmatanui *noun* prima facie [W.453 'open, public, without disguise']

tūmatanui *adjective* public [W.453 'open, public, without disguise']

tūmatarau *noun* magic [tūmatapōngia, tūmatawarea W.453 'a charm to render oneself invisible to one's foes' rau W.328 'hundred, multitude']

tūmau *noun (mathematics, set theory)* identity [tūmau 'fixed', constant']

tūmau kano *noun (colour-fixing)* mordant [tūmau W.453 'fixed, constant, permanent' kano W.94 'colour']

tumu *noun* manager [W.454 'main post in the palisading of a pā']

tumu *noun (cricket)* stump [W.453 'stump, stake, field of battle']

tumu *noun (strip of ground)* wicket [W.453 'field of battle']

tumu waipēhi *noun* hydraulic brake [tumu TM 'brake' waipēhi TM 'hydraulic']

tumu whakahaere *noun* board of governors [tumu W.454 'foundation, main post in the palisading of a pā' whakahaere TM 'control']

tumu whakahaere *noun* board of trustees [tumu W.454 'foundation, main post in the palisading of pā, 'whakahaere TM 'control']

tumu whakahaere *noun (employment)* management [tumu W.454 'main post in the palisading of a pā' whakahaere TM 'manage, administer']

tumuaki tuarua *noun* vice-president [tumuaki W.454 'head, president' tua W.444 'prefix used with numerals to form ordinals' rua W.349 'two']

tumuringa *noun* handbrake [tumu W.454 'halt suddenly' ringa W.341 'hand']

tumutumu *noun (stump)* wicket [tumu W.453 'stump, stake, field of battle']

tumuwae *noun* footbrake [tumu W.454 'halt suddenly' wae W.472 'foot']

tūnga pahi *noun* bus stop [tūnga W.443 'circumstance, time etc. of standing' pahi < Eng. 'bus']

tūnga puoto kakīroa *noun (chemistry)* retort stand [tūnga W.443 'circumstance, time etc. of standing' puoto kakīroa TM 'retort']

tūnga tāhapa *noun* angle park [tūnga waka TM 'carpark' tāhapa W.358 'at an acute angle']

tūnga waka *noun* carpark [tūnga W.443 'circumstance, time etc. of standing' waka common usage 'vehicle']

tūnga wakatono *noun* taxi rank [tūnga W.443 'circumstance, time etc. of standing' wakatono TM 'taxi']

tungi *noun* ignition [W.455 'set a light to, kindle']

tuohunga *noun* rest home [W.455 'dwelling place, house']

tūpana *transitive verb* bounce [W.456 'spring up, recoil']

tūpanapana *transitive verb* (*basketball*) dribble [tūpana TM 'bounce']

tūpanapana rua *noun* double dribble [tūpanapana TM 'dribble' rua W.349 'two']

tupe *transitive verb* disarm [W.456 'a charm for depriving one's enemies of power, and arresting their weapons']

tupe *noun* disarmament [W.456 'a charm for depriving one's enemies of power, and arresting their weapons']

tūpeke *noun* (*event*) high jump [W.456 'jump, leap']

tūpiki *noun* handcuffs [W.457 'bind securely']

tūponotanga *noun* (*statistics*) probability [tūpono W.457 'chance to hit']

tūponotanga *noun* (*probability*) odds [tūpono W.457 'chance to hit']

tūpou *noun* (*diving*) pike [W.457 'bow the head, stoop down, fall or throw oneself headlong, dive']

tūraparapa *noun* trampoline [turapa W.458 'spring, rebound, recoil, spring up']

ture *noun* precept [W.459 'law']

ture *noun* (*legal*) justice [W.459 'law']

ture *noun* statute [W.459 'law']

ture *noun* (*legal*) justice system [W.459 'law']

ture *adjective* legal [W.459 'law']

ture ārahi *noun* standing order [ture W.459 'law' ārahi W.14 'lead, conduct']

ture ārahi *noun* regulation [ture W.459 'law' ārahi W.14 'lead, conduct']

ture kāwanatanga *noun* constitutional law [ture W.459 'law' kāwanatanga < Eng 'government']

ture o te ao *noun* international law [ture W.459 'law' ao W.11 'world']

ture tohatoha *noun* (*mathematics*) distributive law [ture W.259 'law' tohatoha W.429 'distribute, disperse']

ture whakatikatika *noun* (*justice*) amendment [ture W.459 'law' whakatika W.417 'correct']

ture-ā-rohe *noun* by-law [ture W.459 'law' ā-rohe TM 'regional']

turi tāmaki *noun* knee-jerk [turi W.459 'knee' tāmaki W.375 'start involuntarily']

tūringa *noun* handstand [tū W.443 'stand, be erect' ringa W.341 'hand']

tūroro *noun* patient [W.460 'sick person']

tūroro noho hōhipera *noun* inpatient [tūroro W.460 'sick person' noho W.223 'remain, stay' hōhipera < Eng. 'hospital']

tūroro noho kāinga *noun* outpatient [tūroro W.460 'sick person' noho W.223 'remain, stay' kāinga W.81 'place of abode']

turuki *adjective* ancillary [W.461 'anything supplementary or by way of support']

turumata *noun* eyedropper [turu W.460 'leak, drip' mata W.185 'eye']

tūtakarerewa *adjective* (*colloquial*) on edge [W.462 'alert, unsettled, apprehensive']

tūtanga *noun* (*property*) equity [W.462 'portion, division']

tūtika *adjective* perpendicular [W.462 'upright']

tūtohi auau *noun* frequency chart [tūtohi W.462 'point out, indicate' auau TM 'frequency']

tūtohi tatau *noun* tally chart [tūtohi W.462 'sign, indication' tatau W.395 'count']

tūtohinga *noun* (*document*) charter [tūtohi W.462 'indication, point out, direct']

tūtoko *noun* (*sport*) pole vault [Best *Games and Pastimes* 20]

tutukai *noun* toss, toss-up [Best *Games and Pastimes* W.117]

tūwaewae *noun* guest [W.463 'visitors, company']

tūwhanga *noun* (*exercise*) split [tūwhangawhanga W.463 'diverging wide apart']

U

ū ki te haora i whakaritea *adjective* punctual [ū W.464 'be firm, be fixed' haora < Eng. 'hour' whakaritea W.343 'arrange']

ua *noun* muscle [uaua W.465 'sinew, strenuous, vigorous']

ua hiki pākoukou *noun* levator scapulae muscle [ua TM 'muscle' hiki W.49 'lift up, raise' pākoukou W.255 'shoulderblade']

ua ihu *noun* nasalis muscle [ua TM 'muscle' ihu W.75 'nose']

ua kaokao *noun* serratus anterior muscle [ua TM 'muscle' kaokao W.94 'ribs, side of the body']

ua karu *noun* orbicularis oculi muscle [ua TM 'muscle' karu W.102 'eye']

ua kati waha *noun* orbicularis oris muscle [ua TM 'muscle' kati W.103 'shut, close up' waha W.473 'mouth']

ua kawiti *noun* brachioradialis muscle [ua TM 'muscle' kawititanga o te ringaringa' W.111 'wrist']

ua kōnui toro *noun* extensor pollicis longus muscle [ua TM 'muscle' kōnui W.134 'thumb', great toe' toro W.438 'stretch forth, extend']

ua kōnui whati *noun* flexor pollicis brevis muscle [ua TM 'muscle' kōnui W.134 'thumb, great toe' whawhati W.491 'bend at an angle, fold']

ua kōtore *noun* gluteus maximus muscle [ua TM 'muscle' kōtore W.150 'buttocks']

ua kumu *noun* gluteus medius muscle [ua TM 'muscle' kumu W.156 'posterior, buttocks']

ua mati whati *noun* flexor digitorum superficialis muscle [ua TM 'muscle' mati W.193 'finger' whawhati W.491 'bend at an angle, fold']

ua matitoro *noun* digitorum muscle [ua TM 'muscle' mati W.193 'finger' toro W.438 'stretch forth, extend']

ua ngaungau *noun* masseter muscle [ua TM 'muscle' ngau W.230 'bite, ngaw']

ua pāpāringa *noun* buccinator muscle [ua TM 'muscle' pāpāringa W.260 'cheek']

ua paemanu *noun* trapezius muscle [ua TM 'muscle' paemanu W.246 'collarbone']

ua pakihiwi *noun* deltoid muscle [ua TM 'muscle' pakihiwi W.254 'shoulder']

ua rae *noun* occipitofrontalis muscle [ua TM 'muscle' rae W.320 'forehead']

ua rahirahinga *noun* temporalis muscle [ua TM 'muscle' rahirahinga W.320 'temple of the head']

ua rara *noun* latissimus dorsi muscle [ua TM 'muscle' rara W.326 'rib']

ua rei *noun* pectoralis major muscle [ua TM 'muscle' rei W.335 'breast, chest']

ua rūrū māhunga *noun* sternocleidomastoid muscle [ua TM 'muscle' rūrū W.349 'wave about' māhunga W.165 'head']

ua takakaha *noun* tibialis anterior muscle [ua TM 'muscle' takakaha W.368 'shinbone']

ua tengi *noun* triceps muscle [ua TM 'muscle' tengi W.412 'three']

ua tōpū *noun* muscular system [ua TM 'muscle tōpū W.437 'assembled, in a body']

ua tuaiwi *noun* erector spinae muscle [ua TM 'muscle' tuaiwi W.445 'back, backbone']

ua tūturi *noun* sartorius muscle [ua TM 'muscle' tūturi W.459 'bend the legs, draw up the knees' turi 'knee']

ua whā *noun* quadriceps muscle [ua TM 'muscle' whā W.484 'four']

uakawa *noun* acid rain [ua W.465 'rain' waikawa TM 'acid']

uapare *transitive verb* pass the blame, shift the blame [W.465 'attribute to another what is charged to oneself']

uapare *noun* (*justice*) denial of liability [W.465 'attribute to another what is charged to oneself']

uara *noun* (*mathematics*) value [W.465 'value']

uara mata *noun* (*mathematics*) face value [uara TM 'value' mata W.185 'face']

uara pū *noun* (*mathematics*) absolute value [uara TM 'value' pū W.300 'base, foundation']

uara tū *noun* place value [uara TM 'value' tū W.443 'stand']

uarua *noun* biceps [ua TM 'muscle' rua W.349 'two']

uarua *noun* raincoat [W.465 'cloak with a cape to it']

uarua kātete *noun* (*anatomy*) leg biceps [uarua TM 'biceps' kātete W.103 'leg']

uatoru *noun* triceps [ua TM 'muscle' toru W.441 'three']

uaua *noun* degree of difficulty [W.465 'difficult']

uehā *noun* axle [W.465 'support']

uepū *noun* caucus [W.465 'company, party']

uhi tīpāta *noun* tea-cosy [uhi W.471 'cover, covering' tīpāta < Eng. 'teapot']

uhikaramea *noun* carrot [uhi W.471 'root crops' karamea W.98 'red ochre']

uhikura *noun* radish [uhi W.471 'root crops' kura W.157 'red, glowing']

uhitea *noun* parsnip [uhi W.471 'root crops' tea W.410 'white, light in colour']

uhono *noun* preposition [W.466 'connected, join']

uiui matewhawhati *noun* inquest [uiui W.466 'inquire for, interrogate' matewhawhati TM 'unexpected death']

ukauka *noun* cash [W.466 'hard']

ukiuki *adjective* (*occupation*) full-time [W.466 'lasting, continuous']

ūkui *transitive verb* erase [W.466 'scour, wipe, efface']

ūkui pepa *noun* paper towel [ūkui W.466 'scour, rub, wipe' pepa < Eng. 'paper']

umanga *noun* (*enterprise*) business [W.467 'pursuit, occupation, business']

umanga *noun* (*commercial enterprise*) company [W.467 'pursuit, occupation, business']

umanga taunaha tāpui limited liability company [umanga TM 'company' taunaha TM 'liability' tāpui W.385 'set aside, reserve']

umaraha kaiao *noun* ecological diversity [umaraha W.467 'extended, wide' kaiao TM 'organism']

umu *noun* oven, stove [W.467 'earth oven']

umu kapuni *noun* gas cooker [umu TM 'stove' kapuni TM 'natural gas']

umu pongipongi *noun* nuclear warfare [W.292 'an incantation and rite to cause death']

unahi *noun* parabola [W.467 'scale of fish etc.']

unu *intransitive verb* (*sport*) retire [W.467 'slip out of a crowd']

ūngutu *noun* (*electricity*) junction [W.468 'place with the ends touching or converging, meet together, converge']

ūngutu *noun* kiss [W.468 'place with the ends touching or converging' ngutu W.236 'lip']

upa *adjective* (*physics, chemistry*) stable [W.468 'fixed, settled, at rest']

upane *noun* (*procedure*) step [W.468 'terrace of a hill']

ūpoko mārō *adjective* pig-headed [idiom ūpoko W.468 'head' mārō 'W.183 'unyielding, headstrong']

ūpoko reta *noun* letterhead [ūpoko W.468 'head, upper part' reta < Eng. 'letter']

upokotaua *noun* head-high tackle [W.468 'surprise attack']

upokotaua *noun* coup d'etat [W.468 'surprise attack']

ura *adjective* reddish-brown [W.468 'red, brown, glowing']

uru *intransitive verb* qualify [W.469 'enter, participate in']

uru matū *noun* chemical family [uru W.469 'grove of trees' matū TM 'chemical']

uru tiwha *noun* toupee [uru W.469 'hair of the head' tiwha W.427 'patch, spot, applied to a bald patch on the head']

uru whakapīwari *noun* wig [uru W.469 'hair of the head' whakapīwari W.285 'bedeck, ornament']
urumaranga *noun* (*rugby*) drop goal [W.470 'surprise in war']
urungi *noun* (*vehicle*) driver [W.470 'steer, steering, paddle, rudder']
urungi *transitive verb* navigator [W.470 'rudder, steering paddle, steer']
urupounamu *noun* general enquiry [W.470 'question']
urupū *adjective* self-disciplined [W.470 'diligent, persevering']
ururua *noun* (*golf*) rough [W.470 'overgrown with bushes, fresh growth, brushwood']
urutā *noun* plague [W.470 'epidemic']
urutapu *noun* virgin forest [W.470 'untouched in a state of nature']
urutapu *adjective* (*unrefined, in natural state*) crude [W.470 'untouched, in a state of nature, chaste, pure']
urutau *intransitive verb* adapt [uru W.469 'enter' tau W.396 'settle down']
urutaunga *noun* adaptation [urutau TM 'adapt']
urutaunga tinana *noun* (*biology*) structural adaptation [urutaunga TM 'adaptation' tinana 'body']
urutaunga whaiaroaro *noun* physiological adaptation [urutaunga TM 'adaptation' whaiaroaro TM 'physiological']
urutaunga whanonga *noun* behavioural adaptation [urutaunga TM 'adaptation' whanonga W.487 'conduct, behaviour']
uruuru *noun* propeller [W.469 'blade of a weapon, urge, hasten']
uruuru *noun* turbine blade [W.469 'blade of a weapon' uru 'enter, reach a place']
uruwhenua *noun* passport [uru W.469 'enter, reach a place, arrive' whenua W.494 'land, country']
uruwhetū *noun* galaxy [W.469 'grove of trees, appear above the horizon' whetū W.496 'star']
uta *noun* (*softball*) home base [W.470 'land, as opposed to the sea or water']
uta *noun* (*softball*) home plate [W.470 'land, as opposed to the sea or water']

utauta *noun* equipment [W.471 'property, accoutrements']
utu *transitive verb* pay [W.471 'return for anything, price']
utu *noun* cost [W.471 'price']
utu *noun* pay [W.471 'return for anything, price']
utu *noun* fee [W.471 'price']
utu āwhina hunga whara *noun* ACC levy [utu W.471 'price' āwhina W.25 'assist' hunga W.70 'people' whara W.489 'be struck, be hit accidentally']
utu karere *noun* postage [utu W.471 'price' karere W.100 'messenger']
utu tāpui *noun* (*finance*) allowance [utu W.471 'reward' tāpui W.385 'set aside, reserve']
utu tōmua *transitive verb* prepay, *noun* prepayment [utu TM 'pay' tōmua W.435 'early']
utu tūturu *noun* historical cost [utu W.471 'price' tūturu W.460 'fixed, permanent']
utu whakahaere *noun* administrative cost [utu W.471 'price' whakahaere TM 'administer']
utu whakamatuatanga *noun* holiday pay [utu TM 'pay' whakamatuatanga TM 'holiday']
utu whakamutu mahi *noun* redundancy payment [utu W.471 'reward, price' whakamutu W.215 'leave off, cause to cease' mahi W.163 'work']
utu whakamutu mahi *noun* severance pay [utu W.471 'reward, price' whakamutu W.215 'leave off, cause to cease' mahi W.163 'work']
utu whakatakoto take *noun* (*justice*) filing fee [utu TM 'cost' whakatakoto W.374 'lay down' take TM 'claim']
utu whakauru *noun* membership fee [utu TM 'fee' whaka- W.486 'causative prefix' to make uru W.469 'associate oneself with, participate in']
utu whakawā *noun* (*justice*) court cost [utu W.471 'price' whakawā TM 'judge']
utukore *adjective* free, gratis [utu W.471 'price' kore W.140 'no, not']
utukore *adjective* (*unpaid*) amateur [utu 'pay' kore 'no']

W

wā *noun* (*time*) period [W.472 'time']

wā kaute *noun* accounting period [wā W.472 'time, interval' mahi kaute TM 'accounting']

wā tāpiri *noun* extra time [wā W.472 'time' tāpiri W.384 'anything added or appended']

wā whara *noun* injury time [wā W.472 'time' whara W.489 'be hit, be struck accidentally']

wae *noun* unit [W.472 'divide, part, portion']

wae hōpara *noun* sightseer [wae W.472 'foot, leg' hōpara TM 'sightseeing']

wae iahiko *noun* ampere [waeine TM 'unit of measurement' ia W.74 'current' hiko common usage 'electricity']

wae kōpere *noun* sprinter [wae W.472 'leg, foot' kōpere TM 'sprint']

wae ngaohiko *noun* volt [wae TM 'unit' ngao W.229 'energy' hiko common usage 'electricity']

wae taipana *noun* (*physics*) newton [wae TM 'unit' taipana TM 'force']

wae tāpoi *noun* tourist [wae W.472 'leg, foot' tāpoi TM 'tourism']

wae tauārai *noun* steeplechaser [wae W.472 'leg, foot' oma tauārai TM 'steeplechase']

wae tūtuki *phrase* leg before wicket [wae W.472 'leg' tūtuki W.450 'strike against an object']

wae whana *noun* kicker [wae W.472 'leg, foot' whana W.486 'kick']

waea ki tawhiti *noun* toll-call [waea < Eng. 'wire' ki W.116 'to' tawhiti W.409 'a distant locality']

waea pūkoro *noun* cellular phone [waea common usage 'phone' pūkoro W.308 'pocket']

waea tuhi *noun* telex [waea < Eng. 'wire' tuhi W.448 'write']

waea whakaahua *noun* facsimile machine [waea common usage 'telephone' whakaahua TM 'picture']

waeine *noun* unit of measurement [wae W.472 'divide, part, portion' ine W.78 'measure']

waeine aro whānui *phrase* standard unit of measurement [waeine TM 'unit of measurement' aro W.16 'turn towards, be inclined, favour' whānui W.487 'broad, wide']

waeine aronga kē non-standard unit of measurement [waeine TM 'unit of measurement' aronga kē TM 'non-standard']

(waeine) mahana C *adjective* Celsius [waeine TM 'unit of measurement' mahana W.162 'warm']

(waeine) mahana F *adjective* Fahrenheit [waeine TM 'unit of measurement' mahana W.162 'warm']

waekape *noun* hooker [wae W.472 'foot' kape W.96 'pick out']

waenga *noun* (*sport*) centre line, half-way line [W.472 'dividing line']

waengero *noun* myriapod [wae W.472 'leg' ngero W.233 'very many']

waepere *noun* flick kick [wae W.474 'foot' pere W.278 'throw an arrow or dart']

waeraka *intransitive verb* hike [wae W.472 'foot' raka W.321 'go, spread abroad, agile, adept']

waerau *noun* (*chemistry*) polymer [wae TM 'unit' rau W.328 'multitude, number']

waerau *adjective* polymeric [wae TM 'unit' rau W.328 'multitude, number']

waerewa *noun (foot)* arch [wae W.172 'foot, the middle' rewa W.339 'elevated, raised up']

waetahi *noun (chemistry)* monomer [wae TM 'unit' tahi W.359 'one, single']

waetea *noun (person)* runner [W.473 'good runner, one strong of foot']

waetea hauroa *noun* long-distance runner [W.473 'good runner, one of strong foot' hauroa W.41 'long']

waetea taitua *noun* middle-distance runner [waetea W.473 'good runner, one strong of foot' taitua W.365 'distant']

waetea taumano *noun* marathon runner [waetea W.473 'good runner, one strong of foot' taumano W.399 'for a long time']

waetohu *noun (work completed towards university qualification)* credit [wae TM 'unit' tohu TM 'degree']

waetoru *noun* tripod [wae W.472 'leg' toru W.441 'three']

waha kōrero *noun (justice)* counsel [waha W.473 'mouth, voice' kōrero W.141 'speak, address']

waha mautohe *noun* protestor [waha W.473 'voice, raise up, carry on the back' mautohe W.198 'oppose persistently']

waha whare tangata *noun* cervix [waha W.473 'mouth, entrance' whare tangata common usage 'womb']

wāhanga *noun* session [TM 'division']

wāhanga *noun (mathematics)* sector [wāhi 'break, split, part, portion']

wāhanga *noun (university)* faculty [TM 'division']

wāhanga *noun (part of larger unit)* division [wāhi W.474 'part, portion']

wāhanga *noun* compartment [wāhi W.474 'part, portion']

wāhanga *noun* section [wāhi W.474 'part, portion']

wāhanga paki *noun* fiction section [wāhanga TM 'section' pakiwaitara W.254 'fiction, folk lore']

wāhanga pakimaero *noun* fiction section [wāhanga TM 'section' pakimaero W.254 'fiction']

wāhanga (pouaka whakaata) *noun* television channel [wāhanga TM 'division' pouaka whakaata common usage 'television']

wāhanga tio *noun* freezer compartment [wāhanga TM 'compartment' whakatio TM 'freeze']

wāhanga tuarua *noun* second half [wāhanga TM 'division' tua W.444 'prefix used with numerals to form ordinals' rua W.349 'two']

wāhanga tuatahi *noun* first half [wāhanga TM 'division' tua W.444 'prefix used with numerals to form ordinals' tahi W.359 'one']

wāhanga whāomoomo *noun* intensive care [wāhanga TM 'unit' whāomoomo W.239 'tend an invalid']

wahapū *noun* reporter [W.473 'eloquent']

wahapū *noun* narrator [waha W.473 'voice' wahapū W.473 'eloquent']

wahapū *adjective* articulate [W.473 'eloquent']

wāhi *noun* segment [W.474 'part, portion']

wāhi tū *noun (sport)* position [wāhi W.474 'place, locality' tū W.443 'stand']

wāhi whakahoki *noun (library)* returns desk [wāhi W.474 'place, locality' whakahoki W.57 'cause to return, give back']

wahine *noun* female gender [W.474 'female']

wāhine kōkiri mana pōti *noun* suffragette movement [wāhine W.474 'women' kōkiri W.130 'rush forward, charge' mana W.172 'authority, control' pōti < Eng. 'vote']

wahine moe tāne *noun* heterosexual woman [wahine W.474 'woman, female' moe W.205 'sleep together' tāne W.377 'male']

wahine moe wahine *noun* homosexual woman, lesbian [wahine W.474 'female' moe W.205 'sleep together' wahine W.474 'female']

wahine takāpui *noun* homosexual woman, lesbian [wahine W.474 'female' takāpui TM 'homosexual']

wāhirutu *noun (judo)* contest area [wāhi W.474 'place, locality' rutu W.353 'dash down, overcome']

wāhituku *noun (library)* issues desk [wāhi W.474 'place, locality' tuku W.451 'allow, let']

wai ewaro *noun* methylated spirits [wai W.474 'water, liquid' ewaro TM 'ethane']

wai hōrū *noun* red ink [wai W.474 'water, liquid' renga hōrū W.336 'fine powder of red ochre used as a pigment']

wai ngārahu *noun* black ink [W.229 'pigment for tattooing']

wai petipeti *noun* (*dessert*) jelly [wai W.474 'water' petipeti W.278 'jellyfish']

wai pukepoto *noun* blue ink [wai W.474 'water, liquid' pukepoto TM 'dark blue']

wai tātari *noun* filtrate [wai W.474 'water, liquid' tātari TM 'filter']

wai tātea *noun* sperm [W.394 'semen']

wai tinana *noun* body fluid [wai W.474 'water' tinana W.419 'body']

waihā *noun* hydroxide [wai W.474 'water' hāora TM 'oxygen']

waihā ewaro *noun* ethanol [waihā TM 'hydroxide' ewaro TM 'ethane']

waihā mewaro *noun* methanol [waihā TM 'hydroxide' mewaro TM 'methane']

waihā pēwaro *noun* pentanol [waihā TM 'hydroxide' pēwaro TM 'pentane']

waihā pōwaro *noun* propanol [waihā TM 'hydroxide' pōwaro TM 'propane']

waihā pūwaro *noun* butanol [waihā TM 'hydroxide' pūwaro TM 'butane']

waihanga *adjective* synthetic [TM 'artificial, man-made']

waihanga *adjective* man-made [waihanga W.485 'make, build, construct']

waihanga *adjective* artificial [waihanga W.485 'make, build, construct']

waihāro *noun* soup [W.38 'a sort of soup made by mixing meal of hīnau berries with water and boiling same']

waiho *intransitive verb* (*computer*) exit [W.475 'let be']

waiho kia tārewa *phrase* adjourned sine die [waiho W.475 'let be' tārewa W.391 'hanging, unsettled']

waiho mō raurangi *intransitive verb* procrastinate [waiho W.475 'let be' raurangi W.330 'another time, another day']

waikahu *noun* amniotic fluid [wai W.474 'water' kahu W.84 'membrane enveloping foetus']

waikanaetanga *noun* equilibrium [W.475 'peace, tranquility']

waikawa *noun* acid [wai W.474 'water liquid' kawa W.109 'bitter, sour, unpleasant to the taste']

waikawa ewaro *noun* ethanoic acid [waikawa TM 'acid' ewaro TM 'ethane']

waikawa marohi *noun* strong acid [waikawa TM 'acid' marohi W.183 'strong']

waikawa mewaro *noun* methanoic acid [waikawa TM 'acid' mewaro TM 'methane']

waikawa ngako *noun* fatty acid [waikawa TM 'acid' ngako TM 'fats']

waikawa ngori *noun* weak acid [waikawa TM 'acid' ngori W.235 'weak, listless']

waikawa pōwaro *noun* propanoic acid [waikawa TM 'acid' pōwaro TM 'propane']

waikawatanga *noun* acidity [waikawa TM 'acid']

waikura *intransitive verb* corrode, *noun* corrosion [W.476 'rust, redden']

waikuruwhatu *noun* whey [wai W.474 'water, liquid' kurukuruwhatu W.159 'curdled, as milk']

wainehu *noun* aerosol [wai W.474 'water, liquid' nehu W.220 'fine powder, dust, spray']

wainene *noun* (*drink*) cordial [W.476 'sweet' wai W.474 'water, liquid']

waipē rēmana *noun* lemon squash [wai W.474 'water, liquid' pēpē W.274 'crushed, mashed' rēmana < Eng. 'lemon']

waipēhi *adjective* hydraulic [wai W.474 'water, liquid' pēhi W.274 'press, weigh down']

waipupuru *noun* yoghurt [waiū pupuru W.315 'curdled milk' pupuru 'thick, stiff, semi-solid']

wairaka *noun* parka [W.476 'a kind of rough rain cloak']

wairākau *noun* compost [W.476 'manure']

wairanu *noun* sauce [W.476 'gravy, juice']

wairanu huamata *noun* salad dressing [wairanu TM 'sauce' huamata TM 'green salad']

wairanu huamata *noun* mayonnaise [wairanu TM 'sauce' huamata TM 'green salad']

wairenga *noun* (*food*) stock [W.477 'gravy or broth from cooked meat']

wairewa *noun* solution [wai W.474 'water, liquid' rewa W.339 'be or become liquid, melt']

wairewa kukū *noun* concentrated solution [wairewa TM 'solution' kukū TM 'concentrate']

wairewa meha *noun* dilute solution

wakatauā

[wairewa TM 'solution' memeha W.200 'weak, pass away']

wairori *noun (bottle-opener)* corkscrew [W.477 'turn round, twist']

wairua auaha *adjective* innovative [wairua W.477 'spirit' auaha W.21 'create, form, fashion, throb, thrill with passion']

wairua kōhuki *noun* mental stress [wairua W.477 'spirit' kōhukihuki TM 'stress']

wairua tōkeke *noun (justice)* equity [wairua W.477 'spirit' tōkeke W.433 'just, impartial']

wairua tuakoi *noun* schizophrenia [wairua W.477 'spirit, unsubstantial image, shadow' tuakoi W.445 'divide, separate, misconceive, imagine, be deceived']

wairua tuakoi *noun, adjective* schizophrenic [TM 'schizophrenia']

wairuatoa *noun* loser [W.477 'unlucky']

waitara *noun* difficult task [W.477 'project or scheme of a fanciful or difficult nature']

waitara *noun* pipedream [W.477 'project or scheme of a fanciful or difficult nature']

waitī *noun* glucose [W.477 'sweet, sweet sap of tī']

waitinana *noun* lymph [wai W.474 'water, liquid' tinana W.419 'body']

waitohu *noun, transitive verb* brand [W.477 'mark, signify, indicate']

waitohu *noun* ranking [W.477 'mark, signify, indicate']

waitohu *noun* signature [W.477 'mark, signify, indicate']

waitohu *noun* prognosis [W.477 'prognosticate']

waitohu *noun* logo [W.477 'mark, signify, indicate']

waiū pupuru *noun* junket [W.315 'curdled milk' pupuru W.315 'thick, stiff, semi-solid']

waiwaro *noun* hydrocarbon [wai W.474 'water' waro TM 'carbon']

waiwaro rua *noun* alkene [waiwaro TM 'hydrocarbon' rua W.349 'two']

waiwaro tahi *noun* alkane [waiwaro TM 'hydrocarbon' tahi W.359 'one']

waiwaro toru *noun* alkyne [waiwaro TM 'hydrocarbon' toru W.441 'three']

waka kōpiko *noun* ferry [waka common usage 'boat' kōpiko W.137 'go alternately in opposite directions']

waka kōpiko *noun (vehicle)* shuttle [waka common usage 'vehicle' kōpiko W.137 'go alternately in opposite directions']

waka kōpiko tuarangi *noun* space shuttle [waka kōpiko TM 'shuttle' tuarangi TM 'outer space']

waka rereangi *noun* hang-glider [waka rererangi common usage 'aeroplane' rere W.337 'fly' angi W.11 'move freely, float']

waka ruarangi *noun (aviation)* jumbo [waka rererangi common usage 'aeroplane' ruarangi W.350 'large, robust']

waka tauihi *noun* glider [waka rererangi common usage 'aeroplane' tauihi W.398 'glide in the air, soar']

waka tautō *noun* cable car [waka common usage 'vehicle' tautō W.404 'drag']

waka topaki *noun* hovercraft [waka common usage 'vehicle' topaki W.437 'hover, as a bird']

waka tuarangi *noun* spacecraft [waka rererangi common usage 'aeroplane' tuarangi TM 'outer space']

waka tukituki *noun* stock car [waka common usage 'vehicle' tukituki W.450 'demolish, knock to pieces, batter, dash']

waka tūroro *noun* ambulance [waka common usage 'vehicle' tūroro W.460 'sick person']

waka whakatakere *noun (vessel)* submarine [waka common usage 'boat' whakatakere W.371 'bottom of a channel or of deep water, bed of a river']

wakahiki *noun (machine)* crane [waka common usage 'vehicle' hiki W.49 'lift up, raise']

wakapana *noun* bulldozer [waka common usage 'vehicle' pana W.256 'drive away, expel']

wakapū *noun* alphabet [waka W.478 'canoe' wakawaka 'row' pū TM 'letter of alphabet']

wakareretai *noun* seaplane [waka rererangi common usage 'aeroplane' tai W.361 'the sea']

wakatauā *noun* naval ship [waka common usage 'boat' tauā W.397 'hostile expedition, army']

wakatauā *noun* frigate [waka W.478 'canoe in general' tauā W.397 'hostile expedition, army']

wakatauā *noun* warship [waka W.478 'canoe in general' tauā W.397 'hostile expedition, army']

wakatauā karihi *noun* nuclear-armed ship [wakatauā TM 'naval ship' karihi TM 'nuclear']

wakatauā whakatakere *noun* submarine warship [wakatauā TM 'frigate' whakatakere W.371 'bottom of a channel or of deep water, bed of a river']

wakatō *noun* tugboat [waka W.478 'canoe in general' tō W.428 'drag, haul']

wakatono *noun* taxi [waka common usage 'vehicle' tono W.436 'bid, command']

wakuwaku *noun* friction [waku W.478 'rub, scrape, abrade']

wara waipiro *noun* alcoholic (person) [waranga TM 'addiction' waipiro common usage 'alcohol']

wara waipiro *noun* alcoholism [waranga TM 'addiction' waipiro common usage 'alcohol']

waranga *noun* addiction, habit [W.479 warawara 'crave, craving, ravenous']

warawara (ki) *adjective* addicted [TM 'addiction']

-waro (*used as suffix*) alkane [waiwaro TM 'hydrocarbon']

waro *noun* carbon [W.480 'charcoal']

waro *noun* mine [W.480 'deep hole or pit, abyss']

warowaihā *noun* carbohydrate [waro TM 'carbon' wai W.474 'water' hāora TM 'oxygen']

waruoro *noun* octave [waru W.480 'eight' orotahi TM 'note']

wātaka *noun* timetable [wā W.472 'time' taka W.366 'come round, as a date or period of time']

wātea *adjective* available [W.480 'unoccupied, free']

wati tumu *noun* stop watch [wati < Eng. 'watch' tumu W.454 'halt suddenly']

wauwau *noun* mattock [W.480 'a pole used to loosen the earth for making earthworks, cultivation etc.']

wāwāhi *noun* spanner [W.473 'split, lay open']

wāwāhi *noun* wrench [W.473 'break, split']

wāwāhi tikanga *adjective* radical [wāwāhi W.473 'break, split, break open' tikanga W.416 'anything normal or usual, rule, plan']

wāwaro *noun* octane [waru W.480 'eight' waro TM 'alkane']

wē waewae *phrase* (*hockey*) between feet [wē W.481 'the middle, the midst' waewae W.472 'foot']

wēanga *noun* (*statistics*) central tendency [wē W.481 'the middle' anga W.10 'move in a certain direction']

wēanga *noun* centre [wē W.481 'the middle']

wehe *adjective* (*marital status*) separated [W.481 'detach, divide']

wehe whārangi *noun* (*word-processing*) page break [wehe W.481 'detach, divide' whārangi W.489 'page of a book']

weherua *transitive verb* bisect [weherua W.481 'divided']

weherua *noun* diameter [W.481 'dividing, separating, midnight']

weherua tapatoru *noun* (*triangle*) median [weherua TM 'bisect' tapatoru TM 'triangle']

weheruatanga ao *adjective* equatorial [weherua W.481 'dividing, separating' weherua pō W.481 'midnight' ao W.11 'world']

weheruatanga o te ao *noun* equator [weherua W.481 'dividing, separating' weherua pō W.481 'midnight' ao W.11 'world']

wehewehe *transitive verb* differentiate [W.481 'sort out, arrange']

weku *adjective* tuft [wekuweku W.481 'tufted, in tufts']

weritai *noun* bristleworm [weriweri W.482 'centipede' tai W.361 coast, sea']

wero *transitive verb* inject, *noun* injection [W.482 'pierce, spear, sting of an insect']

weropepa *noun* hole punch [wero W.482 'pierce' pepa < Eng. 'paper']

weru hunahuna *noun* camouflage clothing [weru W.482 'garment' hunahuna W.69 'concealed, seldom seen']

wete hihi *noun* spectroscope [wete W.483 'untie, unravel' hihi W.48 'ray']

wetekupu *noun* morphology [wete W.483 'untie, unravel' kupu W.157 'word']

wetenga *noun* morpheme [wete W.483 'untie, unravel']

weteoro *noun* phonology [wete W.483 'untie, unravel' oro TM 'phoneme']

wetereo *noun* syntax [TM 'grammar']

wetereo *noun* grammar [wete W.483 'untie, unravel' reo W.336 'language']

wetonoa switch off automatically [weto

W.483 'be extinguished' noa W.222 'spontaneously']

wētoto *noun* (*medicine*) plasma [wē W.481 'water, liquid' toto W.441 'blood']

wī *noun* (*cricket*) crease [TM 'line' see W.284 piro 'out, in games']

wī *noun* (*sport, athletics etc.*) line [Best Games and Pastimes 165 'a circle marked on the ground around which players stand']

wī epa *noun* (*cricket*) bowling crease [wī TM 'crease' epa TM 'bowl']

wī hoki *noun* return crease [wī TM 'crease' hoki W.57 'return']

wī ngapunga *noun* starting-line ['Best Games and Pastimes 165 'a circle marked on the ground around which players stand' ngapunga TM 'starting-gate']

wī tarapeke *noun* popping crease [wī TM 'crease' tarapeke W.388 'spring, leap, jump']

wī tuatuku *noun* (*athletics*) throwing arc [wī TM 'line' tuatuku W.447 'let go']

wiri *noun* screwdriver [W.483 'bore, twist, gimlet']

Wh

whāhauhau *noun* air-conditioning [whā W.484 'causative prefix' hauhau W.38 'cool']

whai mātauranga *transitive verb* (*learn*) study [whai W.484 'follow, pursue, go in search of' mātauranga common usage 'knowledge']

whai tikanga *adjective* formal [whai W.484 'possessing, acquiring the shape or character of' tikanga W.417 'correct, right']

whaiaro *adjective* personal [W.485 'self, person']

whaiaroaro *noun* physiology, *adjective* physiological [W.485 'self, person']

whaihanga *transitive verb* simulate, *noun* simulation [W.485 'make, construct, busy oneself with, manipulate']

whaihua *adjective* beneficial [whai W.484 'possessing, equipped with' huanga W.64 'advantage, benefit']

whaihua *adjective* useful [whai W.484 'possessing, equipped with' huanga W.64 'advantage, benefit']

whaihua *adjective* worthwhile [whai W.484 'possessing, equipped with' huanga W.64 'advantage, benefit']

whaihua *adjective* informative [whai W.484 'possessing, equipped with' huanga W.64 'advantage, benefit']

whaikano *adjective* (*paper*, *etc.*) coloured [whai W.484 'possessing, equipped with' kano W.94 'colour']

whaimana *adjective* (*law*) valid [whai W.484 'possessing, equipped with' mana W.172 'authority, power, influence']

whāinga *noun* (*objective*) goal, objective, purpose, aim [whai W.484 'follow, pursue, aim at']

whāinga poto *noun* short-term objective [whāinga TM 'objective' poto W.297 'short']

whāinga roa *noun* long-term objective [whāinga TM 'objective' roa W.344 'long']

whaipua *noun* angiosperm [whai W.483 'possessing' pua W.301 'flower']

whaitake *adjective* valid [whai W.484 'possessing, equipped with' take W.370 'well founded, firm lasting']

whaitua *noun* (*sport*) outfield [W.485 'region, space']

whaitua *noun* (*building*) block [W.485 'region, space']

whaitua hāparapara *noun* surgical block [whaitua TM 'block' hāparapara TM 'to perform surgery']

whaitua inuinu *noun* (*hotel*) saloon [whaitua W.485 'space' inuinu W.78 'drink frequently']

whaitua matau *noun* right outfield [W.485 'side, region, space' matau W.192 'right, on the right hand']

whaitua mauī *noun* left outfield [whaitua W.485 'side, region, space' mauī W.196 'left, on the left hand']

whaitua noho *noun* apartment block [whaitua W.485 'region, space' noho W.223 'dwell']

whaitua whakawai *noun* (*practice area*) range [whaitua W.485 'region, space' whakawai TM 'practise']

whaiutu *noun*, *adjective* professional [whai W.484 'possessing, equipped with' utu TM 'pay']

whaiwhai-ā-kapa *noun* team pursuit [whaiwhai W.484 'chase, hunt' ā W.1 'after the manner of' kapa TM 'team']

whakaae-ā-tuhi *noun* written consent [whakaae W.2 'consent' ā-tuhi TM 'written']

whakaahua *transitive verb* photocopy [W.4 'acquire form']

whakaahua *transitive verb* delineate, describe [W.4 'acquire form']

whakaahua *noun* picture, photograph, diagram [W.4 'acquire form']

whakaahua *noun* (*photography*) shot [TM 'picture']

whakaahua hiko-manawa *noun* electrocardiogram [whakaahua 'picture' iahiko TM 'electrical current' manawa W.174 'heart']

whakaahua huinga *noun* Venn diagram [whakaahua TM 'picture' huinga TM 'set']

whakaahua karihika *noun* pornographic picture [whakaahua TM 'picture' karihika W.101 'lewd, immoral, copulation']

whakaako *transitive verb* coach [W.7 'teach']

whakaako *transitive verb* educate [W.7 'teach']

whakaakoranga *noun* doctrine [whakaako W.7 'teach']

whakaara wairua auaha *noun* creative therapy [whakaara W.13 'raise, rouse, wake' wairua W.477 'spirit' auaha TM 'creative']

whakaari *noun* (*theatre*) play, drama [W.15 'show, expose to view']

whakaari ataata *noun* video programme [whakaari W.15 'show, expose to view' ataata TM 'video']

whakaari paki *noun* (*theatre*) sketch [whakaari TM 'play' paki W.253 'tales']

whakaari pūoru *noun* opera [whakaari TM'drama' pūoru TM 'music']

whakaata *transitive verb* (*mathematics*) reflect [W.18 'reflect, as water']

whakaata *noun* (*mathematics*) reflection [W.18 'reflection']

whakaata *noun* mirror [W.18 'reflect, as water']

whakaata aorangi *noun* (*device*) planetarium [whakaata W.18 'reflect, simulate by gesture, pretend' aorangi TM 'planet']

whakaata hakoko *noun* concave mirror [whakaata TM 'mirror' hakoko W.32 'concave']

whakaata koropuku *noun* convex mirror [whakaata TM 'mirror' koropuku W.145 'convex']

whakaata muri *noun* rear mirror [whakaata TM 'mirror' muri W.214 'the rear']

whakaata nekehanga *noun* (*mathematics*) glide reflection [whakaata TM 'reflect' nekehanga TM 'translation']

whakaata roto *noun, transitive verb* x-ray [whakaata W.18 'reflect, look, peer into' roto W.348 'the inside']

whakaata ū *noun* mammogram [whakaata roto TM 'x-ray' ū W.464 'breast']

whakaatu *transitive verb* display [W.40 'point out, show']

whakaatu *transitive verb* (*clothing*) model [whakaatu W.20 'call attention to, show']

whakaatu pāpāho media coverage [whakaatu W.20 'point out, show, call attention to' pāpāho TM 'media']

whakaatu tōrua *noun* (*ice skating etc.*) duet routine [whakaatu TM 'display' tōrua TM 'duet']

whakaaturanga *noun* television programme [whakaatu W.20 'point out, show, call attention to']

whakaaturanga *noun* display [whakaatu W.40 'point out, show']

whakaauraki *transitive verb* rehabilitate [whaka- W.486 'causative prefix' *to make* auraki W.22 'turn aside, return']

whakaauraki *noun* rehabilitation [TM 'rehabilitate']

whakaauraki whanonga *noun* behaviour modification [whaka- W.486 'causative prefix' *to make* auraki W.22 'turn aside' whanonga W.487 'behaviour, conduct']

whakaawhiwhi *transitive verb* (*mathematics*) round [whaka- W.486 'causative prefix' *to make* āwhiwhi W.25 'near, approximate']

whakaawhiwhitanga *noun* approximation [whaka- W.486 'causative prefix' *to make* āwhiwhi W.25 'approximate, resemble']

whakaehu *transitive verb* emulsify, *noun* emulsifier [W.26 'disperse']

whakahā *intransitive verb* respire [W.29 'breathe, emit breath']

whakahā *intransitive verb* (*breathe out*) expire [W.29 'emit breath']

whakahaere *transitive verb* (*manage*) administer [W.30 'conduct any business']

whakahaere *transitive verb* (*manage*) control [W.30 'conduct, lead']

whakahaere *noun* (*institution*) organisation [W.30 'conduct any business, execute']

whakahanumi *noun* (*kitchen appliance*) blender [W.34 'mix, cause to be swallowed up']

whakahanumi *transitive verb* homogenise [W.34 'mix, cause to be swallowed up']

whakahāngai *transitive verb* (*make relevant*) apply [whaka- W.486 'causative prefix' *to make* hāngai TM 'relevant']

whakaharahara *adjective* (*extraordinary occurrence*) phenomenal [W.36 'extraordinary, marvellous']

whakaharatau *intransitive verb* rehearse [W.37 'practise, acquire dexterity']

whakahau *noun* (*grammar*) imperative [W.38 'command, order, direct']

whakahaumako *noun* (*horticultural*) fertiliser [whaka- W.486 'causative prefix' *to make* haumako W.40 'rich, fertile']

whakahiato *transitive verb* (*formulate*) develop [W.48 'collect together']

whakahiato *transitive verb* (*idea, policy*) formulate [W.48 'collect together, reduce in size']

whakahiato *transitive verb* aggregate [W.48 'collect together']

whakahiku *noun* sequel [W.50 'to follow on']

whakahirihiri *noun* (*sport*) reserve [W.53 'assist, relieve']

whakahirihiri *noun* (*basketball*) substitute [W.53 'assist, relieve']

whakahoe *transitive verb* repel [W.55 'wave the hand in token of refusal, etc., reject']

whakahoho *noun* fire alarm [W.55 'a sort of trill to call attention']

whakahoki *transitive verb* repeat [W.57 'turn back, cause to return']

whakahōtaetae *noun* injunction [W.62 'prevent, obstruct']

whakahou *noun* renew [whaka- W.486 'causative prefix' *to make* hou W.62 'new, recent, fresh']

whakahou tikanga pūtea *noun* financial reform [whaka- W.486 'causative prefix' *to make* hou W.62 'new' tikanga W.416 'plan, method' pūtea TM 'financial']

whakaineine *transitive verb* spreadeagle [W.78 'extend']

whakaipurangi *noun* resource centre [W.79 'head or source of a stream, small storehouse on a single post']

whakaipurangi rongoā *noun* (*dispensary*) pharmacy [whakaipurangi W.79 'a small storehouse on a single post, head or source of a stream' rongoā W.346 'remedy, medicine']

whakairoiro *noun* graphics [W.80 'ornamented']

whakakā *noun* (*electrical*) switch [whaka- W.486 'causative prefix' *to make* kā W.81 'take fire, be lighted, burn']

whakakā *transitive verb* (*machinery etc.*) turn on [TM 'switch on']

whakakā *transitive verb* switch on [whaka- W.486 'causative prefix' *to make* kā W.81 'take fire, be lighted, burn']

whakakakapa manawa *noun, adjective* (*aerobics*) cardio routine [whaka- W.486 'causative prefix' *to make* kakapa W.95 'throb, palpitate' manawa W.174 'heart']

whakakaurapa *transitive verb* disable [W.108 'put out of action, unable to swim, cramp in the legs']

whakakēkerewai *noun* local anaesthetic [whaka- W.486 'causative prefix' *to make* kēkerewai W.114 'numb, numbness']

whakakeko pū *noun* marksman [W.113 'take aim']

whakakeko pū *noun* markswoman [W.113 'take aim']

whakakikorua *transitive verb* pluralize [whaka- W.486 'causative prefix' *to make* kikorua TM 'plural']

whakakoi māripi *noun* knife-sharpener [whakakoi W.127 'sharpen' māripi W.182 'knife']

whakakoi pene *noun* pencil-sharpener [whaka- W.486 'causative prefix' *to make* koi W.127 'sharp' pene < Eng. 'pen']

whakakōkī *noun* (*chemistry*) catalyst [whaka- W.486 'causative prefix' *to make* kōkīkī W.130 'fast']

whakakōmau *noun* muffler [W.132 'repress, stifle']

whakakopa *noun* clamp [W.135 'clasp, clutch']

whakakopa pūaho *noun* (*science*) bulb holder [whakakopa W.135 'clasp, clutch' pūaho TM 'bulb']

whakakore *transitive verb* cancel [W.141 'cause not to be']

whakakore *transitive verb* (*computer*) undo [W.141 'cause not to be']

whakakukū *transitive verb* (*substance*)

whakamaroke makawe

concentrate [whaka- W.486 'causative prefix' to make kukū TM 'concentrate']

whakakurepe noun (building) extension [W.159 'extend']

whakamāhunga noun, intransitive verb experiment [W.165 'make trial of a new crop']

whakamāhunga noun dummy-run [W.165 'make trial of a new crop']

whakamāmore whenua noun deafforestation [whaka- W.486 'causative prefix' to make māmore W.172 'without accompaniments or appendages, bare' whenua W.494 'land, country']

whakamāngina noun cannabis, marijuana [W.178 'floating, fleeting, unreliable']

whakamāori transitive verb translate [W.179 'explain, elucidate'] e.g. whakamāori(hia) ki te reo Wīwī 'translate into French'

whakamāori-ā-kupu noun literal translation [whakamāori TM 'translation' ā W.1 'after the manner of' kupu W.157 'word']

whakamāori-ā-wairua noun free translation [whakamāori TM 'translation' ā W.1 'after the manner of' wairua W.477 'spirit']

whakamārama transitive verb account for [W.180 'make clear, explain']

whakamārama noun justify [whakamārama W.180 'illuminate, explain'] e.g. Tēnā whakamārama mai he aha i pau ai tērā nui o te moni. 'Justify spending that amount of money.'

whakamārama transitive verb describe [W.180 'illuminate, explain']

whakamārō poho noun, adjective (exercise) press-up [whakamārō W.183 'extend, stretch' mārōrō W.183 'strong, sturdy' poho W.287 'chest']

whakamātau intransitive verb, noun experiment [W.192 'make to know, make trial of']

whakamātautau tahua tāpiri noun bursary examination [whakamātautau common usage 'examination' tahua tauira tāpiri TM 'bursary']

whakamātau tika noun (science) fair test [whakamātautau W.192 'test' tika W.417 'correct, straight, right']

whakamātau whakatina noun control experiment [whakamātau TM 'experiment' whakatina W.419 'confine, put under restraint']

whakamahana noun (appliance) heater [W.162 'warm']

whakamahana noun (heating device) radiator [W.162 'warm']

whakamahine transitive verb (wood etc.) sand [W.164 'make smooth, polish']

whakamahiri noun assistant [W.164 'assist']

whakamahuki transitive verb simplify [whakamahuki W.165 'explain' mahuki 'clear, plain']

whakamahuru transitive verb pacify [W.165 'appease, soothe']

whakamakaka intransitive verb (exercise) warm down [W.168 'bend the body and stretch oneself to relieve the muscles when weary']

whakamakoha transitive verb inflate [W.170 'cause to expand']

whakamamae noun (birth) labour [W.162 'feel pain']

whakamana transitive verb confirm [W.172 'give effect to']

whakamana noun warrant [W.172 'give effect to, make effective']

whakamana haurapa noun search warrant [whakamana TM warrant' haurapa W.41 'search diligently for']

whakamana herepū rawa noun warrant to seize property [whakamana TM 'warrant' herepū W.46 'seize, catch and hold firmly' rawa W.331 'goods, property']

whakamana hopu tangata noun arrest warrant [whakamana TM 'warrant' hopu W.59 'catch, seize' tangata W.379 'human being']

whakamana mau herehere noun committal warrant [whakamana TM 'warrant' mau herehere TM 'imprison']

whakamana waka noun warrant of fitness [whakamana TM 'warrant' waka common usage 'vehicle']

whakamana wehenga noun separation order [whakamana W.172 'give effect to, make effective' wehe TM 'separated']

whakamaroke noun dehydrator [whakamaroke W.183 'cause to wither']

whakamaroke makawe noun hair-dryer [whaka- W.486 'causative prefix' to make maroke W.183 'dry' makawe W.169 'hair']

whakamatara *transitive verb (problem)* solve [W.190 'unravel, loosen, undo']

whakamatuatanga *noun (sport etc.)* half time [W.195 'rest, pause, after an effort']

whakamatuatanga *noun* holiday [whakamatua W.195 'rest, pause after an effort']

whakamatuatanga-ā-tau *noun* annual leave [whakamatua W.195 'rest, pause, after an effort' ā-tau TM 'annual']

whakamemeke *noun* poliomyelitis [W.200 'wasting, shrivelling of the limbs']

whakamohiki *noun, transitive verb (volleyball)* set [whaka- W.486 'causative prefix' *to make* mohiki W.205 'raised up, lifted up']

whakamōhinu *transitive verb* varnish [whaka- W.486 'causative prefix' *to make* mōhinuhinu W.205 'shiny, glistening, glossy']

whakamōhio *transitive verb (direct)* refer [whaka- W.486 'causative prefix' *to make* mōhio W.205 'know, recognise']

whakamōhou kiri *noun* plastic surgery [whakamōhou W.206 'renew' mohou 'fresh, new' kiri W.119 'skin']

whakamua *adjective, adverb (direction)* forward [whaka- W.485 'in the direction of' mua W.213 'the front']

whakamua *adverb* forwards [whaka- W.485 'towards, in the direction of' mua W.213 'the front, the fore part']

whakamuri *adverb* backwards [whaka- W.485 'towards, in the direction of' muri W.214 'the rear, the hind part']

whakamutu *transitive verb* quit [W.215 'leave off, cause to cease']

whakamutunga *adjective* last [W.215 'concluding']

whakanā *noun (sport)* bye [W.216 'rest, remain still']

whakanako *noun, adjective* cosmetic [W.217 'adorn with fine markings']

whakanao *transitive verb (coinage)* mint [TM 'produce']

whakanao *transitive verb* manufacture [W.218 'make, manipulate, operate on']

whakanao *transitive verb* produce [W.218 'make, manipulate, operate on']

whakangā *noun (breathe)* inspiration [W.225 'take breathe']

whakangaku pepa *noun* paper-shredder [whaka- W.486 'causative prefix' *to make* ngakungaku W.228 'reduced to shreds' pepa < Eng. 'paper']

whakangā-riro *intransitive verb (work)* retire [W.225 'take breath' riro W.343 'intensive']

whakangotangota *noun* nuclear fission [whaka- W.486 'causative prefix' *to make* ngota W.235 'fragment, particle' TM 'atom' ngotangota W.235 'smashed to atoms']

whakangote *noun* lactation [W.235 'suckle, cause to suck']

whakangote *noun* mammal [W.235 'suckle, cause to suck']

whakangungu *transitive verb (teach)* train [W.236 'defend, protect, parry, shield']

whakangungu *noun* training [W.236 'defend, protect, parry, shield']

whakaoho *transitive verb (computer)* start up [W.238 'startle, rouse']

whakaora *noun* resuscitate [W.241 'save alive']

whakaora manawa *noun* cardiopulmonary resuscitation CPR [whakaora W.241 'save alive, restore to health' manawa W.174 'heart']

whakaora whawhati tata *noun* first aid [whakaora W.241 'save alive, restore to health' mate whawhati tata TM 'emergency']

whakaoti *transitive verb (mathematics)* solve [W.242 'finish']

whakapā *intransitive verb (person)* refer [W.243 'cause to touch']

whakapā hē *noun (justice)* charge [W.243 'accuse, bring a charge of wrongdoing against anyone']

whakapā tinana *noun (sport)* physical contact [whakapā W.243 'cause to touch, touch' tinana W.419 'body']

whakapae *transitive verb (put forward an idea)* contend, hypothesise [W.245 'make an accusation']

whakapae *intransitive verb* suspect [W.245 'accuse, make an accusation']

whakapae *noun* hypothesis [TM 'contend']

whakapae *noun (justice)* complaint [W.245 'accuse, make an accusation']

whakapāhare *transitive verb (chemistry)* neutralise [whaka- W.486 'causative prefix' *to make* pāhare TM 'salt']

whakapahoho *noun (of people)* inertia [W.248 'remain listless and inactive']

whakapahoho *adjective* stationary [W.248 'remain listless and inactive']

whakapahuhu *transitive verb* sue [W.248 'use charms to induce shame in an ill-doer']

whakapahū *transitive verb* detonate [whaka- W.486 'causative prefix' *to make* pahū TM 'explosive']

whakapahūnga *noun* detonation [whaka- pahū TM 'detonate']

whakapai ake *transitive verb* improve [W.249 'make good, set in order' ake W.7 'upwards']

whakapai ake *transitive verb* revise [whakapai W.249 'make good, set in order' ake W.6 'intensifying the force']

whakapai whare *noun* house cleaning [whakapai W.249 'make good, set in order' whare W.489 'house']

whakapākeka *transitive verb* (*earth*) leach [whaka- W.486 'causative prefix' *to make* pākeka W.252 'land that has been exhausted by cultivation']

whakapapa *transitive verb* give a history *phrase* [W.259 'recite in proper order genealogies, legends etc.']

whakaparuhi *noun* godparent [whaka- W.486 'causative prefix' *to make* paruhi W.269 'favourite, darling']

whakapati *noun* bribe [W.271 'induce by means of gifts']

whakapau kaha *intransitive verb* (*effort*) give one's all [whakapau W.273 'exhaust' kaha W.82 'strength']

whakapaunga *noun* expenditure [whaka- W.486 'causative prefix' *to make* pau W.273 'consumed, exhausted']

whakapeto *noun* (*ecology*) consumer [whaka- W.486 'causative prefix' *to make* peto W.278 'be consumed']

whakapiere *noun* fission [whaka- W.486 'causative prefix' *to make* piere W.279 'fissure, crack, chink']

whakapineke *transitive verb* compress [whaka- W.486 'causative prefix' *to make* pineke W.281 'compressed']

whakapohewa *noun* hallucinogen [whaka- W.486 'causative prefix' *to make* pohewa W.287 'mistaken, confused, imagine']

whakapōauau *noun* (*narcotic*) drug, narcotic [whaka- W.486 'causative prefix' *to make* pōauau W.286 'mistaken, confused']

whakapongi *noun* (*cooling device*) radiator [whaka- W.486 'causative prefix' *to make* pongi W.292 'cool']

whakapopo *transitive verb* break down, decompose [whaka- W.486 'causative prefix' *to make* popo W.292 'rotten, decayed, worm-eaten']

whakapopo *noun* decomposer [whaka- W.486 'causative prefix' *to make* popo W.292 'rotten, decayed, worm-eaten']

whakapuango *noun* crash diet [W.302 'starve']

whakapuango *noun* hunger strike [W.302 'starve']

whakapuru waha *noun* mouth guard [whakapuru W.314 'cram, protect with a pad' waha W.473 'mouth']

whakaputa *transitive verb* publish [W.316 'cause to come forth']

whakaputa uri *intransitive verb* (*biology*) reproduce [whakaputa W.316 'cause to come forth' uri W.469 'offpring']

whakaputa uri *noun* (*biology*) reproduction [TM 'reproduce']

whakapūhoi *intransitive verb* (*gear*) change down [whaka- W.486 'causative prefix' *to make* pūhoi W.305 'slow']

whakapūioio puku *noun* (*sport*) abdominal exercise [whaka- W.486 'causative prefix' *to make* pūioio W.306 'strong, muscular, sinewy' puku W.308 'abdomen, stomach']

whakapūioio remu *noun, adjective* (*aerobics etc.*) buttock exercise [whakapūioio W.306 'strong, muscular' remu W.335 'posterior, buttocks']

whakapūkara *noun* marinade [whaka- W.486 'causative prefix' *to make* pūkarakara W.307 'fragrant, well flavoured']

whakapūwharu *noun* hors-d'oeuvre [W.318 'dainty morsel, titbit']

whakarahi *transitive verb* enlarge [whaka- W.486 'causative prefix' *to make* rahi W.320 'great']

whakarahinga *noun* enlargement [whaka- W.486 'causative prefix' *to make* rahi W.320 'great']

whakarākei *noun* (*theatre*) set [W.321 'adorn, decorate']

whakarāpopoto *noun* synopsis [whaka- W.486 'causative prefix' *to make* rāpopoto W.326 'be assembled' whakarāpopoto common usage 'summarise']

whakarara *adjective* parallel [W.326 'mark in parallel lines']

whakarārangi *transitive verb* catalogue [W.324 'draw up or arrange in a line or row']

whakarārangi-ā-pū *transitive verb* alphabetise [whakarārangi W.324 'arrange in a line or row' ā W.1 'after the manner of' pū TM 'letter of alphabet']

whakararo *adjective* lower [whaka- W.485 'towards, in the direction of' raro W.327 'the bottom, the underside']

whakararo *adverb* downwards [whaka- W.485 'towards, in the direction of' raro W.327 'the bottom, the underside']

whakararo *adjective* northwards [whaka- W.485 'towards, in the direction of' raro W.327 'north, the north']

whakarau *noun* multiplication [W.328 'multiply']

whakarau harangotengote *noun* periodic detention [whakarau W.328 'take captive' harangotengote W.37 'do piecemeal or by instalments']

whakarau Kīngi *noun* chess [whakarau W.328 'take captive' Kīngi < Eng. 'King']

whakaraupapa *transitive verb* (*sequence*) order [whaka- W.486 'causative prefix' *to make* raupapa W.330 'put in order, ordered, completed']

whakaraupapa (*dispute*) remain neutral [W.330 'remain tranquil']

whakarauwaka tuhinga *noun* typesetter [whakarauwaka W.331 'lay off in beds or divisions' tuhinga TM 'text']

whakarawe *noun* (*accompanying item*) accessory [W.332 'fitting, furnishing']

whakarea *noun* multiplication [whaka- W.486 'causative prefix' *to make* rea W.333 'multiply']

whakarehu *noun* condiment [W.334 'give a relish to, flavour' rehu W.334 'fine dust']

whakareke *transitive verb* (*rugby*) mark [whakarekenga W.335 'mark made by stamping on the ground' rekereke W.335 'heel']

whakarere *transitive verb* abandon [W.338 'cast away, reject, leave, forsake']

whakarewa *transitive verb* defrost [whaka- W.486 'causative prefix' *to make* rewa W.339 'melt, be or become liquid']

whakarewa *noun* solvent [whaka- W.486 'causative prefix' *to make* rewa W.339 'be or become liquid']

whakarihariha *adjective* despicable [W.340 'disgusting']

whakarīroa *transitive verb* mainstream [whaka- W.486 'causative prefix' *to make* rīroa TM 'mainstream']

whakaripa *transitive verb* tabulate [whaka- W.486 'causative prefix' *to make* ripa W.341 'row, rank, line, furrow']

whakaripanga *noun* tabulation [whaka- W.486 'causative prefix' *to make* ripa W.341 'row, rank, line, furrow']

whakaroha *transitive verb* (*arithmetic*) expand [whaka- W.486 'causative prefix' *to make* roha W.344 'spread out, expanded']

whakarongo pīkari *adjective* attentive [W.280 '(listen) like nestlings awaiting the parent bird']

whakarōpū *transitive verb* classify [whaka- W.486 'causative prefix' *to make* rōpū W.347 'company of persons, clump of trees']

whakaroto *adverb* inwards [whaka- W.485 'towards, in the direction of' roto W.348 'the inside']

whakaruhi ārai mate *noun* human immuno-deficiency virus HIV [whakaruhi W.350 'enervate, weaken, cause anything to exhaust itself' ārai mate TM 'immunity']

whakarunga *adjective* upper [whaka- W.485 'towards, in the direction of' runga W.352 'the top, the upper part']

whakarunga *adverb* upwards [whaka- W.485 'towards, in the direction of' runga W.352 'the top, the upper part']

whakarunga *adverb* southwards [whaka- W.485 'towards, in the direction of' runga W.352 'the south, the southern parts']

whakataetae *noun* (*sport*) match [W.356 'try strength, contend']

whakataetae *noun* tournament [W.356 'try strength, contend']

whakataetae *noun* competition [W.356 'try strength, contend']

whakatāhei tohutoa *noun* medal presentation [whaka- W.486 'causative prefix' *to make* tāhei W.358 'wear anything suspended from the neck' tohutoa TM 'medal']

whakatairite *transitive verb* compare [whaka- W.486 'causative prefix' *to make* tairite W.365 'like, on a level with']

whakatairitenga *noun* comparison [whakatairite TM 'compare']

whakatakataka tūpāpaku *noun* funeral director, undertaker [whakatakataka W.366 'set anyone on his way, send forth' takataka 'make ready' tūpāpaku W.456 'corpse']

whakatakere *adjective* submarine [W.371 'bottom of a channel or of deep water, bed of a river']

whakatakoto *transitive verb* (*reports etc.*) submit [whaka- W.486 'causative prefix' *to make* takoto W.374 'lay down']

whakatakupe *noun* (*sport etc.*) full time [W.374 'at ease, pack up']

whakatanga *noun* (*vehicle*) clutch [whakatangatanga W.378 'release from restraint, disengage']

whakatara *adjective* (*difficult*) challenging [W.386 'challenge, put on one's mettle']

whakatata *noun* approach run [W. 393 'approach']

whakatata *noun* (*gymnastics*) run-up [W.393 'approach']

whakatau *transitive verb* (*decide*) conclude, decide, determine [whaka- W.486 'causative prefix' *to make* tau W.396 'come to rest, settle down']

whakatau *noun* conclusion, decision, ruling [whaka- W.486 'causative prefix' *to make* tau W.396 'come to rest, settle down']

whakatau *transitive verb* diagnose, *noun* diagnosis [TM 'conclude']

whakatau *noun*, *intransitive verb* role-play [W.396 'imitate, make believe, simulate']

whakatau *noun* mimicry [W.396 'imitate, make believe, simulate']

whakatau a te nuinga *noun* majority rule, consensus [whakatau TM 'decision' nuinga W.224 'majority, larger part']

whakatau ārai mamae *noun* non-molestation order [whakatau TM 'ruling' ārai W.14 'keep off, ward off' mamae W.162 'feel pain or distress of body or mind']

whakatau atua *noun* fate [whakatau TM 'decision' atua W.20 'supernatural being']

whakatau tangomoni *noun* attachment order [whakatau TM 'decision, settlement' tango W.380 'remove' moni < Eng.'money']

whakatau tata *transitive verb*, *noun* estimate [whakatau TM 'conclude' tata W.393 'near']

whakatauira *transitive verb* (*give example*) illustrate [whaka- W.486 'causative prefix' *to make* tauira W.398 'pattern, copy']

whakatāuke *transitive verb* segregate [whaka- W.486 'causative prefix' *to make* tāuke W.399 'apart, separate']

whakatāuke *noun* segregation [TM 'segregate']

whakatāuke tangata *noun* apartheid [whaka- W.486 'causative prefix' *to make* tāuke W.399 'apart, separate' tangata W.379 'human being']

whakataunga tata *noun* estimation [whakatau tata TM 'estimate']

whakataurite *transitive verb* compare [whaka- W.486 'causative prefix' *to make* taurite W.403 'alike, matching']

whakataurite *transitive verb* (*mathematics*) rearrange [whaka- W.486 'causative prefix' *to make* taurite W.403 'opposite, alike, matching']

whakatauritenga *noun* comparison [whakataurite TM 'compare']

whakatāupe *noun* narcissism [W.401 'regard oneself with admiration, i.e. bend over the wai whakaata']

whakatāupe *noun* vanity, *adjective* vain [W.401 'regard oneself with admiration, i.e. bend over the wai whakaata']

whakatautau *noun* charades [whakatau W.396 'imitate, simulate']

whakatautika *transitive verb* (*printing*) justify [whaka- W.486 'causative prefix' *to make* tautika W.404 'even, level, boundary']

whakatautika katau *transitive verb* (*printing*) right justify [whaka- W.486 'causative prefix' *to make* tautika W.404 'even, level, boundary' katau W.103 'right']

whakatautika maui *transitive verb* (*printing*) left justify [whaka- W.486 'causative prefix' *to make* tautika W.404 'even, level, boundary' maui W.196 'left']

whakatauwehe *transitive verb* factorise [whaka- W.486 'causative prefix' *to make* tauwehe TM 'factor']

whakateka noun flying tackle [W.410 'fly headlong']

whakatere transitive verb accelerate [whaka- W.486 'causative prefix' to make tere W.412 'swift, moving quickly, active, hasty']

whakatere noun (vehicle) accelerator [whaka- W.486 'causative prefix' to make tere W.412 'swift, moving quickly, active, hasty']

whakatere matūriki iraruke noun linear accelerator [whakatere TM 'accelerate' matūriki TM 'particle' irarukeTM 'radiation, radioactive']

whakatewhatewha noun investigator [W.413 'investigate, examine']

whakatewhatewha noun inspector [W.413 'investigate, examine']

whakatieke intransitive verb exert oneself [W.415 'exert one's strength to the full']

whakatika transitive verb discipline [W.417 'straighten, correct']

whakatika transitive verb (correct) fix [W.417 'correct']

whakatika i te takoto phrase format transitive verb (word-processing) [whakatika W.417 'straighten, correct' takoto W.373 'lie']

whakatika niho tāpiki noun orthodontics [whakatika W.417 'straighten, correct' niho W.221 'tooth' tāpiki W.384 'be entangled, doubled over' niho tāpiki 'a tooth overriding another']

whakatiki hārukiruki noun anorexia [whakatiki W.418 'keep short of food' hārukiruki W.38 'intensive']

whakatiko noun laxative [whaka- W.486 'causative prefix' to make tiko W.418 'evacuate the bowels']

whakatina noun safety-belt [W.419 'fasten, fix, confine, put under restraint']

whakatina tamariki noun child restraint [whakatina W.419 'fasten, fix, confine, put under restraint' tamariki W.376 'child']

whakatinana transitive verb (policy etc.) implement [whaka- W.486 'causative prefix' to make tinana W.419 'actual, real']

whakatio transitive verb freeze [whaka- W.486 'causative prefix' to make tio W.420 'ice, sharp, piercing, of cold']

whakatio noun freezer [whaka- W.486 'causative prefix' to make tio W.420 'ice, sharp, piercing, of cold']

whakatipu-ā-wai noun hydroponics [whakatipu W.458 'cause to grow' ā W.1 'after the manner of' wai W.474 'water']

whakatiriwhana noun crowbar [W.424 'prise with a lever']

whakatītaha transitive verb (mathematics) shear [whaka- W.486 'causative prefix' to make tītaha TM 'shear']

whakatīwhara transitive verb (chemistry) precipitate [tīwharawhara TM 'precipitate']

whakatīwheta transitive verb harass, hassle [W.428 'make to writhe, torment']

whakatō transitive verb transplant [W.428 'plant, introduce, insert']

whakatō transitive verb (reproduction) fertilise [W.428 'cause to conceive, plant']

whakatō kākano noun (reproduction) fertilisation [whakatō TM 'fertilise' kākano TM 'egg']

whakatō kano ārai mate transitive verb immunise [whakatō W.428 'introduce, insert' kano W.94 'seed' ārai W.14 'ward off, obstruct' mate W.192 'sickness']

whakatō kano ārai mate noun immunisation [TM 'immunise']

whakatō wairua auaha noun creative therapy [whakatō W.428 'introduce, insert, cause to conceive' wairua W.477 'spirit' auaha TM 'creative']

whakatoihara transitive verb (justice) prejudge [W.432 'disparage']

whakatoihara noun (justice) prejudice [W.432 'disparage']

whakatoihara iwi noun racism [whakatoihara W.432 'disparage' iwi W.80 'nation, people']

whakatoka transitive verb solidify [W.433 'make solid']

whakatoki noun chemical bleach [W.343 'bleach']

whakatonu noun safety-rail [W.436 'cautious, careful']

whakatū transitive verb appoint [W.443 'set up']

whakatūaho noun poker machine [W.444 'deceive, beguile']

whakatuaki transitive verb accuse, implicate [W.445 'blame']

whakatuaki noun defendant, accused [W.445 'blame' TM 'accused']

whakatuaki *noun* accusation [TM 'accuse']
whakatukutahi *noun* (*music*) synthesiser [whaka- W.486 'causative prefix' *to make* tukutahi W.452 'together, simultaneous']
whakatutukitanga *noun* achievement [whaka- W.486 'causative prefix' *to make* tutuki W.450 'be finished, be completed']
whakatūturu *transitive verb* verify [whaka- W.486 'causative prefix' *to make* tūturu W.460 'fixed, permanent']
whakatuwheratanga *noun* opening ceremony [whakatuwhera W.464 'open, set open']
whakaū *transitive verb* confirm [W.464 'make firm, establish']
whakaū *transitive verb* enforce [whaka- W.486 'causative prefix' *to make* ū W.464 'reach its limit, strike home']
whakaū *transitive verb* affirm [whakaū W.464 'make firm']
whakaū *noun* enforcement [whaka- W.486 'causative prefix' *to make* ū W.464 'reach its limit, strike home']
whakaū mahana *noun* thermostat [whakaū W.464 'make firm' mahana W.162 'warm']
whakaū pono *noun* affirmation [whakaū W.464 'make firm' pono W.291 'true']
whakauenuku *noun* tape recorder [W.465 'keep, retain']
whakauenuku *noun* (*audio*) recorder [W.465 'keep, retain']
whakauru *intransitive verb, transitive verb* enrol [whaka- W.486 'causative prefix' *to make* uru W.469 'enter, participate in']
whakauru atu *transitive verb* (*mathematics*) substitute [whaka- W.486 'causative prefix' *to make* uru W.469 'join, insert' atu W.20 'to indicate a direction away from speaker']
whakawātea *intransitive verb* (*cricket*) declare [whaka- W.486 'causative prefix' *to make* wātea W.480 'clear, free, open']
whakawātea *transitive verb* stand down [whaka- W.486 'causative prefix' *to make* W.480 'clear, free']
whakawaho *adverb* outwards [whaka- W.485 'towards, in the direction of' waho W.474 'the outside']
whakawaho *adjective* centrifugal [whaka- W.485 'towards, in the direction of' waho W.474 'the outside']
whakawai *intransitive verb, transitive verb* (*training*) practise [W.474 'practise the use of weapons']
whakawai *noun* (*training*) drill [W.474 'practise the use of weapons']
whakawai riri *noun* military exercise [W.474 'practise the use of weapons']
whakawaiwai *noun* (*training*) practice [W.475 'practise the use of weapons']
whakawaiwai reo *noun* language laboratory [whakawai TM 'practise' reo W.336 'language']
whakawao *transitive verb* reafforest [whaka- W.486 'causative prefix' *to make* wao W.479 'forest']
whakawehe *transitive verb* (*mathematics*) divide [whaka- W.486 'causative prefix' *to make* wehe W.481 'detach, divide']
whakawehe *noun* (*mathematics*) division [whaka- W.486 'causative prefix' *to make* wehe W.481 'detach, divide']
whakawera wai *noun* water-heater [whaka- W.486 'causative prefix' *to make* wera W.482 'heated, hot' wai W.474 'water']
whakaweto *transitive verb* (*machinery etc.*), switch off, shut down, turn off [whaka- W.486 'causative prefix' *to make* weto W.483 'be extinguished']
whakawhāititanga *noun* specialisation [whakawhāiti W.485 'put into small space, compress']
whakawhānau *noun* (*birth*) labour [W.487 'come to the birth']
whakawhārangi *transitive verb* paginate [whaka- W.486 'causative prefix' *to make* whārangi W.489 'page of a book']
whakawhena *transitive verb* (*anatomy*) flex [whaka- W.486 'causative prefix' *to make* whena W.494 'stiffen, make taut']
whakawhena wae *phrase* flex the foot [whakawhena TM 'flex' wae W.472 'foot']
whakawhenumi *transitive verb* absorb [whaka- W.486 'causative prefix' *to make* whenumi W.494 'be out of sight, be eclipsed, be consumed' whakawhenumi 'mix up one thing with another']
whakawhiti *transitive verb* transfer [W.497 'convey across, exchange']
whakawhiti *noun* (*soccer*) cross [whakawhiti W.497 'convey across']
whakawhiti pito *intransitive verb* change ends [whakawhiti W.497 'cross over' pito W.284 'end. extremity']

whakawhiti whakaaro *intransitive verb* negotiate [whakawhiti W.497 'exchange' whakaaro W.16 'thought, opinion']

whakawhiwhi *transitive verb* award [W.499 'give, present']

whakawhiwhi-ā-ōrau *noun* proportional representation [whakawhiwhi TM 'award' ā W.1 'after the manner of' ōrau TM 'percentage']

whāmutu *transitive verb* curtail [W.215 'leave off, cause to cease']

whana *noun* rebellion [W.486 'revolt, rebel']

whana *noun* (*device*) spring [W.486 'spring of a trap, recoil']

whana *noun* (*archery*) bow [Best *Games and Pastimes* 183]

whana *noun* (*violin*) bow [Best *Games and Pastimes* 183]

whana *noun* mutiny [W.486 'revolt, rebel']

whana autaki *noun* indirect free kick [whana W.486 'kick' autaki W.23 'roundabout, circuitous']

whana aweawe *noun* (*sport*) chip kick [whana W.486 'kick' aweawe W.24 'out of reach']

whana koko *noun* (*soccer*) corner kick [whana W.486 'kick' koko W.130 'corner']

whana kōkiri *noun* (*rugby*) drop out [whana W.486 'kick' kōkiri W.130 'body of men rushing forward']

whana korowhiti *noun* bicycle kick [whana W.486 'kick' korowhiti W.146 'bent round, like a hoop']

whana korowhiti *noun* overhead kick [TM 'bicycle kick']

whana pātea *noun* free kick [whana W.486 'kick' pātea W.270 'unencumbered, free from burdens']

whana ripi *noun* grubber kick [whana W.486 'kick' ripi W.341 'glance off, skim along the surface']

whana roa *noun* (*soccer*) long ball [whana W.486 'kick' roa W.344 'long']

whana tāwhe *noun* round-the-corner kick [whana W.486 'kick' tāwhe W.408 'go round, turn a corner']

whana taka *noun* drop kick [whana W.486 'kick' taka W.366 'fall off']

whana tautopenga *noun* goal kick [whana W.486 'kick' whakatautopenga TM 'goalkeeper']

whana tautuku *noun* penalty kick [whana W.486 'kick' tautuku TM 'penalty']

whana tike *phrase* high kick [whana W.486 'kick' tike W.417 'lofty, high']

whana tōkiri *noun* torpedo kick [whana W.486 'kick' tōkiri W.434 'thrust lengthwise']

whana tū-ā-nuku *noun* place kick [whana W.486 'kick' tū W.443 'stand' ā W.1 'after the manner of nuku W.225 'the earth']

whana turuki *noun* (*rugby etc.*) conversion [whana W.486 'kick' turuki W.461 'come as a supplement, follow']

whana whakatau *noun* tap kick [whana W.486 'kick' whakatau W.396 'feign, simulate']

whanake *intransitive verb* (*organism*) develop [W.487 'grow, spring up']

whānako rupe *noun* aggravated robbery [whānako W.487 'steal' rupe W.352 'shake violently, treat with violence']

whānau a tākaru *noun, adjective* pinniped [whānau W.487 'offspring, family group' a W.1 'of, belonging to' tākaru W.369 'splash about, flounder']

whānau kōaro *noun* breech birth [whānau W.487 'be born' kōaro W.122 'inverted, turned right around']

whānau whaiaro *noun* nuclear family [whānau W.487 'family' whaiaro W.485 'self, person']

whānui *noun* range [W.487 'broad, wide']

whānui *noun* width [W.487 'broad, wide']

whānui, whāroa *phrase* length and breadth [whānui W.487 'broad, wide' whāroa W.490 'long-continued']

whāngai *transitive verb* (*give to patient for consumption*) administer [W.488 'feed']

whāngai hē *noun* (*rugby*) incorrect feed [whāngai W.488 'feed' hē TM 'incorrect']

whāngai toto *noun* blood transfusion [whāngai W.488 'nourish, feed' toto W.441 'blood']

whāomo wai *noun* water conservation [whāomoomo W.239 'tend, use sparingly, husband' wai W.474 'water']

whāparo-tahi *noun* aldehyde [whā W.484 'causative prefix' paro W.268 'dry' tahi W.359 'one']

whārahi *transitive verb* enlarge [whā W.484 'causative prefix' rahi W.320 'great']

whārahi irahiko *noun* electron microscope

[whārahi TM 'enlarge' irahiko TM 'electron']

whārangi *noun* (*stationery*) sheet [W.489 'leaf or page of a book']

whārangi tārua *noun* carbon paper [whārangi W.489 'page of a book' tārua W.392 'tattoo a second time']

wharau *noun* pavilion [W.489 'temporary shed or booth']

wharau hoko *noun* kiosk [wharau W.489 'temporary shed or booth' hoko W.57 'sell']

whare haumanu *noun* clinic [whare W.489 'house' haumanu W.40 'restore to health, revive']

whare horoi kākahu *noun* laundromat [whare W.489 'house, hut, shed' horoi W.61 'cleanse, wash' kākahu W.84 'garment']

whare kahu *noun* (*childbirth*) delivery room [W.84 'shed erected for childbirth']

whare kōhanga *noun* maternity ward [W.124 'house to which mother and newborn child were removed']

whare koropū *noun* weatherboard house [whare W.489 'house' koropū W.145 'built with wrought timber']

whare maita *noun* (*lawn bowls*) bowling centre [whare W.489 'house' maita TM 'lawn bowls']

whare pītakataka *noun* gymnasium [whare W.489 'house' pītakataka TM 'gymnastics']

whare punanga *noun* women's refuge [punanga W.310 'any place used as a refuge for noncombatants in troubled days. Hence kāinga punanga, whare punanga, pā punanga']

whare rīhi *noun* (*accommodation*) flat [whare W.489 'house, habitation' rīhi < Eng. 'lease' common usage 'rent']

whare tāwhai *noun* caravan [whare W.489 'hut, habitation' tāwhai W.407 'go forth, travel to a distance']

whare takiura *noun* college of education [W.373 'building set apart for instruction in esoteric lore']

whare tapere *noun* theatre [W.383 'house in which the members of the hapū met for amusement']

whare tapere *noun* community centre [W.383 'house in which the members of the hapū met for amusement etc.']

whare tīkoke *noun* skyscraper [whare W.489 'house, habitation' tīkoke W.418 'high up in the heavens']

whare whakarauika *noun* auditorium [whare W.489 'house' whakarauika W.329 'assemble, gather together']

whare whakawā *noun* (*justice*) court [whare W.489 'house' whakawā TM 'judge']

whare whakawā take namunamu *noun* small claims court [whare whakawā TM 'court' take TM 'matter, claim' namunamu W.217 'small, diminutive']

wharehere pupuri *noun* minimum security prison [whare herehere W.46 'prison' pupuri W.314 'detain, press to remain']

wharehere whakaita *noun* medium security prison [whare herehere W.46 'prison' whakaita W.80 'hold fast, restrain']

wharehere whakatiki *noun* maximum security prison [whare herehere W.46 'prison' whakatiki W.417 'tie up, keep in confinement']

wharemoa *noun* (*zoology*) coelenterate [W.490 'hollow']

wharepī *noun* beehive [whare W.489 'habitation' pī < Eng. 'bee']

whārite *noun, transitive verb* (*weighing apparatus*) balance [W.343 'balance by an equivalent']

whārite *noun* (*weighing*) scales [W.343 'compare, liken, balance by an equivalent']

whārite *noun* (*mathematics*) equation [whā W.484 'causative prefix' rite W.343 'alike']

whārite hiko *noun* electric balance [whārite TM 'balance' hiko common usage 'electric']

whārite hiko *noun* electronic balance [whārite TM 'balance' hiko TM 'electronic']

whārite kore *noun* inequation [whārite TM 'equation' kore W.140 'no, not']

whārite whana *noun* spring balance [whārite TM 'balance' whana TM 'spring']

whata mātao *noun* refrigerator [whata W.490 'elevated stage for storing food, be laid, rest' mātao W.189 'cold']

whata pouheni *noun* cloakroom [whata pouheni W.298 'a pole with branches or pegs on which to hang things']

whata pouheni *noun* clothes-rack [W.298 'a pole with branches or pegs on which to hang things']

whata pouheni *noun* hatstand [W.298 'a pole with branches or pegs on which to hang things']

whata pouheni *noun* coat-rack [W.298 'a pole with branches or pegs on which to hang things']

whātika rererangi *noun* tarmac [whātika W.417 'way, path, set out on journey' waka rererangi common usage 'aeroplane']

whātōtō *noun* (*judo*) groundwork [W.491 'wrestle']

whatu *adjective* optic [W.492 'eye, pupil of the eye']

whatu *adjective* optical [W.492 'eye, pupil of the eye']

whatutoto *adjective* (*course, qualification etc.*) advanced [W.492 'red heartwood of tōtara or matai']

whāwhā raraunga ā-rorohiko *noun* electronic data-processing [whāwhā 484 'feel with the hand' raraunga TM 'data' ā W.1 'after the manner of' rorohiko TM 'computer']

whāwhai *adjective* urgent [whāwhai W.484 'be in haste, be hurried, exert oneself'] *E whāwhaitia ana tō whakautu* 'Your response is urgently needed'

whēkau *noun* (*generic*) internal organ [W.493 'internal organs of the body, entrails']

whētuitui *noun* origami [W.496 'fold, double, a garment etc.']

whētuitui *noun* (*origami*) paper-folding [W.496 'fold, double, a garment etc.']

whekewheke *noun* elephantiasis [W.493 'rough, scabrous' fe'efe'e Tongan and Samoan word for elephantiasis]

whenu *noun* cosine [W.494 'strand of a cord, warp of a flax garment']

whenua maru *noun* colony [whenua W.494 'land, country' maru W.184 'shaded, sheltered']

whenua rahi *noun* continent [whenua W.494 'land' rahi W.320 'great']

whenumi *intransitive verb* become absorbed [W.494 'be out of sight, be eclipsed, be consumed']

whenumi *adjective* assimilated [W.494 'be eclipsed, be consumed']

whenguwhengu *noun* moustache [W.494 'tattoo marks on the upper lip']

wheori *noun* virus, *adjective* viral [W.494 'diseased, ill']

whero *adjective* orange-red [W.495 'red, orange']

whetau *noun* reflex action [W.495 'move quiclky to avoid a blow']

whetūriki *noun* asterisk [whetū W.496 'star' riki W.340 'small']

wheua ihu *noun* nasal bone [wheua W.496 'bone' ihu W.75 'nose']

wheua kakaru *noun* cancellate bone tissue [wheua W.496 'bone' kakaru W.102 'spongy matter']

wheua kapu *noun* metacarpus [wheua W.496 'bone' kapu W.97 'hollow of the hand']

wheua kapuwae *noun* metatarsus [wheua W.496 'bone' kapu W.97 'hollow of the hand, sole of the foot' wae W.472 'foot']

wheua kawititanga *noun* carpus [wheua W.496 'bone' kawititanga o te ringaringa W.111 'wrist']

wheua kiato *noun* compact bone tissue [wheua W.496 'bone' W.116 'compact, in small compass']

wheua kōpako *noun* occipital bone [wheua W.496 'bone' kōpako W.135 'back of the head']

wheua ngohe *noun* cartilage [wheua W.496 'bone' ngohe W.234 'supple, soft']

wheua ngohe puata *noun* hyaline cartilage [wheua ngohe TM 'cartilage' puata W.303 'clear, transparent']

wheua pāpāringa *noun* (*anatomy*) yoke bone [wheua W.496 'bone' pāpāringa W.260 'cheek']

wheua puke huruhuru *noun* pubis [wheua W.496 'bone' puke W.307 'pubes, mons veneris' huruhuru W.72 'coarse hair, bristles']

wheua punga *noun* tarsus [wheua W.496 'bone' punga W.311 'ankle']

wheua rahirahinga *noun* temporal bone [wheua W.496 'bone' rahirahinga W.320 'temple of the head']

whiranui *noun* cello [whira < Eng. 'fiddle' nui W.244 'large']

whiringa *noun* (*sport*) round [whiriwhiri W.497 'select, choose']

whiringa aro-ā-kapa *noun* (*sport*) heat [whiriwhiri W.497 'select, choose' aro-ā-kapa W.16 'front rank']

whiringa taiao *noun* natural selection [whiriwhiri W.497 'select, choose' taiao TM 'environment']

whiringa tangata *noun* artificial selection [whiriwhiri W.497 'select, choose' tangata W.379 'man, human being']

whiringa taumātaki *noun* (*race*) preliminary round [whiriwhiri W.497 'select, choose' taumātakitaki W.400 'select a champion for each side in fighting']

whiringa toa *noun* (*competition sport*) medal round [whiriwhiri W.497 'select, choose' toa W.428 'victorious']

whiringa toa *noun* play off [whiriwhiri W.497 'select, choose' toa W.429 'victorious']

whiringa uru *noun* qualifying round [whiriwhiri W.497 'select, choose' uru TM 'qualify']

whirirua *noun* (*electoral system*) mixed member proportional representation [whiriwhiri W.497 'select, choose' rua W.349 'choose']

whiriwhiri *transitive verb* confer [W.497 'select, choose']

whiriwhiri (ko tēhea tēhea) *phrase* distinguish (between two or more things) [whiriwhiri W.497 'select, choose' tēhea W.410 'which' ko tēhea tēhea common usage 'which is which']

whiro *noun* (*cricket*) bat [common usage 'willow']

whītau *noun* (*textile*) felt [W.497 'prepared flax' whīwhiwhi W.499 'entangled']

whiti *noun* pinchbar [W.497 'prise, as with a lever']

whiu *transitive verb* penalise [W.498 'whip, chastise']

whiu *transitive verb* throw [W.498 'a certain throw in wrestling, fling, toss']

whiu *noun, transitive verb* (*justice*) sentence [W.498 'whip, chastise']

whiu tārewa *noun* (*justice*) indeterminate sentence [whiu TM 'sentence' tārewa W.391 'hanging, unsettled']

whiwhinga pūtea ā-whānau *noun* family income [whiwhi W.499 'be possessed of, having acquired' pūtea TM 'fund, finance' ā W.1 'after the manner of' whānau W.487 'family, family group']

Government Departments and Crown Entities

Many Government departments and Crown entities have officially adopted a Māori name which features on their official letterhead. A list of these agencies is provided below. Te Taura Whiri i te Reo Māori did not provide all of the names which appear in this list.

Government Departments

Ministry of Agriculture	Te Manatū Ahuwhenua
Audit Department	Te Tari Arotake o te Motu
Ministry of Commerce	Te Manatū Tauhokohoko
Department of Conservation	Te Papa Atawhai
Department for Courts	Te Tari Kooti
Ministry of Cultural Affairs	Te Manatū Tikanga-ā-Iwi
Customs Department	Te Mana Ārai o Aotearoa
Ministry of Defence	Manatū Kaupapa Waonga
Ministry of Education	Te Tāhuhu o te Mātauranga
Education Review Office	Te Tari Arotake Mātauranga
Ministry for the Enviroment	Manatū mō te Taiao
Ministry of Fisheries	Te Tautiaki i ngā tini a Tangaroa
Ministry of Foreign Affairs and Trade	Manatū Aorere
Ministry of Forestry	Te Manatū Ngāherehere
Government Superannuation Fund Department	Te Pūtea Penihana Kāwanatanga
Ministry of Health	Manatū Hauora
Ministry of Housing	Te Whare Ahuru
Inland Revenue Department	Te Tari Taake
Department of Internal Affairs	Te Tari Taiwhenua
Ministry of Justice	Te Manatū Ture
National Library of New Zealand	Te Puna Mātauranga o Aotearoa
Ministry of Māori Development	Te Puni Kōkiri
Ministry of Research, Science and Technology	Te Manatū Pūtaiao
Serious Fraud Office	Te Tari Hara Tāware
Department of Social Welfare	Te Tari Toko i te Ora
State Services Commission	Te Komihana o ngā Tari Kāwanatanga
Statistics New Zealand	Te Tari Tatau
Department of Survey and Land Information	Te Puna Kōrero Whenua
Ministry of Transport	Te Manatū Waka
The Treasury	Kaitohutohu Kaupapa Rawa
Ministry of Womens Affairs	Minitatanga mō ngā Wāhine
Office of Youth Affairs	Te Tari Taiohi

Crown Entities

Alcohol Advisory Council of New Zealand	Kaunihera Whakatūpato Waipiro o Aotearoa
Arts Council of New Zealand	Toi Aotearoa
Aviation Security Service	Kaiwhakamaru Rererangi
Broadcasting Standards Authority	Te Mana Whanonga Kaipāho
Careers Service	Rapuara
Civil Aviation Authority of New Zealand	Te Mana Rererangi Tūmatanui o Aotearoa
Commissioner for Children	Tiakina ā Tātou Tamariki
Early Childhood Development Unit	Ngā Kaitaunaki Kōhungahunga
Energy Efficiency and Conservation Authority	Te Tari Tiaki Pūngao
Foundation for Research, Science and Technology	Tūāpapa Toha Pūtea, Whakatakoto Kaupapa Rangahau, Pūtaiao
Health Research Council of New Zealand	Te Kaunihera Rangahau Hauora o Aotearoa
Health Sponsorship Council	Te Rōpū Whakatairanga Hauora
Hillary Commission for Sport, Fitness and Leisure	Te Kōmihana Hākinakina a Hillary
Housing Corporation of New Zealand	Te Kaporeihana Whare
Human Rights Commission	Kōmihana Tikanga Tangata
Landcare Research New Zealand Limited	Manaaki Whenua
Land Transport Safety Authority of New Zealand	Te Mana Marutau Waka Whenua o Aotearoa
Law Commission	Te Aka Matua o Te Ture
Learning Media Limited	Te Pou Taki Kōrero
Māori Broadcasting Funding Agency	Te Māngai Pāho
Maori Language Commission	Te Taura Whiri i te Reo Māori
Maritime Safety Authority of New Zealand	Te Mana Ārai Hauata Moana
Meteorological Service of New Zealand Limited	Te Ratonga Tirorangi
The Museum of New Zealand	Te Papa Tongarewa
National Institute of Water and Atmospheric Research Limited (NIWA)	Taihoro Nukurangi
New Zealand Film Commission	Te Tumu Whakaata Taonga
New Zealand Fire Service Commission	Whakaratonga Iwi
New Zealand Institute for Crop and Food Research Limited	Mana Kai Rangahau
New Zealand Lottery Grants Board	Te Poari Rota
New Zealand On Air	Irirangi Te Motu
New Zealand Police	Ngā Pirihimana o Aotearoa
New Zealand Qualifications Authority	Mana Tohu Mātauranga o Aotearoa

The Office of Films and Literature Classification	**Te Tari Whakarōpū Tukuata, Tuhituhinga**
Privacy Commissioner	**Te Mana Mātāpono Matatapu**
Race Relations Office	**Te Tari Whakawhanaunga-ā-Iwi**
Radio New Zealand Limited	**Te Reo Irirangi o Aotearoa**
Special Education Service	**He Tohu Umanga Mātauranga**
Teacher Registration Board	**Te Poari Kairēhita Kaiako**
Transit New Zealand	**Ararau Aotearoa**
Transport Accident Investigation Commission	**Te Kōmihana Tirotiro Aitua Waka**

Days of the Week

The following is a list of alternatives for the days in Māori.

Monday	**Mane** (> Eng.) **Rātahi** (rā W.319 'day' tahi W.359 'one') **Rāhina** (rā W.319 'day' māhina W.164 'moon')
Tuesday	**Tūrei** (> Eng.) **Rārua** (rā W.319 'day' rua W.349 'two') **Rātū** (rā W.319 'day' Tūmatauenga common usage 'God of war', used by some as the Māori name for Mars)
Wednesday	**Wenerei** (> Eng.) **Rātoru** (rā W.319 'day' toru W.441 'three') **Rāapa** (rā W.319 'day' Apārangi W.497 'evil, bad', used by some as the Māori name for Mercury)
Thursday	**Tāite** (> Eng.) **Rāwhā** (rā W.319 'day' whā W.484 'four') **Rāpare** (rā W.319 'day' Pare-arau W.266 'Jupiter')
Friday	**Paraire** (> Eng.) **Rārima** (rā W.319 'day' rima W.340 'five') **Rāmere** (rā W.319 'day' Meremere W.201 'Venus')
Saturday	**Hātarei** (> Eng.) **Rāhoroi** (rā W.319 'day' horoi W.61 'wash')
Sunday	**Rātapu** (rā W.319 'day' tapu W.385 'ceremonial restriction')

Months of the Year

The following is a list of alternatives for the months in Māori.

January	**Hānuere** (> Eng.) **Kohi-tātea** (EB *Māori Division of Time* 19)
February	**Pāpuere** (> Eng.) **Hui-tanguru** (EB *Māori Division of Time* 19)
March	**Māehe** (> Eng.) **Poutū-te-rangi** (EB *Māori Division of Time* 19)
April	**Āperira** (> Eng.) **Paenga-whāwhā** (EB *Māori Division of Time* 19)
May	**Mei** (> Eng.) **Haratua** (EB *Māori Division of Time* 19)
June	**Hune** (> Eng.) **Pipiri** (EB *Māori Division of Time* 19)
July	**Hūrae** (> Eng.) **Hōngongoi** (EB *Māori Division of Time* 19)
August	**Ākuhata** (> Eng.) **Here-turi-kōkā** (EB *Māori Division of Time* 19)
September	**Hepetema** (> Eng.) **Mahuru** (EB *Māori Division of Time* 19)
October	**Oketopa** (> Eng.) **Whiringa-ā-nuku** (EB *Māori Division of Time* 19)
November	**Noema** (> Eng.) **Whiringa-ā-rangi** (EB *Māori Division of Time* 19)
December	**Tīhema** (> Eng.) **Hakihea** (EB *Māori Division of Time* 19)

International Place Names

The following is a list of international place names which have been translated into Māori.

Afghanistan	**Awhekenetāna**
Albania	**Arapeinia**
Algeria	**Aratiria**
American Samoa	**Hāmoa Amerikana**
Amman	**Amāna**
Angola	**Anakora**
Ankara	**Anakara**
Antigua	**Te Moutere Nehe**
Antwerp	**Anatepe**
Argentina	**Āketina**
Armenia	**Āmenia**
Asia	**Āhia**
Athens	**Ātene**
Atlantic	**Te Moana o Ātarānaki**
Australia	**Ahitereiria**
Austria	**Ateria**
Aztec	**Ātiki**
Baghdad	**Pākatata**
Bahamas	**Pāhama**
Bahrain	**Pāreina**
Bangkok	**Pangakoko**
Bangladesh	**Penekāri**
Barbados	**Papatohe**
Basque Country	**Te Whenua Pākihi**
Beijing	**Peihinga**
Belarus	**Pērara**
Belgium	**Pehiamu**
Belize	**Pērihi**
Benin	**Pēnina**
Berlin	**Pearīni**
Bermuda	**Pāmura**
Bethany	**Petane**
Bethlehem	**Peterehema**
Bogotá	**Pokotā**
Bolivia	**Poriwia**
Bonn	**Pono**
Bosnia-Herzegovina	**Pōngia-Herekōmina**
Botswana	**Poriwana**
Brazil	**Parīhi**
Brisbane	**Piripane**
Britain	**Ingarangi**
British Columbia	**Te Taha Rātō**

British Virgin Islands	Ngā Moutere Puhi
Brunei	Poronai
Brussels	Paruhi
Bulgaria	Purukāria
Burkina	Pūkina
Burma	Pēma
Burundi	Puruniti
California	Karapōnia
Cambodia	Kamapōtia
Cameroon	Kamerūna
Canada	Kānata
Canberra	Kānapera
Caribbean	Karipiana
Caspian Sea	Te Moana o Kapiana
Cayman Islands	Ngā Moutere Kāmana
Chad	Kāta
Chile	Hiri
China	Haina
Colombia	Koromōpia
Colombo	Koromo
Cook Islands	Kuki Airani
Cos	Koha
Costa Rica	Koto Rika
Croatia	Koroātia
Cuba	Kūpā
Cyprus	Haipara
Denmark	Tenemāka
Dominica	Tomonaki
Dublin	Tāperene
Ecuador	Ekuatoa
Egypt	Ihipa
England	Ingarangi
Estonia	Etonia
Ethiopia	Etiopia
Fiji	Whītī
Finland	Hinerangi
France	Wīwī
Frankfurt	Parewhiti
Fukuoka	Whukuoka
The Gambia	Te Kamopia
Geneva	Hiniwa
Georgia	Hōria
Germany	Tiamana
Ghana	Kāna
Gibraltar	Kāmaka
Great Britain	Piritene Nui
Greece	Kirihi
Grenada	Kerenara

Guam	Kuamu
Guatemala	Kuatamāra
Guernsey	Kōnihi
Guinea	Kini
Guyana	Kaiana
The Hague	Te Heke
Haiti	Haiti
Hamburg	Hamupēke
Harare	Harāre
Hawaii	Hawai'i
Hokkaido	Hokairo
Holland	Hōrana
Holy See	Te Pāriha Tapu
Honduras	Honotura
Hong Kong	Hongipua
Honiara	Honiara
Hungary	Hanekeria
Iceland	Tiorangi
India	Īnia
Indonesia	Initonīhia
Iran	Īrāna
Iraq	Īrāki
Ireland	Airangi
Israel	Iharaira
Italy	Itāria
Ivory Coast	Te Tai Rei
Jakarta	Tiakāta
Jamaica	Hemeika
Japan	Nipono, Hapanihi
Jeddah	Hera
Jersey	Tōrehe
Jerusalem	Hiruhārama
Jordan	Hōtene
Karachi	Karāti
Kathmandu	Katamarū
Kazakhstan	Katatānga
Kenya	Kenia
Kirghizstan	Kikitānga
Kiribati	Kiripati
Korea	Kōrea
Kuala Lumpur	Kuara Rūpa
Kurd	Kuru
Kurdistan	Kurutānga
Kuwait	Kūweiti
Laos	Rāoho
Latin America	Amerika ki te Tonga
Latvia	Rāwhia
Lebanon	Repanona

Lesotho	**Teroto**
Liberia	**Raipiria**
Libya	**Ripia**
Lima	**Rima**
Lisbon	**Rīpene**
Ljouwert/Leeuwarden	**Rauati**
London	**Rānana**
Los Angeles	**Ngā Ānahera**
Luxembourg	**Rakapuō**
Macau	**Makau**
Macedonia	**Makerōnia**
Malawi	**Marāwi**
Malaysia	**Mareia**
Maldives	**Māratiri**
Mali	**Māri**
Malta	**Mārata**
Manila	**Manira**
Marshall Islands	**Ngā Moutere Māhara**
Mauritius	**Marihi**
Maya	**Māia**
Melbourne	**Poipiripi**
Memphis	**Mēpihi**
Mexico	**Mēhiko**
Mexico City	**Te Tāone o Mēhiko**
Milan	**Mirāna**
Mongolia	**Mongōria**
Montevideo	**Maungaata**
Montreal	**Maungaihi**
Montserrat	**Maungaherai**
Morocco	**Moroko**
Moscow	**Mohikau**
Mozambique	**Mohapiki**
Muskat	**Muhukata**
Myanmar	**Pēma**
Nagoya	**Nakoia**
Nairobi	**Ngāiropi**
Namibia	**Namīpia**
Nauru	**Nauru**
Nepal	**Nepōra**
Netherlands	**Hōrana**
New Caledonia	**Kanaki**
New Delhi	**Nūteri**
New York	**Te Āporo Nui**
New Zealand	**Aotearoa**
Nicaragua	**Nikarāhua**
Niger	**Ngāika**
Nigeria	**Ngāitiria**
Niue	**Niue**

Norfolk Island	Te Moutere Nōpoke
Northern Ireland	Airangi ki te Raki
Norway	Nōwei
Noumea	Noumea
Nuku'alofa	Nuku'aroha
Oman	Omāna
Osaka	Ohaka
Oslo	Ōhoro
Ottawa	Otawa
Pakistan	Pakitāne
Palestine	Pirihitia
Panama	Panama
Pape'ete	Pape'ete
Papua New Guinea	Papua Nūkini
Paraguay	Parakai
Paris	Parī
Peru	Perū
Philippines	Piripīni
Poland	Pōrana
Port Louis	Poi Ruihi
Port Moresby	Poi Moahipi
Port of Spain	Te Poi o Pāniora
Port Vila	Poi Whira
Portugal	Potukara
Puerto Rico	Peta Riko
Qatar	Katā
Quebec (Province of)	Kopeke
Quebec City	Te Kuititanga
Rarotonga	Rarotonga
Rhodes	Rōhoro
Riyadh	Riata
Rome	Rōma
Romania	Romeinia
Russia	Rūhia
Rwanda	Rāwana
Samoa	Hāmoa
San Diego	Hanga Piako
Santiago	Hanatiākō
Sao Paolo	Hao Pāora
Sardinia	Hāringia
Saudi Arabia	Hauri Arāpia
Scandinavia	Te Hauraro o Ūropi
Scotland	Kotarangi
Seattle	Heātara
Sendai	Hēnai
Senegal	Henekara
Seoul	Houra
Seychelles	Heikere

Shanghai	Hangahai
Sierra Leone	Te Araone
Singapore	Hingapoa
Slovakia	Horowākia
Slovenia	Horowinia
Solomon Islands	Ngā Motu Horomona
Somalia	Hūmārie
South Africa	Āwherika ki te Tonga
South America	America ki te Tonga
Spain	Pāniora
Sri Lanka	Hiri Rānaka
St Helena	Hato Hērena
St Kitts	Hato Kete
St Lucia	Hato Rūiha
Stockholm	Tokoomo
Sudan	Hūtāne
Suva	Huwha
Swaziland	Warerangi
Sweden	Huitene
Switzerland	Huiterangi
Sydney	Poihākena
Syria	Hiria
Tahiti	Tahiti
Taiwan	Taiwana
Tajikstan	Takiritānga
Tamuning	Tamuninga
Tanzania	Tānahia
Tarawa	Tarawa
Tehran	Terāna
Thailand	Tairanga
Thessaloniki	Teharoniki
Togo	Toko
Tokyo	Tōkio
Tonga	Tonga
Trinidad and Tobago	Tirinaki-Tōpako
Tunisia	Tūnihia
Turkey	Whenua Korukoru
Turkmenistan	Tukumanatānga
Tuvalu	Tūwaru
Uganda	Ukānga
Ukraine	Ūkareinga
United Nations	Te Kotahitanga o ngā Whenua o te Ao
United States of America	Te Hononga o Amerika
Uruguay	Urukoi
USSR	Rūhia
Uzbekistan	Uhipeketāne
Valletta	Whāreta
Vancouver	Te Whanga-a-Kiwa

Vanuatu	**Whenuatū**
Vatican	**Te Poho o Pita**
Venezuela	**Penehūera**
Vienna	**Whiena**
Vietnam	**Whitināmu**
Wales	**Wēra**
Washington	**Wāhitāone**
Western Samoa	**Hāmoa ki te Uru**
Yangon	**Iangona**
Yemen	**Īmene**
Zambia	**Tāmipia**
Zimbabwe	**Timuwawe**